THE FORMATION OF THE BOOK OF JEREMIAH

THE SOCIETY OF BIBLICAL LITERATURE
MONOGRAPH SERIES

Editor
Terence Fretheim

Number 51
THE FORMATION OF THE
BOOK OF JEREMIAH
Doublets and Recurring Phrases

by
Geoffrey H. Parke-Taylor

THE FORMATION OF THE BOOK OF JEREMIAH
Doublets and Recurring Phrases

Geoffrey H. Parke-Taylor

Society of Biblical Literature
Atlanta, Georgia

THE FORMATION OF THE BOOK OF JEREMIAH
Doublets and Recurring Phrases

by
Geoffrey H. Parke-Taylor

Copyright © 2000 by the Society of Biblical Literature

All rights reserved. No part of this work may be reproduced or transmitted in any form or by any means, electronic or mechanical, including photocopying and recording, or by means of any information storage or retrieval system, except as may be expressly permitted by the 1976 Copyright Act or in writing from the publisher. Requests for permission should be addressed in writing to the Rights and Permissions Office, Society of Biblical Literature, 825 Houston Mill Road, Atlanta, GA 30329.

Library of Congress Cataloging-in-Publication Data

Parke-Taylor, Geoffrey H., 1920–
    The formation of the book of Jeremiah : doublets and recurring phrases / Geoffrey H. Parke-Taylor.
       p. cm. —(Monograph series / The Society of Biblical Literature; no.51)
    Includes bibliographical references and index.
    ISBN 0-88414-003-2 (hardcover : alk. paper)—ISBN 978-1-58983-394-4 (paper : alk. paper)
    1. Bible. O.T. Jeremiah—Language, Style. 2. Bible. O.T. Jeremiah—Criticism, interpretation, etc. I. Title. II. Monograph series (Society of Biblical Literature) ; no. 51.

BS1525.2.P37 2000
224'.2066—dc21   00-027497

Printed in the United States of America
on acid-free paper

To my dear wife Mary, with love and esteem

TABLE OF CONTENTS

Acknowledgements xv
Abbreviations xvii

Chapter One: Doublets and Recurring Phrases:
        Some Preliminary Considerations 1
    Doublets in Jeremiah
    Recent Research in Doublets in Jeremiah
    Studies of Recurring Phrases
    The Septuagint (LXX)
    Methodology
    Jeremiah 8:15=Jeremiah 14:19b
    Jeremiah 26:18b=Micah 3:12
    The Purpose and Organization of this Study
        of Doublets and Recurring Phrases

Chapter Two: Doublets in the Confessions 13
    Jeremiah 11:20=Jeremiah 20:12
    Jeremiah 11:23b=Jeremiah 23:12b
    The Triad ("Sword, Famine, Pestilence")
    Jeremiah 15:13-14=Jeremiah 17:3-4
    Summary

Chapter Three: Additional Doublets in the Confessions 33
    Jeremiah 15:15d=Psalm 69:8a
    Jeremiah 15:20=Jeremiah 1:18-19
    Jeremiah 17:18b=Jeremiah 1:17b
    Jeremiah 18:20a=Jeremiah 18:22b
    Jeremiah 18:23b=Jeremiah 3:37(4:5E)
    Jeremiah 20:10a=Psalm 31:14a
    Jeremiah 20:12=Jeremiah 11:20
    Summary

Chapter Four: Doublets Regarding the Monarchy 55
        Jeremiah 23:5-6=Jeremiah 33:14-16
        Jeremiah and Ideal Monarchy
        Recurring Phrases in Jeremiah 21:12b
            and Jeremiah 4:4b
        Jeremiah 22:4=Jeremiah 17:25
        A Future Restored Monarchy: Jeremiah 30:8-9
            and Jeremiah 30:21
        The Term אַדִּיר in Jeremiah 30:21
        The Strophic Structure of Jeremiah 30-31
        Jeremiah 23:7-8=Jeremiah 16:14-15
        Jeremiah 29:13 and Deuteronomy 4:29
        Summary: Doublets

Chapter Five: Doublets Concerning Prophecy 81
        Denunciation of False Prophets: Jeremiah 23:1-40
        Jeremiah 23:15a=Jeremiah 9:14(15E)
        Jeremiah 23:19-20=Jeremiah 30:23-24
        Three Recurring Phrases in Jeremiah 23
        Jeremiah 23:33-40
        Jeremiah 6:13-15=Jeremiah 8:10b-12
        Jeremiah 28 and 29
        Summary: Doublets

Chapter Six: Recurring Phrases in Jeremiah 25:1-13 101
        Nebuchadrezzar as Yahweh's "Servant"
            (Jer 25:9; 27:6; 43:10)
        The Text of the LXX and the MT Compared
        Jeremiah 25:1-13: Other Parallel Phrases
        Parallel Phrases in Jeremiah 25:3b-6
            and Jeremiah 35:14b-15
        The Position and Order of the OAN
            in the LXX and the MT
        Summary

Chapter Seven: Doublets and Recurring Phrases
            in Jeremiah 46-49 (OAN) 115
        Jeremiah 46:2-26: Egypt

Jeremiah 46:27-28=Jeremiah 30:10-11
Jeremiah 47:1-7MT (29:1-7LXX)
    The Philistines
Jeremiah 48: Moab (Jeremiah 31LXX)
Jeremiah 48:5ab=Isaiah 15:15bc
Jeremiah 48:29-33 and Isaiah 16:6-10
Jeremiah 48:34-39 and Isaiah 15:2-7
Jeremiah 48:40-41 (Moab)
    = Jeremiah 49:22 (Edom)
Jeremiah 48:43-44=Isaiah 24:17-18ab
Jeremiah 48:45-46=Numbers 21:27-29; 24:17c
Recurring Phrases in Jeremiah 49:1-6MT
    (=30:1-5LXX): The Ammonites
Recurring Phrases in Jeremiah 49:7-22MT
    (=29:18-23LXX): Edom
Jeremiah 49:9=Obadiah 5
Jeremiah 49:14-16=Obadiah 1b-4 (Edom)
Jeremiah 49:17; 50:13; 18:16; 19:8
Jeremiah 49:18=Jeremiah 50:40
Jeremiah 49:19-21=Jeremiah 50:44-46
Jeremiah 49:22=Jeremiah 48:40-41
Recurring Phrases in Jeremiah 49:23-27MT
    (=30:12-16LXX): Damascus
Jeremiah 49:26=Jeremiah 50:30
Recurring Phrases in Jeremiah 49:28-33MT
    (=30:6-11LXX): Kedar and "the kingdoms of Hazor"
Recurring Phrases in Jeremiah 49:34-39MT
    (=25:24-26:1LXX): Elam
Summary: Jeremiah 25:1-14
    and Jeremiah 46-49 (OAN)

Chapter Eight: Recurring Phrases in Jeremiah 50-51:
    Oracles Against Babylon 165
    The Content of Jeremiah 50 and 51
        (LXX: 27 and 28): Babylon
    Common Ideas and Vocabulary in Jeremiah 50-51
        and the OAN of Jeremiah 46-49
    Jeremiah 50:16b=Isaiah 13:14b

        Jeremiah 50:23b=Jeremiah 51:41b
        Jeremiah 50:30=Jeremiah 49:26
        Jeremiah 50:32b=Jeremiah 21:14b
        Jeremiah 50:39-40 and Isaiah 13:9-22
        Jeremiah 50:40=Jeremiah 49:18
        Jeremiah 50:41-43=Jeremiah 6:22-24
        Jeremiah 50:44=Jeremiah 49:19-21
        Recurring Phrases and Doublets in Jeremiah 51
        Jeremiah 51:15-19=Jeremiah 10:12-16
        Jeremiah 51:39b=Jeremiah 51:57b
        Jeremiah 51:58d=Habakkuk 2:13b
        Summary: Recurring Phrases
           and Doublets in Jeremiah 50-51

Chapter Nine: Other Doublets Within the Book of Jeremiah 185
        Jeremiah 2:26b=Jeremiah 32:32b
        Jeremiah 2:27b=Jeremiah 32:33a
        Jeremiah 2:28b=Jeremiah 11:13
        Jeremiah 4:5c=Jeremiah 8:14a
        Jeremiah 5:9=Jeremiah 5:29=Jeremiah 9:8 (9:9E)
        Jeremiah 7:6 and Jeremiah 22:3
        Jeremiah 7:7=Jeremiah 25:5
        Jeremiah 7:16=Jeremiah 11:14
        Jeremiah 7:30-32=Jeremiah 19:5-6, 11-12; 32:34-35
        Jeremiah 7:34 and Parallels
           in Jeremiah 16:9; 25:10 and 33:10a, 11a
        Jeremiah 8:2b=Jeremiah 16:4a=Jeremiah 25:33b
        Jeremiah 8:15=Jeremiah 14:19b
        Jeremiah 13:14b=Jeremiah 21:7b
        Jeremiah 17:10b=Jeremiah 32:19b
        Jeremiah 17:26; 32:44; 33:13
        Jeremiah 21:9=Jeremiah 38:2
        Jeremiah 26:3=Jeremiah 36:3
        Jeremiah 32:4=Jeremiah 34:3
        Jeremiah 34:22a=Jeremiah 37:8
        Jeremiah 39:3=Jeremiah 39:13
        Summary

Chapter Ten: Doublets and Phrases in the Book of Jeremiah with Parallels
        in Other Parts of the Old Testament 213
    Doublets in Jeremiah and in Other Books
      of the Old Testament
    Jeremiah and Other Prophets
    Jeremiah 14:10b=Hosea 8:13b
    Jeremiah 49:4-16 and Obadiah 4, 5
    Jeremiah 51:58d=Habakkuk 2:13
    Jeremiah 31:29=Ezekiel 18:2
    Jeremiah 31:35c=Isaiah 51:15b
    Jeremiah and Psalms: Jeremiah 10:25=Psalm 79:6-7
      Jeremiah 15:15d=Psalm 68:8
      Jeremiah 20:10a=Psalm 31:14a
    Jeremiah and 2 Kings: Jeremiah 19:3b=2 Kings 21:12
      Jeremiah 38:3=2 Kings 18:30
    Jeremiah and Deuteronomy
      Jeremiah 7:33=Deuteronomy 28:26
      Jeremiah 19:9=Deuteronomy 28:53
      Jeremiah 22:8-9 and Deuteronomy 29:23-25
      Jeremiah 29:13=Deuteronomy 4:29
      Jeremiah 29:14a and Deuteronomy 30:3
    Jeremiah 18:23b=Nehemiah 3:37 (4:5E)
    Summary and Conclusions
    Recurring Phrases in Jeremiah and Other Books
      of the Old Testament
    Jeremiah and Hosea
    Jeremiah and Amos
    Jeremiah and Isaiah
    Jeremiah and Micah
    Jeremiah and Zephaniah
    Jeremiah and Nahum
    Jeremiah and Habakkuk
    Jeremiah and Ezekiel
    Jeremiah and Psalms
        Jeremiah 17:5-8 and Psalm 1
        Other Parallels with Psalms

          Jeremiah and 2 Kings
          Jeremiah and Deuteronomy
          Recurring Phrases: Summary

Chapter Eleven: Prominent Terms and Phrases in the Book of Jeremiah
          and Phrases that are Unique to Jeremiah 243
          (1) The Triad ("Sword, Famine, Pestilence")
          (2) "To pluck up," "to break down," "to destroy,"
              "to overthrow," "to build," "to plant"
          (3) "My servant"
          (4) "The people of the land"
          (5) "To restore the fortunes"
          Repetitive Words and Phrases that are Unique to Jeremiah
            (A1-A37)
          Summary

Chapter Twelve: Phrases in the Book of Jeremiah with Parallels
          in non-Deuteronomistic Books
          of the Old Testament 257
          Repetitive Words and Phrases Common to Jeremiah
            and Other Parts of the Old Testament
            (excluding Deuteronomy and the
            Deuteronomistic literature [B1-B57])
          Summary

Chapter Thirteen: Recurring Phrases in the Book of Jeremiah: Phrases with
          Parallels in the Deuteronomistic Books
          of the Old Testament (C1–C103) 267
          Covenant (ברית) and the Covenantal Formula
          Repetitive Phrases (C1–C103)
          Conclusions
          A Deuteronomistic Redaction

Chapter Fourteen: Conclusions 293
Bibliography 307
Index of Doublets in the book of Jeremiah 325

ACKNOWLEDGEMENTS

My fascination with the prophet Jeremiah and the book of Jeremiah began many years ago, when I was an undergraduate at the University of Toronto. I was introduced to the Hebrew text of Jeremiah by Dr. Cuyler Young, a professor at Victoria College, a constituent part of the University. He also aroused my interest in critical questions surrounding the book of Jeremiah by inviting me to read John Skinner's book, *Prophecy and Religion* (Cambridge, Cambridge University Press, 1922).

During the years that I was Dean of Theology and Professor of Old Testament and Hebrew at Huron College (University of Western Ontario, London, Ontario) I taught classes on the book of Jeremiah (Hebrew text and exegesis). Some years later, in retirement, I pursued further studies in the vast literature surrounding the book of Jeremiah. I decided that a full-scale study of doublets in the book of Jeremiah needed to be undertaken. This led on to studies of recurring phrases in the book, many of which are found in the doublets. Both the doublets and the recurring phrases helped me to a better understanding of the formation of this complicated prophetic book.

I am indebted to those who have helped me in the preparation of this book. In addition to the two readers appointed for the SBLMS publications, Dr. Terence Fretheim, the editor or the series, has assisted me with many valuable suggestions regarding the content and format of the manuscript. I am deeply grateful to Dr. Fretheim for his guidance and sound advice regarding this project. Leigh Andersen, Production Manager at the Society of Biblical Literature, has also given me most helpful assistance.

I appreciate more than I can readily put into words the help in setting up the camera-ready copy which I have received from my good friend, Dr. John Hurd, Professor Emeritus of New Testament, Trinity College, Toronto. Likewise, I have received encouragement from members of the teaching faculty at Wycliffe College, Toronto, Dr. Marion Taylor, Dr. Glen Taylor and Dr. Alan Hayes.

Finally my warmest thanks fo to my wife, Mary, who has been so patient during the period of my preparation of the manuscript. Her support and encouragement have been invaluable.

ABBREVIATIONS

AB	Anchor Bible
AJSL	*American Journal of Semitic Languages and Literature*
AnBib	Analecta biblica
ATD	Das Alte Testament Deutsch
BASOR	*Bulletin of the American Schools of Oriental Research*
BDB	F.Brown, S. R. Driver and C. A. Briggs, *Hebrew and English Lexicon of the Old Testament*
BETL	Bibliotheca ephemeridum theologicarum lovaniensium
BHS	*Biblia hebraica stuttgartensia*
Bib	*Biblica*
BJRL	*Bulletin of the John Rylands University Library of Manchester*
BKAT	Biblischer Kommentar Altes Testament
BTS	*Bible et terre sainte*
BWANT	Beiträge zur Wissenschaft vom Alten und Neuen Testament
BZAW	Beihefte zur *ZAW*
CBC	Cambridge Bible Commentary
CBQ	*Catholic Biblical Quarterly*
ExpTim	*Expository Times*
FRLANT	Forschungen zur Religion und Literatur des Alten und Neuen Testaments
GKC	*Gesenius' Hebrew Grammar*, ed. E. Kautzsch, transl. A. E. Cowley
HKAT	Handkommentar zum Alten Testament
HTR	*Harvard Theological Review*
HUCA	*Hebrew Union College Annual*
IB	*Interpreter's Bible*
ICC	International Critical Commentary
IDB	G. A. Buttrick (ed.), *Interpreter's Dictionary of the Bible*
Int	*Interpretation*
ITC	International Theological Commentary
JAOS	Journal of the American Oriental Society
JB	Jerusalem Bible
JBL	*Journal of Biblical Literature*
JNES	*Journal of Near Eastern Studies*
JQR	Jewish Quarterly Review

JSOT	*Journal for the Study of the Old Testament*
JSOTSup	*Journal for the Study of the Old Testament, Supplement Series*
JSS	*Journal of Semitic Studies*
JTS	*Journal of Theological Studies*
KAT	Kommentar zum Alten Testament
LD	Lectio Divina
NCB	New Century Bible
NEB	New English Bible
NKZ	*Neue kirchliche Zeitschrift*
OBO	Orbis biblicus et orientalis
OTL	Old Testament Library
OTS	*Oudtestamentische Studiën*
RB	*Revue biblique*
RHPR	*Revue d'histoire et de philosophie religieuses*
SANT	Studien zum Alten und Neuen Testament
SBLDS	SBL Dissertation Series
SBT	Studies in Biblical Theology
TDOT	*Theological Dictionary of the Old Testament*
TWAT	*Theologisches Wörterbuch zum Alten Testament*
TRu	*Theologische Rundschau*
TSK	Theologische Studien und Kritiken
TZ	*Theologische Zeitschrift*
VD	*Verbum domini*
VT	*Vetus Testamentum*
WBC	Word Biblical Commentary
WMANT	Wissenschaftlich Monographien zum Alten und Neuen Testament
ZAW	*Zeitschrift für die altestamentliche Wissenschaft*
ZDMG	*Zeitschrift der deutschen morgenländischen Gesellschaft*
ZDPV	*Zeitschrift des deutschen Palästina-Vereins*

CHAPTER ONE

DOUBLETS AND RECURRING PHRASES:
SOME PRELIMINARY CONSIDERATIONS

The Old Testament abounds in duplications of various kinds. In some cases, extensive passages have been repeated. Isaiah 36-39, an historical appendix, bringing together additional information regarding the prophet Isaiah, is heavily dependent on 2 Kgs 18:13-20:19.[1] The Decalogue, with some variations, appears both in Exod 20:2-17 and in Deut 5:6-21.[2]

The Chronicler, drawing selectively from the books of Samuel and Kings, concentrates attention on Judah as the true Israel, and demonstrates a special interest in cultic personnel and requirements.[3] The Chronicler also shows indebtedness to certain psalms: e.g., 1 Chr 16:8-36, Asaph's hymn of thanksgiving, is dependent on Pss 105; 96; 106.[4] The book of Psalms contains a number of parallels, notably Ps 14=Ps 53.[5] Other parallels are Ps

---

[1] Otto Kaiser (*Isaiah 13-39: A Commentary* [London: SCM, 1974]) gives reasons why "the book of Kings...has the priority" (p. 367). Kaiser (pp. 403-407) also discusses Isa 38:9-20, a psalm of thanksgiving ascribed to Hezekiah. This comes from a source other than Kings. See also P. A. H. de Boer, "Notes on Text and Meaning of Isaiah xxxviii, 9-20," *OTS* 9 (1951) 170-186.

[2] The main difference in the two versions is found in the reasons given for prohibition of work on the sabbath day (Deut 5:15 refers to the exodus from Egypt and the need to treat servants in a humane way; Exod 20:11 refers to the seventh day on which Yahweh rested, after the six days of creation). Martin Noth (*Exodus: A Commentary* [OTL; London: SCM, 1962]) comments aptly, "When a piece, which, like the Decalogue, represents a catechism-like collection of the fundamental requirements of God, has been handed down over a long period and has often been repeated, the secondary appearance of expansions and alterations is not to be wondered at" (p. 20). Brevard S. Childs (*The Book of Exodus: A Critical Theological Commentary* [OTL; Philadelphia: Westminster, 1974] 85-439) discusses the Decalogue in detail and provides a comprehensive bibliography.

[3] Parallel passages are indicated and discussed by Jacob Myers, *I Chronicles: Introduction, Translation and Notes* (AB 12; New York: Doubleday, 1965); *II Chronicles: Translation and Notes* (AB 13; New York: Doubleday, 1965). Selective use of the Deuteronomistic history by the Chronicler is discussed by Myers, *1 Chronicles*, LXII-LXIII.

[4] 1 Chronicles 16:8-22=Ps 105:1-15; 16:23-33=Ps 96:1b-13; 16:34-36=Ps 106:1,47-48. Myers (*1 Chronicles*) states, "Commentators are agreed that the Chronicler used the Psalms and that they are therefore older than his work" (p. 121).

[5] Hans-Joachim Kraus, *Psalmen I* (BKAT 15/1; Neukirchen-Vluyn: Neukirchener Verlag, 1961) 103-109.

31:2–4a(H)=Ps 71:1–3; Ps 40:14–18(H)=Ps 70; Ps 60:8–14(H)=Ps 108:8–14(H). The lengthy Psalm 18 (fifty-one verses) is present in its entirety in 2 Samuel 22, in view of promises made to the Davidic dynasty, 2 Sam 7:7.[6]

Likewise, the book of Jeremiah contains several passages in which parallel material is found. Jeremiah 17:5–8 has affinities with Psalm 1, as has Jer 20:14–18 with Job 3. The historical appendix, Jeremiah 52, duplicates 2 Kgs 24:18–25:30.[7] Duplications also occur within the book itself: e.g., the Temple Sermon in Jeremiah 26 draws on an earlier version in Jeremiah 7; Jer 52:7–16 provides the basis for the historical material in 39:4–10.[8]

The book of Jeremiah also contains an unusually large number of duplicate phrases and "doublets," the area of investigation with which this study is principally concerned.

The word "doublet" is used in more than one sense with regard to double readings in Scripture. The term is used in a restricted sense to designate conflations in which variants from two or more manuscripts are combined in the text, so as to preserve different textual traditions or explanatory glosses.[9] In many instances, when the text was being standardized, the Masoretes, confronted with a word or form which they considered to be incorrect, used the device known as *Qere-Kethib*, so that the consonantal text (*Kethib*) was preserved and supplied with vocalization and a marginal notation (*Qere*) to indicate the correct way in which the form should be read.[10] The intention is always to preserve the text as completely as possible.

A quite different use of the term "doublet" refers to duplicate texts in which a single verse or several verses with a high measure of agreement are

---

[6] See F. M. Cross and D. N. Freedman, "A Royal Song of Thanksgiving: 2 Samuel 22=Psalm 18," *JBL* 72 (1953) 15–34, with important observations regarding orthography; G. Schmuttermayr, *Psalm 18 and 2 Samuel 22. Studien zu einem Doppeltext* (SANT 25; Munich: Kösel, 1971). According to P. Kyle McArter, Jr. (*II Samuel* [AB 9; Garden City, New York: Doubleday, 1984]), both 2 Samuel 22 and Psalm 18 "stem from a single original poem" (p. 473).

[7] William Holladay (*Jeremiah 2: A Commentary on the Book of the Prophet Jeremiah Chapters 26-52* [Minneapolis: Fortress Press, 1989]) claims that the direction of borrowing is from 2 Kings to Jeremiah 52, with some expansions, such as 52:10–11, an expansion of 2 Kgs 25:7 (p. 439).

[8] For the relationship between Jeremiah 7 and Jeremiah 26 (*proclamation* and *response*), see Walter Brueggeman, *Jeremiah 26-52: To Build, To Plant* (ITC; Grand Rapids: Eerdmans, 1991), p. 5. William Holladay (*Jeremiah 2*) points out that Jer 39:1–2, 4–10 "are a duplicate or adaptation of 52:4–16=2 Kgs 25:1–12" (p. 291).

[9] See J. Gerald Janzen, *Studies in the Text of Jeremiah* (HSM 6; Cambridge, Mass.: Harvard University Press, 1973) 10–33.

[10] GKC § 17. The variant textual traditions behind the forms are preserved by means of this device. See also Page H. Kelley, David S. Mynatt, and Timothy G. Crawford, *The Masorah of Biblia Hebraica Stuttgartensia* (Grand Rapids: Eerdmans, 1998) 42.

found within a single book or in different books of the OT. This is the sense in which the term is used in the present study.

Doublets in Jeremiah

Doublets occur with great frequency in the book of Jeremiah, in contexts both of prose and poetry. At least half of these doublets are internal, passages repeated in different places within the book, sometimes almost exactly duplicated, sometimes with variations that may help to explain why such verses have been duplicated. Many of the doublets are external, passages in Jeremiah that occur also in other books of the Hebrew Bible (Isaiah, Micah, Obadiah, Habakkuk, Ezekiel, Psalms, 2 Kings, Deuteronomy), especially in the case of the oracles against foreign nations (Jeremiah 46–51), often with some degree of textual freedom and flexibility.[11] When duplicate texts appear in different contexts, questions must be raised regarding the suitability of the texts within such contexts, as well as the identity of the addressee in each instance.

Recent Research on Doublets in Jeremiah

Relatively little research has been undertaken on the subject of doublets in the book of Jeremiah. The study of Franz Hubmann (1978), who deals comprehensively with Jer 11:18-12:6 (and the doublet 11:20=20:12), as well as with Jer 15:20-21 (and the doublet 15:13-14=17:3-4), leads on to a general survey of some fifty or more doublets altogether (both innerjeremianic and extrajeremianic), with charts provided.[12] This is a penetrating study, in which Hubmann examines carefully the views of nineteenth and twentieth century scholars and states his own views with clarity and well-supported arguments. He is particularly interested in the form of the doublets (whether poetry or prose, or a mixture of both). He also investigates the differences in orthography which occur in the doublets.[13] Hubmann examines passages in which only a single passage is found in the LXX *Vorlage* rather than duplicate passages

---

[11] The oracles against foreign nations will be designated as OAN, in keeping with general practice.

[12] Franz D. Hubmann, *Untersuchungen zu den Konfessionen Jer 11,18-12,6 und Jer 15,10-21* (Forschung zur Bible 30; Würzburg: Echter Verlag, 1978) 217-244; charts 219-220, 225, 235, 239-241.

[13] Hubmann, *Untersuchungen*, 238-241 (with charts). See also D. N. Freedman, A. D. Forbes, and F. I. Andersen, *Studies in Hebrew and Aramaic Orthography* (Biblical and Judaic Studies 2; Winona Lake, Indiana: Eisenbrauns, 1972) 111-124. Attention is drawn to the intra-book and inter-book parallels, but caution is advised because the sample size is small.

(doublets) as in the MT.[14] He raises the question of whether a Deuteronomistic redaction took place, but leaves the question open.[15]

Another important study of doublets in Jeremiah was undertaken by Alfred Marx in 1980.[16] He restricts himself to internal doublets, which appear principally in Jeremiah 1-25. He is interested in the hermeneutical and theological presuppositions of the redactors who were responsible for the editorial placement of text-complexes in which doublets occur or are intentionally reused. This is in keeping with the concern of Albert Condamin that each doublet needs to be considered separately with regard to its origin and meaning.[17] Marx concentrates on the intentionality that lies behind the placement of a duplicated passage, and the efforts made to adapt to a new context. He makes a particularly important contribution by concentrating attention on those to whom each doublet was addressed; quite different addressees occur in different contexts. The second placement of a passage reflects the fact that the exile has taken place and pastoral concerns are now expressed to enable those addressed to take responsibility for their actions and to come to terms with life as it is now experienced. Yahweh is still the God of Israel for those addressed, but is also the Master of the Universe. There is continuity between the past and the present. Yahweh has chastised Israel. Nevertheless, Yahweh chastises the nations as well, and restores Israel.

A more recent study (1997) is that of Jean-Daniel Macchi.[18] He takes account of the earlier studies by Hubmann and Marx. Macchi examines a number of doublets internal to the book of Jeremiah, and comes to the conclusion that three successive major periods of redaction can be inferred. He is prepared to acknowledge different stages of Deuteronomistic redaction, dealing with the theme of the judgment and condemnation of Israel (e.g., 9:14 [9:15E]=23:15; and the Tophet doublets, 7:30-33; 19:5-7; 32:34-35). This period of Deuteronomistic redaction represents the first phase in which doublets appear. A second phase is exilic or post-exilic. The theme of a new exodus now emerges (e.g., 16:14-15=23:7-8), with the assurance of salvation for Israel. A doublet originally addressed to false prophets (23:19-20) is now addressed to Israel's oppressors (30:23-24). In particular, oracles originally

---

[14] See Hubmann, *Untersuchungen,* Excursus, espec. p. 242.

[15] Hubmann, *Untersuchungen,* 244.

[16] Alfred Marx, "A propos des doublets du livre de Jérémie: Reflexions sur la formation d'un livre prophetique," in *Prophecy: Essays presented to Georg Fohrer on his sixty-fifth Birthday 6 September 1980* (ed. J. A. Emerton; BZAW 150; Berlin: Walter de Gruyter, 1980) 106-120.

[17] Albert Condamin, *Le Livre de Jérémie: Traduction et Commentaire* (Echter Bibel; Paris: Gabalda, 1936) 31.

[18] Jean-Daniel Macchi, "Les Doublets dans le Livre de Jérémie," in *The Book of Jeremiah and Its Reception* (ed. A. H. W. Curtis and T. Römer; BETL 128; Leuven: University Press, 1997) 119-150.

addressed to the nations are sometimes readdressed (e.g., 49:19-21 [Edom] is now addressed to Babylon [50:44-46]). The third phase can be seen in the MT, in the case of those doublets for which only a single occurrence appears in the LXX. These additions to the Massoretic text (e.g., 23:5-6=33:14-16, where 33:14-16 is missing in the LXX) are oriented towards Jerusalem and the return of the Davidic monarchy. The entire section, 33:14-26, is missing from the LXX. Jeremiah 33:17-18MT guarantees a permanent monarchy of the line of David as well as a permanent levitical priesthood. Macchi proposes that such hopes belong to hellenistic times.

Macchi's study offers many valuable insights. My own study of the doublets was well advanced when Macchi's helpful article was drawn to my attention. My approach has been to study all the doublets in the book of Jeremiah, with a desire to understand more fully how the book of Jeremiah evolved. In this connection, I have also undertaken a study of the many repeated phrases in the book, both within the doublets and, more frequently, in other parts of the book. Undoubtedly, major changes in Israel's history are reflected in the development of the book, as Macchi has demonstrated. In addition, many piecemeal additions and insertions in the margin were eventually incorporated in the text, before the text was finally standardized. Many of these additions, I believe, were the work of learned scribes who had a good grasp of the Jeremianic tradition and a thorough knowledge of other parts of the OT.

Studies of Recurring Phrases

Phrases and word-strings which recur in the book of Jeremiah have been of considerable interest over the years. Significant contributions have been made in this area of study by a number of scholars. I have found the work of John Bright, William Holladay, Helga Weippert, Winfried Thiel and Louis Stulman a major resource for my own independent study (chapters eleven, twelve and thirteen).[19] Both doublets and recurring phrases need to be considered as primary *data* in seeking to trace the evolution of the book of Jeremiah.

---

[19] John Bright, "The Date of the Prose Sermons of Jeremiah," *JBL* 70 (1951) 15-312; 193-212; William Holladay, "Prototype and Copies: A New Approach to the Poetry-Prose Problem in the Book of Jeremiah," *JBL* 79 (1960) 351-367; Helga Weippert, *Die Prosareden des Jeremiabuches* (Berlin: Walter de Gruyter, 1973); Winfried Thiel, *Die deuteronomistische Redaktion von Jeremia 1-25* (WMANT 41; Neukirchen-Vluyn: Neukirchener Verlag, 1973); *Die deuteronomistische Redaktion von Jeremia 26-45* (WMANT 52; Neukirchen-Vluyn: Neukirchener Verlag, 1981); Louis Stulman, *The Prose Sermons of the Book of Jeremiah* (SBLDS 83; Atlanta: Scholars Press, 1986).

The Septuagint (LXX)

The Septuagint (LXX) has always been of considerable interest in Jeremiah studies, especially since the LXX text is approximately one-eighth shorter than the MT.[20] From the time of a major study by A. W. Streane (1896), the relationship between the LXX and the MT versions of the book of Jeremiah has been of exceptional interest.[21] This has led to the conclusion by some scholars that the LXX text represents a first edition of the book of Jeremiah, followed subsequently by an expanded second edition, represented by the MT.[22] Though the date of the LXX *Vorlage* remains uncertain, in the judgment of most scholars it is a translation of the *primary* Hebrew text, a judgment in which I concur. The LXX text is of great value to those engaged in the task of textual criticism.

In the case of seven doublets (6:13-15=8:10b-12; 15:13-14=17:3-4; 23:5-6=33:14-16; 30:10-11=46:27-28; 39:1-10=52:4-16; 48:40-41=49:22; 48:5-46=Num 21:27-29), one parallel passage is missing in the LXX in each instance.[23] This has been interpreted by Friedrich Giesebrecht and others to be a deliberate deletion on the part of the translator(s), who sought to eliminate unnecessary duplication.[24] But other explanations are possible and will be discussed at the appropriate places in this study, when these particular doublets are examined.[25]

Methodology

In the following chapters, all the doublets in the book of Jeremiah will be examined (some fifty doublets altogether), in an attempt to identify the various stages by which the book of Jeremiah arrived at its present form. My translations of the doublets will be given in parallel columns, so that

---

[20] Otto Eissfeldt, *Einleitung in das Alte Testament unter Einschluss der Apokryphen und Pseudepigraphen* (Tübingen: Mohr, 1934) 391; Janzen, *Studies*, 1.

[21] A. W. Streane, *The Double Text of Jeremiah (Massoretic and Alexandrian) compared, Together with an Appendix on the Old Latin Evidence* (Cambridge: Deighton Bell, 1896).

[22] E. Tov, "Some Aspects of the Textual and Literary History of the Book of Jeremiah," in *Le Livre de Jérémie: Le Prophète et son Milieu, les Oracles et leur Transmission* (ed. P.-M. Bogaert; BETL 54; Leuven: University Press, 1981) 145-167; P.-M. Bogaert, "De Baruch à Jérémie: Les rédactions conservée du livre de Jérémie" in *Le Livre de Jérémie, les Oracles et leur Transmission* (ed. P.-M. Bogaert; BETL 54; Leuven: University Press, 1981) 168-173.

[23] Jeremiah 8:10b-12; 17:3-4; 30:10-11; 33:14-16; 39:1-10; 48:40-41; 48:45-46.

[24] F. Giesebrecht, *Das Buch Jeremia* (HAT; 1st ed.; Göttingen: Vandenhoeck & Ruprecht, 1894) xxxii. Cf. W. Rudolph, *Jeremia* (HAT 12; 3rd ed.; Tübingen: Mohr-Siebeck, 1968) 63; J. Bright, *Jeremiah* (AB 21; New York: Doubleday, 1965) LXXV n. 25.

[25] For some explanations, I am indebted to Janzen, *Studies*, 91-96. See also below, espec. pp. 28; 61 n. 26; 139; 143; 209-210.

Some Preliminary Considerations

comparisons may easily be made. In each case, the MT of *BHS* will be followed without emendation, bearing in mind Otto Kaiser's cautionary observation, "...it is not methodologically correct to take a text handed down in two different places, and to emend one on the strength of the other, when it cannot be proved that the difference came into being only in the course of the tradition of the text."[26] In the "Textual and Translational Notes" which follow, reference will also be made to the LXX text, as well as to readings in other versions.[27] This will lead on to a discussion of the relation of the doublets to one another and of the context in which each occurs.

Two doublets will serve as an illustration. In Jer 8:15=Jer 14:19b, the parallels occur within the book of Jeremiah itself; in the case of Jer 26:18b=Mic 3:12, the parallel to the Jeremiah passage occurs in the book of Micah.

JEREMIAH 8:15=JEREMIAH 14:19b

JEREMIAH 8:15
ᵃ We expected ᵃ well-being, but no good (came) ᵇ for a time ᵇ
ᶜ of healing,ᶜ but look, terror.

JEREMIAH 14:19b
ᵃ We expected ᵃ well-being, but no good (came); [and]
ᵇ for a time ᵇ ᶜ of healing,ᶜ but look, terror.

Textual and Translational Notes

ᵃ...ᵃ קַוֵּה The infinitive absolute is used as a substitute for the finite verb: GKC §113y. This is recognized in the LXX translations (συνήχθημεν; ὑπεμείναμεν).

ᵇ...ᵇ לְעֵת (8:15); וּלְעֵת (14:19b). The copula is missing in many manuscripts (14:19b) and in the translation found in the LXX.

ᶜ...ᶜ מַרְפֵּה (8:15); מַרְפֵּא (14:19b). Many manuscripts (8:15) have מַרְפֵּא.

---

[26] Otto Kaiser, *Isaiah 1-12: A Commentary* (OTL; London: SCM, 1972) 24.

[27] For the LXX text of Jeremiah, the Göttingen edition has been used: Joseph Ziegler, *Jeremias. Baruch. Threni. Epistula Ieremiae* (Septuaginta 15; Göttingen: Vandenhoeck & Ruprecht, 1957). In the case of other OT books, the LXX text is that of Alfred Rahlfs, *Septuaginta: Id est Vetus Testamentum Graece Juxta LXX Interpretes* (2 Vols.; 3rd ed.; Stuttgart: Priviligierte Württembergische Bibelanstalt, 1949).

Comment

For Rudolph, 14:19b is primary, 8:15 is secondary.[28] However, a better case can be made for the reverse situation: 14:19b is borrowed from 8:15.[29] John Berridge believes that 8:15 expresses disappointment that hopes have not been realized, using an older formula; 14:19 is complete without the addition that repeats 8:15.[30] The addition seems to have been triggered by the word מַרְפֵּא in the first half of the verse, 14:19a.

JEREMIAH 26:18b = MICAH 3:12

JEREMIAH 26:18b
[a] This is what Yahweh of hosts has said, [a] "Zion shall be ploughed as a field and Jerusalem shall be rubble [b] and the mountain of the house [c] a wooded height."[c]

MICAH 3:12
[a]"Therefore because of you [a] Zion shall be ploughed as a field and Jerusalem shall be rubble [b] and the mountain of the house [c] a wooded height."[c]

Textual and Translational Notes

[a]...[a] לָכֵן בִּגְלַלְכֶם ("Therefore because of you," Mic 3:12) has been omitted from the quotation in Jer 26:18b. The messenger formula יְהוָה צְבָאוֹת כֹּה־אָמַר has been substituted instead, in order to confirm the authenticity and authority of Micah's prophecy.[31]

[b] עִיִּים, 26:18b; עִיִּין, Mic 3:12. The quotation from Micah is exact, except for the plural ending of עִי, which appears in the Aramaic form עִיִּין in Mic 3:12, but with the regular Hebrew plural ending עִיִּים in 26:18b (cf. Ps 79:1). A few manuscripts read עִיִּים in Mic 3:12. The final *nun* may possibly be due to the following ת, for ease of pronunciation (GKC §§ 44k, 87e). In Jer 33:18LXX, εἰς ἄβατον ("desolation") is an appropriate translation for עִיִּים, but

---

[28] Rudolph, *Jeremia*, 62. Cf. Karl-Friedrich Pohlmann, *Studien zum Jeremiabuch. Ein Beitrag zur Frage nach der Entstehung des Jeremiabuches* (Göttingen: Vandenhoeck & Ruprecht, 1978) 161-162.

[29] William Holladay writes, "they fit poorly in the context of the words of the people" (*Jeremiah 1: A Commentary on the Book of the Prophet Jeremiah Chapters 1-25* [Hermeneia; Philadelphia: Fortress, 1986]) 240. Cf. William McKane, *A Critical and Exegetical Commentary on Jeremiah* (Vol.1; ICC; Edinburgh: T. & T. Clark, 1986) 191-192.

[30] John M. Berridge, *Prophet, People, and the Word of Yahweh* (Basel Studies of Theology 4; Zürich: EVZ-Verlag, 1970) p. 104, n. 175.

[31] In 33:18bLXX צְבָאוֹת is missing, secondarily inserted here in the Hebrew text. See Janzen, *Studies*, 167, 170.

Mic 3:12LXX, ὡς ὀπωροφυλάκιον ("as the hut of a garden-watcher") may reflect Isa 1:8LXX.

ᶜ לְבָמוֹת יָעַר, 26:18b; Mic 3:12; εἰς ἄλσος δρυμοῦ, 33:18bLXX; ὡς ἄλσος δρυμοῦ, Mic 3:12. The substitution of בְּהֵמוֹת ("beasts") for בָּמוֹת, first suggested by Arnold Ehrlich, has been accepted by Rudolph, Holladay and Delbert Hillers, but McKane considers the change unnecessary.[32] The phrase בְּבַהֲמוֹת יָעַר occurs in Mic 5:7 (5:8E), but the context is quite different. This proposed emendation remains debateable; the MT is probably preferable. The LXX translation (ἄλσος "sacred grove" for בָּמוֹת) carries with it overtones of an idolatrous "high place" which deserves destruction; cf. Mic 5:14MT: "I will cut off the groves (τὰ ἄλση) from your midst and I will destroy your cities."

Comment

Three considerations indicate the significance of the quotation from Mic 3:12 in the book of Jeremiah. In the first place, the words quoted are exact.[33] Secondly, the use of the messenger formula in 26:18b is intended to place emphasis on the validity of the message spoken by Micah. A third consideration is that 26:18a is similar to the superscription to the book of Micah, but concentrates attention on king Hezekiah (rather than mentioning Jotham and Ahaz as well). The rhetorical question in 26:19 implies that Hezekiah did not put Micah to death for pronouncing Zion's doom.[34] A translation of the verb נִבָּא in 26:18aMT is not present in the LXX rendering of this verse (33:18aLXX) and may well point to a later insertion in the Hebrew text to establish the fact that Micah is an authentic prophet of Yahweh.[35] The purpose of the quotation from Micah is to establish the fact that Micah was not put to death by Hezekiah for pronouncing the doom of Jerusalem; therefore Jeremiah should not be put to death for similar oracles.

The Purpose and Organization of this Study of Doublets and Recurring Phrases

Chapters two to ten are largely devoted to doublets in the book of Jeremiah, with some discussion of recurring phrases not found in the doublets. The "Confessions" are considered in chapters two and three. They contain references to Jeremiah's life and prophetic role. In thought and language, the "Confessions" are essentially Jeremianic. Some verses have been repeated later

---

[32] Arnold B. Ehrlich, *Randglossen zur Hebräischen Bibel: textkritisches, sprachliches und sachliches*, 5 (Leipzig: Hinrich's, 1912) 280; McKane, *Jeremiah 1-25*, 663.

[33] With the exception of עִיִּין = עִיִּים, discussed on page 9 (note ᵇ).

[34] Note the manuscript support for the *Qere* מִיכָה in 26:18a (cf. Mic 1:1).

[35] The *Niphal* of נבא is faithfully translated in the case of 26:9, 11, 12MT (33:9, 11, 12LXX).

(e.g., 20:12 repeats 11:20), with the intention of reasserting Jeremiah's vocational role against enemies who deserve to come under Yahweh's judgment. In chapter four, the main subject is the monarchy (Jer 21:12-23:8). Jeremiah offered a strong critique of monarchy in his own time and expected the monarchy to come to an end, since principles of justice and freedom from oppression were not upheld. Certain doublets (e.g., 23:5-6=33:14-16) point to a future king of David's line, who would embody Jeremiah's view of what constitutes ideal monarchy. Jeremiah himself did not hold out the promise of a future righteous Davidic king. Those who fostered this hope believed that they were faithful to Jeremiah's view of what monarchy should represent. Jeremiah believed fervently in the hope of an eventual return from exile. This hope was clearly expressed by a later generation of his followers (e.g., 23:7-8=16:14-15).

Chapter five is concerned with the subject of prophecy, particularly as contained in 23:9-40, a passage remarkably free from Deuteronomistic language. This section contains a number of verses dealing with false prophets, which are repeated elsewhere in later passages in the book, indicating that the perils of false prophets continued long after Jeremiah's time. Those who stood in the Jeremiah tradition faithfully followed in the footsteps of the prophet *par excellence* by denouncing "optimistic" prophets who led Yahweh's people astray.

Chapter six considers the recurring phrases in 25:1-13, a key passage introducing the OAN. This passage contains many phrases duplicated elsewhere and provides clues to the evolution of the book, as does the text and order of the OAN in the LXX. The priority of the LXX text is to be asserted; many additions have been made to the Hebrew *Vorlage* subsequently, as well as the decision to place the OAN at the end of the book. The next two chapters examine the OAN; chapter seven (Jeremiah 46-49), the oracles against the nations; chapter eight (Jeremiah 50-51), the oracles against Babylon. There is considerable interaction between Jeremiah 46-49 and Jeremiah 50-51, where oracles against various nations are also applied to the Babylonians. In addition, some verses are repeated elsewhere in the book of Jeremiah, or occur in other books of the OT as well. In some cases, learned scribes have made connections with other parts of the OT in marginal references which were later incorporated in the main text.

Chapters nine and ten examine the remaining doublets in the book: those which occur within the book of Jeremiah itself, and those which have their counterpart elsewhere in the OT. These, too, throw light on the editorial process.

Some of the doublets contain recurring phrases which also appear elsewhere in the book of Jeremiah. Many of the repeated phrases and word-strings are found outside of the doublets, frequently in "preaching passages." In chapter eleven, I have investigated prominent terms and phrases recurring throughout the book and phrases that are unique in the book of Jeremiah. In chapter twelve, I concentrate attention on phrases with parallels in non-Deuteronomistic books of the OT, many of which occur in the prophetic literature. Both Jeremiah and those who composed sections of the book which bear his name, stood firmly in the prophetic tradition. These phrases have been listed in the order of key words, following the Hebrew alphabet for ease of reference. In chapter thirteen, I examine the phrases which are common to the book of Jeremiah and the Deuteronomistic literature, by far the largest group in the book. Some of these phrases are found also in other parts of the OT. They are also listed according to the Hebrew alphabet.

In chapter fourteen, I seek to draw conclusions from the data presented, with an attempt to trace the stages by which the book of Jeremiah developed, so far as this is possible. Such matters as textual, literary and redaction criticism, and stylistic concerns, have been pursued throughout this study, in order to establish possible dates of the component parts of the book and the complicated editorial work involved. Doublets and recurring phrases provide useful clues as to how the book evolved. What is clear is that the book continued to take shape over several centuries, with numerous additions intended to interpret or reinterpret the existing text. The additions were frequently made by scribes interested in upholding the Jeremiah tradition, while demonstrating a wide familiarity with the Hebrew scriptures as a whole.

CHAPTER TWO

DOUBLETS IN THE CONFESSIONS

The so-called "Confessions" of Jeremiah are in the form of laments (or "complaints") and have traditionally included 11:18-12:6; 15:10-21; 17:14-18; 18:18-23; 20:7-18.[1] The precise limits of these units are debateable, similar to the "Servant Songs" in Deutero-Isaiah, about the boundaries of which there has always been debate.

Although a nucleus of the Confessions may indeed be derived from Jeremiah himself, the presence of various doublets lead to the conclusion that these passages have been subject to editorial revision during the process of transmission. The doublets to be investigated in chapters two and three are 11:20=20:12; 11:23b=23:12b; 15:13-14=17:3-4; 15:15d=Ps 69:8a; 15:20=1:18-19; 17:18b=1:17b; 18:20a=18:22b; 18:23b=Neh 3:37(4:5E); 20:10a=31:14a(31:13E), numbered consecutively.

1. JEREMIAH 11:20=20:12

JEREMIAH 11:20
20. ᵃ But, O Yahweh ᵃ
ᵇ of hosts,ᵇ who makes right
judgment, who tests the heart
and mind, ᶜ Let me see ᶜ your
vengeance on them, for to you
ᵈ I have revealed ᵈ my cause.

JEREMIAH 20:12
12. ᵃ O Yahweh ᵃ
ᵇ of hosts,ᵇ who tests the
righteous, who sees the
heart and mind, ᶜ Let me see ᶜ
your vengeance on them,
for to you ᵈ I have revealed ᵈ
my cause.

Textual and Translational Notes

ᵃ⁻ᵃ וַיהוָה The MT: *waw* adversative in 11:20; copulative in 20:12 (20:11 begins with *waw* adversative). The LXX does not translate *waw* in 11:20, but rightly uses the vocative in the address to Yahweh.

ᵇ⁻ᵇ צְבָאוֹת ("of hosts"). "Yahweh of hosts" occurs two hundred and eighty-five times in the OT, mostly in prophetic books, with eighty-two occurrences in the book of Jeremiah. This epithet does not occur in 11:20LXX and

---

[1] For a full discussion of different views concerning the passages generally understood to be "Confessions", see Holladay, *Jeremiah 1*, 358. The term does not adequately describe the contents of these passages, but in view of its general acceptance, I shall use this term without the quotation marks throughout this study.

20:12LXX and is missing frequently in the LXX elsewhere. In twelve instances (5:14; 15:16; 23:16; 25:27; 31:36; 32:14, 18; 33:11; 44:7; 50:34; 51:5, 57), the LXX translates with παντοκράτωρ. Otherwise in Jeremiah צְבָאוֹת is not present in the LXX; in fact, the single word κύριος is often found even when the MT has the extended phrase יְהוָה צְבָאוֹת אֱלֹהֵי יִשְׂרָאֵל (e.g., 28:14; 29:8, 21; 31:23; 35:13, 17, 18; 38:17; 42:15, 18, etc.). Was there a tendency on the part of the LXX translators to abridge the Hebrew text, especially in the case of recurring phrases?[2] Answering this question in the negative, Janzen has argued persuasively that the MT as it now stands is the result of expansionist tendencies, i.e., that צְבָאוֹת was not present in the Hebrew *Vorlage* of the LXX.[3] In the MT, יהוה צבאות is found in all the strata of the book of Jeremiah — concluding or introducing poetic oracles (e.g., 2:19; 6:6, 9; 9:6); introducing prose passages (e.g., autobiography, 27:18, 19; 32:14; biography, 35:17, 18; 38:17; the Book of Consolation, 30:8; 31:23, 25; in the OAN, 46:18, 25; 48:1). The only occurrences in the Confessions are found in 11:20(=20:12) and 11:22. Since the phrase is not found in the book of Deuteronomy, and infrequently in the Deuteronomistic literature, the probability that the phrase belongs to the redactional work of the Deuteronomists is slight. The insertion of צבאות and the more ponderous צבאות אלהי ישראל after the Tetragrammaton would seem to be the result of late scribal activity, perhaps reflecting the emphasis on divine sovereignty made by pious scribes.

c...c אֶרְאֶה ("let me see"; LXX, ἴδοιμι) - cohortative.

d...d גִּלִּיתִי Hitzig's emendation גַּלּוֹתִי (גלל) *Qal*, "I have entrusted, committed"), has been widely followed (Duhm, Volz, Rudolph, *BHS*, RSV, NEB, JB).[4] However, as McKane has indicated, the MT should be retained, in view of solid support from the versions: LXX ἀπεκάλυψα; Vg revelavi; cf. Pesh and Tg.[5]

Jeremiah 11:20bMT is repeated *verbatim* in 20:12bMT, while the LXX has minor variations.[6]

Jeremiah 11:20 in Context

Although McKane (cf. NEB, JB), following Thiel, claims that 11:18-19 is prose, 11:20 poetry, my view is that 11:18-20 is poetry and has affinities

---

[2] Giesebrecht *Jeremia*, XXV. Some two thousand seven hundred words in the MT are missing in the LXX, while only about one hundred words in the *Vorlage* of the LXX are not present in the MT.

[3] Janzen, *Studies*, 80.

[4] F. Hitzig, *Der Prophet Jeremia* (KEH 3; Leipzig: Weidmann, 1841) 95.

[5] McKane, *Jeremiah 1*, 259.

[6] ἐξ αὐτῶν (11:20b) becomes ἐν αὐτοῖς (20:12b); τὸ δικαίωμά becomes τὰ ἀπολογήματά. The translators of the Hebrew OT into Greek did not strive for absolute consistency.

with 12:1-5, also poetry.⁷ In the entire passage 11:18-12:6, only 11:21-23 is prose and is best regarded as a redactional addition which identifies those who "devised schemes" against the prophet (11:19) as the "men of Anathoth." Jeremiah 12:6 is also a redactional addition (poetry), in which "your brothers and the house of your father" (12:6) have "dealt treacherously" with the prophet.

Various attempts have been made to rearrange the position of the verses in 11:18-12:6 to provide a more logical sequence.⁸ Pioneers in this regard are Rowley and Volz.⁹ Volz inserted 12:3 between 11:20a and 11:20b. However, to divide 11:20 is to overlook the fact that this verse finds its parallel without division in 20:12. The order in the MT is followed by the LXX and other versions, and need not be changed. The Hebrew mind was not always concerned with logical consistency.¹⁰ The final form of 11:18-12:6 appears to have been satisfactory to the editors.

Phrases that differ in Jer 11:20=20:12

שֹׁפֵט צֶדֶק ("who makes right judgment," 11:20)=בֹּחֵן צַדִּיק ("who tests the righteous," 20:12). The use of שֹׁפֵט coupled with צֶדֶק introduces forensic language in the prayer of entreaty to God in 11:20.¹¹ This prayer is the response to the schemes devised by the anonymous "they" who are quoted in 11:19b. The language of the lawcourt is present also in the use of רִיבִי ("my cause/case") in 11:20b, providing a link with אָרִיב in 12:1. Another link is present between צֶדֶק in 11:20 and צַדִּיק in 12:1. Yahweh who is righteous (צַדִּיק, 12:1; cf. Ps 119:137) makes right judgment (שֹׁפֵט צֶדֶק, 11:20). בֹּחֵן צַדִּיק (20:12) may be understood as an intentional change on the part of the redactor who inserted 20:12, making a link between צַדִּיק and the synonym אֶבְיוֹן in

---

⁷ Winfrid Thiel, *Die deuteronomistische Redaktion von Jeremia 1-25* (WMANT 41; Neukirchener-Vluyn: Neukirchener Verlag, 1973) 159, considers that 11:20 and 20:12 may represent a fragment of a lament carried down in tradition as an isolated saying (prose) and fitted into 11:18-20 and 20:7-12 by a Deuteronomistic redactor.

⁸ For a useful summary of proposals regarding changes in the position of the text within 11:18-12:6, see Hubmann, *Untersuchungen,* 30-46.

⁹ H. H. Rowley, "The Text and Interpretation of Jer 11:18-12:6," *AJSL* 42 (1926) 217-227; D. Paul Volz, *Der Prophet Jeremia: Übersetzt und Erklärt* (KAT 10; Leipzig: A. Deichert, 1928) 136.

¹⁰ Johannes Pedersen (*Israel: Its Life and Culture 1-II* [Oxford: Blackwell, 1965]) writes: "For the Israelite *thinking* was not the solving of abstract problems. He does not add link to link, nor does he set up major and minor premises from which conclusions are drawn. To him thinking is to grasp a totality" (p. 108).

¹¹ See article on שפט by H. Niehr (*TWAT* 8.4; 408-428). שׁוֹפֵט צֶדֶק is descriptive of God in Ps 9:5; cf. Ps 7:12, אֱלֹהִים שׁוֹפֵט צַדִּיק. See also Deut 1:16, where שֹׁפְטִים are to judge righteously (צֶדֶק).

20:13.[12] In 20:12, the speaker is himself Yahweh's "righteous one," whom Yahweh "tests."[13] The root בחן is used six times in the book of Jeremiah. God is the one who "assays" or "tests" in 20:12; 11:20; 9:6 (9:7E); 17:10. In 6:27, Jeremiah has been made an "assayer" (בָּחוֹן) by God, to "assay" (בחן) the ways of the people. The verb is used in the Psalms predominantly in a profession of innocence, as also in Jer 20:12 (e.g., Ps 7:10; 17:3; 26:2; 139:23).[14] The terms "kidneys and heart" (כְּלָיוֹת וָלֵב, 11:20) occur together in the parallel passage (20:12) as well as in 17:10; cf. Ps 7:10; 26:2. They represent the emotional and intellectual aspects of psychical life, "heart and mind."[15] The use of כְּלָיוֹת in 12:2 provides a catchword link with 11:20. In 20:12, the participle רֹאֶה is substituted for בחן (11:20), since בחן has already been used in place of שֹׁפֵט, at the same time providing a link with אֶרְאֶה in 20:12b.

Jeremiah 11:20 is Prior to 20:12

Although the verb גלה is used in both 11:20 and 20:12, this statement of trust suits the context in Jeremiah 11 better than 20:12b in the context of Jeremiah 20, where already in 20:11 the confidence that Yahweh will deal with persecutors has been expressed.[16] Bright agrees that 20:12 may have been drawn in secondarily from 11:20, but also claims that this may have been a favorite appeal of Jeremiah, employed more than once.[17] However, the view I propose is that 11:20 belongs to the original Jeremianic nucleus of the Confessions and that 20:12 has been added editorially.

Comment

Although the Confessions are similar in form, style and language to Psalms of lament, and have a generality of meaning rather than referring to

---

[12] Marx, "A Propos des doublets," p. 107 n. 4. A few Hebrew manuscripts read צָדָק in 20:12b (cf. LXX δοκιμάζων δίκαια). צַדִּיק, however, is the *lectio difficilior* and should be retained (cf. Vg, probator justi). Artur Weiser, *Das Buch Jeremia: Übersetzt und Erklärt* (ATD 20/21; Göttingen: Vandenhoeck & Ruprecht, 1966) p. 172 n. 1 retains צַדִּיק as basically the same in cultic language as אֶבְיוֹן.

[13] D. H. Bak, *Klagender Gott - klagender Menschen* (BZAW 193; Berlin: Walter de Gruyter, 1990) 203.

[14] For a review of the OT occurrences of the root בחן, see article by M. Tsevat (*TWAT* 1.5; Stuttgart: Kohlhammer, 1972) 588–592. Elsewhere in the prophetic literature, בחן occurs only in Ezek 21:18; Zech 13:9 and Mal 3:10, 15.

[15] Elmer A. Leslie, *Jeremiah: Chronologically Arranged, Translated, and Interpreted* (New York: Abingdon Press, 1954) p. 140 n. 4, "dominant affections."

[16] Cf. Norman Ittmann, *Die Konfessionen Jeremias. Ihre Bedeutung für die Verkündigung des Propheten* (WMANT 54; Neukirchener-Vluyn: Neukirchener Verlag, 1981) p. 153 n. 11.

[17] Bright, *Jeremiah*, 133.

specific events in the life of Jeremiah (*pace* Holladay), this does not necessarily militate against attributing at least a nucleus of the Confessions to the prophet himself.[18] The Confessions (except for redactional additions) are remarkably free of Deuteronomistic language, and should not be regarded as Deuteronomistic compositions.[19] The thesis of O'Connor in her study of the Confessions is that their incorporation into the book of Jeremiah was "not a chance event but a purposeful literary editing."[20] The legitimacy of Jeremiah's prophetic vocation is asserted in the Confessions. Jeremiah's relationship to Yahweh becomes symbolic of the relationship which should exist between Israel and Yahweh.[21]

A striking fact concerning 11:20=20:12 is that the verses appear near the beginning of the first Confession and near the end of the fifth Confession, serving as an *inclusio*, linking the two Confessions together.[22] O'Connor makes the interesting observation that this repetition may have implications for the Confessions as a collection rather than as isolated units. She writes, "Though the framing doublet does not prove literary intentionality, its presence strengthens the hypothesis that the Confessions once circulated as an independent collection of poems. Moreover, the verse's repetition promises that these poems may be interpreted as a collection of poetry rather than only as independent units."[23]

Although the Confessions originated as private reflections on the part of the prophet as he wrestled with his commission and prophetic office, faced with resistance to his message and persecution, these poems were understood later as an essential part of the prophetic message. The prophet's suffering and its meaning has relevance for a suffering nation and indeed for suffering individuals. An editor added 20:12, thereby making an explicit link between the first and fifth Confessions. In shifting the emphasis of 11:20, where Yahweh is described as שֹׁפֵט צֶדֶק ("judging rightly, making right judgment"), to Yahweh

---

[18] Walter Baumgartner, *Jeremiah's Poems of Lament* (Sheffield: The Almond Press, 1987) 16.

[19] Mark S. Smith (*The Laments of Jeremiah and Their Contexts* [SBLMS; Atlanta: Scholars Press, 1990]) states: "Jeremiah's authorship of the laments (discounting discernible additions) cannot be established without doubt, but the placement of the laments within chapters 11–20 and their largely non-Deuteronomistic character support the dating of these compositions to the life of Jeremiah" (pp. xvii-xviii).

[20] Kathleen O'Connor, *The Confessions of Jeremiah: Their Interpretation and Role in Chapters 1-25* (SBLDS 94; Atlanta, Georgia: Scholars Press, 1988) 3.

[21] A. R. Diamond, *The Confessions of Jeremiah in Context* (JSOTSup 45; Sheffield Academic Press, 1987) XX.

[22] So Diamond (*Confessions*, 136) "The doublet of 20:12 with 11:20, whether it is redactional or not, seems to provide an explicit link back to the first unit." Cf. Smith (*Laments*, 2) "Jer 11:20 and 20:12 repeat, forming an envelope around the material within."

[23] O'Connor, *Confessions*, 89.

as בֹּחֵן צַדִּיק ("testing the righteous," 20:12), the editorial concern is to provide a theodicy. Yahweh, who takes up the cause of the righteous (those who suffer unjustly), will bring about their eventual vindication.

2. JEREMIAH 11:23b = 23:12b

These verses have in common the phrases כִּי־אָבִיא רָעָה and שְׁנַת פְּקֻדָּתָם.

JEREMIAH 11:23
23. And they shall have no remnant, [b] for I shall bring disaster [b] to the men of Anathoth, [c] the year of their punishment.[c]

JEREMIAH 23:12
12. Therefore their way shall be like slippery (places) [a] in darkness [a] to them, in which they will be thrust down and will fall. [b] For I shall bring disaster on them,[b] [c] the year of their punishment [c] — Oracle of Yahweh.

Textual and Translational Notes

[a...a] בָּאֲפֵלָה The translation here links "in darkness" with the previous clause, following the punctuation in the MT and the LXX. McKane follows Syr (cf. Duhm, Rudolph, Weiser, NEB) in connecting באפלה with the following phrase.[24] However, there is no difficulty in keeping to the MT, as the LXX does explicitly by introducing καὶ after ἐν γνόφῳ. בה refers back to באפלה in the previous clause.

[b...b] כִּי אָבִיא...רָעָה ("For I will bring...disaster"). The verb בוא (usually Hiphil Participle, preceded by הִנְנִי) followed by רָעָה ("evil" in the sense of "calamity, disaster," i.e., the consequence of "evil") occurs frequently in the book of Jeremiah.[25] בוא Hiphil is followed either by אֶל־ (11:23b) or by עַל (23:12); the prepositions are virtually interchangeable, e.g., 19:15; 36:31.

[c...c] שְׁנַת פְּקֻדָּתָם ("the year of their punishment"). Apart from 11:23b = 23:12b, this precise phrase occurs only in 48:44 (regarding Moab). Volz dismisses 11:23b as a prosaic addition to 11:21-23a, which he regards as poetry, claiming that since הָבִיא רָעָה and פְּקֻדָּתָם are formulaic, Jeremiah himself would hardly use שְׁנַת in this context.[26] However, פְּקֻדָּה is a term

---

[24] McKane, *Jeremiah 1*, 572.
[25] See 6:19; 11:11; 19:3; 19:15(Q); 35:17; 42:17; 45:5. Cf. Moshe Weinfeld, *Deuteronomy and the Deuteronomic School* (Oxford: Oxford University Press, 1972) 25. Weinfeld regards הבִיא רעה על as "a typical opening formula of the deuteronomic oracle of punishment" (p. 24 n. 2); cf. 1 Kgs 14:10; 21:21(Q); 2 Kgs 22:16, 20.
[26] Volz, *Jeremia*, 136. Cf. J. Vermeylen, "Essai de Redaktionsgeschichte des 'Confessions de Jérémie'," in *Le Livre de Jérémie* (ed. P.-M. Bogaert; BETL 54; Leuven:

already used by eighth century prophets, e.g., Hos 9:7 (יְמֵי הַפְּקֻדָּה), Isa 10:3 (יוֹם פְּקֻדָּה; cf. Mic 7:4). The verb פָּקַד (+ עַל) is used in 11:22 and very frequently in the book of Jeremiah in the sense of "to punish."[27] This is not surprising in view of the fact that the central *motif* in Jeremiah's proclamation is Yahweh's judgment on his people, who have forsaken him. Weippert argues that the use of פקד in such passages as 11:22; 27:8; 44:13b does not indicate a Deuteronomistic origin.[28] In any case, the idea of an appointed time for Yahweh's judgmental action (Isa 10:3, "the day of punishment"; Jer 11:23b=23:12b, "the year of their punishment") underlines its inevitability.

Comment

I take the position that Jeremiah 23:12b appears in a context of poetry and is prior to 11:23b, which is in a context of prose (11:21-23).

Jeremiah 23:9-40 comprises a collection of oracles, both in poetry (23:9-15,18-22) and prose (23:16-17, 23-40), under the superscription לַנְּבִאִים ("concerning the prophets").[29] Hyatt considered the collection to be very early, showing "no evidence of Deuteronomic editing."[30] Even Thiel finds no certain trace of editing by D in 23:9-16, apart from 23:15a, which is repeated almost verbally in 9:14H (9:15E), perhaps under the influence of 23:15a.[31]

Although the superscription in 23:9 ("concerning the prophets") has a general application to false prophets in the oracles of 23:9-40, specific reference is made to "both prophet and priest" in 23:11 (cf. 14:18b), to "the prophets of Samaria" (23:13) and to "the prophets of Jerusalem" (23:14). In due time, in "the year of their punishment," the way of false prophet and priest will be like slippery paths in darkness in which they will fall (23:12).

Leuven University Press, 1981) 257-259. He regards 11:23 as a later addition to 11:21-22, just as 23:12 is a later commentary on 23:10-11. In 11:23, the "men of Anathoth" stand for unfaithful Jews.

[27] J. Bright, "The Date of the Prose Sermons of Jeremiah," in *A Prophet to the Nations* (ed. Leo G. Perdue and Brian W. Kovacs; Winona Lake, Indiana: Eisenbrauns, 1984), 193-212 (see p. 211 n. 45); originally published in *JBL* 70 (1951) 15-35. עַל + פקד occurs both in prose (e.g., 9:24; 15:3; 23:2, 34; 25:12; 27:8; 29:32; 36:31; 44:13, 29) and poetry (e.g., 11:22; 21:14; 30:20 etc.). In spite of listing 11:22 as being in a "poetry context," Bright, *Jeremiah*, 84, treats 11:21-23 as prose in his translation.

[28] Helga Weippert, *Die Prosareden des Jeremiabuches* (BZAW 132; Berlin: Walter de Gruyter, 1973) p. 181 n. 337.

[29] The LXX mistakenly attaches ἐν τοῖς προφήταις to the end of 23:6 and transfers 23:7-8 to a position after 23:40. Vg, however, correctly interprets לנבאים as *ad prophetas*. See McKane, *Jeremiah 1*, 567-568 for a full discussion.

[30] James P. Hyatt, *The Book of Jeremiah: Introduction and Exegesis* (IB 5; New York: Abingdon Press, 1956) 989.

[31] Thiel, *Redaktion 1*, 250.

In 11:21-23, disaster will be brought by Yahweh upon "the men of Anathoth" at an indefinite but certain future time, "the year of their punishment." Is it possible to determine with precision the identity of "the men of Anathoth"? Are "both prophet and priest" in mind, as in 23:11? Or is the reference to the prophet's brothers and the house of his father (cf. 12:6)? The "men of Anathoth" are quoted as threatening the prophet with death unless he ceases to prophesy. Here we find a reinforcement of the resolve of the (unnamed) persons who "devised schemes" against Jeremiah, saying "let us cut him off from the land of the living" (11:19). Skinner has sought to locate this incident early in Jeremiah's ministry, when he supported the Josianic reform based on Deuteronomy, which outlawed the local shrines.[32] This rests in part on the assumption that because Jeremiah came from a priestly family in Anathoth (1:1), "the men of Anathoth" are members of his own family, especially in view of 12:6.[33] However, there are not sufficient grounds for establishing a precise time in Jeremiah's life to which Jeremiah's Confession in 11:18-20 refers, together with the response of Yahweh in 11:21-23. One cannot be sure that Jeremiah threw in his support for Josiah's reform or indeed that he was actively engaged in his prophetic ministry at that time.[34] The "men of Anathoth" are simply identified as those who seek the prophet's life (11:21). They wish to silence the prophet once and for all. Whether they are kinsmen or (false) prophets is not clear. The implication in Jer 11:19 is that Jeremiah had been made aware of the mounting danger to be expected from those who planned his death. His struggle with false prophets (and priests, 6:13; 8:10) is a major *motif* of the book of Jeremiah (e.g., 23:9-40; 27-29; cf. the use of the term שֶׁקֶר *passim*).[35]

The intended divine punishment of "the men of Anathoth" will leave them with no remnant (שְׁאֵרִית). In view of such passages as Ezra 2:23; Neh 7:27,

---

[32] John Skinner, *Prophecy and Religion* (Cambridge: Cambridge University Press, 1922) 110-112.

[33] Skinner, *Prophecy and Religion*, 20-21.

[34] Holladay, *Jeremiah 1*, 1, claims that Jeremiah was a boy only five years old at the time of Josiah's reform (622 BCE). According to Holladay (17), the thirteenth year of Josiah (627-626 BCE) referred to in the superscription (1:2) was actually the date of the prophet's birth. He was appointed to a prophetic ministry even before he was formed in his mother's womb (1:5; cf. the Suffering Servant, Isa 49:1; Paul, Gal 1:15). C. F. Whitley, "The Date of Jeremiah's Call," *VT* 4 (1964) 467-483, has set out the arguments which support this view; cf. Hyatt, *Jeremiah*, 779. Even if one accepts 627-626 BCE as the date of Jeremiah's call while still a youth (1:6), few passages in the book of Jeremiah would seem to apply to the circumstances of Josiah's reign. L. G. Perdue ("Jeremiah in Modern Research: Approaches and Issues" in *A Prophet to the Nations* [ed. L. G. Perdue and B. W. Kovacs; Winona Lake, Indiana: Eisenbrauns, 1984]) states categorically that "nowhere in the Jeremiah traditions do we find the prophet specifically referring to the Josianic reform, based on the Deuteronomic law code" (p. 3).

[35] T. W. Overholt, *The Threat of Falsehood* (SBT 2/16; London: SCM Press, 1970).

where "the men of Anathoth" who return from exile are numbered as one hundred and twenty-eight, the reference to "the men of Anathoth" in 11:21 and 11:23 would appear to apply to part of the community only, unless one understands the reference as hyperbolic. A parallel is to be found in 50:26-27, regarding Babylon, a polemical passage entreating that no remnant should be left, at "the time of their punishment."[36]

The Triad ("Sword, Famine, Pestilence")

Considerable interest attaches to the references to חֶרֶב ("sword") and רָעָב ("famine") in 11:22, two of the triad of "sword, famine, and pestilence (דֶּבֶר)" which occurs so frequently in the book of Jeremiah. Another occurrence in the Confessions is in 18:21, where "famine" and "sword" are referred to, in this order, as well as the phrase הֲרֻגֵי מָוֶת, which McKane translates as "mortally wounded," and the phrase מֻכֵּי־חֶרֶב, a second reference in this verse to "the sword."[37] A full discussion of the use of the triad will be undertaken with reference to 21:9=38:2, a doublet of exceptional importance regarding the composition of the book of Jeremiah (see below, chap. nine, p. 201[note ᵇ⁻⁻⁻ᵇ]; chap. eleven, pp. 203-204). However, since 18:21 occurs within a Confessions passage, some preliminary observations concerning the triad are in order.

Poetic passages in the book of Jeremiah refer primarily to "the sword" as the predicted agent of destruction (e.g., 5:17; 9:15; 15:9; 25:31). Specifically, "the sword of Yahweh" (חֶרֶב לַיהוה) is referred to in 12:12 (cf. 47:6, regarding the destruction of the Philistines, and 26:10LXX, where חֶרֶב (46:10MT), perhaps originally חַרְבּוֹ, is translated as μάχαιρα τοῦ κυρίου.[38] In Jeremiah 46-51, apart from 47:6, only "sword" is mentioned (e.g., 46;14, 16; 48:2; 49:37; 50:16, 35, 36, 37).[39]

Other references in poetic sections are 2:30 חַרְבְּכֶם ("your [own] sword"); 5:12, in a quotation from those who claim that they are in no danger of seeing "sword or famine"; 14:18, חַלְלֵי־חֶרֶב ("those slain by the sword") in the field, and תַּחֲלוּאֵי רָעָב ("the diseases of famine") in the city. Holladay has an instructive comment regarding 14:18, "...though the pairs 'pestilence, sword'

---

[36] Holladay draws attention to the fact that 11:23 and 50:26 are the only OT passages where a negative + הָיָה שְׁאֵרִית ל appears (*Jeremiah 1*, 403).

[37] McKane, *Jeremiah 1*, 435. McKane (p. 440) also refers to Kimchi, who glosses מות הרני as ימותו; cf. JB, "die of plague."

[38] Since וְשָׁבְעָה follows, the pronominal ו could have dropped out by haplography. See Robert P. Carroll, *Jeremiah: A Commentary* (OTL; London: SCM Press, 1986) 763.

[39] In 48:10, חַרְבּוֹ ("his sword") comes within a curse (in prose). Volz (*Jeremiah*, p. 405 n. 2) treats this verse as a gloss and finds a parallel in Judg 5:23. The MT in Jer 50:38 reads חֹרֶב ("drought"), which fits the immediate context regarding the drying up of the waters, but could be pointed חֶרֶב ("sword," cf. Syr), completing the series of references to חֶרֶב in the preceding verses, 50:35-37 (see Volz, *Jeremiah*, 430c).

and 'famine, pestilence' appear in pre-Jeremianic passages (Exod 5:3 [JE]; 2 Sam 24:13; Amos 4:10), there is no occurrence before Jer. of the pair 'sword, famine'."[40] The two passages in the Confessions, 11:22 ("sword, famine") and 18:21 ("famine, sword") together with the phrases הֲרֻגֵי מָוֶת and מְכֵי־חֶרֶב are among the few occurrences where just the two terms חֶרֶב and רָעָב are brought together in the book of Jeremiah (see also 5:12; 14:13, 15 [bis], 16, 18; 42:16; 44:18).[41] Elsewhere, the triad חרב, רעב and דֶּבֶר occurs very frequently and mostly in prose passages, e.g., 14:12; 21:9=38:2; 24:10; 27:8, 13; 32:24, 36; 42:17, 22; 44:13. Sometimes the nouns occur in a different order: 21:7 ("pestilence, sword, famine"); 15:2, which adds שְׁבִי ("captivity") as a fourth term; 34:17 ("sword, pestilence, famine"). Jeremiah 28:8 has the sequence "war, famine and pestilence." The triad will be discussed more fully in connection with the doublet 21:9=38:2 (see below, chap. nine, p. 201[note b...b]). Are 11:22 and 18:21 the result of redactional activity? The view taken in this study is that 18:21 is an authentic part of the prayer for vengeance (18:21-22), whereas 11:22 is editorial.[42] There is a reference in Jer 18:21 to "famine, sword and pestilence," but the term הֲרֻגֵי מָוֶת ("those who die by pestilence," literally, "slain by death") is unique and represents a stage in the process leading to a standardizing of the classical formula חֶרֶב, רָעָב and דֶּבֶר. An interesting parallel to this passage is found in 9:20 (9:21E), where "death" is personified but represents "pestilence." McKane has stated convincingly that דַּבֵּר at the beginning of 9:21MT (9:22E) really represents a marginal comment, in the form of the noun דֶּבֶר.[43] This was originally intended to interpret מָוֶת, but when incorporated into the Hebrew text was changed into a *Piel* imperative of the verb דבר.

In the LXX and Syr the phrase דַּבֵּר כֹּה נְאֻם־יְהוָה is missing at the beginning of 9:21. Sept.^OL and Theodotion, with the reading θανάτῳ, provide the

---

[40] Holladay, *Jeremiah 1*, 435.

[41] Weippert's discussion of these pre-forms is illuminating (*Die Prosareden*, 158-160). She observes that in five instances (5:12; 14:13, 15; 42:16; 44:18) they occur in a context of citation.

[42] *Contra* Bernard Duhm, *Das Buch Jeremia* (HKAT 11; Tübingen: J. B. Mohr, 1901) 159 ("Pseudojeremia") and Carl H. Cornill, *Das Buch Jeremia* (Leipzig: Tauchnitz, 1905) 227, who consider 18:21-23 to be redactional. This is also the opinion of Ulrike Eichler in her (unpublished) doctoral dissertation, *Der klagende Jeremia. Eine Untersuchung zu den Klagen Jeremias und ihrer Bedeutung zum Verstehen seines Leiden* (University of Heidelberg, 1971) 71. Diamond (*Confessions*, 91-94), however, puts forward linguistic arguments regarding the vocabulary and expressions used in this passage which occur only here or in Jeremianic poetry (p. 247 n. 19) and concludes (p. 94) that Eichler's argument is not well-founded. He specifically challenges her assumption that the presence of a "doublet" (in this instance, "they have dug a pit") always demonstrates the secondary character of a text.

[43] McKane, *Jeremiah 1*, 208-209.

clue that the word דָּבָר was intended as an interpretation of מָוֶת. McKane also notes that in the case of 18:21, Kimchi glosses הֲרֻגֵי מָוֶת as ימותו בדבר.[44]

The prose passage 11:21-23 is to be regarded as editorial, in some measure influenced by 18:21. Jeremiah's "enemies" (אַנְשֵׁיהֶם, 18:21), referred to in 18:20 ("they have dug a pit for my life," the verb כָּרוּ does not have an antecedent subject), have become more precisely the אַנְשֵׁי עֲנָתוֹת in 11:21; "their youths" (בַּחוּרֵיהֶם) in 18:21 are referred to in 11:22 as those who "shall die by the sword." O'Connor, who regards 11:21-23 as redactional, also observes that "the language of punishment wrought by sword and famine is generally reserved in the book of Jeremiah to describe punishment upon the whole people."[45]

This examination of 11:23b=23:12b in context has led to the conclusion that 23:9-15 has received little editorial modification, and represents Jeremiah's consistent diatribe against false prophets. Within the first Confession, 11:23b editorially reproduces the phrases כִּי־אָבִיא רָעָה and שְׁנַת פְּקֻדָּתָם from 23:12b. Indeed, the prose unit 11:21-23 is best considered as editorial, reflecting the language of the third Confession found in 18:21. The editorial passage 11:21-23 stands within the Jeremiah tradition, but has the purpose of identifying Jeremiah's enemies as "the men of Anathoth." All one knows regarding "the men of Anathoth" is that they sought to silence the prophet, threatening him with death if he failed to cease prophesying. This redactional passage provides a divine response to Jeremiah's prayer for vengeance against his enemies (11:18-21).

3. JEREMIAH 15:13-14 = JEREMIAH 17:3-4

Jer 15:13-14, in the second Confession, appears again in 17:3-4MT, although 17:3-4 and the two preceding verses (17:1-2) do not appear in the LXX.

JEREMIAH 15:13-14
13. Your wealth and ᵃ treasures ᵃ
I will give as plunder
ᵇ without price,ᵇ
ᶜ both for all your sins ᶜ
ᵈ and in all your territories.ᵈ
ᵉ Indeed, I will cause your
enemies to cross over ᵉ
ᶠ into a land ᶠ you do not know.
For a fire ᵍ is kindled ᵍ
in my anger; ʰ against you (pl.) ʰ

JEREMIAH 17:3-4
3. [...in the mountain country]. Your wealth (and)
ᵃ all your treasures ᵃ
I will give as plunder,
ᵇ your high places ᵇ
ᶜ as the price of sin ᶜ
ᵈ in all your territories ᵈ
4. Indeed, you will let your hand drop from your inheritance which I gave you

---

[44] McKane, *Jeremiah 1*, 440.
[45] O'Connor, *Confessions*, 18. In n. 17, she lists the passages: 14:12-15, 18; 15:6, 16; 21:7-9; 27:13; 29:18; 38:2; 42:7, 22; 44:12, 13, 18, 27.

it is kindled.

and ^{e} I will cause you to serve your enemies^e ^{f} in a land ^{f} which you did not know, for ^{g} you have kindled ^{g} a fire; in my anger it will burn ^{h} forever.^{h}

Textual and Translational Notes

$^{a...a}$ וְאוֹצְרוֹתֶיךָ (15:13), כָּל־אוֹצְרוֹתֶיךָ (17:3). The MT of 15:13 is substantiated by the LXX. How does one account for this doublet (15:13-14=17:3-4) and for the variations in the Hebrew text? The most helpful solution is that proposed by Janzen, who notes that 15:11 and 17:1-4 would have stood in adjacent columns in an ancient manuscript.[46] He surmises that a marginal variant to 17:1-4 in another manuscript tradition was wrongly inserted in chap. 15. However, one need not consider 15:12 and 17:1 (which have only the single word בַּרְזֶל in common) to have been part of the marginal variant or correction, which could have represented only the doublet 15:13-14=17:3-4.

$^{b...b}$ בִּמְחִיר לֹא ("without price," 15:13), בָּמֹתֶיךָ ("your high places," 17:3). The reference to בָּמוֹת ("high places"), is quite appropriate in 17:3, in view of the idolatrous practices referred to in 17:2.[47] בָּמֹתֶיךָ בְּחַטֹּאת is translate "your high places as the price of sin,"" i.e., also given by Yahweh as booty.[48] בִּמְחִיר לֹא ("without price," 15:13) is intended to convey the same general sense as לָבַז ("as booty"), and is suitably rendered in the LXX by ἀντάλλαγμα. Holladay offers another possibility, i.e., that לֹא governs all three phrases that follow in the MT.[49]

$^{c...c}$ וּבְכָל־חַטֹּאתֶיךָ (15:13), בְּחַטֹּאת (17:3), בְּ of price. The text in 15:13 has been modified by the addition of the 2d pl. pronominal suffix to match the form of the following בְּכָל־גְּבוּלֶיךָ.

$^{d...d}$ וּבְכָל־גְּבוּלֶיךָ (15:14), בְּכָל־גְּבוּלֶיךָ (17:4). The *waw* before each phrase in 15:13 gives the sequence ו...ו, "both"..."and." The בְּ in this instance is best taken as locative.[50]

---

[46] Janzen, *Studies*, 133.

[47] *Contra* Bright, *Jeremiah*, 118. L. C. Allen ("More Cuckoos in the Textual Nest: At 2 Kings XXIII.5; Jeremiah XVII 3,4; Micah III.3; Vi.16(LXX); 2 Chronicles XX.25(LXX)," JTS NS 24 [1973] 70-71) has suggested that בָּמֹתֶיךָ may have been an exegetical annotation, specifying more precisely the sin for which punishment was to befall the people (p. 71). If indeed Deuteronomistic expansion is present in 17:2, this could have carried over into 17:3.

[48] Ronald J. Williams, *Hebrew Syntax* (University of Toronto Press, 1967) § 246, בְּ of price or exchange.

[49] Holladay, *Jeremiah 1*, 456.

[50] Williams, *Hebrew Syntax*, § 240.

e...e וְהַעֲבַרְתִּי אֶת־אֹיְבֶיךָ ("I will cause your enemies to cross over," 15:14); וְהַעֲבַדְתִּיךָ אֶת־אֹיְבֶיךָ ("I will cause you to serve your enemies," 17:4). The LXX in 15:14, καταδουλώσω σε, coincides with the MT reading in 17:4, suggesting that וְהַעֲבַדְתִּיךָ stood in the Hebrew *Vorlage* of 15:14, from which the LXX translation was made. This supports the view, which will be developed below, that because the pronominal suffix is omitted in וְהַעֲבַרְתִּי we do not have a case of confusion between ר and ד, but rather that a change has been made deliberately in the Hebrew text in the process of redaction.[51]

f...f בְּאֶרֶץ , anarthrous, ("in a land," 15:14); בָּאָרֶץ (17:4). The LXX in 15:14, ἐν τῇ γῇ , uses the definite article, which suggests the possibility that בָּאָרֶץ (as in 17:4) was the reading in the Hebrew *Vorlage*. The LXX translation may reflect the fact that the land in question (Babylonia) was well-known to the translator, rather than an indefinite "land."

g...g קָדְחָה ("it is kindled," 15:14); קְדַחְתֶּם ("you have kindled," 17:4). The sudden change from 2d s. to 2d pl. in 17:4 has been emended in 15:14 to the intransitive קָדְחָה (LXX ἐκκέκαυται). Holladay proposes that the Hebrew text in 17:4 originally read קָדַחְתָּ ("I have kindled against you," i.e., dative of disadvantage), and that a final ךְ was confused with a final ם in the process of transmission.[52]

h...h עֲלֵיכֶם ("against you," 15:14); עַד־עוֹלָם ("forever," 17:4). עֲלֵיכֶם represents an abrupt change from 2d s. to 2d pl. Unless one adopts the reading in 17:4, עַד־עוֹלָם, the MT reading עֲלֵיכֶם should stand.[53] Holladay follows Hubmann in explaining the plural form "over you" as referring to both Jeremiah and his enemies.[54]

Other variations between 15:13-14 and 17:3-4 are as follows: 17:3 begins with הֲרָרִי בַשָּׂדֶה, literally "my mountain in the field," (NEB "in the mountain country," i.e., vocalizing as הֲרָרֵי and attaching the phrase to 17:2; cf. Syr). McKane also connects the phrase with the preceding verse, which deals with idolatrous practices, translating "on solitary(?) mountains."[55] This seems more satisfactory than Holladay's emendation הַר רִיב שָׁדוּד ("the mountain of strife is devastated").[56] A phrase at the beginning of Jer 17:4 is not carried

---

[51] Holladay, *Jeremiah 1*, 447. Holladay, following Hubmann (*Untersuchungen*, 233), holds out the possibility that "...vv 13-14 are an ironic variant of 17:3-4, an adaptation of that passage as an address to Jrm" (p. 448). Diamond (*Confessions*, 52) also retains the reading וְהַעֲבַרְתִּי in 15:14. Cf. Vermeylen, "Redaktionsgeschichte," p. 266 n. 80. Carroll, on the other hand, accepts וְהַעֲבַדְתִּיךָ as correct in 15:14, since this reading does occur in many manuscripts, as well as in 17:4 (*Jeremiah*, 25). This reading, however, could reflect a textual tradition originally taken over from 17:4, and then consciously changed.

[52] Holladay, *Jeremiah 1*, 445.
[53] Cf. McKane, *Jeremiah 1*, 344.
[54] Holladay, *Jeremiah 1*, 447; Hubmann, *Untersuchungen*, 271.
[55] McKane, *Jeremiah 1*, 384-385; cf. *BHS*; Carroll, *Jeremiah*, 348.
[56] Holladay, *Jeremiah 1*, 483, 485.

over to 15:13: וְשִׁמַּטְתָּה וּבְךָ מִנַּחֲלָתְךָ אֲשֶׁר נָתַתִּי לָךְ ("Indeed, you will let your hand drop from your inheritance which I gave you"). This is either a secondary addition, or a phrase omitted in the marginal correction of 17:3-4 which found its way into 15:10-21 as the intrusive 15:13-14. The problem here is וּבְךָ, which is probably best treated as a corruption of an original יָדְךָ, to be translated, "You will lose possession of your inheritance which I gave you."[57]

The Context of Jer 15:13-14

This doublet comes at the conclusion of a prose passage, Jer 15:10-12. The passage begins with an impassioned expression of lament, אוֹי־לִי ("Woe is me!," 15:10), an exclamation found also in 10:19, and in the form אוֹי־נָא לִי in 4:31 and 45:3.[58] Jeremiah's lament is addressed to his mother, deploring the fact that she bore him to become אִישׁ רִיב וְאִישׁ מָדוֹן ("a man of strife and contention"). The phrase רִיב וּמָדוֹן is also found in Hab 1:3. These terms in Hab 1:3 and Jer 15:10 are not necessarily legal terms.[59] Habakkuk 1:3 also contains the couplet שֹׁד וְחָמָס ("destruction and violence"), non-legal terms, found in reverse order חָמָס וָשֹׁד in Amos 3:10 and Jer 6:7. The context in Hab 1:2-4 certainly specifies lawlessness and the perversion of justice. Yet, "lending and borrowing" in 15:10, which the prophet denies as descriptive of his behaviour, seems to have been the basis on which "all of them curse" him. The prophet is probably using a proverbial saying regarding "lending and borrowing" which leads inevitably to unhappy consequences for the person involved.[60]

A crisis in the prophet's vocation is represented in 15:10. Jeremiah feels that he is unjustly the victim of oppression. The divine reply to his lament, 15:11-12, to which 15:13-14 has been added, is similar to 12:5 in its unexpected challenge. A suggested translation for 15:11, 12 is as follows:

11. Surely those of you who are left will benefit;
    (yet) surely I will set the enemy upon you

---

[57] I adopt this proposal of J. D. Michaelis, *Observationes Philologicae et Criticae in Jeremiae Vaticinia et Threnos* (Göttingen: Vandenhoeck & Ruprecht, 1793). He has been followed by virtually all commentators. Cf. the phrase תַּשְׁמֵט יָדְךָ in Deut 15:3.

[58] Although 4:31 and 10:19 represent the voice of the community, the subject of the lament in 45:3 is Baruch. Jeremiah speaks on his own behalf in 15:10, as does Isaiah in Isa 6:5. See also Wanke, *Untersuchungen*, 215-218; E. Gerstenberger, "Jeremiah's Complaints: Observations on Jer 15:10-21," *JBL* 82 (1963) 393-408.

[59] Cf. McKane, *Jeremiah 1*, 346; Diamond, *Confessions*, p. 224 n. 44.

[60] Douglas R. Jones points to the prohibition of lending for interest in Deut 23:19, reflected in Ps 15:5 as one of the requirements for worshippers in the entrance liturgy in the Temple (*Jeremiah* [NCB; Grand Rapids, Michigan: Eerdmans, 1992] 220). In 15:10 the prophet claims that he has fulfilled the conditions for being a faithful follower of Yahweh and has done nothing to incur hostility and cursing.

in a time of calamity and in a time of distress.
12. Can one break iron, iron from the north and bronze?[61]

In vv.11-12 a note of hope is sounded for the remnant, those who will be left when disaster falls, including Jeremiah himself. However, since the prophet is lamenting the personal cost of his vocation, he is now being sternly reminded that he must continue to proclaim a message of inevitable judgment. Yahweh will indeed set (the prophetic perfect is used) the enemy upon his people. The rhetorical question in 15:11, expecting a negative answer, refers to the inevitability of the Babylonian invasion and conquest, "iron from the north," which cannot be broken.[62] Yahweh is reaffirming the message which the prophet has been commissioned to proclaim. He must not shrink from the burden of the message, or accommodate the message to those who would deny it (cf. 15:19). As Yahweh's spokesman, he must remain faithful to the message which has been entrusted to him.

A redactor, confronted with 15:13-14 in the margin at this point, an intrusive passage from 17:3-4, incorporates these verses into Yahweh's answer to the prophet's lament, making a significant change in 15:14 by substituting וְהַעֲבַרְתִּיךָ for the original reading וְהַעֲבַדְתִּיךָ (17:4). This change underlines the fact that Jeremiah is being personally addressed; Yahweh will cause his enemies to pass over into a land "you do not know." This latter phrase is used in Deut 28:33 regarding a nation (עַם) "you have not known."[63]

Already the transition is being made to the final statement in 15:14, "against you [plural] it [i.e., a fire] is being kindled," where the reference seems to be made intentionally to include both Jeremiah and his enemies.[64] Jeremiah will not escape the effect of judgment entirely and indeed, as the redactor well knows, Jeremiah was taken against his will to Egypt (42:19; 43:4-6). The phrase "for a fire is kindled in my anger" (כִּי־אֵשׁ קָדְחָה בְאַפִּי) occurs in Deut 32:22. This use of Deuteronomistic language in 15:14 and 17:4 is in all likelihood an indication of the hand of the redactor.

---

[61] In this translation, I translate אִם־לֹא...אִם־לֹא as "surely...surely," as in 49:20. שֵׁאֲרִיתְךָ is substituted for שֵׁרִיתְךָ (MT), following Vg, Tg and Aquila. שְׁאֵרִיתְךָ also provides a catch-word link with שְׁאֵרִיתָם in 15:9 (cf. אָמֵן in 15:10, a link with אִם in 15:8). פָּגַע ב (Hiphil) is translated as in Isa 53:6. In Jer 15:12, הֲיָרֹעַ (ה interrogative with Qal imperfect of רָעַע II ("to break") is treated as impersonal, "Can one break?").

[62] McKane states convincingly, "...it is improbable that מִצָּפוֹן can be disengaged from 'the enemy from the north' in this short verse" (Jeremiah 1, 349).

[63] Cf. Deut 28:36, a nation (גּוֹי) "that neither you nor your fathers have known"; Jer 5:15; 16:13; Deut 28:64, "other gods" which "neither you nor your fathers have known"; Jer 22:28, Jehoiachin and his children will be hurled into "a land which they do not know."

[64] Hubmann, Untersuchungen, 271.

The Absence in the LXX of 17:1–4

The question as to why 17:1–4 is absent in the LXX is met by Janzen's proposal that this is the result of haplography, an instance of homoioteleuton, since יהוה is the final word in 16:21MT and also in the phrase כֹּה אָמַר יהוה at the beginning of 17:5, which is not present in the LXX.[65] Rather than viewing the absence of 17:1–4 as an example of deliberate omission, Janzen states, convincingly, that "G is marked by a high incidence of haplography, which in many instances can be shown to have occurred in the Hebrew *Vorlage*."[66] Traces of interaction between 15:14 and 17:4 are discernible, as McKane has pointed out, in Sept ^{OL}, in Aquila, Symmachus and Theodotion, as well as in Syr.[67]

The Relationship Between 15:13–14 and 17:3–4

In general, there is a consensus among exegetes that 17:3–4 is the primary passage, secondarily inserted after 15:12. However, Reventlow claims that 15:13–14, interpreted as applying to the community, is a natural continuation of 15:12, and has its original place here.[68] Hubmann, on the other hand, in a careful and detailed study of 15:10–21, interprets 15:13–14 as applicable to Jeremiah himself, rather than to the people, as also in 17:3–4.[69] Holladay adopts a similar view, upholding the integrity of the MT, the rightness of 15:13–14 in the present position, as relating to Jeremiah himself rather than to the nation.[70]

In making an analysis of 15:10–21, much depends on a decision regarding the opening words of 15:11. If one follows LXX γένοιτο δέσποτα (which presupposes אָמֵן יְהוָה as the Hebrew *Vorlage*), Jeremiah continues to be the speaker, and after the plaintive lament of 15:10, addressed to his mother, now addresses Yahweh directly. However, if one follows the MT אָמַר יְהוָה, Yahweh is now replying to the prophet after the complaint voiced in 15:10.

The position taken in this study is as follows: 15:10, the prophet's lament, is followed by Yahweh's reply, 15:11–14. The intrusive verses,

---

[65] Janzen, *Studies*, 117.
[66] Janzen, *Studies*, 120.
[67] McKane, *Jeremiah 1*, 384.
[68] H. Graf Reventlow, *Liturgie und prophetisches Ich bei Jeremia* (Gütersloh: Gerd Mohn, 1963) 215. In his judgment, 17:3–4 may indeed be a second genuine occurrence.
[69] Hubmann, *Untersuchungen*, 233, 267–272. He states (p. 267), "A brief comparison of 17,3f. with 15,13f. shows further that the variations also observed here can in no way go back to arbitrariness or a poor textual tradition, but represent likewise an example of conscious accommodation."
[70] Holladay, *Jeremiah 1*, 455.

15:13–14, have been adapted redactionally, differing from 17:3–4 by substituting וְהַעֲבַרְתִּי (15:14) for וְהַעֲבַדְתִּיךָ (17:4) and עֲלֵיכֶם (15:14) for עַד־עוֹלָם (17:4). The pattern of lament followed by divine answer is repeated in 15:15–21: the lament of the prophet, 15:14–18; Yahweh's reply, 15:19–21.

Jeremiah 15:13–14 in the Context of 15:10–14

In order to interpret 15:13–14 in the context of 15:10–14, a closer examination of this passage is needed. The question must be raised at the outset as to whether the lament in 15:10 is the lament of an individual or a communal lament. Arguments for the latter have been put forward by Reventlow, who claims that a collective interpretation is to be placed on 15:10–18, in which the prophet is acting as intercessor on behalf of the community, in a cultic-liturgical role; i.e., the speaker is the prophet in his official role, representing the community.[71] Although the first person singular is used in 15:10, the contours between individual and community vanish in a statement which is to be interpreted as a collective lament. This is not an expression of the personal distress of Jeremiah in relation to his prophetic call. The personality of the prophet thoroughly recedes behind the characteristic form of the prophet as speaker in his official role. Carroll also takes 15:10 to be a communal lament rather than an individual lament spoken by Jeremiah.[72] He observes that the only identifiable mother in the tradition is the communal one, Rachel (31:15; cf. 50:12).

Conversely, if 15:10 is interpreted in the light of 15:15–21, where 15:15–18 may be understood as an individual lament, especially in the light of the divine reply with its conditional promise that כְּפִי תִהְיֶה ("you shall be as my mouth," 15:19), the prophet being set over against the people (15:20; cf. 1:18) as "a fortified wall of bronze," we are dealing with the outburst of an individual rather than with a lament of the community.[73]

McKane sums up the situation very aptly when he refers to the prophet's reaction to the day of his birth (cf. 20:14; Job 3:3) as having "the appearance of a singular rather than a collective representational activity" and states further, "we should envisage a prophet bowing beneath the burden of his vocation, unable to bear the injustice that he should be caught up in an insoluble conflict with his own people."[74]

---

[71] Reventlow, *Liturgie,* 210–228, esp. pp. 217–218.

[72] Carroll, *Jeremiah*, 326.

[73] Holladay's view that 15:20–21 is a secondary addition does not alter the pattern of dialogue, in which Jeremiah makes an individual lament, to which Yahweh replies (*Jeremiah 1*, 449, 465).

[74] McKane, *Jeremiah 1*, 346. In general, the view that the Confessions contain autobiographical accounts of the prophet's individual struggles is widely held, e.g., Skinner, *Prophecy and Religion*, 201–203; E. A. Leslie, *Intimate Papers of Jeremiah* (Boston

Jeremiah 15:10 is therefore to be regarded as a cry of individual lament from the prophet himself. The Confessions contain many such private utterances, which were presumably not originally intended as a public proclamation. These outpourings, fragmentary in nature, represent the prophet struggling with his vocation at the deepest possible level. The emotional overtones of anguish are powerfully present, not only because of the persecution which the prophet has endured (15:10, "all of them curse me"), but because Yahweh has been "like a deceitful brook, like waters that fail" (15:18).

One can only speculate regarding the history of the Confessions leading up to their present form and final position in the book of Jeremiah. It may well be that the original autobiographical portions of the Confessions were written down by Jeremiah himself. In all probability, they came subsequently into the hands of Baruch, Jeremiah's faithful scribe and amanuensis.[75] Baruch acted as the original custodian of this and other aspects of the Jeremiah tradition. In the course of time, editorial additions were made by others who sought to safeguard and to interpret the prophet's message to later generations. In this way, a new element was added to the prophetic proclamation. The experience of the prophet himself became part of the message. As Smith has stated so well, "Within the context of the divine speeches, the laments with their human complaints and divine responses become part of the portrait of the special relationship between Jeremiah and Yahweh," symbolic of Israel's relationship with Yahweh.[76]

University Press, 1953); Hubmann, "Jer 18,18-23 im Zusammenhang der Konfessionen," in *Le Livre de Jérémie* (ed. P. -M.Bogaert; BETL 54; Leuven: Leuven University Press, 1981) 271-296, esp. 296. Berridge claims that the Confessions were spoken in public, as a part of Jeremiah's proclamation (*Prophet*, 157). O'Connor claims more convincingly that the Confessions have been inserted editorially in the book "to establish the authenticity of Jeremiah's claim to be the true prophet of Yahweh" (*Confessions*, 85).

[75] Cf. James Muilenburg, "Baruch the Scribe" in *Proclamation and Presence: Old Testament Essays in Honour of Gwynne Henton Davies* (ed. J. I. Durham and J. R. Porter; London: SCM, 1970) 215-238. He writes, "He was a person of some eminence, one who was favourably known to his professional colleagues" (p. 228); "...all the speeches reported by Baruch, whether Jeremiah's or those of others, have the same style and terminology" (p. 241). The question of whether or not Baruch played any role in preserving and transmitting material found in the Confessions is not raised by Muilenburg, but he does suggest that Baruch may have had a major hand in compiling and editing the material in 1:1-45:5 (p. 244). Gunther Wanke argues that one can no longer speak of a "Baruch document," although he agrees that Baruch stood in a special relationship of trust to Jeremiah (*Untersuchungen zur sogenannten Baruchschrift* [BZAW 122; Berlin: Walter de Gruyter, 1971] p. 147). Claus Rietzschel earlier identified blocks of tradition that lie behind the book of Jeremiah (*Der Problem der Urrolle: Ein Beitrag zur Redaktionsgeschichte des Jeremiabuches* [Gütersloh: Gerd Mohn, 1966]). In his view, the contents of the original scroll dictated by Jeremiah to Baruch (36:2) are to be found in Jeremiah, chaps. 1-6, which seems very probable.

[76] Smith, *Laments*, 62.

We are not able to pinpoint chronologically the exact moments in the prophet's experience which evoked the Confessions. The purpose in inserting them editorially in Jeremiah 11-20 was not to place emphasis on them as autobiography, but to present a theodicy. This has been aptly summarized by Diamond, "The Confessions serve a distinctly apologetic purpose of constructing a theodicy of Yahweh's judgment upon Judah."[77]

Jeremiah 17:3-4 in Context

Except for the change to the second person, these two verses follow readily on 17:1-2, describing the judgment which will fall upon Judah in view of the sin which is permanently written "on the tablet of their heart" (17:1). However, in 15:13-14, the passage has been adapted in order to make it a meaningful continuation of Yahweh's answer to the prophetic lament in 15:10. The reference in 17:1 to the sin of Judah being inscribed on "the horns of their altars" indicates that the cultic system as practised in Jeremiah's day is far removed from its original intention and function. Rather than symbolizing Yahweh's protection of his people, the horns of the altars now represent syncretistic practices and Baal worship (cf. 2:20-28) which alienate his people from their god. Although Volz emends כִּזְכֹר בְּנֵיהֶם to כְּזִכָּרוֹן בָּהֶם at the beginning of 17:2, there is no need to abandon the MT at this point, since the reference to sons "remembering" their altars and Asherim underlines their continuing idolatrous attitudes, which demonstrate that their sin is written indelibly with a pen of iron, and for which they have incurred Yahweh's permanent anger (17:1, 4).

SUMMARY

The conclusions reached in this chapter may be summarized as follows:

(a) The Confessions are similar to Psalms of Lament in form, style and language.

(b) These passages are remarkably free from Deuteronomistic language; a nucleus may indeed go back to the prophet himself.

(c) The Confessions do not refer to specific events in the life of Jeremiah, but represent in general his struggles with vocation and his reaction to persecution by enemies.

(d) Passages missing in the LXX version of the Confessions were not excised deliberately by the translator(s), although the omission of 17:1-4 may be the result of haplography. The translator(s) did not aim at an abridged version, but faithfully followed the Hebrew *Vorlage* which was available to them. Expansions were made to the Hebrew text from time to time, often many

---

[77] Diamond, *Confessions*, 62.

years later. For example, an expansion of the Tetragrammaton, adding "of hosts," found in all strata of the book of Jeremiah, reflects the emphasis on divine sovereignty made by pious scribes.

(e) The placement of the Confessions is not a matter of chance, but represents intentional literary editing (e.g., the use of *inclusio* in 11:20=20:12).

(f) The doublets are the result of editorial activity aimed at presenting a theodicy of Yahweh's judgment upon Judah.

The three doublets investigated in this chapter yield the following results:

1. Jeremiah 11:20=20:12

Jeremiah 11:20 is prior to 20:12, and suits the context better. Jeremiah 11:20 is part of the original first Confession, whereas Jer 20:12 has been added editorially to provide an *inclusio*, making an explicit link between the first and fifth Confessions. A shift of emphasis is made in Jer 20:12, in that the speaker is himself "the righteous one," whom Yahweh "tests." The editorial concern is to provide a theodicy; Yahweh takes up the cause of those who suffer unjustly, and will bring about their eventual vindication.

2. Jeremiah 11:23b=23:12b

Jeremiah 23:12b, which appears in a poetic context, is prior to 11:23b, in a context of prose. The prose passage, 11:21-23, has been inserted in the first Confession in order to identify "those who devised schemes" against the prophet (11:19). Jeremiah 11:23b refers to "the men of Anathoth," unnamed persons who resolve to bring about the prophet's death. "The men of Anathoth" are not precisely identified, unless they are understood to be the prophet's kinsmen (cf. 12:6), or to be false prophets (and priests?), as in 23:11.

3. Jeremiah 15:13-14=17:3-4

Jeremiah 17:1-4 is not present in the LXX, probably as the result of haplography. Regarding the doublet Jer 15:13-14=17:3-4, 17:3-4MT is the primary passage; 15:13-14 appears to be intrusive, and fits rather awkwardly in the context. The most helpful solution is that Jer 15:11-12 and 17:3-4 stood in adjacent columns in an ancient manuscript. A marginal variant of 17:3-4 (a scribal notation) was eventually incorporated in the text of Jeremiah 15, after 15:11-12. A Deuteronomistic phrase is used regarding the fire kindled in Yahweh's anger (17:4; 15;14; cf. Deut 32:22). The original intention in 17:1-4 was to justify Yahweh's action in sending his people into exile to serve their enemies.

Additional doublets in the Confessions are examined in the following chapter.

CHAPTER THREE

ADDITIONAL DOUBLETS IN THE CONFESSIONS

Additional doublets in the Confessions are Jer 15:15d=Ps 69:8a; 15:20=1:18-19; 17:18b=1:17b; 18:20a=18:22b; 18:23b=Neh 3:37(4:5E); 20:10a=Ps 31:14a. We continue our examination of these remaining doublets in the Confessions in this chapter.

4. JEREMIAH 15:15d=PSALM 69:8a

The doublet 15:15d=Ps 69:8a in the second Confession is additional confirmation that Jeremiah's laments are similar in form and content to individual and communal laments in the book of Psalms. Gunkel's division of the Psalms into *Gattungen* (literary types) on the basis of their form, has dominated study of the Psalms in the twentieth century.[1] *Klagelieder*, songs of lament, represent the form most frequently found in the book of Psalms. Baumgartner, in a monumental study of Jeremiah's songs of lament, has demonstrated the psalm like character of Jeremiah's impassioned laments in the Confessions.[2]

The *genre* of the individual lament is used by Jeremiah.[3] The usual pattern consists of the address to Yahweh, an expression of trust and confidence in him, the complaint (often against adversaries) and a prayer for vindication or request for vengeance.

JEREMIAH 15:15d
15d. Know that for your sake
I bear reproach.

PSALM 69:8a
8...because for your sake
I have borne reproach.

---

[1] H. Gunkel, *Die Psalmen übersetzt und erklärt* (HKAT; Göttingen: Vandenhoeck & Ruprecht, 1926).

[2] Walter Baumgartner, *Die Klagedichte des Jeremias* (BZAW 32; Giessen: Töpelmann, 1917; *Jeremiah's Poems of Lament*, Sheffield: Almond, 1988).

[3] Holladay: "In taking over the genre of the individual lament Jrm has cut that genre loose from its place in the cult. Here, as in so many other ways, Jrm shows himself an innovator in making fresh use of earlier genres" (*Jeremiah 1*, 360).

Textual and Translational Notes

The expression נָשָׂא חֶרְפָּה עַל ("to bear reproach for") occurs also in Zeph 3:18.[4] In these occurrences of the phrase (15:15d; Ps 69:8a; Zeph 3:18), עַל is understood as an עַל of advantage, meaning "on behalf of," "for the sake of," as in Ps 44:23(H).[5] נָשָׂא חֶרְפָּה (without the preposition עַל) also occurs in Jer 31:19 in the phrase כִּי נָשָׂאתִי חֶרְפַּת נְעוּרָי ("because I bore the reproach of my youth").

Comment

The doublet 15:15d = Ps 69:8a raises the question of the relationship between Jeremiah's Confession in 15:15-18 and Psalm 69. Indeed, the wider question of the relationship between the book of Jeremiah and the book of Psalms is of considerable interest. Bonnard identified thirty-three psalms (including Psalm 69) which in his judgment exhibit the literary and spiritual influence of Jeremiah.[6] Holladay comments on a number of Psalms where the influence mayhave been in the other direction and indeed considers the phrase כִּי עָלֶיךָ נָשָׂאתִי חֶרְפָּה (15:15d) to be a citation from Ps 69:8a.[7]

Although the question of relationship will be taken up again in connection with other doublets (e.g., 10:25 and Ps 79:6-7; see below, chap. ten, pp. 217-218) our concern here is to draw attention to features which 15:15-18 and Psalm 69 have in common. Both the prophet and the psalmist have suffered at the hands of enemies (15:15 "my persecutors"; Ps 69:5 "those who hate me without cause," "those who would destroy me"); both call out for Yahweh's vengeance (15:15; Ps 69:23-29); both have borne reproach for Yahweh's sake (15:15d = Ps 69:8a); both speak as individuals rather than voicing the concerns of the community.

The question of the priority of 15:15-18 over Psalm 69 is closely related to one's decision as to the degree to which the laments in Jeremiah have been shaped or augmented editorially. The position taken in this study is that the Confessions contain a basic nucleus of material written down by Jeremiah himself to express his painful agonizing and later incorporated in the book of

---

[4] The MT in Zeph 3:18 presents difficulties, especially in the form of the verb, הָיוּ. The LXX transposes the letters and arrives at הוֹי (οὐαί). Perhaps the best solution to the textual problem is to attach the מ at the beginning of מִמּוֹעֵד as the final letter of הָיוּ and read עָלַי instead of עָלֶיהָ, i.e., אָסַפְתִּי הַיּוֹם שְׂאֵת עָלַי חֶרְפָּה מִמֵּךְ ("Today I have removed from you [any] bearing of reproach for me").

[5] Williams, *Hebrew Syntax*, § 295. This understanding of עַל is to be seen in the LXX translation of עָלֶיךָ: περὶ σοῦ (15:15d); ἕνεκα σοῦ (Ps 68:8a).

[6] Pierre Bonnard, *Le Psautier selon Jérémie. Influence littéraire et spirituelle de Jérémie sur trente-trois psaumes* (LD 26; Paris: Cerf, 1960).

[7] Holladay, *Jeremiah 2*, 68-70.

5. JEREMIAH 15:20 = 1:18-19

JEREMIAH 15:20
And I will make you
[a] to this people [a]
[c] A fortified [c]
[b] wall of bronze.[b]
They will fight against you
But will not overcome you,
For I am with you
[d] To save you and deliver you,[d]
[e] says Yahweh.[e]

JEREMIAH 1:18-19
18. And I, behold, I make
you today [c] a fortified
city,[c] an iron pillar and
[b] bronze walls [b]
[a] against all the land, [a]
against the kings of Judah,
its princes, its priests
and the people of the land.
19. They will fight against
you, but will not overcome
you, for I am with you,
[e] says Yahweh [e]
[d] to deliver you. [d]

Textual and Translational Notes

[a...a] לָעָם הַזֶּה ("to this people," 15:20); עַל־כָּל־הָאָרֶץ ("against all the land," 1:18; missing in the LXX). The reference to "this people" (15:20) makes a link with הֵמָּה (15:9). Cf. רְדָפַי (15:5). עַל־כָּל־הָאָרֶץ (1:18) is defined by the stereotyped list which follows, "against the kings of Judah, its princes, its priests, and the people of the land," with a change in preposition from עַל to לְ. The LXX reads "to *all* the kings of Judah" and makes no reference to "its priests."

[b...b] לְחוֹמַת נְחֹשֶׁת ("wall of bronze," 15:20); וּלְחֹמוֹת נְחֹשֶׁת ("bronze walls," 1:8). Many manuscripts (1:18) have the singular form חוֹמַת, as in 15:20MT. Cf. LXX τεῖχος; Vg *murum*; Tg; which support the singular form. Volz regards the plural form as intensive.[8] The phrase וּלְעַמּוּד בַּרְזֶל ("and for an iron pillar"), not present in the LXX, has been added in the Hebrew text of 1:18.[9]

[c...c] בְּצוּרָה ("fortified," 15:20); לְעִיר מִבְצָר ("a fortified city," 1:18). In 15:20, the passive participle *Qal* is used adjectivally (cf. Isa 2:5; Deut 28:52) to describe the wall of bronze as "fortified," "impregnable," whereas in 1:18 a

---

[8] Volz, *Jeremia*, 11.
[9] S. Talmon, "An Apparently Redundant MT Reading in Jeremiah 1:18," *Textus* 8 (1973) 160-163. He argues that ולעמוד ברזל should be retained: "...it can be reasonably assumed that what the coiner of the phrase עמוד ברזל in Jer 1:18 had in mind when joining it with עיר מבצר and המ(ו)ת was a hefty iron rod used as a bolt to fasten the heavy doors of a city gate, possibly of Jerusalem" (p. 162).

different phrase עִיר מִבְצָר ("a city of fortification," "a fortified city") occurs.[10] ᵈ⁻⁻ᵈ לְהוֹשִׁיעֲךָ וּלְהַצִּילֶךָ ("to save you and deliver you," 15:20); לְהַצִּילֶךָ ("to deliver you," 1:19). The phrase כִּי־אִתְּךָ אָנִי is common both to 15:20 and 1:19 (cf. 46:28=30:11). However, whereas two verbs (ישׁע Hiphil, נצל Hiphil) follow in 15:20MT, only נצל Hiphil is found in 1:19MT. The LXX has only the equivalent of ישׁע Hiphil in 15:20 (τοῦ σώζειν σε). Jeremiah 15:21MT repeats נצל Hiphil (וְהִצַּלְתִּיךָ; LXX ἐξαιρεῖσθαί σε).

ᵉ⁻⁻ᵉ נְאֻם יְהוָה ("says Yahweh"). The formula comes at the end of 15:20bMT (absent in the LXX), but is in a medial position in 1:19bMT (here the LXX places λέγει κύριος at the end, as in 15:20bMT). Jeremiah 30:11a is similar to 1:19b (with נְאֻם יְהוָה in a medial position), but like 15:20b uses ישׁע Hiphil rather than נצל Hiphil, 1:19b.

Comment

The doublet 15:20=1:18-19 is by no means an exact doublet. Features in common include the verb נתן followed by the 2d s. suffix (נְתַתִּיךָ), the reference to the "bronze wall" ("bronze walls" in 1:18), the phrase כִּי־אִתְּךָ אָנִי וְנִלְחֲמוּ אֵלֶיךָ וְלֹא יוּכְלוּ לָךְ and the verb נצל followed by the 2d s. suffix (לְהַצִּילֶךָ). In Jeremiah 15:20 we find the addition of the verb ישׁע followed by the 2d s. suffix (לְהוֹשִׁיעֲךָ) and a different position for the formula נְאֻם יְהוָה.

Jeremiah 1:18 expands 15:20 considerably by adding וַאֲנִי הִנֵּה, the words עַל־כָּל־הָאָרֶץ and וּלְעַמּוּד בַּרְזֶל, לְעִיר מִבְצָר, הַיּוֹם, followed by a stereotyped list of officials.

What is the relationship between the two passages? A substantial group of commentators regard 15:20 as original and 1:18-19 as derivative. On the contrary, others consider 15:20 to be dependent on 1:18-19.

I take the view that 15:20 is prior to 1:18-19 and that the latter passage at the conclusion of Jeremiah 1 has elaborated the more concise statements in 15:20 by supplementary additions. The orientation is somewhat different. In the case of 15:20 the context is Yahweh's response to the lament of the prophet in his vocational crisis, whereas in 1:18-19 the emphasis is on Jeremiah's mission with a direct link to 1:8.[11] In fact, 1:17-19 is closely linked with 1:4-10, skilfully combining the concept of Jeremiah as a "fortified city" with the account of his call.[12] Jeremiah 1 contains a considerable expansion of the call narrative, the purpose of which is to provide an introduction to Jeremiah 2-45.

---

[10] The phrase is found in Josh 19:29 (regarding Tyre); 1 Sam 6:18; 2 Kgs 3:19; 10:2; 17:9; 18:8. The plural, עָרֵי מִבְצָר, ("fortified cities"), occurs in Jer 4:5; 5:17; 8:14; 34:7 (regarding Judah). Cf. Num 32:17, 36; Josh 10:20; 19:35; 2 Chron 17:19. Note also מִבְצָר in Jer 6:27.

[11] Marx, "A propos des doublets," 107.

[12] Cf. Jüngling, "Ich mach dich zu einer ehernen Mauer, Literarkritische überlegungen zum Verhältnis von Jer 1,18-19 zu Jer 15,20-21," Bib 54 (1973) 1-24.

Additional Doublets in the Confessions 37

This is substantiated by the double introduction, 1:1-2 and 1:3.[13] Brueggemann has drawn attention to the "but you" (וְאַתָּה) speeches in 1:17-19 (regarding Jeremiah) and 45:5 (regarding Baruch), which provide an envelope for the entire text as well as a clue to post-Jeremianic editorial activity.[14]

The relationship of 15:20-21 to 15:19 is debateable. Holladay points to the lack of structural connections between 15:20-21 and 15:15-19.[15] On the other hand, Diamond comes to the tentative conclusion that 15:20-21 is "integral and original to the divine oracle."[16] Although וְהִצַּלְתִּיךָ at the beginning of 15:21 might suggest that this verse has been added by catchword association with וּלְהַצִּילֶךָ in 15:20, the use of yet another verb expressing salvation (פדה) and the adjective עָרִיץ (pl.) used as a substantive (parallel to רָעִים in 15:21b) make it more probable that verses 20 and 21 belong together originally.

In 15:20 Yahweh promises to make Jeremiah a fortified wall of bronze "to this people," whereas in 1:18 this phrase is expanded to "against the whole land," defined in terms of "the kings of Judah, its princes, its priests and the people of the land." Extensive stereotyped lists, with variations, are found principally in prose passages elsewhere in the book of Jeremiah.[17]

The four characteristic groups itemized in 1:18 are מְלָכִים ("kings"; cf. 1:1-3); שָׂרִים ("princes," i.e., "officials"); כֹּהֲנִים ("priests"), absent in the LXX; and עַם־הָאָרֶץ ("people of the land").[18] The stereotyped lists elsewhere include

---

[13] For a careful analysis of the complicated syntactical relationships in 1:1-3, see Siegfried Herrmann, *Jeremia* (BKAT 12/1; Neukirchen-Vluyn: Neukirchener Verlag, 1986) 4.

[14] Walter Brueggemann, *To Pluck up, to Tear down; A Commentary on the Book of Jeremiah 1-25* (ITC; Grand Rapids, Michigan: Eerdmans, 1988) 28.

[15] Holladay, *Jeremiah 1*, 449.

[16] Diamond, in a diction analysis of 15:15-21 finds "numerous points of stylistic and thematic contact with Jeremianic poetry," but "nothing distinctive of Dtr. or Jeremianic prose" *Confessions*, p. 234 n. 49).

[17] E.g., 2:26 (poetry); 4:9 (perhaps poetry); elsewhere prose: 8:1; 13:13; 17:25; 21:7; 24:1, 8; 25:19; 26:11, 12, 16; 29:2, 16; 32:32; 34:19, 21; 37:2; 39:3, 13; 44:9, 17, 21.

[18] Various interpretations have been placed on the expression עַם־הָאָרֶץ, e.g., Holladay, "the citizens of the nation outside the orbit of the palace and temple in Jerusalem" (*Jeremiah 1*, 45); Bright, "landed gentry" (*Jeremiah*, 5); Carroll, "landowners," in view of 34:19; 37:2; 44:21 (*Jeremiah*, 108). Jones refers to "influential country landowners," but adds that "the purpose of the list is to suggest the opposition of the whole land" (*Jeremiah*, 79); McKane, "the common people" (*Jeremiah 1*, 23); Thompson, "ordinary citizens" (*Jeremiah*, 157). For a discussion of "people of the land" elsewhere in the OT, see Ernest W. Nicholson, *The Book of the Prophet Jeremiah: Chapters 1-25* (CBC; Cambridge University Press, 1973) 59-66; A. H. L. Gunneweg, "עם הארץ - A Semantic Revolution," *ZAW* 95 (1983) 437-440. In my judgment, the expression in 1:18 is not intended to include "the people of the land" among the ruling classes, but to refer to inhabitants of the land generally, as suggested by the blanket term כָּל־הָאָרֶץ, which is defined by the four categories which follow.

"people of the land" only in 34:19; 37:2 and 44:21. The four categories frequently encountered elsewhere are "kings," "princes," "priests" and "prophets" (e.g., 2:26; 4:9; 8:1; 32:32). "Prophets" are not included in 1:18; indeed, "priests" are not included in the LXX here. Janzen regards the reference to "priests" as intrusive, from 2:26 and 32:32.[19] Apart from the exclusion of "its priests" in 1:18, the LXX follows the MT very closely in all the other instances of stereotyped lists in the book of Jeremiah.

In 15:20 the promise is made by Yahweh to the prophet that he will be made חוֹמַת נְחֹשֶׁת בְּצוּרָה ("a fortified wall of bronze"). Interesting connections are made by Beyerlin between the book of Amos, especially the third vision (Amos 7:7-9), and such passages in the book of Jeremiah as 21:4; 15:20 and 1:18.[20] In an earlier monograph, Beyerlin had argued that the translation of חוֹמַת אֲנָךְ in Amos 7:7 should be "a wall of tin" and that אֲנָךְ does not refer to a "plumbline" but to the metal from which the wall was constructed, and that the "tin" in Yahweh's hand (בְּיָדוֹ אֲנָךְ) implies a potential for weapons.[21] In 21:4 the disturbing prospect of their own weapons of war being turned against God's people themselves (a reversal of the accepted theme of Yahweh's protection in "holy war") is now applied in 15:20 to Jeremiah's role as "a fortified wall of bronze" (חוֹמַת נְחֹשֶׁת בְּצוּרָה) against "this people," who are enemies both of Yahweh and Jeremiah. This description is amplified in 1:18. Jeremiah is not only to be made "wall(s) of bronze" but "a fortified city" (מִבְצָר עִיר) and "an iron pillar" (עַמּוּד בַּרְזֶל) "against all the land." In the context of 1:17-19, the reference is to Jeremiah as "a fortified city."[22] Enemies will fight and not prevail against him; he stands in marked contrast to the city of Jerusalem, whose fate was sealed in 587 BCE. The editorial insertion in all likelihood has been made in the light of that event. According to 52:17, the pillars of bronze (עַמּוּדֵי הַנְּחֹשֶׁת) in the temple were broken in pieces by the Babylonians in 587 BCE. Again, Jeremiah as "an iron pillar" stands in contrast to these bronze pillars. The LXX lacks the phrase וּלְעַמּוּד בַּרְזֶל and also the phrase לְכֹהֲנֶיהָ, which makes it possible that these late additions in the Hebrew text reflect an anti-priestly bias on the part of the editor.

Interestingly, the terms נְחֻשָׁה, מִבְצָר, נְתַתִּיךָ, and בַּרְזֶל are found in both 1:18 and 6:27-28. The latter passage presents textual difficulties.[23] The

---

[19] Janzen, *Studies*, 36.
[20] W. Beyerlin, *Reflexe der Amosvisionen im Jeremiabuch* (OBO 93; Göttingen: Vandenhoeck & Ruprecht, 1989).
[21] W. Beyerlin, *Bleilot, Brecheisen oder was sonst? Revision einer Amosvisionen* (OBO 81; Göttingen; Vandenhoeck & Ruprecht, 1989).
[22] The phrase עָרֵי מִבְצָר appears elsewhere in the book of Jeremiah (e.g., 4:5; 5:17; 8:14; 34:7).
[23] For discussion of the textual problems, see Rudolph, *Jeremia*, 48. Godfrey R. Driver ("Two Misunderstood Passages in the O.T.," *JTS* NS 6 [1955] 82-87) argues that "...וברזל נחשת belong on the grounds of rhythm and sense to the next verse," i.e., 6:29 (p. 85).

probability is that 6:27-28 have been added by a scribe who saw a link between 1:18 and this passage.[24]

Jeremiah 15:20bc and 1:19 clearly represent the use of the salvation *genre*. The phrase in 15:20c, כִּי־אִתְּךָ אֲנִי לְהוֹשִׁיעֶךָ ("for I am with you to save you"), is paralleled in 30:11. A parallel which includes both ישע Hiphil and נצל Hiphil with the object "you" (plural) occurs in 42:11 (אֶתְכֶם וּלְהַצִּיל אֶתְכָם כִּי־אִתְּכֶם אֲנִי לְהוֹשִׁיעַ). The exhortation "Do not fear" (אַל תִּירָא) found in 30:10 (cf. אַל־תִּירְאוּ 42:11), reminiscent of similar salvation-oracles in Deutero-Isaiah (cf. Isa 43:1, 2; 43:5), is not found in 15:20, although the analogous אַל־תֵּחַת occurs in 1:17. However, all these passages carry the assurance of the divine presence. So does 1:8, which also has affinities with 15:20 and 1:19, as well as with Deutero-Isaiah: אַל־תִּירָא מִפְּנֵיהֶם כִּי־אִתְּךָ אֲנִי לְהַצִּילֶךָ. The call narrative (1:4-10) is by no means a uniform composition.[25] The links between 1:8 and 1:17-19 (כִּי־אִתְּךָ אֲנִי לְהַצִּילֶךָ, 1:8, 19), אַל־תֵּחַת מִפְּנֵיהֶם, 1:17; אַל־תִּירָא מִפְּנֵיהֶם, 1:8) indicate editorial activity in which Jeremiah 1 was shaped as a prelude to the chapters which follow. In this respect, 15:20 was a major resource. The use of the formula נְאֻם יְהוָה in 15:20 and in 1:19 differs (see Textual and Translational Notes above, note [e...e], p. 36). This formula occurs 376 times in the prophetic literature, with a preponderance in the book of Jeremiah (176 ocurrences).[26] As noted by Rendtorff, the formula in most cases stands outside the metrical structure in poetic passages.[27] The most frequent use of נְאֻם יְהוָה in the book of Jeremiah is at the conclusion of a Yahweh-word in poetry or prose (e.g., 2:3; 3:10; 9:23; 29:9; 31:14; 34:5; 49:6; etc.) or as an introductory statement, often in conjunction with the formula לָכֵן הִנֵּה יָמִים בָּאִים (e.g., 7:32; 16:14; 19:6; etc.). In 1:19, the formula is a *"Zwischenformel"* (cf. 2:9; 3:12 [bis];

---

[24] Possibly, a scribe who noted the use of נְתַתִּיךָ in both passages to express Yahweh's action with regard to Jeremiah added marginal notes as a cross-reference, including the terms מִבְצָר, בַּרְזֶל and נְחֹשֶׁת. מִבְצָר cannot readily be understood as a gloss interpreting בָּחוֹן, unless vocalized as מְבַצֵּר ("assayer"). The other terms, נְחֹשֶׁת and בַּרְזֶל, would be placed more appropriately in 6:29 (rather than in 6:28), to accompany עֹפָרֶת ("lead").

[25] McKane (*Jeremiah 1*) refers to "its incoherence and lack of integration" (p. 9), since in 1:5 and 1:10 Jeremiah is called to be a prophet to the nations, yet in 1:8 the concern is with the opposition that he will face within his own community, not among foreign nations. The use of the terminal נְאֻם יְהוָה at the end of 1:8 also points to the composite nature of 1:4-10.

[26] Francis I. Andersen & A. Dean Forbes, *The Vocabulary of the Old Testament* (Rome: Editrice Pontificio Istituto Biblico, 1989) 370. The eighth century prophets employed the formula: e.g., Amos (twenty-one times); Hosea (four times); Isaiah, including DI (twenty-five times). Ezekiel also made frequent use of נְאֻם יְהוָה, with eighty-five occurrences.

[27] R. Rendtorff, "Zum Gebrauch der Formel n^{e}um jahwe im Jeremiabuch," *ZAW* 66 (1954) 27-37.

4:1; 5:22; 8:13; etc.).²⁸ Jeremiah 30:11 (כִּי־אִתְּךָ אֲנִי נְאֻם־יְהוָה לְהוֹשִׁיעֶךָ) is of special interest since the formula comes in a medial position, after the formula "for I am with you" (cf. 1:19), but contrary to 1:19 is followed by the verb לְהוֹשִׁיעֶךָ, as in 15:20 (where נְאֻם־יְהוָה comes at the conclusion). Clearly, there is no set pattern in the use of the formula. This is emphasized by the fact that λέγει κύριος (LXX) translates the formula in 102 instances, while the formula is absent in the LXX in 73 cases where it is present in the MT.²⁹ The frequent addition of נְאֻם יְהוָה in the Hebrew text over and above the occurrences common to both the MT and the LXX has never been satisfactorily explained, but as Scholz has suggested, may point to synagogue homiletical practice.³⁰ Possibly נְאֻם יְהוָה in 1:19b originally stood as a conclusion (cf. 1:19bLXX), but was changed to a medial position under the influence of 30:11a by a scribe who was aware of the word order in that passage.

6. JEREMIAH 17:18b = JEREMIAH 1:17b

Although we are not dealing here with a precise *verbatim* doublet, the double use of the verb חתת both in Jeremiah's prayer in the third Confession in Jeremiah 17 (17:18b; note also the use of the noun מְחִתָּה in 17:17) as well as in Yahweh's equipping Jeremiah for his mission in 1:17-19, suggests a degree of correspondence between the two passages.

JEREMIAH 17:18b
18b. Let them be dismayed,
but let me not be discouraged.

JEREMIAH 1:17b
17b. Do not be dismayed by
their presence, lest I make
you dismayed in their presence.

Textual and Translational Notes

Jeremiah 1:17bLXX is of interest because of the use of two different

---

²⁸ See Hans Wildberger, *Yahwewort und prophetischer Rede bei Jeremia* (Diss. Zürich: Zwingli, 1942) 49. F. S. North lists twenty-one occurrences of the phrase in an unusual position in a sentence, of which sixteen occur in Jeremiah: 1:19; 4:1; 19:12; 25:9, 12; 27:22; 28:4; 29:11, 19, 32; 30:11=46:28; 31:17, 34; 48:30; 49:5 ("The Expression 'The Oracle of Yahweh' as an Aid to Critical Analysis," *JBL* 71 [1952]). North claims "...it is probable that the twenty-one abnormal occurrences indicate the presence of secondary material," e.g., as in 1:18 (p. X).

²⁹ Janzen, *Studies*, 83. In eight passages (1:17; 2:2; 2:17; 2:19; 5:1; 16:1; 31:35 [some manuscripts]; 50:20), the LXX has λέγει κύριος whereas the MT lacks נְאֻם יְהוָה.

³⁰ A. Scholz, *Der masoretische Text und die LXX-Uebersetzung des Buches Jeremias* (Regensburg: G. J. Manz, 1875), cited by Janzen, *Studies*, 83.

verbs to translate חתת ("be dismayed") and the addition of the clause ὅτι μετὰ σοῦ ἐγώ εἰμι τοῦ ἐξαιρεῖσθαί σε, λέγει κύριος (cf. 1:8; 1:19b). The MT has the phrase כִּי־אִתְּךָ אֲנִי לְהַצִּלֶךָ only at the end of 1:8 and 1:19b, with the formula נְאֻם יְהוָה at the end in 1:8 and in a medial position in 1:19b. Was the additional phrase, "'for I am with you to deliver you,' says Yahweh," in the Hebrew *Vorlage* of 1:17b on which the LXX translation is based? The question of the *Vorlage* also comes to the fore in that the LXX seems to have read the first part of 1:17b differently from the present MT, e.g., אַל־תִּירָא מִפְּנֵיהֶם וְאַל תֵּחַת לִפְנֵיהֶם. Ziegler argues that this represents the original Hebrew text, followed by כִּי־אִתְּךָ אֲנִי לְהַצִּלֶךָ נְאֻם יְהוָה.[31] Janzen claims that the LXX represents a variant text in the *Vorlage*, but thinks that a secondary change to a more common cliché may have taken place in the course of transmission.[32] Volz and McKane both contend that the LXX translation reflects a change on dogmatic grounds to remove the element of threat.[33]

The textual problem may be approached by raising the question of the purpose of introducing 1:17 after the two "visions" recorded in 1:11-16. The intention seems to be to reinforce Jeremiah's call to act as Yahweh's prophet, with an awareness of the inevitable conflicts involved, but with the assurance of the divine presence to deliver him and to enable him to overcome opposition. He is to gird up his loins (1:17a) and carry out his prophetic commission in complete obedience.[34] Jeremiah 1:17 provides a necessary link with 1:7 (תְּדַבֵּר וְאֵת כָּל־אֲשֶׁר אֲצַוְּךָ). If indeed 1:17b originally read אַל־תִּירָא מִפְּנֵיהֶם, as the LXX (μὴ φοβηθῇς ἀπὸ προσώπου) indicates, there is also a connection with 1:8.

Comment

The following history of the text is proposed:
(1) Originally, 1:17 was added in the form represented by the LXX, based on a *Vorlage* which employed the verbs יָרֵא and חָתַת. These verbs, found together in Deut 1:21 (אַל־תִּירָא וְאַל־תֵּחָת; cf. Deut 31:8; 10:25), would have been used by a Deuteronomistic editor who was well aware of the opposition which

---

[31] J. Ziegler, *Beiträge zur Jeremias-Septuaginta* (Mitteilungen des Septuaginta-Unternehmens der Akademie der Wissenschaften; Göttingen: Vandenhoeck & Ruprecht, 1958) 88-89.
[32] Janzen, *Studies*, 96.
[33] Paul Volz, *Studien zum Text des Jeremia* (BWAT 25; Leipzig: Hinrichs, 1920) 4; McKane, *Jeremiah*, 22.
[34] Cf. Elijah (1 Kgs 18:46) and Job (Job 38:3; 40:7).

Jeremiah faced during his prophetic ministry. Originally, the phrase נְאֻם־יְהוָה כִּי־אִתְּךָ אֲנִי לְהַצִּלֶךָ came at the end of the verse (cf. the LXX), as in 1:8.
(2) At a subsequent stage, a second supplementary passage was added (1:18–19), reflecting Yahweh's promise to the prophet in the second Confession (15:20).
(3) Later still, under the influence of the third Confession (17:18b: אֲנִי יֵחַתּוּ הֵמָּה וְאַל־אֵחַתָּה), 1:17b was changed by the double use of חתת and strengthened by the use of the first person in the phrase פֶּן־אֲחִתְּךָ (cf. Vg *nec enim timere te faciam*). The phrase כִּי־אִתְּךָ אֲנִי לְהַצִּלֶךָ נְאֻם יְהוָה would be an unnecessary duplication in 1:17, if this was now the concluding statement in 1:19b. Jeremiah 1:17–19MT, with the other additions in 1:18 already discussed (see p. 36 above), originally reflected two *Yahweh-Worte*. The unit as it now stands expresses command, encouragement and promise.

Bak observes that the root חתת, which occurs frequently in the book of Jeremiah, is used not only in announcements of doom (8:9; 49:37; 50:36), but also in lament-situations (14:4; 48:1, 20, 39; 51:56) and in connection with words of salvation (1:17[*bis*]; 10:2[*bis*]; 23:4; 30:10=46:27).[35] Although Bak thinks that 17:18b, in which the root is used in an autobiographical context, reflects the command in the account of Jeremiah's call (1:17b), the reverse situation may also be argued: the appeal to Yahweh in 17:18b with regard to persecutors, "let them be dismayed, but let me not be dismayed," has become a conditional promise of salvation in 1:17b, "Do not be dismayed by their presence, lest I make you dismayed in their presence."[36] I adopt this latter view. As Jüngling rightly points out, the element of threat in 1:17b has not been anticipated and contains a sharp warning for the prophet if he fails to comply with the divine command.[37] Implicit, however, is a promise of vindication for obedience. One concludes that the passage 1:17–19 in its final form shows signs of dependency on 17:18 and 15:20.

7. JEREMIAH 18:20a = JEREMIAH 18:22b

In the fourth Confession (Jer 18:18–23) the phrase כִּי־כָרוּ שׁוּחָה ("for they have dug a pit") occurs in Jer 18:20a and recurs in slightly different form in Jer 18:22b.

JEREMIAH 18:20a
20a. Yet [a] they have dug
[b] a pit [b] for my life

JEREMIAH 18:22b
22b. [a] For [a] they have dug [b] a pit [b]
to take me.

---

[35] Bak, *Klagender Gott*, p. 81 n. 5.
[36] Thiel, *Redaktion 1*, 77.
[37] Jüngling, "Ich mache dich...," 15.

Textual and Translational Notes

^{a...a} כִּי in 18:20a is best taken as adversative after the implied negative answer to the question raised in 18:20a.[38] כִּי is causal in 18:22b[39]
^{b...b} שׁוּחָה ooccurs in 18:20a and in many manuscripts of 18:22b, following the *qere*, although the *kethibh* in 18:22b is שִׁיחָה. שִׁיחָה ("pit") follows the verb כָּרָה in Ps 57:7 (57:6E) and in Ps 119:85 (plural). The more usual term for "pit" in Psalms is שַׁחַת (e.g., Ps 7:16; 9:16; 35:7). שׁוּחָה is used as a collective in Jer 2:6. Vulgate has *foveam* ("pit") in both 18:20a and 18:22b. The LXX reads ὅτι συνελάλησεν ῥήματα κατὰ τῆς ψυχῆς μου ("for they have spoken words against my soul," 18:20a); ὅτι ἐνεχείρησαν λόγον εἰς σύλλημψιν μου ("for they have formed a plan to take me," 18:22b). The LXX seems to have read שִׂיחָה ("complaint") rather than שׁוּחָה ("pit") in both instances.

The LXX adds the phrase καὶ τὴν κόλασιν αὐτῶν ἔκρυψαν μοι ("and they have hidden the punishment [meant] for me," 18:20aLXX). The introduction of this phrase cannot easily be explained. ἔκρυψαν occurs also in 18:22bLXX, καὶ παγίδας ἔκρυψαν ἐπ᾿ ἐμέ ("and they have hidden snares for me"), translating the MT וּפַחִים טָמְנוּ לְרַגְלָי, parallel to כִּי־כָרוּ שִׁיחָה לְלָכְדֵנִי. However, the use of the noun κόλασις ("punishment") in 18:20a is puzzling. McKane assumes that the parallel phrase, "and they have concealed their snares to trap me," in 18:22b would have been added in 18:20a, but finds difficulty in Janzen's suggestion that פחם was read in 18:20a in place of פחים in 18:22b.[40] Possibly, פֶּחָים ("coals") was read by the LXX translator in the sense of "coals of fire," as in Ps 11:6, a metaphor for "punishment." In any case, the extra phrase in 18:20aLXX does not occur in any of the other versions.

Comment

Commentators are divided as to whether or not the phrase, "Yet they have dug a pit for my life," in 18:20a should be regarded as an intrusion from 18:22b and should therefore be eliminated. Yet, a case can be made for the retention of the phrase in both verses. The slight differences between 18:20a and 18:22b suggest that the phrase has not simply been inserted editorially in 18:20a as a response to the question, "Is evil a recompense for good?" The doublet has been used intentionally in both instances, not only as a response to the question raised in 18:20a, but to serve as an *inclusio* for the passage 18:20–22, in which the introductory כִּי is adversative in the first instance, causal in the second. Diamond, in his discussion of the passage, argues against the

---

[38] Williams, *Hebrew Syntax* § 447.
[39] Williams, *Hebrew Syntax*, § 444.
[40] McKane, *Jeremiah 1*, 439; Janzen, *Studies*, 27.

view that the presence of a doublet automatically provides evidence for the secondary character of a text.[41]

Relevant to the discussion is the question regarding the antecedent of "they" in the phrase "they have dug a pit." If one accepts the MT in 18:19b, יְרִיבַי ("hearken to the voice of my adversaries"), rather than the emendment רִיבִי ("hearken to my plea," cf. LXX δικαιώματός μου), the reference in 18:23 to "all their plotting to slay me" presumably has the same adversaries in mind. If יְרִיבַי in 18:19b is accepted, then the question raised in 18:20a, "Is evil a recompense for good?," would appear to come from these adversaries, unless one takes the rhetorical question as a reference back to those who plan to "make plots against Jeremiah" (18:18), as suggested by Drinkard.[42] The question would then imply a protest against Jeremiah's prophecy of רָעָה ("disaster") against טוֹבָה ("the good") which has been merited by those who in their own eyes have complied with Yahweh's requirements. Jeremiah, on the other hand, claims that he has held out for "good," "for their sake" (עֲלֵיהֶם; עַל of advantage).[43] The "good," which was his concern in carrying out his office as prophet, standing in the presence of Yahweh, has been rejected (cf. 4:14; 5:3).[44] Jeremiah had high hopes that his people would respond to the message he was commissioned to speak to them, in order to receive "good" and to have Yahweh's wrath turned away from them. The fact that they have repudiated the message confirms that judgment is now inevitable. In this way, Jeremiah puts a different slant on the question, "Is evil a recompense for good?" His enemies have repaid evil for good, "they have dug a pit" for his life (18:20a), although in his prophetic task he had been concerned for their welfare. Now רָעָה ("calamity") may be expected to come upon them (18:21-23), since their actions have not been "good" but evil (note the references to עֲוֹנָם, חַטָּאתָם in 18:23). They have rejected both Yahweh's messenger and Yahweh himself. The imprecatory prayers in 18:21-23 reflect Jeremiah's conviction that divine judgment is imminent, but also in the light of 18:20 vindicate the prophet as having been faithful in proclaiming the message entrusted to him by God. His enemies are not only those who have plotted to slay him (18:23), but people in general (18:21-22).

The question must now be raised as to whether 18:18 is part of the fourth Confession or is redactional. I take the position that this verse in prose is a redactional insertion (cf. Duhm) intended to introduce the Confession which

---

[41] Diamond, *Confessions*, 93-94.

[42] Joel F. Drinkard, Jr., in Peter C. Craigie, Page H. Kelley and Joel F. Drinkard, Jr., *Jeremiah 1-25* (WBC 26; Dallas: Word, 1991) 253.

[43] Williams, *Hebrew Syntax*, § 295.

[44] The phrase עָמְדִי לְפָנֶיךָ is used in the same sense as in 15:19, where "standing before me" (i.e., before Yahweh) has to do with Jeremiah's commission. In my judgment, this is not a reference to Jeremiah in the role of prophetic intercessor, but as one called to proclaim Yahweh's message to his people.

follows (18:19-23) and to provide a link with the preceding verses in Jeremiah 18.[45] The use of the verb קשׁב in 18:18 makes a connection with הַקְשִׁיבָה in 18:19. The use of the root חשׁב (18:18: מַחֲשָׁבוֹת) is found also in 18:8(חָשַׁבְתִּי), 18:11 (וְחֹשֵׁב...מַחֲשָׁבָה), and 18:12 (מַחְשְׁבוֹתֵינוּ).[46] The general statement "they said" (18:18, וַיֹּאמְרוּ) is similar to וְאָמְרוּ in 18:12 (the versions suggest וַיֹּאמְרוּ, i.e., "people have said"). Interpretation of 18:18 requires establishment of the text. The LXX does not include the negative(אַל-) in the final statement of the verse, but reads "and let us hear all his words." German commentators generally accept the LXX rather than the MT here. In this case, the meaning of this phrase would be "let us then listen to his words," i.e., with a view to using them as evidence against him.[47] In keeping with this, Syr reads "with his tongue" (=בִּלְשׁוֹנוֹ) in the preceding phrase.[48] This would imply that Jeremiah's own tongue will convict him. However, the Qumran fragment from Cave 4 (4QJer[a]) would appear to confirm MT in both instances.[49] Jones claims that the sense of 18:18 as a whole is that Jeremiah's enemies *have* Torah and therefore "have confidence to speak and to drive Jeremiah to silence."[50] The groups referred to in 18:18 ("priest," "wise," "prophet") are variously spoken against in 2:8; 5:13; 8:9 and 23:11 (cf. Ezek 7:26); in this passage they conspire against Jeremiah, claiming that they are the true upholders of Yahweh's law, counsel and word. They have rejected Jeremiah's prophecy of doom as unrealistic, hence the urgency of his appeal to Yahweh (18:21-23) to bring about the very disaster his enemies have so readily dismissed.

The reference in 18:21 to coming "famine" and "sword" opposes the widely held false view (cf. 5:12) that no calamity (רָעָה) will come, that sword and famine will not be experienced. At the end of 18:23 the plea, "Deal with them in the time of thine anger" (בְּעֵת אַפְּךָ), points to an unspecified but inevitable time in the future. The verses preceding the fourth Confession (18:13-17) end in 18:17 with a reference to "the day of their calamity" (אֵידָם בְּיוֹם), when Yahweh's people (18:15) will be scattered before the enemy. This appears to be a direct reference to the fall of Jerusalem in 587 BCE (cf. the threefold use of the noun in Obad 13, also referring to 587 BCE). In the third Confession (17:14-18), יוֹם רָעָה ("the day of evil") has twice been mentioned (17:17; 17:18). In the light of such passages as Amos 5:18 and Isa 2:11-17,

---

[45] Duhm, *Jeremia*, 156.

[46] Hubmann (*Untersuchungen*) claims that "...v. 18 is connected with v.11f both stylistically and theologically and belongs to the *same stage* in the development of the text" (p. 292).

[47] Cf. Holladay, *Jeremiah 1*, 527, 530.

[48] Holladay accepts Syr here and suggests that the suffix may have been dropped by haplography in the MT (*Jeremiah 1*, 527).

[49] See McKane, *Jeremiah 1*, 436.

[50] Jones, *Jeremiah*, 263.

Weiser finds an allusion to the eschatological "Day of Yahweh."[51] However, Jeremiah in the Confessions (17:16-17; 18:23) points rather to a coming judgment of Yahweh upon his people in the near future, a judgment which cannot be evaded. The delay of this coming judgment creates a problem; in the third Confession this has given the occasion for his adversaries, who deny the danger altogether, to declare, "Where is the word of Yahweh? Let it come!" (17:15). For Jeremiah there has been a growing conviction that Yahweh's judgment cannot be averted. This is categorically asserted in such a passage as 6:22-26, where the catastrophic invasion of the foe from the north is described.

8. JEREMIAH 18:23b = NEHEMIAH 3:37(4:5E)

JEREMIAH 18:23b
23b. [a] Do not forgive [a] their iniquity and [b] do not not blot out their sin from thy sight. [b]

NEHEMIAH 3:37(4:5E)
37. [a] Do not cover [a] their iniquity and [b] do not let their sin be blotted out from their sight. [b]

Textual and Translational Notes

[a...a] אַל־תְּכַפֵּר ("do not forgive," 18:23); וְאַל־תְּכַס ("do not cover," Neh 3:37). This is the only occurrence of כפר Piel in Jeremiah (+ עַל, cf. Ps 79:9). Although most occurrences of the root כפר are found in the Torah (as the technical term for "atone"), כפר Pual + עָוֹן is found in Isa 22:14; 27:9 in the sense of "to forgive sin." כָּסָה + עַל in Neh 3:37 conveys the same meaning, i.e., "to cover over," "forgive." In both instances, God is the subject.

[b...b] אַל־תֶּמְחִי ("do not blot out," 18:23); אַל־תִּמָּחֶה ("do not let...be blotted out," Neh 3:37). This is the only occurrence of the root מחה in Jeremiah (Hiphil jussive) and in Nehemiah (Niphal jussive). The yodh in תֶּמְחִי is usually regarded as otiose and תֶּמְחֶה is to be read. Rudolph regards תֶּמְחִי as a "Schreibfehler" (cf. 3:6b, וַתִּזְנִי, which also occurs in Ezek 16:17, as noted by Rashi).[52] In GKC § 75ii, attention is drawn to these Lamedh He verb variations (the Mil'el tone probably points to תֶּמְחֶה as the correct reading in 18:23). Volz claims that the superfluous yodh really belongs to what follows, i.e., the next clause should begin with יהיו.[53] מחה followed by חַטָּאת also occurs in the imprecatory Ps 109:14 (cf. the use of the verb מחה in the imprecation in Ps 69:29 [69:28E]). The clause "do not let their sin be blotted out from their sight" is missing in the LXX in Neh 3:37 (2 Esdras 13:37). However, Vg follows the MT closely, both in 18:23b and 2 Ezra 4:5 (=Neh 3:37MT).

---

[51] Weiser, *Jeremia*, 149.
[52] Rudolph, *Jeremia*, 124.
[53] Volz, *Jeremia*, 198.

Comment

The phrase וְאַתָּה יְהוָה יָדַעְתָּ at the beginning of 18:23 occurs also with minor variations in 12:3 (first Confession) and 15:5 (second Confession).[54] The prophet, who realizes that Yahweh is aware of the murderous plans of enemies, prays an imprecatory prayer that the enemies should not be forgiven. The prayer is repeated with modifications in Neh 3:37. We are not dealing with a precise quotation in the book of Nehemiah (תְּכַס takes the place of תְּכַפֵּר and תִּמָּחֶה *Niphal* is read instead of תֶּמְחִי *Hiphil*).

Since 2 Esdras 13:37LXX (=Neh 3:37MT) contains a translation only of the first clause, "Do not cover their iniquity," this suggests that the Hebrew *Vorlage* consisted of this clause only, unless the translator simply omitted the second clause. Possibly, a scribe noted the similarity of Neh 3:37MT to Jer 18:23b and added the second clause, which became the final standard form of Neh 3:37MT. Much depends on how Neh 3:36-38 was composed. Myers thinks that the Chronicler, or the compiler of the material in the book of Nehemiah, sometimes "copied the sources much as he found them, sometimes he rewrote them, and sometimes he doubtless composed freely (in the case of speeches and prayers)."[55]

The situation of enemies (Sanballat, governor of Samariah and Tobiah the Ammonite) confronting Nehemiah, governor of Judah, evokes Nehemiah's imprecatory prayer (Neh 3:36-38). Myers draws a parallel between the reaction of Nehemiah to Sanballat and Tobiah, and that of Jeremiah against his enemies.[56] Both in Jer 18:23 and Neh 3:36-38, opposition to the work undertaken at the command of Yahweh (proclaiming Yahweh's word and building the wall of Jerusalem) may be viewed as tantamount to opposition to Yahweh himself. The imprecatory prayer in each case is concerned with vengeance upon enemies but also is a prayer for vindication, both of Yahweh's word and the spokesman who has proclaimed it.

---

[54] The verb ידע is a key word in the Confessions (e.g., 11:18, 19; 12:3; 15:15; 17:16; 18:23), referring both to Yahweh's revelation to Jeremiah and to Yahweh's knowledge of Jeremiah and his situation. Cf. Smith, *Laments*, 17.

[55] Jacob Myers, *Ezra-Nehemiah* (AB 14; New York: Doubleday, 1965) lii. However, L. W. Batten takes a more conservative view: "The brief prayers and imprecations scattered through the document make the impression of a narrative originally written for the author's eye alone" (*The Books of Ezra and Nehemiah* [ICC; Edinburgh: T. & T. Clark, 1913] 14). Rolf Knierim assumes dependency of Neh 3:37 on Jer 18:23b, but suggests that the scribe of the Nehemiah passage is quoting freely from memory (*Die Hauptbegriffe für Sünde im Alten Testament* [Gütersloh: Gerd Mohn, 1965]) p. 224 n. 100.

[56] Myers, *Ezra-Nehemiah*, lii.

9. JEREMIAH 20:10a = PSALM 31:14a

JEREMIAH 20:10a
10a. ^a For ^a I have heard
^b the disparagement ^b of many,
^c "Terror on every side." ^c

PSALM 31:14a
14a. ^a For ^a I have heard
^b the disparagement ^b of many,
^c "Terror on every side." ^c

Textual and Translational Notes

^{a...a} כִּי Causal in 20:10a (cf. 20:8, twice); asseverative in Ps 31:14a.[57] McKane states, "...it should be noted that in Ps 31:14 כִּי is a more convincing connection than it is at Jer 20:10."[58] However, the causal use of כִּי in 20:8 and 20:10a is to give reasons for the situation described in 20:7. An apt connection with the preceding verses is provided by 20:10, since the subject matter in each case is the message which the prophet has been called to proclaim, and its effect upon those who have responded to it with mockery and denunciation.

^{b...b} דִּבַּת — The noun דִּבָּה may be taken here, with Holladay, in the sense of "defamation," "disparagement," rather than "whispering."[59]

^{c...c} מָגוֹר מִסָּבִיב — the phrase is found also in 6:25; 20:3; 46:5; 49:29 (cf. Lam 2:22, מְגוּרַי מִסָּבִיב). Volz regards the phrase as intrusive in Jer 20:10, a superscription or marginal note to provide a link with 20:1-6 (cf. 20:3).[60] However, this interjection is intrinsic to the Confession. The LXX derives מָגוֹר from גּוּר I ("to sojourn"), rather than from גּוּר III ("to dread, be afraid").

Comment

The identical phrase, כִּי שָׁמַעְתִּי דִּבַּת רַבִּים מָגוֹר מִסָּבִיב, occurs in Jer 20:10a and in Ps 31:14a (31:13E). Commentators have argued that 20:10a is dependent upon Ps 31:14a, or conversely that Ps 31:14a is derived from 20:10a. The date of Psalm 31 cannot be determined with certainty, but common liturgical language may be present both in Jer 20:10a and Ps 31:14a. מִסָּבִיב מָגוֹר could have been a common figure of speech or a proverbial saying used in both passages.

I believe that מָגוֹר מִסָּבִיב probably originates with Jeremiah himself and that the phrase in Ps 31:14a is derived from Jer 20:10a.[61] Since the phrase occurs also in 6:25; 20:3; 46:5; 49:29, and in modified form (מְגוּרַי מִסָּבִיב) in Lam 2:22, these passages should be investigated in order to discover the way

---

[57] Williams, *Hebrew Syntax*, § 444, 449.
[58] McKane, *Jeremiah 1*, 476.
[59] Holladay, *Jeremiah 1*, 555.
[60] Volz, *Jeremia*, 211.
[61] Cf. A. M. Honeyman, "Magôr Mis-sabîb and Jeremiah's Pun," *VT* 4 (1954) 424–426. He states, "...Jeremiah...is often credited with having coined the expression" (p. 424).

in which the phrase is to be understood. For Holladay, the principal passage is 20:3, where Jeremiah renames Pashhur as Magor–missabib.[62] Elaborate paranomasia is involved in 20:3–6. The שָׁחוּר part of the name פַּשְׁחוּר is related to the Aramaic word סְחוֹר ("surrounding").[63] According to Holladay, a threefold meaning of מָגוֹר is present in 20:4–6, based on three homonyms, "terror" (from גּוּר III), "enmity" (from גּוּר II) and "sojourning in exile" (from גּוּר I).[64] The name Pashhur, originally heard or twisted as pas sᵉḥôr, "fruitful on every side," has undergone a theological reversal, magôr missabîb, in which various interpretations find expression in 20:4–6.

Vermeylen draws attention to the fact that "Terror on every side" in 20:10 is used very differently from 20:3, by putting this phrase in the mouth of adversaries.[65] Diamond indicates that 20:3 is the only occurrence of מָסָבִיב מָגוֹר in a prose context, and "appears to be a redactional expansion for the editorial linking of 20:1–6 to vv.7–13."[66] In any case, מָגוֹר מִסָּבִיב in 20:10 calls for further consideration, as both here and in the other occurrences in a poetic context (6:25; 46:5; 49:29) we are dealing with an exclamatory interjection.[67] Bright imaginatively suggested some years ago that Jeremiah had used the expression "Terror All Around" so often that it was becoming a nickname, so that one man in the crowd would nudge another as Jeremiah passed, whispering "there goes old Magor-Missabib."[68]

I propose that מָגוֹר מִסָּבִיב here is an interjection which summarizes Jeremiah's message of doom, so unpalatable to his hearers, who preferred the optimistic message of false prophets. מָגוֹר מִסָּבִיב in 20:10 would then be an indignant renunciation of the judgment that Jeremiah had been proclaiming (e.g., 6:25, "Terror on every side, indeed!"). Even his familiar friends, שְׁלוֹמִי כָּל אֱנוֹשׁ (20:10, cf. אַנְשֵׁי שְׁלֹמְךָ in 38:22), cry out "Let us denounce him!" Such

---

[62] William Holladay, "The Covenant with the Patriarchs Overturned. Jeremiah's Intention in 'Terror on Every Side' (Jer 20:1-6)," JBL 91 (1972) 305–320.

[63] This view finds support in the Tg מְסָחוֹר סָחוֹר and from most scholars since Michaelis, Observationes (1793).

[64] Holladay, "The Covenant...," 306.

[65] Vermeylen, "Essai de Redaktionsgeschichte...," p. 268 n. 85.

[66] Diamond, Confessions, p. 253 n. 34. Cf. J. M. Ward ("Passhur" [IDB 3; 1962]), "The play on words in the Hebrew of vs.3 is absent in the Greek and may show assimilation to vs.10" (p. 662). The absence of κυκλόθεν in 20:3LXX leads Janzen to a similar conclusion (Studies, 73). McKane, Jeremiah 1, 462, explains 20:4–6 as "secondary exegesis of מָגוֹר." O'Connor claims that "20:1-6 can be understood as a midrash developed around this catch-word" (Confessions, 111).

[67] McKane, "an asyndetic interjection" (Jeremiah 1, 476). Berridge suggests that originally the words were shouted by Israel "at the beginning, or during the course of, a holy war" (Prophet, 90).

[68] Bright, Jeremiah, 132. Carroll, however, finds Bright's view unpersuasive, because the use of מָגוֹר מִסָּבִיב in the tradition is quite otherwise (Jeremiah, 400). He concludes that the phrase in 20:10, if not a gloss from the lament psalms, is most likely due to 20:3.

an interpretation is strengthened by the fact that the theme which runs through 20:7-10 is the mockery and reproach which the prophet has suffered in seeking to proclaim the word of Yahweh. The introductory כִּי in 20:10 adds yet another reason to supplement the reasons for his distress already given in 20:8, where כִּי is used twice. The verbs פתח and יכל used in 20:7 ("Yahweh, you have deceived me... you have prevailed") are used again in 20:10 ("Perhaps he will be deceived, then we can overcome him").[69]

The phrase חָמָס וָשֹׁד in 20:8 is also of special interest here. "Violence and destruction" could also be understood as belonging to the prophet's message. The phrase occurs in 6:7 regarding Jerusalem, "חָמָס וָשֹׁד are heard within her" (cf. Amos 3:10). The phrase is best taken in 6:7 as a hendiadys, in view of the verb in the singular(יִשָּׁמַע).[70]

Berridge, in discussing the word-pair חָמָס וָשֹׁד in prophetic writings (e.g., in Jer 6:7; 20:8; Amos 3:10; Hab 1:3; Ezek 45:9; cf. the two words used separately in Hab 2:17 and Isa 60:18), concludes, "The combination of the two words undoubtedly refers to a violation of social justice."[71] This is the sense in which 20:8a is taken in the Tg, "For at the time when I prophesy, I lift up my voice, weeping and crying out; and I prophesy against violent men and plunderers."[72] Jones has a similar understanding of the phrase: "Context suggests that the slogan serves as a summary of Jeremiah's message from which he cannot escape."[73] Carroll refers to Rudolph's reference to a threefold understanding of the phrase, in which an act of violence and oppression could be: a) the punishment announced by Jeremiah in his preaching of judgment; b) the sins denounced by Jeremiah (*Scheltrede*, cf. 6:7); and c) the ill-treatment with which Jeremiah is threatened.[74] Rudolph prefers the third interpretation, as does McKane, who finds here "an explosive verbal expression of inner

---

[69] Holladay (*Jeremiah 1*, 552-553) draws attention to the sexual connotation of the verbs פתח and חזק in 20:7, implying "seduction" (cf. Exod 22:15H) and "rape" (cf. חזק Hiphil in Deut 22:25). This view has been put forward by Abraham Heschel, *The Prophets* (New York: Harper & Row, 1962) 113-114. This is a powerful way of expressing the "attraction and coercion of God." Carroll finds this image "too grotesque and modern to be the likeliest reading of the text" (*Jeremiah*, 398).

[70] Holladay (*Jeremiah 2*) suggests that חֲמָסִי וְשֹׁארִי in 51:35 should be read "The violence and destruction done to me" (p. 399).

[71] Berridge, *Prophet*, 153. Cf. Weiser, *Jeremia*, 170.

[72] The translation given by Hayward, *The Targum of Jeremiah* (The Aramaic Bible 12 [1987]) 104. Cf. McKane, *Jeremiah 1*, 471. McKane also quotes Rashi, "For whenever I speak to them, I am compelled to shout and raise my voice, and I never proclaim good to them but prophecies of חמס and שׁד."

[73] Jones, *Jeremiah*, 273.

[74] Carroll, *Jeremiah*, 399; Rudolph, *Jeremia*, 130. Cf. חָמָס in Job 19:7, in which Job finds no answer to his cry of "Violence!" and is left with a bitter feeling of having been dealt with unjustly by God.

desperation (חמס ושד אקרא)."[75] Even if this interpretation is to be preferred, we are dealing basically with the result of the prophetic proclamation which has brought his message denouncing "violence and destruction!" unjustly back upon himself.

"Violence and destruction!" and "Terror on every side!" have been central to Jeremiah's proclamation to his people. This is borne out by 6:7, which points to oppression, and 6:25, in which judgment is declared. Although מסביב מגור in 6:25 is rendered παροικεῖ κυκλόθεν (LXX), with מגור treated as a verbal form derived from גור I, with ῥομφαία (חֶרֶב) as subject, "for the sword of enemies dwells round about," Vg follows the MT with *pavor in circuito*, "terror all around."

In addition to 20:3 and 20:10, the phrase occurs also in the OAN, 46:5 (Egypt) and 49:29 (Kedar). In 46:5, the LXX (26:5) has περιεχόμενοι κυκλόθεν, again presupposing גור I and failing to understand מגור מסביב as an exclamatory interjection. The Vg again translates literally, *terror undique*. In the case of 49:29MT, the LXX (30:7) renders ἀπώλειαν κύκλοθεν, "destruction all around," whereas the Vg follows the MT closely with *formidinem in circuito*, "terror all around."

Apart from Ps 31:14a, the only passage outside of the book of Jeremiah with a phrase similar to מָגוֹר מִסָּבִיב is found in Lam 2:22, where מְגוּרַי מִסָּבִיב occurs, usually translated "my terrors on every side." Hillers prefers the translation "my attackers" (from גור III, with a similar derivation in the case of בִּמְגוּרָיו in Job 18:19).[76] Gottwald, following the LXX (παροικίας μου κυκλόθεν), derives מְגוּרַי from גור I, and translates "sojourners from round about."[77] The reference in Lam 2:22 to "the day of the anger of Yahweh" (cf. "the day of thy anger" in Lam 2:21) obviously regards the Day of Yahweh as having taken place at the time of the destruction of Jerusalem in 587.[78]

The "enemy" (Lam 2:22) is clearly Babylonia; Zion is the speaker addressing Yahweh, as in Lam 1:14-16; 1:18-22, whereas in 20:10a the prophet's enemies and detractors include his familiar friends. The translation for מְגוּרַי מִסָּבִיב in Lam 2:22 would appear tentatively to be "those who terrify

---

[75] McKane, *Jeremiah 1*, 472. Stanley B. Morrow ("Hamas ['violentia'] in Jer 20:8," *VD* 43 [1965] 241-255) notes the use of חֲמָסִי in Gen 16:5 ("the wrong done to me"). He understands חָמָס in 20:8 as an accusation by Jeremiah of wrong done to him by Yahweh: "Defensio sui et accusatio directa est ad Jahweh oppressorem suum et iudicem, adversarium et vindicem" (p. 255). See also Clines and Gunn, "'You tried to persuade me' and 'Violence! Outrage!' in Jeremiah XX 7-8," *VT* 28 (1978) 20-27 (esp. 25-26).

[76] Delbert R. Hillers, *Lamentations* (AB 7A; New York: Doubleday, 1972) 41.

[77] Norman K. Gottwald, *Studies in the Book of Lamentations* (SBT 14; London: SCM, 1954) 84.

[78] L. Cerny (*The Day of Yahweh and Some Relevant Problems* [Prague: Nákladam Filosofické Fakulty University Karlovy, 1948]) states, "...this is the only example where the Day of Yahweh is spoken of as already being past!" (p. 20).

me round about" (cf. Vg, *qui terrerent me de circuitu*). In any case, that Lam 2:22 has been influenced by Jer 20:10a seems more probable than the reverse situation.

10. JEREMIAH 20:12=JEREMIAH 11:20

This doublet has already been discussed above (chapter two, pp. 13–18), where the conclusion was reached that 20:12 is an editorial addition serving as an *inclusio* for the first and fifth Confessions, with the purpose of providing a theodicy. Jeremiah and those like him who commit their cause to Yahweh will be eventually vindicated. The verse is appropriately inserted here, since the subject of vengeance (נְקָמָה) occurs elsewhere in the Confessions (15:15) and in 20:12b provides a catchword link with 20:10. Those who denounce Jeremiah plan to take revenge on him. The editorial insertion of 20:12 is intended to reverse this situation. Revenge upon Jeremiah's persecutors is sought, in keeping with the expectation already expressed in 20:11, "my persecutors will stumble, they will not overcome me."

צַדִּיק is the key-word in 20:12a, as is אֶבְיוֹן ("the poor, the needy") in the doxology which follows in 20:23. These are not terms which Jeremiah would be expected to apply to himself.[79] Although Harrelson detects "a ring of mocking irony" in 20:13, the call to praise, with its imperatives in the plural (הַלְלוּ, שִׁירוּ), is better understood as the spontaneous response of a reader whose comment in the margin was eventually incorporated in the text.[80] An alternative explanation cannot be discounted. Lament psalms, indeed, often include "resolution in praise" and for this reason arguments may be advanced that 20:13 is intrinsic to 20:7-13, with regard to both form and diction.[81] However, the term אֶבְיוֹן is more likely to be used by someone else in this doxology, rather than by Jeremiah to describe himself. We would expect נֶפֶשׁ rather than נֶפֶשׁ אֶבְיוֹן, if Jeremiah were himself the speaker.

---

[79] McKane (*Jeremiah 1*) writes, "...the most important question to be asked about v.13 [is] whether אביון is to be regarded as a suitable or even credible designation of the prophet Jeremiah" (p. 481).

[80] Walter Harrelson, *Interpreting the Old Testament* (New York: Holt, Rinehart and Winston Inc., 1964) 268; Cf. McKane, *Jeremiah 1*, 481.

[81] So Brueggemann, *To Pluck Up*, 178. See Clines and Gunn, "Form, Occasion and Redaction in Jeremiah 20," ZAW 88 (1976) 390–409; O'Connor (*Confessions*), "It is characteristic of the psalms of individual lament to move from statements of distress in tragic predicaments to sudden bursts of confidence and trust in the midst of suffering" (p. 69).

SUMMARY

The conclusions reached in chaps. two and three may be summarized as follows:
1. Jeremiah 11:20=20:12. See chapter two, pp. 13-19.
2. Jeremiah 11:23b=23:12b. See chapter two, pp. 19-22.
3. Jeremiah 15:13-14=17:3-4. See chapter two, pp. 25-34.
4. **Jeremiah 15:15d=Psalm 69:8a.** The appeal of the prophet to Yahweh is reflected in Psalm 69.
5. **Jeremiah 15:20=1:18-19.** Yahweh's assurance to his prophet that he will be made "a fortified wall of bronze" is taken up and expanded editorially in 1:18-19 as an introduction to the chapters which follow.
6. **Jeremiah 17:18b=1:17b.** The double use of חתת ("to be dismayed") has also been incorporated editorially in the introductory chapter of the book of Jeremiah.
7. **Jeremiah 18:20a=18:22b.** The phrase, "for they have dug a pit," rightly belongs twice in the passage, intentionally used in response to the question of adversaries in 18:20a, "Is evil a recompense for good?", and serving as an *inclusio* for the passage 18:20-22.
8. **Jeremiah 18:23b=Nehemiah 3:37(4:5E).** The imprecatory prayer, "Do not forgive their iniquity, *etc.*," in the fourth Confession, provides the model for the prayer in Neh 3:37, with slight modifications such as might be expected if the writer were quoting from memory.[82]
9. **Jeremiah 20:10a=Psalm 31:14a(31:13E).** The identical phrase, "For I have heard the disparagement of many, 'Terror on every side'," belongs to the fifth Confession and has been derived from 20:10a by the author of Ps 31:14a.
10. **Jeremiah 20:12=11:20.** See chapter two, pp. 13-19.

One cannot with confidence assign the Confessions to particular historical moments during Jeremiah's prophetic ministry. The Confessions have been inserted editorially with some skill into various contexts. They serve the purpose of validating Jeremiah as a true prophet of Yahweh. For the editor, they justify the prophet's appeal for vengeance.

---

[82] Another explanation has been proposed by B. M. Levinson, "Recovering the Lost Original Meaning of ולא תכסה עליו (Deuteronomy 13.9)," *JBL* 115 (1996) 601–620. He suggests that Nehemiah avoided the technical priestly language of Jer 18:23 (אל תכפר) and "substituted lay terminology to express the idea of divine forgiveness: כסה על" (p. 612).

CHAPTER FOUR

DOUBLETS REGARDING THE MONARCHY

Jeremiah 21:12-23:8 consists of a series of prophetic sayings on the subject of monarchy, both in poetry and prose. Two doublets conclude this group of oracles: 23:5-6=33:14-16 and 23:7-8=16:14-15. The hope of a restored monarchy (the coming of a righteous Branch) is expressed in 23:5-6=33:14-16. Jeremiah 23:7-8=16:14-15 look forward to a new exodus of the house of Israel out of the north country to dwell in their own land, an event which will surpass in significance even the exodus from Egypt in popular memory. Other passages in the book of Jeremiah which have some bearing on attitudes towards the monarchy are 17:25 (reminiscent of 22:4), 30:8-9 and 30:21. We are confronted with the question as to how much of this material comes directly from Jeremiah himself and how much has been added subsequently.

We shall consider first 23:5-6=33:14-16.

1. JEREMIAH 23:5-6=JEREMIAH 33:14-16

JEREMIAH 23:5-6
5. [a] Behold, the days are coming,[a] says Yahweh, when I shall raise up for David [c] a righteous Branch [c] And he shall reign as king and deal wisely and execute justice and righteousness in the land.
6. [d] In his days Judah will be kept safe And Israel shall dwell securely [d] and this is the name by which he will be called: [e] "Yahweh is our righteousness."

JEREMIAH 33:14-16
14. [a] Behold, the days are coming,[a] when I shall perform the good word which I have spoken to the house of Israel and the house of Judah.
15. In those days and at that time I will cause[c] a Branch of righteousness [c] for David to spring forth will execute justice and righteousness in the land.
16. [d] In those days, Judah will be in safety and Jerusalem will dwell securely. [d] And this is the name by which it will be called: [e] "Yahweh is our righteousness" [e]

Jeremiah 33:14-16 is missing in the LXX. Jeremiah 40:1-13LXX translates 33:1-13MT, but 33:14-16 is absent.

Textual and Translational Notes

a...a הִנֵּה יָמִים בָּאִים (23:5 and 33:14). This formula, usually followed by יְהוָה נְאֻם, occurs fifteen times in the book of Jeremiah. It is frequently introduced by לָכֵן (e.g., 7:32=19:6; 16:14=23:7; 48:12; 49:2; 51:47; 51:52). The formula without לָכֵן is found in 9:24; 23:5=33:14; 30:3; 31:27; 31:31; 31:38(Q). The phrase also occurs in Amos 4:2; 8:11; 9:13; Isa 39:6=2 Kgs 20:17; 1 Sam 2:31. The formula introduces an oracle of doom in 7:32=19:6; 9:24; 48:12 (Moab); 49:2 (Ammon); 51:47 (Babylon); 51:52 (Babylon); Amos 4:2 (Samaria); Amos 8:11 (Israel); Isa 39:6=2 Kgs 20:17 (Hezekiah); 1 Sam 2:31 (Eli). An oracle of salvation is introduced in 23:5=33:14; 16:14=23:7; 30:3; 31:27; 31:38(Q); Amos 9:13. In the LXX, the phrase occurs in all the passages in Jeremiah with the exception of 33:14 and 51:47, both of which are within larger sections absent in the LXX (33:14-26 and 51:44b-49a).

b...b וַהֲקִמֹתִי This is a *Stichwort* linking 23:5 with the preceding verse, 23:4, which is introduced by the same form of the verb קוּם. In 23:5 the object of the verb is צֶמַח צַדִּיק, whereas in 33:14 the verb is followed by a lengthy object clause: אֶת־הַדָּבָר הַטּוֹב אֲשֶׁר דִּבַּרְתִּי אֶל־בֵּית יִשְׂרָאֵל וְעַל־בֵּית יְהוּדָה. The reference to צֶמַח צַדִּיק and to David (לְדָוִד) in 23:5 is postponed accordingly to 33:15 (צֶמַח צְדָקָה). Jeremiah 33:15 is introduced by two other temporal phrases: הָהֵם בָּעֵת הַהִיא and בַּיָּמִים.

c...c צֶמַח צַדִּיק ("a righteous Branch," 23:5); צֶמַח צְדָקָה ("a Branch of righteousness," 33:15). The phrase ולצמח צדק occurs in line 11 of the Larnax Lapethos 2 Phoenician inscription, dated in the third century BCE.[1] G. A. Cooke translates "and to the legitimate offspring" and adds "צדק here may be either an adj צַדִּיק or more likely a noun צֶדֶק."[2] For Holladay, "the nuance of 'rightful' is central" in 23:5.[3] Yet the emphasis on "righteousness" is also prominent in the phrase וְעָשָׂה מִשְׁפָּט וּצְדָקָה (23:5; 33:15); cf. צֶמַח צְדָקָה (33:15) and the name יְהוָה צִדְקֵנוּ (23:6; 33:16). צֶמַח (23:5) is translated here and in Zech 3:8; 6:12 by ἀνατολή in the LXX, indicating that צֶמַח in these passages

---

[1] G. A. Cooke, *A Text-Book of North-Semitic Inscriptions* (Oxford: Clarendon Press, 1903) 82-88. Further bibliography relating to the Larnaca Inscription and to צמח as a technical term is supplied by Holladay, *Jeremiah 1*, 616.

[2] Cooke, *North-Semitic Inscriptions*, 86. See also James Swetnam, "Some Observations on the Background of צדיק in Jeremias 23,5a," *Bib* 46 (1965) 29-40. This inscription and other inscriptions are examined, exhibiting an overall pattern which supports the meaning of "legitimate" for צדק.

[3] Holladay, *Jeremiah 1*, 618. He translates צֶמַח צַדִּיק as "a scion, a rightful one." Mowinckel (*He That Cometh* [Oxford: Blackwell, 1956]) states, "the adjective means 'rightful' as well as 'righteous', 'just'" (p. 161).

Doublets Regarding the Monarchy   57

was regarded at the time of translation as a technical term, with messianic significance.[4]

d...d תּוּשַׁע יְהוּדָה וְיִשְׂרָאֵל יִשְׁכֹּן לָבֶטַח ("Judah will be kept safe and Israel shall dwell securely," 23:6); תִּוָּשַׁע יְהוּדָה וִירוּשָׁלַ͏ִם תִּשְׁכּוֹן לָבֶטַח ("Judah will be in safety and Jerusalem will dwell securely," 33:16). Although בֵּית יִשְׂרָאֵל and בֵּית יְהוּדָה are referred to in 33:14, the reference to יִשְׂרָאֵל (23:6) has been changed to יְרוּשָׁלַ͏ִם in 33:16. Codex Sinaiticus substitutes Ιερουσαλημ for Ισραηλ in 23:6 (cf. 30:22LXX =49:2MT).

e...e יְהוָה צִדְקֵנוּ (23:6; 33:16). The 1st pl. suffix is in contrast with the 1st s. suffix in Zedekiah's name, צִדְקִיָּהוּ ("My righteousness is Yahweh"). Jeremiah 23:6LXX understands the name as Ιωσεδεκ.[5] Additional words, ἐν τοῖς προφήταις, are added to 23:6LXX. In view of the fact that the unit 23:7–8LXX has been transferred to a position after 23:40, the additional words at the end of 23:6LXX were perhaps originally a superscription to 23:9LXX, corresponding to לַנְּבִאִים 23:9MT; cf. ἐν τοῖς προφήταις Σαμαρείας, 23:13LXX; ἐν τοῖς προφήταις Ιερουσαλημ, 23:14LXX.

Comment

Before discussing the additions to 23:5–6 in 33:14–16 and the emphasis on Jerusalem in 33:16, we should first examine 23:5–6 more closely.

When the phrase הִנֵּה יָמִים בָּאִים is preceded by לָכֵן (see Textual and Translational Notes above), as in 7:32=19:6; 48:12; 49:2; 51:47; 51:52, an oracle of judgment usually follows.[6] The phrase without לָכֵן, 23:5=33:14 and also 30:3; 31:27; 31:31; 31:38(Q), usually introduces an oracle of salvation.[7]

There are not sufficient grounds for making a distinction regarding the element of time implied by the use of the formula preceding pronouncements of judgment or salvation. Holladay claims that this stock phrase in Jeremiah

---

[4] See Raymond E. Brown, *The Birth of the Messiah* (New York: Doubleday, 1977) 390. He comments on Luke 1:78: "...ἀνατολή was a term used among Greek-speaking Jews to describe the expected king of the house of David."

[5] The name Ιωσεδεκ occurs elsewhere in the OT in the LXX only in Zech 6:11 (the father of Joshua, the high priest). Regarding 23:6, E. Lipinski ("Études sur les textes 'messianiques' de l'Ancien Testament," *Semitica* 20 [1970] 41-57) claims that Ιωσεδεκ is the exact equivalent to the name of Zedekiah, on the basis that the theophoric element in the name may come either at the beginning or the end, as in the case of Zedekiah's predecessor, יְהוֹיָכִן (52:31) and כָּנְיָהוּ (22:24).

[6] An exception is in the pericope which follows 23:5–6, where 23:7–8 (=16:14–15) introduces the "new Exodus" *motif*. לָכֵן in 23:7 provides a link with 23:3, while עוֹד וְלֹא־יֹאמְרוּ is reminiscent of וְלֹא־יֵאָמְרוּ in 7:32 (cf. Holladay, *Jeremiah 1*, 622).

[7] An exception is 9:24MT, an oracle of judgment, as in Amos 4:2; 8:11. In Amos 9:13, the formula precedes an oracle of salvation. Janzen (*Studies*) comments, "About half the time, the formula is הנה ימים באים in Jer., the other half of the time it is הנה ימים באים לכן" (p. 220 n. 16).

should not be understood as eschatological, but "simply that there will be a profound reversal in the near future."[8] McKane, on the other hand, discussing 23:5 specifically, notes: "Most commentators have rightly supposed (cf. Duhm) that הנה ימים באים is indicative of a distant rather than an immediate future."[9] This is not to be thought of as "eschatological" in the way that Rudolph and Weiser have understood it, because "the portrayal is not that of a Messianic kingdom beyond the end of the present age."[10] Thiel assumes that the formula is used predominantly by the Deuteronomists.[11] However, the formula as a prelude to oracles of judgment appears to indicate an imminent threat, whereas oracles of salvation are oriented towards a more distant future.

The only use of the term צֶמַח in the book of Jeremiah is found within the phrase וַהֲקִמֹתִי לְדָוִד צֶמַח צַדִּיק in 23:5 and the parallel phrase לְדָוִד צֶמַח צְדָקָה אַצְמִיחַ in 33:15. The somewhat similar but much more extensive pericope in Isa 11:1 uses quite different terminology (חֹטֶר; נֵצֶר). In Isa 4:2 (צֶמַח יהוה) and in Isa 61:11 (צְמָחֶיהָ), צֶמַח occurs in a context of the fertility of the earth.[12] The term is found also in two passages in the book of Zechariah, Zech 3:8 and 6:12. Although Joshua the high priest is addressed (Zech 3:6), "my servant the Branch" (עַבְדִּי צֶמַח) in Zech 3:8 seems to be a reference to Zerubbabel.[13] In Zech 6:9-14, Joshua is to have a crown set on his head (Zech 6:11). However, "the man whose name is the Branch" (Zech 6:12) is usually taken to be Zerubbabel, whose task it was to "build the temple of Yahweh" (cf. Zech 4:9).[14] The relationship between the Jeremiah צֶמַח passages (23:5; 33:15) and the Zechariah passages (3:8; 6:12) needs to be explored. Much depends on

---

[8] Holladay, *Jeremiah 1*, 268-269.

[9] McKane, *Jeremiah 1*, 560.

[10] McKane, *Jeremiah 1*, 561.

[11] Thiel, *Redaktion 1*, 249. Cf. his assignment to D of 30:3, within the introduction to Jeremiah 30-31, chapters which nevertheless contain Judaean texts which do not stem from D (Thiel, *Redaktion 2*, 21). Jones (*Jeremiah*, 371-372) discusses the formula in the book of Jeremiah and concludes that "this phrase marks the introduction within the prose tradition of passages referring to the ultimate future from the perspective of the sixth century" (p. 372).

[12] See Joyce G. Baldwin, "Semah as a Technical Term in the Prophets," *VT* 14 (1964) 93-97. She claims that in Isa 4:2 "...the striking phrase 'shoot of Yahweh' does not seem to be sufficiently explained by the vegetation which he causes to grow," "...the phrase is beginning to be used in a messianic sense" (pp. 93-94).

[13] H. G. Mitchell, in H. G. Mitchell, J. M. P. Smith, and J. A. Bewer, *A Critical and Exegetical Commentary on Haggai, Zechariah, Malachi and Jonah* (ICC; Edinburgh: T. & T.Clark, 1912) 156. McKane is more cautious about the identification of צֶמַח with Zerubbabel, "...it is not evident that צמח functions as a metaphor at Zech 3:8 differently from צמח at Jer 23:5 and חטר at Isa 11:1" (*Jeremiah 1*, 562).

[14] Baldwin draws attention to the omission of the definite article before אִישׁ in Zech 6:12 (cf. LXX ἀνήρ; Vg *vir*) and concludes that "someone other than either Joshua or Zerubbabel is meant" ("Semah as a Technical Term," 95). However, the omission may be the result of haplography, since ה is the final letter of the preceding word, הִנֵּה.

whether the unit 23:5-6 comes from Jeremiah himself. Bright, drawing attention to the "similarity of the future Davidide's name to that of Zedekiah," ascribes these words to a period early in Zedekiah's reign.[15] Dynastic hopes were revived when Nebuchadrezzar established Zedekiah as ruler after the deportation of his nephew, Jehoiachin. However, the "true Shoot" would not be Zedekiah, but a future king of the line of David. Rudolph holds a similar view, but does not believe that the word צֶמַח is to be taken as a *terminus technicus* for Messiah in 23:5.[16] Cornill detected in צִדְקֵנוּ a play on the name of Zedekiah in the ascription of this name to the צֶמַח in 23:6.[17] Some scholars claim that an intentional contrast has been made between Zedekiah's name and the name by which the צֶמַח will be called.[18]

Among those who consider 23:5-6 to be post-Jeremianic and late are Duhm, Volz, Carroll, McKane and Jones. Perhaps under the influence of Jer 23:5, interest in Zerubbabel (the son of Shealtiel [Ezra 3:2, 8], grandson of Jehoiachin [1 Chr 3:17-19]) in the book of Zechariah (e.g., Zech 4:6-10; 6:12; cf. Hag 1:1), indicates the hope that the Davidic line might be restored.

If 22:28-30 is indeed Jeremianic, the prophet did not expect a descendant of Jehoiachin to "succeed in sitting on the throne of David and ruling again in Judah" (22:30 RSV).[19] Jeconiah's seven sons are listed in 1 Chr 13:17-18; the word "childless" (עֲרִירִי) in 22:3 is not necessarily to be taken literally, but implies that no descendant will reign again in Judah.[20] In view of the death of

---

[15] Bright, *Jeremiah*, 143.

[16] Rudolph, *Jeremia*, 145-147.

[17] See John Skinner, *Prophecy and Religion* (Cambridge University Press, 1922), p. 312 n. 1.

[18] Drinkard (*Jeremiah 1*) states, "The name of this new king reverses the elements of Zedekiah's name (צִדְקִיָּהוּ, 'Zedekiah'; צִדְקֵנוּ יהוה, 'Yahweh is our righteousness'), indicative perhaps that all the aspects of Zedekiah are here reversed" (p. 329).

[19] Holladay (*Jeremiah 1*, 609) interprets 22:28 as a question raised by the people, who do not believe that Jehoiachin is "a smashed puppet or vessel no one cares for," to which Jeremiah responds with a word of judgment on Jehoiachin (22:29-30). McKane believes that the references to Jehoiachin's offspring in 22:28, 30 are secondary (*Jeremiah 1*, 551); cf. Carroll, *Jeremiah*, 440.

[20] See Rudolph, *Jeremia*, 143. He claims that Jehoiachin's sons would not be registered in the list of citizens in Jerusalem, and as children born in exile would have no justification for succeeding to the throne. Cf. W. J. Wessels, "Jeremiah 22,24-30. A Proposed Ideological Reading," *ZAW* (1989) 232-249. He makes a careful analysis of 22:24-30, in which he concludes that 22:28-30 contains genuine Jeremianic words spoken at the time of Jehoiachin's consecration as king. Jeremiah was speaking vehemently against Jehoiachin, who represented Egyptian control of the state (p. 245). The term "childless" may represent an over-reaction or is to be understood as hyperbole, but in any event, children born in a strange land would not appear in the register of citizens of Jerusalem (p. 243). Cf. G. R. Driver, "Linguistic and Textual Problems. Jeremiah," *JQR* NS (1937-1938) 97-129. He claims (p. 115) that the real meaning of עֲרִירִי is "disgraced," "stripped of honour" (cf. LXX ἐκκήρυκτον; O.L. *abdicatum*).

Zedekiah's sons in 587 BCE and Zedekiah's deportation to Babylon (39:1-10; cf. 34:2-5) and death in exile (52:11), the royal line (apart from Jehoiachin and his sons) has come to an end.[21] The fact that the book of Jeremiah ends with an appendix (Jeremiah 52) which concludes with Jehoiachin's rehabilitation (52:31-34), as does also 2 Kgs 25:27-30, may suggest that a flicker of hope for the Davidic dynasty was kept alive in Jehoiachin (cf. 28:4) and his descendants, but there is nothing to indicate that 23:5 has any connection with Jehoiachin.

Jeremiah and Ideal Monarchy

There is an interesting possibility, however, that 23:5-6 may represent a later expansion of words of Jeremiah that were originally intended to portray the standards of ideal monarchy. A king should וְעָשָׂה מִשְׁפָּט וּצְדָקָה בָּאָרֶץ ("execute justice and righteousness in the land," 23:5). This is a phrase which appears with minor variations in 22:3 (מִשְׁפָּט וּצְדָקָה עֲשׂוּ) and in 22:15, describing the reign of Josiah (וְעָשָׂה מִשְׁפָּט וּצְדָקָה). An editorial catchword link is found in the recurrence of this phrase which sets out Jeremiah's ideal for monarchy, an ideal preserved in the Jeremiah tradition. Although Jeremiah was intensely critical of the monarchy, as Jeremiah 22 clearly indicates, he had high praise for Josiah, who came closest to his ideal by executing justice and righteousness and by judging the cause of the poor and needy (22:15, 16). Doubtless, Jeremiah approved of Josiah's Deuteronomic reform, although he became disillusioned when he realized that legislative changes do not guarantee the transformation of the heart which alone could bring about the religious and social changes that were so desperately needed.[22]

In 21:11, the king of Judah (unspecified) is addressed "O house of David" (22:1), "O king of Judah, who sit on the throne of David." The ideals which should be exemplified in monarchy are set forth: justice and righteousness; freedom from oppression; concern for the alien, the fatherless and widow. Could it be that Jeremiah challenged Zedekiah with such ideals, expressly since his theophoric throne-name ("my righteousness is Yahweh") should have been a constant reminder that Yahweh demanded righteousness? At a much later date

---

[21] See Leslie, *Jeremiah*, 217-218. He points out that "there are other members of the Davidic house of another line" (e.g., Ishmael "of the seed royal," 41:1, using the same term applied to Zedekiah in Ezek 17:13) and that Jeremiah in 23:5-6 looks forward to a future ruler of the house of David whose reign will be in contrast to Zedekiah. Ishmael himself, the murderer of Gedaliah (41:2), would certainly not be the future king expected in 23:5. The name Jerahmeel, "the king's son" (36:26), appears on a *bulla* which would date from the time of Jeremiah; see Nahman Avigad, *Hebrew Bullae from the Time of Jeremiah. Remnants from a Burnt Archive* (Jerusalem: Israel Exploration Society, 1986) 27. Philip J. King states: "According to Avigad, persons bearing this title were assigned to the royal family, without being natural sons of the king" (*Jeremiah. An Archaeological Companion* [Louisville, Kentucky: Westminster Press, 1993]) 95.

[22] Cf. Henri Cazelles, "Jérémie et le Deutéronome," *RSR* 38 (1984) 5-36.

among the custodians of the Jeremianic tradition hopes were revived that the monarchy would be restored, in keeping with the concept of the Davidic monarchy as permanent (2 Sam 7:13). Jeremiah's ideals were projected into the future and expressed in the expectation of a king of the royal line of David, yet to come, in whom they would be realized. The righteous Branch to be raised up by Yahweh would also have a theophoric name, "Yahweh is our righteousness," indicating that both king and people will demonstrate Yahweh's righteousness. At this time (perhaps late in the period of the exile) צֶדֶק־צְדָקָה vocabulary will also have taken on overtones of vindication and salvation. צִדְקֵנוּ יְהוָה means virtually, "Yahweh is our salvation."[23]

In 33:16, the theophoric name, יְהוָה צִדְקֵנוּ, will be the name by which Jerusalem will be called.[24] The emphasis on Jerusalem serves as a prelude to the three units which follow: 33:17-18; 33:19-21; 33:23-26, which have as their focus the permanence of the royal line of David and the Levitical priesthood in a united kingdom. Jeremiah 33:26 contains the phrase "I will restore their fortunes" (אָשׁוּב אֶת־שְׁבוּתָם) which not only provides a catchword link with 33:7 and 33:11, but an *inclusio* with 30:3.[25]

Jeremiah 33:14-26, dated by Holladay towards the end of the 5th. century, is missing in the LXX.[26] Rudolph describes these verses as a broadsheet reflecting apologetic tendencies.[27] The author is interested in the

---

[23] See Norman Snaith, *The Distinctive Ideas of the Old Testament* (London: Epworth Press, 1944) 87-88. He attributes this soteriological understanding of צדק to Deutero-Isaiah, but detects in Jer 23:6 a connection between "Judah shall be saved" and the new name, "Yahweh is our righteousness." Cf. B. Johnson, regarding 23:6, "Yahweh is the salvation, the deliverance of his people" ("צֶדֶק־צְדָקָה"), *TWAT* VI.8; [Stuttgart: W. Kohlhammer, 1989] 911).

[24] Cf. Isa 1:26, "Afterward you shall be called the city of righteousness" (עִיר הַצֶּדֶק).

[25] The recurrence of the phrase in 30:3; 31:23; 33:7; 33:11 and 33:26 suggests that the same hand which provided 30:1-4 as a prologue to the Book of Consolation (Jeremiah 30-31) added 31:23-40. This is a parallel version to the biographical accounts in 32:1-33:13 and the future hopes later expressed in 33:14-26. The two passages have various themes in common: building and planting (31:28 and 32:41); renewed covenant (31:31; 32:40; 33:19-22); the covenantal formula (31:33; 32:38); and a people in a permanent relationship with Yahweh (31:35-36; 33:17, 23-26). In both sections, geographical indications of the extent of the territories affected are given: 31:38-40; 32:44; 33:12-13, with the emphasis on Jerusalem in 31:38-40 and on Judah in 32:44; 33:12-13.

[26] Holladay, *Jeremiah 1*, 230. As Janzen points out, 33:14-26 is the largest single block of the MT material absent in the LXX (*Studies*, 122-123). He argues that the translator did not omit it intentionally, even although 33:15-16 duplicates 23:5-6, since 33:17-18, 21-22 do not have parallels elsewhere in the book. He concludes that the pericope was added to the MT after the divergence of the two text traditions. E. Tov claims that the shorter LXX version of the book of Jeremiah *in toto* was an earlier edition of the book (*The Text-Critical Use of the Septuagint in Biblical Research* [Jerusalem Biblical Studies 3; Jerusalem: Simor, 1981] 296).

[27] Rudolph, *Jeremia*, 217-219.

continuity of the restored Davidide monarchy along the lines of Nathan's prophecy in 2 Sam 7:16. "In his days" (23:6, regarding the righteous Branch) has been changed to the more general "in those days and at that time"(33:15).²⁸ The reference to Yahweh's covenant with day and night (33:25) and "the fixed orders" (חֻקּוֹת) of heaven and earth are similar to the statements in the poetic passage, 31:35-37.²⁹ Rudolph discusses at length the references to Levitical priests in 33:18, 21, 22 and concludes that these may indicate a date as late as the time of Ezra and Nehemiah.³⁰

The collection of sayings concerning the monarchy, 21:11-23:6, begins in 21:11 (cf. 22:1) with the command to the prophet to speak the word of Yahweh regarding "the house of the king of Judah," using the address, "O house of David!" (21:11; cf. 22:2, "O king of Judah, who sit on the throne of David"). No particular king is identified.³¹ This supports the view that the collection contains general statements of Jeremiah regarding the ideals of monarchy, which have been amplified and revised editorially. A connecting link between the recurring phrase וְהַצִּילוּ גָזוּל מִיַּד עוֹשֵׁק ("deliver from the hand of the oppressor him who has been robbed," 21:12 and 22:3) suggests that 22:1-5, 6-7 are related editorially to 21:11-12, 13-14 (note also the reference to אֵשׁ ["fire"] in 22:7 and 21:12, 14).³²

Recurring Phrases in Jeremiah 21:12b and Jeremiah 4:4b

In Jer 21:12a, the "house of David" is exhorted to "Execute justice" and "deliver from the oppressor anyone who has been robbed." An interesting link exists between 21:12b and 4:4. Jeremiah 21:12b is a phrase which repeats 4:4b

---

²⁸ See Thiel, *Redaktion 1*, 97. He claims that the eschatological phrase "in those days" belongs as a rule to late passages (e.g., not only 33:15, but also 33:16; 3:18; 50:4, 20; all regarded as post-Deuteronomistic).

²⁹ Cf. also the use of the phrase כָּל־הַיָּמִים in 33:18 and 31:36.

³⁰ Rudolph, *Jeremia*, 219. Cf. Carroll, *Jeremiah*, 639. He claims that "sources in the Persian period" are reflected here. Jones *(Jeremiah)* refers to Deut 10:8-9 and the sacrificial function of the Levitical priests (33:18) as an indication that the statements made in Jeremiah 33 regarding the Levitical priests are prior to the resolution of the precise nature of the priesthood, therefore "this passage is unlikely to be later than the fifth century and might well be late sixth" (p. 423). For a full discussion of the origins and evolution of the priesthood, especially in relation to the second temple, see Raymond Abba, "Priests and Levites" *(IDB* 3; New York: Abingdon Press, 1962) 876-889; George Buchanan Gray, *Sacrifice in the Old Testament* (Oxford: Clarendon, 1925) 179-270.

³¹ In the phrase לְבֵית מֶלֶךְ יְהוּדָה, ל may be taken as a *lamedh* of specification (Williams, *Hebrew Syntax* § 273). The phrase serves as an introduction to the oracles regarding monarchy which follow in 21:11-23:8.

³² Nicholson draws attention to the repetition of the phrase and notes, "...the word translated *victim* [גָּזוּל] occurs in the book of Jeremiah only in these two passages. This favours the view...that 22:1-5 is an expansion of 21:11-12" *(Jeremiah 1*, 183).

verbatim, except for the final word מַעַלְלֵיכֶם, for which the 3d pl. suffix is substituted: פֶּן־תֵּצֵא כָאֵשׁ חֲמָתִי וּבָעֲרָה וְאֵין מְכַבֶּה מִפְּנֵי רֹעַ מַעַלְלֵיהֶם. The LXX translates the final phrase in 4:4b (מִפְּנֵי רֹעַ מַעַלְלֵיכֶם) as ἀπὸ προσώπου πονηρίας ἐπιτηδευμάτων ὑμῶν, but the phrase is missing in 21:12bLXX. The collection of sayings, 2:2b-4:4, is introduced editorially by 2:1-2a and concludes with an oracle, 4:3-4, addressed to "the men of Judah and to the inhabitants of Jerusalem" (4:3a). The entire introduction in the MT (2:1-2a): יְרוּשָׁלִַם לֵאמֹר וַיְהִי דְבַר־יְהוָה אֵלַי לֵאמֹר הָלֹךְ וְקָרָאתָ בְאָזְנֵי is represented by only two words in the LXX: καὶ εἶπε. Although Rudolph claims that the LXX had abbreviated the MT at this point, Janzen argues against this view on the grounds that if the LXX translator had to deal with the MT in its present form the abbreviation would have been καὶ εἶπεν ιερεμιας.[33] In any case, the MT should be retained, as 2:1MT provides a link with 1:4; 1:11; 1:13. The emphasis on Jerusalem (2:2) and on Judah and Jerusalem (4:3) in a collection of sayings largely addressed to "Israel" (2:4; 2:14; 2:26; 3:20; 4:1) points to a late redaction.[34] McKane, following Rudolph and Weiser, nevertheless sees a connection between 2:1-2 and the event recorded in Jeremiah 36, "Another explanation of the appearance of 'Jerusalem' and a more positive estimate of its function associates it with the reading of the scroll by Baruch in the Jerusalem temple in 605."[35] The scroll read in the temple by Baruch would then contain oracles such as those now recorded in Jeremiah 2-6. However, this collection of Jeremianic oracles has been subject to editorial additions such as 2:1-2a; 4:3-4.

The superscription in 4:3 ties in well with the opening words of 4:5 ("Declare in Judah, and proclaim in Jerusalem") which introduce the collection of oracles, 4:5-6:30, in relation to the "foe from the north." There is a link also with the preceding oracles; 4:3-4 provides, as Carroll observes, "an appropriate

---

[33] Rudolph, *Jeremia,* 14; Janzen, *Studies,* 113. Holladay, *contra* Janzen, follows Rudolph here and claims that "each introductory rubric has its own integrity" (*Jeremiah 1,* 81).

[34] Carroll, "The formulaic introduction is typical of the late redaction of the tradition (lacking in G)" (*Jeremiah,* 119). Thiel regards the phrase "men of Judah and inhabitants of Jerusalem" in 4:3, 4 (cf. 11:2; 11:9; 17:25; 18:11; 32:32) as a typical Deuteronomistic phrase (*Redaktion 1,* 95; cf. Carroll, *Jeremiah,* 158-159). Holladay (*Jeremiah 1*) argues that "an inner core was expanded both at the beginning and the end by material destined for Jerusalem" (p. 63). Cf. R. Albertz, "Jer 2-6 und die Frühzeitverkündigung Jeremias," *ZAW* 94 (1982) 452-467. Pohlmann (*Studien*), on the other hand, criticizes this view, concluding that "house of Jacob" (i.e., "house of Israel") does not refer specifically to the northern kingdom of Israel, and that "this complex is in no way the early proclamation of Jeremiah, indeed, it does not reflect the historical Jeremiah anyway" (p. 116). To regard the entire collection of oracles in Jeremiah 2-6 as post-Jeremianic does not seem to be convincing (e.g., in the light of the repeated references to "the foe from the north" in 4:5-6:30). For the view that Jeremiah 2-6 contains mostly genuine Jeremianic material from his early prophetic activity, see R. Liwak, *Der Prophet und die Geschichte*(BWANT 121; Berlin: Kohlhammer, 1987).

[35] McKane, *Jeremiah 1,* 26.

conclusion to the liturgy of turning in 3:21-4:2."³⁶ Jeremiah 4:3b begins with the phrase נִירוּ לָכֶם נִיר ("Break up your fallow ground"), a phrase found also in Hos 10:12b. Whether or not this is a direct quotation from Hosea (Holladay) or the employment of a popular proverb by both Hosea and Jeremiah (Duhm), clearly the context in each case establishes a different use of the imagery.³⁷ Hosea is concerned with the quality of the seed sown and the subsequent harvest to be reaped, whereas Jer 4:3 expresses the need for well-prepared soil. The imagery regarding circumcision of the heart in 4:4 reflects the admonition in Deut 10:16 (cf. the reference to "the uncircumcised heart" in Lev 26:41), with the addition of ליהוה and the use of the verb הָסִרוּ.³⁸ The ideas expressed in 4:3-4 are in accord with Jeremiah's emphasis on the need for radical change, although the address in 4:4, "O men of Judah and inhabitants of Jerusalem," may have been added by the redactor at the same time as the superscription in 4:3a.

The warning in 4:4b finds its counterpart in 21:12b, except for the replacement of the single word מַעַלְלֵיכֶם (4:4b) by מַעַלְלֵיהֶם (21:12b). The absence of a translation for מִפְּנֵי רֹעַ מַעַלְלֵיהֶם in 21:12bLXX indicates that only the first part of 4:4b was repeated in 21:12b, and the final phrase "because of the evil of their doings" (in which the 3d pl. suffix is substituted for the 2d pl. suffix of 4:4b) was added to the Hebrew text later. A plausible explanation of the textual situation is offered by McKane, "The phrase, as a marginal comment, explained why the threat was being issued and the commentator was no doubt influenced by 4:4."³⁹

The prose passage 22:1-5, addressed to an unnamed king of Judah, appears to be a prose variant of 21:11-12.⁴⁰ Jeremiah 22:3a not only stresses the role the king must play in the dispensing of justice (מִשְׁפָּט), already stated in 21:12a, but contains the phrase וְהַצִּילוּ גָזוּל מִיַּד עָשׁוֹק which also occurs in 21:12.⁴¹

Also to be noted is the parallelism between 22:4 and 17:25, where the text is sufficiently close to enable us to classify these verses as doublets.

---

³⁶ Carroll, *Jeremiah*, 157.
³⁷ Holladay, *Jeremiah 1*, 129; Duhm, *Jeremia*, 46; see also McKane, *Jeremiah 1*, 87.
³⁸ Jeremiah 4:4 also uses the phrase עָרְלוֹת לְבַבְכֶם, although many MSS, LXX and Syr read עָרְלַת (as in Deut 10:16).
³⁹ McKane, *Jeremiah 1*, 510.
⁴⁰ Holladay, *Jeremiah 1*, 580; cf. Nicholson, *Jeremiah 1*, 181.
⁴¹ In 21:12, עוֹשֵׁק is found rather than עָשׁוֹק (22:3). The LXX, Syr and Tg read עשׁקו in both instances. McKane (*Jeremiah 1*, 514), following Duhm, considers עשׁוק to be a scribal error, but draws attention to Kimchi's view that this form, on the analogy of קרוב, would have the same sense as עושׁק ("oppressor").

2. JEREMIAH 22:4 = JEREMIAH 17:25

JEREMIAH 22:4
4.[a] For if you indeed carry out this word,[a] then kings who sit on David's throne [b] will enter the gates of this house,[b] riding in chariots and on horses, [c] they and their servants and their people.[c]

JEREMIAH 17:25
25. [b] Then shall enter through the gates of this city [b] kings [d] and princes[d] who sit on the throne of David, riding in chariots and on horses, [c] they and their princes, men of Judah and the inhabitants of Jerusalem, [e] [e] and this city shall be inhabited for ever.

Textual and Translational Notes

[a...a] The introductory conditional phrase in 22:4 אִם־עָשׂוֹ תַּעֲשׂוּ אֶת־הַדָּבָר הַזֶּה כִּי has its counterpart in 17:24a: וְהָיָה אִם־שָׁמֹעַ תִּשְׁמְעוּן אֵלַי נְאֻם־יְהוָה, using the infinitive absolute of the verb in each case for emphasis.

[b...b] בְּשַׁעֲרֵי הַבַּיִת הַזֶּה ("the gates of this house," 22:4); בְּשַׁעֲרֵי הָעִיר הַזֹּאת ("the gates of this city," 17:25). The reference is to the royal palace in 22:4 and to the city of Jerusalem in 17:25.

[c...c] הוּא וַעֲבָדָיו וְעַמּוֹ (22:4). In this phrase, the reference back to מְלָכִים (pl.), as in 22:2, is made applicable to an individual king, whereas the LXX uses plural forms (cf. Vg). In 17:25, the plural is used in a different phrase (with אִישׁ as collective): הֵמָּה וְשָׂרֵיהֶם אִישׁ יְהוּדָה וְיֹשְׁבֵי יְרוּשָׁלִָם.

[d...d] וְשָׂרִים (17:25). Probably included by dittography; the following word is יֹשְׁבִים. וְשָׂרֵיהֶם occurs later in the sentence.[42] Both the LXX (καὶ οἱ ἄρχοντες) and Vg (*et principes*) follow the MT, as does Tg.

[e...e] וְיָשְׁבָה הָעִיר־הַזֹּאת לְעוֹלָם (17:25). The additional phrase, "and this city shall be inhabited forever," makes a promise that is contingent upon keeping the sabbath day holy.

Comment

In 22:4, a specific but unnamed king of Judah is addressed, together with his servants and the people who enter the gates of the palace (22:1-2). The content of the prophetic message emphasizes the administration of justice especially towards those who need their rights to be recognized and defended, he "who has been robbed," "the alien, the fatherless and the widow" (22:3).

---

[42] Carroll, *Jeremiah*, 366.

The shedding of innocent blood "in this place" is prohibited (22:3; cf. 7:6).⁴³ The close parallelism between 22:3 and 7:5-7 is obvious. The conditional sentences in 22:4, 5 differ slightly from those in 7:5, 6, but in the context "executing justice" (22:3; 7:5) is a key issue.

The parallel passage, 17:24-25, stresses keeping holy the sabbath day by doing no work on it and bringing in no burden by the gates of Jerusalem. In the context, those addressed are "you kings of Judah, and all Judah, and all the inhabitants of Jerusalem, who enter by these gates" (17:20).⁴⁴ The entire pericope, 17:19-27, underlines the importance of Sabbath day observance. The passage is very similar to Neh 13:15-22, in which Nehemiah takes action to stop commercial activities on the Sabbath day involving many kinds of merchandise being brought into Jerusalem for sale. The use of the term מַשָּׂא, "burden," in Neh 13:15 finds a parallel in the repeated use of מַשָּׂא in 17:21, 22, 24, 27. Jeremiah 17:19-27 is therefore usually regarded as post-Jeremianic, reflecting a period when observing the Sabbath was a paramount concern.⁴⁵ W. Emery Barnes, on the other hand, accepts the passage as Jeremianic, and assigns the incident to "the middle point of Jeremiah's activity."⁴⁶ He draws attention to 22:13, the condemnation of Jehoiakim, who built his grandiose palace with slave labour. To rest on the Sabbath day was a charter of freedom for the labourer; "keep the Sabbath" means "cease from oppression." Rather

---

⁴³ "In this place" (22:3) would presumably refer to the palace area, although the same phrase connoting the temple area in 7:6 (cf. 7:3) is expanded in 7:7 to mean "the land that I gave of old to your fathers for ever" (cf. 25:5b). In 7:20, "in this place" also has a frame of reference wider than the temple area. Kilpp refers to הַמָּקוֹם הַזֶּה as "a favourite dtrjer expression" occurring frequently in the book of Jeremiah, e.g., 7:3, 6, 7, 20; 14:13; 19:3, 4(*bis*),6, 7, 12; 22:3, 11; 24:5; 27:22; 29:10; 32:37; 40:2; 42:18; 44:29 (*Niederreissen und aufbauen*, p. 27 n. 1). Kilpp regards the occurrences in 33:10, 12 as post-Deuteronomistic. The remaining six occurrences are in 28:3(*bis*), 6 ("a biographical passage") and in 16:2, 3, 9 ("an autobiographical passage"). The expression occurs in prose passages only. In general, the reference is to the city of Jerusalem, often as *pars pro toto* for the whole land (cf. Thiel, *Redaktion 1*, 108).

⁴⁴ According to 17:19MT, Jeremiah is instructed to stand בְּשַׁעַר בְּנֵי־עָם to make his proclamation. Volz, *Jeremia*, 191, proposes the emendation בְּשַׁעַר בִּנְיָמִין on the basis of 37:13; 38:7 (*Jeremia*, 191). Cf. Arnold B. Ehrlich, *Randglossen zur Hebräischen Bibel: textkritisches, sprachliches und sachliches*, V (Leipzig: J. C. Hinrich's, 1912) 288. Holladay argues for the retention of the MT because of the support of the versions and the reference to "all the gates of Jerusalem" in 17:19b, but believes that a temple gate rather than a city gate is referred to, especially if 17:19-27 is modeled on 7:1-12 (*Jeremiah 1*, 510).

⁴⁵ For example, Giesebrecht, *Jeremia*, 101. He regards the passage as unauthentic; cf. Volz, "not Jeremianic" (*Jeremia*, 190); Holladay (*Jeremiah 1*) "neither the diction nor the subject matter can be identified with anything authentic to him [Jeremiah]" (p. 509); McKane (*Jeremiah 1*), "the passage reflects the importance attached to the Sabbath commandment in the post-exilic community" (p. 419).

⁴⁶ W. Emery Barnes, "Prophecy and the Sabbath (A Note on the Teaching of Jeremiah)," *JTS* 29 (1928) 390.

than adopt this speculative view, one is inclined to admit the possibility that keeping the Sabbath was of importance to Jeremiah, but that 17:9-27 emanates from those who sought to apply their understanding (or misunderstanding?) of Jeremiah's words in a post-exilic situation.[47]

Thiel regards the form of the passage, 17:19-27, as an example of "Alternativ-Predigten," typical of D, as in 7:1-15 and especially 22:4, 5.[48] Each of these prose passages (7:1-15; 17:19-27; 22:1-5) has been inserted after a poetic passage. Why has 17:19-27 been inserted at this point, after the so-called "Confession," 17:14-18? Holladay sees a catchword connection (יוֹם in 17:16, 17, 18; cf. 17:21, 24, 27) but this in itself seems an insufficient explanation, since "day of disaster," "day of evil," does not correspond to "Sabbath day."[49] Smith concentrates attention on the superscription in 17:19 (כֹּה־אָמַר יְהוָה אֵלַי), which has its exact counterpart in 13:1.[50] He regards this superscription as designed to give order to the material, seeming to have been added in the post-exilic period. The fact that אֵלַי is missing in the LXX in both 13:1 and 17:19 may also point to a late date for the superscription. A thorough study of the superscriptions in the book of Jeremiah would assist in an understanding of how the book was compiled.

In both 22:4 and 17:25 the consequence of right actions (22:3, executing justice; 17:25, keeping the Sabbath day holy) will lead to "kings who sit on the throne of David, riding in chariots and on horses" entering through the palace gates (22:4) or "by the gates of this city" (17:25). Jeremiah 17:25 runs parallel to 22:4 in holding out this promise, although "they and their princes (שָׂרֵיהֶם), the men of Judah and the inhabitants of Jerusalem" seems to reflect 17:20, just as the singular forms in 22:4 (הוּא וַעֲבָדָיו וְעַמּוֹ) point back to 22:2.[51]

---

[47] Bright, *Jeremiah*, 120. Cf. Niels-Erik Andreasen, *The Old Testament Sabbath: A Tradition-Historical Investigation* (SBLDS 7; Missoula: Scholars Press, 1972). He states, "It is possible that we are dealing with words and ideas of the prophet, as they were understood or misunderstood by his disciples" (p. 34). According to Nicholson (*Preaching to the Exiles*), 17:19-27 "must be understood as the work of those who developed the Jeremianic tradition" (p. 66). Cf. Jones (*Jeremiah*), "The passage...has a distant but substantial link with the teaching of Jeremiah, but in its elaborated form belongs to the exilic or post-exilic period" (p. 249). See also Michael Fishbane, "Revelation and Tradition. Aspects of Inner-Biblical Exegesis," *JBL* 99 (1980) 343-361. He cites 17:19-27 as an example of the way in which "protective restrictions were added to biblical laws so as to safeguard them from infraction" (p. 348).

[48] Thiel, *Redaktion 1*, 204. Cf. Carroll, *Jeremiah*, 367; Nicholson, *Preaching to the Exiles*, 65. Nicholson gives examples of this Deuteronomistic homiletical form: Deut 6:1-19; 7:1-15; 8:1-20; Josh 23; 2 Kgs 17:7-20.

[49] Holladay, *Jeremiah 1*, 509. Cf. כִּסֵּא in 17:12, 25 as another catchword association; Holladay, *Architecture*, 158.

[50] Smith, *Laments*, 34, 35, 37.

[51] McKane (*Jeremiah 1*), "...what is intended is kings with their retinue of שָׂרִים" (p. 415).

The phrase "who sit on the throne of David" occurs several times in the book of Jeremiah, e.g., not only in 17:25 and 22:4, but in 13:13; 22:2; 22:30. Jeremiah 22:30 states categorically that none of Jehoiachin's offspring shall sit on the throne of David. In 29:16, Zedekiah and the people of Jerusalem will be pursued with sword, famine, and pestilence.[52] In 36:30, "He (Jehoiakim) shall have none to sit upon the throne of David." Jeremiah 22:30; 29:16; 36:30 imply the end of the monarchy; on the other hand, 33:17 ("David shall never lack a man to sit on the throne of the house of Israel") restates the promise of 2 Sam 7:16 and 1 Kgs 8:25. Jeremiah 17:25 and 22:4 hold out the hope of the restoration of the monarchy, when "kings who sit on the throne of David, riding in chariots and on horses" will again enter the city of Jerusalem (17:25, "the gates of this city") or the royal palace (22:4, "the gates of this house"). This suggests that 22:1-5 is a late addition, based on 21:11-12. Jeremiah 17:19-27 is later still, reflecting not only the picture of Davidic kings returning victoriously to Jerusalem, but stating that "this city (Jerusalem) shall be inhabited for ever" (17:25).[53]

A Future Restored Monarchy: Jeremiah 30:8-9 and Jeremiah 30:21

In the "Book of Consolation" (Jeremiah 30-31) other references to a future restored monarchy are found in the prose passage 30:8-9 (cf. Hos 3:5; Ezek 34:23, 24) and in 30:21. The theme of liberation and independence under a monarch raised up by Yahweh (30:8-9) is based on the final phrase in 30:7, understood as a statement of future salvation, "yet he (Jacob, i.e., Israel) shall be saved out of it."[54] Although "breaking the yoke" and "bursting the bonds" are phrases used in 5:5 (cf. 2:20, where different vocabulary expresses these ideas), 30:8 changes the concept entirely from the idea of Israel's repudiation

---

[52] Jeremiah 29:16-20(MT) is missing in the LXX. This could be explained by homoioteleuton, since בְּבָלָה occurs in the MT at the end of both 29:15 and 29:20.

[53] Cf. McKane (*Jeremiah 1*), "...in agreement with prophecy from Ezekiel on, hope for the future is centred in Jerusalem" (p. 419).

[54] Holladay (*Jeremiah 2*, 150) translates this phrase as interrogative, "and out of it shall he be saved?," and considers it "an ironic rhetorical question" (p. 173). See also Holladay, "Style, Irony and Authenticity in Jeremiah," *JBL* 81 (1962) 44-54, esp. 53-54; cf. Watson, "Gender-Matched Synonymous Parallelism in the Old Testament," *JBL* 99 (1984) 307. However, the versions (LXX, Vg and Tg) uniformly treat the phrase as a statement. The basic question is whether these words have been added editorially, as suggested by Hyatt (*Jeremiah*, 1023); Sigmund Böhmer, *Hiemkehr und neuer Bund. Studien zu Jeremia 30-31* (Göttinger Theologische Arbeiten; Göttingen: Vandenhoeck & Ruprecht, 1976) 58. The phrase as it stands acts to preserve the balance in the poetic structure of 30:7.

of Yahweh (2:20 and 5:5) to that of their liberation by Yahweh from the bonds of enemies.[55]

The Term אַדִּיר in Jeremiah 30:21

The poetic reference to their "prince" (אַדִּיר) in 30:21, envisages a future ruler, "one of themselves," yet avoids the term מֶלֶךְ.[56] The context, 30:18-22, deals with a future restoration of the fortunes of Jacob, in which the city of Jerusalem will be rebuilt. Both 30:8-9 and 30:21 are to be interpreted in the context of the Book of Consolation (30-31) and its place in the development of the book of Jeremiah.

The Strophic Structure of Jeremiah 30-31

Lohfink regards seven strophes from Jeremiah 30 and 31 as probably stemming from the prophet himself: 30:5-7; 30:12-15; 30:18-21; 31:2-6; 31:15-17; 31:18-20; 31:21-22.[57] The references to "Jacob" (30:7; 30:18), "Israel" (31:4; 31:21); "Rachel" (31:15); and "Ephraim" (31:6; 31:9; 31:18; 31:20) point to the northern kingdom. Especially in 30:18-21, Jacob's restored land and community will be built again.[58] According to Lohfink, Jeremiah acts

---

[55] Although 30:8 is introduced by the phrase בַּיּוֹם הַהוּא (cf. 4:9; 25:33; 34:16, 17; 48:41=49:22; 44:26=50:30), the oracle in 30:8-9 changes the theme of distress connected with "that day" (30:7) to that of future salvation. Jeremiah 4:9, on the other hand, uses the introductory בַּיּוֹם הַהוּא to continue the proclamation of destruction in 4:5-8, by asserting that "courage shall fail both king and princes; the priests shall be appalled and the prophets astounded" (cf. 2:26, where the same groups are specified). See also note on בַּיּוֹם הַהוּא regarding the doublets 48:41=49:22; 49:26=50:30 (chap. seven, p. 138 [d...d]; p. 158 [c...c]). A precise date cannot easily be determined for the hope expressed in 30:8-9. Nicholson (*Jeremiah 2*) asserts "... it is possible that hopes for the re-establishment of the Davidic dynasty sprang up already in the late period of the exile; perhaps prompted by the release of Jehoiachin from prison in exile in 562BCE [52:31-4]" (p. 54). Cf. Böhmer, *Heimkehr*, 60.

[56] Deuteronomy 17:15 states specifically that the king must not be a foreigner (נָכְרִי) but מִקֶּרֶב אַחֶיךָ, one "from among your brethren." See Barbara Bozak, *Life 'Anew.' A Literary Study of Jer.30-31*(AnBib 122; Roma: Editrice Pontificio Istituto Biblico, 1991) 63. She interprets מִמֶּנּוּ ("from him") to mean "from 'Jacob' and his progeny." Clements (*Jeremiah*) writes, "'The prince' of verse 21 is certainly a reference to a future ruler, or governor, and quite evidently the title 'king' has been avoided deliberately for political or religious reasons" (p. 183).

[57] Norbert Lohfink, "Der junge Jeremia als Propagandist und Poet, zum Grundstock von Jer 30-31," in *Le Livre de Jérémie: Le Prophète et son Milieu; Les Oracles et leur Transmission* (ed. P.-M. Bogaert; BETL 54; Leuven: Leuven University Press, 1981) 357. Cf. Holladay (*Jeremiah 2*, 156) who "depends heavily on his analysis" and designates these passages as "The Early Recension to the North." Jeremiah 30:10-11; 30:16-17 and 31:7-9a comprise "The Recension to the South."

[58] Lohfink, "Der junge Jeremia," 360.

as propagandist for Josiah, who expanded his territory and sought to unite north and south. Lohfink claims that the reference to "their אַדִּיר" (30:21) indicates Josiah, who will extend his boundaries (now that a power vacuum exists with the collapse of Assyria) and act as ruler over north as well as south. Yet, the view that אַדִּירוֹ must necessarily point to Josiah is to be challenged if one takes into account the statement in 30:21b, "I will make him draw near (וְהִקְרַבְתִּיו) and he shall approach me," which puts the emphasis on a cultic role (cf. the use of the term עֵדָה, "congregation," in 30:20).[59] The coming leader is "a cultic figure rather than a king."[60] Political and cultic roles will be combined in the אַדִּיר, whose leadership will be exercised in the coming theocracy, when the city (30:18), Jerusalem (cf. Tg), with its fortress (אַרְמוֹן), is rebuilt.[61] Holladay considers "the tents of Jacob" (אָהֳלֵי יַעֲקוֹב, 30:18) to be a reference to the temple, which would be in keeping with the cultic references in 30:20, 21.[62] The viewpoint of Lohfink (and Holladay) that "Jacob" in 30:18 represents the northern kingdom (cf. 30:7; "virgin Israel," 31:4, 21; "mountains of Samaria," 31:5; "Ephraim," 31:18, 20) is of crucial importance if one is to locate these oracles in their original form in the time of Jeremiah's prophetic ministry in the latter years of the reign of Josiah. According to this approach, as Holladay develops it, a recension to the south was made between 588 and 587BCE, which includes 30:10-11 (where "Jacob" and "Israel" are equated); 30:16-17 (where "Zion" is referred to in 30:17); 31:7-9a (a reversal of 6:21-22).[63] Odashima claims that the words in 30:10-11 and 30:16-17 are addressed to "Israel" understood in a comprehensive way, including both inhabitants of the former northern kingdom of Israel and also former inhabitants of the state of Judah, as well as their descendants.[64] These passages are the work of a pre-Deuteronomistic author, who (like Deutero-Isaiah) looks to a future when "Gesamtisrael" will be restored and in which the name "Jacob" will take on new meaning in a re-ordered world.[65]

In Deutero-Isaiah, "Jacob" and "Israel" are equivalent terms; cf. Isa 42:1LXX; 43:1; 44:1; 45:4; 48:12; 49:5 — passages ascribed to an anonymous

---

[59] קרב Hiphil (30:21b) has the sense of "make an offering," e.g., Num 7:2, of "the leaders of Israel" (נְשִׂיאֵי יִשְׂרָאֵל). The use of נגשׁ "approach" in 30:21b also has cultic overtones (cf. Ezek 44:13).

[60] Carroll, Jeremiah, 583.

[61] Rudolph understands both עִיר and אַרְמוֹן in a collective sense, in which case עִיר would include Jerusalem (Jeremia, 193).

[62] Holladay, Jeremiah 2, 177. Although a translation for אָהֳלֵי is missing in the LXX, Vg translates as tabernaculorum Jacob.

[63] Holladay, Jeremiah 2, 160-162.

[64] Von Taro Odashima, Heilsworte im Jeremiabuch. Untersuchungen zu ihrer vordeuteronomistischen Bearbeitung (BWANT 125; Stuttgart: Kohlhammer, 1989) 299.

[65] Odashima, "the author is not the prophet Jeremiah" (Heilsworte, 298).

prophet in the latter part of the Babylonian exile.[66] The cultic terminology used in Jer 30:18-21, especially עֲרָה in 30:20a, and the reference to punishment of "Jacob's" enemies (30:20b), lead Böhmer to assign for this oracle a date in the post-Jeremianic period.[67] Whether or not the substance of this prophetic utterance goes back to Jeremiah himself, as Lohfink has argued, the oracle in its present form would appear to express hopes in the period of the exile for a restored Israel (as in Deutero-Isaiah) with massive rebuilding, growth in population, and the assurance of a worthy leader.[68]

Bozak, in her thorough analysis of 30:18-22 and 30:23-31:1, regards these passages as constituent parts of one poem, thematically related in declaring positive and negative aspects of the action of Yahweh.[69] In her essentially synchronic approach to Jeremiah 30 and 31, she allows a place for a redactional process, seen as "meaningful and not haphazard."[70] Although the original oracles were intended for exiles from the Northern Kingdom, "the historical context of the final redaction is seen to be the Babylonian Exile."[71] This seems to be a balanced view.

The extensive treatment of the subject of monarchy in 21:11-23:6 concludes with a further oracle, 23:7-8 (=16:14-15). This text does not deal with monarchy directly, but declares that "days are coming" when the memory of the action of Yahweh in bringing the people of Israel out of Egypt will be overshadowed by another action of Yahweh in bringing the descendants of the house of Israel out of all the countries of the diaspora.

---

[66] Ernst Sellin and Georg Fohrer, *Introduction to the Old Testament* (New York: Abingdon, 1968) 374-377.

[67] Böhmer, *Heimkehr*, 64, 65. Böhmer postulates the priority of "P" ("der Priesterschrift") and the post-Jeremianic hope regarding the punishment of Israel's enemies (30:20b; cf. 25:12; 50:18, 31; 51:44, 47, 52) as criteria for dating 30:18-21 during the exile: "All in all the origin of Jer 30 18ff is to be understood more easily as from the time of the exile" (p. 65).

[68] Lohfink denies only 30:20b and 30:21b to Jeremiah ("Der junge Jeremia," p. 351 n. 5). Cf. Lohfink, "Die Gotteswortverschachtelung in Jer 30-3," in *Künder des Wortes. Beiträge zur Theologie des Propheten: Josef Schreiner zum 60 Geburtstag* (ed. Lothar Ruppert, Peter Weimar und Erich Zeuger; Würzburg: Echter, 1982) 106.

[69] Bozak draws attention to הִנְנִי (30:18) and הִנֵּה (30:23) at the beginning of each section and the covenant formula (30:22 and 31:1) at the end (*Life 'Anew,'* 59). Jeremiah 31:1 also serves as the introduction to 31:1-22 (p. 69).

[70] Bozak, *Life 'Anew,'* 173.

[71] Bozak, *Life 'Anew,'* 31. Cf. Jones (*Jeremiah*), "...chapters 30-31...represent an independent effort to collect together material, held within the Jeremiah tradition, concerning the future" (p. 371).

3. JEREMIAH 23:7-8 = JEREMIAH 16:14-15

JEREMIAH 23:7-8

7. [a] "Therefore, behold, days are coming,[a] says Yahweh, [b] when the people will no longer say, [b] 'As Yahweh lives who brought up the people of Israel from the land of Egypt,'
8. but 'As Yahweh lives [c] who (brought up) and led [c] [d] offspring of (the house of) Israel[d] [e] from the land of the north,'[e] [f] indeed, from all the lands where I had driven them. [f] [g] Then they shall dwell [g] in their (own) land."

JEREMIAH 16:14-15

14. [a] "Therefore, behold, days are coming,[a] says Yahweh, [b] when it shall no longer be said,[b] 'As Yahweh lives who brought up the people of Israel from the land of Egypt,' 15. but 'As Yahweh lives [c] who brought up [c] [d] the people of Israel [d] [e] from the land of the the north[e] [f] and from all the lands where he had driven them.'[f] [g] Then I will bring them back [g] to their (own) land that [h] I gave to their fathers." [h]

Textual and Translational Notes

[a...a] לָכֵן הִנֵּה־יָמִים בָּאִים. This phrase has already been discussed (see above p. 62 note [a...a]).

[b...b] וְלֹא־יֹאמְרוּ עוֹד ("people shall no longer say," 23:7). Cf. 3:16; 31:29. עוֹד וְלֹא־יֵאָמֵר ("it shall no longer be said," 16:14). Cf. 7:32 and יֵאָמֵר in 4:11. In both passages, the LXX reads καὶ οὐκ ἐροῦσιν ἔτι (cf. 3:16LXX; 7:32LXX).

[c...c] אֲשֶׁר הֶעֱלָה וַאֲשֶׁר הֵבִיא ("who brought up and led," 23:8); אֲשֶׁר הֶעֱלָה ("who brought up," 16:15). ὃς ἀνάγαγε in 16:15LXX refers back to ὁ ἀναγαγὼν in 16:14, but a translation for the phrase אֲשֶׁר הֶעֱלָה (23:8) is missing in the LXX in most manuscripts, where ὃς συνήγαγεν probably represents אֲשֶׁר הֵבִיא.[72] Vg follows the MT: *qui eduxit et adduxit* (23:8).

[d...d] אֶת־זֶרַע בֵּית יִשְׂרָאֵל ("offspring of the house of Israel," 23:8; cf. Ezek 20:5; 44:2; LXX ἅπαν τὸ σπέρμα Ισραηλ; אֶת־בְּנֵי יִשְׂרָאֵל, "the Israelites," 16:15; LXX τὸν οἶκον Ισραηλ). Although ἅπαν (23:8) may well be secondary, as Janzen claims, בֵּית is not translated in the Greek translation of 23:8, אֶת־זֶרַע בֵּית יִשְׂרָאֵל (τὸ σπέρμα Ισραηλ), whereas in 16:15 בֵּית is presupposed in the phrase τὸν οἶκον Ισραηλ, although בֵּית is not present in 16:15MT (אֶת־בְּנֵי יִשְׂרָאֵל).[73] The history of the text and its transmission appears to be very complicated; for further comments, see below, p. 75).

---

[72] Janzen, "It would seem simplest to take συναγω = הביא, with העלה אשר an inner manuscript conflation from 16:15" (*Studies*, 12).

[73] Janzen, *Studies*, 67.

Doublets Regarding the Monarchy

e...e   Differences in orthography are found in צָפוֹנָה (23:8); צָפוֹן (16:15); שָׁם (23:8); שָׁמָּה (16:15). The differences are minimized by Herrmann.[74]

f...f   הִדַּחְתִּים ("I had driven them," 23:8); הִדִּיחָם ("he [Yahweh] had driven them," 16:15). Although RSV, NEB, JB and most commentators prefer the 3d s. of the verb, הִדִּיחָם, in both passages (cf. LXX ἔξωσαν αὐτούς, "he had driven them out," 23:8), McKane points out that "תדיחם is a possible reading only if the words of the oath are assumed to extend to שמה (שם)."[75] The first person singular is used in both הִדַּחְתִּים (23:8; cf. 8:3b) and הֲשִׁבֹתִים (16:15) in clauses which have been added subsequently, in each case referring back to נְאֻם יהוה. הִדַּחְתִּים (23:8) is also supported by Vg *eieceram* and Tg.

g...g   וְיָשְׁבוּ ("then they shall dwell," 23:8); וַהֲשִׁבֹתִם ("then I will bring them back," 16:15). Marx draws attention to the change in verb.[76] יָשַׁב Hiphil in 23:8 has been changed to שׁוּב in 16:15, with Yahweh as subject; the return has been placed in explicit relationship to the patriarchal promise.

h...h   The phrase אֲשֶׁר נָתַתִּי לַאֲבוֹתָם ("that I gave to their fathers") has been added in 16:15; cf. 24:10; 25:5; 35:15.

Comment

The position of 23:7-8 in the LXX, following 23:40, is not readily explained. However, Janzen makes the interesting proposal that the MT order of 23:1-8 was at one time 1-4, 7-8, 5-6.[77] Jeremiah 23:3, "Then I myself will gather the remnant of my flock out of all the lands where I have driven them" (the phrase מִכֹּל הָאֲרָצוֹת אֲשֶׁר־הִדַּחְתִּי אֹתָם שָׁם occurs in both 23:3 and 23:8) is expanded in 23:7-8 into a statement that this new exodus and *Heimkehr* will be more prominent in people's memories than the exodus from Egypt and will give rise to a new form of oath. Jeremiah 23:4, which refers to caring shepherds, is made concrete by 23:5-6, the promise of a righteous Branch. Janzen's view also helps to explain how the phrase ἐν τοῖς προφήταις came to be added to 23:6LXX, which would have been placed originally before 23:9, from which the superscription לַנְּבִאִים has been wrongly incorporated into 23:6 in the LXX.[78] Because of the introductory phrase הִנֵּה יָמִים בָּאִים in 23:5 and 23:7,

---

[74] Siegfried Herrmann, *Die prophetischen Heilserwartungen in Alten Testament. Ursprung und Gestaltwandel* (BWANT 5; Stuttgart: Kohlhammer, 1965) 170. Note the comment by Freedman, Forbes, and Andersen (*Orthography*), "If material was duplicated some time into the transmission process, the recently introduced version might betray its origins by its spelling. Of course, it is also possible that a copy of the book was made with a change of scribe somewhere along the way or that one part was copied from one manuscript and the rest from another manuscript" (p. 118).

[75] McKane, *Jeremiah 1*, 375; cf. Volz, *Jeremia*, p. 232 n. 1.

[76] Marx, "A Propos des doublets," 110.

[77] Janzen, *Studies*, 93.

[78] Cf. McKane, *Jeremiah 1*, 566.

23:7-8 was omitted by haplography, but was later written in the margin.⁷⁹ At yet a later stage, Janzen proposes, "The subsequent marginal restoration...was received into the text at different points in the archetypes of M and G."⁸⁰

The oath-formula in 23:7-8 and 16:14-15 begins with the conventional חַי־יְהוָה.⁸¹ The phrase "people shall no longer say" (23:7; cf. "it shall no longer be said," 16:14) is of special interest, since the oath is to be replaced by another oath in which the emphasis will shift to the expected return of the people of Israel not only from the north country, but also from other lands of the diaspora.⁸²

Herrmann considers 23:7-8 and 16:14-15 to be Deuteronomistic in language and thought.⁸³ The idiomatic use of the *Hiphil* of עלה in the sense of leading "upwards" from Egypt is found in Deuteronomistic passages such as Judg 6:13; 1 Sam 8:8; 10:18; 12:6 (cf. Gen 50:24), whereas the *Hiphil* of יצא occurs frequently in similar phrases in the book of Deuteronomy.⁸⁴ Herrmann contends that the reference to a leading out of the north country and out of "all the countries" (23:8; 16:15) will include Egypt and that the developed stage of the diaspora reflected in these passages represents *vaticinia ex eventu*.

In general, 23:7-8 suits the context better than does 16:14-15.⁸⁵ The abrupt transition in 16:14 after the harsh language of 16:1-13 is striking. Jeremiah 16:13 announces deportation into a land "that neither you nor your ancestors have known," with no possibility of divine grace. By contrast, 16:14-15 promise a return from the north country and all the countries where

---

⁷⁹ Holladay, "perhaps vertically between two columns of the archetype of M and G" (*Jeremiah 1*, 621).

⁸⁰ Janzen, *Studies*, 93.

⁸¹ The expression occurs forty-three times in the OT; eight times in the book of Jeremiah: 4:2; 5:2; 12:16; 16:14, 15; 23:7, 8; 38:16 (cf. 44:26, חַי־אֲדֹנָי יְהוִה; 22:24; 46:18, חַי־אָנִי). Cf. Moshe Greenberg, "The Hebrew Oath Particle Hay/He," *JBL* 76 (1957); he claims: "The evidence seems to require taking *hay* as a noun 'life', the singular of the otherwise attested plural *hayyim*" (p. 37). Yahweh swears בְּנַפְשִׁי (51:14), the equivalent to the oath חַי־יְהוָה on the part of human speakers.

⁸² See also 3:16, a reference to a time when people will no longer mention the ark of the covenant of Yahweh; 31:29 (cf. Ezek 18:2, 3, when people will no longer say, "The parents have eaten sour grapes, and the children's teeth are set on edge"). Holladay regards 3:16 and 31:29-30 as late passages (*Jeremiah 1*, 622).

⁸³ Herrmann, *Heilserwartungen*, 169-172. Cf. Thiel, *Redaktion 1*, 199, 248.

⁸⁴ E.g., Deut 1:27; 4:20, 37; 5:6, 15; 6:12, 21, 23; 8:14; 9:12, 26, 28; 13:6, 11; 16:1; 26:8. An exception is found in Deut 20:1, where עלה (*Hiphil* participle) occurs + מִצְרַיִם מֵאֶרֶץ, avoiding יצא which has already been used at the beginning of the sentence.

⁸⁵ McKane lists among those who hold this point of view Giesebrecht, Duhm, Rudolph, Weiser, Bright, Nicholson and Thiel (*Jeremiah 1*, 373). Cf. also Holladay, *Jeremiah 1*, 621; Carroll, *Jeremiah*, 447; Jones, *Jeremiah*, 300. However, Macchi ("Les Doublets," 132-133) thinks that the doublet could have been inserted in both Jeremiah 23 and 16 at about the same time, in the exilic or post-exilic period (["ancestors"] in 16:15 provides a link with 16:11, 12, 13).

the people of Israel had been driven. According to Marx, the passage has been inserted from 23:7-8 to alleviate the harshness of the preceding prose passages (16:5-9; 16:10-13).[86] Volz also regards the passage as an insertion which completely contradicts the purpose of the threat in the previous verses.[87] This late insertion, he claims, is to meet the needs of the synagogue community, bringing consolation when the prophetic texts were read in services of worship by adding words of salvation to the words of threat.[88]

Bright raises the question regarding doublets as to whether one should look for another explanation for duplicated material rather than postulating that we are dealing with a passage that is original in one place and secondary in another.[89] Sayings transmitted separately, whether orally or in writing, would readily be drawn into different complexes of material. This view of a repeated anchorage is amplified by Hubmann, who finds this explanation of doublets more satisfactory than the view that duplicate formulations (where there is a minimum of change, except insofar as context or change in speaker calls for some modification) reflect the work of redaction.[90]

In the case of 23:7-8 = 16:14-15 both processes may have contributed to the texts in their present form. Initially, a brief saying contrasting the original exodus from Egypt with the more significant exodus from the north country became part of different tradition complexes, i.e., as the conclusion to 21:11-23:4 (with 23:5-6 inserted later) and added to 16:1-13.

In the earliest form, the verb הֶעֱלָה was used in both parts of the saying. However, two versions of the second oath were known, one using הֶעֱלָה, the other הֵבִיא. These have been conflated in the present text of 23:8. In the course of time, other changes were introduced. בְּנֵי יִשְׂרָאֵל, which occurs in both 16:14 and 16:15, is found only once in 23:7-8 (23:7). Jeremiah 23:8 reads בֵּית יִשְׂרָאֵל זֶרַע, a phrase which occurs also in Ezek 20:5 in a context regarding exodus

---

[86] Marx also draws attention to רִאשׁוֹנָה ("first") in 16:18, a term missing in the LXX, but which in his judgment could proceed from the same hand as 16:14-15, in order to indicate the sequence of events ("A Propos des doublets," p. 110 n. 13). Cf. Bright, *Jeremiah*, 108; Holladay, *Jeremiah 1*, 479. They interpret רִאשׁוֹנָה as a gloss, inserted after 16:14-15 was in place. This seems a preferable view in the light of the fact that the LXX translates 16:14-15 but does not translate רִאשׁוֹנָה in 16:18.

[87] Volz, *Jeremia*, p. 178 n. 2.

[88] Volz explains the illogical לָכֵן as the usual introduction of added salvation sayings (*Jeremia*, 179). But 23:7=16:14 is the only instance in the book of Jeremiah where בָּאִים לָכֵן הִנֵּה־יָמִים introduces a "salvation" promise. Weiser (*Jeremia*) seeks to justify לָכֵן on the basis of the content of this passage, "the introductory 'therefore' confirms the entire sharpness of the fate of the exile" (p. 140). Janzen (*Studies*), states, "לָכֵן...may be secondary from the longer form [i.e., in 23:7]" (p. 220 n. 16). Yet, the abrupt use of לָכֵן to introduce an unexpected change in the flow of thought is found also in 30:16 (cf. 37:16LXX; διὰ τοῦτο=לָכֵן).

[89] Bright, *Jeremiah*, LXXV-LXXVI.

[90] Hubmann, *Untersuchungen*, 227-229.

from the land of Egypt. The occurrence of τὸν οἶκον Ισραηλ in 16:15LXX suggests that at least בית ישראל was present in the *Vorlage* from which the LXX translation was made. The additional term זֶרַע ("descendants, offspring") in 23:8 sets up (perhaps intentionally) a contrast with the statement in 22:30 that none of the זֶרַע of Jeconiah will rule again in Judah. Although no descendant of Jeconiah will reign, זֶרַע "of the house of Israel" will return to the homeland. Indeed, they will return from "all the countries where I have driven them" (23:8MT, following 23:3), at which time Yahweh will set shepherds over them (23:4). The change in subject of the verb נדח to the third person singular (16:15) makes this phrase part of the new oath.[91]

Orthographic changes (see Textual Note ᵉ and n. 77) would have been made during the course of transmission: צָפוֹנָה (23:8) צָפוֹן (16:15); שָׁם (23:8); שָׁמָּה (16:15). As already indicated (see Textual Note ᵍ), different verbs (ישׁב 23:8; שׁוּב 16:15) have been used in the added phrase concerning "their (own) land," with a further statement in 16:15, "that I gave to their ancestors," making an explicit link with the patriarchal promise. Jeremiah 16:16-18 reverts to the theme of inescapable judgment; at some stage in the transmission of the text, רִאשׁוֹנָה was added in 16:18 to make it clear that the action of the "fishers" and "hunters" was prior to the return from exile (16:15).

In both 23:7 and 16:14 the saying is introduced by לָכֵן הִנֵּה־יָמִים בָּאִים לָכֵן. is appropriate in the case of 23:7, even if this originally followed 23:4. Mutual interaction between 23:7-8 and 16:14-15 during the course of transmission could account for לָכֵן in 16:14, unless one accepts Pedersen's suggestion that the particle does not necessarily imply logical sequence but means "under these circumstances."[92]

Admittedly, this attempt at tracing the textual history and transmission of 23:7-8 = 16:14-15 is conjectural and tentative. Since the theme of return from the exile is prominent in the book of Jeremiah (e.g., 3:18; 24:4-7; 27:22; 29:10-14; 30:10=46:27; 31:7-9; 32:15), the important question is whether or not this hope was part of the future expectation of Jeremiah himself. The key passages in this regard have to do with Jeremiah's purchase of Hanamel's field at Anathoth (Jeremiah 32) and his letters to the exiles in Babylon (Jeremiah 29).[93] These are both prose passages in narrative style, with strong homiletic overtones. Yet there is no overwhelming reason why they should not be based on a sound tradition regarding Jeremiah's purchase of the field and

---

[91] McKane, "The assumption that the oath ran as far as שמה (שם) was what produced הדיחם at 16:15" (*Jeremiah 1*, 375).

[92] Pedersen, "it does not indicate consequence, but connection" (*Israel I-II*, 16). Cf. 16:21.

[93] According to Holladay, "the chapter [32] has had a complicated history of expansions" (*Jeremiah 2*, 206). Cf. Carroll, "a heavily edited chapter" (*Jeremiah*, 620). Thiel claims, "An authentic autobiographical report is present in the oldest part of the chapter" (*Redaktion 2*, 31).

correspondence with the exiles. The statement in 32:15b may be seen as expressing a genuine hope of the prophet, "Houses and fields and vineyards shall again be bought in this land." The time element is left indeterminate, but the care with which the deeds are preserved in an earthenware vessel "that they may last for a long time" (32:14) suggests that a considerable period of time will elapse before this promise becomes a reality. Likewise, in the case of a letter to the exiles, the exhortation is made: "Build houses and live in them; plant gardens and eat what they produce" (29:5).[94] Shemaiah, a false prophet within the community of exiles in Babylon, has quoted with disapproval Jeremiah's words, "It will be a long time (אֲרֻכָּה); build houses and live in them" (29:28).

A period of "seventy years" is mentioned in 29:10 (cf. 25:11, 12) as the period of time which will elapse before the return from exile.[95] Rather than take this as a precise figure, with exact dates to be determined for a *terminus a quo* and a *terminus ad quem* the better solution is to regard "seventy years" as a round figure, a life-time, as in Ps 90:10.[96] Jeremiah thought of the period of exile as God's inevitable judgment upon his people. Those in exile in Babylon must come to terms with their situation, build homes, marry and have progeny, and seek the welfare of Babylon.

The note of hope expressed in 29:10-14 is in keeping with the action taken by Jeremiah in purchasing land in Anathoth, a tangible sign that "Houses and fields and vineyards shall again be bought in this land" (32:15b). In the book of Jeremiah, the striking phrase וְשַׁבְתִּי אֶת־שְׁבוּת occurs for the first time in 29:14. The verb שׁוּב has a dominant place in Jeremiah, with a variety of

---

[94] Thiel considers 29:5-7 to be free from Deuteronomistic influence and to be close to the authentic words of Jeremiah (*Redaktion 2*, 11-12). The letter in its present form contains a number of additions, but reflects the tradition that Jeremiah expected the exile to be lengthy.

[95] The literature on this subject is very extensive. For a useful bibliography, see Peter Ackroyd, *Exile and Restoration* (OTL; London: SCM, 1968) p. 240 n. 27. The seventy-year period referred to in the book of Jeremiah is taken up again by writers in post-exilic times: e.g., Zech 1:12; 7:5; 2 Chron 36:21, where Jeremiah is specifically mentioned and where Lev 26:34 may also be in the Chronicler's mind; Dan 9:2, again with a reference to Jeremiah and followed by an interpretation in Dan 9:24, "seventy weeks of years" (i.e., 490 years); Epistle of Jeremy, verse 3 (Syr "seventy years"; Greek, "seven generations" ἕως γενεῶν ἑπτά). Seitz regards the seventy years of 29:10 and 25:12 as a secondary reflective elaboration on the less specific word of Jeremiah in 27:22 (*Theology in Conflict*, p. 107 n. 6).

[96] Cf. Robert Carroll, *From Chaos to Covenant* (London: SCM, 1981) 204. He writes, "...the most reasonable approach to the motif is to treat it as a conventional figure for a period of divine judgment." Cf. 27:7, where the period of Babylonian captivity will span the period of the rule of Nebuchadrezzar, his son and his grandson. This verse is missing from the LXX; Janzen regards 27:7 as a late secondary addition (*Studies*, 101-103).

meanings, including "to turn," "to repent," and "to return" (from exile).[97] In this particular phrase, which occurs with variations in the book of Jeremiah eleven times, the reference is usually to a return from exile, but is sometimes a more general reference to the restoration of fortunes of the land of Judah and its cities.[98] This major *motif* in the oracles of hope is used not only with regard to the exiles, but also in the OAN (Moab, 48:47; the Ammonites, 49:6 [missing in the LXX]; Elam, 49:39). The phrase occurs elsewhere in the OT in Hos 6:11, Amos 9:14 (a late addition), as well as in Ezek 16:53 (Sodom and Gomorrah) and in Ezek 29:14 (Egypt). Weiser draws attention to the phrase שׁוּב שְׁבוּת in the Psalms (e.g., Ps 85:2MT; 126:1, 4), originally a phrase with cultic significance, which later took on new meaning for the exilic community in their return from exile.[99] A significant use of the phrase is found in Deut 30:3, preceded by the use of שׁוּב in the sense of "return to Yahweh, your God" in Deut 30:2. The verb קבץ occurs both in Deut 30:3 and in Jer 29:14, but the vocabulary otherwise differs (e.g., עַמִּים, פּוּץ in Deut 30:3; גּוֹיִם, נדח in Jer 29:14; see below, chapter thirteen, C62 and C81).

JEREMIAH 29:13 and DEUTERONOMY 4:29

A closer correspondence exists between 29:13 and Deut 4:29, where the former is a slightly abbreviated but almost identical version of the latter. Although the basic idea of an eventual return from exile after a lengthy period of time may well have been a genuine hope of Jeremiah, 29:10-14 in its present form has much in common with Deut 30:3; 4:29. The extracts from Jeremiah's letters in Jeremiah 29 are unlikely to reflect throughout the precise words of the prophet, but are rather an expansion and interpretation of the prophet's words, especially in 29:10-14, 15-23, 24-28, 29-32.[100] For Jeremiah 29:13 and Deuteronomy 4:29, see also chap. ten, pp. 226-227.

We conclude that 23:7-8 = 16:14-15, like 29:14, contains elements of the Jeremianic tradition of an eventual return from exile, inserted editorially in extended form probably at a time during the exile.

---

[97] William Holladay, *The Root SUBH in the Old Testament, with Particular Reference to its Usages in Covenantal Contexts* (Leiden: Brill, 1958) 128-129 (esp. 110-114).

[98] For example, 31:23; 32:44; 33:11; cf. Kilpp, *Niederreissen und aufbauen*, p. 130 n. 130. The original meaning of שׁוּב שְׁבוּת ("return from exile") has come to mean "restore the fortunes"; see Seitz, *Theology in Conflict*, p. 210 n. 8.

[99] Weiser, *Jeremia*, p. 254 n. 4.

[100] Jeremiah 29:16-20 is missing from the LXX since the Hebrew *Vorlage* did not contain vv. 16-19 and v. 20 was omitted by *homoioteleuton* (בְּבָלָה occurs at the end of both v. 15 and v. 20). These verses in the Hebrew text have been added by an editor who reflects the view regarding the "vile figs" (29:17) set forth in 24:8-10.

SUMMARY: DOUBLETS

We may now summarize the doublets regarding monarchy as follows:

1. Jeremiah 23:5–6 = 33:14–16
Jeremiah's concept of ideal monarchy is preserved in 23:5–6, but the oracle in its present form is an adaptation of an earlier oracle, pointing to a future king of the royal line of David in whom these ideals will be realized. Jeremiah himself did not expect the monarchy to continue, but in his critique of monarchy set out the ideals of monarchy which later prophets incorporated in their hopes for the future. Jeremiah 33:14–16 applies the theophoric name "Yahweh is our righteousness" (i.e., "vindication," "salvation") to the city of Jerusalem.

2. Jeremiah 22:4 = 17:25
Jeremiah 21:11-12 (Jeremianic), regarding the responsibility of the monarch to execute justice, has been expanded at a later date in 22:1–5 (post-Jeremianic), in which the hope of restoration of the monarchy is expressed (22:4). Later still, in 17:25, this hope of Davidic kings returning victoriously to Jerusalem is also expressed, with special emphasis on the expectation that "this city will be inhabited forever."

3. Jeremiah 23:7–8 = 16:14–15
This oracle does not refer to monarchy directly, but rather to a time when the descendants of the house of Israel will be brought back from the countries of the diaspora to their own land. Jeremiah 23:7–8 suits the context better than does 16:14–15. Jeremiah's hope for the future (32:14) points to a distant future after a lengthy period of exile (29:5, 28). This hope, in its later developed form as expressed in this doublet, was editorially inserted probably during the exile.

CHAPTER FIVE

DOUBLETS CONCERNING PROPHECY

The subject of prophecy is uppermost in 23:9–40, with parallels (doublets) such as 23:12b=11:23b; 23:15=9:14MT (9:15E) and 23:19-20=30:23-24. Another significant doublet is 6:13-15=8:10b-12, Jeremiah's denunciation of false prophets who offer soothing words and refuse to face imminent divine judgment upon their people. In addition to these doublets, other passages which require consideration include Jeremiah 28, the account of the contest between Jeremiah and Hananiah, and 29:15-32, especially with regard to Ahab, Zedekiah and Shemaiah, who were among those exiled to Babylonia by Nebuchadrezzar in 597 BCE.

Denunciation of False Prophets: Jeremiah 23:9–40

The section 23:9-40 has the superscription: "Concerning the prophets." False prophets are denounced as well as priests (23:11; 23:33). The phrase כִּי־גַם־נָבִיא גַם־כֹּהֵן occurs both in 23:11 and 14:18, followed by the verb חנף ("to be profane, godless") in 23:11, and by סחר ("to wander about") in 14:18. Jeremiah 23:10 is reminiscent of Jeremiah 14, referring to the effects of drought; in 23:10, "the land mourns" (אָבְלָה); in 14:1, "Judah mourns" (אָבְלָה). The close parallel between 23:12b and 11:23b has already been discussed above (see chap. two, pp. 18-21), where the conclusion was reached that 23:12b has been drawn upon in a prose insertion in the first Confession. The prophets of Samaria (23:13) are condemned for prophesying by Baal, but even more reprehensible are the prophets of Jerusalem (23:14-14) who "commit adultery and walk in lies."[1]

Although the verb נאף in 23:14 may be understood metaphorically as referring to apostasy, yet in 29:23 the false prophets Ahab and Zedekiah "have committed adultery (נאף) with their neighbors' wives."[2] Jeremiah 23:14 seems to go beyond reference only to the prophets to include the inhabitants of

---

[1] Cf. 3:11, "Faithless Israel has shown herself less guilty than false Judah." Note that *qere* שַׁעֲרוּרִיָּה ("horrible thing") in Hos 6:10 has to do with "the house of Israel"; cf. Jer 18:13, "The virgin Israel has done a very horrible thing." The term שַׁעֲרוּרָה in Jer 23:14 is applied only to "the prophets of Jerusalem"; the same term is used, however, in 5:30 in the indictment against prophets and priests "in the land" generally.

[2] Cf. the use of מְנָאֲפִים in 9:1 (9:2E) as the prophet's description of "my people."

Jerusalem generally - "all of them have become like Sodom to me, and its inhabitants like Gomorrah." The Sodom and Gomorrah *motif* (כִּסְדֹם...כַּעֲמֹרָה) occurs elsewhere in the book of Jeremiah: e.g., 49:18 (Edom); 50:40 (Babylon; cf. Isa 13:19b) and also in 20:16, although in this case the cities are not specifically named. The destruction of Sodom and Gomorrah (Gen 19:24; cf. Deut 29:22) is referred to frequently in the prophets: Isa 1:9, 10; 3:9; 13:19b; Amos 4:11; Zeph 2:9 (Moab and the Ammonites) and in Ezek 16:46-56 (*passim*). רָעָה ("wickedness," 23:11; 23:14) will bring divine judgment, destruction such as that of Sodom and Gomorrah. In these references in the prophets, wickedness in general is the reason for judgment; "rebellion" is emphasized in Isaiah, "lewdness and abominations" by Ezekiel. In Jer 23:13 the prophets of Samaria are upbraided for prophesying by Baal; in 23:14 the prophets of Jerusalem are condemned for committing adultery and walking in lies (בַּשֶּׁקֶר).[3]

After the condemnation of the prophets of Samaria and the prophets of Jerusalem, an oracle (23:15) follows concerning the prophets in general, closely parallel to a similar statement regarding "this people" in 9:14 (9:15E).

1. JEREMIAH 23:15a = JEREMIAH 9:14(15E)

JEREMIAH 23:15a
15a. Therefore thus says
[a] Yahweh of hosts [a] [b] concerning prophets: [b] "Behold, I will feed [c] them [c] with wormwood, and give them [d] poisoned water [d] to drink".

JEREMIAH 9:14 (15E)
14. Therefore thus says
[a] Yahweh of hosts,[a] the God the of Israel: "Behold, I will feed [c] this people [c] with wormwood, and give them [d] poisoned water [d] to drink".

Textual and Translational Notes

[a...a] יְהוָה צְבָאוֹת Both in 23:15a and 9:14, the LXX has only κύριος, but in 9:14 the LXX follows the MT with ὁ θεὸς Ἰσραηλ (אֱלֹהֵי יִשְׂרָאֵל). The complete phrase כֹּה־אָמַר יְהוָה צְבָאוֹת אֱלֹהֵי יִשְׂרָאֵל occurs thirty-one times in the book of Jeremiah (MT) but is always incomplete in the LXX. For Janzen, the frequent use of צְבָאוֹת reflects expansionist activity.[4] Elsewhere, צְבָאוֹת occurs regularly in the post-exilic prophets, Haggai, Zechariah and Malachi.

---

[3] Overholt ("The Falsehood of Idolatry," 87) has drawn attention to the thirty-six occurrences of the term שֶׁקֶר in the book of Jeremiah, especially in relation to false prophets. In other parts of the OT (Pentateuch, Psalms, Proverbs) the legal sense of the term predominates (cf. Jer 37:14), but the שֶׁקֶר of the prophets consists in their sense of false security and in their reliance upon the worship of "other gods."

[4] Janzen, *Studies*, 75-79 and Appendix B, Table B.2.

b...b עַל־הַנְּבִאִים ("concerning the prophets," 23:15a) is missing in the LXX (23:15a). The frame of reference is extended in 9:14 to "this people" (missing in the LXX).

c...c אֶת־הָעָם הַזֶּה seems to have been an explanatory addition in 9:14, since the 3d pl. suffix attached to the participle (מַאֲכִילָם) already provides an object, equivalent to מַאֲכִיל אוֹתָם (23:15a).[5]

d...d מֵי־רֹאשׁ 23:15a; 9:14. 23:15aLXX ὕδωρ πικρόν; 9:15LXX ὕδωρ χολῆς. The term also occurs in 8:14 (LXX ὕδωρ χολῆς).

The terms לַעֲנָה ("wormwood") and מֵי־רֹאשׁ ("poisoned water") are coupled together in 23:15a and 9:14. רֹאשׁ and לַעֲנָה are also found in Amos 6:12b (cf. Deut 29:17b; 18E), while the phrase לַעֲנָה וָרֹאשׁ occurs in Lam 3:19. Both concepts appear to have a botanical background.[6]

מֵי־רֹאשׁ is found only in the book of Jeremiah (23:15a=9:14; 8:14). Since the term means literally "waters of the head," i.e., "tears," this is the translation adopted by Craigie in 8:14.[7] However, the versions (e.g., LXX ὕδωρ χολῆς, cf. 9:15; Vg *aquam fellis*) translate in keeping with the concept of "poisoned water." The use of the term מֵי־רֹאשׁ is metaphorical in Jeremiah, "far removed from the limited area of trial by ordeal indicated in the Numbers passage [Numbers 5] and the clauses in the Code of Hammurabi."[8] Numbers 5:11-31, however, provides an appropriate background in the context of Jer 23:9-15, in the light of such phrases as "the land is full of adulterers" (23:10), "they commit adultery" (23:14).

Weinfeld makes the observation that the reference to "poisoned water" in 8:14 is "not worded in stereotyped deuteronomical phraseology."[9] However, he regards 9:10-15 as a "deuteronomic accretion"; 23:15a also constitutes "the same stereotyped malediction of the deuteronomic type."[10] Thiel, on the other hand, finds no trace of Deuteronomistic editing in 23:9-16, but believes that the

---

[5] Janzen (*Studies*, 11 n. 7) regards 9:14MT as the conflation of variants הַזֶּה / מַאֲלִילִם מַאֲכִיל אֶת הָעָם.

[6] For לַעֲנָה, see Holladay (*Jeremiah 1*, 308); McKane (*Jeremiah 1*, 205), "a poisonous herb." G. Fleischer ("רֹאשׁ" *TWAT* VII.3 [Stuttgart: Kohlhammer, 1990] 284-286) finds the clearest indication of the meaning of רֹאשׁ in Hos 10:4, "an agricultural crop"; cf. Deut 29:17b.

[7] Peter C. Craigie, Page H. Kelley and Joel F. Drinkard, Jr., *Jeremiah 1-25* (WBC 26; Dallas, Texas: Word Books, 1991) 14. See Mitchell Dahood, "Hebrew-Ugaritic Lexicography II," *Bib* 45 (1964) 393-412, esp. 402 (reference to Ugar. 125:27); Holladay, *Jeremiah 1*, 291-292.

[8] McKane, *Jeremiah 1*, 191.

[9] Moshe Weinfeld, *Deuteronomy and the Deuteronomic School* (Oxford: Oxford University Press, 1972) 143.

[10] Weinfeld, *Deuteronomic School*, p. 142 n. 3; p. 143 n. 1. Weinfeld also draws attention to an extra-biblial parallel, "may Ea...give you deadly water to drink, may he fill you with dropsy" (see D. J. Wiseman, "The Vassal Treaties of Esarhaddon," *Iraq* 20 [1958] 521-522).

word-flow of 23:15a has been taken over in the D-passage (9:11-15) in which 9:14 occurs.¹¹

Untranslated words in the LXX (צְבָאוֹת in both 23:15a and 9:14; עַל־הַנְּבִאִים in 23:15a; אֶת־הָעָם הַזֶּה in 9:14) lead to the conclusion that the Hebrew *Vorlage* on which the LXX is based did not contain these words. צְבָאוֹת is regularly a feature of expansionist activity (see Textual Note ᵃ⁻⁻ᵃ above). עַל־הַנְּבִאִים in the MT reinforces נְבִיאֵי יְרוּשָׁלַם in 23:15b and makes a closer connection with 23:14 in view of the suffix in יֹשְׁבֶיהָ (23:14), which includes the people of Jerusalem generally.¹² אֶת־הָעָם הַזֶּה interprets the suffix in מַאֲכִילָם, without removing the suffix which this phrase defines.

Comment

In 23:17, false prophets give encouragement to "those who despise the word of Yahweh" by saying continually, "It shall be well with you" (יִהְיֶה לָכֶם שָׁלוֹם). This phrase is also found in 4:10, where Yahweh is accused of deceiving "this people and Jerusalem" by saying "It shall be well with you," presumably through the mouth of false prophets.¹³ McKane rightly draws attention to the prose form of 4:10, and argues for the retention of the first person singular form of the verb, וָאֹמַר, which introduces the verse.¹⁴

A long tradition of the inviolability of Jerusalem could well contribute to the optimism of the false prophets.¹⁵ Micah 3:12 (cf. 26:18) however, represents another tradition, which asserts that "Jerusalem shall become a heap of ruins." This is reinforced by Jeremiah's awareness that there can be no escape from "the foe from the north"; it is now apparent that "a sword has reached the throat" (4:10); judgment cannot be averted. The address in 4:10, "Ah, Lord God" (אֲהָהּ אֲדֹנָי יְהוִה) appears also in 14:13, another passage

---

¹¹ Thiel, *Redaktion 1*, 136-137, 250. Cf. Rudolph (*Jeremia*), "9:14 is a copy" (p. 151).

¹² McKane (*Jeremiah 1*) states, "...a retention of עַל הנבאים (v. 15) is not incompatible with וישביה (v. 14), because it is the guilt of the prophets for the state of general corruption which is the particular point of v. 15" (p. 576).

¹³ See Holladay, *Jeremiah 1*, 150, 155. Cf. 5:12, the false assumption that Yahweh "will do nothing, no evil will come upon us, nor shall we see sword or famine."

¹⁴ For a full treatment of 4:10, see McKane, *Jeremiah 1*, 93-95. Although the LXX (Alexandrinus) reads καὶ εἶπαν ("and they said," i.e., "people say" ואמרו), a reading followed by German commentators beginning with Duhm, nevertheless, the LXX generally and the other OT versions follow the MT (וָאֹמַר), which should stand; cf. 14:13.

¹⁵ Commenting on Sennacherib's campaign of 701 BCE, Bright (*Jeremiah*) states "...some dramatic deliverance of Jerusalem must be assumed to have taken place, if only to explain the popular belief in the inviolability of Zion which subsequently hardened into a fixed dogma, as well as the fact that oracles of Isaiah predicting such a deliverance were cherished and preserved" (p. 299). Cf. Seitz, *Theology in Conflict*, p. 30 n. 47; John H. Hayes, "The Tradition of Zion's Inviolability," *JBL* 82 (1963) 419-426.

referring to prophets who have promised שָׁלוֹם.[16] "Ah, Lord God" also occurs in 1:6 (Jeremiah's response to his call) and in 32:17 (Jeremiah's prayer after giving the deed of purchase of Hanamel's field to Baruch for safe-keeping). These autobiographical passages may indeed exhibit traces of redaction, but as McKane rightly indicates, Jeremianic vocabulary from other parts of the *corpus* may well have been used, thereby preserving "an authentic recollection of his [i.e.,Jeremiah's] polemical encounter with the שָׁלוֹם prophets."[17] The phrase "Ah, Lord God" appears in the Deuteronomistic history (e.g., used by Joshua in Josh 7:7 and by Gideon in Judg 6:22), as well as four times in the book of Ezekiel (4:14; 9:8; 11:13; 21:5=20:49E), in autobiographical passages. The phrase occurs in contexts where a deep emotional response may be expected.[18]

The Contexts of Jeremiah 23:19-20 and Jeremiah 30:23-24

Before discussing in detail the doublet regarding "the storm of Yahweh" (23:19-20=30:23-24), attention must be given to the contexts in which this doublet is found. McKane regards 23:16-22 as a single unit.[19] Holladay, on the other hand, identifies 23:16-20 as a unit which introduces a paranetic appeal, followed by a separate unit, in which Yahweh speaks (note the transition from 3d s. to 1st s.).[20] In any event, there is a connecting link between 23:18 and 23:22 in the use of a phrase in which the verb עמד is followed by בְּסוֹד יְהוָה (23:18) or בְּסוֹדִי (23:22). סוֹד also occurs in 6:11 and 15:17a in the sense of "intimate circle."[21] Whether one understands in 23:18

---

[16] שָׁלוֹם in 14:13 is described as שְׁלוֹם אֱמֶת, literally "peace of trustworthiness" (Holladay, *Jeremiah 1*, 420). Some Hebrew manuscripts and Syr read שָׁלוֹם וֶאֱמֶת. Holladay (*Jeremiah 2*, 222) treats the expression in 33:6 (a hendiadys) as a gloss from 14:13 to explain עֲתֶרֶת. The LXX in 14:13 uses the conjunction καὶ but reverses the nouns, i.e., ἀλήθειαν καὶ εἰρήνην, to express the same idea, "assured peace."

[17] Regarding 14:11-16, see Thiel, *Redaktion 1*, 193; McKane, *Jeremiah 1*, 326.

[18] Reventlow (*Liturgie*) detects a note of intercession in some passages introduced by אֲהָהּ, e.g., 4:10; 14:13; Ezek 9:8; 11:13 (pp. 71, 123). But as Berridge (*Prophet*) has indicated regarding 4:10, "V.10 is closely analogous to the earliest form of OT lamentation, which consists solely of a brief and intense reproach directed against Yahweh,...this verse contains a spontaneous and impassioned outcry spoken by Jeremiah himself" (p. 108). The LXX translates אֲהָהּ as Ὁ Ὤν in 4:10 (cf. 1:6; 14:13; 39:17=MT32:17), misunderstanding this interjection and associating it with אֶהְיֶה in Exod 3:14, translated in LXX as Ὁ Ὤν. See H. St.John Thackeray, *The Septuagint and Jewish Worship* (2d ed.; Oxford: Oxford University Press, 1923) 33-34; Janzen, *Studies*, p. 216 n. 27. The LXX translator was concerned to make a connection between the call of Jeremiah and the call of Moses.

[19] McKane, *Jeremiah 1*, 577.

[20] Holladay, *Jeremiah 1*, 633.

[21] See Ludwig Köhler, *Hebrew Man* (London: SCM, 1956) 102-104. Köhler refers to the evening circle of men, among whom news is exchanged and plans for the future are

and 23:22 a reference to the "heavenly council" or understands סוֹד as a revelation of "secret counsel," the emphasis is on the fact that the שָׁלוֹם prophets have not received a direct communication from Yahweh. These false prophets have offered false assurances to "those who despise the word of Yahweh" (23:17). Pohlmann considers that for the author of 23:17 such a prophetic assurance is "fully perverse, because moreover future acts of judgment are excluded by Yahweh's unrestricted promise of salvation."[22] Kilpp claims that 30:23-24 does not readily fit the context, unless one makes a connection between "the wicked" in 30:23 and "the nations" in 30:11.[23] Thiel regards these two verses as an isolated saying of doubtful origin, not thematically suitable in the context.[24] The saying is not to be attributed to D and, because of its generality (judgment over the wicked), could be inserted in various contexts. Marx observes that 30:23-24 is a passage inserted between 30:22 and 31:1, each a form of the covenantal formula.[25] Bozak notes further that the use of הִנֵּה as the introduction of the oracles in 30:18 and 30:23, each ending with a covenantal formula, contributes to a definite structure demonstrable in three poems in Jeremiah 30. Each poem consists of two stanzas expressing a contrast: (1) 30:5-7; 30:8-11; (2) 30:12-15; 30:16-17; (3) 30:18-22; 30:23-31:1.[26] The contrast in the first poem is between a picture of distress and destruction (30:5-7) and Yahweh's saving presence (30:8-11); in the second poem, between the incurable wound of the people (30:12-15) and the promise of healing (30:16-17); in the third poem, between Yahweh's caring presence (30:18-22) and his chastising presence (30:23-31:1). Although the theme in the third poem differs somewhat from the theme in the first two poems and in the order of presentation, a good case has been made for justifying the position of 30:23-24 in context.

A more detailed treatment of 23:19-20=30:23-24 now follows:

2. JEREMIAH 23:19-20=JEREMIAH 30:23-24

JEREMIAH 23:19-20	JEREMIAH 30:23-24
19. Behold, the storm of Yahweh!	23. Behold, the storm of Yahweh!
ᵃ Wrath ᵃ has gone forth!	ᵃ Wrath ᵃ has gone forth!
ᵇ Even a whirling gale;ᵇ	ᵇ A whirling gale; ᵇ
on the head of the wicked	on the head of the wicked
ᶜ it will whirl.ᶜ	ᶜ it will whirl. ᶜ
20. ᵈ The anger of Yahweh ᵈ	ᵈ The fierce anger ᵈ of Yahweh

---

discussed.

[22] Pohlmann, *Studien*, p. 73.
[23] Kilpp, *Niederreissen und aufbauen*, 132.
[24] Thiel, *Redaktion 2*, 21 (cf. *Redaktion 1*, 251).
[25] Marx, "A Propos des doublets," 113.
[26] Bozak, *Life 'Anew,'* 33-70, esp. 67-68.

will not turn back
Until he has carried out and
achieved the intents of his mind.
In the latter days
ᵉ you will (fully) understand this.ᵉ

will not turn back
Until he has carried out and
achieved the intents of his mind.
In the latter days
ᵉ you will understand this.ᵉ

Textual and Translational Notes

ᵃ⁻⁻⁻ᵃ חֵמָה ("wrath," 23:19 and 30:23). Although חֵמָה is viewed as a gloss or variant reading by Rudolph, Bozak retains this noun as in apposition to יְהוָה סָעֲרַת.²⁷ Retention of חֵמָה does not overload the line. חֵמָה + יָצָא are found together in the OT only in the book of Jeremiah (here and in 4:4=21:12).²⁸

ᵇ⁻⁻⁻ᵇ וְסַעַר (23:19); סַעַר (30:23). The וְ is perhaps explicative, "even a whirling gale" (23:19), but is omitted in 30:23 as unnecessary.²⁹ The use of the masculine סַעַר after the feminine סָעֲרַת־יְהוָה is typical of gender-contrastive variants found in Jeremiah and elsewhere in the OT.³⁰

ᶜ⁻⁻⁻ᶜ מִתְחוֹלֵל (23:19); מִתְגּוֹרֵר (30:23). The change in verb in 30:23 may be intentional, although the LXX (συστρεφομένη, 23:19; στρεφομένη, 30:23) does not seem to have found a change in verb in the Hebrew *Vorlage*.³¹

ᵈ⁻⁻⁻ᵈ אַף־יְהוָה (23:20); חֲרוֹן אַף־יְהוָה (30:24). The expression חֲרוֹן אַף occurs frequently in the OT, always in connection with Yahweh's anger; in Jeremiah eight times (4:8; 4:26; 12:13; 25:37, 38; 30:24; 49:37; 51:45).³² In view of its frequent use elsewhere, חֲרוֹן אַף (30:24) would readily be substituted for אַף (23:20). The LXX supports the MT in both 23:20 and 30:24.

ᵉ⁻⁻⁻ᵉ בִּינָה (23:20), cognate accusative, is missing in the LXX and Syr, as well as in 30:24. If the MT is retained (cf. Vg *consilium*; Tg), the sense is "fully understand."³³

---

²⁷ Rudolph, *Jeremia*, 152. Bozak (*Life 'Anew'*), "specifying its content as negative rather than positive" (p. 67 n. 219). Driver also retains חמה, but suggests a different vocalization, חַמָּה ("heat"), i.e., with סערת יהוה ("a scorching wind"). See Driver, "Linguistic and Textual Problems," 115.

²⁸ Holladay, *Jeremiah 1*, 635. For 4:4b=21:12b, see also above, chap. four, pp. 62–64.

²⁹ Williams draws attention to this use of *waw*, but does not cite 23:19 as an example (*Hebrew Syntax*, § 434).

³⁰ Wilfred G. E. Watson, "Gender Matched Synonymous Parallelism in the Old Testament," *JBL* 99 (1980) 321-341. Cf. 16:4; 46:12; 48:46.

³¹ Holladay (*Jeremiah 2*), "quite possibly a deliberate change" (p. 180). Marx ("A Propos des Doublets") makes the interesting suggestion that 25:32, in which the image of "a great storm" (סַעַר גָּדוֹל) appears, contains the verb עוּר (Niphal יֵעוֹר "is stirred up") and suggests that (presumably by an *Ohrfehler*) a scribe wrote מִתְגּוֹרֵר where מִתְעוֹרֵר was intended (p. 113 n. 21).

³² חֲרוֹן occurs altogether forty-one times; thirty-five times with אַף.

³³ So Drinkard, *Jeremiah 1*, 342. Georg Fischer draws attention to the fact that the double use of the root בִּין (23:20) parallels the double use of the root חוּל (23:19); cf. the

Comment

Who are "the wicked" (רְשָׁעִים) referred to in 23:20 and 30:24? Although the adjective רָשָׁע (used as a noun in the singular, or in the plural, רְשָׁעִים) occurs 263 times in the OT, only five occurrences appear in the book of Jeremiah: 5:26; 12:1; 23:20=30:24; 25:31.[34] In 5:26, "wicked men are found among my people," these רְשָׁעִים typify the people as a whole, when one considers the total pericope 5:20-29, addressed to "the house of Jacob," "Judah" (5:20).[35] Berridge comments, "Although the רשעים of 5:26 are certainly a specific group of people, the word could also be applied to the people as a whole (cf. for example, Jer 23:19)."[36] The two verses (5:30-31), appended to 5:20-29, single out the prophets who prophesy falsely, and the priests who rule at their direction. Again, in 12:1, where the question is raised "Why does the way of the wicked prosper?," the additional question "Why do all who are treacherous (כָּל־בֹּגְדֵי בָגֶד) thrive?" also has a wide application. However, in the context (11:21-12:6), the specific reference is to "the men of Anathoth" (11:21-23).[37]

In the case of 23:19, the context (23:16-22) in which the statement is made that the storm of Yahweh "will burst upon the head of the wicked" relates to false, "optimistic" prophets. However, the doublet in 30:23-24 has within its wider context specific reference to "the nations," among whom the people are scattered (30:11=46:28). If, however, the reference within the more immediate context is to "the tents of Jacob" (30:18), the editorial insertion (30:23-24) has been made to underline the fact that the fortunes of Jacob will be restored only after the tempest of Yahweh's wrath has wrought its devastation. Only then can the covenantal promise (30:22; 31:1) be fulfilled.

The remaining passage in which רְשָׁעִים come under judgment is 25:31: "Yahweh has an indictment against the nations; he is entering into judgment with all flesh." As in 23:19=30:23, a tempest (סַעַר, 25:32) from "the farthest parts of the north" is stirring (יֵעוֹר), which in this case will have disastrous effects "from nation to nation" (cf. "all the inhabitants of the earth," 25:29, 30).

---

double use of the roots נבא and חלם in 23:25. See Fischer, *Das Trostbüchlein. Text, Komposition und Theologie von Jer 30-31* (Stuttgarter Biblische Beiträge 26; Stuttgart: Verlag Katholisches Bibelwerk, 1993) 170-172.

[34] Andersen and Forbes, *VOT*, 424. For a discussion of the term, with its forensic background, signifying "the guilty," and its opposite, צַדִּיק, "the innocent," see K. Hj. Fahlgren, *Sᵉdaka, nahestehende und entgegengesetze Begriffe im Alten Testament* (Uppsala: Almquist & Wiksells, 1932) 1-7. The majority of the occurrences are found in the Wisdom literature (e.g., eighty-two in Psalms, seventy-eight in Proverbs, twenty-six in Job). "רָשָׁע is rare before exile" (BDB:957).

[35] Note also "this people" (5:23); "a nation such as this" (5:29). McKane (*Jeremiah 1*) regards 5:26-29 as "a further spelling out of v. 25" (p. 132).

[36] Berridge, *Prophet*, p. 163 n. 260.

[37] Diamond, *Confessions*, 46.

In 23:19, then, "the wicked" are primarily false prophets; whereas in 30:23, the reference appears to be to "Jacob" (30:18). The wider context points to "all the nations" (30:11). In 25:31, "the nations" include Jerusalem and Judah (25:18), as well as the foreign nations listed in 25:19-26.

The אַף־יְהוָה ("anger of Yahweh," 23:20) usually appears in a more complete phrase, חֲרוֹן אַף־יְהוָה ("the fierce anger of Yahweh," 30:24).[38] The latter expression is used in 25:37 and 25:38, in the context of Yahweh's judgment against the "shepherds."

The judgment expected in 23:19-20=30:23-24 is also at an unspecified time, although the statement is made that "in the latter days (בְּאַחֲרִית הַיָּמִים) you will understand it clearly" (23:20=30:24).[39] Lipinski argues that God's intervention will be within history, "in the days to come" rather than "at the end of days" in an apocalyptic sense, as in Dan 10:24.[40] The remaining references in the book of Jeremiah to בְּאַחֲרִית הַיָּמִים (48:47; 49:39) have to do with the restoration of the fortunes of Moab and Elam.

According to 23:20c=30:24c only "in the latter days" will Yahweh's judgment be understood clearly. The "optimistic" prophets and those who have accepted their false assurances that no judgment will come will only understand Yahweh's purposes after judgment has taken place (23:20). This reference to "the latter days" in 30:24, in keeping with the new frame of reference, in which the judgment applies both to Yahweh's people and to "all the nations" (30:11), points to the post-exilic period, but still to an event within history. There are purposes for Israel beyond this time of judgment (30:11=46:28; 31:2-6). The oracle of judgment (23:19-20) has been thoroughly adapted to a later situation by its insertion in Jeremiah 30, followed by the hope expressed in 31:1.

---

[38] See Textual Note d...d above. The expression, which always refers to Yahweh's anger (not human anger) occurs frequently throughout the OT: e.g., Exod 32:12; Deut 13:8; Hos 11:9; Isa 13:9, 13.

[39] The expression "in the latter days" occurs fourteen times in the OT: four times in the Pentateuch: Gen 49:1; Num 24:14; Deut 4:30; 31:29; eight times in the Prophets, including four in Jeremiah: 23:20=30:24; 48:47; 49:39 (regarding Moab); 49:39 (regarding Elam); Hos 3:5; Isa 2:2=Mic 4:1; Ezek 38:16; twice in the book of Daniel: 2:23 (Aram.); 10:14.

[40] E. Lipinski, "באחרית הימים dans les textes pre-exiliques," *VT* 20 (1970) 445-450. Cf. G. W. Buchanan, "Eschatology and the 'End of Days'," *JNES* 20 (1961) 188-193. Buchanan makes a careful examination of the thirty-five occurrences of אַחֲרִית in the OT, concluding that באחרית הימים "does not by itself have any eschatological overtones" (p. 190). Regarding 23:20=30:24 Buchanan concludes: "The future may hold prosperity for Israel (Isa 2:2; Jer 23:20; 37[30]:24; Mic 4:1) or hardship to be followed by prosperity for Israel, Moab, or Edom (Jer 48:47; 49:39 [25:10]; Ezek 38:16)" (p. 189). Weiser (*Jeremia*) states that in 23:20, "The expression 'at the end of days' cannot here possibly be meant absolutely eschatologically in the sense of the end-time" (p. 206 n. 1). Similarly, Cerny (*The Day of Yahweh*) makes a distinction between "the latter days" and "the day of Yahweh" (p. 25).

Three Recurring Phrases in Jeremiah 23

Three recurring formulations in Jeremiah 23 need consideration: (a) עַם־חָזֶה (23:32); (b) הַנְּבִאִים בִּשְׁמִי שָׁקֶר (23:25); (c) מֵרֹעַ מַעַלְלֵיהֶם (23:22).

(a) Jeremiah 23:22 brings a charge against the prophets who have not stood in Yahweh's council. They have failed to proclaim Yahweh's words to "my people" and so have not turned them "from the evil of their doings" (מֵרֹעַ מַעַלְלֵיהֶם, cf. 25:5). A similar phrase (מִפְּנֵי רֹעַ מַעַלְלֵיכֶם) occurs in 4:4b=21:12b(*Qere*); 26:3; 44:22.[41]

Thiel has argued for the originality of the phrase מֵרֹעַ מַעַלְלֵיהֶם in 23:22, as over against other occurrences in Jeremiah with מִפְּנֵי in prose passages which are to be ascribed to D, in the light of Deut 28:20.[42] He acknowledges that early texts in the OT contain the phrase with minor adaptation: e.g., Isa 1:16; Hos 9:15 (עַל רֹעַ מַעַלְלֵיהֶם); Ps 28:4 (כְּמַעַלְלֵיהֶם).[43]

The phrase has its roots in earlier prophetic tradition before its use by Jeremiah himself (23:22). Such passages as 26:3 and 44:22 stand within this prophetic tradition.[44]

(b) הַנְּבִאִים בִּשְׁמִי שָׁקֶר הַנִּבְּאִים (23:25). The phrase occurs also in 14:14 (with a different word order); cf. 29:9, 21. The false prophets inveighed against in 23:25 have claimed validity for their message on the basis of dreams (cf. 23:32; 29:9). In 11:21, Jeremiah is forbidden by the "men of Anathoth" to "prophesy in the name of Yahweh" or else to be put to death (the penalty for false prophecy, Deut 13:5); cf. 26:8–9, when the penalty of death is pronounced by "the priests and the prophets and all the people" in view of Jeremiah's proclamation that Yahweh will make the temple "like Shiloh" (cf. Uriah, 26:20; Deut 18:20).

Although some scholars (e.g., Holladay and McKane) assert that in 23:23–32 there are two distinct units, 23:23–24 and 23:25–32, a good case can be made for the view that these verses constitute a single unit which expands 23:16–22, specifying those characteristics of "false" prophets which make them unreliable.[45] The first rhetorical question in 23:23 places the emphasis on

---

[41] Note also אֶת־רֹעַ מַעַלְלֵיכֶם in 23:2.

[42] Thiel (*Redaktion 1*, 252), with 25:5 dependent upon 23:22.

[43] Thiel (*Redaktion 1*, 252) considers Psalm 28 to be early.

[44] Cf. Jones (*Jeremiah*, 106), commenting on 4:4. Similarly, the phrase "according to the fruit of his (evil) doings" (כִּפְרִי מַעֲלָלָיו, 17:10; 21:14; 32:19; cf. 6:19) belongs within the prophetic tradition (cf. Hos 10:13; Mic 7:13; Isa 3:10, "fruit of [good] deeds").

[45] For example, Rudolph, *Jeremia*, 153. Jones (*Jeremiah*, 311) points to structural considerations: the three-fold rhetorical questions of 23:23–24 and the three-fold pronouncement of judgment in the phrase, "Behold, I am against the prophets, says Yahweh, who..." (23:30, 31, 32). Cf. the repeated admonition, "Do not listen to" (אַל־תִּשְׁמְעוּ) the

Yahweh's remoteness (i.e., transcendence), followed by two further questions as to the inability to hide from his scrutiny and his omnipresence.[46] The polemic is directed towards self-deluded prophets who prophesy שֶׁקֶר in Yahweh's name, on the basis of dreams (23:25). Overholt argues that although dreams as a means of revelation are well attested elsewhere in the OT, e.g., Num 12:6; Joel 3:1 (2:28E), dreams may be misused (Deut 13:1-5; Jer 23:32, "lying dreams"; cf. 27:9; 29:8).[47]

(c) עָם־הַזֶּה ("this people," 23:33), refers to the people as a whole.[48] In the second Confession, the term עָם־הַזֶּה (15:20) could refer to הֵמָּה in 15:19, i.e., those opposed to Jeremiah. However, Diamond sees in 15:20 a reference to the nation as a whole, a departure from the stereotyped reference to the prophet's opponents in the preceding verses of this Confession (e.g., רֹדְפַי in 15:15).[49] In 15:10, Jeremiah has become "a man of strife and contention to the whole land." "This people" in 5:14; 14:10; 16:5, 10 applies to the people as a whole; cf. 27:16, כָּל־הָעָם הַזֶּה.

JEREMIAH 23:33-40

A final prose passage, 23:33-40, concluding the section dealing with prophecy (23:9-40), contains the term מַשָּׂא יְהוָה, "burden of Yahweh," which occurs six times, in 23:33; 23:36 (twice); 23:38 (three times), while the single word מַשָּׂא occurs in 23:33 and 23:36.[50] The catchword connection with the preceding unit is provided by the reference to הָעָם הַזֶּה (25:33); cf. לָעָם הַזֶּה in 23:32. The subject of conflict between true and false prophecy continues as a main concern in 23:33-40, although vv. 34-40 may well be regarded as coming from a post-exilic period.[51]

---

prophets, 27:9, 14, 16, 17. Carroll (*Jeremiah*, 469-470) also treats 23:25-32 as a single unit, "heavily edited" (p. 470); e.g., 23:32 shows Deuteronomistic influence.

[46] The LXX and Syr, however, reverse the meaning of the question by vocalizing ה as the definite article, rather than as the interrogative particle, thereby affirming that God is near and accessible, not distant. See Werner E. Lemke, "The Near and the Distant God. A Study of Jer 23:23-24 in its Biblical Theological Context," *JBL* 100 (1981) 541-555. He interprets 23:23MT to mean that God is not only a near God (קָרֹב), but also distant (רָחֹק). The emphasis is on God as transcendent (רָחֹק, "distant").

[47] Overholt, *The Threat of Falsehood*, 64-68. Cf. K. Seybold, *Der Prophet Jeremia. Leben und Werk* (Stuttgart: Kohlhammer, 1993) 101-102, regarding 23:28.

[48] The additional words in 23:33, אוֹ־הַנָּבִיא אוֹ־כֹהֵן, are best taken as a gloss from 23:34. Cf. Rudolph, *Jeremia*, 154.

[49] Diamond, *Confessions*, 76.

[50] The term מַשָּׂא in the literal sense of "burden" (BDB מַשָּׂא II:672) occurs four times in Jeremiah 17 (vv. 21, 22, 24, 27).

[51] E.g., Holladay (*Jeremiah 1*) assigns a date "well into the post-exilic period" (p. 649). J. Lindblom, *Prophecy in Ancient Israel* (Oxford: Basil Blackwell, 1963), following Rudolph, sees 23:34-40 as "a specimen of Talmudic learning" (p. 290). Jones (*Jeremiah*),

Jeremiah 23:33 seems to be an isolated unit, in which an unnamed addressee (presumably Jeremiah) is instructed by Yahweh that the answer to the question, "What is the מַשָּׂא of Yahweh?" should be "You are the מַשָּׂא."[52] In his magisterial treatment of this verse and the appended verses, 23:34–40, McKane discusses very fully the text and the various views held regarding the interpretation of the passage.[53] In the case of the two homonyms, מַשָּׂא ("load," "burden") and מַשָּׂא ("utterance," "oracle") no nuance of "burden" is regularly found in מַשָּׂא ("utterance").[54] There is a play on words in 23:33; the question is derisory on the part of the questioners, who find Jeremiah's oracles to be burdensome. In his sharp reply, the prophet accepts the play on words and turns the question against his interrogators, "You are the מַשָּׂא." The intention of the question, then, is "What is your latest burdensome word from Yahweh?," to which Yahweh's answer to his prophet is "'You' [referring to the people] are the burden and I am about to unburden myself of you."[55]

Jeremiah 23:33–40 represents later attempts to interpret the conflict between Jeremiah and the שָׁלוֹם prophets, in support of Jeremiah, whose prophecies of doom have been fulfilled. A key verse is 23:36, which indicates that the term מַשָּׂא is no longer to be used, since it has been subject to perversion.[56] A part of 23:36 and most of 23:37 is missing in the LXX, יהוה... והפכתם. Janzen raises the possibility that the missing words in 23:36–37LXX may have been the result of the accidental loss of a line in the LXX *Vorlage*.[57] Textual problems and grammatical questions make translation of 23:36 difficult.[58] McKane translates 23:36 as follows: "You shall make no further

---

however, claims that "this section expresses and strengthens the fundamental insights of the Jeremiah tradition" and "is itself authentic prophecy" (p. 317).

[52] By revocalizing מַשָּׂא אֶת־מַה־מַשָּׂא (MT) to אַתֶּם הַמַּשָּׂא; cf. also LXX: Ὑμεῖς ἐστε τὸ λῆμμα; Vg *quid vobis onus*. See Tov, "Some Aspects," 281–282. The proposal has been made to treat מַה as an interrogative pronoun, but this would be unusual in this construction. The best solution is to follow the LXX.

[53] William McKane, "משׂא in Jeremiah 23 35-40," in *Prophecy, Essays Presented to Georg Fohrer on His Sixty-Fifth Birthday, 6 September 1980* (ed. J. S. Emerton; BZAW 150; Berlin: Walter de Gruyter) 15–54.

[54] BDB:672. Both homonyms are derived from נָשָׂא ("to lift, bear, carry, lift up [utter]").

[55] McKane, "משׂא in Jeremiah 23:35–40," 45.

[56] מַשָּׂא as a *terminus technicus* in the sense of "prophetic oracle" appears frequently elsewhere in the prophetic literature: Isa 13:1; 14:28; 15:1; 17:1; 19:1; 21:1, 11, 13; 22:1; 23:1; 30:6; Nah 1:1; Hab 1:1; Zech 9:1; 12:1; Mal 1:1. Seybold (*Der Prophet Jeremia*, 101) suggests that these oracles were mostly of a political nature. Cf. 2 Kgs 9:25; 2 Chron 24:27. Lam 2:14 has to do with מַשְׂאוֹת that are "false and misleading."

[57] Janzen, *Studies*, p. 223 n. 35.

[58] Ehrlich (*Randglossen*, 305) proposes reading ה interrogative in place of the definite article and changing דְּבָרִי to דְּבָרוֹ, so that the phrase in 23:36 would read יִהְיֶה לְאִישׁ דְּבָרִי הַמַּשָּׂא ("Is my word a burden to anyone?"). Rudolph (*Jeremia*, 154) follows Ehrlich's proposal regarding ה interrogative, but retains דְּבָרוֹ. דְּבָרוֹ leaves open the question as to

mention of 'Yahweh's burden,' for that 'burden' is what he entrusts to the man who bears his word. You twist the words of the living God, Yahweh Sabaoth, our God."[59] The play on words continues in this polemical assertion that the prophet of doom is the true prophet, as over against the one who twists Yahweh's words (i.e., the שָׁלוֹם prophet). The reference to "the city" in 23:39 is an indication that the destruction of Jerusalem was regarded as a vindication of Jeremiah's "doom" prophecy. However, the term מַשָּׂא is no longer to be used (23:38), since its misuse by pseudo-prophets brings only "everlasting reproach and perpetual shame." The precise date when this prohibition of the use of the term מַשָּׂא was made remains uncertain, but presumably a late date is probable, in view of its use in such books as Zechariah (9:1; 12:1) and Malachi (1:1).[60]

Another doublet, which also includes false prophets in the prophetic indictment, is 6:13-15=8:10b-12 (cf. 14:13-16).

3. JEREMIAH 6:13-15=JEREMIAH 8:10b-12

JEREMIAH 6:13-15
13. ⁿᵃ For from the least
to the greatest of them ᵃ
ᵇ Every one is greedy ᵇ
for unjust gain;
ᶜ Even from prophet to priest, ᶜ
ᵇ Every one ᵇ practises falsehood.
14. ᵇ They have healed ᵇ
the wound of
ᵈ my (dear) people ᵈ superficially
saying, 'Peace, peace',
ᵉ when there is no peace. ᵉ
15. ᵇ They should be ashamed ᵇ
because they have behaved
abominably.
ᵇ They are by no means ashamed,ᵇ
ᶠ Nor do they know how to feel
disgraced.ᶠ Therefore ᵍ they shall
among those who fall;ᵍ
ʰ At the time that I punish them ʰ
shall be thrown down",
ⁱ says Yahweh.ⁱ

JEREMIAH 8:10b-12
10b."...because ᵃ from the least
to the greatest ᵃ
ᵇ Every one is greedy ᵃ
for unjust gain;
ᶜ From prophet to priest ᶜ
ᵇ Every one ᵇ practises falsehood.
11. ᵇ They have healed ᵇ
the wound of
ᵈ my (dear) people superficially
saying, 'Peace, peace',
ᵉ when there is no peace. ᵉ
ᵇ They should be ashamed ᵇ
because they have behaved
abominably.
ᵇ They are by no means ashamed,ᵇ
ᶠ Nor do they know how to feel
disgraced. ᶠ Therefore ᵍ they shall be
be among those who fall; ᵍ
ʰAt the time that I punish themʰ they
they shall be thrown down",
ⁱ says Yahweh.ⁱ

---

whether the reference is to a man's own word (by relating the pronominal suffix to אִישׁ , cf. Tg, or to Yahweh's word given to a man). McKane (*Jeremiah 1*, 600) argues for the latter view (cf. NEB).

[59] McKane, *Jeremiah 1*, 597. Yahweh is described as "the living God" (אֱלֹהִים חַיִּים) only in 23:36 and in 10:10 in the book of Jeremiah (cf. Deut 5:23; 1 Sam 17:26, 36), although the concept is present in 2:13, where Yahweh is described as מְקוֹר מַיִם חַיִּים.

[60] Perhaps as late as the 3d Cent. BCE, according to Sellin-Fohrer, *Introduction*, 468.

Jeremiah 8:10b-12 does not occur in the LXX.

Textual and Translational Notes

a...a מִקְּטַנָּם וְעַד־גְּדוֹלָם ("from the least to the geatest of them," 6:13); וְעַד־גָּדוֹל מִקָּטֹן ("from the least to the greatest," 8:10b). The LXX combines both versions: ἀπὸ μικροῦ αὐτῶν = מִקְּטַנָּם; καὶ ἕως μεγάλου = וְעַד־גָּדוֹל. With minor variations the phrase is also found in 16:6 (reverse order); 31:34; 42:1, 8; 44:12.

b...b Differences in orthography: כֻּלֹּה (6:13 *bis*); כֻּלֹּה (8:10b *bis*); בּוֹצֵעַ (6:13); בֹּצֵעַ (8:10b); וַיְרַפְּאוּ (6:14); וַיְרַפּוּ (8:11; cf. מַרְפֵּה, 8:15); הֹבִישׁוּ (6:15); הֹבִשׁוּ (8:12); יֵבוֹשׁוּ (8:12); הַכְּלִים (6:15); וְהִכָּלֵם (8:12). Unlike the random orthographic differences in 23:8=16:15; 46:27=30:10; 51:16=10:13, there is in 6:13-15 (at variance with the context in Jeremiah 6) a consistent employment of *scriptio plena*, wherever the form differs from that in 8:10b-12. Although 6:13-15 may represent "an orthographically more advanced text than 8:10b-12" (Janzen), the sample is too small to allow a firm decision to be made.[61] For other examples of כֻּלֹּה (8:10b), see 2:21; 8:6; 20:7.

c...c וּמִנָּבִיא וְעַד־כֹּהֵן ("Even from prophet to priest," 6:13). The initial *waw* is missing in 8:10b, but is found in some Hebrew manuscripts, as well as in Arabic and Syriac versions. The *waw* may be considered as explicative.[62] The LXX (6:13) reverses the order of the MT: ἀπὸ ἱερέως καὶ ἕως ψευδοπροφήτου (cf. 14:18; 23:11). The LXX interprets נָבִיא as ψευδοπροφήτης (cf. the description of Hananiah as ψευδοπροφήτης in 35:1LXX=28:1MT).

d...d עַמִּי ("my people," 6:14[MT and LXX]); בַּת־עַמִּי ("my [dear] people," [literally] "daughter of my people," 8:11). Many Hebrew manuscripts, as well as Syr and Vg, read בַּת־עַמִּי at 6:14. בַּת־עַמִּי occurs in both contexts: 6:26; 8:19, 21, 22, 23, as well as at 4:11; 9:6.[63] The pronominal suffix "my" could indicate either Yahweh or the prophet as speaker (see discussion below).

e...e וְאֵין שָׁלוֹם ("when there is no peace," 6:14; 8:11). The LXX (6:14) reads καὶ ποῦ ἐστιν εἰρήνη ("and where is peace?," i.e., וְאַיֵּה שָׁלוֹם, probably through misreading final *nun* as ה).[64] Other occurrences of אֵין שָׁלוֹם are found in 12:12; 30:5 (cf. Isa 48:22).

---

[61] Janzen, *Studies*, p. 232 n. 3. However, see Freedman, Forbes and Andersen, *Studies in Hebrew and Aramaic Orthography*, 119, 121; cf. Hubmann, *Untersuchungen*, 242.

[62] Williams, *Hebrew Syntax* § 434.

[63] Janzen (*Studies*, 38) claims that בַּת in 8:11 has entered the text under the influence of 8:21, שֶׁבֶר בַּת־עַמִּי. Holladay (*Jeremiah 1*, 156) regards the genitive to be appositional, literally "my daughter people," a term of endearment, "my fair people" (hence the translation above, "my dear people)."

[64] Holladay (*Jeremiah 1*, 211) notes that the LXX reading is preferred by Duhm and Cornill, but the other versions consistently follow the MT.

f...f נַם־הֹכְלִים (6:15); יִכָּלְמוּ (8:12); i.e., infin. constr. *Hiphil* at 6:15; infin. constr. *Niphal* at 8:12 (cf. 3:3). *Niphal* makes better sense, "to be ashamed," and is the usual parallel with בּוֹשׁ, *Qal*, elsewhere in the book of Jeremiah.[65]
g...g יָפְלוּ בַנֹּפְלִים is followed by יִכָּשְׁלוּ (6:15; 8:12). These two verbs, "fall" and "stumble" are closely associated (in reverse order) in the oracles against Egypt, e.g., 46:12, 16.
h...h בְּעֵת־פְּקַדְתִּים (6:15); בְּעֵת פְּקֻדָּתָם (8:12). The use of the 1st sing. *Qal* in 6:15 is defended by Holladay, as the *lectio difficilior*.[66] The LXX, however, has ἐν καιρῷ ἐπισκοπῆς; בְּעֵת פְּקֻדָּתָם (8:12) occurs also elsewhere in the book of Jeremiah, e.g., 10:15=51:18; 46:21; 50:27.
i...i אָמַר יְהוָה (6:15; 8:12; 6:15LXX, εἶπε κύριος). The appropriateness of this indication of Yahweh as speaker in 6:13-15 is denied by McKane, although in view of אָתֵּן in 8:10, where Yahweh is clearly the speaker, אָמַר יְהוָה is retained in 8:12.[67] The phrase אָמַר יְהוָה occurs a number of times, both in the book of Jeremiah, as well as elsewhere in the OT (e.g., Isa 48:22; 49:5; 54:1; 57:19; 59:21; 66:20, 21, 23; Amos 1:15; 2:3; 5:17, 27; 7:3; Mal 1:2, 13; 3:13).[68]

To define the relationship between 6:13-15 and 8:10b-12 is difficult in view of the differences in text and orthography, the fact that 8:10b-12 is missing in the LXX, and the question as to whether Yahweh or the prophet is the speaker. Janzen makes the claim that the passage originally was situated in Jeremiah 6 and then secondarily inserted in Jeremiah 8, in view of the similarity in context.[69] Carroll treats the doublet as a unit "independent of its present contexts," inserted editorially.[70] Either explanation is possible.

Jeremiah 6:13-15 and Jeremiah 8:10b-12 in Context

The context needs to be examined carefully, especially the immediate context. Jeremiah 6:12a and 8:10a have some features in common, but 6:12b is not duplicated in 8:10. Jeremiah 6:12 refers to a judgment in which לַאֲחֵרִים וְנָסַבּוּ בָתֵּיהֶם ("their *houses* shall be turned over to others"); cf. 8:10, לַאֲחֵרִים לָכֵן אֶתֵּן אֶת־נְשֵׁיהֶם ("Therefore I will give their *wives* to others"); 6:12, יַחְדָּו

---

[65] E.g., 3:3; 22:22; 31:19; cf. Holladay, *Jeremiah 1*, 211. Because of the differences in orthography in 6:13-15=8:10b-12, perhaps the form in 6:13 was originally הִכָּלֵים (*Niphal*). Cf. McKane, *Jeremiah 1*, 147.
[66] Holladay, *Jeremiah 1*, 211.
[67] McKane, *Jeremiah 1*, 148, 188.
[68] Janzen, *Studies*, 159, Appendix B, Table B.3.
[69] Janzen, *Studies*, 95-96 (cf. Duhm, Cornill, Giesebrecht, Rudolph, and Holladay, *Jeremiah 1*, 274). Janzen surmises that the passage dropped out of Jeremiah 6 by *homoioteleuton*, v. 12 נאם יהוה to v. 15 אמר יהוה, and was subsequently wrongly inserted in Jeremiah 8 because of the similarity in context (6:12 and 8:10a), later reinserted in Jeremiah 6, but as a conflation from a manuscript with full orthography.
[70] Carroll, *Jeremiah*, 198; cf. Jones, *Jeremiah*, 135.

שָׂדוֹת וְנָשִׁים "their fields and wives as well"); 8:10, שְׂדוֹתֵיהֶם לְיוֹרְשִׁים ("and their fields to conquerors"). In the Decalogue (Deut 5:21), a neighbour's wife, house and field are to be protected, since coveting them is prohibited.[71] However, in the pronouncement of judgment in Jer 6:12, houses, fields and wives are now no longer protected, but are subject to judgment. Similarly, in 6:12b (not paralleled in 8:10), Yahweh's judgment runs counter to his action in Deut 26:8 in bringing his people out of Egypt בְּיָד חֲזָקָה וּבִזְרֹעַ נְטוּיָה ("with a mighty hand and an outstretched arm").[72] The phrase used in 6:12 (כִּי־אַטֶּה אֶת־יָדִי) is found also in 15:6 (וָאַט אֶת־יָדִי עָלַיִךְ), expressing Yahweh's judgment.[73] In 15:6, judgment upon Jerusalem has already taken place in the mind of the prophet.[74]

Jeremiah 6:12 rightly concludes the unit 6:9–12, which consists of a dialogue between Yahweh and the prophet.[75] Yahweh's words are quoted in 6:9, a command to glean thoroughly as a vine שְׁאֵרִית ("the remnant") of Israel.[76] Even if one accepts Yahweh's command as positive, i.e., a second gleaning will save at least a few, Jeremiah's disheartened response in 6:10–11a indicates his sense of hopelessness in appealing to those who will not listen. Nevertheless, in Yahweh's rejoinder (6:11b–12), judgment is pronounced, with a wide application to children, youths, husbands, wives, "old folk and the very

---

[71] In the alternative form (Exod 20:17), "field" is not specifically mentioned.

[72] The phrase בְּיָד נְטוּיָה וּבִזְרוֹעַ חֲזָקָה, with minor variations, occurs in the book of Jeremiah in 21:5, where Yahweh fights against his own people. In 27:5, the reference is to Yahweh's power in creation, which gives him the sovereign right to deal with what he has made according to his will (cf. 32:17, 21, where appeal is made to Yahweh's actions in creation and the exodus, yet because of Israel's disobedience, רָעָה has come upon them, 32:23). The phrase occurs frequently in the book of Deuteronomy (e.g., 4:34; 5:15; 7:19; 9:29; 11:2; 26:8) and usually denotes deliverance and redemption (cf. also Exod 6:16; Ps 136:12). However, the phrase is used in Ezek 20:33, 34 to express judgment.

[73] Cf. the refrain in Isa 5:25; 9:12; 10:4.

[74] An example of "the language of prophetic anticipation." See Paul Joüon, *A Grammar of Biblical Hebrew,* Part III, *Syntax* (rev. T. Muraoka; Rome: Editrice Pontificio Istituto Biblico, 1991) 363 § 112h; Williams, *Hebrew Syntax,* § 165, perfect of certainty ("prophetic perfect").

[75] Rudolph, *Jeremia,* 44–45.

[76] Jeremiah 6:9 contains the only reference to "the remnant of Israel" in the book of Jeremiah. For "remnant of Judah," see 40:11, 15; 42:15, 19; 44:12, 14, 28, all referring to the post-587 BCE period. For a discussion of the post-587 BCE remnant, see Seitz, *Theology in Conflict,* 273–278. Note also "all the remnant of the people," 41:10, 16; "all this remnant," 42:2; "the remnant of Jerusalem" (among the bad figs), 24:8. See also the reference to a remnant "of this evil family," widely dispersed, 8:3; no remnant of the men of Anathoth (referred to in 11:23); שְׁאֵרִיתָם ("the remnant of them," i.e., of the inhabitants of Jerusalem, 15:9). Regarding 6:9, Carroll considers the image of the thoroughly gleaned vine to be pointing to the utter destruction of Israel (*Jeremiah,* 195). Cf. Holladay, "the harvest is judgment" (*Jeremiah 1,* 213) and Brueggemann (*To Pluck Up,* 68). For an interpretation that envisages some survivors, see Berridge, *Prophet,* 79; McKane, *Jeremiah 1,* 145, "try to save a few."

aged." This comprehensive judgment is maintained in the unit which follows (6:13–15), "from the least to the greatest" (6:13), although prophet and priest are singled out as especially blameworthy.

In Jeremiah 8, in the immediate context (8:8–9), the emphasis falls on scribes who have falsified the *torah* of Yahweh (8:8) and "wise men" who have rejected Yahweh's word. Jeremiah 8:10 begins with לָכֵן ("therefore"), in justification of the judgment pronounced at the end of the unit, 8:8–10a (cf. לָכֵן in 8:12b, at the end of the unit 8:10b–12). I take the view that the doublet is limited to 6:13–15=8:10b–12 and that 6:12 and 8:10a are not part of the doublet *per se*. Jeremiah 6:12 belongs to the preceding unit, 6:9–12; 8:10a is part of the preceding unit 8:8–10a. There is sufficient similarity between 6:12a and 8:10a to account for the insertion of the doublet, which is more intrusive in Jeremiah 8.[77] The fact that 8:10b–12 is missing in the LXX indicates that these verses were not present in the Hebrew *Vorlage*. This is a preferable explanation, rather than the assumption that the doublet was consciously omitted by the translators.[78]

Comment

Jeremiah 6:13–15=8:10b–12 begins with a general condemnation; "from the least to the greatest" all are greedy for unjust gain (בּוֹצֵעַ בָּצַע, participle followed by cognate accusative). בָּצַע also occurs in the accusation brought against Jehoiakim in 22:17.[79] A significant word in 6:14=8:11 is שֶׁבֶר ("fracture, destruction, wound"), frequently found in the book of Jeremiah.[80] שֶׁבֶר גָּדוֹל in 4:6 will come "from the north" (cf. 6:1; 51:54, "from the land of the Chaldeans"). Pohlmann claims that the שֶׁבֶר event reflected in the doublet (6:13–15=8:10b–12) is the catastrophe of 587 BCE.[81] That event has already taken place; those proclaiming peace and prosperity are false prophets who have refused a conscious act of penitence and shame for their previous guilty acts, and are therefore still to face a future day of visitation (6:15=8:12). Pohlmann believes that this passage reflects a temporal distance from

---

[77] Jeremiah 6:12b (...כִּי־אַטֶּה אֶת־יָדִי), for which there is no parallel in 8:10, should be retained as part of the unit 6:11b–12 (*pace* McKane, *Jeremiah 1*, 144, 146), rather than seeking to accommodate 6:12 and 8:10 to one another as part of the doublet.

[78] See Janzen's treatment of this, *Studies*, 95–96.

[79] The only other occurrence of בָּצַע in the book of Jeremiah is in 51:13, regarding Babylon. If one follows the MT, אַמַּת בִּצְעֵךְ could be a metaphor from the weaving trade, literally "the cubit of your cutting off," parallel to בָּא קִצֵּךְ, "your end has come" (see Carroll, *Jeremiah*, 839).

[80] E.g., 4:6, 20; 6:1; 8:21; 10:19; 14:17; 30:15; 48:3, 5; 50:22; 52:54. The term most often used is שֶׁבֶר גָּדוֹל (4:6; 6:1; 14:17; 48:3; 50:22; 51:54).

[81] Karl-Friedrich Pohlmann, *Die Ferne Gottes. Studien zum Jeremiabuch* (BZAW 179; Berlin: Walter de Gruyter, 1989) 90–93.

Jeremiah's time. However, both 597 BCE and 587 BCE may be understood as שֶׁבֶר events. Seitz insists that, in general, insufficient attention is given by exegetes to the significance of the 597 BCE event.[82] If the conflict between Jeremiah and the שָׁלוֹם prophets extended over a considerable period of time, one could argue that these false prophets were unable to admit the seriousness of the 597 BCE historical situation and the threat of further destruction after 597 BCE. A decade later, the concern with the prophet who prophesies שָׁלוֹם is still reflected in 28:9, the post-587 BCE situation in which Hananiah prophesied the return of the temple vessels, as well as Jeconiah and the exiles from Babylon "within two years" (28:3).

In prophesying שָׁלוֹם, the false prophets have committed תּוֹעֵבָה (6:15=8:12; cf. Lev 18:27; 20:13). Six other references to תּוֹעֵבָה in the book of Jeremiah emphasize idolatrous behaviour as the main reason for Yahweh's judgment.[83] Here the emphasis is on עָשָׂה שֶׁקֶר ("dealing falsely"), by the misuse of the prophetic and priestly office, with the blithe assumption that all is well.[84] McKane regards 6:13-15 as from Jeremiah himself; consequently, עַמִּי in 6:14 "should be taken as a mark of the intensity of the prophet's identification with his people and should be compared with 8:23 (חֲלָלֵי בַת עַמִּי אֶת)."[85] "They have healed the wound of my people (שֶׁבֶר עַמִּי) superficially" (6:14=8:11). However, this would mean emending פְּקֻדָּתִים in 6:15 to פְּקֻדָּתָם (as in 8:12) and the elimination of אָמַר יְהוָה at the end of 6:15. If one stays with the MT, then Yahweh is the speaker who speaks of "my people."[86] In view of the verb אָתֵן in 8:10a, where Yahweh is speaker, I assume that the added doublet 8:10b-12, in spite of the form פְּקֻדָּתָם in 8:12, also implies that Yahweh is the speaker, as indicated by the concluding אָמַר יְהוָה.[87]

This discussion of the content of the doublet 6:13-15=8:10b-12 shows that there is not sufficient evidence for maintaining that this unit is a redactional composition; rather, this is part of the Jeremiah tradition which redactors have felt free to insert in appropriate contexts.

---

[82] Seitz (*Theology in Conflict*), "...the impact 597 events had on the community in Judah and especially on those deported to Babylon is not given its full force" (p. 101).

[83] Jeremiah 2:7; 7:10; 16:18; 32:35; 44:4, 22.

[84] See Berridge (*Prophet*), "The תּוֹעֵבָה which the 'false' prophets have committed is not their optimism...but rather the misuse or abuse of their prophetic office" (p. 35 n. 52). תּוֹעֵבָה also occurs forty-three times in the book of Ezekiel, both in the sense of idolatry and of moral turpitude.

[85] McKane, *Jeremiah 1*, 147.

[86] Cf. 8:7, and the covenantal formula in 7:23; 11:4; 24:7; 30:22; 31:1, 33; 32:38 (לְעָם לִי).

[87] The suffix in פְּקֻדָּתָם is objective, literally "their visitation," "their punishment," i.e., "the punishment that falls on them."

Jeremiah 28 and 29

Other passages regarding false prophets are found in Jeremiah 28 and 29. Jeremiah 28 records Jeremiah's conflict with Hananiah. Although Jeremiah would have welcomed Hananiah's prediction (if this were true prophecy) that the period of exile would last only two years (28:6), he was constrained to declare the falsity of such optimism. Jeremiah 28:9 appeals to the Deuteronomic criterion that the word of the true prophet is authentic when fulfilled by events in the course of time (Deut 18:21-22).[88] The difficulties surrounding this criterion are discussed by Overholt, who also draws attention to another criterion in Deut 13:1-6 (12:31-13:5E), the teaching of rebellion (סָרָה) against Yahweh.[89] This is the basis for Jeremiah's prediction of Hananiah's death (28:15-17). Teaching rebellion and causing his hearers to trust in a lie (שֶׁקֶר) indicate that a prophet has not been sent by Yahweh, and is to be put to death; e.g., Shemaiah, 29:30-32; cf. Ahab and Zedekiah, 29:21. The cycle, Jeremiah 27-29, has many unique features and a complicated textual history.[90] No attempt is made here to analyse this cycle in a detailed way, only to point to the Deuteronomistic viewpoint which dominates the treatment of prophecy in these chapters.

SUMMARY: DOUBLETS

1. Jeremiah 23:15a = 9:14(15E)

Judgment is pronounced upon (false) prophets, who will be fed with wormwood and caused to drink poisoned water. The oracle, which is original in 23:15a, has been taken over in the Deuteronomistic passage, 9:11-15.

2. Jeremiah 23:19-20 = 30:23-24

The storm of Yahweh which will "whirl on the head of the wicked" is seen in the context of Jeremiah 23 as judgment upon false prophets, whereas in 30:23-24 this is a judgment upon "Jacob" (30:18), viewed in the wider perspective of judgment upon "all the nations." With Rudolph, I conclude that

---

[88] The word שָׁלוֹם does not appear in Deut 18:21-22, but otherwise this passage is accurately reflected in 28:9. Holladay (*Jeremiah 1*, 129) notes the possible connection with Mic 3:5, which has to do with prophets who lead the people astray by declaring שָׁלוֹם.

[89] Overholt, *The Threat of falsehood*, p. 39 n. 18. Cf. D. Lys, "Jérémie 28 et le problème du faux prophète ou la circulation du sens dans le diagnostique prophétique," *RHPR* 59 (1974) 453-482.

[90] See Theodor Seidl, *Texte und Einheiten in Jeremia 27-29*, (Arbeiten zu Text und Sprache im Alten Testament 2; St.Ottilien: EOS, 1977); Tov, "Some Aspects," 145-167.

the version in 23:19-20 is original.[91] However, in a careful analysis of 30:23-24, Talmon, in reviewing and summarizing the opinions of various commentators, sounds a note of caution.[92] The genuineness of either 23:19-10 or 30:23-24 (or both) cannot be decided without attention to both stylistic-structural phenomena and literary-historical considerations. Phrases such as "from the evil of their doings" (23:22), "the prophets who prophesy lies in my name" (23:25), and the reference to "this people" (23:32) are appropriate in the mouth of Jeremiah and have been transmitted by those who safeguarded the Jeremiah tradition.

The oracles concerning prophecy in 23:9-40 contain material reflecting Jeremiah's conflict with false prophets, in which authentic words have been expanded editorially.[93] The prose conclusion to Jeremiah 23 (23:33-40), which contains the term מַשָּׂא eight times, appears to be a late addition.

3. Jeremiah 6:13-15 = 8:10b-12

A general condemnation of those who are greedy for unjust gain is applied specifically to שָׁלוֹם prophets. Jeremiah 6:12 and 8:10a are not part of the doublet, but are sufficiently similar to account for the insertion of the doublet in somewhat different contexts. The doublet (not present in the LXX in Jeremiah 8 presumably because it did not occur in the Hebrew *Vorlage*) does not appear to be a redactional composition, but rather words spoken by the prophet which have been inserted redactionally in appropriate places.

Jeremiah 27-29 contain little duplicated material, but faithfully reflect the viewpoint regarding false prophecy which is found in such passages as Deut 18:20-22; 13:1-6 (12:31-13:5E).

---

[91] Rudolph, *Jeremia*, 153. Cf. Volz, *Jeremia*, 279. Volz considers 30:23-24 as a repetition of 23:19-20.

[92] S. Talmon, "The Textual Study of the Bible — A New Outlook," in *Qumran and the History of the Biblical Text* (ed. F. M. Cross and S. Talmon; Cambridge, Mass.: Harvard University Press, 1975) 367.

[93] Meyer, *Jeremia und die Falschen Propheten*, 140.

CHAPTER SIX

RECURRING PHRASES IN JEREMIAH 25:1–13

Oracles directed against foreign nations (OAN) in Jeremiah 46–51MT (25:14–31:34LXX) contain a large number of doublets, parallels within the book of Jeremiah itself and also parallels with other books of the OT. Jeremiah 46:1 is a general editorial introduction to the OAN, using the phrase "The word of Yahweh came to Jeremiah the prophet," עַל־הַגּוֹיִם ("concerning the nations"), continuing in 46:2 with the oracle לְמִצְרַיִם ("with respect to Egypt").[1]

"Everything written in this book" (25:13MT and LXX) points to the strong possibility that the OAN were brought together originally in a separate collection and were inserted at first at this mid-point in the corpus, as in the *Vorlage* of the LXX. This is the pattern in other prophetic books, e.g., Isaiah 13–23 and Ezekiel 25–32, where the OAN are placed at an intermediate point rather than as a special collection at the end.

In the present form of the MT, the list of nations under judgment is given in 25:17–26, although the actual OAN (Jeremiah 46–51) are appended after Jeremiah 45.[2]

---

[1] The formula which introduces Jeremiah 46, אֲשֶׁר הָיָה דְבַר־יְהוָה אֶל־יִרְמְיָהוּ הַנָּבִיא (absent in the LXX), differs slightly from the usual stereotyped formula found elsewhere in the book of Jeremiah, i.e., הַדָּבָר אֲשֶׁר הָיָה אֶל־יִרְמְיָהוּ מֵאֵת יְהוָה (7:1; 11:1; 18:1; 21:1; 30:1; 32:1; 34:1, 8; 35:1; 40:1). The syntax in 46:1 finds parallels in 1:2 and 14:1 (see discussion by Holladay, *Jeremiah 2*, 14, 429). Cf. 47:1; 49:34, where the formula also occurs. The reference עַל־הַגּוֹיִם ("concerning the nations," 46:1) goes back to 25:13 (עַל־כָּל־הַגּוֹיִם). The original location of the OAN was immediately after 25:13, as evidenced by the LXX. The LXX changes the order in which the oracles appear (e.g., 25:14–19LXX=49:34–39MT), beginning with the oracle against Elam, where the heading Ἃ ἐπροφήτευσεν Ιερεμιας ἐπι τὰ ἔθνη τὰ Αιλαμ replaces 25:13bMT, יִרְמְיָהוּ עַל־כָּל־הַגּוֹיִם אֲשֶׁר־נִבָּא. Jeremiah 25:14MT is not present in the LXX, and is best taken as a secondary addition (cf. 27:7b and 50:29); see Janzen, *Studies*, 122, and Rietzschel, *Der Problem der Urrolle*, 86–87.

[2] Walter Brueggemann finds in the reference to כָּל־הָאָרֶץ ("the whole earth," 45:5) a transnational scope which serves a transitional function from Jeremiah 45 to the OAN which follow. See *To Build, to Plant: A Commentary on Jeremiah 26–52* (ITC; Grand Rapids: Eerdmans, 1991) 207, 210. Jeremiah 45:4 relates to 1:10 (cf. 1:5), in which Jeremiah is set over nations and over kingdoms. The phrase at the end of 45:4, וְאֶת־כָּל־הָאָרֶץ הִיא ("that is, the whole land"), missing in the LXX, should perhaps be taken as an explanatory gloss (see Jones, *Jeremiah*, 483).

In all probability the placement of the OAN by the LXX after 25:13 represents the original position of these oracles in the structure of the book of Jeremiah.³ The alternative placement after Jeremiah 45 in the final form of the book (MT) underlines the theological *motif* that Yahweh is sovereign over all the nations, including the Babylonians (Jeremiah 50-51), who were the instrument of his purposes in exercising judgment upon the nations spoken against in Jeremiah 46-49.⁴

A summary of historical events follows the OAN in Jeremiah 52 (based on 2 Kgs 24:18-25:30), which covers the period from Zedekiah's rebellion against Babylon up to the time when Jehoiachin was given preferential treatment in exile by Evil-Merodach, king of Babylon.

Nebuchadrezzar as Yahweh's "Servant" (Jeremiah 25:9; 27:6; 43:10)

Nebuchadrezzar is described as Yahweh's עַבְדִּי ("servant") in 25:9; 27:6; 43:10.⁵ עַבְדִּי does not appear in 25:9LXX. In 27:6 (34:5LXX) the LXX gives the translation δουλεύειν αὐτῷ = לְעָבְדוֹ. An extensive literature has developed regarding this textual situation and its exegetical and theological implications.⁶

---

³ This view is upheld by Holladay, *Jeremiah 2*, 313. See also Rudolph, Rietzschel, Boadt, Carroll, McKane, and Clements. Jeremiah 25:14-31:44LXX(=46-51MT) rearranges the order of the OAN, and is then followed by 32:1-24LXX(=25:25-38MT).

⁴ Jeremiah 25:9; 46:13, 26; 49:28, 30. Cf. Isa 10:5, where Assyria is the rod of Yahweh's anger against Israel.

⁵ The spelling with *resh*, נְבוּכַדְרֶאצַּר (or נְבֻכַדְרֶאצַּר) is the usual spelling in the book of Jeremiah and also in Ezekiel, whereas elsewhere in the OT the spelling is with *nun*, נְבֻכַדְנֶאצַּר (or נְבוּכַדְנֶאצַּר). There is no reference to Nebuchadrezzar by name in Jeremiah 1-20; the first occurrence is in 21:2; the name appears subsequently many times in the book. However, the spelling with *nun* is found in Jeremiah 27-29 (except for 29:21), appearing in this form eight times. The name is frequently missing in the LXX (for example in LXX 34-36 [27-29], with the exception of 34:5bα=27:6MT) and frequently (fifteen times) elsewhere. The LXX always transliterates the name as Ναβουχοδονοσορ. The form with *nun* has been seen as an example of dissimilation of ר to נ (e.g., Janzen, *Studies*, 7). Perhaps the change in names is to express ridicule. For further discussion of the two forms of the name, see Rudolph, *Jeremia*, 134; Holladay, *Jeremiah 1*, 571; *Jeremiah 2*, 114. In the many passages where the name is missing in the LXX, the best explanation is that the name is a late insertion in the hebrew text, perhaps related to the liturgical reading of short passages in the synagogue.

⁶ See especially: Curt Lindhagen, *The Servant Motif in the Old Testament* (Uppsala: 1950) 288; Werner E. Lemke, "Nebuchadnezzar, my servant," *CBQ* 28 (1966) 45-50; T. W. Overholt, "King Nebuchadnezzar in the Jeremiah Tradition," *CBQ* 30 (1968) 39-48; Ziony Zevit, "The Use of עֶבֶד as a Diplomatic Term in Jeremiah," *JBL* 88 (1969) 74-77; Adrian Schenker, "Nebukadnezzars Metamorphose vom Unterjocher zum Gottesknecht. Das Bild Nebukadnezzars und Einige mit Ihm zusammenhängende Unterschiede in der Beide Jeremia-Rezensionen," *RB* 89 (1982) 498-527; William McKane, "Jeremiah 27,5-8, especially 'Nebuchadrezzar, my servant,'" in *Prophet und Prophetenbuch. Festschrift für*

Lemke argues that "my servant" is inappropriate as a description of Nebuchadrezzar, and concludes that the reading was originally לְעָבְדוֹ in 27:6, secondarily transferred to 25:9 and 43:10.[7] Zevit, on the other hand, claims that עֶבֶד is a diplomatic term ("vassal") which occurs also in extra-biblical texts.[8] He believes that in a context where foreign envoys are addressed (Jeremiah 27), the term would be appropriate. However, in his judgment, the LXX translators did not understand the term; hence, its omission.

Schenker examines the two recensions of the book of Jeremiah represented by the MT and the LXX and the textual differences which exist between them.[9] Jeremiah 27:5-6MT is to be understood in the light of the creation-narrative (Gen 1:26-30; Ps 8:6-9; Gen 2:17), in which a cosmic aetiological origin-myth is now made to apply to a political figure, Nebuchadrezzar. The message to the foreign envoys who have come to Zedekiah to enlist his aid in rebelling against Nebuchadrezzar is that "men and animals" (27:5) are now under the sovereignty of the king of Babylon. Just as animals had been placed under the dominion of mankind (Gen 1:28), now "lands" and "beasts of the field" have been placed under Nebuchadrezzar's sovereignty (27:6). Schenker concludes that the designation of Babylon's king as the servant of Yahweh is indeed possible and not unreasonable in the light of the total context.[10] He points to the "Babylonizing" tendency in 25:1-14MT. The four-fold reference to Nebuchadrezzar in this passage (25:1, 9, 11, 12) is typical of the MT and is absent in the LXX. A theological intention is present in the longer recension, in which Nebuchadrezzar is named as "my servant" (25:9). Likewise, in 43:10-13MT, where reference is made to the setting up of Nebuchadrezzar's throne at Tahpanhes, the king of Babylon is named as "my servant" (43:10), an expression missing in the LXX (50:10LXX=43:10MT). Other textual differences in the two recensions suggest that the LXX text is

---

Otto Kaiser zum 65 Geburtstag (ed. Volkmar Fritz, Karl-Friedrich Pohlmann and Hans Christoph Schmitt; *BZAW* 185; Berlin: Walter de Gruyter, 1989) 98-110.

[7] Lemke ("Nebuchadnezzar, my servant"): "To be an instrument of God's activity is one thing, to be his servant is quite another" (p. 46). Note also 25:12 (Nebuchadrezzar's "iniquity"). Lemke accounts for the reading עַבְדִּי in 25:9 as the result of a simple w/y confusion (since these letters are virtually indistinguishable in the Aramaic script), and a haplography of the letter *l*, "i.e., the scribe accidentally wrote *mlk bbl 'bdy*, instead of *mlk bbl l'bdw*" (p. 48). Although he interprets the textual evidence differently, Janzen (*Studies*) comes to a similar conclusion (p. 209 n. 60).

[8] Zevit, "עֶבֶד as a Diplomatic Term."

[9] Schenker,"Nebukadnezzars Metamorphose," 498-527. Qumran manuscript fragments bear witness to the text represented in the two recensions. 4QJer[a] is approximately equivalent to the MT; 4QJer[b] to the LXX. See Janzen, *Studies*, 173; E. Tov, "L'Incidence de la critique textuelle sur la critique littéraire dans le livre de Jérémie," *RB* 79 (1972) 189-199.

[10] Schenker, "Nebukadnezzars Metamorphose," 508.

based on a Hebrew *Vorlage* more original than that reflected in the MT.[11] The present Hebrew text of 43:10-13 has literary and theological affinities with 25:9 and 27:6. Schenker concludes that the title "my servant" is a later addition, expressing the view that Yahweh has made Nebuchadrezzar a world ruler much in the same vein as in Dan 2:37-38, which may be considered as an exegesis of 27:5-6MT. In both 27:5-6MT and Dan 2:37--38, Nebuchadrezzar is given lordship over men and the beasts of the earth.

McKane also regards עַבְדִּי in 25:9; 27:6; 43:10 as a late addition.[12] Its absence from the LXX is not to be considered as a deliberate omission by a translator who found this term offensive (*contra* Rudolph, Volz and Bright).[13] Rather, according to McKane, "...עבדי is a late characterization of Nebuchadnezzar and is secondary in MT."[14] From a text-critical point of view, "where a Greek text shorter than MT is explained on the basis of its Hebrew *Vorlage*, the pluses in MT should in general be regarded as later expansions."[15]

I concur in the conclusion that עַבְדִּי in 25:9; 27:6; 43:10 is a late addition, but the question that comes to mind immediately is, How late? At what point would this theologically motivated description of Nebuchadrezzar be appropriate? To attempt to answer such questions involves a careful comparison of the LXX and the MT versions of 25:1-14; 27:1-7; 43:8-13.

The Text of the LXX and the MT Compared

With regard to the textual history of the book of Jeremiah, Tov claims that the text of the Hebrew *Vorlage* represented in the LXX should be considered edition I, while the MT is an expanded edition, edition II.[16] Only the Hebrew text of the shorter edition I was available to the Greek translators in Egypt; edition II was perhaps produced in a different geographical locale.[17] In edition II changes were made in text-arrangement (e.g., the transfer of the OAN to their present position in Jeremiah 46-51) and by the addition of headings to prophecies (e.g., 2:1-2; 7:1-2; 27:1).[18] The process by which the MT assumed its final form may have been even more complicated than this,

---

[11] Note especially וְשַׂמְתִּי כִסְאוֹ in 43:10MT, in which Yahweh himself will set up Nebuchadrezzar's throne, whereas in 53:10LXX the king is responsible (καὶ θήσει αὐτοῦ τὸν θρόνον).

[12] McKane, *Jeremiah 2*, 688-689.

[13] McKane, "Jeremiah 27,5-8," 101. Regarding 27:6, see Rudolph, *Jeremia*, 177 ("too offensive"); Volz, *Jeremia*, 259 ("on dogmatic grounds"); Bright, *Jeremiah*, 200.

[14] McKane, "Jeremiah 27,5-8," 101.

[15] McKane, "Jeremiah 27,5-8," 107.

[16] Tov, "L'Incidence de la critique textuelle," 189-199; cf. Gosse, "Le malédiction contre Babylone," 383-399.

[17] Tov, "Some Aspects," 149.

[18] Tov, "Some Aspects," 152.

with not only editorial activity, but with many scribal expansions incorporated in the final text.[19]

Jeremiah 25:1-13MT

Jeremiah 25:1-13MT gives evidence of many additions to the Hebrew *Vorlage* utilized by the LXX. However, in each case there is a reference to "everything written in this book" (25:13MT: אֵת כָּל־הַכָּתוּב בַּסֵּפֶר הַזֶּה; LXX πάντα τὰ γεγραμμένα ἐν τῷ βιβλίῳ τούτῳ). In the light of Jeremiah 36, the reference could be to the scroll, in its original (36:2) or expanded form (36:32), containing Yahweh's words against Israel and Judah and "all the nations" (36:2).[20] On the other hand, the reference may be specifically to the OAN, as McKane surmises.[21] Rietzschel restricts the reference to the oracles against Babylonia (50-51MT).[22] Jones sees a reference in 25:13 to the passages which follow, rather than to earlier material in the book of Jeremiah or just to Jeremiah 50-51, when he concludes, "The 'book'... must include at least the oracle on the cup of wrath (vv. 15-29) which includes 'all the kings of the north'(25:26) and, as a climax, 'after them the king of Babylon'(25:26b), and possibly it includes the oracles against Babylon in chapters 50-51; indeed it may be the book explicitly referred to in 51:60."[23]

A possible explanation of the way in which the text of 25:1-13LXX and the amplifications in 25:1-14MT came about is as follows. Originally, the emphasis was on Jeremiah's message of judgment upon "all the people of Judah and all the inhabitants of Jerusalem" (25:2), summarizing the content of Jeremiah 1-24. The passage in a more extended form was also to provide an introduction to the oracles of judgment upon the surrounding peoples, "against all these nations round about" (25:9). Jeremiah 25:1-13LXX at no point specifically mentions the king of Babylon or the Babylonians. "A family from the north" (πατριὰν ἀπὸ βορρα, 25:9LXX; cf. 25:9MT אֶת־כָּל־מִשְׁפְּחוֹת צָפוֹן and 1:15) will be responsible for carrying out the impending judgment which will fall upon "this land," as well as upon the surrounding nations. After a period of seventy years, Yahweh will also take vengeance on "that nation" (25:12).[24]

---

[19] Cf. McKane, *Jeremiah 1*, li. He suggests the idea of a rolling *corpus*. The scribal expansions "...have exegetical, interpretative, harmonizing functions, and they do not look beyond the small pieces of text to which they are attached, in some cases, individual verses" (p. li).

[20] Cf. Holladay, *Jeremiah 1*, 664; Bright, *Jeremiah*, 163; Drinkard, *Jeremiah 1*, 368.

[21] McKane, *Jeremiah 1*, lxxxvi, 627.

[22] Rietzschel, *Der Problem der Urrolle*, 42. This alternative possibility is also considered by Carroll, *Jeremiah*, 492-493; cf. Jeremiah 51:60.

[23] Jones, *Jeremiah*, 328.

[24] No mention is made in 25:1-13LXX of "the king of Babylon" or "the land of the Chaldeans."

Some of the additions in the expanded Hebrew text (25:1-14MT) carry theological implications. In this final form of the text, the emphasis is placed on Nebuchadrezzar the king of Babylon, and upon the Babylonians. A correlation is made between the fourth year of Jehoiakim and the first year of Nebuchadrezzar king of Babylon (25:1). The phrase "the tribes of the north" (25:9) is made concrete by direct reference to "Nebuchadrezzar the king of Babylon, my servant," a phrase missing in the LXX. Whereas 25:11LXX refers to the exile as a time of servitude "among the nations" (ἐν τοῖς ἔθνεσιν), for seventy years, 25:11MT reads "these nations shall serve the king of Babylon seventy years." After the seventy years, Yahweh will take vengeance on τὸ ἔθνος ἐκεῖνο ("that nation," 25:12LXX).

Jeremiah 25:12MT is much more specific, "I will punish the king of Babylon and that nation, the land of the Chaldeans, for their iniquity."

Jeremiah 27:1-7MT = Jeremiah 34:2-7LXX

In the case of 27:1-7MT, the LXX version (34:2-7) is more closely parallel, although lacking the superscription (27:1) and stating (34:5LXX=27:6MT), "I have given the earth (τὴν γῆν; MT אֶת־כָּל־הָאֲרָצוֹת הָאֵלֶּה) to Nebuchadrezzar to serve him (δουλεύειν αὐτῷ; MT, עָבְדִי) and the beasts of the field to labour for him" (ἐργάζεσθαι αὐτῷ; MT לְעָבְדוֹ).[25]

Jeremiah 43:8-12MT = Jeremiah 50:8-13LXX

The LXX translation of 43:8-12MT (50:8-13LXX) includes the name Nebuchadnezzar as king of Babylon (50:10), but עַבְדִּי ("my servant," 43:10MT) is missing. Jeremiah 50:10LXX continues, "he (Nebuchadnezzar) shall set his throne upon these stones which you (i.e., Jeremiah) have hid," whereas 43:10MT reads "I (i.e., Yahweh) will set his throne above these stones which I (Yahweh) have hid."[26] Similarly, 50:12LXX reads "He (i.e., Nebuchadnezzar) shall kindle a fire in the houses of their gods," while 43:12MT uses the first person וְהִצַּתִּי ("I shall kindle"). The MT underlines the action of Yahweh throughout this narrative prose section. The emphasis is on

---

[25] McKane ("Jeremiah 27:5-8"), "...δουλεύειν αὐτῷ is an inner-Greek phenomenon — a misplaced doublet of ἐργάζεσθαι αὐτῷ — ...LXX, lacking any representation of עבדי, preserves an earlier stage of the text than MT" (p. 101). See also Janzen, *Studies*, 56. Janzen, however, questions whether Nebuchadnezzar was mentioned by name in 34:5LXX, in view of the fact that the name is missing in some manuscripts and also uniformly missing in the other eight instances in the MT of Jeremiah 27-29: 27:8, 20; 28:3, 11, 14; 29:1, 3, 21 (p. 57).

[26] Jeremiah 50:10LXX: κατέκρυψας. This is in keeping with Yahweh's instruction to Jeremiah (43:9MT=50:9LXX) to hide the stones in the mortar in the pavement.

Yahweh's sovereignty; the Babylonian king is Yahweh's agent in performing his will.

In all three passages (25:1-14; 27:1-7; 43:8-13) the MT makes explicit the decisive role of Yahweh in world events. Unknowingly, Nebuchadrezzar is the agent of Yahweh's purposes to be carried out against Yahweh's own people and in a wider spectrum, against the other nations. The loss of independence, the tragic fate of Jerusalem, and especially the fact of the exile are to be understood against this background of the sovereignty of Yahweh. Profound theological reflection during the period of the exile, particularly by those who were the custodians of the Jeremiah tradition, would lead to the conclusion that Nebuchadrezzar was indeed Yahweh's servant in fulfilling Yahweh's will. Anti-Babylonian attitudes were not easily changed. Jeremiah's letter to the exiles (see especially 29:7) may have assisted in bringing about a more positive attitude towards Babylonia. However, 25:12-14 sets forth the view that in due time even the Babylonian empire will inevitably fall.[27] Jeremiah 25:1-14, with a twofold reference to Nebuchadrezzar's role in carrying out Yahweh's judgment upon Israel and the nations round about (25:8-11), as well as to the eventual fate of the Babylonians (25:12-14), follows the pattern of Isaiah 10:5-15, in which Assyria is described as the rod of Yahweh's anger (10:5), but will also finally come under Yahweh's judgment (10:12-19). Yahweh is the sovereign lord of history; all nations are subject to him.

Jeremiah 25:1-13: Other Parallel Phrases

Jeremiah 25:1-13 contains a number of phrases which are paralleled in other parts of the book of Jeremiah. In successive verses, 25:3 and 25:4, Jeremiah states "I have spoken persistently (אַשְׁכִּים וְדַבֵּר) to you" and "Yahweh has persistently sent (הַשְׁכֵּם וְשָׁלֹחַ) to you all his servants the prophets," but the people have not listened or inclined their ears to hear. The *Unermüdlichkeitformel* in its two forms, "rising up early and speaking," "rising up early and sending," occurs frequently in the book of Jeremiah, although the only other occurrence in the OT is found in 2 Chron 36:15 (הַשְׁכֵּם וְשָׁלֹחַ), where the Chronicler seems to be dependent on Jeremiah, rather than on Kings.[28]

---

[27] This is underlined in 25:14MT, a verse missing in the LXX. Jeremiah 25:26MT is also missing in the LXX, regarding drinking from the cup of Yahweh's wrath, "after them the king of Babylon shall drink." However, the LXX includes the oracles against Babylonia in the OAN (27-28LXX=50-51MT). These oracles may well have been drawn from a separate collection (see Holladay, *Jeremiah 2*, 313; Jones, *Jeremiah*, 520). The prose narrative, 51:59-64, appended to the oracles against Babylonia, whatever its origin, claims that "Jeremiah wrote in a book all the evil that should come upon Babylon" (51:60).

[28] הַשְׁכֵּם וְדַבֵּר occurs within prose passages in 7:13b; 25:3; 35:14. In each case the phrase is followed by וְלֹא שְׁמַעְתֶּם. The phrases "you did not listen, and when I called you

The two formulae occur in succeeding verses in 25:3, 4 and 35:14, 15, but in 42:15LXX (35:15MT) the formula הַשְׁכֵּם וְשָׁלֹחַ is missing.[29]

The stereotyped phrase "my/his servants the prophets" appears several times in the book of Jeremiah, but also in Deuteronomistic passages, as well as in Amos, Ezekiel, Ezra, Zechariah and Daniel.[30] In 25:5, the exhortation to Yahweh's people has always been for them to "turn (שׁוּבוּ) from their evil way," a phrase found seven times in the book of Jeremiah, as well as in the book of Ezekiel and elsewhere in the OT.[31] In the context of Jeremiah passages where these various phrases are used, there is frequently an additional statement that those addressed "have not listened" (שׁמע + לא) and "have not inclined their ear" (אזן + נטה + לא), phrases which also occur elsewhere in the OT, usually without the negative and with the verb in the imperative, often in prayers of entreaty.[32]

Weippert has made an intensive study of these phrases, with careful tabular charts to indicate their occurrences both in the book of Jeremiah and in other OT passages.[33] The primary passage from which she undertakes her investigation is 35:15, in which the waywardness and inconstancy of the men of Judah and the inhabitants of Jerusalem stands in strong contrast to the fidelity of the Rechabites to their vows, 35:18-19. Attention is drawn to the fact that the phrases introduced by the *Hiphil* infinitive absolute form הַשְׁכֵּם are

---

did not answer" (7:13b) are reflected in 35:17b as a gloss (Janzen, *Studies*, 37; Holladay, *Jeremiah 1*, 236). הַשְׁכֵּם וְשָׁלֹחַ occurs in 7:25; 25:4; 26:5; 29:19 (missing in the LXX); 35:15 (missing in the LXX); 44:4. Cf. 11:7, הַשְׁכֵּם וְהָעֵד, "warning persistently" (missing in the LXX); 32:33 (וְלַמֵּד), הַשְׁכֵּם, "teaching persistently"). Helga Weippert provides a chart indicating the various phrases introduced by שׁכם *Hiphil* (note the phrase וְשָׁלוֹחַ הַשְׁכֵּם in 2 Chron 36:15), but points out that there is no connection with Deuteronomistic literature (*Die Prosaredendes Jeremiabuches* [BZAW 132; Berlin: Walter de Gruyter, 1973] 126). Since הַשְׁכֵּם וְשָׁלֹחַ in 29:19 and 35:15 is missing in the LXX, the probability is that this *cliché*, found so frequently in other prose passages, was added subsequently to the Hebrew text. Weippert also draws attention to the dependency of the Chronicler on the book of Jeremiah. "Jeremiah" is specifically mentioned in 2 Chron 36:12, 21. Cf. A. Graeme Auld ("Prophets and Prophecy in Jeremiah and Kings," *ZAW* 96 [1984]), "...since this phrase is paralleled only in Jeremiah, and since the Chronicler uses it just after his only mention of Jeremiah (36:12) it is likely that he has drawn the theme from Jeremiah, not Kings"p. 76).

[29] See Streane, *The Double Text of Jeremiah*. He regards the formula in 35:15 as secondary from 25:4; cf. Holladay, "a gloss from 25:4" (*Jeremiah 2*, 245).

[30] See Jer 7:25; 25:4; 26:5; 29:19; 35:15; 44:4; 2 Kgs 9:7; 17:13, 23; 21:10; 24:2; Amos 3:7; Ezek 38:17 ("my servants the prophets of Israel"); Ezra 9:11; Zech 1:6; Dan 9:10.

[31] Jeremiah 18:11; 23:22; 25:4; 26:3; 35:15; 36:2, 7. Cf.1 Kgs 13:33 (Jeroboam); 2 Kgs 17:13; Ezek 3:19; 13:22; 33:11; Jon 3:8, 10; Zech 1:4; 2 Chron 7:14.

[32] Jeremiah 7:24, 26; 11:8; 17:23; 25:4; 34:14; 35:15; 44:5. Cf. 2 Kgs 19:16 (=Isa 37:17); Isa 55:3; Pss 17:6; 31:3H; 45:11H; 49:5H; 71:2H; 78:1; 86:1; 88:3H; 102:3H; 116:2; Prov 4:20; 5:1, 13; 22:17; Dan 9:18.

[33] Weippert, *Die Prosareden*, 121-148.

found uniquely in the book of Jeremiah, with the exception of 2 Chron 36:15, with no relationship to the Deuteronomistic literature.³⁴ In the case of נשה + אזן, the phrase is always preceded by לא, and the perfect tense of the verb occurs exclusively; the phrase is used in this distinctive way only in the book of Jeremiah.³⁵ Although the contemporary prophets are treated negatively and in polemical fashion throughout the book, in the phrase "my/his servants the prophets" Jeremiah's predecessors are assessed positively. Jeremiah, in his pronouncements, stands within this line of prophets which extends back into the past. The phrase is always followed by the הַשְׁכֵּם phrase in the book of Jeremiah, whereas in the books of Kings the phrase כִּדְבַר יְהוָה אֲשֶׁר דִּבֶּר בְּיַד (with slight variations) always precedes it.

Weippert also studies formulaic phrases in 34:17-20, 18:7-10 and 32:29b-32.³⁶ She concludes that the formulaic expressions which occur in these prose discourses do not show traces of a Deuteronomistic revision.³⁷ The total sphere of redaction must be considered to be much more modest than it has previously seemed to some scholars. Holladay accepts Weippert's conclusion that the prose discourses, in which the phrases under discussion are found, stand near enough to Jeremiah to be designated as "jeremianische Tradition."³⁸ McKane, however, is more cautious in his approach.³⁹ Although he commends Weippert for her demonstration that "correspondences between patterns of prose in the book of Jeremiah and those of Deuteronomic/Deuteronomistic prose are sometimes looser than has been represented," nevertheless, "since the prose of the book of Jeremiah is the product of the ongoing growth and development of a prophetic book, we should expect it to have its own character and themes."⁴⁰ Since a considerable number of recurring phrases are examined later in this present study (see below, chaps. eleven to thirteen), many of which have parallels with Deuteronomic/Deuteronomistic prose, conclusions will be postponed for the time-being, other than to indicate that those who safeguarded the Jeremiah tradition were also strongly influenced by Deuteronomistic ideas, language and style.⁴¹ The prose sermons and discourses, as well as the accounts of incidents in the life of the prophet related to contemporary historical events, are theological and didactic in their present form. A major purpose was "to

---

[34] Weippert, *Die Prosareden*, 126.
[35] Weippert, *Die Prosareden*, 128. Imperative forms of the verb occur in the passages in Psalms and Proverbs.
[36] Weippert, *Die Prosareden*, 148-227.
[37] Weippert (*Die Prosareden*), "One cannot evaluate them as traces of a deuteronomistic editing" (p. 234).
[38] Holladay, *Jeremiah 2*, 13.
[39] McKane, *Jeremiah 1*, 629.
[40] See McKane's comments on 23:25-32, in *Jeremiah 1*, 596.
[41] See Nicholson, *Preaching to the Exiles*, 117.

interpret the meaning of the exile for those in exile," since "the so-called 'Jeremiah tradition' was not a static thing but a living testimony to the creative genius of a man like Jeremiah."[42]

Parallel Phrases in Jeremiah 25:3b–6 and Jeremiah 35:14b–15.

Both 25:3b–6 and 35:14b–15 contain a number of phrases in common, with minor variations. One example is "I have spoken to you persistently" (25:3 [reading הַשְׁכֵּם וְדַבֵּר with Tg and some Hebrew manuscripts]; 35:14); other examples include שׁוּבוּ־נָא אִישׁ מִדַּרְכּוֹ הָרָעָה ("Turn now every one of you from his evil way," 25:5; 35:15); "dwell upon the land which Yahweh has given to you and your fathers" (25:5; 35:15); "do not go after other gods to serve them" (25:6; 35:15). In his discussion of these parallel formulaic phrases, Thiel finds in the correspondences between these passages (and Jeremiah 7) a good example of the methodology of the Deuteronomist, to whom they should be attributed, in his judgment.[43] He considers the total unit 25:3b–7 to have undergone a further post-deuteronomic editing, in which what was originally a Yahweh saying has been changed stylistically into a saying of the prophet.[44]

Knights, in his analysis of the structure of Jeremiah 35, comes to the conclusion that 35:13–15 is a redactional insertion between 35:1–12 and 35:16–19.[45] Although his primary purpose is to demonstrate Jeremianic authorship of most of Jeremiah 35, and to draw attention to the links with 18:1–11 and 13:1–11 (acts of prophetic symbolism), his conclusion regarding the redactional nature of 35:13–15 carries weight.[46] The phrase "other gods" (אֱלֹהִים אֲחֵרִים, 35:15) occurs eighteen times in prose passages in the book of Jeremiah, and frequently in Deuteronomy.[47] "Amend your doings" (מַעַלְלֵיכֶם הֵיטִיבוּ, 35:15) is found elsewhere in the book of Jeremiah in the form וּמַעַלְלֵיכֶם

---

[42] T. R. Hobbs, "Some Remarks on the Composition and Structure of the Book of Jeremiah," *CBQ* 34 (1972), 257–275.

[43] See the chart in Thiel, *Redaktion 1*, 267, and Thiel's comments (pp. 265–267).

[44] Thiel, *Redaktion 1*, 265. Note especially the phrase in 25:5, "the land which *Yahweh* has given you"; LXX: ἐπὶ τῆς γῆς, ἧς ἔδωκα ὑμῖν ("the land which I gave to you," 42:15LXX=35:15MT).

[45] C. H. Knights, "The Structure of Jeremiah 35," *ExpTim* 106:5 (1995) 142–144.

[46] Knights finds distinctive (non-Deuteronomistic) language in such phrases as "that you may live many days in the land *where you sojourn*" (35:7, אֲשֶׁר אַתֶּם גָּרִים שָׁם); "we, our wives, our sons and our daughters" (35:8); "vineyard or field or seed" (35:9). For a contrary view, see McKane, "Jeremiah and the Rechabites," *ZAW* Supplement 100 (1988) 106–123.

[47] Jeremiah 1:16; 7:6, 9, 18; 11:10; 13:10; 16:11, 13; 19:4, 13; 22:9; 25:6; 32:29; 35:15; 44:3, 5, 8, 15. Cf. Deut 7:4; 11:16; 17:3; 28:36, 64; 29:25H; 31:18, 20. See Bright, "The Date of the Prose Sermons," 207; Weinfeld, *Deuteronomy and the Deuteronomic School*, 320–324 (Appendix A). The phrase אֱלֹהֵי נֵכָר occurs in Jeremiah only in 5:19 (cf. Deut 31:16).

דַּרְכֵיהֶם + יֹשֵׁב *Hiphil*.[48] Many of the phrases in 35:15 occur in the temple sermon in Jeremiah 7; e.g., "I have sent to you all my servants the prophets, sending them persistently" (7:13, 25); "amend your doings" (7:3, 5); "other gods" (7:18); "you shall dwell in the land which I gave to you and your fathers" (7:7); "you did not incline your ear or listen to me" (7:26).

Stock phrases, such as are found in the temple sermon in Jeremiah 7 and 26, and also elsewhere in the book of Jeremiah (e.g., Jeremiah 25, 26, 29, 36 and 44) are brought together in this redactional addition within Jeremiah 35.[49] Jeremiah 25:3b-6 also draws upon these stock phrases. In 25:5, the promise has been made insistently that the reward of obedience is to continue dwelling for ever on the land given by Yahweh; "I will do you no harm" (לֹא אָרַע לָכֶם, 25:6) is the assurance given, but disobedience has been "to your harm" (לָכֶם לְרָע, 25:7). Failure to obey will bring destruction and ruin to the land (25:8-11), as well as to the surrounding nations and finally to the Babylonians, whose land will be made "an everlasting waste" (25:12).[50] Jeremiah 25:1-7 appropriately introduces the judgment which is to come upon Judah and upon the nations. In 35:15, the phrase וּשְׁבוּ אֶל־הָאֲדָמָה אֲשֶׁר־נָתַתִּי לָכֶם וְלַאֲבֹתֵיכֶם (differing from 25:5 only in the use of אֲשֶׁר־נָתַתִּי for נָתַן יְהוָה) has close parallels elsewhere in the book of Jeremiah and also in Deuteronomistic passages.[51] The purpose of the redactional addition, 35:13-15, is not only to provide a homiletic reminder of the consequences of disobedience, but also to place emphasis on the land ("then you shall dwell in the land," 35:15), carrying with it a note of hope for those in exile, a hope which is made explicit in such passages as 16:15(=23:8) and 30:3.

The Position and Order of the OAN in the LXX and the MT

Jeremiah 25:8-13LXX serves as an introduction to the OAN (25:14-31:44LXX), oracles which have been transferred in the MT to a new position (Jeremiah 46-51).[52] Although Holladay regards the MT order of the

---

[48] Jeremiah 7:3, 5; 18:11; 26:13; cf. 25:5. The two nouns occur together also in Judg 2:19. However, יָשַׁב "amend" (*Hiphil*) is not a term used by the Deuteronomist. See also Weippert, *Die Prosareden*, 137-148.

[49] See the chart and discussion by Nicholson, *Preaching to the Exiles*, 56. A common pattern (cf. 2 Kgs 17:13-18) is recognized: (a) Yahweh warns Israel by "his servants the prophets" (b) Israel rejects the words of the prophets (c) Yahweh's judgment upon Israel follows.

[50] שִׁמְמוֹת עוֹלָם; cf. 51:26, 62 (Babylon); Ezek 35:9 (Edom).

[51] Jeremiah 7:7, 14; 16:15; 23:39; 24:10; 30:3; cf. 11:5; 32:22 (see also Deut 26:15; Ezek 20:15). Deuteronomistic passages include Deut 3:19, 20; 9:23; 1 Kgs 9:7; 2 Kgs 21:8. Cf. Ezek 36:28.

[52] The order of the oracles differs in the LXX from that of the MT. Holladay (*Jeremiah 2*) comments, "It is likely ...that the turmoil of the Maccabean revolt is the setting both for the reordering of the oracles in G, and the shift of the oracles to the end of the book in the

oracles as original, rather than that of the LXX, Carroll holds to the contrary view, "The position of the OAN in G, with its list of nations in no particular order, must be regarded as original and the arrangement of them in MT as a secondary development of the tradition."[53] The order of the nations differs yet again in 25:15-26 (32:1-12LXX). The MT order in 46-51 is closer than the LXX to the order of this list. Nevertheless, the correspondences are not close enough to establish any clear principle by which the order in the MT and in the LXX was reached.[54] The LXX reflects a later viewpoint of the geographical situation; for example, "all the kings of Elam, and all the kings of Persia" (32:11LXX).[55] One can only speculate regarding the order of the OAN in the *Vorlage* on which the section 25:14-31:44LXX is based. Whereas the LXX translation elsewhere in the book of Jeremiah seems to have followed the Hebrew *Vorlage* closely, considerable freedom seems to have been exercised by the translator(s) in establishing the order of the OAN in the LXX.[56] When the OAN were appended as Jeremiah 46-51 in the present form of the MT, the oracles against Babylon (Jeremiah 50-51), possibly from a separate collection which was later greatly expanded, made a fitting climax to the book. Interspersed with the oracles against Babylonia are passages which promise restoration for Israel (e.g., 50:17-20, 33-34; 51:5, 10, 19).

Parallel Phrases in Jeremiah 25:8-13

The section 25:8-13, which announces coming destruction at the hands of Nebuchadrezzar for Yahweh's people and their land, as well as for "all the nations round about" (25:9), also contains phrases which occur elsewhere in the

---

text tradition behind M" (p. 314).

[53] Carroll, *Jeremiah*, 759. Cf. Janzen, *Studies*, 115-116 (Excursus). Holladay (*Jeremiah 2*, 313) follows Rietzschel (*Urrolle*, 82-84) in explaining the LXX placement of the oracle against Elam at the head of the list (the MT has Egypt in first place) on the grounds that the LXX understood Elam as the Parthian Empire, a major threat to Antiochus Epiphanes (during 175-163 BCE).

[54] For example, 25:21MT=32:21LXX gives the order: Edom, Moab, Ammon. Jeremiah 46-51 has the sequence: Moab (48), Ammon (49:1-6); Edom (49:7-22); whereas the LXX order is Edom (29:8-23), Ammon (30:1-5) and Moab (31:1-44), with Kedar and Damascus intervening. The order in 9:26 is Edom, Ammon, Moab (cf. Amos 1:11-2:3). However, as Boadt (*Jeremiah 26-52*) points out, the order of the oracles in 46-51 moves from far west to east, "an order that far excels the mixed-up one within the Septuagint" (p. 119).

[55] McKane (*Jeremiah 1*), "It would appear that the Greek translator understood MT as a reference to the components of imperial Persia rather than to the earlier history of Elamites and Medes before the period of the Persian empire" (p. 645). Oracles against the Medes (or against the Persians) are not included in the MT or the LXX.

[56] Whereas Volz is unwilling to say whether the LXX order is intentional or accidental, Rietzschel claims that the LXX has changed the order of the OAN in such a way that a definite constellation of powers of the Hellenistic period is reflected (Volz, *Jeremia*, 382; cf. Rietzschel, *Urrolle*, 82).

book of Jeremiah. Jeremiah 25:9b states וְשַׂמְתִּי לְשַׁמָּה וְלִשְׁרֵקָה וּלְחָרְבוֹת עוֹלָם ("I will make them a horror, a hissing and an everlasting reproach").[57] שַׁמָּה is coupled with שְׁרֵקָה both in poetry and prose: שְׁרוּקַת in 18:16 (poetry); שְׁרֵקָה in 19:8; 25:18; 29:18 (prose). שַׁמָּה is a characteristic word in the book of Jeremiah, occurring both in poetic and prose passages twenty-four times.[58] שְׁרֵקָה, קְלָלָה, אָלָה and זַעֲוָה, חֶרְפָּה, חָרְבָּה are all used in conjunction with שַׁמָּה in the book of Jeremiah.[59] Although חָרְבָּה, חֶרְפָּה, and שְׁרֵקָה are not characteristic Deuteronomistic terms, קְלָלָה and אָלָה are used frequently in the book of Deuteronomy to express the consequences of disobedience, while זַעֲוָה (see n. 59 above regarding the transposed form) occurs in Deut 28:25.[60] The terms מָשָׁל ("by-word") and שְׁנִינָה ("taunt"), used together with חֶרְפָּה and קְלָלָה, regarding the "bad figs," are reminiscent of Deut 28:37.[61] "My people" are addressed; they have made "their land a horror (שַׁמָּה), a thing to be hissed at (שְׁרוּקַת) for ever" (18:16; cf. 19:8 regarding Jerusalem; 24:9 concerning "the bad figs"). Similar statements are made with regard to Edom (49:17) and Babylon (50:13). Jeremiah 25:9 appropriately summarizes the judgment and its consequences for "this land and its inhabitants and against all these nations round about."

Jeremiah 25:10 contains expressions found elsewhere in the book of Jeremiah, but not in the Deuteronomistic literature: "the voice of mirth (שָׂשׂוֹן), the voice of the bridegroom (חָתָן) and the voice of the bride (כַּלָּה)." This precise series occurs also in 7:34; 16:9; 33:11.[62] Two of the terms, שָׂשׂוֹן and שִׂמְחָה, are coupled together in the Second Confession (15:16), describing Yahweh's "word."[63] Diamond rejects the view of Ahuis that 15:15-16 is a

---

[57] Following the LXX; see Weinfeld, *Deuteronomy and the Deuteronomic School*, p. 348 n. 1.

[58] Jeremiah 2:15; 4:7; 5:30; 8:21; 18:16; 19:8; 25:9, 11, 18, 38; 29:18; 42:18; 44:12, 22, and in the OAN: 46:19; 48:9; 49:13, 17; 50:3, 23; 51:29, 37, 41, 43. Cf. also Isa 13:9 (oracle against Babylon); Hos 5:9 (Ephraim); Deut 28:37; 2 Kgs 22:19 (לְשַׁמָּה וְלִקְלָלָה), cf. Jer 42:18; 44:12, 22; 49:13).

[59] אָלָה ("execration") occurs with שַׁמָּה in 29:18; 42:18; 44:12. זַעֲוָה occurs in 15:4; 24:9; 29:18 and 34:17. In all four passages, זַעֲוָה ("object of trembling, terror") follows the verb נתן and adds the phrase לְכֹל מַמְלְכוֹת הָאָרֶץ; cf. Deut 28:25, לְכֹל מַמְלְכוֹת הָאָרֶץ וְהָיִיתָ לְזַעֲוָה. The transposed form זְוָעָה occurs only in Deut 28:25 and Ezek 23:46 (cf. 2 Chron 29:8 Qere), and appears as the Qere in the Jeremiah passages (i.e., לִזְוָעָה); cf. Isa 28:19. For a further discussion of זַעֲוָה + לְכֹל מַמְלְכוֹת הָאָרֶץ see chap. thirteen, C29.

[60] קְלָלָה occurs in Deut 11:26, 28; pl. 28:15, 45; אָלָה (pl.) in Deut 29:20(H); 30:7. See Weippert for a discussion of these terms (*Die Prosareden*, 140).

[61] Cf. Thiel, *Redaktion*, 258. מָשָׁל and שְׁנִינָה are also combined in 1 Kgs 9:7.

[62] Hubmann (*Untersuchungen*) notes that the translation in LXX differs in each instance (p. 242). However, one need not presuppose a text different from the MT in the *Vorlage*. In Jer 33:11MT=40:11LXX, a promise of restoration is made.

[63] דְּבָרֶיךָ ("your word," see Qere); LXX ὁ λόγος σου; Vg *verbum tuum*. Cf. Ezekiel's scroll (Ezek 3:3), which he "ate" (cf. אכל Jer 15:16) and which became "sweet as honey."

Deuteronomistic expansion and claims that authentic Jeremianic language is to be found in the Second Confession.[64] The extended series, שָׂשׂוֹן, שִׂמְחָה, חָתָן and כַּלָּה, is an appropriate description of wedding festivities. Jeremiah 16:9 is particularly suitable in the context of Jeremiah 16, in which Jeremiah is forbidden to take a wife (16:2). A prohibition is also made against entering "the house of mourning" (16:5) and "the house of feasting" (16:8), referring to funerals and weddings. Jeremiah 16:1-9 could be considered in many aspects as an extended commentary on 15:17, alluding to the loneliness of the prophet. The major purpose of 16:10-13 is to place emphasis on the disaster that has fallen on "this people" (16:10); they have forsaken Yahweh, who has in turn forsaken them by sending them into exile (16:13). Jeremiah 16:14-15 (=23:7-8) introduces a note of hope for the future, announcing a second exodus and homecoming from exile.[65] In 7:34, the voice of mirth, gladness, bridegroom and bride will be made to cease from "the cities of Judah and from the streets of Jerusalem," a situation which is to be reversed in 33:10-11. The cultic emphasis dominates in 33:11, with the addition, "the voices of those who sing, as they bring thankofferings to the house of Yahweh." Jeremiah 33:10-11 reflects a post-exilic situation, in which the temple has been rebuilt. Jeremiah 33:10-11 not only provides a close link with 32:43 (note the phrase אָדָם וּבְהֵמָה מֵאֵין in both 33:11 and 32:43), but by using the series שָׂשׂוֹן, שִׂמְחָה, חָתָן and כַּלָּה indicates how closely and skilfully this late passage has been integrated into the book as a whole.

Jeremiah 25:1-14: Summary

This survey of phrases in Jer 25:1-13 which recur elsewhere in the book of Jeremiah and in some cases in other books of the OT, especially in the book of Deuteronomy, leads to the conclusion that a circle of traditionists not only safeguarded the Jeremiah tradition, but applied this tradition to historical situations well beyond the time of Jeremiah himself. These traditionists demonstrate a special interest in making theological judgments regarding the significance of the exile for Yahweh's people and with an emphatic assertion of Yahweh's sovereignty over the nations, including the Babylonians. The relationship between the book of Jeremiah and the Deuteronomistic literature will be explored in greater detail at a subsequent stage in this study (see especially chapter thirteen).

---

[64] See Ferdinand Ahuis, *Der klagende Gerichtsprophet. Studien zur Klage in der Überlieferung von den alttestamentlichen Gerichtspropheten* (Calwer Theologische Monographien 12; Stuttgart: Calwer Verlag, 1982) 90-91; Diamond, *Confessions*, pp. 69-70; p. 234 n. 9).

[65] See above, chap. four, pp. 72-77.

CHAPTER SEVEN

DOUBLETS AND RECURRING PHRASES IN JEREMIAH 46–49 (OAN)

In this section and the next chapter, we shall examine recurring phrases and doublets in the OAN (Jeremiah 46–51). A long tradition of such oracles precedes these OAN in the book of Jeremiah, as is made clear when Jeremiah confronts Hananiah in 28:8. Earlier prophets had prophesied מִלְחָמָה ("war"), רָעָה ("disaster"), and דֶּבֶר ("pestilence") "against many countries and great kingdoms." Hayes states, "The recognition of warfare as an original *Sitz im Leben* for Israelite oracles against foreign nations is supported by the use of oracles and curses against the enemy during military undertakings in other Near Eastern cultures."[1] This *genre* doubtless originated early on in Israel's history. However, the collections of oracles in Isaiah 13–23, Jeremiah 46–51 and Ezekiel 25–32 have been developed and supplemented over a long period of time. Editorial introductions in the book of Jeremiah (46:1, 13; 47:1; 49:34; 50:1) ascribe the OAN to Jeremiah himself, in keeping with 1:5, 10.[2] The following study of Jeremiah 46–51, with particular attention to recurring phrases and doublets, throws some light on the process by which the OAN in the book of Jeremiah reached their present form.

Jeremiah 46:2–26: Oracles Against Egypt

After the general introduction to the OAN (46:1), Jeremiah 46 consists of two magnificent poems (46:3–12; 46:14–24) directed against Egypt, in each case preceded by a prose superscription (46:2; 46:13). An oracle in prose (46:25–26) follows, in which punishment (הִנְנִי פוֹקֵד) by Yahweh on Egypt through Nebuchadrezzar is promised, ending in 46:26b with a further promise that "afterward" (אַחֲרֵי־כֵן) "Egypt shall be inhabited as in the days of old."

---

[1] See John H. Hayes, "The Usage of Oracles Against Foreign Nations in Ancient Israel," *JBL* 87 (1968) 81–92. He claims that proclamation of oracles against the nations was part of the royal court procedure in Israel (p. 91).

[2] Jeremiah 27:1LXX has only the brief heading λόγος κυρίου ὃν ἐλάλησεν ἐπὶ Βαβυλῶνα instead of the lengthy introduction of 50:1MT. The MT introductions have undergone expansion (see Janzen, *Studies*, 114). See also Watts, "Text and Redaction in Jeremiah's Oracles Against the Nations," *CBQ* 54 (1992) 432–447.

Jeremiah 46 then ends with 46:27-28 (=30:10-11), in which a coming peaceful return of "Jacob" from exile is announced.

The prose superscription (46:2) to the first poem (46:3-12) refers directly to the battle of Carchemish (605 BCE), at which Pharoah Neco II with his Egyptian army was defeated by the Babylonians.[3] The poem is divided into three stanzas: 46:3-6, 7-10, 11-12. Although the Babylonians are not specifically mentioned, the references to the north (46:6, צָפוֹנָה; 46:10, צָפוֹן בְּאֶרֶץ) and the location "by the river Euphrates" (46:6, עַל־יַד נְהַר־פְּרָת; 46:10, אֶל־נְהַר־פְּרָת) are in keeping with the superscription.[4]

Certain words and phrases in this poem call for comment, in view of their use elsewhere in the book of Jeremiah. מַדּוּעַ רָאִיתִי ("What do I see?," 46:5JB; cf. 30:6, and the fourfold repetition of רָאִיתִי in 4:23-26) does not necessarily imply a visionary experience, but may rather express poetic imagination at work.[5] The familiar phrase מָגוֹר מִסָּבִיב also occurs in 46:5, best taken as an exclamatory interjection "Terror all around!," a Jeremianic phrase (e.g., 6:25) which also appears in the oracle against Kedar, 49:29.[6] The verbs כָּשַׁל and נָפַל in 46:6 and 46:12 are also combined in the second poem (46:16).[7]

Jeremiah 46:10 refers specifically to הַיּוֹם הַהוּא ("that day") as "belonging to the Lord Yahweh of hosts," "a day of vengeance" (יוֹם נְקָמָה).[8] Jeremiah

---

[3] The Egyptian defeat is dated "in the fourth year of Jehoiakim" (46:2), a significant date in the book of Jeremiah (cf. 25:1; 36:1; 45:1).

[4] See Rudolph, *Jeremia*, 270. He regards the death of Josiah at the hands of the Egyptians at Megiddo in 609 BCE as the situation which prompted Jeremiah's anti-Egyptian stance. The vengeance (נְקָמָה) of Yahweh (46:10) against a political enemy, Egypt, is reminiscent of Jeremiah's plea for vengeance against his personal enemies (e.g., 11:20=20:12).

[5] רָאִיתִי in 46:5 is missing in the LXX. In the MT, one would expect an object after רָאִיתִי, as in 30:6. For these reasons, רָאִיתִי has been regarded as secondary. Holladay (*Jeremiah 2*, 315, 320) notes also that this is the only first-person singular reference in the poem. However, Vg and Tg support the MT. "Poetic imagining" is just as possible as "a visionary view" (Rudolph, *Jeremia*, 269).

[6] For מָגוֹר מִסָּבִיב, see above, chap. three, pp. 48-52. Holladay (*Jeremiah 2*, 316) omits מִסָּבִיב in 46:5 as a gloss, but this is unlikely in view of its retention in the versions. מָגוֹר מִסָּבִיב (6:25) and indeed the unit 6:22-24 (=50:41-43) have influenced the formation of this oracle in the OAN; see Volz, *Jeremia*, 386.

[7] These verbs are also combined in Isa 31:3 (Egypt) and Isa 3:8 (Jerusalem and Judah). In the OAN, in 50:32, זָדוֹן ("the proud one," i.e., Babylon) will "stumble and fall." The verb כָּשַׁל occurs often elsewhere in the book of Jeremiah, e.g., 6:21; 18:15; 18:23 (Third Confession); 20:11 (Fourth Confession); 31:9. נָפַל also appears frequently, especially in the OAN: 48:44 (Moab)=Isa 24:18; 49:12 (Edom); 50:15; 51:8, 44, 49 (Babylon).

[8] Isaiah 34:8 contains the term יוֹם נָקָם ("day of vengeance"), referring to the judgment on Edom. Isaiah 34 is reflected elsewhere in the OAN; see Volz, *Jeremia*, 386. Cf. also the term יוֹם אֵידָם ("the day of their calamity"), in 46:21. יוֹם אֵידָם also occurs in 18:17, regarding "my people" (cf. Obad 13, *tris*; Ezek 35:5, אֵידָם בְּעֵת אֵיד is a term used several times in the OAN: 48:16 (Moab); 49:8, אֵיד עֵשָׂו (regarding Edom); 49:26 (Hazor).

46:3-12 may indeed be a poem from Jeremiah himself, but even if this is the case, the passage has been edited and expanded.⁹

Jeremiah 46:11, "Go up to Gilead and take balm," is reminiscent of 8:22. צֳרִי, גִּלְעָד ("balm") and the root רפא appear in both passages. In addition, בַּת־עַמִּי ("the daughter of my people," 8:22), finds a counterpart in בַּת־מִצְרַיִם in 46:11.¹⁰ רְפֻאוֹת ("medicine") and the phrase תְּעָלָה אֵין לָךְ ("there is no healing for you") occur in both 46:11b and 30:13. The second poem (46:14-24) has a number of connecting links with the first poem (46:3-12): e.g., the use of the verbs כשל and נפל in 46:16 (cf. 46:6, 12); the use of the verb פנה in 46:21 (cf. 46:5); the epithet "Yahweh of hosts" in 46:18 (cf. 46:10); the reference to the north (צָפוֹן) in 46:20, 24 (cf. 46:6, 10). Yahweh is designated הַמֶּלֶךְ ("the King") in 46:18, the supreme sovereign, as over against Pharoah (מֶלֶךְ מִצְרַיִם) in 46:17.

The phrase, "the King, whose name is the Lord of hosts" (46:18), occurs also in 48:15, in the oracle against Moab, as well as in 51:57b (regarding Babylon). The phrase, עֵת־פְּקֻדָּתָם ("the time of their punishment") in 46:21 appears also elsewhere in the OAN (with various pronominal endings): 49:8; 50:27; 51:18=10:15, as well as in the doublet 6:15=8:12.

---

⁹ See Schwally, "Die reden des Buches Jeremia gegen die Heiden, XXV, XLVI-LI," *ZAW* 8 (1888) 177-217. He claims that the OAN contain no authentic words of Jeremiah. Others have come to the same conclusion: e.g., Volz (*Jeremia*, 379-390) assigns them to another author, Deuterojeremia. Cf. Skinner, *Prophecy and Religion*, p. 239 n. 3. Carroll (*Jeremiah*) states, "...nothing in the poem necessitates identifying the speaker as Jeremiah" (p. 754). On the other hand, Holladay (*Jeremiah 2*), while acknowledging the variety of form in the OAN, concludes that "the basic material gives every evidence of the diction and outlook of Jrm," and dates many of the OAN prior to the fall of Jerusalem (p. 313). Rudolph (*Jeremia*, 265-268) assigns a nucleus of the OAN to Jeremiah, while recognizing many additions and insertions. In particular, the poems 46:2-12 and 46:14-24 have been attributed to Jeremiah by a number of commentators. Nicholson (*Jeremiah 26-52*) believes that 46:2-12 was composed by Jeremiah himself just before or after the battle of Carchemish, and concludes that "the composition of verses 13-24 is to be connected with Jeremiah's prophecy in 43:8-13" (p. 165). Jones (*Jeremiah*) states that "throughout the poems against the nations, there are phrases characteristic of the Jeremiah tradition" (p. 487). Certainly, use is made of the Jeremianic tradition in the case of the doublets 50:41-43=6:22-24 and 51:15-19=10:12-16 (see below, chap. eight, pp. 202-208) and many Jeremianic words and phrases occur in the OAN, although this in itself does not settle questions of authorship. The position of Rudolph (outlined above) seems very balanced (cf. Weiser, *Jeremiah*, 381).

¹⁰ The vocative בְּתוּלַת בַּת־מִצְרַיִם (46:11) has a direct parallel in בְּתוּלַת בַּת־עַמִּי (14:17). בְּתוּלַת is missing in 14:17LXX, yet the noun παρθένος occurs in 46:11 for בְּתוּלָה, and always in other passages: 2:32; 18:13; 31:4, 13, 21 (38:4, 13, 21LXX); 51:22 (28:22LXX). Cf. Isa 7:14LXX. Volz (*Jeremia*, 380) regards 46:11 as an example of the way in which a later author is able to use a citation from Jeremiah as a generalized formula, now applied to Egypt.

A possible clue to the date of the second poem may be found in 46:17, if this verse contains a pun on the name of the Egyptian Pharaoh, Hophra.[11] The verb הֶעֱבִיר, according to this view, is a play on the name Hophra (in Egyptian, w'h-ib-r'), the Pharaoh mentioned in 44:30.[12] The LXX simply transliterates שָׁאוֹן הֶעֱבִיר הַמּוֹעֵד as Σαων εσβι εμωηδ and identifies the Pharaoh as Νεχαω (26:17aLXX). However, the internal references in the poem to Migdol and Tahpanhes (46:14) and to Memphis (46:14, 19) would indicate a Babylonian invasion of Egypt (cf. the superscription, 46:13). A campaign against Egypt by Nebuchadrezzar in his thirty-seventh year (i.e., 568 BCE) is recorded in a Babylonian source, but by this time Hophra had been replaced by Amasis.[13] Whether or not there is a reference to Hophra in 46:17, the best solution seems to be that the poem is to be understood as the threat of inevitable Babylonian invasion, with which the superscription concurs.

A prose oracle against Egypt (46:25–26) is appended, confirming the punishment of Egypt at the hands of Nebuchadrezzar. Jeremiah 46:26b makes it clear, however, that Egypt will survive.[14] This promise of hope for Egypt's future (cf. Isa 19:25, "Blessed be Egypt my people"; Ezek 29:14, "I will restore the fortunes of Egypt") reflects a universalizing tendency found also in the phrase "I will restore the fortunes of Moab in the latter days" (48:47a), with its parallels in 49:6 (the Ammonites) and 49:39 (Elam). Jeremiah 46:26b; 48:47a and 49:6 are missing in the LXX.[15] Such late passages as Isaiah 60, Pss

---

[11] See H. Ewald, *Die Propheten des Alten Bundes* (Stuttgart: Krabbe, 1841); Duhm, *Jeremia*, 340; Cornill, *Jeremia*, 453.

[12] Holladay, *Jeremiah 2*, 330. Holladay argues that a pun is involved; he translates שָׁאוֹן הֶעֱבִיר הַמּוֹעֵד as "Loudmouth missed his chance." In 46:17a, שָׁם (MT) is read as שֵׁם ("name," cf. 26:17LXX, τὸ ὄνομα; Vg *nomen*). As to the Egyptian name of Hophra, Hyatt (*Jeremiah*) states, "The word-play...is not close" (p. 1109). Carroll (*Jeremiah*) finds the word-play to be over-subtle, "and may be more imaginary than real" (p. 765).

[13] Pritchard, *Ancient Near Eastern Texts*, 308.

[14] In a passage in Isaiah (19:16-24), regarded as late by Kaiser (*Isaiah 13-39*, 97-112), Egypt will eventually turn to Yahweh (19:21-22) and receive Yahweh's blessing (19:24-25). The promise in Jer 46:26b that Egypt will eventually "be inhabited as in the days of old" is not present in the LXX (see Janzen, *Studies*, 41-42). The promise is regarded by Holladay (*Jeremiah 2*) as "a late addition" (p. 324).

[15] In the case of 49:39 (Elam), 25:19LXX translates *Qere* אָשִׁיב אֶת־שְׁבוּת as ἀποστρέψω τὴν αἰχμαλωσίαν, cf. 31:23 (38:23LXX). The phrase שׁוּב שְׁבוּת in the MT is either in passages missing in the LXX (e.g., 29:14MT; 33:26MT) or translated ἀποστρέψω τὴν ἀποικίαν (30:3; 32:44; 33:7). In any case, the meaning in the LXX implies the return of exiles from captivity. Curiously, 49:39 is apparently the only passage in the *Vorlage* used by the translators of the LXX offering hope for the future for a foreign nation (in this case, for Elam). The other passages in the MT: Egypt (46:26b); 48:47a (Moab); the Ammonites (49:6), are late additions to the text.

72:11; 86:9; 102:22 reflect a more fully developed hope that all peoples and kingdoms would eventually worship Yahweh, the god of Israel.[16]

Jeremiah 46 ends with an additional poetic oracle, 46:27-28 (=30:10-11), in which "Jacob" is promised "quiet and ease" after a period of chastening.

1. JEREMIAH 46:27-28 = JEREMIAH 30:10-11

JEREMIAH 46:27-28
27. But you, O my servant
[b] Jacob,[b] [a] do not be afraid and
do not be discouraged, [a]
O Israel. For look I
[b] will save you [b] from afar
and your offspring from the
land of their captivity.
[b] Jacob [b] shall return and
have quiet and ease, without
anyone making him afraid.
28. You, O my servant [b] Jacob,[b]
do not be afraid, [c] says Yahweh,[c]
[d] for I am with you. [d]

For [e] I will make a full end [e]
of all the nations [b] among whom [b]
[f] I have driven you.[f]
[e] But I will not make a full
end of you.[e] I will chasten you
in fairness; I will not leave you
entirely unpunished.

JEREMIAH 30:10-11
10. But you, O my servant
[b] Jacob, [b] [a] do not be afraid,
says Yahweh and [a] do not be
discouraged, [a] O Israel; For look I
[b] will save you [b] from afar
and your offspring from the
land of their captivity.
[b] Jacob [b] shall return and
have quiet and ease, without
anyone making him afraid.

11. [d] For I am with you, [d]
[c] says Yahweh, [c] to save you.
[e] I will make a full end [e]
of all the nations [b] among whom [b]
[f] I have scattered you [f]
[e] Yet I will not make a full
end of you.[e] I will chasten you
in fairness; I will not leave you
entirely unpunished.

The LXX omits 30:10-11.

Textual and Translational Notes

a...a אַל־תִּירָא ... וְאַל תֵּחָת ("do not be afraid ... and do not be discouraged," 46:27; 30:10). אַל־תִּירָא is a characteristic feature of salvation oracles in Deutero-Isaiah (e.g., Isa 41:10, 13, 14; 43:1, 5; 44:2). In Isa 44:2, as in Jer 46:27 (=30:10), the oracle is addressed to עַבְדִּי יַעֲקֹב. The verb ירא followed by חתת (cf. Jer 23:4) is not a combination found in the DI oracles, but rather in the Deuteronomistic history (e.g., Deut 1:21; 31:8; Josh 8:1; 10:25). The second occurrence of the phrase אַתָּה אַל־תִּירָא עַבְדִּי יַעֲקֹב (46:28) is omitted in 30:11.

---

[16] See Gerhard Von Rad, *Old Testament Theology 2* (London: Oliver and Boyd, 1965) 292-297.

b...b Orthographic differences in the two passages are as follows: יַעֲקֹב (46:27); יַעֲקוֹב (46:27); יַעֲקֹב (46:28); יַעֲקוֹב (30:10); יַעֲקֹב (30:10); the third occurrence of the name "Jacob" does not appear in 30:11; מוֹשִׁעֲךָ (46:27); מוֹשִׁיעֲךָ (30:10); שָׁמָּה (46:28); שָׁם, (30:11).[17] No consistent pattern of orthography has been maintained in either passage. Therefore, orthography does not provide a clue regarding an earlier date for either of the two passages.

c...c נְאֻם־יְהוָה Although this expression does not occur in 46:27, but only in 46:28, it appears in both 30:10 and 30:11. In Jeremiah 46, the preceding prose oracle, 46:25-26, ends with נְאֻם־יְהוָה, whereas in the case of 30:10-11, as Böhmer observes, the use of the *Gottesspruchformel* is to mark the beginning of a new unit, following a prose passage (30:8-9) without this formula.[18] מוֹשִׁיעֲךָ (30:10) and לְהוֹשִׁיעֶךָ (30:11) do indeed have a direct link with the final verb in 30:7b (יִוָּשֵׁעַ), but there is also a catchword association between the noun עֶבֶד in 30:10 and the use of the verb עבד in 30:8, 9, i.e., Jacob is Yahweh's servant (30:10), no longer in servitude to "strangers" (30:8), but serving Yahweh (30:9).[19]

d...d כִּי אִתְּךָ אָנִי, 46:28; 30:11 (cf. 1:8; 15:20=1:19). This assurance of Yahweh's presence is also found in Isa 43:5, אַל־תִּירָא כִּי אִתְּךָ־אָנִי. However, in Isa 41:10, the expression is כִּי עִמְּךָ־אָנִי (cf. Exod 3:12; Deut 31:8).

e...e אֶעֱשֶׂה כָלָה ... לֹא אֶעֱשֶׂה כָלָה, 46:28; 30:11. A contrast is made between Yahweh making a full end of the גּוֹיִם and not making a full end of his people. כלה + עשׂה with a negative occurs in 4:27; 5:10, 18. These passages are discussed below (pp. 122-123).

f...f הִדַּחְתִּיךָ (46:28); הֲפִצוֹתִיךָ (30:11). These verbs appear frequently in the books of Jeremiah and Deuteronomy; e.g., נדח *Hiphil*: Jer 8:3; 16:15; 23:2, 3, 8; 24:9; 27:10, 15; 29:14, 18; 32:37; 40:12; 43:5; 50:17; Deut 13:14; 30:1, 4; פוץ *Hiphil*: Jer 9:15; 13:24; 18:17; 23:1, 2; Deut 4:27; 28:64; 30:3. Both verbs occur in Jer 23:2 as virtual synonyms (cf. Deut 30:1-4, where both verbs are used).

Salvation-oracles

The form of the doublet 46:27-28=30:10-11, beginning with אַל־תִּירָא, is analogous to the form of the salvation oracles in Deutero-Isaiah. According

---

[17] The *daghesh* in שָׁם is *daghesh forte conjunctivum*.

[18] Böhmer, *Heimkehr*, 60. Cf. Holladay (*Jeremiah 2*, 150); he claims that the expression in 30:10 may have been added later.

[19] In the only other reference to Israel as עֶבֶד in the book of Jeremiah (2:14), the term is used in the negative sense of "one who lacks freedom" (cf. the parallelism with בֵּית יְלִיד).

to Begrich, DI was consciously using priestly oracles of salvation as a model.[20] Conrad argues for the war oracle as the model for salvation oracles in DI.[21] In the case of Jeremiah, because of the repetition of אַל־תִּירָא in 46:27 and 46:28 (אַל־תִּירָא occurs only in 30:10 in the parallel passage), he concludes that two distinct war oracles appear in 46:27-28 (cf. Isa 43:1-7), whereas only a single war oracle is found in 30:10-11.

Whatever solution is adopted regarding the origin of the *Heilsorakel*, a further problem to be addressed has to do with the relationship between this doublet in Jeremiah (46:27-28=30:10-11) and the salvation-oracles in DI. According to Holladay, who regards these verses as authentic to Jeremiah, Jeremiah is the innovator, with DI providing variations (e.g., Isa 41:8-13).[22] Böhmer, on the other hand, thinks that the doublet in Jeremiah shows the influence of DI.[23] Those addressed are living in exile, having already suffered for some time under compulsory rule; the saying should be dated in the second half of the time of exile.[24]

Comment

Before coming to conclusions, closer attention needs to be given to the language employed in the doublet. אַל־תִּירָא, so characteristic of DI, occurs also in Jer 1:8 in the account of Jeremiah's call, followed by כִּי אִתְּךָ אָנִי, as in 46:28=30:11 (cf. Isa 43:5; pl. forms in Jer 42:11). אַל־תֵּחָת occurs elsewhere in the book of Jeremiah only in 1:17 and in plural form in 10:2 (אַל־תֵּחָתּוּ), and not at all in DI. Both verbs, ירא and חתת, occur as synonyms in 23:4, and are found together frequently in D (e.g., Deut 1:21; 31:8; Josh 8:1; 10:25; 1 Sam 17:11). עַבְדִּי יַעֲקֹב occurs only in 30:10; 46:27, 28 in the book of Jeremiah. The phrase also occurs in DI; e.g., Isa 44:1; 45:4, as well as in Ezek 37:25.[25]

---

[20] J. Begrich, "Das priesterliche Heilsorakel," *ZAW* 52 (1934) 81-92. A critique of Begrich's view is made by Thomas M. Raitt, *A Theology of Exile. Judgment/Deliverance in Jeremiah and Ezekiel* (Philadelphia: Fortress Press, 1977) 152-158. Raitt claims that "the salvation oracle was not original in Second Isaiah within the prophetic tradition, but built upon a deliverance oracle tradition from Ezekiel, Jeremiah, and earlier prophets" (p. 157). For a study of prophetic oracles of salvation in general, see Claus Westermann, *Prophetic Oracles of Salvation* (Louisville: John Knox Press, 1991).

[21] E. W. Conrad, *Fear not Warrior: A Study of 'al tîra Pericopes in the Hebrew Scriptures* (Brown Judaic Studies 75; Chico: Scholars Press, 1985).

[22] Holladay, *Jeremiah 2*, 173. Berridge (*Prophet*) asks: "Has Deutero-Isaiah...been directly influenced by Jeremiah?" (p. 185 n. 12).

[23] Böhmer (*Heimkehr*), "It is...more probable that Jer 30,10a is an echo of deuteroisaianic proclamation, than that Deuteroisaiah is oriented towards Jer 30,10a" (p. 61). Cf. Westermann (*Prophetic Oracles of Salvation*), "This oracle is in the tradition of Second Isaiah and presupposes that tradition" (p. 139).

[24] Böhmer, *Heimkehr*, 62.

[25] Isaiah 42:1LXX reads Ιακωβ ὁ παῖς μου.

Yahweh as מוֹשִׁיעֵךְ ("your savior," 46:27; 30:10) is also so described in Isa 43:10. מֵרָחוֹק ("from afar," 46:27; 30:10) also occurs in DI, referring to Yahweh's people in exile: e.g., Isa 43:6; 49:1, 12. זַרְעֲךָ ("your offspring," 46:27; 30:10) also recurs in DI: Isa 43:5; 44:3; 48:19. אֶרֶץ שִׁבְיָם ("the land of their captivity," 46:27; 30:10) is also found in 2 Chron 6:37, 38 (Solomon's prayer). The verbs שָׁקַט וְשַׁאֲנַן ("have quiet and ease," 46:27; 30:10) also occur (in reverse order) in 48:11, regarding Moab. The phrase וְאֵין מַחֲרִיד ("without anyone making [him] afraid") appears in 7:33, as well as elsewhere in the OT.[26]

"I will (not) make a full end"

The formulae אֶעֱשֶׂה כָלָה and לֹא־אֶעֱשֶׂה כָלָה are of special interest. כָלָה אֶעֱשֶׂה ("I will make a full end," 46:28; 30:11) announces Yahweh's action against the nations. In Isa 10:23, in the context of the return of a remnant (10:20-23), a total destruction is decreed "in the midst of all the earth," presumably involving the nations (cf. Isa 28:22; 24:1-13).[27] In Nah 1:8, Yahweh "will make a full end" of his adversaries, and in Zeph 1:18, Yahweh will make a full end "of all the inhabitants of the earth."[28] לֹא־אֶעֱשֶׂה כָלָה ("I will not make a full end," 46:28; 30:11) is a phrase used elsewhere in the book of Jeremiah in 4:27; 5:10, 19:12[29] In these three passages, the pronouncement of judgment is mitigated by the promise that Yahweh will not make a full end of his people.[30] In the case of 4:27, if לָהּ is substituted for לֹא, i.e., "I will make a full end with respect to it," then 4:27b is in harmony with 4:27a.[31]

---

[26] Cf. Deut 28:26; Lev 26:6; see also chapter thirteen, C34. Cf. also Isa 17:2; Ezek 34:28; 39:26; Mic 4:4; Nah 2:13 (2:11E); Zeph 3:13; Job 11:19.

[27] Kaiser (*Isaiah 1-12*) regards 10:20-23 as "a secondary interpolation" (p. 147).

[28] The text of Nah 1:8 is best based on the LXX and Tg (rather than the MT מְקוֹמָהּ), taking into account the reference to אֹיְבָיו in the second half of the verse. See J. M. P. Smith, W. H. Ward and J. A. Bewer, *A Critical and Exegetical Commentary on Micah, Zephaniah, Nahum, Habakkuk, Obadiah and Joel* (ICC; Edinburgh: T. & T. Clark, 1911) 292.

[29] Note also Ezekiel's entreaty at Ezek 11:13, in which he recoils in horror at the thought that Yahweh would "make a full end of the remnant of Israel." Ezekiel 20:17 looks back to the fact that Yahweh did not make a full end (לא + עשה + כלה) of his people in the wilderness.

[30] A similar passage regarding "the house of Jacob," but using the verb שמד, is found in Amos 9:8. James L. Mays (*Amos* [OTL; London: SCM, 1969]) states, "The opinion expressed in 8b is doubtless that of a Judean redactor who notes in the light of Judah's experience in the sixth century that Yahweh did not intend to obliterate all of Israel in spite of its sin" (p. 160).

[31] Rudolph, *Jeremia*, 36; cf. McKane, *Jeremiah 1*, 109. Other proposals have been made, for example, the suggestion of Holladay (*Jeremiah 1*) that וְכָלָה MT should be read as וְכַלֵּה followed by לֹא, i.e., "and none of it will I remake" (p. 143). See also J. Soggin,

Berridge stays with the MT (לֹא), but claims that 4:27a applies to the land, 4:27b to the people.[32] As for 5:10, וְכָלָה אַל־תַּעֲשׂוּ also has the support of the versions and אַל should therefore not be eliminated. "Strip away her branches" (5:10b, הָסִירוּ נְטִישׁוֹתֶיהָ) implies a thorough pruning, but not necessarily complete destruction.[33] The prose unit 5:18-19 is introduced by בַּיָּמִים הָהֵמָּה ("in those days") and the assurance that Yahweh "will not make a full end of you" is set in the context of a question and answer relating to the necessity of the exile as Yahweh's judgment on the apostasy of his people. Thiel draws attention to the use of עָשָׂה (perfect) in 5:19, referring to the catastrophe of the exile as having already taken place, as well as to the *Frage-Antwort-Form*, in which a reason (idolatry) is given for Yahweh's judgment.[34] This form of community instruction is attested in Deut 29:23-26 and in 1 Kgs 9:8-9 (D). Jeremiah 5:18-19 affirms that the judgment of exile did not mean the end of Yahweh's people, a conviction that is reflected in 4:27; 5:10. In each instance, we meet with later insertions in the text.

נדח *Hiphil* and פוץ *Hiphil*

The verbs נדח *Hiphil* and פוץ *Hiphil* (*46:28*, הִדַּחְתִּיךָ; 30:11, הֲפִיצוֹתִיךָ) occur frequently in the books of Jeremiah and Deuteronomy, relatively infrequently elsewhere in the OT.[35] וְיִסַּרְתִּיךָ לַמִּשְׁפָּט ("I will chasten you in just measure" [RSV], 46:28; 30:10) is reminiscent of 10:24, יַסְּרֵנִי יהוה אַךְ־בְּמִשְׁפָּט ("Correct me, O Yahweh, but in just measure").[36] לַמִּשְׁפָּט, literally "according to justice," seems to imply "in fairness."[37] The final phrase וְנַקֵּה לֹא אֲנַקֶּךָ ("I will not leave you entirely unpunished," cf. a similar phrase in 25:29), is found in the form וְנַקֵּה לֹא יְנַקֶּה in Exod 34:7, where Yahweh's justice is understood

---

"La negazione in Geremia 4,27 e 5,10a, cfr. 5,18b," *Bib* 46 (1965) 59. He reads לֹאעֲשֶׂה וכלה, claiming that ל is *emphaticum* and that the א in לֹא MT came into the text through dittography. Jeremiah 4:27b would coincide in meaning with 4:27a, i.e., "I will certainly make the destruction complete." Robert Althann (*A Philological Analysis of Jeremiah 4-6 in the Light of Northwest Semitic* [Biblica et Orientalia 38; Rome: Biblical Institute Press, 1983]) states, "In v.27, the difficulty caused by MT לֹא disappears if it is vocalized לֻא, 'the Omnipotent'," pointing to Canaanite antecedents for this divine title (p. 103). These suggestions do not find support in the versions.

[32] Berridge, *Prophet*, 191.
[33] Bright, *Jeremiah*, 40.
[34] Thiel, *Redaktion 1*, 97-99. Cf. also 9:11-15 (12-15E); 16:10-13; 22:8-9. עזב is a key verb in these passages.
[35] See textual note [f...f] above.
[36] McKane (*Jeremiah 1*), "...the 1st. person sing. form is indicative of the completeness of the prophet's identification with his community" (p. 234).
[37] Rudolph, "in Billigkeit" (*Jeremia*, 74, 190). See further: H. W. Herzberg, "Die Entwicklung des Begriffes מִשְׁפָּט in A. T.," *ZAW* 40 (1922) 256-257; 41 (1923) 16-76; Berridge, *Prophet*, 194.

in the context of divine mercy; the iniquity of the fathers will be punished to the third and fourth generation, whereas Yahweh's חֶסֶד will be extended to the thousandth (generation).[38] Both the justice and mercy of Yahweh are indicated in 46:27-28; 30:10-11.

Jeremiah 46:27-28=30:10-11: Summary

From this survey of the vocabulary and phrases found in 46:27-28=30:10-11, demonstrating linguistic features appearing elsewhere in the book of Jeremiah, as well as language found also in the Deuteronomistic books and DI, we conclude that the author of these verses stands in the Jeremianic tradition, but has come under the influence of the Deuteronomist and Deutero-Isaiah.[39]

The fact that 30:10-11 is missing in the LXX is explained by Holladay on the basis that in the LXX ordering of the chapters, 46:27-28MT (26:27-28LXX) precedes Jeremiah 30MT (37LXX): "LXX has thus included the material in their first occurrence and omitted them in their second."[40] However, there is a considerable distance between Jeremiah 26 and 37(LXX), especially when one considers that in the case of 49:18=50:40MT (in reverse order in the LXX: 29:29=27:40) and 49:19-21=50:44-46 (also in reverse order in the LXX: 29:20-22=27:44-46), i.e., in passages close together, these doublets are retained in the LXX. It is more probable that verses 30:10-11MT were missing in the *Vorlage* used by the translator of the LXX.

The explanation offered by Janzen is that the oracles against Egypt and against Babylon (now separated in the MT), originally came immediately after one another, as in the *Vorlage* of the LXX. Jeremiah 46, 50-51 MT appear as Jeremiah 26, 27, 28 LXX. Janzen claims that a marginal gloss on 50:2-5 (oracle against Babylon) became incorporated in the text of the oracle against Egypt, which later (as Jeremiah 46MT) was placed in a different sequence within the OAN.[41] A different suggestion is made by Marx who finds the

---

[38] לָאֲלָפִים is the counterpart of וְעַל־רִבֵּעִים עַל־שִׁלֵּשִׁים. Umberto Cassuto (*A Commentary on the Book of Exodus* [The Hebrew University, Jerusalem: The Magnes Press, 1967]) writes, "He [Yahweh] continues to shew his lovingkindness even for thousands of generations, to the distant descendants of those to whom the promises were made" (p. 400).

[39] Janzen (*Studies*), "We have to do with a self-contained oracle which probably existed independently before its inclusion in either context" (p. 93). For Fischer (*Das Trostbüchlein*, 63) the question regarding the original place of this oracle, whether in Jeremiah 30 or 46 or independently of both, must remain open.

[40] Holladay, *Jeremiah 2*, 160. Cf. Bright (*Jeremiah*), "LXX habitually omits doublets in their second occurrence" (p. cxxiii).

[41] Janzen, *Studies*, 93, 116.

present placement of 46:27-28 in Jeremiah 46 appropriate, as an oracle of salvation applied to Jewish refugees in Egypt.⁴²

I take the view that these verses, expressing hope for Israel, were inserted first in Jeremiah 46, at the end of the chapter as a subsequent insertion, and on a later occasion in Jeremiah 30. The LXX translators did not omit this unit from Jeremiah 30; the verses were not in the *Vorlage* from which the translation was made.

The doublet does not fit easily into the context of either chapter. However, the insertion in Jeremiah 46 could have been made in the light of 46:26b, which offers the promise that Egypt "shall be inhabited as in the days of old." Likewise, hope for the future is held out to Israelites in exile. When the time of punishment is over, they will return to the homeland. On the other hand, "I will make a full end of all the nations to which I have driven you" (46:28) is intended to negate 46:26b. The unit 30:10-11 was eventually inserted in Jeremiah 30, on the basis of the catchwords יַעֲקֹב and יִוָּשֵׁעַ in 30:7 (cf. יַעֲקֹב, מוֹשִׁיעֲךָ and לְהוֹשִׁיעֲךָ in 30:10-11), as well as in the desire to spell out the promise in 30:7 in greater detail.⁴³

"Jacob" and "Israel"

Another matter to be considered is the precise meaning of "Jacob" and "Israel" in the doublet 46:27-28=30:10-11. In 46:27-28, both names relate to the people of Israel as a whole.⁴⁴

---

⁴² Marx, "A Propos des doublets," 109. If the passage rightly belongs to Jeremiah 46, this is confirmed by its presence in the *Vorlage* of the LXX.

⁴³ See Kilpp, *Niederreissen und aufbauen*, 113-115. In advancing reasons for retaining 30:10-11MT, Kilpp claims that the doublet is more appropriate to Jeremiah 30 than to Jeremiah 46. The repetition of "Fear not" etc. in 46:28a militates against 46:27-28 representing a more original text than 30:10-11 (p. 115 n. 57). However, the repetition of נְאֻם יְהוָה (30:10, 11) suggests that the doublet consists of two separate units, as in 46:27, 28. Much depends on the translation of the phrase in 30:7, וּמִמֶּנָּה יִוָּשֵׁעַ. Possibly, an ironical rhetorical question is being raised, "and out of *this* he shall be *saved*??!!" For Holladay, 30:10-11 has been inserted on a quite different understanding of the phrase, i.e., that it is to be understood as a note of hope, expressly stated, "and out of this, he shall be saved." See Holladay, *Jeremiah, Spokesman Out of Time* (New York: The Pilgrim Press, 1974) 111; *Jeremiah 2*, 173). According to Holladay, Jeremiah himself has given a fresh interpretation to the doom-oracle (30:5-7) in 30:10-11. More probable, however, is the view that 30:10-11 is a late insertion expressing hope, with catchword associations, that make this a suitable insertion in the little book of Consolation.

⁴⁴ According to tradition, Jacob's name became "Israel" (Gen 32:28). Jacob was father of twelve sons from whom the twelve tribes of Israel descended (Genesis 49). 1 Kings records the division of Solomon's kingdom into northern and southern kingdoms ("house of Israel, "house of Judah," 1 Kgs 12:21). The "house of Israel" applies to the northern kingdom, whereas the designation "all Israel" (e.g., 1 Kgs 12:16) applies to the people as a whole. The exiles in Babylonia are addressed as "Jacob" and as "Israel" (e.g., Isa 43:1),

Lohfink identifies seven strophes in Jeremiah 30–31 (30:5–7; 30:12–15; 30:18–21; 31:2–6; 31:15–17; 31:18–20; 31:21–22), which he believes were addressed to the people of the northern kingdom at the time when Josiah was seeking to expand his kingdom to the north.[45] Holladay accepts Lohfink's thesis, with the claim that 30:10–11 (together with 30:16–17; 31:7–9a) is part of a recension to the south, offering "compensation for the words of disaster spoken over the south."[46] If the prose introduction (30:1–3) is taken into account, as well as the superscription (30:4) to the strophe 30:5–7, the editorial understanding was that the collection of oracles that follows applies to Israel and Judah, i.e., to the people as a whole.[47] There is much to suggest that the collection of oracles of hope in Jeremiah 30–31 reached their final form only after a long period of time.[48] Jeremiah 30:10–11 is a unit incorporated at a late stage in this process, when the return of exiles had become a genuine possibility and a realistic hope.

Jeremiah 47:1–7MT (29:1–7LXX) Oracle Against the Philistines

The superscription (47:1MT) states that the destruction of the Philistines, which is the subject of the oracle that follows, was soon to take place. Since the superscription in the LXX (29:1LXX) gives the heading simply as ἐπὶ τοὺς ἀλλοφύλοις (literally "concerning the strangers"), the original superscription may have been לִפְלִשְׁתִּים, in keeping with לְמוֹאָב (48:1), לִבְנֵי עַמּוֹן (49:1), לֶאֱדוֹם (49:7), לְדַמֶּשֶׂק (49:23). The expanded superscription could well have been added out of historical interest, although the precise occasion can only be

---

where the reference is to the creation of Israel as a nation. See Claus Westermann (*Isaiah 40–66*, London: SCM, 1969) 117.

[45] Lohfink, "Der junge Jeremia," 351–368.

[46] Holladay, *Jeremiah 2*, 161.

[47] See Rudolph, *Jeremia*, 188, 189. He regards וִיהוּדָה (30:3) and וְאֶל־יְהוּדָה (30:4) as supplementary expansions of the text (cf. *BHS*). For Holladay (*Jeremiah 2*), the words וִיהוּדָה and וְאֶל־יְהוּדָה should not be excised, "The words are appropriate: 'Israel and Judah' suggests the presence in this recension to the south of the earlier recension to the north" (p. 171). But as McKane (*Jeremiah 2*) rightly points out, "...'Jacob'...is a more appropriate model for all-Israel than for the northern kingdom — Jacob being the 'father of the twelve tribes'" (p. clix).

[48] A wide range of views is held regarding the composition and date of Jeremiah 30–31. While Lohfink, "Die junge Jeremia," (cf. Holladay) attributes seven oracles to the young Jeremiah, acting as propagandist for king Josiah, Carroll (*Jeremiah*) draws attention to "many disparate elements" in Jeremiah 30–31, and concludes that "only in the final redaction is the cycle incorporated into the Jeremiah tradition" (p. 572). Siegfried Herrmann, comparing the opinions of Lohfink and Carroll, opts for an intermediate position: "The truth surely lies in the middle, older material has been added to, expanded, and finally revised," a view with which I concur. See Herrmann, *Jeremia. der Prophet und das Buch* (Erträge der Forschung 271; Darmstadt: Wissenschaftliche Buchgesellschaft, 1990) 156.

conjectured.[49] Certainly, the emphasis in the poem is on the threat "from the north" (47:2, מִצָּפוֹן).[50] This would point to the Babylonians, described as "waters rising out of the north," "an overflowing torrent."[51] The phrase in 47:2b, וְיִשְׁטְפוּ אֶרֶץ וּמְלוֹאָהּ עִיר וְיֹשְׁבֵי בָהּ ("they shall overflow the land and all that fill it, the city and those who dwell in it") is similar to the phrase in Jer 8:16 (only the verb at the beginning of the phrase in 8:16 differs). In both instances, the reference to "the city" is best understood collectively. The verbs זעק ("cry out") and ילל Hiphil ("wail," 47:2) occur also (in reverse order) in 25:34. The vocabulary in 47:3, פַּרְסוֹת and גַּלְגִּלָּיו, "their wheels," referring to horses and chariotry, is found also in Isa 5:28, describing the horses and chariots of the Assyrians. In 47:3b, the feebleness of the hands of the fathers (מֵרִפְיוֹן יָדַיִם) in their inability to protect their children is reminiscent of רָפוּ יָדֵינוּ ("our hands fall helpless") in 6:24.[52]

The editor who supplied the superscription (47:1) ascribes the oracle to Jeremiah. As we have demonstrated, much of the language in the poem is used elsewhere in preceding chapters in the book of Jeremiah. Whether the poem comes from Jeremiah himself or from an author who consciously uses the language of Jeremianic oracles (for example, regarding the foe from the north) as a model, cannot readily be determined in the space of a few short verses. However, the OAN which follow in Jeremiah 48-51 contain extensive parallels with other books of the OT and indicate elaborate supplementation.

---

[49] The superscription reads, "The word of Yahweh that came to Jeremiah the prophet concerning the Philistines, before Pharoah smote Gaza" (47:1MT; Vg; Tg). In the OAN, other references to Jeremiah "the prophet" are found in 46:1, 13; 47:1; 49:34; 50:1; 51:59. Jeremiah is described as הַנָּבִיא thirty-one times in the book of Jeremiah (see chart in Janzen, *Studies*, 145-148, Appendix A). Except for 20:2 and 25:2, the occurrences are found in the latter half of the book, in which scribal additions are frequent. The LXX describes Jeremiah as προφήτης only in 49:2LXX (42:2MT); 50:6LXX (43:6MT); 51:31LXX (45:1MT); 28:59LXX (51:49MT). Scribes responsible for the additions in the Hebrew text considered Jeremiah to be *the* prophet, *par excellence*. See also Auld, "Prophets and Prophecy," 66-82.

[50] For מִצָּפוֹן see also 46:20; 50:3; 50:41=6:22, and עַם־צָפוֹן (46:24); מֵאֶרֶץ צָפוֹן (50:9), as well as many other references to the north elsewhere in the book of Jeremiah, e.g., 1:14; 4:6b; 6:1; 10:22; 13:20; 25:9. See Aare Lauha, "ZAPHON: Der Norden und die Nordvölker im Alten Testament," in *Annales Academiae Scientarium Fennicae* (Helsinki: Suomalainen Tiedeakatemia, 1944) 1-96. Lauha claims that a historical-geographical identification of the foe from the north is impossible. The northern enemy is the mysterious, irresistible power, which fills the whole earth with horror and death and brings divine judgment over this age (66-67).

[51] Cf. 6:23 "the roaring sea." The verb שׁטף, used twice in 47:2, occurs also in the description of Assyria in Isa 8:7-8. See Brueggemann, *To Build, to Plant*, 231. Nebuchadrezzar conquered the city of Ashkelon in Dec. 604 BCE (Wiseman, *Chronicles*, 69).

[52] Volz (*Jeremia*, 386) draws attention to the creative use of 6:22-24 in the OAN. For the doublet 50:41-43=6:22-24, see below, chap. eight, pp. 174-176.

Jeremiah 48: Moab (Jeremiah 31LXX)

Although Edom, Moab, and the sons of Ammon are simply mentioned in 25:21, considerable space is given to them in the OAN, where the order differs, i.e., 48:1-47 (Moab); 49:1-6 (the Ammonites); 49:7-22 (Edom).[53]

Jeremiah 48 begins with a powerful poem against Moab (48:1-9), followed by a curse (48:10).[54] A series of poems follow: a second poem (48:11-17), containing a prose insertion (48:12-13); a third poem (48:18-28), also containing a prose insertion (48:21-27); a fourth poem (48:29-33), based on Isa 16:6-10; and a passage in prose (48:34-39) with many parallels to Isaiah 15-16. Additional poems follow in 48:40-47, summarizing the message of judgment and its consequences, with parallels to other passages (48:40-41=49:22, Edom; 48:43-44=Isa 24:17-19; 48:45-46 has correspondences with Num 21:27-29; 24:17bβ). The length of the chapter results from the many additions; learned scribes have borrowed extensively from Isaiah 15-16, 24 and Numbers 21, 24. Their knowledge of Moabite geography is incorporated in 48:21-24 and 48:34 (cf. Isa 15:4), which include place names found on the Moabite Stone.[55]

The theme of שֹׁדֵד ("the destroyer"), who is never identified, occurs with frequency throughout the poems: 48:8, 15, 18, 32; cf. שֻׁדְּדָה ("is laid waste"), 48:1, 20.

The verb שָׁדַד ("to destroy," found elsewhere in the book of Jeremiah), the concept of exile, and references to Chemosh (the national god of the Moabites) help to bring a degree of unity to the various disparate sections regarding Moab.[56] The phrase שֹׁד וָשֶׁבֶר ("desolation and destruction," 48:3) occurs in Isa 59:7; 60:18 (cf. Isa 51:9, with the definite article). שֶׁבֶר גָּדוֹל is found in Jer 4:6; 6:1; 14:17; 50:22; 51:44. צַעֲקַת־שֶׁבֶר ("the cry of destruction,"

---

[53] The LXX order: 29:8-23 (=49:7-22MT) Edom; 30:1-5 (=49:1-6 MT) the Ammonites; 31 (=48MT) Moab, also differs from 25:21MT (32:7LXX), but coincides with 9:26.

[54] Although Jer 48:10 begins with the passive participle of אָרוּר, which occurs elsewhere in the book of Jeremiah: 11:3; 17:5; 20:14, 15 (cf. Mal 1:14 and the imperative "Curse Meroz" in Judg 5:23), this semi-poetic verse lies outside of the metrical pattern of the poem and is best taken as a later addition. Jeremiah 48:10 reflects an attitude entirely different from the sympathetic view of 48:36, "My heart moans for Moab like a flute" (cf. Isa 16:11). The phrase מְלֶאכֶת יְהוָה ("work of Yahweh") finds a parallel in 50:25, Yahweh's מְלָאכָה "in the land of the Chaldeans."

[55] The text of the Moabite Stone (Mesha inscription) is found in Pritchard, *Ancient Near Eastern Texts*, 320-321.

[56] The verb שׁדד occurs in 4:30 (missing in the LXX); 5:6; 6:26 (הַשֹּׁדֵד); 10:20; 25:36 (Yahweh as destroyer); in the OAN 47:4 (the Philistines); 49:10 (Edom); 49:28 ("the people of the east"); 51:55 (Yahweh as "destroyer" of Babylon). For the concept of exile, see 48:7, 11 (גּוֹלָה); 48:46 (שְׁבִי). Cf. 1:3; 28:6; 29:1, 4, 20, 31; 52:27 and in the OAN, 46:19; 49:3.

48:5) is similar to זְעָקַת־שֶׁבֶר in Isa 15:5, from which the entire verse (48:5) is taken.[57] Of the forty-six occurrences of שֶׁבֶר ("fracture, destruction") in the OT, nine are found in Isaiah, fifteen in Jeremiah, a keyword in both books.[58] The phrase שַׁמָּה ... מֵאֵין יוֹשֵׁב ("a desolation without any inhabitant," 48:9) occurs several times in the book of Jeremiah, especially in the OAN.[59]

In the second poem, the verbs שׁאן and שׁקט (48:11) have already been encountered together in reverse order in 46:27 = 30:10.[60] הִנֵּה־יָמִים בָּאִים ("Behold, days are coming," 48:12) has been discussed in chap. four, p. 62. Attention should be drawn to the fact that the phrase occurs three times in the book of Amos (4:2; 8:11; 9:13) and that the majority of occurrences in the book of Jeremiah are in collections such as Jeremiah 30-31 and the OAN, which suggests that the use of this formula became a standard way of introducing oracles of judgment (OAN) or oracles of hope (30-31), soon to be realized.[61] Stylistically, אֵיךְ תֹּאמְרוּ ... אֲנָחְנוּ (48:14) is reminiscent of 8:8 (cf. 2:23). Jeremiah 48:15 (missing in the LXX) ends with the phrase שְׁמוֹ צְבָאוֹת נְאֻם־הַמֶּלֶךְ יְהוָה, already encountered in 46:18, and occurring also in 51:57b.[62] The phrase "Yahweh of hosts is his name" (cf. "Yahweh is his name," Amos 5:8; 9:6; Jer 33:2) is rooted in the prophetic tradition, e.g., Amos 4:13; 5:27; Isa 47:4; 48:2; 51:15; 54:5. The phrase is found also in the OAN in 50:34; 51:19 (=10:16), as well as in 31:35; 32:18, which may account for this addition in the Hebrew text of 46:18 and 48:15 (missing in the LXX).

The verb נוד ("shake one's head in mourning, bemoan," 48:17) occurs frequently in passages in the book of Jeremiah referring to lamentation: e.g., 15:5; 16:5; 22:10; 31:18.[63] Holladay's observation regarding turns of phrase distinctive to Jeremiah, "... their shape in the present material is not a slavish imitation but fresh usage," coupled with the fact that the OAN also draw on phrases and vocabulary found elsewhere in the prophetic literature, support the view that much of the material collected in the OAN stems from sources in

---

[57] See below, pp. 130-131, for discussion of the doublet Jer 48:5 = Isa 15:5.

[58] Andersen and Forbes, *VOT*, 430.

[59] Jeremiah 4:7; 46:19; 51:29, 37. Cf. 2:15; 34:22; 44:22, and for מֵאֵין יוֹשֵׁב 26:9; 33:10; Isa 5:9; 6:11; Zeph 2:5; 3:6. Such stereotyped phrases belong to the prophetic vocabulary in general use.

[60] שׁקט Hiphil also occurs in 47:6, 7 and in 49:23.

[61] Jeremiah 30:3; 31:27, 31, 38; 49:2; 51:47, 52. Cf. the doublets 7:32 = 19:6; 23:5 = 33:14; 23:7 = 16:14. Although the oracles in Amos and in the OAN are poetic, the oracles with this formula in Jeremiah 30-31 and Jeremiah 23 are in prose. The prose oracles generally express hope for the future. Jeremiah 23:5-6 and 23:7-8, appended to oracles denouncing the monarchy, express hope for the eventual restoration of the monarchy; the oracles in Jeremiah 30-31 reinforce the predominant note of hope for Israel's future.

[62] Jeremiah 26:18LXX reads λέγει κύριος ὁ θεός. Holladay (*Jeremiah 2*, 342) claims that the phrase in the MT is imported from 46:18.

[63] Cf. Isa 51:19; Nah 3:7. Cf. also נוד Hithpolel ("the wagging of the head [in derision]"): 48:27; 18:16.

which both the Jeremianic tradition and the prophetic tradition in general are used sometimes stereotypically, sometimes creatively.[64]

In the third poem (48:18-20), the imperative forms רְדִי and שְׁבִי (48:18) are also found in Isa 47:1, addressed to Babylon.[65] The noun יֹשֶׁבֶת ("inhabitress," 48:18, 19) is used as a collective elsewhere in the book of Jeremiah: 21:13, "inhabitant of the valley"; 22:23, "inhabitant of Lebanon."

Some further correspondences should be noted, in addition to the doublets which make up most of the rest of Jeremiah 48. For example, the phrase regarding breaking Moab, כִּכְלִי אֵין־חֵפֶץ בּוֹ ("like a vessel no one cares for," 48:38b) is parallel to the phrase in the question raised regarding Jehoiachin in 22:28: אִם־כְּלִי אֵין חֵפֶץ בּוֹ (cf. Hos 8:8 regarding Israel). The nouns שְׂחֹק ("derision") and מְחִתָּה ("horror, object of terror," 48:39) are of interest: שְׂחֹק has already appeared in 48:26, 27 (cf. the fourth Confession, 20:7); מְחִתָּה occurs in the third Confession, 17:17 (cf. Isa 54:17).

The doublets to be considered are 48:5 = Isa 15:5; 48:29-33 = Isa 16:6-10; parallels between 48:34-38a and Isaiah 15, 16; 48:40-41 = 49:22 (Edom); 48:43-44a = Isa 24:17-18a; parallels between 48:45-46 and Num 21:27-29; 24:17.

2. JEREMIAH 48:5ab = ISAIAH 15:5bc

JEREMIAH 48:5ab
5. Truly, (at) the ascent of
ᵃ Luhith,ᵃ people go up upon
ᵇ it with weeping;ᵇ truly,
ᶜ at the descent ᶜ of Horonaim,
ᵉ they hearᵉ ᵈ (distresses of) ᵈ
ᶠ a cry ᶠ of destruction.

ISAIAH 15:5bc
5bc. Truly, (at) the ascent of
ᵃ Luhith,ᵃ people go up upon
ᵇ it with weeping;ᵇ truly,
ᶜ on the way ᶜ to Horonaim,
ᵉ they raise ᵉ
ᶠ a cry ᶠ of destruction.

Textual and Translational Notes

ᵃ…ᵃ הַלֻּחוֹת, 48:5; הַלּוּחִית, Isa 15:5b. Qere in 48:5 is supported by Syr, Tg, Vg, Isa 15:5bMT and the LXX (Λουιθ).

ᵇ…ᵇ בְּכִי, 48:5; בּוֹ, Isa 15:5b. בּוֹ is the superior reading; בְּכִי is to be explained by dittography with the following כִּי and is a repetition of בְּכִי already present in 48:5a.[66]

ᶜ…ᶜ בְּמוֹרַד, 48:5; דֶּרֶךְ, Isa 15:5b. Although מוֹרַד would be a good antonym for מַעֲלֶה, the use of the noun ὁδός in both 31:5LXX (=48:5MT) and Isa 15:5bLXX gives support to the reading דֶּרֶךְ.

---

[64] Holladay, *Jeremiah 2*, 387. This, for Holladay, is a mark of authenticity.
[65] Carroll, *Jeremiah*, 786.
[66] Volz, *Jeremia*, 405; Holladay, *Jeremiah 2*, 341.

d...d צָרֵי, 48:5 (missing in the LXX); Isa 15:5b (misssing in both the MT and the LXX). Most commentators simply delete צָרֵי from 48:5.[67] Perhaps צָרֵי is a corruption of וְצֹעַר (and Zoar), in view of the reference to Zoar in 48:4, where צֹעַר (צֹעֲרָה + ה locative) is preferable to צְעִירֶיהָ ("her little ones"), especially since Isa 15:5a also refers to Zoar (עַד־צֹעַר).

e...e שָׁמְעוּ, 48:5; יְעֹעֵרוּ, Isa 15:5b. יְעֹעֵרוּ may have been originally יְעַרְעֵרוּ, Pilpel of עור ("they raise"). The form כַּעֲרוֹעֵר ("like Aroer," 48:6) may have come into the text from Isa 15:5b and was understood differently by the LXX: ὥσπερ ὄνος ἄγριος ("like a wild ass," i.e., כְּעָרוֹד; cf. ὄνον ἄγριον for עָרוֹד, Job 39:5). The verb שמע (48:5) appears also in 48:4 (Hiphil).

f...f צַעֲקַת, 48:5; זַעֲקַת, Isa 15:5b. Isaiah 15:4 has already employed the verbal form זְעָקָה. תִּזְעַק occurs in Jer 48:4. Is צַעֲקַת an Ohrfehler?

Comment

How does one account for these textual problems? At least two possibilities may be suggested. A scribe may have broken the continuity of 48:4 and 48:6 by inserting a verse (48:5) taken from the oracle against Moab in Isaiah (Isa 15:5b), in view of the references to Horonaim (48:3) and (probably) Zoar (48:4). Alternatively, since 48:34a runs parallel to Isa 15:4a (see below, pp. 135-137 for the parallels between 48:34-39 and Isaiah 15), the original position of 48:5 (=Isa 15:5b) could have been at the beginning of this series of verses (48:34-39), based on their counterparts in Isaiah 15.[68] Volz's suggestion that Jer 48:5ab (=Isa 15:5bc) was originally written in the margin as part of the Isaiah material in 48:34-36 and then wrongly inserted by a scribe in the text between 48:4 and 48:6 is therefore quite plausible.[69]

3. JEREMIAH 48:29-33 and ISAIAH 16:6-10

JEREMIAH 48:29-33
29. [a] We have heard of the pride of Moab, excessive pride![a]
his loftiness,[b] his pride,[b]

his arrogance and the haughtiness of his heart. 30. I know
[c] his insolence, [c] says Yahweh;
[d] indeed his boasts are invalid;[d]
he has not done such things.

ISAIAH 16:6-10
6.[a] We have heard of the pride of Moab, excessive pride![a]
[b] his arrogance,
his pride [b]
[c] and his insolence;[c]

[d] his boasts are invalid[d]

---

[67] E.g., Volz, *Jeremia*, 409; Bright, *Jeremiah*, 313.
[68] The introductory כִּי in 48:5 (=Isa 15:5b), or immediately before 48:34 (if this is the correct original position) in either instance is best understood as כִּי asseverative; see Williams, *Hebrew Syntax*, § 449, "truly," "indeed"; Holladay, "yes."
[69] Volz, *Jeremia*, 405.

31.ᵉ Therefore I wail over Moab;
I cry out for all Moab ᵉ and

ᶠ for the men of Kir-heres
I moan. ᶠ
32.ᵍ O fountains of Jazer!
I weep for you, O vine of Sibmah! ᵍ

ʰ Your branches are extended
to the sea,ʰ ⁱ as far as Jazer
they reached; ⁱ upon your summer
ʰ her shoots have spread abroad
ʰ fruits and your vintage the
destroyer has fallen.

33.ᵏ Gladness and joy have been
taken away from the fruitful
land,ᵏ indeed from the land of Moab;
ˡ I have made the wine cease from
the wine presses, no one treads
(them) with shouts of joy; the
shouting is not the shout of joy.ˡ

ᵉ Therefore let Moab wail;
let everyone wail for Moab. ᵉ
ᶠ You shall moan,
utterly stricken,
for the raisin-cakes of
Kir-hareseth. ᶠ
8. For the fields of Heshbon languish,
O vine of Sibmah. The overlords of the
nations have struck down ʰ
her branches ⁱ (which)
extended as far as
Jazer,ⁱ (which) wandered to the desert;
and extended to the sea.
9.ᵍ Therefore I weep
with the weeping of Jazer, O vine
of Sibmah.ᵍ I will drench you with
my tears, O Heshbon and Elealeh,
for upon your summer fruits and
your crops the shout
(of battle) has fallen.
10. ᵏ Gladness and joy
have been taken away
fruitful land; ᵏ in the
vineyards no ringing
shout shall be given, no
shout (of joy) be raised;
ˡ no treader shall tread
out wine in the wine-
presses. I have silenced
the (vintage) shout of joy. ˡ

Textual and Translational Notes

ᵃ⋯ᵃ שָׁמַעְנוּ גְאוֹן־מוֹאָב גֵּאֶה מְאֹד, 48:29a;
שָׁמַעְנוּ גְאוֹן־מוֹאָב גֵּא מְאֹד, Isa 16:6a.
1QIsᵃ (Qumran) and two manuscripts read גֵּאֶה in Isa 16:6a; גֵּא appears to be a scribal error. Although the MT of both 48:29a and Isa 16:6a begins with שָׁמַעְנוּ ("We have heard," cf. ἠκούσαμην, Isa 16:6LXX), 31:29LXX=48:29MT has ἤκουσα ("I have heard," cf. Zeph 2:8, "I have heard the taunt of Moab"), perhaps to bring the form of the verb (1st sing.) into conformity with the following אֲנִי יָדַעְתִּי (48:30), an emphatic phrase not found in Isaiah 16.
ᵇ⋯ᵇ וּגְאוֹנוֹ וְגַאֲוָתוֹ (48:29); גַּאֲוָתוֹ וּגְאוֹנוֹ (Isa 16:6). The two terms "his pride and his arrogance" appear in reverse order. Jeremiah 48:29 adds two more terms: גָּבְהוֹ ("his loftiness") and וְרֻם לִבּוֹ ("and the haughtiness of his heart").
ᶜ⋯ᶜ וְעֶבְרָתוֹ ("and his insolence," 48:30; Isa 16:6), preceded in 48:30 by the phrase אֲנִי יָדַעְתִּי נְאֻם־יְהוָה (not paralleled in Isaiah 16). נְאֻם־יְהוָה (missing in the LXX) occurs only here in 48:29-33, but not at all in Isa 16:6-10.

d...d   וְלֹא כֵן בַּדָּיו ("his boasts are invalid," 48:30; "his boasts are false," Isa 16:6, without *athnah* pause). Jeremiah 48:30 includes וְלֹא־כֵן in the preceding clause, followed by בַּדָּיו לֹא־כֵן עָשׂוּ ("his boastings have wrought nothing well-founded").[70] However, most commentators ignore the *athnah* pause in 48:30.

e...e   עַל־כֵּן עַל־מוֹאָב אֲיֵלִיל וּלְמוֹאָב כֻּלֹּה אֶזְעָק, 48:31a
        לָכֵן יְיֵלִיל מוֹאָב לְמוֹאָב כֻּלֹּה יְיֵלִיל, Isa 16:7a.

Jeremiah 48:31 changes 3d s. to 1st s. and substitutes the verb זעק for the second occurrence of ילל Hiphil imperf. 3d s. in Isa 16:7a (cf. Isa 15:2, 3). For the forms יְיֵלִיל, אֲיֵלִיל, see GKC § 70d.

f...f   אֶל־אַנְשֵׁי קִיר־חֶרֶשׂ יֶהְגֶּה, 48:31b
        לַאֲשִׁישֵׁי קִיר־חֲרָשֶׂת תֶּהְגּוּ, Isa 16:7.

אַנְשֵׁי קִיר־חֶרֶשׂ (48:31b; in the LXX, ἄνδρας Κιρ Αδας) has been substituted for אֲשִׁישֵׁי קִיר־חֲרָשֶׂת "raisin-cakes of Kir-hareseth" (Isa 16:7b). This is a good example of what Holladay describes as "the result of the misreading or carelessness of copyists."[71] For אֶל־אַנְשֵׁי קִיר־חֶרֶשׂ see also 48:36 (Isa 16:11 also has the form קִיר חֶרֶשׂ). For קִיר־חֲרָשֶׂת (Isa 16:7b), see also 2 Kgs 3:25. The LXX place names are Κιρ Αδας (48:31) and Δεσεθ (Isa 16:7). In a careful treatment of these various forms, Holladay suggests that the name was originally קִיר־חָדָשׁ Kir-hadash ("new city"), mockingly deformed to קִיר חֶרֶשׂ ("city of potsherds").[72] If תֶּהְגּוּ (Isa 16:7) requires modification, אֶהְגֶּה (Q^or) rather than יֶהְגֶּה (48:31) would be in keeping with the use of the first person singular in the immediate context in Jeremiah 48. אַךְ־נְכָאִים ("utterly stricken," Isa 16:7) is not carried over into 48:31.

g...g   מִבְּכִי יַעְזֵר אֶבְכֶּה־לָּךְ הַגֶּפֶן שִׂבְמָה, 48:32a
        עַל־כֵּן אֶבְכֶּה בִּבְכִי יַעְזֵר גֶּפֶן שִׂבְמָה, Isa 16:9a.

The suggestion of Landes that מַבְּךְ ("fountain"), based on *mbk* (Ugaritic) should be read for מִבְּכִי 48:32a, is accepted by most commentators (e.g., Rudolph, Bright, Holladay, Thompson, Jones); "fountain" may be ironic.[73] Although גֶּפֶן שִׂבְמָה ("the vine of Sibmah") is mentioned also in Isa 16:8, 48:32a more closely approximates Isa 16:9a. In any case, גֶּפֶן שִׂבְמָה (without the definite article) should be read in 48:32a (cf. the LXX: ἄμπελος Σεβημα).

h...h   שְׁלֻחוֹתַיִךְ נִטְּשׁוּ עָבְרוּ יָם, 48:32b; נְטִישֹׁתַיִךְ עָבְרוּ יָם, Isa 16:8d.

Jeremiah 48:32b indicates a selective use of Isa 16:8, which is substantially abbreviated, with no reference to the בַּעֲלֵי גוֹיִם ("lords of the nations") as the agents of destruction. Isaiah 16:8 LXX, καταπίνοντες τὰ ἔθνη, understands "the nations" as victims rather than destroyers.

---

[70] H. Freedman, *Jeremiah: Hebrew Text & English Translation and Commentary* (rev. A. J. Rosenberg; New York: The Soncino Press, 1985) 308.

[71] Holladay, *Jeremiah 2*, 346. Cf. Volz, *Jeremia*, 407.

[72] Holladay, *Jeremiah*, 361.

[73] G. M. Landes, "The Fountain at Jazer," *BASOR* 144 (1956) 34. See also Holladay, *Jeremiah 2*, 361.

i...i עַד־יָם יַעְזֵר נָגָעוּ ,48:32b; עַד־יַעְזֵר נָגָעוּ, Isa 16:8c. Jeremiah 48:32b changes the order of Isa 16:8cd and in doing this repeats יָם, which should be deleted. θάλασσα occurs only once in the LXX translation of 48:32b (31:32bLXX) and is missing in two manuscripts.

j...j עַל קֵיצֵךְ וְעַל־בְּצִירֵךְ שֹׁדֵד נָפָל, 48:32c
כִּי עַל־קֵיצֵךְ וְעַל־קְצִירֵךְ הֵידָד נָפָל, Isa 16:9c.

The substitution of בְּצִירֵךְ ("your vintage," 48:32c) for קְצִירֵךְ ("your grain harvest," Isa 16:9c) and שֹׁדֵד ("the destroyer," 48:32c) for הֵידָד ("the battle shout," Isa 16:9c) may point to carelessness on the part of scribes in the course of transmission.[74] However, as Jones indicates, in the case of שֹׁדֵד "the alteration is entirely in line with the author's purpose."[75]

k...k וְנֶאֶסְפָה שִׂמְחָה וָגִיל מִן־הַכַּרְמֶל, 48:33a
וְנֶאֱסַף שִׂמְחָה וָגִיל מִן־הַכַּרְמֶל, Isa 16:10.

Jeremiah 48:33 omits Isa 16:10b, but adds וּמֵאֶרֶץ מוֹאָב, another indication of the freedom with which the Isaiah 16 poem is treated in Jeremiah 48.

l...l וְיַיִן מִיקָבִים הִשְׁבַּתִּי לֹא־יִדְרֹךְ הֵידָד הֵידָד לֹא הֵידָד, 48:33b
יַיִן בַּיְקָבִים לֹא־יִדְרֹךְ הַדֹּרֵךְ הֵידָד הִשְׁבַּתִּי, Isa 16:10c.

In the adaptation of Isa 16:10c in 48:33b, the verb הִשְׁבַּתִּי is attached to the first clause, הַדֹּרֵךְ is omitted and הֵידָד occurs three times. Whereas הֵידָד refers to the exultant shout of grape-treaders in Isa 16:10c, "battle-shout" is implied in the second occurrence of הֵידָד in 48:33b.[76] Thompson emends the first occurrence of הֵידָד to הַדֹּרֵךְ (in keeping with Isa 16:10c), "the grape-treader does not tread"; הֵידָד לֹא הֵידָד then means "no glad shout goes forth."[77] However, in spite of the awkwardness of the MT, the LXX confirms the MT with the threefold use of αιδεδ; RSV translates, "no one treads them with shouts of joy; the shouting is not the shout of joy." Isaiah 16:10b is omitted, as are Isa 16:8ab and Isa 16:9c, regarding Heshbon; 48:45 draws on Num 21:27-28 for the poetic passage dealing with Heshbon.

Comment

Hubmann raises the possibility that the extra-Jeremianic parallel passages upon which Jeremiah 48 draws may have been textually less different from the present MT at the time they were taken over, and that the texts have suffered in transmission.[78] This may well be the result of carelessness of scribes before the text became standardized. In any case, the comparison between 48:29-33 and Isa 16:6-10 indicates that the text of Isa 16:6-10 has been used with freedom and is an addition and adaptation made by an editor who is aware of

---

[74] Holladay, *Jeremiah 2*, 346.
[75] Jones, *Jeremiah*, 508. Isaiah 16:4b also refers to שֹׁדֵד, a particular "destroyer."
[76] Carroll (*Jeremiah*, 791) draws attention to the pun. Cf. הֵידָד ("battle-shout") in 51:14.
[77] Thompson, *Jeremiah*, 709.
[78] Hubmann, *Untersuchungen*, 236.

the parallel poem in Isaiah 16 and incorporates selectively most of Isa 16:6–10. Both passages begin with שָׁמַעְנוּ (" **we** have heard"), implying Israel and Moab's other neighbours, while the consistent use of the first person singular form of the verbs in 48:30-33 (הִשְׁבַּתִּי; אָבְכָּה; אֶהְגֶּה; אֶזְעָק; אֵילִיל; יָדַעְתִּי) makes Yahweh the speaker throughout the remainder of the poem. Jeremiah 48:29-30, the indictment of Moab, is followed in 48:30-33 with a lament on Moab in which battle shouts now take the place of vintage shouts of joy, in view of the devastation of the land.

4. JEREMIAH 48:34-39 and ISAIAH 15:2-7

JEREMIAH 48:34-39

34.[a] Because of the cry of Heshbon they have uttered their voice even unto Elealeh, even unto Jahaz, [a] [b] from Zoar even unto Horonaim (and) Eglath-shelishiyah,[b] [c] for the waters of Nimrim also have become desolate. [c] 35.[d] And I will bring to an end in Moab, says Yahweh, him who offers sacrifice on a high place and burns offerings to his god.[d] 36.[e] Because of this my heart moans for Moab like a flute [e] [f] and my heart moans (like a flute) for the men of Kir-heres; because of this the wealth they have gained has perished. 37.[h] For every head is made bald and every beard is cut off; upon every hand are gashes and on the loins is sackcloth.[h] 38.[i] On all the housetops of Moab and in the squares there is wholesale lamentation,[i] for I have broken Moab [j] like a vessel for which no one cares, says Yahweh.[j] 39. How it is broken! [k] (How) they do wail! How Moab has turned her back in shame![k] Moab has become [l] a derision and a horror[l] to all that are round about him.

ISAIAH 15:2-7

2. The daughter of Dibon has gone up to the high places to weep; over Nebo and over Medeba Moab wails, [h] on every head of his is baldness, every beard is cut off; 3. In his streets they gird on sackcloth;[h] [i] on the housetops and in the squares every one wails, melting into tears.[i] 4. [a] Heshbon and Elealeh cry out, their voice is heard as far as Jahaz, [a] therefore the warriors of Moab shout a war-alarm, his soul shudders. 5. [e] My heart cries out for Moab [e] [b] whose fugitives (flee) to Zoar, to Eglath-Shelishiyah [b] For at the ascent of Luhith they go up weeping; on the road to Horonaim they raise a cry of destruction, 6.[c] the waters of Nimrim are a desolation;[c] the grass withers, the new growth fails, the verdure is no more. 7. Therefore the abundance they have gained and [m] their store [m] they carry off across the wadi of the Arabim.

Textual and Translational Notes

a...a   48:34a, מִזַּעֲקַת חֶשְׁבּוֹן עַד־אֶלְעָלֵה עַד־יַהַץ נָתְנוּ קוֹלָם
       Isa 15:4a, וַתִּזְעַק חֶשְׁבּוֹן וְאֶלְעָלֵה עַד־יַהַץ נִשְׁמַע קוֹלָם.

The change from וַתִּזְעַק, Isa 15:4a to מִזַּעֲקַת, Jer 48:34a (מִן causal) and from נִשְׁמַע, Isa 15:4a to נָתְנוּ are indications that the editor who added 48:34–39 to the preceding verses in Jeremiah 48 may have been quoting from memory.[79] The arrangement and sequence of ideas in Isa 15:2–7 is not followed closely in 48:34–39 and Isa 16:11–12 is also in mind (e.g., in 48:35, 36).

b...b   48:34a, מִצֹּעַר עַד־חֹרֹנַיִם עֶגְלַת שְׁלִשִׁיָּה
       Isa 15:5a, בְּרִיחֶהָ עַד־צֹעַר עֶגְלַת שְׁלִשִׁיָּה.

Jeremiah 48:34–39 has no mention of Moab's fugitives (בְּרִיחֶהָ), but the place names occur in both 48:34–39 and Isa 15:2–7; צֹעַר in 48:34a and Isa 15:5a; חֹרֹנַיִם in 48:34a and Isa 15:5c; עֶגְלַת שְׁלִשִׁיָּה is found only in 48:34a and Isa 15:5 and may be, as Holladay suggests, a gloss on צֹעַר.[80]

c...c   48:34b, כִּי גַם־מֵי נִמְרִים לִמְשַׁמּוֹת יִהְיוּ:
       Isa 15:6a, כִּי־מֵי נִמְרִים מְשַׁמּוֹת יִהְיוּ.

The fact that 48:34b picks up Isa 15:6a, while the intervening lines Isa 15:5bc are closely parallel to 48:5ab, makes the explanation given by Volz (an insertion from the margin) altogether reasonable.[81]

d...d   Although 48:35 has no direct parallel in Isaiah 15 or 16, the noun מַעֲלֶה occurs in both 48:35 and Isa 15:5b; בָּמָה (48:35) finds a parallel in Isa 16:12 (cf. הַבָּמוֹת Isa 15:2a). The formula נְאֻם־יְהוָה 48:35 (cf. 48:38) is substantiated by the LXX but has no counterpart in Isaiah 15 and 16. The phrase occurs with great frequency in the book of Jeremiah (176 times) and is frequently the mark of redaction.[82]

e...e   48:36, עַל־כֵּן לִבִּי לְמוֹאָב כַּחֲלִלִים יֶהֱמֶה
       Isa 15:5a, לִבִּי לְמוֹאָב יִזְעָק.

The additional words כַּחֲלִלִים יֶהֱמוּ in 48:36 are repeated again in this sentence (see f...f below) and are reminiscent of Isa 16:11, עַל־כֵּן מֵעַי לְמוֹאָב כַּכִּנּוֹר יֶהֱמוּ. The same thoughts are expressed with different vocabulary in 48:36, although the introductory עַל־כֵּן and the verb הָמָה are retained. This reinforces the view that excerpts from Isaiah 15 and 16 are quoted from memory in 48:34–39.

---

[79] Weiser, *Jeremia*, 395.

[80] Holladay, *Jeremiah 2*, 344. עֶגְלַת שְׁלִשִׁיָּה (the third Eglath), is so named probably to distinguish this town from two other towns in the vicinity, named "Eglath"; see Nicholson, *Jeremiah 2*, 187. Isaiah 15:5aLXX translates δάμαλις...τριετής ("a heifer three years old"). A reference to אֶגְלַיִם in Isa 15:8 finds no parallel in Jer 48:34–39.

[81] See the discussion of the doublet 48:5ab=Isa 15:5bc above (pp. 130-131) and Volz, *Jeremia*, 405.

[82] Andersen and Forbes, *VOT*, 370. See Seybold, *Jeremia*, 28.

Jeremiah 46-49 (OAN)

$^{f...f}$ 48:36, וְלִבִּי אֶל־אַנְשֵׁי קִיר־חֶרֶשׂ כַּחֲלִילִים יֶהֱמֶה
This repetitious statement (see $^{e...e}$ above) concentrates on "the men of Kirheres," employing the phrase also used in 48:31, אֶל־אַנְשֵׁי קִיר־חָרֶשׂ.
$^{g...g}$ 48:36, עַל־כֵּן יִתְרַת עָשָׂה אָבֵדוּ
עַל־כֵּן יִתְרָה עָשָׂה, Isa 15:7
For יִתְרַת in 48:36, some manuscripts read יִתְרַת (see also GKC § 80g).
$^{h...h}$ 48:37, כִּי כָל־רֹאשׁ קָרְחָה וְכָל־זָקָן גְּרֻעָה
עַל כָּל־יָדַיִם גְּדֻדֹת וְעַל־מָתְנַיִם שָׂק:
בְּכָל־רָאשָׁיו קָרְחָה כָּל־זָקָן גְּרוּעָה, Isa 15:2c
בְּחוּצֹתָיו חָגְרוּ שָׂק, Isa.15.3a
Jeremiah 48:37 is quoting freely from Isa 15:2c3a. The verb גדד (48:37) does not occur in Isaiah 15, but is found (*Hithpael*) in 16:6 and 41:5, in contexts where the signs of mourning are described.
$^{i...i}$ 48:38, עַל כָּל־גַּגּוֹת מוֹאָב וּבִרְחֹבֹתֶיהָ כֻּלֹּה מִסְפֵּד
עַל גַּגּוֹתֶיהָ ..., Isa 15:3a
וּבִרְחֹבֹתֶיהָ כֻּלֹּה יְיֵלִיל יֹרֵד בַּבֶּכִי, Isa 15:3b
Jeremiah 48:38 is quoting freely from Isa 15:3ab, probably from memory. Elsewhere in the book of Jeremiah, the housetops (גַּגּוֹת) are associated with idolatrous worship (19:13; 32:29).
$^{j...j}$ 48:38, כִּכְלִי אֵין־חֵפֶץ בּוֹ נְאֻם יְהוָה
There is no direct parallel in Isaiah 15 or 16, but Coniah (Jehoiachin) is described in 22:28 as כְּלִי אֵין חֵפֶץ בּוֹ. See also below (chap. ten, p. 232) regarding 22:28 (Jehoiachin) and Hos 8:8 (Israel).
$^{k...k}$ 48:39, אֵיךְ חַתָּה הֵילִילוּ אֵיךְ הִפְנָה־עֹרֶף מוֹאָב בּוֹשׁ
Jeremiah 48:39 is an adaptation of 48:20; הֵילִילוּ חַתָּה occurs in both; מוֹאָב בֹּשׁ (48:39) is reminiscent of הֹבִישׁ מוֹאָב (48:20; cf. 48:1, הֹבִישָׁה הַמִּשְׂגָּב וָחָתָּה); הִפְנָה־עֹרֶף as a metaphor for apostasy occurs in 2:27 and 32:33.
$^{l...l}$ לִשְׂחֹק וְלִמְחִתָּה ("a derision and a horror"). שְׂחֹק also occurs in 48:26, 27. Interestingly, each of the terms שְׂחֹק and מְחִתָּה occurs in the quite different context of the Confessions; Jeremiah refers to himself as a שְׂחֹק ("laughingstock") in 20:7; he implores Yahweh not to be a מְחִתָּה ("terror") in 17:17. The author of 48:34-39 not only draws on Isaiah 15 and 16, but is familiar with vocabulary found elsewhere in the book of Jeremiah, e.g., אֵין־חֵפֶץ בּוֹ (48:38; 22:28); הִפְנָה־עֹרֶף (48:39; 2:27; 32:33); as well as the terms שְׂחֹק and מְחִתָּה.
$^{m...m}$ וּפְקֻדָּתָם ("their store," Isa 15:7). Although this term does not appear in 48:34-39, the term appears frequently in the book of Jeremiah in an entirely different sense, "their punishment," 6:15=8:12; 10:15; 49:8 (Edom); cf. פְּקֻדָּתָם שְׁנַת, 48:44c.

5. JEREMIAH 48:40-41 (MOAB)=JEREMIAH 49:22 (EDOM)

JEREMIAH 48:40-41
40. ᵃ For thus says Yahweh: ᵃ
ᶜ Behold, like an eagle he flies swiftly and spreads his wings against Moab.ᶜ
41. ᵇ The cities have been captured and the strongholds seized.ᵇ
ᵈ The heart of the warriors of Moab shall be on that day like the heart of a woman in labour

JEREMIAH 49:22
22. ᵃ Behold like an eagle he mounts up and flies swiftly and spreads his wings against Bozrah, ᶜ
ᵈ and the heart of the warriors of Edom shall be on that day like the heart of a woman in labour.ᵈ

Textual and Translational Notes

ᵃ⋯ᵃ 48:40, כִּי־כֹה אָמַר יְהוָה

The formula introduces a new unit (48:40MT; 31:40LXX), which originally consisted of 48:40b, 41b, 42 (=31:40-42LXX).

ᵇ⋯ᵇ 48:41a, נִלְכְּדָה הַקְּרִיּוֹת וְהַמְּצָדוֹת נִתְפָּשָׂה

The original reference may have been to Kerioth (קְרִיּוֹת, 48:24; Καριωθ, 31:24LXX; Ακκαριωθ, 31:40LXX). The initial ה in הַקְּרִיּוֹת could be explained by dittography or by later accommodation to הַמְּצָדוֹת, in which case the place name became "the cities," but was still understood as a topographical reference by the LXX translator. The verb תָּפַשׂ ("lay hold of, seize") occurs frequently in the book of Jeremiah: *Niphal* 34:3; 38:23; *Qal* 26:8; 37:13, 14; 40:10 and in OAN: *Qal* 46:9 (in the special sense of "handle," cf. 2:8); 49:16; *Niphal* 50:24, 46; 51:32, 41.

ᶜ⋯ᶜ 48:40b, הִנֵּה כַנֶּשֶׁר יִדְאֶה וּפָרַשׂ כְּנָפָיו אֶל־מוֹאָב

49:22a, הִנֵּה כַנֶּשֶׁר יַעֲלֶה וְיִדְאֶה וְיִפְרֹשׂ כְּנָפָיו עַל־בָּצְרָה

Jeremiah 48:40b is missing in the LXX. וְ יַעֲלֶה is missing in Jer 29:23LXX(=49:22MT); LXX reads יִרְאֶה (ὄψεται) instead of יִדְאֶה, due to the similarity of ד and ר. וְ יַעֲלֶה is probably the result of conflation; an alternative textual tradition was derived from Isa 40:31. In the case of אֶל־מוֹאָב and עַל־בָּצְרָה, אֶל and עַל (adversative) are interchangeable as elsewhere in the book of Jeremiah (e.g., 1:7; 21:13; 33:26). בָּצְרָה in 49:22 refers back to 49:13. Jeremiah 29:14LXX (=49:13MT) does not mention Bozrah, but reads instead ἐν μέσῳ αὐτῆς (?בְּעֶרָה). Bozrah is not mentioned in 29:23LXX (=49:22MT); for עַל־בָּצְרָה (MT) the LXX reads ἐπ' ὀχυρώματα αὐτῆς (cf. τὰ ὀχυρώματα in 31:40LXX=48:41aMT), suggesting that the Hebrew text known to the translator of the LXX was עַל־מִצְרוֹתֶיהָ.

ᵈ⋯ᵈ 48:41b, וְהָיָה לֵב גִּבּוֹרֵי מוֹאָב בַּיּוֹם הַהוּא כְּלֵב אִשָּׁה מְצֵרָה׃

49:22b, וְהָיָה לֵב גִּבּוֹרֵי אֱדוֹם בַּיּוֹם הַהוּא כְּלֵב אִשָּׁה מְצֵרָה׃

Jeremiah 48:41b is missing in the LXX. In 49:22b, אֱדוֹם is found (cf. the LXX), whereas מוֹאָב appears in 48:41b. בַּיּוֹם הַהוּא occurs also in the OAN

doublet 48:41=49:22; the usual term elsewhere in the book of Jeremiah is
חִיל כַּיּוֹלֵדָה (e.g., חִיל כַּיּוֹלֵדָה, 6:24; 22:23; 50:43).

Comment

The fact that 48:40b, 41b are missing in 31:40, 41LXX has been explained by Volz as deliberate, since in the LXX order 29:23LXX precedes 31:40, 41LXX (=48:40, 41MT); there was no need to repeat the eagle metaphor.[84] However, in view of the fact that 48:41a comes between 48:40b (=49:22a) and 48:41b (=49:22b), another more probable explanation of the way in which this doublet is handled in Jeremiah 48 may be given. Janzen proposes that the couplet came into Jeremiah 48 secondarily inserted as a gloss on 48:24 (where a Moabite Bozrah is mentioned) and was taken into the wrong column of the manuscript (48:40, 41), with names appropriately changed.[85] The allegory (מָשָׁל) of the great eagle (הַנֶּשֶׁר הַגָּדוֹל) in Ezek 17:3 points to Nebuchadrezzar as the aggressor against Jerusalem (Ezek 17:12); likewise, an unnamed conqueror will devastate Moab (48:40-41) and Edom (49:22).

6. JEREMIAH 48:43-44 = ISAIAH 24:17-18ab

JEREMIAH 48:43-44
43. [a] Terror and trench and trap are upon you, O inhabitant of Moab![a] [b] says Yahweh.[b]
44. [c] He who flees from the terror shall fall into the trench, and he who climbs [d] out of[d] the trench shall be caught in the trap.
[e] For I will bring these things upon Moab in the year of their punishment,[e] [b] says Yahweh.[b]

ISAIAH 24:17-18ab
17.[a] Terror and trench and trap are upon you, O inhabitant of the earth! [a]
18.[c] He who flees at the sound of the terror [c] shall fall into the trench; and he who climbs [d] out of [d] the trench shall be caught in the trap.

Textual and Translational Notes

[a...a] פַּחַד וָפַחַת וָפָח עָלֶיךָ יוֹשֵׁב מוֹאָב, 48:43
פַּחַד וָפַחַת וָפָח עָלֶיךָ יוֹשֵׁב הָאָרֶץ:, Isa 24:17
The nouns פַּחַד, פַּחַת, פָּח are repeated in the following verse in each case: 48:44ab; Isa 24:18ab. The vocabulary occurs occasionally elsewhere in the book of Jeremiah: פַּחַד, 30:5; 49:5; פָּח, 18:22 (Fourth Confession); פַּחַת (in a different sense) in 48:28, addressed to יֹשְׁבֵי מוֹאָב (cf. יוֹשֵׁב מוֹאָב in 48:43). Holladay draws attention to the striking assonance of these three nouns as

---

[84] Volz, *Jeremia*, 410.
[85] Janzen, *Studies*, 59, 94.

worthy of Jeremiah.⁸⁶ Isaiah 24:17 universalizes יֹשֵׁב מוֹאָב in the address הָאָרֶץ יוֹשֵׁב ("O inhabitant of the earth!").

ᵇ⁻ᵇ נְאֻם יְהוָה, 48:43, 44c.⁸⁷ The formula is missing in the LXX in both cases, and does not appear in Isa 24:17, 18. Since no equivalent to 48:44c is found in Isaiah 24, the double use (editorial?) of נְאֻם יְהוָה in Jer 48:43, 44c suggests that separate units have been combined in Isa 24:17-18.

ᶜ⁻ᶜ הַנָּס מִפְּנֵי הַפַּחַד, 48:44a
וְהָיָה הַנָּס מִקּוֹל הַפַּחַד, Isa 24:18a

הַנָּס (Qere) in 48:44a is surely correct.⁸⁸ An introductory וְהָיָה (Isa 24:18a) appears elsewhere in Isaiah 24-27 (24:2, 21; 27:12, 13). In 30:5, פַּחַד is parallel to קוֹל חֲרָדָה; in 48:44a מִקּוֹל (rather than מִפְּנֵי) may have been the original reading, as in 48:44 Syr and Isa 24:18a.

ᵈ⁻ᵈ מִן, 48:44b; מִתּוֹךְ, Isa 24:18b. מִתּוֹךְ occurs in 48:44b in some manuscripts, Syr, and Tg.

ᵉ⁻ᵉ Jeremiah 48:44c, a separate unit, is not taken up in Isa 24:18. אֵלֶיהָ is better read as אֵלֶה (LXX ταῦτα; cf. Syr). שְׁנַת פְּקֻדָּתָם occurs also in 11:23 (regarding "the men of Anathoth," first Confession); 23:12 (regarding "prophet and priest"). This phrase suggests that 48:44c was added by a scribe who was familiar with these passages.

Comment

The change in address from "O inhabitant of Moab!" (48:43) to "O inhabitants of the earth!" (Isa 24:17) implies that 48:43-44ab have been taken over in the Isaiah Apocalypse and given a universal application. Although Isa 24:17-18 is undoubtedly late, the date of 48:43-44 is uncertain and may even go back to Jeremiah himself.⁸⁹

7. JEREMIAH 48:45-46 = NUMBERS 21:27-29; 24:17c

JEREMIAH 48:45-46
45. In the shadow of Heshbon ᵃ the fugitives ᵃ stand without strength; ᵇ For a fire has gone forth from Heshbon and a flame

NUMBERS 21:27-29
27. Therefore the ballad singers say: "Come to Heshbon, let it be built; let the city of Sihon

---

⁸⁶ Holladay, *Jeremiah 2*, 349.
⁸⁷ Vg and Tg follow the MT.
⁸⁸ *Kethib* הַנִּיס is a scribal error; Holladay, *Jeremiah 2*, 345.
⁸⁹ Isaiah 24:17-18 probably goes back to the 4th C. BCE (Kaiser, *Isaiah 13-39*, 179), or even earlier (Sellin-Fohrer *Introduction to the Old Testament*, 369). See also Hans Wildberger, *Jesaja* (BKAT 10/2; Neukirchen-Verluyn: Neukirchener Verlag, 1978) 911. Wildberger believes that the so-called Isaiah Apocalypse developed in different phases between 500 BCE and 300 BCE (27:6-11, regarding Samaria, for example, is a late supplement).

ᵃ the fugitives ᵃ stand without strength; ᵇ For a fire has gone forth from Heshbon and a flame from the house of Sihon.ᵇ ᶜ It has destroyed the forehead of Moab and the crown of the sons of tumult.ᶜ
46. ᵈ Woe to you, O Moab! The people of Chemosh have perished;ᵈ ᵉ for you have been taken into exile and your daughters into captivity. ᵉ

singers say: "Come to Heshbon, let it be built; let the city of Sihon be established.
28. ᵇ For fire has gone forth from Heshbon, flame from the city of Sihon.ᵇ ᶜ It has devoured Ar of Moab, the lords of Bamoth of the Arnon. ᶜ
29.ᵈ Woe to you, O Moab! You have perished, O people of Chemosh! ᵈ
ᵉ He has made his sons fugitives and his daughters (have gone) into captivity ᵉ to an Amorite king, Sihon".

NUMBERS 24:17c

17c. ᶜ "It shall crush the forehead of Moab and the crown of all the sons of Seth." ᶜ

Jeremiah 48:45-46 is missing in the LXX.

Textual and Translational Notes

ᵃ...ᵃ נָסִים ("fugitives," 48:45a). Jeremiah 48:45a is without a parallel in Num 21:27-29, other than the place name Heshbon (Num 21:27,28), but נָסִים provides a catchword association with הַנָּס (Qere) in 48:44. חֶשְׁבּוֹן appears earlier at 48:2, 34, and also in 49:3 (oracle against the Ammonites), which suggests that Hebron, near the border, was at one time under Ammonite control.⁹⁰

ᵇ...ᵇ 48:45b, כִּי־אֵשׁ יָצָא מֵחֶשְׁבּוֹן וְלֶהָבָה מִבֵּין סִיחוֹן

Num 21:28a, כִּי־אֵשׁ יָצְאָה מֵחֶשְׁבּוֹן לֶהָבָה מִקִּרְיַת סִיחוֹן

Many manuscripts read יָצְאָה in 48:45b, in agreement with Num 21:28a. סִיחוֹן מִבֵּין ("from the midst of Sihon") is followed by Vg (de medio Seon), but some manuscripts support מִבֵּית ("from the house of"). Numbers 21:28a has סִיחוֹן מִקִּרְיַת ("from the city of Sihon"); cf. Num 21:26, כִּי חֶשְׁבּוֹן עִיר סִיחֹן ("for Heshbon was the city of Sihon").

ᶜ...ᶜ 48:45c, וַתֹּאכַל פְּאַת מוֹאָב וְקָדְקֹד בְּנֵי שָׁאוֹן׃

Num 21:28b, אָכְלָה עָר מוֹאָב בַּעֲלֵי בָּמוֹת אַרְנֹן׃

Num 24:17c, וּמָחַץ פַּאֲתֵי מוֹאָב וְקַרְקַר כָּל־בְּנֵי־שֵׁת

Apart from the use of the verb אכל, 48:45c corresponds more closely with Num 24:17c than with Num 21:28b. The Num 21:27-29 passage, which is credited

---

⁹⁰ Bright, Jeremiah, 325; Rudolph, Jeremia, 289. Volz, Jeremia, 415, eliminates חֶשְׁבּוֹן as an intrusion into the text from 48:45.

to הַמֹּשְׁלִים ("the ballad singers"; LXX οἱ αἰνιγματισταί, "those who speak riddles") is concerned with Moabite cities in 21:28: חֶשְׁבּוֹן (cf. Num 21:26,27); עָר (cf. Num 21:15; Isa 15:1) and the river Arnon, אַרְנֹן (cf. Num 21:14, 26, 28). בָּמוֹת in 21:28b may also be taken as a place-name (cf. Num 21:19, 20). Jeremiah 48:45c borrows metaphorical language: פְּאַת מֹאָב ("forehead of Moab") from Balaam's oracle regarding a star from Jacob, a sceptre from Israel, which will crush (מָחַץ) Moab's forehead. The Samaritan Pentateuch (Num 24:17c) reads וְקַרְקַר instead of וְקַרְקַר, another instance of confusion between ר and ד. קָרְקֹד ("scalp, crown," 48:45c) sustains the imagery (cf. 2:16), and may well have been the original reading in Num 24:17c.[91] בְּנֵי שָׁאוֹן ("sons of tumult," 48:45c) takes the place of כָּל־בְּנֵי־שֵׁת ("all the sons of Seth").[92] This perhaps reflects Amos 2:2, where the phrase וּמֵת בְּשָׁאוֹן מוֹאָב ("and Moab shall die amid uproar") is found.[93]

d...d אוֹי־לְךָ מוֹאָב אָבַד עַם־כְּמוֹשׁ, 48:46a
       אוֹי־לְךָ מוֹאָב אָבַדְתָּ עַם־כְּמוֹשׁ, Num 21:29a

These "woe-sayings," which are virtually identical, find a counterpart in 13:27, אוֹי לָךְ יְרוּשָׁלִַם ("Woe to you, O Jerusalem!"). Other woe-sayings in the book of Jeremiah introduced by אוֹי are 4:13, 31; 6:4; 45:3, and in the Confessions אוֹי לִי (10:19; 15:10). For similar pronouncements of woe in other prophets, see Isa 3:9; 6:5; Hos 7:13; 9:12; Ezek 24:6, 9. The reference to the Moabite god Chemosh (cf. 48:7, 13) is in keeping with references to other foreign deities in the OAN: Apis, 46:15 (Egypt); Milcom, 49:1, 3 (the Ammonites); Bel, 50:2; 51:44 (Babylon).

e...e כִּי לֻקְּחוּ בָנֶיךָ בַּשֶּׁבִי וּבְנֹתֶיךָ בַּשִּׁבְיָה, 48:46b
       נָתַן בָּנָיו פְּלֵיטִם וּבְנֹתָיו בַּשְּׁבִית, Num 21:29b

The two lines have in common the fact that sons and daughters have been taken into captivity, but 48:46b indicates that the Numbers passage has been freely adapted. Num 21:30, which completes the unit Num 21:27–30, has not been carried over into Jeremiah 48.

Comment

Although there can be no certainty regarding the dating of the passages from Numbers, both the song of the ballad-singers celebrating Moab's defeat (Num 21:27–30) and Balaam's oracles (Num 23:7–10, 18–24; 24:3–9, 15–24) must have been early and well-known to later generations.[94]

---

[91] George Buchanan Gray, *Numbers* (ICC; Edinburgh: T. & T. Clark, 1903) 371.

[92] שֵׁת, son of Adam (Gen 4:25).

[93] The vocabulary of Amos 2:2 has other points in common with 48:45; e.g., the noun אֵשׁ and the verb אָכַל.

[94] See Martin Noth, *Numbers* (OTL; London: SCM, 1968) 161. He considers Num 21:27–30 to be older than the narrative into which this song has been inserted, requiring an explanatory introduction, 21:25–26. Noth regards 24:17b–18 as applicable to David's

Why is Jeremiah 48:45-46 missing in the LXX?

The fact that 48:45-46 is missing in the LXX points to the probability that these verses have been added in the Hebrew text at a late date by a scribe who was familiar with early passages in Numbers and Amos, in which the fate of Moab is announced, in order to supplement the collection of oracles regarding Moab.

Jeremiah 48:47, looking forward to the restoration of Moab's fortunes, is also missing from the LXX. The phrase וְשַׁבְתִּי שְׁבוּת ("I will restore the fortunes," 48:47a) recurs in the OAN in 49:6 (the Ammonites) and 49:39 (Elam).[95] Only in the case of Elam (25:19LXX=49:39MT) is there the promise of the restoration of fortunes in the OAN oracles in the LXX.[96] Jeremiah 48:47 and 49:6 appear to be later additions to the MT. Jeremiah 48:47b, עַד־הֵנָּה מִשְׁפַּט מוֹאָב ("Thus far is the judgment on Moab") is an editorial rubric similar to that which concludes Jeremiah 50-51 (Babylonia): 51:64, עַד־הֵנָּה דִּבְרֵי יִרְמְיָהוּ.[97]

Recurring Phrases in Jer 49:1-6 MT (30:1-5LXX): THE AMMONITES

Within the book of Jeremiah, in addition to 49:1-6, references to the Ammonites are found in 9:26; 25:21; 27:3 (they are among the envoys planning revolt against Babylonia); 40:11, 14 (Baalis, king of the Ammonites, plans to assassinate Gedaliah); 41:10, 15 (Ishmael is supported by the Ammonites). In all probability, the Ammonites are also included among the "evil neighbours" of 12:14.

In spite of their prominence generally in the OT (Judg 11:4; 1 Samuel 11; 1 Kgs 11:1-8; among the OAN: Amos 1:13-15; Zeph 2:8-11; Ezek 21:20, 28-32; 25:1-7), the Ammonites are the object of only two brief oracles among the OAN in the book of Jeremiah: 49:1-2 (judgment); 49:3-5 (lament), followed by a promise of restoration, 49:6. North reduces these oracles considerably, claiming only 49:1b,2b (omitting בְּנֵי עַמּוֹן and מִלְחָמָה), 49:2d (omitting אָמַר יְהוָה, missing in the LXX), 49:3a (omitting the references to Heshbon and Ai), as the essential core, to which editorial additions were

---

[95] Although the phrase שַׁבְתִּי שְׁבוּת is not used in 46:26b (but is applied to Egypt in Ezek 29:14), the promise is made that Egypt shall be inhabited again. Jeremiah 46:26 is missing in the LXX.

[96] In the LXX order of the OAN, Elam is in first place.

[97] וַיַּעֲפוּ, immediately before this phrase, is an indication that the concluding words really belong at the end of 51:58 (where the final word is וְיָעֵפוּ), and that 51:59-64 is an insertion. The final phrase in 51:64 is missing from 28:64LXX, since in the LXX the Babylonian oracles (Jeremiah 50-51MT) have been incorporated (27-28LXX) immediately after the oracles against Elam and Egypt, rather than as a climax to the series of OAN, as in the MT order.

subsequently made.⁹⁸ However, Holladay excludes only 49:2a, pointing to the metrical regularity of the poems, and suggesting that the summer of 587 BCE (when Baalis, king of the Ammonites, sponsored Ishmael as the assassin of Gedaliah) would provide an appropriate occasion for these verses.⁹⁹

The series of rhetorical questions in 49:1, introduced by ה, אִם and מַדּוּעַ, a stylistic feature found elsewhere in the book of Jeremiah (e.g., 2:14, 31; 8:4-5, 19, 22; 14:19; 22:28), has been studied by Brueggemann. He examines Judg 11:25-26; Job 21:4 and Mal 2:10 and the developed form as it is used in the Jeremiah passages, concluding that both in frequency and the disciplined manner of its use the form is almost unique to Jeremiah.¹⁰⁰

The familiar phrase לָכֵן הִנֵּה יָמִים בָּאִים (49:2), which occurs throughout the book of Jeremiah, appears also in the OAN in 48:12; 51:47, 52 (cf. 47:4, הַיּוֹם הַבָּא).¹⁰¹ The LXX supports the MT in these passages, except in the case of 51:47, which belongs to a lengthy passage, 51:44b-49a, missing in the LXX, perhaps by haplography.¹⁰² The support of the LXX and the versions for 49:2MT makes it less likely that this is a later addition. The phrase does not necessarily imply events to take place in a distant future.

The use of the verb ירש (49:1 *bis*, 49:2 *bis*), especially in the sense "dispossess," underlines the fact that Israel's inheritance, territory across the Jordan which rightly belongs to Gad (Deut 3:12; Josh 13:24-28), has been usurped by Milcom (god of the Ammonites). A similar situation is reflected in Judg 11:24, "Will you not possess what Chemosh your god gives you to possess? And all that Yahweh our God has dispossessed before us, we will possess." The situation will be reversed when Israel dispossesses those who dispossessed it (49:2).¹⁰³ Jeremiah 49:2 refers to the תְּרוּעַת מִלְחָמָה ("battle cry") which will be heard, a phrase which occurs elsewhere only in 4:19.¹⁰⁴ וּבְנֹתֶיהָ in the phrase וּבְנֹתֶיהָ בָּאֵשׁ תִּצַּלְנָה (49:2), literally "her daughters," refers to the satellite villages of the capital city of the Ammonites, Rabbah.¹⁰⁵

---

⁹⁸ F. S. North, "The Oracle Against the Ammonites in Jeremiah 49:1-6," *JBL* 65 (1946) 37-43.

⁹⁹ Holladay, *Jeremiah 2*, 366-367.

¹⁰⁰ Walter Brueggemann, "Jeremiah's Use of Rhetorical Questions," *JBL* 92 (1973) 358-374.

¹⁰¹ See above, chap. four, pp. 56, 58, for references and discussion.

¹⁰² Another possibility, suggested by Janzen (*Studies*, 119) is that 51:44b-49a and 51:49b-53, with similar phraseology, are old variants, conflated in the MT.

¹⁰³ For the concept of "the house of Jacob" repossessing their own possessions, see Obad 17. Obadiah 15 envisages justice exercised against "the nations": "As you have done, it shall be done to you; your deeds shall return on your own head." Rudolph (*Jeremia*) regards 49:2b as "only a pipe-dream of later Judaism" (p. 289).

¹⁰⁴ Holladay, *Jeremiah 2*, 367.

¹⁰⁵ Cf. בְּנוֹת רַבָּה (49:3) and the phrase וּבְכָל־בְּנֹתֶיהָ in Num 21:25 (Heshbon).

בָּאֵשׁ תִּצַּתְנָה is reminiscent of וְהִצַּתִּי אֵשׁ ("I will kindle a fire," Amos 1:14).[106] The verb ילל Hiphil ("wail") in 49:3, recurs in the OAN (47:2; 48:20, 31, 39; 51:8) and is also found in 4:8; 25:34. The final phrase in 49:3, כֹּהֲנָיו וְשָׂרָיו יַחְדָּיו כִּי מַלְכָּם בַּגּוֹלָה יֵלֵךְ has a counterpart in 48:7b, where only the name of the deity (Chemosh) differs and is similar to Amos 1:15, בַגּוֹלָה הוּא וְשָׂרָיו יַחְדָּו וְהָלַךְ מַלְכָּם, where the reference to "their king" in all probability accounts for the vocalization מַלְכָּם in 49:2, 3. The inclusion of כֹּהֲנָיו ("his priests," 49:3c; 48:7b) is followed in the LXX.[107] In the case of הַבַּת הַשּׁוֹבֵבָה ("O faithless daughter," 49:4; cf. 31:22 regarding Israel), Rudolph, following Duhm, changes the participial adjective to הַשַּׁאֲנַנָּה ("complacent," cf. 48:11) as a more suitable description in the context.[108] Smothers argues for the retention of הַשּׁוֹבֵבָה as an appropriate designation for Ammon, carrying political overtones of a vassal violating treaty obligations (49:1).[109] However, in this separate oracle 49:3-5, the charge against Ammon is that of trusting in her treasures (49:4); it is similar to the charge against the Moabites (48:7a), where the same combination of בטח and אוֹצָרוֹת is found. Jeremiah 49:5 begins with the participial phrase הִנְנִי מֵבִיא עָלַיִךְ, often found elsewhere in the book of Jeremiah: e.g., 5:15; 6:19; 11:11; 19:3. In 49:5, פַּחַד ... מִכָּל-סְבִיבָיִךְ ("terror ... from all who are round about you") is to be brought upon the Ammonites, "a variation of the expression *magôr-missabîb*" i.e., "terror on every side."[110]

SUMMARY: JEREMIAH 49:1-5; 49:6

This survey of 49:1-5 demonstrates that much of its vocabulary and phraseology is duplicated in other OAN in the book of Jeremiah, with a number of points of contact with earlier oracles (the interrogative triad in 49:1; מִלְחָמָה תְּרוּעָה, 49:2; הִנְנִי מֵבִיא and פַּחַד, 49:5), and with dependency on phrases in the oracle against the Ammonites in Amos 1:13-15. The conclusion of Jones that this is "the work of a prophet in the tradition" appears to be justified.[111]

A promise of future restoration of the fortunes of the Ammonites (49:6MT, missing in the LXX) has been added, with a slight variation from the similar promise to Moab (48:47) by the use of וְאַחֲרֵי־כֵן ("afterward," cf. 46:26)

---

[106] In the oracles of judgment in Amos 1-2, this phrase is used only in the case of Rabbah; in the other cases (1:4, 7, 10; 2:2, 5) the phrase is וְשִׁלַּחְתִּי אֵשׁ.

[107] The reference to "priests" in the MT of 1:18; 34:19 is missing in the LXX and indicates expansion in the Hebrew text to make the list more inclusive, as in 29:1, where priests are included among the first group of exiles (in both the MT and the LXX).

[108] Rudolph, *Jeremia*, 286; Duhm, *Jeremia*, 353.

[109] Keown, Scalise and Smothers, *Jeremiah 26-52*, 324-325.

[110] Holladay, *Jeremiah 2*, 369. For מָנוֹר מִסָּבִיב in the OAN see 46:5; 49:29 (cf. 6:25; 20:3, 4, 10). The phrase is discussed above, chap. three, pp. 48-52, regarding 20:10, fifth Confession.

[111] Jones, *Jeremiah*, 510.

rather than בְּאַחֲרִית הַיָּמִים ("in the latter days," cf. 48:47; 49:39).[112] Rudolph thinks that the addition may have been made as late as Hellenistic times, when the city of Philadelphia (in former Ammonite territory) experienced a new blossoming.[113] Of special interest is the fact that the prose passage 12:14-17 offers hope to "evil neighbors" (12:14) in that after due punishment ("I will pluck them up," 12:14), Yahweh will show compassion (12:15) to these bordering nations and build them up, conditional upon their learning "the ways of my people" (12:16). The catchword נַחֲלָה ("heritage") links this passage with the poetic passage 12:7-13, where נַחֲלָה is a key word (12:7, 8, 9). נתש, which occurs five times in 12:14-17, בנה (12:16), and אבד (12:17) are three of the verbs used in 1:10, Jeremiah's commission עַל־הַגּוֹיִם ("over the nations".[114] McKane has undertaken a careful study of 12:14-17, relating the passage not only to 1:10, but also to 48:47 (Moab) and 49:6 (Ammon).[115] For him, "... v.15 is one exegesis of (ושבתי שבות עמון (מואב and vv.16-17 is another."[116] The passage must be regarded as very late: "vv.14-15 are post-exilic and vv.16-17 are post-exilic *a fortiori*," presupposing the call narrative and the promises of restoration in the OAN.[117]

Although Zeph 2:9d looks forward to repossession of Moab and Ammon by "the survivors of my nation," Höffken believes that the promises to Moab (48:47) and Ammon (49:6) in the OAN in the book of Jeremiah reflect a more restricted concept of the ideal Israel of the future, in which the Deuteronomistic circle waives rights to part of the territory in Jordan and anticipates the revival of Moab and Ammon.[118] In any case, these additions are much later than the oracles to which they have been attached.[119]

Recurring Phrases and Doublets in Jer 49:7-22MT (29:18-23LXX): EDOM

The Edomites are frequently the target of prophetic OAN: e.g., Amos 1:11-12; Isa 34:5-14; Ezek 35:1-15; Obad 1-14; Mal 1:2-5. These oracles reflect animosity against Edom for their treachery during the siege of Jerusalem, never forgiven by Israel (Lam 4:21-22 ["Rejoice and be glad" is ironic, in view of the context]; Ps 137:7; Ezek 25:12-14).

---

[112] For the meaning of בְּאַחֲרִית הַיָּמִים see the discussion of 23:20=30:24 above, chap. five, p. 89, espec. n. 39.
[113] Rudolph, *Jeremia*, 290.
[114] Volz (*Jeremia*) describes 12:14-17 as "a sermon on the programmatic words of 1:10" (p. 147).
[115] McKane, *Jeremiah 1*, 269-283.
[116] McKane, *Jeremiah 1*, 284.
[117] McKane, *Jeremiah 1*, p. 284.
[118] Peter Höffken, "Zu den Heilszusätzen in der Völkerorakelsammlung des Jeremiabuches," *VT* 27 (1977) 398-412.
[119] Jeremiah 49:39 is also a late addition; see below, p. 162.

Judgment upon Edom is the theme of Jer 49:7-22, which consists largely of a series of doublets: 49:9ab=Obad 5ca; 49:14-16=Obad 1-4; 49:18=50:40; 49:19-21=50:44-46; 49:22=48:40-41.

Jeremiah 49:9-16, a poem with many similarities to Obad 1-14, is interrupted by insertions: 49:11 and a prose passage, 49:12-13, in which 49:12 reflects 25:15-16 (cf. 25:27; 48:26).[120] כָּל־הַגּוֹיִם ("All the nations," 25:25), including Edom, are to drink of Yahweh's cup. The prose passage which follows, 49:17-22, is a pastiche of doublets.

The poem has features in common with the book of Obadiah, in addition to the doublets 49:9ab=Obad 5ca; 49:14-16=Obad 1b-4. The tradition of Edomite wisdom is reflected in 49:7 and in Obad 8 (cf. the book of Job). Teman represents the whole land of Edom (cf. 49:20) as does Bozrah in 49:13. Dedan (49:8) is not specifically mentioned in Obadiah, but is under judgment in Ezek 25:13 (cf. Isa 21:13).[121] נָסוּ ("flee," 49:8) is not found in Obadiah, but occurs frequently in the OAN: 48:6; 49:30; 51:6. פנה Hiphil + the verb נוס ("turn and flee") occur in 46:5; 46:21; 49:24. The phrase אֵיד עֵשָׂו ("calamity of Esau," 49:8, cf. Judah's day of calamity) is ominously repeated three times in Obad 13, when Edom "gloated over his disaster," "looted his goods" and (Obad 14) "cut off his fugitives." A doublet is found in 49:9ab=Obad 5ca, in which "grape-gleaners" and "thieves" are in reverse order in Obadiah.

8. JEREMIAH 49:9 = OBADIAH 5

JEREMIAH 49:9
9. ª If grape-gatherers come to you, they would not leave gleanings.ª If thieves
ᶜ by night,ᶜ ᵉ they would destroy as much as they want (literally, "their sufficiency").ᵉ

OBADIAH 5
5. if thieves ᵇ come to you,ᵇ if destroyers ᶜ by nightᶜ ᵈ — how you have destroyed!— ᵈ ᵉ would they not steal only enough for themselves? ᵉ ª If grape-gatherers came to you, would they not leave gleanings? ª

---

[120] Jeremiah 49:11 has been understood as a quotation from neighbours (49:10) who are ready to help Edomite orphans and widows (Holladay, *Jeremiah 2*, 376; Smothers, *Jeremiah 2*, 330). However, a more likely explanation is that this verse has been added as an indication of Yahweh's mercy (cf. Deut 10:18; 23:7, 8; Ps 68:5), with Yahweh as speaker, to mitigate the harshness of the total destruction announced in 49:10 (cf. Carroll, *Jeremiah*, 803; Jones, *Jeremiah*, 515). This would then be a late addition, somewhat in the spirit of 49:6, 39, reflecting and extending the concern for the widow and orphan expressed in 7:6; 22:3.

[121] Kaiser (*Isaiah 13-39*, 133-135) gives the oracle Isa 21:13-15 the heading, "In the desert" (RSV "Concerning Arabia"). The caravans of the Dedanites are urged to avoid the caravan-routes; the inhabitants of Tema are called upon to supply the fugitives with water and bread. The exact date of this oracle remains an open question.

Textual and Translational Notes

a...a   Except for orthographic differences (49:9a עוֹלְלוֹת, יַשְׁאִרוּ, לוֹא; יַשְׁאִירוּ, עֹלֵלוֹת Obad 5c) and the addition of the interrogative הֲ in Obad 5c, 49:9a and Obad 5c are exact parallels.

b...b   Obadiah 5 contains the phrase בָּאוּ־לָךְ twice, descriptive of the actions both of thieves and grape-gatherers.

c...c   In 49:9b, thieves came בַּלַּיְלָה ("by night"), whereas in Obad 5a an additional term is introduced, אִם־שׁוֹדְדֵי before לַיְלָה ("if despoilers by night").

d...d   An additional ejaculatory phrase appears in Obad 5b, אֵיךְ נִדְמֵיתָה ("how you have been destroyed!"). דמה II (*Niphal*) occurs in OAN: 47:5 (Ashkelon); Isa 15:1 (Moab), as well as in Jer 6:2 ("the daughter of Zion"), but not in 49:9.

e...e   הִשְׁחִיתוּ דַיָּם, literally "they would destroy 'their sufficiency'" (i.e., "as much as they want"), 49:9; הֲלוֹא יִגְנְבוּ דַיָּם ("would they not steal only what they want?,") Obad 5. In the LXX translation of 49:9 (29:10LXX), ἐπιθήσουσι χεῖρα αὐτῶν presupposes יָשִׁיתוּ יָדָם (transposing *daleth* and *yodh*) "they would lay their hands upon ...," but without an object. Obadiah 5LXX, οὐκ ἂν ἔκλεψαν τὰ ἱκανὰ ἑαυτοῖς, faithfully translates הֲלוֹא יִגְנְבוּ דַיָּם.

Comment

The differences between 49:9 and Obad 5 raise doubts about direct dependency of either passage on the other. Whereas Obadiah's questions (Obad 5) indicate that thieves steal only what they need and grape-gatherers customarily leave gleanings behind (Lev 19:9–10; Ruth 2:2), in 49:9 we have statements rather than questions, indicating that contrary to usual custom there will be no gleanings, nothing will be left by thieves. This accounts for the harsher language in 49:10; Esau (Edom) will be stripped bare (חָשַׂפְתִּי) by Yahweh, whereas in Obad 6, שׂ and פ are transposed: אֵיךְ נֶחְפְּשׂוּ עֵשָׂו ("How Esau has been searched out!"). The differences between 49:14–16 and Obad 1–4 are discussed below (pp. 149-152), leading to the conclusion that a common source (perhaps oral) has been drawn upon and used in different ways.[122] Both 49:14–16 and Obad 1–4 have also suffered in transmission.

The prose verses 49:12-13, placed between the first and second strophes of the poem, point back to 25:15-16, 27-29 (cf. Obad 16), implying that although some who did not deserve to drink of Yahweh's cup had to do so, Edom *a fortiori* must not go unpunished. Bozrah, an Edomite fortress city, and "all her cities" (49:13) is specifically mentioned (cf. 49:22) in a curse formula

---

[122] See Weiser, *Jeremia*, p. 408 n. 4. He considers Obad 5–6 to be closer to the original than 49:9–10; the verb גנב ("steal," Obad 5) is more appropriate than שׁחת *Hiphil* ("destroy," 49:9); חפשׂ *Niphal* ("search out," Obad 6) is preferable to חשׂף ("strip bare," 49:10). Perhaps the use of חשׂף in 13:26 has influenced the text of 49:10.

which contains three of the terms (חָרְבָּה, קְלָלָה, שַׁמָּה) also found in 25:18 with regard to "Jerusalem and the cities of Judah."

The second strophe of the poem, 49:14-16, is a doublet, parallel to Obad 1-4.

9. JEREMIAH 49:14-16 = OBADIAH 1b-4 (EDOM)

JEREMIAH 49:14-16

14. [a] I have heard[a] a report from Yahweh and a [b] messenger has been sent [b] among the nations (saying): [c] "Gather yourselves together and come against her, and rise up for battle."[c] 15. [d] Look,[d] I will make you small among the nations, [e] despised among mankind.[e] 16. [f] Horror at you! The arrogance of your heart has deceived you,[f] you who live in the clefts of [g] the rock,[g] [h] who hold the height of the hill.[h] [j] Though[j] you make [k] your nest [k] as high as an eagle's, I will bring you down from there — Oracle of Yahweh.

OBADIAH 1b-4

1b. [a] We have heard [a] a report from Yahweh and a [b] messenger has been sent[b] among the nations (saying): [c] "Arise, let us come up against her for war." [c] 2. [d] Look,[d] I will make you small among the nations, [e] you are utterly despised.[e] 3.[f] The arrogance of your heart has deceived you, [f] you who live in the clefts of [g] the rock,[g] who say in your heart "Who will bring me down to the ground?" 4. Though you soar like an eagle [i] though your nest is set among the stars,[i] I will bring you down from there — Oracle of Yahweh.

Textual and Translational Notes

Whereas there are variations in orthography in 49:9 = Obad 5, the doublet 49:14-16 = Obad 1b-4 is remarkably consistent in agreement in orthography. There are several textual differences, however.

[a...a] שָׁמַעְתִּי (49:14); שָׁמַעְנוּ (Obad 1b). For שְׁמוּעָה שָׁמַעְתִּי (49:14), cf. 31:18, where Yahweh is the speaker. However, שָׁמַעְנוּ 1st pl. (as in Obad 1b), whether referring to "hearing" or "obeying," is more usual in the book of Jeremiah: e.g., 3:25; 6:24; 30:5, and in the OAN, 48:29 (=Isa 16:6), and 51:51 (cf. 3:25). Nevertheless, the LXX has the first person sing. (ἤκουσα) in both passages, pointing to שָׁמַעְתִּי as the original form in the *Vorlage*.

[b...b] שָׁלוּחַ (49:14); שֻׁלַּח (Obad 1b). Obadiah uses the perfect of the verb, in keeping with the previous שָׁמַעְנוּ; 49:14 uses the passive participle, in apposition with צִיר. The LXX in both passages uses the past tense of the verb: ἀπέστειλε (29:15), ἐξαπέστειλεν (Obad 1b).

[c...c] הִתְקַבְּצוּ וּבֹאוּ עָלֶיהָ וְקוּמוּ לַמִּלְחָמָה (49:14b)
קוּמוּ וְנָקוּמָה עָלֶיהָ לַמִּלְחָמָה (Obad 1c)

The statement in 49:14b is more elaborate, with the additional verbs קבץ (*Hithpael*) and בוא.

d...d כִּי־הִנֵּה (49:15; missing in 29:16LXX); הִנֵּה (Obad 2). Perhaps כִּי־ in 49:15, after the quotation of the messenger's words to the nations in the account of the audition, is intended to introduce direct speech, with Yahweh as speaker.[123]

e...e בָּזוּי אַתָּה מְאֹד (49:15); בָּזוּי בָּאָדָם (Obad 2). The MT is supported by the LXX and the other versions.

f...f תִּפְלַצְתְּךָ (49:16a) is not in Obadiah; both 49:16 and Obad 3 have the phrase זְדוֹן לִבְּךָ ("the arrogance of your heart"), preceded by הִשִּׁיא אֹתְךָ in 49:16a and followed by הִשִּׁיאֶךָ in Obad 3a. The *hapax legomenon* תִּפְלֶצֶת has caused difficulty for the translators of the versions. The feminine form + suffix, תִּפְלַצְתְּךָ ("your horror"; RSV, "the horror you inspire") would require a feminine form of נָשָׁא II *Hiphil* ("deceive"); the reading may have been הִשִּׁיאַתְךָ originally.[124] Another possibility is to treat תִּפְלַצְתְּךָ as an exclamation, "horror at you!" (BDB:814a), in which case the rest of 49:16a would remain unchanged, with זְדוֹן לִבְּךָ as the subject of the verb: "the arrogance of your heart has deceived you."

g...g הַסֶּלַע (49:16b); סֶלַע (Obad 3b). The definite article has been omitted in Obad 3b. It is probable that the phrase בְּחַגְוֵי הַסֶּלַע means "in the cleft of the rock" rather than "in places of concealment of Sela"; cf. 29:17LXX, τρυμαλιὰς πετρῶν (cf. 13:4LXX), Vg, *in cavernis petrae*; Obad 3LXX, ἐν ταῖς ὀπαῖς τῶν πετρῶν, Vg, *in scissuris petrae*. 2 Kings 14:7, however, refers to Sela, a fortress city of the Edomites captured by Amaziah; the account in 2 Chron 25:12 refers to רֹאשׁ־הַסֶּלַע ("the top of the rock"), but this may be a play on the name Sela. Whether or not the placename is intended in 49:16b and Obad 3b remains uncertain.

h...h תֹּפְשִׂי מְרוֹם גִּבְעָה (49:16b); מְרוֹם שִׁבְתּוֹ (Obad 3b). תֹּפְשִׂי (cf. שְׁכְנִי in 49:16b) is an example of *hireq campaginis*, an archaic genitive form (GKC § 90k). The phrases in 49:16b have only the noun מְרוֹם (construct form) in common, although both phrases reflect the fact that Edomite territory was well defended by a series of fortresses.

i...i The phrase אֹמֵר בְּלִבּוֹ מִי יוֹרִדֵנִי אָרֶץ ("saying in his heart 'who will bring me down to the ground?'," Obad 3c) has no parallel in 49:16.

j...j כִּי (49:16c); אִם (Obad 4a). Both כִּי and אִם are concessive, "though."[125]

k...k קִנֶּךָ (49:16c). The direct object of the verb occurs in the next phrase in Obad 4a (see l...l).

---

[123] Similar to ὅτι *recitatif* in Greek; see Williams, *Hebrew Syntax*, § 452.
[124] Smothers, *Jeremiah 2*, 327.
[125] Williams, *Hebrew Syntax*, §§ 448, 454.

[...] וְאִם־בֵּין כּוֹכָבִים שִׂים קִנֶּךָ ("and though your nest is set among the stars," Obad 4a) is missing in 49:16c.[126]

Comment

Both 49:14-16 and Obad 1b-4 end with the phrase נְאֻם יְהוָה, indicating that this passage was considered to be an authentic prophetic word from Yahweh. A messenger has summoned the nations (גּוֹיִם, 49:14; Obad 1b) to prepare for battle "against her" (i.e., Edom). Yahweh will make Edom small and despised; Edom's proud boasts of being invulnerable to attack are groundless. Obadiah 7 speaks of "allies" and "confederates" who have turned against Edom.[127] The major indictment against Edom (Obad 10-14) is that Edom (Esau) has treacherously done violence "to your brother Jacob" (cf. Amos 1:11; Ezek 35:5; Joel 3:19). A day of judgment is near (Obad 15) for "all the nations," including Edom; "there shall be no survivor to the house of Esau" (Obad 18). The unit Jer 49:14-16 points only to the pride of Edom as the basis for impending judgment.

Although both Rudolph and Weiser suggest that 49:14-16 is dependent on Obad 1b-4, a stronger case can be made that each drew on a common oral source, with adaptations and inevitable divergencies arising during transmission.[128] There is sufficient difference between 49:14-16 and Obad 1b-4 to make it unlikely that either is directly dependent on the other. The date of the original oracle must remain uncertain. The traditional rivalry between Edom and Israel has a long history, reflected in the patriarchal narratives (e.g., Genesis 27), with bitterness on Israel's part exacerbated by Edom's acts of treachery at the time of Nebuchadrezzar's conquest of Jerusalem (Ps 137:7; Obad 10-14; Ezek 25:12-14). This is not the emphasis in 49:14-16=Obad 1b-4, however, where attention is concentrated on Edom's arrogance and inevitable downfall.

Further prose oracles against Edom have been added in 49:17-22, consisting mostly of doublets which run parallel to other OAN in Jeremiah 48-50.

---

[126] Watts, *Obadiah*, 34, considers the phrase to be a gloss. J. A. Bewer, *Obadiah*, 35, argues that such expressive phrases as "saying in his heart,'Who will bring me down to the ground?'" and "though your nest is set among the stars" would not have been omitted if 49:14-16 is quoted from Obad 1b-4.

[127] J. R. Bartlett (*Edom and the Edomites* [JSOTSup 77; Sheffield: JSOT Press, 1989]) states, "...for Obadiah the allies and confederates of v.7 can hardly be any other than the Babylonians" (p. 159). Bartlett sees no occasion for punitive action from the Babylonians until perhaps 552 BCE, the campaigns of Nabonidus.

[128] See T. H. Robinson, "The Structure of the Book of Obadiah," *JTS* 17 (1916) 403. He states, "It is hardly to be doubted that the two texts represent two forms of the same original" (p. 403).

Jeremiah 49:17 is of special interest, not only because of the parallel poetic passage in 50:13, in which a similar destiny to that of Edom is in store for Babylon, but because of the parallels with 16:16 and 19:8, spoken against Israel ("their land" 18:16) and Jerusalem ("this city" 19:8). An examination of these texts will demonstrate the phrases which they have in common.

10. JEREMIAH 49:17; 50:13; 18:16; 19:8

JEREMIAH 49:17
17. Edom shall become[a] a horror;[a]
[b] every one who passes by it
shall be horror-struck [b] [c] and
shall whistle in amazement at
all her wounds.[c]

JEREMIAH 50:13
13. Because of Yahweh's
wrath she shall be
[a] uninhabited;[a] [b] every
one who passes by Babylon
shall be horror-struck [b] and
shall whistle in amazement
at all her wounds. [c]

JEREMIAH 18:16
16. ... so as to make their land
[a] a horror,[a] a perpetual occasion
for whistling in amazement;
[b] every one who passes by it
shall be horror-struck [b]
[c] and shall shake his head.[c]

JEREMIAH 19:8
8. I shall make this city
[a] a horror,[a] an occasion
for whistling in amazement;
[b] every one who passes by it
shall be horror-struck [b]
[c] and shall whistle in
amazement at all her wounds.[c]

Textual and Translational Notes

[a...a] שַׁמָּה ("horror," i.e., "that which evokes horror," 49:17 [Edom]); 18:16 ("their land"); 19:8 ("this city," i.e., Jerusalem). Jeremiah 50:13 uses the term שְׁמָמָה ("devastation") of Babylon. Both terms are translated in the LXX by ἀφανισμός, except for 29:18 (=49:17MT), where שַׁמָּה is translated by ἄβατος. שַׁמָּה occurs twenty-four times in the book of Jeremiah, in all strata, either in the sense of "devastation" or of "an occasion for horror." Jeremiah 18:16 adds שְׁרִיקֹת עוֹלָם ("a perpetual occasion for whistling in amazement"); the Qere represents an intensive plural.[129]

[b...b] כֹּל עֹבֵר עָלֶיהָ יִשֹּׁם, 49:17; 18:16; 19:8.

כֹּל עֹבֵר עַל־בָּבֶל יִשֹּׁם, 50:13. Cf. 1 Kgs 9:8 and 2 Chron 7:21 (the temple); Zeph 2:15 (Nineveh, with the verb יִשְׁרֹק).

[c...c] וְיִשְׁרֹק עַל־כָּל־מַכּוֹתֶהָ ("and will whistle in amazement because of all her wounds," 49:17; 50:13; 19:8). The phrase does not occur in 18:16, which has instead וְיָנִיד בְּרֹאשׁוֹ ("and shall shake his head").

The LXX translation of 49:17MT (29:18LXX) has only συριεῖ; יִשֹּׁם and עַל־כָּל־מַכּוֹתֶהָ are not translated. This suggests that the original text of 49:17 was

---

[129] Holladay, *Jeremiah 1*, 519.

כֹּל עוֹבֵר עָלֶיהָ יִשְׁרֹק. וְהָיְתָה אֱדוֹם לְשַׁמָּה כֹּל עֹבֵר עָלֶיהָ יִשְׁרֹק. The phrase also occurs in Zeph 2:15, regarding Nineveh.[130] The verb יָשֹׁם takes the place of יִשְׁרֹק in 18:16, whereas the parallel passages 49:17, 50:13 and 19:8 use יִשֹּׁם, followed by the phrase וְיִשְׁרֹק עַל־כָּל־מַכּוֹתֶיהָ.

Any explanation of the relationship between the various texts cannot be other than tentative. The *cliché* כֹּל עֹבֵר עָלֶיהָ followed by יָשֹׁם (18:16) or by יִשְׁרֹק (Zeph 2:15 and Jer 49:17 in its original form) was a traditional prophetic phrase.[131] The earliest occurrences are in Zeph 2:15 and Jer 18:16.[132] The phrases כֹּל עֹבֵר עָלֶיהָ יָשֹׁם and וְיִשְׁרֹק עַל־כָּל־מַכּוֹתֶיהָ have been combined in 19:8, which sets the pattern for 49:17 in its final form and for 50:13.[133] The Targum of 49:17 also shows the influence of 18:16 ("shake his head") and is a good example of the interaction between these parallel texts.[134]

11. JEREMIAH 49:18 = JEREMIAH 50:40

JEREMIAH 49:18
18. [a] As when Sodom and Gomorrah and their neighbour (cities) were overthrown,[a] [b] says Yahweh,[b]
[c] no one shall live there, no human being shall dwell in her.[c]

JEREMIAH 50:40
40. [a] As when God overthrew Sodom and Gomorrah and and their neighbour (cities)[a]
[b] — Oracle of Yahweh — [b]
no one shall live there, no human being shall dwell in her.[c]

Textual and Translational Notes

[a...a] 49:18, כְּמַהְפֵּכַת סְדֹם וַעֲמֹרָה וּשְׁכֵנֶיהָ

50:40, כְּמַהְפֵּכַת אֱלֹהִים אֶת־סְדֹם וְאֶת־עֲמֹרָה וְאֶת־שְׁכֵנֶיהָ

The traditional comparative phrase referring back to the overthrow of Sodom and Gomorrah occurs in 23:14b (regarding the prophets of Jerusalem)

---

[130] Janzen (*Studies*) states, "That the cliché כל עובר עליה ישם וישרק may occur with only one of the verbs is shown by 18:16, Zeph 2:15" (p. 60).

[131] The phrase is also contained in 1 Kgs 9:8 and 2 Chron 7:21, regarding the destruction of the temple. In both cases, the phrase is followed by יָשֹׁם. 1 Kings 9:8 adds וְשָׁרַק (a few manuscripts have וְיִשְׁרֹק). Holladay (*Jeremiah 1*, 540) claims that 1 Kgs 9:8 may be dependent on Jer 19:8. Cf. John Gray (*1 & 2 Kings. A Commentary* [OTL; London: SCM]). Gray states (with respect to 1 Kgs 9:6-9), "...the threat of the destruction of people and Temple (vv.6-9) indicates the post-exilic Deuteronomic revision" (p. 219).

[132] The indictment in 18:13-17 (poetry) has been skilfully added to the prose passage 18:1-12, where connections are made by following שָׁרְרוּת (18:12) with the somewhat similar sounding שַׁעֲרִירִית (18:13), as noted by Brueggemann (*To Pluck up, to Tear down*, 162) and by the use of וְנַחְשְׁבָה and מַחֲשָׁבוֹת (18:18), referring back to וְחֹשֵׁב and מַחֲשָׁבָה (18:11), מַחְשְׁבוֹתֵינוּ (18:12).

[133] Cf. Vg, Syr; Thiel, *Redaktion 1*, p. 223 n. 14.

[134] Robert Hayward, *The Targum of Jeremiah* (The Aramaic Bible 12; Edinburgh: T. & T.Clark, 1987) 177.

and elsewhere in the prophets: Amos 4.11 (Israel); Isa 1:9 (the daughter of Zion, 1:8); 13:19b (Babylon); cf. Zeph 1:9 (Moab and the Ammonites), as well as in Deut 29:22 (29:23E). וּשְׁכֵנֶיהָ ("and their neighbour [cities]") refers to Admah and Zeboim.[135] Jeremiah 50:40 differs from 49:18 in introducing אֱלֹהִים and the particle אֶת־ (the sign of the accusative) before the nouns that follow. This conforms to the text of Isa 13:19b.[136] Rudolph claims that 50:40, dependent on Isa 13:19b, provided the pattern for 49:18.[137] The relationship between 49:18, 50:40 and Isa 13:19b is complicated by the addition of וּשְׁכֵנֶיהָ in the Jeremiah texts, which may have been introduced from 49:10. In any case, 49:17-22 and 50:39-40 must be considered as late additions to the text. An interesting feature is the use of Elohim, the generic name for deity, in 50:40 (cf. Isa 13:19b), rather than the name Yahweh. Apart from such phrases as אֱלֹהֵי יִשְׂרָאֵל, which occurs frequently, אֱלֹהִים חַיִּים ("the living God," 10:10; 23:36); אֱלֹהִים אֲחֵרִים ("other gods," designated as לֹא אֱלֹהִים, 2:11, 5:7), the only occurrence of אֱלֹהִים as the name of God in the book of Jeremiah comes in 50:40. This lends weight to the view that 50:40 has been borrowed from Isa 13:19b.

b...b אָמַר יְהוָה, 49:18 (29:19LXX=49:18MT, εἶπε κύριος + παντοκράτωρ);

נְאֻם יְהוָה, 50:14 (27:40LXX=50:40MT, εἶπε κύριος). The same alternation appears after phrases regarding the restoration of fortunes in 32:44 (נְאֻם יְהוָה) and 33:11 (אָמַר יְהוָה).[138] παντοκράτωρ(= צְבָאוֹת, e.g., 5:14) is an unusual addition in the text of the LXX, in which צְבָאוֹת is usually missing (e.g., in the OAN, in 26:10LXX=46:10MT, *bis* and in 27:25LXX=50:25MT). One can only conjecture that at one stage 49:18 read אָמַר יְהוָה צְבָאוֹת. Janzen points out that the occurrence of צְבָאוֹת in the MT is usually secondary.[139] The descriptive title "Yahweh of hosts" has undergone a long process of evolution in meaning in the OT, from an original "Yahweh of armies" (i.e., Israel's fighting forces) to "Yahweh of hosts," asserting Yahweh's lordship over all powers in heaven and on earth. This concern with the sovereignty of Yahweh perhaps accounts for the many additions of צְבָאוֹת as part of the divine title at a late stage in the expansion of the Hebrew text of the book of Jeremiah.

c...c Jeremiah 49:18b and 50:40c are precise equivalents, as is also 49:33b (a secondary addition). Jeremiah 51:43b is a similar statement concerning Babylon. בֶּן־אָדָם in all these instances means "human being."

---

[135] J. A. Loader, *A Tale of Two Cities. Sodom and Gomorrah in the Old Testament, early Jewish and early Christian Tradition* (Kampen: J. H. Kok, 1990) 62; cf. Gen 14:8; Deut 29:22 (29:23E); Hos 11:8.

[136] וְאֶת־שְׁכֵנֶיהָ is missing in Isaiah 13:19b.

[137] Rudolph, *Jeremia*, 305.

[138] Marx, "A Propos des doublets," 117.

[139] Janzen, *Studies*, 80. The title יְהוָה צְבָאוֹת appears frequently in Isaiah (e.g., 1:24; 2:12; 3:1; 5:7, 9, 16; 6:3; 13:4, 13). The LXX uniformly transliterates as σαβαωθ in these instances.

Jeremiah 46-49 (OAN)

The remaining verses in Jeremiah 49 regarding Edom, 49:19-22, contain two doublets: 49:19-21=50:44-46 and 49:22=48:40-41, in which the agent of disaster is compared to a lion and an eagle.

12. JEREMIAH 49:19-21=JEREMIAH 50:44-46

JEREMIAH 49:19-21 (EDOM)
19. See,ª like a lionª that comes upᵇ from the jungle of Jordanᵇ to a perennial pasture ᶜ So shall I suddenly make them run away from her,ᶜ and I will appoint over her whomever is chosen. For who is like me? Who will call me to trial? What shepherd can stand before me? 20. Therefore, hear Yahweh's plan which he has madeᵈ for Edomᵈ and ᵉ his purposes that he has devisedᵉ ᶠ against the inhabitants of Teman.ᶠ Surely the shepherd boys shall drag them away and ᶠ their pastureᶠ shall be appalled because of them. 21.ᵍ At the sound of their fall the earth shall tremble;ᵍ ʰ the sound of their cry will be heard at the Red Sea.ʰ

JEREMIAH 50:44-46(BABYLON)
44. See,ª like a lionª that comes up ᵇ from the jungle of the Jordan ᵇ to a perennial pasture ᶜ so shall I suddenly make them run away from her ᶜ and whomever is chosen I shall appoint over her. For who is like me? Who will call me to trial? What shepherd can stand before me? 45. Therefore, hear Yahweh's plan which he has made ᵈ for Babylon ᵈ ᵉ and his purposes that he has devised ᵉ ᵈ against the land of the Chaldeans.ᵈ Surely the shepherd boys shall drag them away and ᶠ (their) pasture ᶠ shall be appalled because of them. 46. ᵍ At the sound of the capture of Babylon the earth shall tremble ᵍ ʰ and (her) cry shall be heard among the nations.ʰ

Textual and Translational Notes

There are slight orthographic and vocalic differences in 49:19-21=50:44-46: נְוֵה (construct), 49:19; נָוֶה, 50:44; אַרְגִּיעָה, 49:19; אַרְגִּעָה, 50:44; אֲרִיצֶנּוּ, 49:19; אֲרוּצֵם, 50:44; יִעֲרָנִי, 49:19; יוֹעֲרֵנִי, 50:44; נְוֵהֶם, 49:20; נָוֶה, 50:45.

ᵃ...ᵃ כְּאַרְיֵה ("like a lion," 49:19; 50:44). Yahweh, the agent of destruction, likens himself to a lion; cf. the use of אַרְיֵה in 4:7; 5:6. In 50:17, "Israel is a hunted sheep driven away by lions."

ᵇ...ᵇ מִגְּאוֹן הַיַּרְדֵּן, literally "from the majesty of the Jordan," 49:19; 50:44 (cf. 12:5). Zechariah 11:3 also uses this phrase and in the same context refers to lions (כְּפִירִים).

ᶜ...ᶜ אֲרִיצֶנּוּ מֵעָלֶיהָ, 49:19; אֲרוּצֵם, 50:44. Holladay proposes an emendation to אָרִיצָה עֲלֶיהָ ("I shall chase her sucklings"), i.e., cohortative form of the verb, with the *he* misread as *nun-waw* in 49:19, and as *mem* in 50:44 (*qere* אֲרִיצֵם).[140] However, a better case can be made for final *mem* as the correct reading, being misread as *nun-waw* in 49:19.[141] This is supported by the LXX, ἐκ διώξω αὐτούς ἀπ'αὐτῆς in both 29:20LXX=49:19MT and 27:44LXX=50:44MT, as well as by Syr and Pseudo-Jonathan in 49:19. מֵעָלֶיהָ אֲרִיצֵם would then be the correct reading in both verses.

^{d...d} אֶל־אֶרֶץ כַּשְׂדִּים, 49:20b; אֶל־יֹשְׁבֵי תֵימָן, 50:45a; אֶל־בָּבֶל, 49:20d; אֶל־אֱדוֹם, 50:45b. Both Edom and Teman occur in 49:7. In 27:45LXX=50:45MT, ἐπὶ τοὺς κατοικοῦντας Χαλδαίους indicates אֶל־יֹשְׁבֵי כַשְׂדִּים as the original text; cf. 51:24, 35MT=28:24, 35LXX. For אֶל־בָּבֶל and כַשְׂדִּים אֶל־אֶרֶץ in 50:45, see the superscription, 50:1.

^{e...e} וּמַחְשְׁבוֹתָיו אֲשֶׁר חָשַׁב, 49:20b; 50:45b.
The combination of חשב and מחשבה occurs also in 11:19; 18:11, 18; 29:11; 49:30 (cf. 2 Sam 14:14; Ezek 38:10; Dan 11:24, 25; Esth 8:3; 9:25). Jeremiah 11:19; 18:18 refer to the plans of enemies directed against Jeremiah; 49:30b to Nebuchadrezzar's plans against "Hazor"; 18:11 to Yahweh's plans against Judah and Jerusalem; 49:20b=50:45b to Yahweh's plans against Edom; 29:11 to Yahweh's plans for the welfare of the exiles. According to Graupner, 11:19 and 18:18 do not represent Deuteronomistic language.[142] The author of 49:19-21=50:44-45b draws freely from Jeremianic vocabulary and phraseology.

^{f...f} נְוֵהֶם ("their pasture," 49:20c); נָוֶה, 50:45c.
Syr, Tg, and Vg support נְוֵהֶם in both instances; the final *mem* has been dropped in 50:45c by haplography, since 50:46=49:21 begins with מִקּוֹל.

^{g...g} מִקּוֹל נִפְלָם רָעֲשָׁה הָאָרֶץ, 49:21;
מִקּוֹל נִתְפְּשָׂה בָבֶל נִרְעֲשָׁה הָאָרֶץ, 50:46.
Jeremiah 50:46 differs from 49:31 in the use of נִתְפְּשָׂה rather than נִפְלָם, by introducing בָּבֶל, and by using the *Niphal* of רעש. The verb תפשׂ (= לכד) occurs in 50:24, 46 and 51:32, 41 regarding the capture of Babylon. נרעשה (50:46) continues the use of the *Niphal*.

^{h...h} צְעָקָה בְּיַם־סוּף נִשְׁמַע קוֹלָהּ, 49:21;
וְזַעֲקָה בַּגּוֹיִם נִשְׁמָע, 50:46.
צְעָקָה is considered to be an older form of זְעָקָה (BDB:858). Both terms are found elsewhere in the book of Jeremiah: צְעָקָה in 25:36; 48:3, 5; זְעָקָה in 18:22; 20:16; 48:4, 34; 51:54. The terms are interchangeable in 48:3-5. The only reference to יַם־סוּף in the book of Jeremiah appears in 49:21 (cf. 1 Kgs 9:26, in which the site of Solomon's fleet-building is located "on the shore of יַם־סוּף in the land of Edom"). In 50:46, Babylon's cry of distress will be heard

---

[140] Holladay, *Jeremiah 2*, 371.
[141] Raphael Weiss, "On Ligatures in the Hebrew Bible (נו = ם)," *JBL* 82 (1963) 188-194.
[142] Graupner, *Auftrag und Geschick*, p. 33 n. 24.

בַּגּוֹיִם ("among the nations"). קוֹלָהּ (49:21), missing in 29:22LXX, is probably a gloss, interpreting צְעָקָה as צַעֲקָתָהּ ("her cry").[143]

Comment

Holladay maintains that 49:19-21 is the primary passage and that 50:44-46 is secondary, a reversal of the judgment of many other commentators.[144] The strongest argument for the priority of 50:44-46 is that earth would tremble at the sound of the capture of Babylon (50:46), but that the fall of Edom (49:21) would hardly be considered an earth-shaking event.[145] The text in 50:44 is preferable to that in 49:19 (see $^{c...c}$ above), but the latter could have suffered in transmission. An open mind may be kept on the question of priority. The passage, however, seems to be an editorial addition in each case.

13. JEREMIAH 49:22 = JEREMIAH 48:40-41   See above, pp. 137-139.

RECURRING PHRASES IN JEREMIAH 49:23-27MT (30:12-16LXX): DAMASCUS

Various considerations make it probable that 49:23-27 is made up of late additions to the OAN. Damascus is not included in the list of those who are to drink of the cup of the wine of Yahweh's wrath, 25:17-26. Presumably, the insertion of 49:23-27 was intended to include the Arameans among other neighbours whose borders were close to those of Israel.[146] The *hapax legomenon* רָפָה in 49:24 is an Aramaic word; Weiser regards this as evidence for a post-exilic origin.[147]

Jeremiah 49:23-25 contains some phrases which occur elsewhere in the OT or in the book of Jeremiah. Hamath and Arpad (49:23) are likened to the turbulent sea (הַשְׁקֵט לֹא יוּכָל, "which cannot be quiet"). Both the imagery and this phrase occur in Isa 57:20 as a description of "the wicked."[148] The phrase צָרָה וַחֲבָלִים אֲחָזַתָּה כַּיּוֹלֵדָה ("anguish and sorrows have taken hold of her as of

---

[143] Rudolph, *Jeremia*, 290.
[144] Holladay, *Jeremiah 2*, 372, 404.
[145] Rudolph (*Jeremia*), "eine gewaltig Übertreibung" (p. 292). However, a similar exaggeration is found in 8:16, where at the neighing of the stallions as the enemy approaches Israel רָעֲשָׁה כָּל־הָאָרֶץ ("the whole earth trembles"). Hyperbolic language is characteristic of prophecy: e.g., 2:20b; 13:19b.
[146] Nicholson, *Jeremiah 2*, 196.
[147] Weiser (*Jeremia*), "the saying against Damascus is of post-exilic origin."
[148] Freedman, *Jeremiah*, 321.

a woman in travail," 49:24b) is missing from the LXX, and has in common with 6:24 and 50:43b the words צָרָה and כַּיּוֹלֵדָה, and with Isa 13:8, חֲבָלִים and כַּיּוֹלֵדָה. Jeremiah 49:25 probably represents a taunt similar to those found in 48:39, introduced by אֵיךְ.[149] The phrase עִיר תְּהִלָּה ("famous city," 49:25) is also used of Moab (48:2); cf. תְּהִלַּת כָּל־הָאָרֶץ in the taunt-song against Babylon (51:41).

The doublet 49:26=50:30 and the following verse 49:27 (with echoes of Amos 1:4, 14) are probably additions by a later hand.[150]

14. JEREMIAH 49:26=JEREMIAH 50:30

JEREMIAH 49:26 (DAMASCUS)
26. [a] Therefore [a] her young men shall fall in her squares and [b] all (her) fighting men [b] shall be destroyed [c] on that day[c] [d] — Oracle of Yahweh of hosts.[d]

JEREMIAH 50:30 (BABYLON)
30.[a] Therefore[a] her young men shall fall in her squares and [b] all her her fighting men[b] shall be destroyed [c] on that day[c] [d] — Oracle of Yahweh. [d]

Textual and Translational Notes

[a...a] לָכֵן, 49:26; 50:30. "Therefore" is entirely appropriate in 50:30, following 50:29, in which Babylon's proud defiance of Yahweh merits judgment. לָכֵן is inappropriate in 49:26, suggesting that 50:30 has been duplicated here.[151]

[b...b] הַמִּלְחָמָה, 49:26; מִלְחַמְתָּהּ, 50:30. The personal pronoun in 50:30 is in keeping with the personal pronouns already used (בִּרְחֹבֹתֶיהָ, בַּחוּרֶיהָ) and is reflected in the threefold use of αὐτῆς in 27:30LXX.

[c...c] בַּיּוֹם הַהוּא, 49:26; 50:30. The phrase is missing in both verses in the LXX. De Vries claims that the expression has probably been added as a gloss.[152] Cf. 39:16, where בַּיּוֹם הַהוּא is also missing in the LXX.

[d...d] צְבָאוֹת, 49:26 (missing in the LXX). The absence of צְבָאוֹת in 50:30 (cf. the LXX) adds weight to the view that this title has been added here to the Hebrew text, as elsewhere in the book of Jeremiah.[153]

---

[149] Jeremiah 49:25 contains a problematic negative לֹא (literally, "the famous city is *not* forsaken") which is explained by Rudolph (*Jeremia*, 292) as a note in the margin by an indignant reader who thinks that only Jerusalem should be recognized as "famous," with the negative לֹא later incorporated in the text. Another explanation is that לֹא is an example of an emphatic *lamedh*; see F. Nötscher, "Zum emphatischen Lamed," *VT* 3 (1953) 372-380.

[150] Weiser, *Jeremia*, 413.
[151] Nicholson, *Jeremiah 2*, 197.
[152] De Vries, *Yesterday, Today and Tomorrow*, 296.
[153] Janzen, *Studies*, 159 (Appendix B).

Comment

The vocabulary employed in 49:26=50:30 occurs in such passages as 6:11 (בַּחוּרִים); 9:20 (בַּחוּרִים מֵרְחֹבוֹת) and 8:14; 25:37 (דמם). In 49:27, "I will kindle a fire in the wall of Damascus and it shall devour the strongholds of Benhadad," the phrase in 49:27a (... וְהִצַּתִּי אֵשׁ בְּחוֹמַת) has its counterpart in Amos 1:14a (cf. הִצִּית אֵשׁ in Jer 11:16 and 49:2, "its villages shall be burned with fire"). וְאָכְלָה אַרְמְנוֹת בֶּן־הֲדָד (49:27b) duplicates Amos 1:4b.

The authors of 49:23-27 are familiar not only with other passages in Jeremiah, but with Amos and Isaiah.

Recurring Phrases in JEREMIAH 49:28-33MT (=30:6-11LXX): Kedar and "the kingdoms of Hazor"

Jeremiah 49:28-33, an OAN poem against the Arab tribes, consists of two strophes ending with the formula נְאֻם יְהוָה, 49:28b-30a, concerning nomadic Bedouin tribes, and 49:31-32, concerning semi-nomadic tribes, followed by a summary in 49:33.[154] Each strophe begins with Yahweh's exhortation to the conquering armies, קוּמוּ עֲלוּ ("rise up, advance," 49:28c, 31a).

Jeremiah 25:23 itemizes Arab tribes who are to drink from Yahweh's cup of the wine of wrath: Dedan, Tema, Buz and אֵת כָּל־קְצוּצֵי פֵאָה ("all who cut the corners of their hair"). The latter phrase (קְצוּצֵי פֵאָה) occurs in 49:32b as well as in 9:25 (9:26E). For the tribes listed in 25:23, Kedar and Hazor are substituted in 49:28, described also as "the people of the east."[155] Kedar is mentioned in 2:10, as well as in Isa 21:16, 17; 42:11 and Ezek 27:21. Hazor (49:28, 30, 33) is clearly not the royal city so prominent in Josh 11:1, 10, 11, 13 and Judg 4:2, 17, but may be considered as a collective name for semi-nomadic Arabs or preferably as referring to those who dwell in unwalled villages.[156] In the present form of the MT, Hazor is treated as a place name,

---

[154] The formula נְאֻם יְהוָה occurs three times in the poem, at 49:30a, 49:31a and 49:32c. Only one occurrence is found in the LXX (30:10LXX=49:32cMT). The formula at 49:31a breaks the continuity of thought and should be deleted.

[155] For בְּנֵי־קֶדֶם (49:28c), see also Gen 29:1; Judg 6:3, 33; Isa 11:14; Ezek 25:4, 10.

[156] Volz, *Jeremia*, 420. For חֲצֵרִים, see Lev 25:31; cf. Isa 42:11, חֲצֵרִים תֵּשֵׁב קֵדָר ("the villages that Kedar inhabits"). Cf. Holladay *Jeremiah 2*, 382-383; H. Orlinsky, "Haser in the Old Testament," *JAOS* (1939) 22-37. Both undertake a careful study of the etymologies of חָצֵר ("an enclosed courtyard, settlement, village"). חָצֵר occurs one hundred and twenty times in prophetic writings in the OT; fifteen times in Jeremiah.

but in view of the probability of the reference to unwalled villages, Carroll prefers to translate "the kingdoms of Hazor" as "village chieftains."[157]

"Nebuchadrezzar, king of Babylon" is specifically mentioned in the superscription, 49:28, and in 49:30b, as the agent of destruction. The reference may be to Nebuchadrezzar's campaign of 599-598 BCE, although there can be no certainty about this.[158]

There are no doublets in 49:28-33, although vocabulary and phrases occur elsewhere in the book of Jeremiah, and in the case of 49:31, in Ezek 38:11. In 49:29, יְרִיעוֹת ("tent-curtains") is also found in 4:10 and 10:20; the phrase מָגוֹר מִסָּבִיב ("terror on every side," cf. 6:25; 20:3, 10; 46:5) is either "the shout of raiders as they pounce on their victims" or a call of distress on the part of the Kedarites.[159] מַחֲשָׁבָה + חָשַׁב ("has formed a plan," i.e., regarding Nebuchadrezzar, 49:30) is a description of Yahweh in his action against Edom in 49:20.[160] Jeremiah 49:31 has parallels in Ezek 38:11, e.g., יוֹשֵׁב לָבֶטַח ("dwelling securely," cf. Ezek 38:11, יֹשְׁבֵי לָבֶטַח); לֹא־דְלָתַיִם וְלֹא־בְרִיחַ לוֹ ("with no gates or bars," cf. Ezek 38:11, וּבְרִיחַ וּדְלָתַיִם אֵין לָהֶם).[161]

As Jones has pointed out, there are several parallels between 49:28-33 and the preceding oracles against Edom: e.g., נֻסוּ ... הֶעְמִיקוּ לָשֶׁבֶת, 49:30 and 49:8; חָשַׁב + מַחֲשָׁבָה, 49:30 and 49:20; אֵידָם ("their calamity," 49:32); אֵיד, 49:8 (cf. 46:21; 48:16); 49:33b and 49:18b, לֹא־יֵשֵׁב שָׁם וְלֹא־יָגוּר בָּהּ בֶּן־אָדָם ("no one shall live there"; "no human being shall dwell in her").[162] Jeremiah 49:33a has the conventional phrase מְעוֹן תַּנִּים ("a haunt of jackals," cf. 9:10; 10:22; 51:37); שְׁמָמָה ("desolation") occurs frequently elsewhere: e.g., 4:27; 6:8; 9:10; 10:22; 12:10; 32:43; 34:22; 49:2; 50:13, usually together with a statement about lack of inhabitants.

---

[157] Carroll, *Jeremiah*, 810. See 30:6LXX, τῇ βασιλίσσῃ τῆς αὐλῆς ("the queen of the palace"). Smothers (*Jeremiah 2*) states, "LXX's rendering of ממלכות as מַלְכַּת 'queen' is not as strange as it may seem because the Assyrian records mention several queens of the Arabs who apparently were the heads of their respective tribes or states" (p. 339).

[158] D. J. Wiseman, *Chronicles of Chaldaean Kings (625-556 BCE) in the British Museum* (London: British Museum Publications Ltd., 1956) 31-32, 71.

[159] See Bright, *Jeremiah*, 336; Holladay, *Jeremiah 2*, 383.

[160] The use of the first person in the verbal forms in 49:32 refers to Yahweh's activity rather than to the actions of Nebuchadrezzar. Apart from the superscriptions, Nebuchadrezzar is not mentioned in the OAN, except in 49:30.

[161] Ezekiel 38:11 also contains the phrase יֹשְׁבִים בְּאֵין חוֹמָה ("dwelling without walls"). This description is in keeping with the view that in 49:30-32 semi-nomadic tribes are seen as under attack. Note also the references to Sheba and Dedan in Ezek 38:13. The prophecies against Gog and Magog appear to be unfulfilled prophecies which have now taken on an eschatological form; see John Wevers, *Ezekiel* (The Century Bible; London: Thomas Nelson, 1969) 283.

[162] Jones, *Jeremiah*, 519-519. Jones claims that "the author belongs firmly in the Jeremiah tradition" (p. 518).

Recurring Phrases in JEREMIAH 49:34-39MT (25:14-26:1LXX): ELAM

The position of 49:34-39MT, at the end of the series of oracles, immediately prior to the oracles directed against Babylon (Jeremiah 50-51), matches 25:25, in which "the kings of Elam" come at the end of the list of nations destined to drink of Yahweh's cup of the wine of wrath, 25:17-25. The LXX, on the other hand, begins the OAN with the oracle against Elam (25:14-26:1LXX) and lists the nations (32:4-12LXX) only at the conclusion of the OAN.

The superscription (49:34) consists of a syntactically awkward phrase found also in 14:1; 46:1; 47:1 (cf. 1:2), together with a statement that the date of the oracle was the accession year of Zedekiah's reign.[163]

The inclusion of the oracle(s) (49:34-39) against Elam in the OAN is to underline the fact that even a nation as distant as Elam would come under Yahweh's judgment "against the nations" (25:31), which included "all the inhabitants of the earth" (25:29).[164] The coming judgment is expressed in an impressive series of nine verbs in the first person singular, denoting Yahweh's purposes against Elam. "I will break the bow of Elam" (49:35) invites comparison with "I will break the bow of Israel" in Hos 1:5.[165] The רוחות ארבע ("four winds," 49:36) occur also in other contexts elsewhere in the OT: Ezek 37:9; Zech 2:6; 6:5; Dan 8:8, implying the action of Yahweh. "I will scatter" (זרה) them to all those winds (49:36) provides a link with 49:32. In 49:37, the phrase מבקשׁי נפשׁם ("those who seek their life") is reminiscent of 19:7; 21:7 (cf. 44:30); "I will bring evil upon" occurs frequently in the book of Jeremiah: 4:6; 6:19; 11:11; 19:3, 15; 23:12; 35:17; 36:31; 44:2; 45:5. For

---

[163] There are no oracles recorded against "the kings of Zimri" or "the kings of Media" (25:25). "All the kings of the north" and "all the kingdoms of the world" are listed in a summarizing statement in 25:26, to which is added וּמֶלֶךְ שֵׁשַׁךְ יִשְׁתֶּה אַחֲרֵיהֶם (missing in the LXX) in order to include Babylon and make the list all-inclusive. שֵׁשַׁךְ is the *athbash* cipher for בָּבֶל (cf. 51:41, where in 28:41LXX the *athbash* is missing in the LXX). In 25:25, זִמְרִי, if emended to זִמְכִּי, could be an *athbash* cipher for עילם (see Felix Perles, "A Miscellany of Lexical and Textual Notes on the Bible," *JQR* NS 2 [1911-1912] 97-132). Regarding the form זִמְכִּי, Perles states, "We need not...be surprised that this unknown word which has certainly an un-Hebrew sound, was at an early period replaced by the otherwise unknown זמרי which as the name of a king was also graphically quite similar. Now we may understand why the four words ואת כל מלכי זמרי are wanting in the Septuagint, being nothing other than a doublet of ואת כל מלכי עילם" (p. 103). Holladay (*Jeremiah 1*, 671) regards 25:25 as a conflate text. Carroll (*Jeremiah*, 503) suggests that "Sheshak" may be a cipher for whatever the great power of the period may have been.

[164] Note the repetition of נְאֻם־יְהוָה in 49:37, 38, 39. Jeremiah 25:19LXX (49:39MT) concludes the passage with λέγει κύριος; the formula is not present in the preceding verses.

[165] See Weinfeld, *Deuteronomy and the Deuteronomic School*, 136. He draws attention to the use of the phrase "break the bow" (שבר + קשׁת) in the treaty literature. However, there is no indication of broken treaty arrangements with distant Elam.

חֲרוֹן אַף ("fierce anger," 49:37), cf. 4:8, 26; 25:37, 38. The phrase כָּלוֹתִי אוֹתָם וְשִׁלַּחְתִּי אַחֲרֵיהֶם אֶת־הַחֶרֶב עַד (49:37) has an exact counterpart in 9:15b. כִּסְאִי ("my throne," 49:38), as Holladay points out, has cosmic connotations in such passages as 1 Kgs 22:19=2 Chron 18:18; Isa 66:1; Ezek 43:7; Ps 9:8; 89:15; 93:2; 97:2; Lam 5:19.[166] מֶלֶךְ וְשָׂרִים ("king and princes," 49:38MT; 25:18LXX; cf. 4:9) becomes *reges et principes* in the Vg (cf. Syr), in keeping with the plural "kings of Elam" in 25:25.[167]

The conventional language, especially the inclusion of a phrase from 9:15b in 49:37, and the reference to Yahweh's throne (49:38), suggest that the oracles against Elam are post-Jeremianic, originating later within the Jeremianic tradition. Elam is included among the OAN to demonstrate the scope of Yahweh's sovereignty over the nations.

An additional verse 49:39MT(=25:19LXX) promises the restoration of Elam's fortunes; for the phrase שׁוּב שְׁבוּת cf. 29:14; 30:3, 18; 31:23; 32:44; 33:7, 11, 26; and in the OAN 48:47 (Moab) and 49:6 (the Ammonites); cf. 46:26, where the phrase is not used, but a similar promise is made regarding Egypt.[168] The universalizing tendency which allows the restoration of the fortunes of foreign nations would appear to be redactional, reflecting a late viewpoint (cf. Isa 19:19–25).[169]

SUMMARY: JEREMIAH 25:1–14 and JEREMIAH 46–49 (OAN)

In all probability Jeremiah 46–49MT represents a separate collection, originally inserted immediately after 25:13 as in the LXX, but later transferred so as to follow Jeremiah 45. The Hebrew text of Jer 25:1–14 contains many additions when compared with the LXX. Jeremiah 46–49 is essentially post-Jeremianic.

RECURRING PHRASES

In both Jer 25:1–14 and Jeremiah 46–49 many phrases are paralleled in other parts of the book of Jeremiah and of the OT. When parallels are missing in the LXX, we are usually dealing with phrases added later to the Hebrew text. Many stereotyped phrases indicate that the additions were made by scribes familiar with the prophetic writings and the Deuteronomistic literature. Although phrases from all parts of the book of Jeremiah appear, leading to the conclusion that editors were well acquainted with the Jeremianic tradition and

---

[166] Holladay, *Jeremiah 2*, 388.

[167] Holladay (*Jeremiah 2*, 387) suspects that "kings" was the original reading and that "kings and princes (i.e., officials)" is a substitution derived from 4:9.

[168] Jeremiah 46:26, 48:47 and 49:6 are not in the LXX text, but represent later additions to the Hebrew text.

[169] Westermann, *Prophetic Oracles of Salvation*, 156–157; 260–261.

were concerned to safeguard the tradition, some of the additions (e.g., hopes of restoration of nations: 46:26b, Egypt; 48:47a, Moab; 49:6, the Ammonites) are very late or address later situations. In order to underline the theme of Yahweh's sovereignty over the nations, the title "Lord of hosts" is added frequently at a time later than the primary LXX translation of the Hebrew text.

DOUBLETS IN THE OAN: JEREMIAH 46-49

Many of the doublets represent late additions to the text, confirming McKane's view of a rolling *corpus*.[170]

1. JEREMIAH 46:27-28=JEREMIAH 30:10-11
This doublet does not fit easily into the context of either chapter; 30:10-11MT is missing in the LXX and was a later addition in the text of Jeremiah 30 to spell out the promise in 30:7. The author of this *Heilsorakel* stands in the Jeremianic tradition, but has come under the influence of the Deuteronomist and Deutero-Isaiah.

2. JEREMIAH 48:5ab=ISAIAH 15:5bc
Volz's suggestion that Jer 48:5ab (=Isa 15:5bc) was originally written in the margin as part of the Isaiah material used in 48:34-36 and then wrongly inserted in the parallel column between 48:4 and 48:6 seems plausible to me.[171]

3. JEREMIAH 48:29-33 and ISAIAH 16:6-10
The Isaiah passage has been used selectively and has been inserted in Jeremiah 48 as an additional oracle against Moab. Copyists have been somewhat careless prior to the standardization of the text. The texts have suffered in transmission.

4. JEREMIAH 48:34-39 and ISAIAH 15:2-7
The author of 48:34-39 not only draws on Isaiah 15 and 16, but is thoroughly familiar with vocabulary found elsewhere in the book of Jeremiah.

5. JEREMIAH 48:40-41 (MOAB)=JEREMIAH 49:22 (EDOM)
Janzen's proposal that the couplet came into Jeremiah 48, secondarily inserted as a gloss on 48:24 and taken into the wrong column of the manuscript (48:40, 41), with names appropriately changed, seems to provide the best explanation.[172]

6. JEREMIAH 48:43-44=ISAIAH 24:17-18ab
The date of Jer 48:43-44 is uncertain and may be early (Jeremianic?). The couplet has been inserted in the Isaiah Apocalypse and given a universal application.

---

[170] McKane, *Jeremiah 1*, lxxxiii.
[171] Volz, *Jeremia*, 405.
[172] Janzen, *Studies*, 59, 94.

7. JEREMIAH 48:45-46=NUMBERS 21:27-29; 24:17c

The fact that 48:45-46 is missing in the LXX makes it probable that this unit has been added to the Hebrew text at a late date by a scribe who was familiar with early passages in Numbers (and in Amos), in which the fate of Moab is announced.

8. JEREMIAH 49:9=OBADIAH 5

A common source (perhaps oral) has been drawn upon and used in different ways.

9. JEREMIAH 49:14-16=OBADIAH 1-4 (EDOM)

This doublet (of uncertain date) has probably been drawn from a common source and has suffered during transmission.

10. JEREMIAH 49:17; 50:13; 18:16; 19:8

Traditional prophetic phrases have been combined and interaction among parallel texts has taken place.

11. JEREMIAH 49:18 (EDOM)=JEREMIAH 50:40 (BABYLON)

This doublet may have been borrowed from Isa 13:19b and applied to both Edom and Babylon.

12. JEREMIAH 49:19-21 (EDOM)=JEREMIAH 50:44-46 (BABYLON)

An open mind may be kept on the question of priority, but in each case this unit is an editorial addition.

13. JEREMIAH 49:22=JEREMIAH 48:40-41 (see #5 above).

14. JEREMIAH 49:26 (DAMASCUS)=JEREMIAH 50:30 (BABYLON)

Jeremiah 49:26 has borrowed 50:30 to describe the fate of Damascus.

CHAPTER EIGHT

RECURRING PHRASES AND DOUBLETS IN JEREMIAH 50–51: ORACLES AGAINST BABYLON

The Content of Jeremiah 50 and 51 (LXX: 27 and 28): BABYLON

Two lengthy chapters (110 verses) contain oracles directed against Babylon proclaiming Babylon's destruction, to be brought about by a nation "out of the north" (50:3). A direct reference to the Medes is made in 51:11 and a summons to the nations in 51:27, 28 in the phrase (twice repeated): עֲלִיהָ גוֹיִם קַדְּשׁוּ ("hallow the nations for war against her," NEB), in which the Medes are again specifically mentioned (51:28; cf. Isa 13:17).[1] The name of Cyrus does not appear, whereas DI (Isa 44:28; 45:1) names Cyrus as Yahweh's shepherd, anointed to subdue nations. Since the conquest of Babylon by Cyrus (539 BCE) was not accompanied by widespread destruction and slaughter, we may assume that the oracles against Babylon in Jeremiah 50 and 51 were collected together about the middle of the sixth century BCE, at a time before Cyrus had conquered the Medes.[2] Subsequently, many scribal additions were made to the original collection, as will be demonstrated in the discussions which follow.

Repetitions occur in the "Song of the Sword" (50:35–38), where חֶרֶב is repeated five times, and in the "Hammer-Song" (51:20–23), in which נִפַּצְתִּי ("I

---

[1] Jeremiah 51:27 names Ararat, Minni and Ashkenaz as nations preparing for war against Babylon. The Minni are the Mannaeans, according to H. W. F. Saggs, *The Greatness That Was Babylon* (London: Sidgwick & Jackson, 1988) 108. Ashkenaz probably should be understood as "the Scythians." Holladay discusses these kingdoms in detail (*Jeremiah 2*, 426–427). The Medes are accompanied by אֶת־פַּחוֹתֶיהָ וְאֶת־כָּל־סְגָנֶיהָ ("their governors and all their prefects," 51:28; cf. 51:23, 57).

[2] Jones, *Jeremiah*, 521.

break in pieces") occurs nine times. These "songs" vehemently express the expected utter destruction of Babylon. As in Ps 137:8, the theme of requital (שׁלם *Piel*) for what Babylon has done in Zion is prominent (50:29; 51:6, 24, 56). Babylon's pride (50:29, זדה; 50:32, זָדוֹן) and idolatry (50:2, 38; 51:17, 44, 47) merit Yahweh's vengeance.[3]

Interspersed among the oracles directed against Babylon and usually regarded as late additions are assurances that Israel/Judah will be restored: 50:4-7, 17-20; 51:5, 10.[4] Certain ideas in these units are paralleled in other oracles of hope in the book of Jeremiah: e.g., 50:4, וּבְכוֹ יֵלֵכוּ ("weeping as they come," cf. 31:9); 50:5, בְּרִית עוֹלָם ("an everlasting covenant," cf. 32:40). Yahweh is Israel's מִקְוֵה ("hope") in 50:7 (cf. 14:8, 22). עָוֹן ("iniquity") and חַטֹּאת ("sins") will no longer be found in Judah (50:20; cf. 31:34), because of Yahweh's pardon (סלח, 50:20; 31:34). Yahweh is "the Holy One of Israel" (51:5; cf.50:29), who has not forsaken Israel and Judah.

Boadt asserts: "Probably words of Jeremiah make up the bulk of the material" in Jeremiah 50-51.[5] A major problem with this view, however, is the fact that elsewhere Jeremiah's stance is always strongly pro-Babylonian in the sense that the Babylonians are regarded as Yahweh's agent in bringing about the catastrophes of 597 and 587 BCE. The harsh statements against Babylon in Jeremiah 50-51 are not readily harmonized with the contents of Jeremiah's letter to the exiles, especially his counsel to pray to Yahweh for Babylon, "for in its welfare you will find your welfare" (29:7). Carroll expresses the difficulty clearly: "It is difficult to see how Jeremiah could have been advocating submission (27) or surrender (38) to the Babylonians and yet *at the same time* (cf. 51:59) have been proclaiming 51:14 or 51:25-40."[6] Jeremiah may well have believed that the exiles would eventually return to the homeland many years later, a view reflected in such passages as 27:7; 29:10. This expectation involved the inevitable destruction of Babylon for the authors of

---

[3] The noun נְקָמָה occurs in 50:15, 28; 51:6, 11, 36; cf. 46:10; 11:20=20:12. The reference is always to the vengeance of Yahweh. Cf. the verb נקם in 5:9, 29; 9:9.

[4] Westermann, *Prophetic Oracles of Salvation*, 155. Holladay (*Jeremiah 2*, 403), however, considers 50:4-7, 17-20 to be authentic to Jeremiah.

[5] Lawrence Boadt, *Jeremia 26-52, Habakkuk, Zephaniah, Nahum* (Wilmington: Michael Glazier, 1982) 139. Cf. Holladay (*Jeremiah 2*), "...eighty-two verses or portions of verses are genuine to Jrm" (p. 401).

[6] Carroll, *Jeremiah*, 816. On the other hand, Smothers (*Jeremiah 26-52*) claims: "It is possible to find room in Jeremiah's preaching for both submission to Babylon according to the Lord's plan for Judah in the short term and for preaching encouragement to the exiles through the oracles against Babylon" (p. 364). However, this view does not do justice to the malicious and vengeful character of the oracles against Babylon, e.g., 51:34-37. Cf. Ronald Clements, *Jeremiah* (Atlanta: John Knox, 1988) 263.

25:12-14, 26 (25:14, 26bMT are missing in the LXX) and are best taken as editorial additions.[7]

The prose passage at the conclusion of Jeremiah 50-51 (51:59-64; cf. 50:1) attributes these oracles to Jeremiah. Seraiah, the brother of Baruch, as שַׂר מְנוּחָה ("quartermaster," 51:59), accompanied Zedekiah to Babylon in 594 BCE, in all probability to pay tribute to Nebuchadrezzar.[8] In this account, Jeremiah has entrusted Seraiah with a scroll, in which Jeremiah has written oracles against Babylon.[9] In a symbolic action, Seraiah is to read "all these words" and then throw the scroll, weighted down with a stone, into the Euphrates, to symbolize Yahweh's intention that Babylon will likewise sink, never to rise again (59:61-64). Questions are left unanswered regarding whether the symbolic action was to be performed (perhaps secretly) in the presence of the deportees alone or as a direct prophetic challenge to the might of Babylon, a rebellious act which could hardly have taken place without being followed by swift punishment. Of all the symbolic actions (13:1-11; 18:1-12; 19:1-15; 32:9-15; 43:8-13), this particular action does not involve the physical presence of Jeremiah.

Jeremiah 51:59, the superscription, is a longer text in the LXX than in the MT. Yahweh (κύριος) commands Jeremiah to speak (εἰπεῖν) to Seraiah.[10] The Greek text is in conformity with 51:62, which expresses Yahweh's intention to destroy Babylon. Wanke draws attention to the verbal similarity of 51:59 to 45:1, which introduces Jeremiah's response to Baruch's lament (45:3).[11] Jeremiah 45:1 refers to Baruch having written "these words" in a scroll at Jeremiah's dictation (cf. 51:60, "Jeremiah wrote in a scroll"). According to Taylor "these words" (45:1) point to 36:2 ("Take a scroll") and 36:32 ("Jeremiah took another scroll") and provide a link with the immediately

---

[7] Carroll (*Jeremiah*) refers to the "lateness of the material" (p. 493).

[8] Vg, *cum Sedekia*, supports the MT reading אֶת ("with"). McKane (*Jeremiah 2*, 1351) maintains that Zedekiah went with Seraiah to Babylon, to renew his pledge of loyalty. See also Holladay, *Jeremiah 2*, 433-434.

[9] סֵפֶר אֶחָד (51:60) probably implies "a single leaf" according to Wanke, *Untersuchungen*, 137. W. D. Stacey (*Prophetic Drama in the Old Testament* [London: Epworth Press, 1990] 167-171) sees 51:59-64 as a drama in two acts: (a) the production of the scroll; (b) casting the scroll into the Euphrates. For Stacey, the most probable hypothesis is "that an anti-Babylonian enthusiast produced the first act under the influence of the incident recorded in Jer 36. Subsequently, he, or someone of the same persuasion, gilded the lily by adding verses 63-64a with the second act and the curse formula" (p. 170). Robert M. Paterson ("Reinterpretation in the Book of Jeremiah," *JSOT* 28 [1984] 37-46) claims that the original intention of casting the weighted scroll into the Euphrates was to negate the prophecies against Babylon. Only later was the symbolic action interpreted as a prediction of the doom of Babylon.

[10] The longer LXX reading is supported by Holladay, *Jeremiah 2*, 432-433.

[11] Wanke, *Untersuchungen*, 133-136.

preceding Jeremiah 44.[12] The significant reference to the "fourth year of Jehoiakim" (45:1; cf. 25:1; 36:1; 46:2) "functions as a code-word for judgment," and has its counterpart in 51:59, which has its setting in the fourth year of the reign of Zedekiah.[13] Dearman, in a careful study of Jeremiah 36, discusses the importance of scribal activity in the culture of Judah, especially the role of scribes in "the reading, preservation *and interpretation* of Yahweh's word."[14] Identification of the scribes with "those circles known as Deuteronomistic historians" is not a foregone conclusion. There is good reason to believe that scribes, especially Baruch, played a prominent role in Jeremiah's lifetime.[15] Scribes were among those responsible for shaping and preserving "Jeremianic" traditions throughout the period of the exile and subsequently. Many of the doublets in the OAN demonstrate a knowledge of prophetic literature, while the historical appendix, Jeremiah 52, is clearly based on 2 Kings. These are good examples of the way in which scribal activity is expressed in the book of Jeremiah in maintaining the continuity of the "Jeremianic" tradition.

So far as 51:59-64 is concerned, we may view this prose unit as a late addition to the oracles of Jeremiah 50 and 51, embodying a tradition that the scribe Seraiah performed the action ascribed to him. The purpose of this narrative unit is to establish the authenticity of the oracles by claiming that Jeremiah was directly responsible for them. Jeremiah 28:59LXX (=51:59MT) goes even beyond this, claiming that Yahweh commanded Jeremiah to speak to Seraiah and instruct him to carry out the symbolic action of reading the scroll and casting it into the Euphrates.[16]

A later generation of scribes, who considered Jeremiah to be responsible for every oracle recorded in a book that was still in the process of composition, would not be disturbed, as modern scholars are, by discrepancies and inconsistencies between Jeremiah's pro-Babylonian attitude and what they

---

[12] Marion A. Taylor, "Jeremiah 45: The Problem of Placement," *JSOT* (1987) 79-98.

[13] Taylor, "Jeremiah 45," p. 88. The fourth year of Jehoiakim (605/604 BCE) was the year in which the critical battle of Carchemish took place, establishing Babylonian ascendancy over the nations of the middle East and Egypt. The fourth year of Zedekiah (594 BCE) may have been the year when envoys from Edom, Moab, the Ammonites, Tyre and Sidon, came to Jerusalem prepared to rebel against Babylon. For the superscription to this account (27:1), see the reconstruction proposed by Holladay, *Jeremiah* 2, 112.

[14] J. A. Dearman, "My Servants the Scribes; Composition and Content in Jeremiah 36," *JBL* 109 (1990) 403-421, esp. 411.

[15] Dearman, "My Servants the Scribes," 403.

[16] See Holladay, *Jeremiah* 2, 432-433. He claims that 51:59MT represents a damaged text.

regarded as the inevitability of Babylon's ultimate destruction.[17] As a prophet to the nations (1:10), Jeremiah would be expected to proclaim such a message.

Common Ideas and Vocabulary in Jeremiah 50-51 and the OAN of Jeremiah 46-49

As noted by Jones, certain ideas and vocabulary are common to Jeremiah 50-51 and the OAN of Jeremiah 46-49.[18] Babylon is described as זָדוֹן ("the proud one") in 50:32 (cf. 49:16, Edom), who "shall stumble and fall" (verbs כשל and נפל; cf. 46:6, 12). A nation "out of the north" (50:3; cf. 50:41=6:22) or "a company of great nations" (50:9) will be the agent of Babylon's destruction.[19] A key-word is חֶרֶב ("sword," 50:16, 35-38), found also in 46:10, 14, 16; 47:6; 48:2; 49:37.[20] Especially interesting is the phrase הַיּוֹנָה מִפְּנֵי חֶרֶב ("because of the sword of the oppressor," 50:16; cf. 46:16).[21] The LXX (27:16; 26:16) translates the phrase in both instances as ἀπὸ προσώπου μαχαίρας Ἑλληνικῆς.[22] Does this suggest that the translator, from a different historical perspective, is thinking of the campaigns of Alexander the Great?[23]

The authors of these oracles were also familiar with vocabulary occurring elsewhere in the book of Jeremiah. Jeremiah 50:13 has a number of parallels: קֶצֶף יְהוָה ("the wrath of Yahweh," cf. 10:10; 21:5; 32:37); שְׁמָמָה ("desolation," cf. 6:8; 9:10; 12:10); 50:13b parallels 19:8 (cf. 49:17); צֳרִי ("balm," 51:8) also occurs in 8:22. The formula לָכֵן הִנֵּה יָמִים בָּאִים ("behold, days are coming," 51:47, 52) is found in 7:32=19:6 and 16:14=23:7, as well as in the OAN at 48:12 and 49:2. The *athbash* שֵׁשַׁךְ, Sheshak (=Babylon), is introduced at 51:41a and at 25:26, but is absent from the LXX in both passages. We can only speculate regarding this intrusion. Carroll suggests the use of magical spells against Babylon.[24] A codeword for "Babylon" is inappropriate in

---

[17] At an even later date, the book of Daniel envisages Yahweh's lordship over history, in which successive empires are all doomed to ultimate destruction. As Macchi ("Les doublets") has observed, the placement in the MT of the OAN at the end of the book of Jeremiah, rather than in the earlier position in the LXX, testifies to a late stage (Hellenistic) in the formation of the book of Jeremiah, governed by an apocalyptic theology, where Babylon becomes the symbol "de l'empire du mal" (p. 143 n. 74).

[18] Jones, *Jeremiah*, 521.

[19] References to "the north" occur in 46:6, 10, 20, 24; 47:2; 51:48.

[20] חֶרֶב often occurs in the triad "sword, famine, pestilence" elsewhere in the book of Jeremiah.

[21] Note also מִפְּנֵי חֲרוֹן הַיּוֹנָה ("because of the *anger* of the oppressor," 25:38), where some manuscripts, LXX and Tg read חֶרֶב.

[22] Reading הַיְּוָנִיָּה for הַיּוֹנָה.

[23] Alexander entered Egypt in 332 BCE and Babylon in 331 BCE.

[24] Carroll, *Jeremiah*, 500, 846. Carroll also explains the *athbash* in 51:1 (קָמָי =כַּשְׂדִּים-לֵב) as the vestige of an incantatory practice (pp. 837-838). This interpretation, however, is considered "dubious" by McKane, *Jeremiah 2*, 1296. Cf. Bernard Gosse, "Le

51:38-44, where Babylon is directly mentioned several times. Perhaps an original marginal ejaculation (Sheshak!), incantatory in intention, was later taken into the text.

Jeremiah 50-51 contains a number of doublets 50:16b=Isaiah 13:14b; 50:23b=51:41b; 50:32b=21:14b; 50:39b-40a=Isa 13:19b; 50:41-43=6:22-24; 50:44-46=49:19-21; 51:15-19=10:12-16; 51:39b=51:57b; 51:58d=Hab 2:13b.

1. JEREMIAH 50:16b=ISAIAH 13:14b

JEREMIAH 50:16b
16b. Every one shall turn to his own people, and every one ^{b} shall flee^b ^{a}to his own land.^{a}

ISAIAH 13:14b
14b. Every one shall turn to his own people, and every one ^{b} shall flee^b ^{a}to his own land.^{a}

Textual and Translational Notes

a...a לְאַרְצוֹ, 50:16b; אֶל־אַרְצוֹ, Isa 13:14b.
b...b יָנֻסוּ, 50:16b; יָנוּסוּ, Isa 13:14b.

Except for these minor changes, Jer 50:16b and Isa 13:14b are identical. Many manuscripts in 50:16b read אֶל־אַרְצוֹ, in conformity with Isa 13:14b.

Comment

Is it possible to establish the relationship between the two passages, in view of the fact that the unit 50:39-40 also has points in common with Isa 13:19b-22 and Isa 34:11-17? In the case of 50:39-40, the redactor appears to have drawn on the Isaiah passages.[25] The situation is more complicated in the case of 50:16b=Isa 13:14b. Isaiah 13, מַשָּׂא בָּבֶל ("the oracle concerning Babylon"), may be divided into three units: Isa 13:2-8; 13:9-16; 13:17-22. Isaiah 13:17-22 refers to the Medes as the agent of Babylon's destruction (cf. Jer 51:11). However, the first two units envisage "the day of Yahweh" (Isa 13:6, 9), a day of judgment for the whole earth (Isa 13:5; cf. vv. 9, 13). Within the second unit, Isa 13:14b states, "like a hunted gazelle ... every one shall turn to his own people, and every one shall flee to his own land" (cf. Jer

---

malédiction contre Babylone de Jérémie 51,59-64 et les rédactions du livre de Jérémie," *ZAW* 98 (1986) 383-389. Gosse does not suggest incantation as such; he regards the oracles against Babylon in Jeremiah 50-51 as turning back against Babylon oracles originally pronounced against Jerusalem (e.g., 50:41-43=6:22-24).

[25] See below, pp. 172-173. Jeremiah 49:18 is probably dependent on 50:40 (see above, chap. seven, pp. 153-155). Jeremiah 49:33b (regarding Hazor) also parallels 49:18b), while 49:33a contains the phrase מְעוֹן תַּנִּים ("a haunt of jackals"), present in 9:10; 10:22; 51:37 (cf. נְוֵה תַנִּים, Isa 34:13).

50:16b). It is clear that this flight to the homeland is understood quite differently in the two passages. Isaiah 13:14b refers to the desperate flight of foreigners, in which many who escape temporarily will still be destroyed. On the other hand, Jer 50:16b sees the fall of Babylon as liberation for exiles, the occasion for them to return home (cf. 50:8). Jeremiah 50:17-20 is a prose insertion which looks to the restoration of Israel (50:19). The historical perspective is that of Israel, devoured first by Assyria and then Babylon. These nations become the object of Yahweh's punishment, prior to the idealized future (50:20) which is in store for Israel. In its final form, Isaiah 13 universalizes the doom of Babylon, now a symbol for world-judgment.[26] Since Isaiah 13 in its final form is undoubtedly late, the relationship between this chapter and Jeremiah 50-51 is ambiguous.[27] The most likely view is that selective borrowing from an earlier form of Isaiah 13 is found in Jer 50:16b (=Isa 13:14b) and in Jer 50:39-40 (cf. Isa 13:20a-21; 34:14a).

2. JEREMIAH 50:23b=JEREMIAH 51:41b

How Babylon has become a spectacle of horror among the nations![28]

Comment

The doublet 50:23b=51:41b appears in identical form, with slight variations in the LXX translation, and is in each case coupled with another אֵיךְ saying (50:23a and 51:41a). Babylon, which has caused other nations to be seen as a spectacle of horror, has now herself become a שַׁמָּה, in an ironic, mocking lament. Jeremiah 51:41a(MT) contains the *athbash* שֵׁשַׁךְ, unexpected in a context in which בָּבֶל is named several times. In Jeremiah 28:41aLXX the *athbash* is missing; cf. 32:26LXX, which parallels 25:26MT, except for the final words containing the *athbash*, וּמֶלֶךְ שֵׁשַׁךְ יִשְׁתֶּה אַחֲרֵיהֶם. In each case, שֵׁשַׁךְ is best taken as a secondary intrusion.[29]

3. JEREMIAH 50:30=JEREMIAH 49:26.
See above, chap. seven, pp. 158-159.

---

[26] Isaiah 13:2 begins with the call to שְׂאוּ־נֵס ("raise a signal"). נשׂא followed by נֵס is found also in Isa 5:26; 11:12; 18:3, as well as in Jer 50:2; 51:12, 27, always pointing to impending judgment.

[27] Kaiser (*Isaiah 13-39*, 2) claims that the older, probably post-exilic prophecy, has now become proto-apocalyptic.

[28] McKane's translation, 1996: 1271, 1275. שַׁמָּה appears elsewhere in the OAN in the sense of "a spectacle of horror," e.g., 49:12, 17 (Edom); cf. 5:30; 25;9; 29:18; 44:12.

[29] Janzen, *Studies*, p. 230 n. 3.

4. JEREMIAH 50:32b=JEREMIAH 21:14b

JEREMIAH 50:32b
32b. ª I will kindle a fire ª
ᵇ in her cities ᵇ and it shall
devour ᶜ all that is round
about him.ᶜ

JEREMIAH 21:14b
14b. ª I will kindle a fireª
ᵇ in her forest ᵇ and it
shall devour ᶜ all that is
round about her. ᶜ

Textual and Translational Notes

ª...ª וְהִצַּתִּי אֵשׁ, 50:32b; 21:14b; cf. 17:27; 21:14; 32:29; 43:12; 49:27; 50:32 and Amos 1:14.

ᵇ...ᵇ בְּעָרָיו ("in his cities," 50:32b); בְּיַעְרָהּ ("in her forest," 21:14b). The use of masc. pronom. suffixes in 50:32b (unusual in addressing a city, where fem. suffixes would be expected) is to be explained by the masc. זָדוֹן ("the proud one"), as the addressee. Although Carroll and Jones regard the reference in 21:14b to "her forest" as poetical or proverb-like imagery, a good case can be made that the allusion was originally to the royal palace in Jerusalem, made of cedars of Lebanon (cf. 1 Kgs 7:2; 10:17, 21; Isa 22:8).³⁰ The LXX uses the phrase ἐν τῷ δρυμῷ αὐτῆς both in 21:14b and 27:32b (=50:32bMT), which militates against any emendation of בְּיַעְרָהּ and suggests that בְּיַעְרָהּ was the reading in both texts in the Hebrew *Vorlage*, but was later changed to בְּעָרָיו in 50:32b.

ᶜ...ᶜ כָּל־סְבִיבֹתָיו ("all that is round about him," 50:32b);
כָּל־סְבִיבֹתֶיהָ ("all that is round about her," 21:14b).
The masc. suffix in 50:32b refers to זָדוֹן. The LXX translates as πάντα τὰ κύκλῳ αὐτῆς in each instance, which makes improbable the suggestion that an emendation using the noun סְבֹךְ ("thicket"), with appropriate suffixes, should be made.³¹

Comment

Jeremiah 50:32b (וְהִצַּתִּי אֵשׁ בְּעָרָיו וְאָכְלָה כָּל־סְבִיבֹתָיו) is best taken as drawn from 21:14, since the unit 50:31-32 is an amalgam of quotations found elsewhere in the book of Jeremiah: (a) הִנְנִי אֵלֶיךָ ("behold, I am against you," 50:31; cf. 21:13); (b) עֵת פְּקַדְתִּיךָ ("the time when I will punish you," 50:31;

---

³⁰ Carroll, *Jeremiah*, 415; Jones, *Jeremiah*, 284. Nicholson (*Jeremiah 2*, 180) points out that the descriptions in 21:13 do not fit Jerusalem and that an anonymous poem originally concerning another city has been inserted here and applied to Jerusalem.

³¹ Rudolph, *Jeremiah*, 138. Rudolph is following Cornill.

cf. 6:15; 49:8); (c) וְנָפַל ... וְכָשַׁל ("shall stumble and fall," 50:32; cf. 46:6, 16).³²

5. JEREMIAH 50:39-40 and ISAIAH 13:19-22

Although 50:39-40 and Isa 13:9-22 are not exact doublets, they share many phrases in common.

JEREMIAH 50:39-40
39. Therefore ᵃ desert beasts ᵃ shall dwell with ᵇ hyenas,ᵇ and ᶜ desert owls ᶜ shall dwell in her; ᵈ she shall be inhabited no more for ever and no one shall dwell (there) for all generations.ᵈ
40. ᵉ As when God overthrew Sodom and Gomorrah and their neighbour (cities)ᵉ — Oracle of Yahweh — ᶠ no one shall live there, no human being shall dwell in her.ᶠ

ISAIAH 13:19-22
19. And Babylon, the glory of kingdoms, the splendour and pride of the Chaldeans, ᵉ will be like Sodom and Gomorrah when God overthrew them.ᵉ 20. ᵈ She shall never be inhabited and no one shall dwell (there) for all generations;ᵈ no Arab shall pitch his tent there no shepherds shall make (their flocks) lie down there. 21. But ᵃ hyenas ᵃ shall lie down there and her houses shall be full of howling creatures; ᶜ desert owls ᶜ shall dwell there and demons shall dance there; 22. ᵈ desert beasts ᵈ shall cry out in her citadels (reading בְּאַרְמְנוֹתֶיהָ; cf. LXX) and jackals in the pleasant palaces. Her time is close at hand; and her days will not be prolonged.

Textual and Translational Notes

ᵃ⁻ᵃ   צִיִּים ("desert beasts," 50:39; Isa 13:21; 27:39LXX(=50:39MT) ἰνδάλματα ("apparitions"); Isa 13:21LXX θηρία ("wild beasts").³³

---

³² The phrase וְהִצַּתִּי אֵשׁ ("I will kindle a fire") is a phrase originally found in Amos 1:14.
³³ McKane (*Jeremiah 2*, 1284) translates צִיִּים as "desert beasts." Cf. Nicholson (*Jeremiah 2*, 210), "marmots." See also Bright (*Jeremiah*, 355), "goblins" ("not animals but uncanny beings of some sort").

b...b אִיִּים (אוֹה III) "jackals," "hyenas" (50:39; Isa 13:22).³⁴ Jeremiah 27:39LXX has taken אִיִּים to be a reference to "islands" (אוה I); Isa 13:22LXX, ὀνοκένταυροι ("demons," cf. Isa 34:11, 14LXX).

c...c בְּנוֹת יַעֲנָה ("desert owls," 50:39; Isa 13:21; 34:13).³⁵ 27:39LXX θυγατέρες σειρήνων, literally "daughters of Sirens"; Isa 13:21LXX, σειρῆνες ("monsters").

Selective borrowing has taken place; the Jeremiah passage does not include אֹחִים ("howling creatures," Isa 13:21), שְׂעִירִים ("satyrs, demons," Isa 13:21; 34:14) or תַּנִּים ("jackals," Isa 13:22; 34:13; cf. Jer 9:10; 10:22; 49:33). The thought in Isaiah oscillates between wild animals and monstrous beings of some kind; in any case, no human beings will dwell in such terrifying places (50:39b, 40c; Isa 13:20).

d...d Jeremiah 50:39b duplicates Isa 13:20, but adds עוֹד before לָנֶצַח. In 27:39LXX, the second phrase (וְלֹא תִשְׁכּוֹן עַד־דּוֹר וָדוֹר) is missing, although present in Isa 13:20LXX. This phrase, if not present in the Hebrew *Vorlage* of LXX (Jeremiah), may have been subsequently added to the Hebrew text by a scribe who wished to add the balancing phrase from Isa 13:20.

e...e כְּמַהְפֵּכַת אֱלֹהִים אֶת־סְדֹם וְאֶת־עֲמֹרָה וְאֶת־שְׁכֵנֶיהָ (50:40a=Isa 13:19b; cf. Jer 49:18a; 23:14b). See chap. five, p. 82.

f...f לֹא־יֵשֵׁב שָׁם אִישׁ וְלֹא־יָגוּר בָּהּ בֶּן־אָדָם׃ (50:40b=49:18b, 33b). See chap. seven, p. 154 (note ᶜ⋯ᶜ).

6. JEREMIAH 50:40=JEREMIAH 49:18 has been discussed fully above; see chap. seven, pp. 153-155.

Comment

Janzen sets out 50:39-40 and Isa 13:19-22 in parallel columns for comparison.³⁶ He draws attention to the way selection has been made from the Isaiah material and reshaped, so that "... Jer.v.39 is a literary production, and not just a scribal gloss reminiscent of Isa 13."³⁷ This is in keeping with the view put forward in the present study that a learned scribe, familiar with the text of Isaiah (e.g., Isa 13:19-22 and probably Isa 34:13-14), as well as with the OAN oracles in Jeremiah (50:40=49:18 Edom; 49:33 Hazor), has composed and appended this near-doublet.

The remainder of Jeremiah 50 consists of two other added doublets (50:41-43=6:22-26 and 50:44-46=49:19-21), both introduced by הִנֵּה.

---

³⁴ JB "jackals"; Holladay (*Jeremiah 2*, 395), "ghouls."
³⁵ "Ostriches" RSV, JB; cf. Vg.
³⁶ Janzen, *Studies*, 60.
³⁷ Janzen, *Studies*, p. 210 n. 71.

7. JEREMIAH 50:41-43 = JEREMIAH 6:22-24

JEREMIAH 50:41-43
41. Look, a people is coming [b] from the north;[b] a great nation [c] and many kings[c] are stirring from the farthest parts of the earth. 42. They lay hold of bow and spear;[d] they [d] are cruel and show no mercy. Their sound roars like the sea, they ride upon horses,[e] every soldier deployed for battle,[e] against you, [f] O daughter of Babylon.[f] 43. [g] The king of Babylon has heard the report of them,[g] [h] and his hands have fallen helpless;[h] [i] anguish has seized him, writhing as of a woman in travail.[i]

JEREMIAH 6:22-24
22. [a] This is what Yahweh has said:"Look, a people is coming [b] from a northern land,[b] a great nation is stirring from the farthest parts of the earth. 23. They lay hold of bow and spear, [d] they [d] are cruel and show no mercy. Their sound roars like the sea, they ride upon horses, [e] every soldier deployed for battle,[e] against you, [f] O daughter of Zion!"[f] 24.[g] We have heard the report of it; [g] [h] our hands have fallen helpless; [h] [i]anguish has seized us, writhing as of a woman in travail. [i]

Note the orthographic differences, e.g., יֵעֹרוּ, 50:41; יֵעוֹר, 6:22; וְכִידֹן, 50:41; וְכִידוֹן, 6:23. Jeremiah 6:22-24 shows a preference for *matres lectiones*.

Textual and Translational Notes

[a...a] כֹּה אָמַר יְהוָה, 6:22. The introductory formula applies only to 6:22-23 in the larger unit 6:22-26. Jeremiah 6:22-23 continues the series of dire warnings concerning the threat from the north (4:5; 5:13; 6:1-8). The address is to the "daughter of Zion" (6:23; cf. "O daughter of my people," 6:26), but the change to the first person plural in 6:24 (שָׁמַעְנוּ; cf. also עָלֵינוּ, 6:26) is rather awkward. Since 6:22-24 has been adapted in 50:41-43 to apply to the "daughter of Babylon," with a transition to the third person singular in 51:43, the introductory formula has not been taken over.[38]

[b...b] מִצָּפוֹן (50:41); מֵאֶרֶץ צָפוֹן (6:22)— a minor adaptation. The "foe from the north" remains anonymous in Jeremiah 4-6, and is designated as עַם ... מִצָּפוֹן ("a people ... from the north") in 50:41. Rowley, partly to establish an early date for the oracles of Jeremiah 4-6, supported the view that the Scythians were the

---

[38] Macchi ("Les Doublets") draws attention to the careful way in which the oracle in 6:22-24 has been reapplied in 50:41-43, so that בַּת־צִיּוֹן (6:23) becomes בַּת־בָּבֶל (50:42).

original "foe from the north" described in these chapters.³⁹ As early as 1913, Wilke had raised doubts about the Scythian hypothesis.⁴⁰ Modern commentators have largely abandoned this hypothesis, either in favour of the view that the reference is not geographical or that the Babylonians are definitely in mind.⁴¹

ᶜ⁻⁻⁻ᶜ The remainder of 50:41=6:22 is in verbal agreement except for an additional phrase וּמְלָכִים רַבִּים ("and many kings") in 50:41, perhaps reflecting 50:9, קְהַל־גּוֹיִם גְּדֹלִים ("a company of great nations"), an amplification of גּוֹי גָּדוֹל (50:41; 6:22). The 50:41 reference may be to Cyrus and his allies (cf. 51:27–29). For יֵעוֹר מִיַּרְכְּתֵי אָרֶץ see also 25:32c.

ᵈ⁻⁻⁻ᵈ הֵמָּה (50:42); הוּא (6:23). The plural form in 50:42 is necessary after "many kings" (50:42). If הוּא refers to גּוֹי גָּדוֹל, this does not coincide with the third plural form of the verbs in 6:23a.

ᵉ⁻⁻⁻ᵉ עָרוּךְ כְּאִישׁ מִלְחָמָה (50:42c; 6:23c). Emerton eliminates כְּ, the result of dittography after the preceding ךְ, and translates: "every soldier deployed for battle."⁴² Other similes in the passage (כְּיוֹלֵדָה; כַּיָּם) may account for the introduction of *kaph* (כְּאִישׁ) in 50:42c=6:23c.

ᶠ⁻⁻⁻ᶠ בַּת־בָּבֶל (50:42c); בַּת־צִיּוֹן (6:23c). This adaptation in 50:42c is ironic in the extreme; Babylon, the agent of Zion's destruction, is now herself the victim of aggression. בַּת־צִיּוֹן, which appears first at Isa 22:4, occurs also at Jer 8:11, 19, 21, 22, 23; 9:6 (cf. 14:17); Lam 3:48; 4:3, 6, 10.

ᵍ⁻⁻⁻ᵍ שָׁמַע מֶלֶךְ־בָּבֶל אֶת־שִׁמְעָם ("the king of Babylon has heard the report of them," 50:43a) is an explicit adaptation of 6:24, שָׁמַעְנוּ אֶת־שָׁמְעוֹ ("we have heard the report of it").

ʰ⁻⁻⁻ʰ רָפוּ יָדָיו ("his hands have fallen helpless," 50:43) is adapted from יָדֵינוּ רָפוּ ("our hands have fallen helpless," 6:24).

ⁱ⁻⁻⁻ⁱ צָרָה הֶחֱזִיקַתְהוּ חִיל כַּיּוֹלֵדָה ("anguish has seized him, writhing as of a woman in travail," 50:43); the only change is the singular suffix in place of the plural הֶחֱזִיקַתְנוּ (6:24). The phrase חִיל כַּיּוֹלֵדָה occurs also in 22:23; כְּיוֹלֵדָה occurs in 30:6 and in 49:24 (Damascus). Jeremiah 49:24 includes the verbs רפה and חזק, as well as the noun צָרָה; all three are found in 50:43=6:24. Carroll refers to "the stereotyped nature of this material."⁴³

---

³⁹ H. H. Rowley, "The Early Prophecies of Jeremiah in Their Setting," *BJRL* 45 (1962) 178–234.

⁴⁰ F. Wilke, "Das Scythenprobleme in Jeremiabuch," *Altestamentliche Studien für Rudolf Kittel* (BWANT 13; Leipzig: Hinrichs, 1913) 222–254.

⁴¹ See also Richard P. Vaggione, "Over All Asia? The extent of the Scythian domination in Herodotus," *JBL* 92 (1973) 523–530. He has demonstrated conclusively that the references in Herodotus cannot support the Scythian hypothesis.

⁴² See J. A. Emerton, "A Problem in the Hebrew Text of Jeremiah 6:23 and 50:42," *JTS* NS 23 (1972) 106–113. He states, "The clause refers, not to the attacking army as a whole, but to each individual member of it" (p. 112).

⁴³ Carroll, *Jeremiah*, p. 202. Cf. Jones (*Jeremiah*, 138), who draws attention to the conceptual similarities in Isa 5:26–30 and concludes that the description is conventional.

8. JEREMIAH 50:44-46 = JEREMIAH 49:19-21.

See above, chap. seven, pp. 155-157.

RECURRING PHRASES AND DOUBLETS IN JEREMIAH 51

As in the case of Jeremiah 50, Jeremiah 51 has some vocabulary and phrases found elsewhere in the book of Jeremiah and other parts of the OT, as well as a few doublets: 51:15-19 = 10:12-16; 51:39b = 51:57b; 51:41b = 50:23b; 51:47 = 51:52; 51:58b = Hab 2:13b.

The verb נוס ("flee," 51:6) is used several times in the OAN (46:6; 48:6, 44; 50:8) and is coupled with the concept of Yahweh's נְקָמָה ("vengeance," i.e., vengeance for Yahweh's temple, 50:28, a theme also in 51:11). Jeremiah 51:8 may be a quotation, while the reference to צֳרִי ("balm," cf. 8:22; 46:11) is probably ironic in relation to Babylon.[44] For שְׂאוּ־נֵס ("raise a standard," 51:12), cf. 51:27. This phrase also occurs in 4:6, while תִּקְעוּ שׁוֹפָר ("blow the trumpet," 4:5) is repeated in 51:27. הֵידָד ("shout of victory," 51:14), occurs in 25:30; 48:33.[45] פַּחוֹת וּסְגָנִים ("governors and commanders," 51:23) is found again in 51:28 (cf. Ezek 23:6, 12, 23). קַדְּשׁוּ ("prepare for war," 51:27b) occurs also in 6:4. גַּלִּים ("a heap of ruins") and מְעוֹן־תַּנִּים ("a lair of jackals," 51:37) occur in 9:10 (9:11E).[46] שַׁמָּה ("a horror") and שְׁרֵקָה ("an occasion for whistling and amazement," 51:37) are also found in 18:16 = 19:8; 25:9, 18; 29:18.[47] The phrase חֲרוֹן אַף־יְהוָה ("the fierce anger of Yahweh," 51:45) is reminiscent of 4:8, 26; 12:13; 25:37, 38; 30:24; 49:37.

Vocabulary and phrases used in the OAN (46-51) and in the early chapters of Jeremiah indicate that those who composed the oracles in Jeremiah 50 and 51 were familiar with the OAN in Jeremiah 46 to 49 and stand within the Jeremiah tradition.

9. JEREMIAH 51:15-19 = JEREMIAH 10:12-16

JEREMIAH 51:15-19	JEREMIAH 10:12-16
15. He who made the earth by his power, setting the world in order by his wisdom, and by his understanding stretched out the heavens. 16. At his thunderous command (there is) a tumult of	12. He who made the earth by his power, setting the world in order by his wisdom, and by his understanding stretched out the heavens. 13. At his thunderous

---

[44] Holladay, *Jeremiah 2*, 409, 422. Cf. McKane, *Jeremiah 2*, 1301. McKane considers the phrase אוּלַי תֵּרָפֵא to be ironic.

[45] See above, chap. seven, p. 134 (note 1...).

[46] Many manuscripts read מֵאֵין יוֹשֵׁב rather than מִבְּלִי יוֹשֵׁב in 9:10; cf. מֵאֵין יוֹשֵׁב in 51:37.

[47] For comments on 18:16 = 19:8; 49:17 and 50:13, see above, chap. seven, pp. 152-153.

waters in the heavens and he makes mists ᵃ riseᵃ ᵇ from the ends of the earth.ᵇ He makes ᶜ sluices ᶜ for the rain and brings forth ᵈ the wind ᵈ from his storehouses. 17. Every man is stupid and without knowledge; every goldsmith is put to shame by (his) idol; for his image(s) are false, there is no breath in them. 18. They are of no value, a work of mockery; ᵉ at the time of their punishment they shall perish.ᵉ 19. Not like these is the portion of Jacob, for he is the maker of all things, and Israel is the tribe of his inheritance; Yahweh of hosts is his name.

command (there is) a tumult waters in the heavens and and he makes mists ᵃ rise ᵃ ᵇ from the ends of the earth.ᵇ He makes ᶜ sluicesᶜ for the rain and brings forth ᵈ the wind ᵈ from his storehouses. 14. Every man is stupid and without knowledge; every goldsmith is put to shame by (his) idol; for his image(s) are false, there is no breath in them. 15. They are of no value, a work of mockery; ᵉ at the time of their punishment they shall perish.ᵉ 16. Not like these is the portion of Jacob, for he is the maker of all things, and ᶠ Israel ᶠ is the tribe of his inheritance; Yahweh of hosts is his name.

Textual and Translational Notes

Differences in orthography are as follows: וַיֹּצֵא, 51:16; וַיּוֹצֵא, 10:13; צֶרֶף, 51:17, צוֹרֵף, 10:14; יַעֲקֹב, 51:19, יַעֲקֹב, 10:16. Minimal variations in the text are noted below. The two passages are almost identical.

ᵃ⋯ᵃ וַיַּעַל (51:16); וַיַּעֲלֶה (10:13). The conclusion that 51:15-19 represents a repetition of the unit 10:12-16 is supported by the correction of the rare form וַיַּעֲלֶה to וַיַּעַל.[48]

ᵇ⋯ᵇ מִקְצֵי־אֶרֶץ (51:16); מִקְצֵה אֶרֶץ (10:13). Originally, the phrase was probably מִקְצֵה הָאָרֶץ. Note also 25:33 (cf. Deut 13:8; 28:64; Ps 135:7) and (without the definite article) 12:12.

ᶜ⋯ᶜ בְּרָקִים (51:16; 10:13). Kissane proposes the substitution of בְּקָרִים (confusion of ר and ד), "sluices," as more appropriate than "lightnings."[49]

---

[48] Marx, "A propos des doublets," 112.

[49] E. J. Kissane, "Who Maketh Lightnings for the Rain?," *JTS* NS 3 (1952) 214-216. He bases his view on the grounds that lightning and rain do not always accompany one another, especially in Palestine; "...rain was a token of God's blessing, while lightning was the agent of His wrath (cf. Job 36:31; 37:11-13)" (p. 215).

d...d רוּחַ (51:16; 10:13). LXX has φῶς in both instances. Tov surmises that אוֹר (rather than רוּחַ) stood in the Hebrew *Vorlage* on which the LXX is based, which differed from the MT; e.g., 28:16LXX=51:16MT has εἰς φωνὴν for תִּתּוֹ לְקוֹל, whereas the phrase is missing in 10:13LXX.[50] The MT is awkward as it stands. McKane emends to לְתִתּוֹ ("at his thunderous command").[51]

e...e בְּעֵת פְּקֻדָּתָם ("at the time of their punishment they shall perish," 10:15; 51:18). בְּעֵת פְּקֻדָּתָם also occurs in 8:12; the parallel verse 6:15 uses a verbal form פְּקַדְתִּים (cf. 49:8; 50:31).[52] A similar phrase שְׁנַת פְּקֻדָּתָם ("the year of their punishment") is found in 11:23b=23:12b; 48:44.[53] The idea of Yahweh's retributive justice runs through all these passages.

f...f וְיִשְׂרָאֵל, only in 10:16. שֵׁבֶט is missing in 28:19LXX=51:19MT, as is יִשְׂרָאֵל in 10:16. The name "Israel" is missing in 51:19MT (=28:19LXX), but is found in a number of manuscripts, as well as in the Lucianic recension, Tg, and Vg. Note the use of κύριος in 10:12LXX (cf. Syr), referring to Yahweh. It is improbable that יְהוָה was originally present in the *Vorlage*, as the metre would then have been overloaded. The translator probably intended to make a strong contrast between θεοί ("the pagan deities," 10:11LXX) and the God of Israel.[54]

Comment

The composition of 10:1-16 has been the subject of intense investigation.[55] Although in 2:26-28 Jeremiah attacks the idolatry of the house

---

[50] Tov, *The Text-Critical Use of the Septuagint*, 157.
[51] McKane, *Jeremiah 1*, 216, 225; cf. Peter R. Ackroyd, "Jeremiah 10:1–16," *JTS* NS (1963) p. 307 n. 12. נתן + קוֹל occurs also in Prov 8:1. In Psalm 29, the repeated יְהוָה קוֹל even sounds like the reverberation of thunder.
[52] See above, chap. five, p. 95 (note h...h).
[53] See above, chap. two, pp. 18-19 (note c...c).
[54] Jeremiah 10:11 (Aramaic) is faithfully translated in the LXX. Originally, this single Aramaic verse was probably a marginal comment, summarizing 10:12-16, which was later incorporated into the text; cf. Bright, *Jeremiah*, 79. McKane's comments (*Jeremiah 1*) are valuable with regard to the history of the transmission of the text: "The Aramaic gloss, which is common to MT, 4QJer^b and which is represented by Sept., belongs to an earlier stage of the history of the text than does vv.6-8, 10, which are not represented by Sept. and 4QJer^b. Hence, if the Aramaic gloss is to be dated in the fifth century, these additions to the Hebrew text, present in MT, were made not earlier than in the fifth century" (p. 218). The fifth century date is derived from Walter Baumgartner, "Das Aramäische im Buche Daniel," *ZAW* 45 (1927) 101.
[55] E.g., Ackroyd, "Jeremiah X.1-16," 385-390. Ackroyd finds a Jeremianic kernel in 10:1-16 (p. 389). Cf. T. W. Overholt, "The Falsehood of Idolatry. An Interpretation of Jer 10:1-16," *JTS* NS 16 (1965) 1-12; M. Margoliot, "Jeremiah X 1-16. A Re-examination," *VT* 30 (1980) 295-308. B. N. Wambacq ("Jérémie, X.1-16," *RB* 81 [1974] 57-62) attributes only 10:2 to Jeremiah. Cf. Maurice E. Andrew, "The Authorship of Jer 10 1-16," *ZAW* 94 (1982) 128-130. He states, "...the attempts to reclaim Jer 10 for Jeremiah cannot be said to

of Israel in following Canaanite idolatrous practices, the polemic in 10:1-16, directed against דֶּרֶךְ הַגּוֹיִם ("the way of the nations," 10:2), has much in common with DI (e.g., Isa 40:18-20; 44:9-20; 46:5-7).[56]

The liturgical character of 10:1-16 has been emphasized by Weiser.[57] Certainly, the language of certain psalms is reflected in 10:12-16=51:15-19. For example, בְּכֹחוֹ and מֵכִין (10:12; 51:15) occur in Ps 65:7(H); כּוּן + תֵּבֵל Niphal (10:12; 51:15) in Ps 93:1; and above all, 10:13=51:16 and Ps 135:7 contain very similar phrases.

The most probable conclusion is that the passage 10:12-16 was composed by an author who stood in the Jeremianic tradition, but was aquainted with the DI polemic against idolatry and with Psalms praising Yahweh as the creator of the world, controlling winds and waves. The phrase מֵכִין תֵּבֵל בְּחָכְמָתוֹ ("setting the world in order by his wisdom," 10:12=51:15) is reminiscent of Prov 8.[58]

The passage (51:15-19) has been inserted in Jeremiah 51 to declare the incomparability of Yahweh.[59] Jeremiah 51:19(=10:12) ends with the emphatic assertion יְהוָה צְבָאוֹת שְׁמוֹ ("Yahweh of hosts is his name," cf. 31:35; 32:18; in the OAN: 46:18; 48:15; 50:34; 51:57; Isa 47:4; 48:2; 51:15; 54:5), a phrase which belongs to the prophetic tradition and cannot indicate a precise date for the passages in which it occurs.[60] The content of 51:15-19 points to the exile (or later); 10:12-16 has been quoted here to declare the almighty power of the creator god, Yahweh, denouncing idolatry and asserting that Israel has a secure future.

---

be convincing" (p. 130).

[56] According to Overholt ("The Falsehood of Idolatry"), "There is...a real similarity of both content and function between the polemics of Jeremiah and Deutero-Isaiah" (p. 3). Cf. McKane (Jeremiah 1), "We are here in the presence of a genre with which we are principally acquainted from its appearances in Deutero-Isaiah (40:18-20; 41:6f.; 44:9-20) and this is why Jer 10:1-16 has been widely regarded as exilic or post-exilic...in provenance" (p. 219). Margoliot ("Jeremiah X 1-16," 306) concludes that the passage in Jeremiah was not written by DI, but is less convincing in his view that this is an authentic Jeremianic composition.

[57] Weiser, Jeremia, 87. He regards 10:1-16 to be a Yahweh hymn, placed in its present position in the light of 9:23.

[58] Note חָכְמָה (Prov 8:1); תֵּבֵל (8:26); כּוּן (8:27).

[59] See C. J. Labuschagne, The Incomparability of Yahweh in the Old Testament (Pretoria Oriental Series 5; Leiden: E. J. Brill, 1966) 67-70. He states, "The fact that Jer 10:12-16 is repeated in 51:15-19, proves that the passage was regarded as part of the Jeremiah tradition at the time of the writing of Jer 51" (p. 67). Labuschagne's conclusion (p. 68) that Jeremiah is himself the author of the passage is not an inevitable conclusion, however.

[60] The phrase in its expanded form יהוה אלהי צבאות שְׁמוֹ goes back to Amos 4:13; 5:27, abbreviated to יְהוָה שְׁמוֹ in Amos 5:8 (cf. Jer 33:2). See also Janzen, Studies, p. 216 n. 22.

10. JEREMIAH 51:39b=JEREMIAH 51:57b

JEREMIAH 51:39b
They shall sleep a perpetual
sleep and not wake up —
ᵃ Oracle of Yahweh ᵃ

JEREMIAH 51:57b
57b. They shall sleep a
perpetual sleep and not wake
up— ᵃ Oracle of the King,
whose name is Yahweh of hosts. ᵃ

Textual and Translational Notes

ᵃ⋯ᵃ נְאֻם יְהוָה (51:39b); נְאֻם־הַמֶּלֶךְ יְהוָה צְבָאוֹת שְׁמוֹ (51:57b).
Except for these concluding formulae, 51:39b and 51:57b are identical. For the concluding formula in 51:57b, "oracle of the King, whose name is Yahweh of hosts," cf. 46:18; 48:15.[61] Yahweh is addressed as "King" in 10:7 ("King of the nations") and in 10:10 ("the everlasting King"). Jeremiah 10:1-16 may well have been known to the redactor who inserted 51:57, to whom "the nations" include the Babylonians (cf. the use of 10:13-16 in the unit 51:15-19). The concluding formulae are faithfully rendered in the LXX translation.

Comment

Although Rudolph places 51:39b after 51:40, so as to conclude the unit 51:38-40 with the formula נְאֻם יְהוָה, the formula may occur in an intermediate position and need not necessarily be placed at the end.[62]

The prose verse 51:57 is best taken as an insertion after 51:54-56, a section made up of repetitions from other parts of the book of Jeremiah. In 51:57, not only is 51:39b used, but parts of 50:35-36 from the Song of the Sword (50:35-38), as well as 51:23 (cf. 51:58), are repeated. Of the five groups listed, three have already been mentioned in 50:35-36, "her princes" (שָׂרֶיהָ, LXX τοὺς ἡγεμόνας αὐτῆς), "her wise men" (חֲכָמֶיהָ, LXX τοὺς σοφοὺς αὐτῆς), "her warriors" (גִּבּוֹרֶיהָ, LXX τοὺς στρατηγοὺς αὐτῆς). The remaining two groups, פַּחוֹתֶיהָ וּסְגָנֶיהָ ("her governors and her commanders"), based on 51:23, but missing in 28:57LXX, have been inserted between "her wise men" and "her warriors." This is a good example of the way in which Jeremiah 50 and 51 have been subject to constant additions by learned scribes.

---

[61] See Marc Zvi Brettler, *God is King: Understanding an Israelite Metaphor* (JSOTSSup 76; Sheffield Academic Press, 1989) 31. He states that the substantive מלך ("king") is used of God forty-seven times in the Bible; the list of occurrences is given (p. 172 n. 2) and includes Jer 8:19; 10:7, 10; 46:18; 48:15; 51:57. In the LXX the phrase is missing in 26:18(=46:18MT) and 31:15 (=48:15MT), but the phrase is retained in 28:57b(=51:57bMT). Cf. Janzen, *Studies*, p. 216 n. 22.

[62] Rudolph, *Jeremia, 312*. Other examples of *Zwischenformeln* include 1:15; 5:9; 13:25.

11. JEREMIAH 51:58d=HABAKKUK 2:13b

JEREMIAH 51:58d
Peoples [a] labour [a] for nothing
and nations [c] wear themselves out [c]
[b] only for fire. [b]

HABAKKUK 2:13b
Peoples [a] labour [a]
[b] only for fire [b] and
nations [c] wear themselves
out [c] for nothing.

Textual and Translational Notes

[a...a] וְיִגְעוּ (51:58d); וְיִיגְעוּ (Hab 2:13b). The difference is merely in orthography. Both of these forms (*Qal* imperfect) are found in Isaiah (40:31; 65:23).

[b...b] בְּדֵי־אֵשׁ (51:58d, preceded by בְּדֵי־רִיק; in Hab 2:13b, followed by בְּדֵי־רִיק). ἐν ἀρχῇ (28:58LXX) is based on a misreading of *daleth* and *resh*, i.e., בְּרֹאשׁ instead of בְּדֵי־אֵשׁ, understood correctly in Hab 2:13LXX, ἐν πυρί. Jeremiah 28:58LXX also uses the negative οὐ before κοπιάσουσι, thereby giving a meaning opposite to that of the Hebrew text. אֵשׁ also occurs in 51:58c.

[c...c] וְיָעֵפוּ (51:58d); יִעָפוּ (Hab 2:13b). The *waw* in וְיָעֵפוּ (51:58d) should be changed to *yodh*, i.e., יִיעָפוּ, a difference only in orthography and vocalization.[63] This reading also has the support of the LXX (ἐκλείψουσιν), Theod., and Syr. The unnecessary repetition of וְיָעֵפוּ in 51:64 leads to the conclusion that the final phrase עַד־הֵנָּה דִּבְרֵי יִרְמְיָהוּ originally came at the end of 51:58 and that 51:59–64a was added later.[64]

Comment

A comparison of 51:58d with its doublet Hab 2:13b carries with it the probability either that Habakkuk is being quoted from memory, since בְּדֵי־אֵשׁ and בְּדֵי־רִיק (Hab 2:13b) appear in reverse order in 51:58d, or that both are based on a popular proverb.[65]

Habakkuk 2:13 is part of Hab 2:12–14, the third of five "woes" (Hab 2:6–8; 2:9–11; 2:12–14; 2:15–17; 2:18–19). Building a town with blood and founding a city on iniquity generalizes the language of Mic 3:10, where "Zion" and "Jerusalem" are specifically named. "Peoples" and "nations" are for nothing, if destruction ("fire") is the eventual outcome. In the case of 51:58, where there is a direct statement regarding the "wall of Babylon" (reading חוֹמַת with many manuscripts, LXX τεῖχος, Vg *murus*), some exegetes have argued that

---

[63] Rudolph, *Jeremia*, 312.

[64] For a full discussion of the process, which also offers an explanation of how the form וְיָעֵפוּ came into 51:58d, see McKane, *Jeremiah 2*, 1350.

[65] The reversal in order in these two verses suggests a quotation from memory. A popular proverb may be in mind; cf. Thompson, *Jeremiah*, 769.

the "peoples" and "nations" are those whose tribute money or slave labor helped to build the wall.[66] However, a preferable view is that this is an expression of the futility of the labour of "peoples" and "nations" in any enterprise undertaken in their own power. The statement is added at the end of the oracles in Jeremiah 50-51 to summarize what has been the dominant theme in the OAN: Yahweh is the Sovereign Lord who controls the destiny of "peoples" and "nations."

SUMMARY: RECURRING PHRASES AND DOUBLETS IN JEREMIAH 50-51

Many of the oracles in Jeremiah 50-51 were composed by learned scribes who were familiar with the OAN in Jeremiah 46-49 and with phrases found within the Jeremiah tradition. The doublets of the OAN demonstrate a knowledge of prophetic literature and Jeremianic vocabulary. Scribes of a period later than that of Jeremiah would regard him as a prophet to the nations (1:10) who would inevitably proclaim the ultimate destruction of Babylon.

SUMMARY OF DOUBLETS IN JEREMIAH 50-51

1. JEREMIAH 50:16b=ISAIAH 13:14b
The most likely view is that Jer 50:16b is dependent on the late passage Isa 13:14b.

2. JEREMIAH 50:23b=JEREMIAH 51:41b
An ironic saying, coupled in each case with an אֵיךְ saying (50:23a; 51:41a).

3. JEREMIAH 50:30=JEREMIAH 49:26
See chap. seven, pp. 158-159. This oracle against Babylon (50:30) has also been applied to Damascus (49:26).

4. JEREMIAH 50:32b=JEREMIAH 21:14b
Jeremiah 50:32b is drawn from 21:14b, since the unit 50:31-32 is an amalgam of quotations found elsewhere in the book of Jeremiah.

5. JEREMIAH 50:39-40 and ISAIAH 13:19-22
Jeremiah 50:39-40 borrows selectively from Isaiah 13, also directed against Babylon.

6. JEREMIAH 50:40=JEREMIAH 49:18
See chap. seven, pp. 153-155.

7. JEREMIAH 50:41-43=JEREMIAH 6:22-24
Jeremiah 50:41-43 is an ironic adaptation of 6:22-24.

---

[66] See Leslie, *Jeremiah*, 312; H. Cunliffe-Jones, *The Book of Jeremiah* (TBC; London: SCM, 1960) 280.

8. JEREMIAH 50:44-46=JEREMIAH 49:19-21

See chap. seven, pp. 155-157. The question of priority is not easily answered. Both are editorial additions in the context where each occurs.

9. JEREMIAH 51:15-19=JEREMIAH 10:12-16

Jeremiah 10:12-16 (a late passage) has been inserted in Jeremiah 51 by one who stood in the Jeremianic tradition, and was also acquainted with the DI polemic against idolatry and with Psalms praising Yahweh as the creator of the world.

10. JEREMIAH 51:39b=JEREMIAH 51:57b

Jeremiah 51:54-58 combines other material, including 50:35-36, 51:39b and 51:23.

11. JEREMIAH 51:58d=HABAKKUK 2:13b

Either 51:58d is a quotation from Habakkuk (from memory?) or both are based on a popular proverb.

The dominant theme in Jeremiah 50-51 (as in Jeremiah 46-49) is the sovereignty of Yahweh in controlling the destiny of "peoples and nations."

CHAPTER NINE

OTHER DOUBLETS WITHIN THE BOOK OF JEREMIAH

The doublets discussed so far have been found in the Confessions, in passages dealing with royalty and prophecy, and in the OAN. Additional doublets are found elsewhere in the book of Jeremiah, both within the book itself (the subject of this chapter) and with other parts of the OT (see the following chapter).

The poetic passage **JER 2:26-28** contains three phrases which recur in prose passages: 2:26b=32:32b; 2:27b=32:33; 2:28b=11:13a.

1(a) JEREMIAH 2:26b=JEREMIAH 32:32b

JEREMIAH 2:26b
They, their kings,[a] their princes,[a] their priests and their prophets.

JEREMIAH 32:32b
They, their kings, their priests and their prophets, [a] the men of Judah and the inhabitants of Jerusalem.[a]

1(b) JEREMIAH 2:27b=JEREMIAH 32:33a

JEREMIAH 2:27b
[a] Indeed,[b] they have turned their back to me and not their face.

JEREMIAH 32:33a
They have turned their back to me and not their face.

1(c) JEREMIAH 2:28b=JEREMIAH 11:13

JEREMIAH 2:28b
Surely, as many as your cities are your gods, O Judah.

JEREMIAH 11:13
Surely, as many as your cities are your gods, O Judah, [c] and as many as the streets of Jerusalem are the altars you have set up to shame, altars to burn incense to Baal. [c]

Textual and Translational Notes

[a...a] All three passages, 2:26-8; 11:9-13; 32:26-35, in which these phrases are found, have to do with apostasy and idolatry. To make the list of those who have been guilty of forsaking Yahweh all-inclusive, the oracle in 32:26-35 adds "the men of Judah and the inhabitants of Jerusalem" (cf. 17:25; 44:21) to "they, their kings, their princes, their priests and their prophets." Retribution for their actions will be meted out in due time (8:1-3). The same fourfold list ("kings, princes, priests and prophets") occurs in 4:9. These four categories in 2:26b may well have been added to define more closely the word הֵמָּה ("they"), amplified further in 32:32b to include not only leaders, but all the people (cf. 44:17, 21).[1]

b...b   The phrase "they have turned their back to me and not their face" (2:27b; 32:33a) differs only in the introductory כִּי with פנה (perfect) in 2:27b, rather than with *waw consec.* with פנה (imperfect) as in 32:33a.[2] This figure of speech representing apostasy occurs only in this doublet in Jeremiah, although the figure of Yahweh showing his back, not his face (18:17), is a powerful metaphor for rejection.

c...c   "Surely, as many as your cities are your gods, O Judah" (2:28b) is amplified in 11:13 by the addition of "as many as the streets of Jerusalem are the altars you have set up to shame, altars to burn incense to Baal." This addition (minus an equivalent of the phrase שַׂמְתֶּם מִזְבְּחוֹת לַבֹּשֶׁת מִזְבְּחוֹת) occurs in 2:28bLXX, suggesting that וּמִסְפַּר חֻצוֹת יְרוּשָׁלַיִם לְקַטֵּר לַבָּעַל stood in the Hebrew *Vorlage*.[3] McKane has argued for the retention of 2:28bMT, but where the LXX has a phrase not present in the MT, there is a greater likelihood that this phrase was present in the Hebrew *Vorlage*.[4]

Comment

Thiel discusses 2:27b-28 and 11:11b-13 at length, making comparisons with Deut 32:37, 38 and Judg 10:13b-14.[5] He appears to be correct in his view that 11:13 (with a sudden change from from 2d s. to 2d pl.) is an insertion from 2:28, and that Deuteronomistic phrases are present. The reference to both "cities" and "streets" often occurs in the formula "cities of Judah and streets of Jerusalem" (7:17, 34; 11:6; 33:10; 44:6, 17, 21). We conclude that 11:13 has borrowed from 2:28, with the added complication (perhaps originally a phrase in the margin) which associates בֹּשֶׁת and בָּעַל.

---

[1] Holladay, *Jeremiah 1*, 103.

[2] כִּי asseverative,"indeed"; Williams, *Hebrew Syntax*, § 449.

[3] The substitution of בֹּשֶׁת ("shame") for בָּעַל ("Baal") elsewhere (3:34; cf. Hos 9:10) would account for the reference to בֹּשֶׁת in this additional clause in 11:13MT; note, also, the use of the verbal form הֹבִישׁוּ ("shall be shamed") in 2:26.

[4] Janzen, *Studies,* 121.

[5] Thiel, *Redaktion 1*, 153-156. See Table 5 (p. 155) for precise correspondences in the texts.

2. JEREMIAH 4:4b=JEREMIAH 21:12b.

See above, chap. four, pp. 62-64.

3. JEREMIAH 4:5c=JEREMIAH 8:14a

JEREMIAH 4:5c	JEREMIAH 8:14a
Say "Let us gather together and go to the fortified cities!"	Why do we sit still? Let us gather together and go into the fortified cities; let us perish there.

Comment

If we delete the first וְאָמְרוּ in 4:5a, Yahweh as speaker summons the people to assemble and seek refuge in the fortified cities, in view of the impending disaster from the north.[6] In 8:14a, the people themselves, in a cry of despair, call out for retreat to fortified cities, with the expectation that they will eventually perish there. The words in 4:5c have been taken up in 8:14a with the deepest irony; the fortified cities will offer no protection. The unit 8:14-15 echoes other passages, e.g., מֵי־רֹאשׁ ("poisoned water," 23:15a; 9:14H). Jeremiah 8:14 has a catchword connection with 8:13 (the verb אָסֹף); the use of שָׁלוֹם in 8:15 makes a link with 8:11.[7]

4. JEREMIAH 5:9=JEREMIAH 5:29=JEREMIAH 9:8 (9:9E)

Ought I [a] not [a] punish [b] (them)[b] for these things?, oracle of Yahweh; should I not avenge myself [c] on a nation[c] such as this?

Textual and Translational Notes

[a...a] לוֹא (5:9); לֹא (5:29; 9:8). The MT preserves this difference in orthography.
[b...b] Jeremiah 9:8 adds בָּם־, as do some manuscripts 5:9 and 5:29.
Note also: וְאִם (5:9); אִם (5:29; 9:8). Some manuscripts (5:29) read וְאִם.
[c...c] בְּגוֹי (5:9, 29; 9:8); ἐν ἔθνει (5:9 and 5:29LXX); ἐν λαῷ (9:9LXX).

Comment

A careful study of this rhetorical question (which appears as a refrain in 5:9, 29 and 9:8) has been made by Brueggemann.[8] Although the form may be

---

[6] See Rudolph, *Jeremia*, 32.
[7] For "poisoned water," see above, chap. five, pp. 82-85; for 8:15=14:19b, see chap. one, pp.7-8.
[8] Walter Brueggemann, "Jeremiah's Use of Rhetorical Questions," *JBL* 92 (1973) 358-374.

sapiential in origin, prophetic style has brought about a transformation, confirmed by the use of נְאֻם יְהוָה.⁹ Brueggemann claims, "Its threefold use attests that it may have been a free-floating tradition in the Jeremiah materials."¹⁰ The refrain is used structurally after passages in which Yahweh's people are indicted for their transgressions (5:7-8; 5:20-28; 9:1-8). Pohlmann suggests the possibility that Jeremiah 7-8 have been inserted supplementarily, disturbing the close relationship between the passages which end with the refrain.¹¹ In any case, the threefold use of the refrain indicates the care with which the material in these early chapters has been brought together in a unified way.¹²

The version of the Temple sermon in Jeremiah 7 (cf. Jeremiah 26) has a number of doublets and parallel phrases elsewhere in the book of Jeremiah: 7:6=22:3 (cf. 21:12); 7:7=25:5b; 7:13b=35:17b; 7:16=11:14; the covenantal formula in 7:23, which occurs a number of times elsewhere; 7:30b-33=19:5-7=32:34-35a; 7:34=16:9=25:10=33:11a.

5. JEREMIAH 7:6 and JEREMIAH 22:3

JEREMIAH 7:6
6.(If) you do not oppress the alien, the orphan and the widow and do not shed innocent blood ᵃ in this place ᵃ and (if) you do not go after ᶜ other gods ᶜ to your own hurt ... ill-treat or do violence to

JEREMIAH 22:3
3. Thus says Yahweh: Do ᵇ justice and righteousness ᵇ and deliver the one who has been robbed from the hand of the oppressor. Do not the alien, the orphan and the widow and do not shed innocent blood ᵇ in this place.ᵇ

The two passages have in common reference to the triad גֵּר יָתוֹם וְאַלְמָנָה ("the alien, the orphan and the widow"; cf. Deut 14:29; 24:19, 20, 21; 26:12, 13; 27:19; Ezek 22:7; Zech 7:10; Ps 146:9), as well as the phrase בַּמָּקוֹם הַזֶּה וְדָם נָקִי אַל־תִּשְׁפֹּכוּ ("and do not shed innocent blood in this place").¹³ Jeremiah 22:3 contains a phrase also found in 21:12: וְהַצִּילוּ גָזוּל מִיַּד עָשׁוֹק ("and deliver the one who has been robbed from the hand of the oppressor").

---

⁹ Cf. the rhetorical questions in Amos 8:8; Isa 57:6; 64:11 (64:12E).
¹⁰ Brueggemann, "Rhetorical Questions," 364.
¹¹ Pohlmann, *Studien*, 161.
¹² Cf. Jack R. Lundbom, *Jeremiah. A Study in Ancient Hebrew Rhetoric* (SBLDS 18; Missoula, Montana: Scholars Press, 1975).
¹³ For דָּם נָקִי, see also 26:15 (putting Jeremiah to death will bring "innocent blood" upon "yourselves and upon this city and its inhabitants"). Cf. 22:17, שׁפך + דָּם הַנָּקִי. The phrase is also found in Deuteronomy and Deuteronomistic passages: Deut 21:8 (cf. Deut 19:10, 13); 1 Sam 19:5; 2 Kgs 21:16; cf. Isa 59:7; Ps 106:38; Prov 6:17.

Textual and Translational Notes

ᵃ⁻ᵃ בַּמָּקוֹם הַזֶּה ("in this place," 7:6; 22:3). In view of the same phrase in 7:3 and 7:7, the reference in 7:6 could be either to the temple or to Judah; in 22:3, to the palace or Jerusalem.

ᵇ⁻ᵇ מִשְׁפָּט וּצְדָקָה ("justice and righteousness," 22:3). Cf. Jer 9:23 (9:24E); 22:15; 23:5=33:15; Ezek 45:9; Ps 99:4, as in 22:3 with עשׂה. See also 1 Kgs 10:9; Isa 9:6 (9:7E). See above, chap. four, pp. 56, 62, and below, chapter thirteen, C59.

ᶜ⁻ᶜ אֱלֹהִים אֲחֵרִים ("other gods," 7:6). See chap. thirteen, C8.

Comment

The exhortation to "the king of Judah" (22:1) in 22:2-5 (an expansion of 21:12) sets out the expectations of how a monarch should exercise his kingship. In 7:5-7, within the Temple "sermon," the same insistence on ethical behaviour is made for the people in general; true amendment of life will be marked by the execution of justice (מִשְׁפָּט, 7:5; cf. 22:3), protection of aliens, orphans and widows, and no shedding of innocent blood. The only element missing in 22:3 is forbidding going after "other gods." Although the triad, "the alien, the orphan, the widow," is central in the concerns of the book of Deuteronomy, such concerns are already reflected in Isa 1:17, where exhortation is made to "seek מִשְׁפָּט," and to protect the orphan and widow.

Another parallel within the unit 7:5-7 exists between 7:7 and 25:5.

6. JEREMIAH 7:7=JEREMIAH 25:5

JEREMIAH 7:7	JEREMIAH 25:5
ᵇ Then I shall let you dwell ᵇ in this place, ᶜ in the land which I gave to your fathers ᶜ ᵈ from of old and for ever.ᵈ	5 ... saying, 'Turn now, every one (of you) ᵃ from his evil way and from the evil of your doings ᵃ and dwell ᶜ upon the land which Yahweh has given to you and to your fathers ᶜ ᵈ from of old and for ever.' ᵈ

Textual and Translational Notes

ᵃ⁻ᵃ 25:5, מִדַּרְכּוֹ הָרָעָה וּמֵרֹעַ מַעַלְלֵיכֶם. Note דַּרְכֵיכֶם וּמַעַלְלֵיכֶם in 7:3, 5. For רֹעַ מַעַלְלֵיכֶם ("the evil of your doings"), see above, chap. five, p. 90 n. 42, regarding Thiel's observation that the phrase in 25:5 is dependent upon 23:22 (see also chap. thirteen, C92a).

ᵇ⁻ᵇ וְשִׁכַּנְתִּי ("I shall let you dwell," 7:7) provides another link with 7:3 (וַאֲשַׁכְּנָה).

c...c בָּאָרֶץ אֲשֶׁר נָתַתִּי לַאֲבוֹתֵיכֶם (7:7);
(25:5). עַל־הָאֲדָמָה אֲשֶׁר נָתַן יְהֹוָה לָכֶם וְלַאֲבוֹתֵיכֶם
Jeremiah 25:5LXX, ἧς ἔδωκα ὑμῖν (= אֲשֶׁר נָתַתִּי לָכֶם), suggests the possibility that originally the Hebrew text of 25:5 coincided more closely with 7:7 than the present MT. The change to 3d s. in 25:5MT would have been made in the light of the reference to Yahweh in 25:4MT (וְשָׁלַח יְהֹוָה, but LXX ἀπέστελλον). The phrase "the land which I gave to you and to your fathers" occurs also with slight variations in 7:14 (מָקוֹם); 23:39 (עִיר); 24:10 (אֲדָמָה); 35:15 (אֲדָמָה), cf. Exod 13:11 (אֶרֶץ־הַכְּנַעֲנִי); 2 Chron 6:25 (אֲדָמָה). In 16:15 and 30:3 the promise is made by Yahweh to bring his people back to the land (16:15, אֲדָמָה; 30:3, הָאָרֶץ) given to the forefathers. The gift of the land by Yahweh to his people is a prominent theme in Deuteronomistic literature: Deut 3:20; 9:23; 26:15; 1 Kgs 9:7; 2 Kgs 21:8.

d...d לְמִן־עוֹלָם וְעַד־עוֹלָם (7:7; 25:5). The phrase in this precise form is found only in this doublet.

Comment

Jeremiah 25:3-7, a summary of Jeremiah's proclamation to Judah and its rejection, contains many phrases which occur elsewhere in the book of Jeremiah, especially in Jeremiah 7. In addition to those mentioned in 25:7=7:7, note also 25:3 and 7:13; 25:4 and 7:25; 25:6 and 7:6. The temple sermon in Jeremiah 7 is the main source from which 25:3-7 has been composed.

7. JEREMIAH 7:16=JEREMIAH 11:14

JEREMIAH 7:16
[a] As for you, do not pray for this people and do not lift up cry or prayer on their behalf, [a] [b] and do not entreat me, [b] [c] for I will not listen to you.[c]

JEREMIAH 11:14
[a] As for you, do not pray for this people and do not lift up cry or prayer on their behalf[a] [c] for I will not listen at the time of their calling to me [c] [d] on account of (? at the time of) their disaster. [d]

Jeremiah is prohibited by Yahweh from interceding on behalf of "this people" in the doublet 7:16=11:14, which should be considered in relation to 14:11 and 15:11.[14]

---

[14] Overholt ("The Falsehood of Idolatry"), "Intercession is a part of every prophet's function; ...the intercessory function of the prophet is frequently mentioned in Jer." (p. 37 n. 24).

Textual and Translational Notes

a...a   The identical phrase: אַל־תִּתְפַּלֵּל בְּעַד־הָעָם הַזֶּה וְאַל־תִּשָּׂא בַעֲדָם רִנָּה וּתְפִלָּה וְאַל־תִּפְגַּע־בִּי occurs in both 7:16 and 11:14, in each case in a context of idolatrous behaviour on the part of the people (7:17-20; 11:12-13, 17). Another prohibition of intercession occurs in 14:11: אַל־תִּתְפַּלֵּל בְּעַד־הָעָם הַזֶּה לְטוֹבָה. Regarding לְטוֹבָה, cf. לְטוֹב in 15:11, at the end of a phrase which is textually uncertain, and טוֹבָה in 18:20.

Jeremiah's intercessory activity is alluded to not only in 7:16 = 11:14; 14:11; but in 37:3; 42:2, 4. רִנָּה and תְּפִלָּה are coupled together in Ps 17:1; 61:2 (61:1E); 88:3 (88:2E).

b...b   וְאַל־תִּפְגַּע־בִּי ("and do not entreat me," 7:16). Cf. 15:11, אִם־לוֹא הִפְגַּעְתִּי בְךָ ("have I not entreated you?").

c...c   כִּי־אֵינֶנִּי שֹׁמֵעַ אֹתָךְ ("for I will not listen to you," 7:16). Cf. 11:11, אֲלֵיהֶם וְלֹא אֶשְׁמָע. In place of אֹתָךְ, 11:14 has a longer phrase בְּעֵת קָרְאָם אֵלַי בְּעַד רָעָתָם ("at the time of their calling to me, on account of their disaster!").

d...d   בְּעַד רָעָתָם 11:14. A good case can be made for reading בְּעֵת רָעָתָם, the reading in many manuscripts, the LXX (and other versions, Vg, Syr, Tg) as well as בְּעֵת רָעָתָם in 11:12, 14. A scribe has repeated בְּעַד (from the phrase בְּעַד־הָעָם) instead of בְּעֵת.

Comment

What is the relationship between 7:16; 11:14; 14:11 and 15:11? For Ittmann, 7:16 and 11:14 must be regarded as "Einzelsprüche," introduced in a later (Deuteronomistic?) editorial phase.[15] Jeremiah's intercessory activity is alluded to frequently elsewhere: 17:16; 18:20; 21:2; 37:3; 42:2, 4, 20. The abrupt prohibition of intercession in 7:16; 11:14; 14:11 raises questions concerning its purpose. The prohibition is connected with the inevitability of a judgment which cannot be averted by intercession. In the Confessions, Jeremiah alludes to his intercessory function; he has repeatedly sought the welfare of his people (15:11; 17:16; 18:20). The prophetic role of intercession is indeed powerful (15:1), but judgment is certain. The Jeremiah tradition understands that Jeremiah was a faithful intercessor until Yahweh forbade further intercessory action. Although Jeremiah is prohibited from interceding לְטוֹבָה ("for the welfare") "of this people" (14:11-12; cf. 21:10), hope remains for the "good figs" in exile, upon whom Yahweh sets his eyes לְטוֹבָה ("for good").[16]

The covenantal formula in 7:23 ("I will be your God and you shall be my people"), which recurs frequently elsewhere in the book of Jeremiah and in

---

[15] Ittmann, *Konfessionen*, 152; Thiel, *Redaktion 1*, 119.
[16] Ivor Meyer, *Jeremia und die Falschen Propheten* (OBO 13; Göttingen: Vandenhoeck & Ruprecht, 1977) 53-54.

other parts of the OT, will be examined in chap. thirteen, pp. 269-270. We note here that 7:22-23 contains a number of verbal correspondences with 11:3-5, and 7:24-26 with 11:7-8, e.g., "in the day I brought them out of Egypt" (7:22; 11:4, 7); the covenantal formula (7:23; 11:4); "they did not obey or incline their ear, but walked in ... the stubbornness of their evil hearts" (7:24; cf. 11:8).[17]

The concluding section of Jeremiah 7 (7:30-34), has statements and phrases duplicated elsewhere in the book. For example, the references to Topheth in 7:30-32 (cf. 19:5-6, 11-12; 32:34-35), the fate of dead bodies (7:33; 16:4; 19:7; 34:20) and the cessation of mirth and gladness (cf. 7:34; 16:9; 25:10; 33:10a, 11a).[18] We now examine 7:30-32 and parallel passages.

8. JEREMIAH 7:30-32=JEREMIAH 19:5-6, 11-12=JEREMIAH 32:34-35

JEREMIAH 7:30-32
30. ª For the sons of Judah have done evil in my sight ª ᵇ — oracle of Yahweh;ᵇ ᶜ they have put their detested (idols) in the house which is called by my name, to defile it.ᶜ
31. ᵈ They have built the high places of Topheth which are in the Valley of the sons of Hinnom, to burn their sons and daughters in the fire,ᵈ
ᵉ which I did not command nor did it come into my mind.ᵉ 32. ᶠ Therefore, look, the days are coming ᵇ — oracle of Yahweh— ᵇ when it will no longer be called Topheth or the Valley of the son of Hinnom, but the Valley of Slaughter,ᶠ ᵍ and they will bury in Topheth because there is no place (elsewhere).ᵍ

JEREMIAH 19:5-6, 11-12
5. They have built the high places of Baal to burn their sons in the fire as burnt-offerings to Baal,ᵈ ᵉ which I did not command or decree, nor did it come into my mind.ᵉ 6. ᶠ Therefore, look, days are coming ᵇ — oracle of Yahweh— ᵇ when this place will no longer be called Topheth or the Valley of the sons of Hinnom, but the Valley of Slaughterᶠ
....
11. You shall say to them, Thus says Yahweh of hosts: So will I break this people and this city, as one breaks a potter's vessel so that it cannot be mended.
ᵍ In Topheth, they will bury because there is no place (elsewhere).ᵍ 12. So will I do to this place ᵇ — oracle of Yahweh— ᵇ

---

[17] Janzen (*Studies*), "...the two passages are not strictly doublets, but only substantially similar prose sections" (p. 94).

[18] Charts are provided by Thiel, *Redaktion 1*, 131; Hubmann, *Untersuchungen*, 219; Weippert, *Die Prosareden*, 185.

and to its inhabitants, so as to
make this city like Topheth.

JEREMIAH 32:34-35

34. ᶜ They have put their detested (idols) in the house which is called by my name, to defile it.ᶜ 35. ᵈ They have built the high places of Baal which are in the Valley of the sons of Hinnom to offer up their sons and daughters to Molech,ᵈ ᵉ which I did not command nor did it come into my mind,ᵉ that they should do this abomination, so as to make Judah sin.

Textual and Translational Notes

ᵃ⋯ᵃ כִּי־עָשׂוּ בְנֵי־יְהוּדָה הָרַע בְּעֵינַי ("For the sons of Judah have done evil in my sight," 7:30a). Although this phrase does not occur directly in the parallel passages, a similar phrase is found in 32:30 in the unit in which 32:34-5 is found. Jeremiah 32:30-35 deals with Baal worship, with strong condemnation of "the sons of Israel and the sons of Judah" and "this city" (32:31), i.e., Jerusalem. Note also 52:2 (regarding Zedekiah) and 18:10. This Deuteronomistic phrase (Deut 4:25; 9:18; 17:2; 31:2, 9) regarding doing evil in the sight of Yahweh appears over forty times in Kings (e.g., 1 Kgs 11:6; 15:26; 16:9; 2 Kgs 13:11), a recurring refrain summarizing the conduct of a succession of kings from Solomon on (cf. 1 Kgs 14:22 regarding "Judah"). The phrase also occurs in Isa 65:12; 66:4.

ᵇ⋯ᵇ נְאֻם יְהוָה ("oracle of Yahweh," 7:30, 32; 19:6; cf. 19:12). נְאֻם (sic) in 7:30 represents the unusual *kethib* in the Leningrad MS (B19ᴬ), with the *qere* vocalization. The formula, which does not occur in 32:34-35, is found in 32:30MT, but not in the LXX translation (39:30LXX). Jeremiah 7:30, 32 retains the formula, which was present in the *Vorlage*, intending to underline the authenticity of these oracles. If 7:30-35 is an *addendum*, the theme of the earlier part of the chapter is preserved in 7:30 (desecration of the temple by syncretistic worship, involving Baal, 7:9) and amplified in 7:31-35 by condemnation of idolatrous worship and human sacrifice in the Valley of Ben-Hinnom.

ᶜ⋯ᶜ שָׂמוּ שִׁקּוּצֵיהֶם בַּבַּיִת אֲשֶׁר־נִקְרָא שְׁמִי עָלָיו לְטַמְּאוֹ ("they have put their detested (idols) in the house which is called by my name, to defile it," 7:30; 32:34). Regarding שִׁקּוּצֵיהֶם, cf. שִׁקּוּץ (4:1; cf. 13:27; 16:18). The term also occurs frequently in Ezek (e.g., 5:11; 11:18, 21; 20:7, 8, 30; 37:23).

ᵈ⋯ᵈ In the phrase וּבָנוּ בָּמוֹת הַתֹּפֶת ("they have built the high places of Topheth," 7:31), 19:5 and 32:35 substitute הַבַּעַל for הַתֹּפֶת. Jeremiah 7:31LXX (τὸν βωμὸν τοῦ Ταφεθ) uses the singular form (cf. Tg) in place of בָּמוֹת. The plural is appropriate in 19:5, and would be suitable also in 7:31 if וּבָנוּ is frequentative, as Holladay suggests.[19] As for וּבָנוּ ... בָּאֵשׁ (7:31), the phrase is

---

[19] Holladay, *Jeremiah 1*, 264, 267, 534.

repeated, with variations, in 19:5 and 32:34. In the parallel phrase, 19:5 does not refer to הַתֹּפֶת and its location, but does so in 19:6. Jeremiah 32:35 follows 7:31 more closely, substituting for Topheth references to Baal and Molech, and using the verb עבר *Hiphil* "offer up" (see [e...e] below), rather than שרף ... באש (7:31; 19:5; cf. Ezek 20:31).[20] הַתֹּפֶת appears as well in 2 Kgs 23:10, where Molech also is mentioned, in connection with Josiah's reforms, and in Isa 30:33 (תָּפְתֶּה), in the sense of a "burning-place" (note the absence of the definite article). As to the fate of the Assyrian king, מֶלֶךְ ("king") may also provide a wordplay on Molech (cf. מֹלֶךְ, Jer 32:35), so that the place where sacrifices were offered to Molech becomes the very place where Yahweh will destroy the Assyrian king.[21]

[e...e] אֲשֶׁר לֹא־צִוִּיתִים וְלֹא עָלְתָה עַל־לִבִּי ("which I did not command nor did it come into my mind," 7:31; 19:5; 32:35). Child-sacrifice is expressly forbidden in Deut 18:10, where the *Hiphil* participle of עבר is used.

[f...f] לָכֵן ... הַהֲרֵגָה, regarding the change in name to the Valley of Slaughter, is found both in 7:32, and with slight variations, in 19:6 (יִקָּרֵא for יֵאָמֵר; and the omission of לַמָּקוֹם הַזֶּה). Stylistically, the statement is similar to 23:7–8 = 16:14–15. For the phrase לָכֵן הִנֵּה־יָמִים בָּאִים, see above regarding 23:5 = 33:14, chap. four, p. 57.

[g...g] וְקָבְרוּ בְתֹפֶת מֵאֵין מָקוֹם ("and they will bury in Topheth because there is no place [elsewhere]," 7:32; 19:11, with slight changes). Jeremiah 19:11LXX does not include this phrase, which has been added to the Hebrew text as an interpolation.[22] Jeremiah 19 puts these sayings in the context of a symbolic action (Jeremiah breaking a בַּקְבֻּק, "flask"), with its primary emphasis on the destruction of Jerusalem, in which (19:12) "this city" will be made like Topheth.

Comment

McKane has argued cogently that the reference to הַמָּקוֹם הַזֶּה ("this place," 19:3) is to Jerusalem, and that the references to Topheth are secondary.[23] He states, "... it was as a paradigm of ruin and desolation that תפת made its entry at the end of v.12 in order to underline the terror of

---

[20] Whereas 19:5 refers only to burning "sons" in the fire, the reference in 7:31 to "sons and daughters" is reminiscent of Deut 12:3 (cf. "sons and daughters" offered to Molech, Jer 32:35).

[21] See Kaiser, *Isaiah 13–39*, 310. He traces the development of the name of the deity, probably originally מֶלֶךְ, but changed to מֹלֶךְ, using the vowels of בֹּשֶׁת ("shame"), as happens also in the substitution of בֹּשֶׁת ("shame") for בַּעַל (Jer 3:24; cf. 11:13). Kaiser (p. 305) considers Isa 30:33 to be a later interpolation (reflecting the Seleucid kingdom, the "Assyria" of the time).

[22] McKane, *Jeremiah 1*, 446.

[23] McKane, *Jeremiah 1*, 451.

Jerusalem's devastation."[24] At a later stage in development, 19:5-6 (dependent on 7:30-31) was added, in a lengthy process of adding material. Jeremiah 19 offers strong support for the view of McKane that prose sections of the book of Jeremiah have triggered further prose additions in the course of time.[25]

Jeremiah 32:34-35 follows 7:30-31 without specifically introducing the Topheth tradition. A phrase has been added at the end of 32:35: הַחֲטִי אֶת־יְהוּדָה לַעֲשׂוֹת הַתּוֹעֵבָה הַזֹּאת לְמַעַן ("to do this abomination, so as to make Judah sin," cf. 7:10; 44:4, 22).[26] The noun תּוֹעֵבָה (s. and pl.) occurs 117 times in the OT.[27] Other occurrences in Jeremiah are 2:7; 6:15=8:12; 16:18. The term appears frequently in Deuteronomy and Proverbs.

In comparing 7:30-32, 19:5-6 and 32:34-35, Hubmann comes to the conclusion that none provides a *Vorlage* for the others, in that the three texts clearly diverge in the designation of the cult.[28] However, the texts have sufficient phraseology in common to lead to the conclusion that 19:5-6 and the references to Topheth in 19:11, 12 show that use has been made of 7:30-31 and also, in abbreviated form, in 32:34-35.[29] Jeremiah 32:30-35, as Holladay has indicated, is "a pastiche from genuine paranetic material elsewhere."[30]

Jeremiah 7:34, the final verse in 7:30-34 at the end of Jeremiah 7, has its parallels in 16:9; 25:10, where the message of doom envisages the cessation of mirth and gladness, and the voice of the bridegroom and bride. However, this situation will be reversed (33:10a, 11a) when the fortunes of the land are eventually restored.

9. JEREMIAH 7:34 (and parallels in 16:9; 25:10 and 33:10a, 11a)

JEREMIAH 7:34
I will make to cease from the cities of Judah and from the streets of Jerusalem the voice of mirth and the voice of gladness, the voice of the bridegroom and the voice of the bride; for the land shall become a waste.

Comment

These phrases do not belong to the Deuteronomistic literature, and have already been discussed above (chap. six, pp. 113-114). The sequence is

---

[24] McKane, *Jeremiah 1*, 454. Note also: "The Topheth theme is more firmly embedded in chapter 7 than it is in chapter 19."
[25] McKane, *Jeremiah 1*, lxxxvi.
[26] The final א at the end of הַחֲטִיא has been dropped by haplography.
[27] Andersen and Forbes, *VOT*, 444.
[28] Hubmann, *Untersuchungen*, 227.
[29] See Macchi, "Les Doublets," 126, and n. 23.
[30] Holladay, *Jeremiah 2*, 207. Note also Marx, "A propos des doublets," 117. He claims, "The résumé of Jer 32:26-35 knows ch. 7 in its actual form and takes up again from it the sequence of the accusations" (p. 117).

faithfully followed in 16:9; 25:10; 33:11a, with some differences in introducing the series (וְהִשְׁבַּתִּי, 7:34; הִנְנִי מַשְׁבִּית, 16:9; וְהַאֲבַדְתִּי, 25:10). Jeremiah 16:9 has the phrase מִן־הַמָּקוֹם הַזֶּה לְעֵינֵיכֶם וּבִימֵיכֶם, and 25:10, מֵהֶם, in place of יְרוּשָׁלִָם. קוֹל רֵחַיִם וְאוֹר נֵר (7:34). Jeremiah 25:10 adds to the series מֵעָרֵי יְהוּדָה וּמֵחֻצוֹת ("the voice [i.e., sound] of the handmill and the light of the lamp").[31] Jeremiah 25:11a begins with the words: וְהָיְתָה כָּל־הָאָרֶץ הַזֹּאת לְחָרְבָּה (cf. תִּהְיֶה הָאָרֶץ כִּי לְחָרְבָּה in 7:34, where some manuscripts, the LXX [πᾶσα ἡ γῆ], Syr, point to כָּל־הָאָרֶץ as the original wording).

The repetition of these phrases, adapted to different contexts, is an indication of the way in which the sermonic passages have been built up. Thiel regards 16:9, where Jeremiah is addressed and forbidden to take a wife, as the basic passage from which 7:34 and 25:10 have been drawn.[32] However, I believe a good case can be made for regarding 7:34 as the primary passage (7:33 speaks of death; 7:34, of weddings; all life is affected and prospects for the future are grim in the extreme). Whatever the precise relationships between these passages may be, we can conclude that in the process of redaction freedom was exercised in using well-known stereotyped formulae, considered to be part of the Jeremiah tradition.

Another example is to be found in the parallel phrases in Jer 8:2b; 16:4a and 25:33b (cf. 9:21 [9:22E]).

10. JEREMIAH 8:2b = JEREMIAH 16:4a = JEREMIAH 25:33b

JEREMIAH 8:2b
[a] They shall not be gathered or buried; [a] [b] they shall become dung on the face of the ground.[b]

JEREMIAH 16:4a
[a] They shall not be mourned or buried;[a] [b] they shall become dung on the face of the ground.[b]

JEREMIAH 25:33b
[a] They shall not be mourned, or gathered, or buried;[a] [b] they shall become dung on the face of the ground.[b]

Textual and Translational Notes

[a...a] לֹא יֵאָסְפוּ וְלֹא יִקָּבֵרוּ ("they shall not be gathered or buried," 8:2b); יִקָּבֵרוּ. לֹא יִסָּפְדוּ וְלֹא יֵאָסְפוּ וְלֹא ("they shall not be mourned or buried," 16:4a); יִקָּבֵרוּ לֹא יִסָּפְדוּ וְלֹא ("they shall not be mourned or gathered or buried," 25:33b). Note also the phrase לֹא יִקָּבֵרוּ וְלֹא־יִסָּפְדוּ in 16:6. The LXX has οὐ κοπήσονται καὶ οὐ ταφήσονται in both 8:2b and 16:4a. This raises questions concerning the Hebrew verbs in the *Vorlage*, which would be expected to be the same in both

---

[31] LXX ὀσμὴν μύρου, which probably represents רֵיחַ מוֹר ("the perfume of myrrh"), is more appropriate in this context; cf. McKane, *Jeremiah 1*, 624.

[32] Thiel, *Redaktion 1*, 197.

cases (i.e., יִסָּפְדוּ followed by יִקָּבְרוּ); but there is nothing to account for the difference in the present Hebrew text, although the fact that יֵאָסְפוּ and יִסָּפְדוּ have the two consonants סד in common may suggest an error in transmission in 8:2b. In any case, all three verbs appear in 25:33bMT, drawing on both 8:2b and 16:4a. Since only one verb is found in the LXX (32:19b=25:33bMT), we may conclude that לֹא יִסָּפְדוּ וְלֹא יֵאָסְפוּ is a late addition in the Hebrew text, for which 16:4a is the primary source.[33]

b...b לְדֹמֶן עַל־פְּנֵי הָאֲדָמָה יִהְיוּ. All three texts (8:2b; 16:4a; 25:33b) coincide in this instance. However, παράδειγμα in 8:2bLXX; 16:4aLXX (cf. 9:21LXX) indicates that דֹּמֶן was misunderstood (perhaps thought to be derived from דמה I ("to be like, resemble"). κόπρια in 25:33b is the appropriate equivalent in Greek. We should take into consideration also 9:21(22E), where the phrase כְּדֹמֶן עַל־פְּנֵי הַשָּׂדֶה is a duplicate of the phrase in 2 Kgs 9:37 (regarding the corpse of Jezebel).[34] The words ascribed to Elijah in announcing the destiny of Jezebel are repeated in 9:21(H) in a Jeremianic poetic section which follows a prose section (9:12-15H) in which Baal worship is denounced and seen as the grounds for judgment.[35] Holladay regards 9:21 as the prototype for 8:2; 16:4; 25:33, but in any case 9:21 is indebted to 2 Kgs 9:37 for its phraseology.[36]

11. JEREMIAH 8:15=JEREMIAH 14:19b
See chap. one, pp. 7-8.

12. JEREMIAH 13:14b=JEREMIAH 21:7b

JEREMIAH 13:14b
I will not spare or show pity or have compassion by not destroying them.

JEREMIAH 21:7b
He will not pity them or spare (them) or have compassion.

Textual and Translational Notes

The three verbs חמל, חוס and רחם (13:14b) appear in the order חוס, חמל and רחם in 21:7b. The 1st s. forms in 13:14b have been changed to 3d s. in 21:7b. Jeremiah 21:7bLXX, however, retains 1st s. forms, and leaves out the verb חמל.

---

[33] Janzen, *Studies*, 45.
[34] Cf. Ps 83:11 (10E), regarding the fate of Sisera and Jabin, where the phrase is לָאֲדָמָה הָיוּ דֹמֶן, similar to the other Jeremiah passages.
[35] Holladay (*Jeremiah 1*), "quoting the old phrase" (p. 57). Cf. Thiel, *Redaktion 1*, 130.
[36] Holladay, "Prototype and Copies: A New Approach to the Poetry-Prose Problem in the Book of Jeremiah," *JBL* 79 (1960) 351-367 (p. 359). For a critique, see Thiel, *Redaktion 1*, p. 130 n. 76.

The final word in 13:14b, מֵהַשְׁחִיתָם ("away from destroying them") is not repeated in 21:7bMT (and is also missing in the LXX). The verb שחת is the connecting link between 13:14 and 13:1-11 (cf. שחת in 31:9, 10).

Comment

The symbolic action of the loincloth (13:1-11) and the saying "Every jar shall be filled with wine" (13:12) are more closely linked together by 13:14, which should be regarded as an addition.[37] McKane draws attention to the fragility of jars and the thought of "shattering."[38]

In the case of 21:7b, McKane has noted that 21:6 looks to "a great pestilence" as the cause of death of the inhabitants of Jerusalem (נדול ימתו בדבר), in keeping with 52:4-6(=2 Kgs 25:1-3). Jeremiah 21:7 has been added, referring to the well-known triad of pestilence, sword and famine (in this order, so as to connect with דבר in 21:6) and with the repetition of the phrase 21:7b=13:14b.[39] Since 21:7bLXX uses the 1st s. form of the verbs, the probability is that the *Vorlage* was similar to that of 13:14b, although one verb in the LXX is missing (חמל). Subsequently, the Hebrew verbs were changed to the 3d s., and made to apply to Nebuchadrezzar.

The most satisfactory explanation of the data is that 13:14b was later added to 13:12-14a, as was 21:7 to 21:3-6 (drawing upon the vocabulary of 13:14b in 21:7b). This is a good example of piecemeal addition at a later stage in the evolution of prose sections of the book, probably the work of learned scribes.

13. JEREMIAH 17:10b=JEREMIAH 32:19b

JEREMIAH 17:10b	JEREMIAH 32:19b
[a] ... to give to everyone [a] according to his way(s),[a] [b] according to the fruit of his deeds.[b]	... to give to each [a] according to his ways [a] [b] and according to the fruit of his doings. [b]

Textual and Translational Notes

[a...a] כִּדְרָכָו (17:10b); כִּדְרָכָיו (32:19b). Jeremiah 17:10b(LXX), κατὰ τὰς ὁδοὺς, supports the plural (*qere*) rather than the singular (*kethib*). However, 4QJer[a] (כדרכו) attests the singular (cf. Vg *viam*). The plural (כִּדְרָכָיו) in 32:19bMT is

---

[37] Holladay (*Jeremiah 1*), "Evidently v.14 is a later addition to vv.12aβ-13: the images of 'drunkenness' and 'smashing' are difficult to bring together" (p. 402). Nevertheless, Holladay (p. 401) regards 13:14 as authentic.
[38] McKane, *Jeremiah 1*, 297.
[39] McKane, *Jeremiah 1*, 500.

in the singular in the LXX, but is supported by Vg *vias suas*. Jeremiah 32:19a already contains the plural (עַל־כָּל־דַּרְכֵי, cf. LXX εἰς τὰς ὁδοὺς). In all likelihood, plural forms eventually prevailed in the Hebrew text, so that דרכיו and מעלליו would match one another.

[b...b] כִּפְרִי מַעֲלָלָיו (17:10b); וְכִפְרִי מַעֲלָלָיו (32:19b). The copula וְ is found in 17:10bLXX (καὶ) and could easily have fallen out by haplography. The phrase is missing in 39:19bLXX. A phrase linking פרי and מעלל (pl.) is found in Isa 3:10 and in Mic 7:13. Note also דַּרְכֶּךָ וּמַעֲלָלַיִךְ in Jer 4:18; as well as מַעַלְלֵיכֶם כִּפְרִי (21:14).

Comment

The poetic unit 17:9-10 is somewhat similar to 11:20=20:12 and "may represent a stage in Jeremiah's spiritual pilgrimage."[40] Jeremiah 32:19b comes within Jeremiah's prayer (32:17-25, in prose). According to Bright, the original prayer consisted only of 32:17a ("Ah, Lord Yahweh!") and 32:24-25, with the section concerning the incomparability of Yahweh (32:17b-23) as a later insertion.[41] Jeremiah 32:19b shows indebtedness to 17:10b. The addition of the final phrase in 32:19b (missing in the LXX) is another indication of the way in which learned scribes completed passages that were already in part parallel.

Three verses (17:26; 32:44 and 33:13), each in a context of prose, list political and geographical areas in the restored land of Judah; all may be considered late, for reasons given below. The LXX follows the MT closely in all three passages.[42]

14. JEREMIAH 17:26; JEREMIAH 32:44; JEREMIAH 33:13

JEREMIAH 17:26	JEREMIAH 32:44
People shall come [a] from the cities of Judah [a] and [b] from the environs of Jerusalem,[b] [c] from the land of Benjamin,[c] [d] from the Shephelah,[d] [e] from the hill country,[e] and [f] from the Negeb,[f] bringing burnt offerings and sacrifices, cereal offerings and frankincense, and bringing thankofferings to the	People shall buy for money and sign and seal deeds and witnesses witness [c] in the land of Benjamin[c] and [b] in the environs of Jerusalem, [b] [a] in the cities of Judah, [a] [e] in the cities of the hill country, [e] [d] in the cities of the

---

[40] McKane, *Jeremiah 1*, 397.

[41] Bright, *Jeremiah*, 298. Jones (*Jeremiah*) demonstrates that 32:20-23 are "a conglomerate of Deuteronomic phrases adapted to their present purpose" (p. 412).

[42] Note, however, that for 17:26MT וּמִן־הַנֶּגֶב, the LXX has ἐκ τῆς πρὸς νότον ("from the [country] to the south"), whereas for וּבְעָרֵי הַנֶּגֶב (32:44; 33:13), the LXX has ἐν πόλεσι τῆς Ναγεβ. The formula נְאֻם־יְהוָה is missing at the end of 32:44 in the LXX version.

house of Yahweh.

Shephelah [d] and [f] in the cities of the Negeb;[f] for I shall restore their fortunes — oracle of Yahweh.

JEREMIAH 33:13
[e] In the cities of the hill country,[e] [d] in the cities of the Shephelah [d] and [f] in the cities of the Negeb,[f] [c] in the land of Benjamin,[c] [b] in the environs of Jerusalem,[b] and [a] in the cities of Judah,[a] flocks shall again pass by the hands of the one who counts (them), says Yahweh.

Comment

All six regions appear in a different order in each of the texts: 17:26 abcdef, 32:40 cbaedf, 33:13 edfcba. The order in 17:26 is logical: first, the political divisions (cities of Judah, environs of Jerusalem, land of Benjamin), then geographical areas (the Shephelah, the hill county, the Negeb). The order in 32:44 is to some extent dictated by the need to mention the land of Benjamin first, since this is where the field sold by Hanamel was located. Jeremiah 33:13 goes back to וּבְכָל־עָרָיו in 33:12, but in the elaboration of this the order is reversed, with geographical areas being named before the political regions. Of interest is the fact that the phrase in 32:43, שְׁמָמָה הִיא מֵאֵין אָדָם וּבְהֵמָה ("It is a desolation without man or beast"), appears in slightly different form in 33:12, הֶחָרֵב מֵאֵין־אָדָם וְעַד־בְּהֵמָה (cf. 33:10).[43] Both 32:44 and 33:11 contain the שְׁבוּת שׁוּב formula regarding Yahweh restoring fortunes (cf. 33:7). In spite of the emphasis on the north country in Jeremiah 30 and 31 (i.e., the references to Israel, Jacob and Ephraim and the inclusion of Judah and Israel in 33:7), 32:44 and 33:13 focus attention on Judah, with "the land of Benjamin" (32:44; 33:13; 17:26) encompassing only a limited area to the north of Jerusalem.

Any attempt at reconstructing the process by which these verses were added is admittedly conjectural. In all probability, 32:44 was added first, as an amplification of 32:43, with "the land of Benjamin" (where the field redeemed by Jeremiah was located) in first position. This was followed by 33:13, filling out "in all of its cities" (33:12), and finally by 17:26, an addition within 17:24-27, in which interest shifts from keeping the sabbath to the temple and the resumption of sacrificial offerings in the post-exilic community. Freedom was exercised in making the additions, as the different order in which the regions are named demonstrates, but these passages illustrate the way in which expansions contain specific details (cf. 31:38-40).

We now turn to the doublet 21:9=38:2, where the triad "sword, famine and pestilence" appears (see above, chap. two, pp. 21-23).

---

[43] Thiel, *Redaktion 2*. He states, "V.44 is imitated in 33:13" (p. 37). Jeremiah 33 is dependent on Jeremiah 32 (cf. 33:2 and 32:17; "I will restore their fortunes" in 32:44; 33:7, 11, 26).

15. JEREMIAH 21:9=JEREMIAH 38:2

JEREMIAH 21:9
He who stays in this city [b] shall die by the sword and by famine and by pestilence;[b] but he who goes out [c] and surrenders [c] to the Chaldeans [d] who are besieging you[d] shall live [e] and shall have his life as a prize of war.[e]

JEREMIAH 38:2
[a] Thus says Yahweh:[a] He who stays in this city [b] shall die by the sword, by famine and by pestilence;[b] but he who goes out to the Chaldeans shall live; [e] He shall have his life as a prize of war,[e] [f] and live.[f]

Textual and Translational Notes

[a...a] כֹּה אָמַר יְהוָה, 38:2; cf. 21:8, where the context is "the way of life and the way of death," reminiscent of Deut 30:15, 19. However, whereas faithfulness to Yahweh, "walking in his ways," and renunciation of other gods is the Deuteronomic basis on which "life" depends, "life" in 21:9=38:2 results from surrender to the Babylonians, but seems to imply more than mere survival (see [e...e] below).

[b...b] יָמוּת בַּחֶרֶב וּבָרָעָב וּבַדָּבֶר 21:9; 38:2 omits *waw* before בָרָעָב, (as do many manuscripts, 21:9). Here is the familiar triad, "sword, famine, pestilence" (cf. 21:7 "pestilence, sword, famine"). דֶּבֶר ("pestilence") is missing in the LXX in both 21:9 and 38:2. The LXX uses θάνατος as the equivalent of דֶּבֶר in 14:12; 21:6; 24:10, and is without דֶּבֶר in 27:8 (34:6LXX), as well as in 32:24 (39:24LXX); 42:17 (49:17LXX); 42:22 (49:22LXX); 44:13 (51:13LXX). The entire verse 27:13 is missing in the LXX, perhaps by haplography. In the case of 32:36 (39:36LXX), ἐν ἀποστολῇ ("by banishment") is substituted for בַּדֶּבֶר, which may point to בַּשְּׁבִי.[44] The Greek text in all these instances indicates a Hebrew *Vorlage* which contained only the two terms חֶרֶב and רָעָב. Other examples where only the two terms חֶרֶב and רָעָב occur in MT are 5:12; 11:22; 14:13, 15 (*bis*), 16, 18; 16:4; 42:16; 44:12 (*bis*), 18, 27.[45] Jeremiah 21:6 stresses "a great pestilence" in the city of Jerusalem at the time of the Babylonian siege (cf. 52:6=2 Kgs 25:3), which accounts for the order "pestilence, sword, famine" in 21:7. In course of time, the triad "sword, famine, pestilence" became normative and stereotypical in the Hebrew text (as in 21:9=38:2). However, sometimes the triad occurs in a context where only "sword" and "famine" are otherwise mentioned; e.g., 14:12 (cf. 14:13, 15, 16,

---

[44] Jeremiah 15:2MT includes a fourth category, שְׁבִי ("captivity"), but the LXX translates as αἰχμαλωσία here.

[45] See Janzen, *Studies*, 43–44, and p. 205 n. 19.

18); 42:17 (cf. 42:16); 44:13 (cf. 44:12, 18, 27). This indicates that חֶרֶב and רָעָב are the primary terms; the triad is an editorial expansion.⁴⁶

ᶜ⁻⁻⁻ᶜ וְנָפַל (21:9); προσχωρῆσαι (21:9LXX). The verb is not duplicated in 38:2, and is explained in 21:9 by Holladay as "a clarifying gloss."⁴⁷ For נָפַל עַל ("surrender") see also 37:14; 39:9; 52:15=2 Kgs 25:11.

ᵈ⁻⁻⁻ᵈ הַצָּרִים עֲלֵיכֶם ("who are besieging you," 21:9) does not occur in 38:2, and was probably added from 21:4.

ᵉ⁻⁻⁻ᵉ וְהָיְתָה־לּוֹ נַפְשׁוֹ לְשָׁלָל ("and shall have his life as a prize of war," 21:9; 38:2). This phrase, which occurs only in the book of Jeremiah, is found also in 39:18 (Yahweh's word to Ebed—melech, "you shall have your life as a prize of war") and in 45:5 (Yahweh's word to Baruch, "I will give your life as a prize of war"). The only other occurrences of שָׁלָל ("prize of war, booty") in Jeremiah are in the OAN: 49:32, concerning "camels"; 50:10, "the Chaldeans." For שָׁלָל in Deuteronomy, see Deut 3:7; 13:17 (13:16E); 20:14.

The phrase "to have one's life as a prize of war" is considered by Bright to have originated in a military setting and to indicate that the only "booty" in some cases was the preservation of one's life, barely to escape alive.⁴⁸ Jeremiah 21:9LXX translates לְשָׁלָל as εἰς σκῦλα ("as booty"), but 45:2LXX (=38:2MT), εἰς εὕρημα ("as a windfall"), comes closer to this point of view.⁴⁹ In all probability, the phrase reflects an authentic saying of Jeremiah, but a question remains concerning the precise menaing in the various contexts in which it occurs in the book of Jeremiah.⁵⁰ Kilpp maintains that 45:5 is the basic passage.⁵¹

Although there is an implied rebuke to Baruch in 45:5a ("do you seek great things for yourself?"), Yahweh's promise to give him his life as a prize of war is surely more than a promise of survival, and the additional phrase "in all places to which you may go" carries with it the assurance of protection.⁵² Yahweh's promise to Ebed-melech (39:18) is in a context (39:16-18) where the verbs נצל Hiphil (39:17; cf. the promise to Jeremiah in 1:8, "I am with you to

---

⁴⁶ McKane (*Jeremiah 2*),"...the preponderance of the threefold formula in MT is due to editorial processes of expansion and systematization which were largely incomplete when the Septuagint translation was made" (p. 948).

⁴⁷ Holladay, *Jeremiah 1*, 573.

⁴⁸ Bright, *Jeremiah*, 184–185. Volz(*Jeremia*, 219) points to the ironic nature of this proverbial saying.

⁴⁹ McKane (*Jeremiah 1*), "bare survival is a 'windfall'" (p. 502).

⁵⁰ See Hubmann, *Untersuchungen*, 226. He finds in both 21:0 and 38:2 "a genuine kernel."

⁵¹ Kilpp, *Niederreissen und aufbauen* (Biblisch-Theologische Studien 13; Neukirchen-Vluyn: Neukirchener Verlag, 1990), p. 87 n. 12; cf. Thiel, *Redaktion 2*, 86.

⁵² Cf. Taylor, "Jeremiah 45." She claims, "'The great things' might be a position of influence which he had hoped to occupy by the side of Jeremiah in the reconstruction of the new Israel" (p. 81).

deliver you") and מלט Piel (39:18 "I will surely save you") occur; a reward "because you have put your trust in me."

Jeremiah 21:8, the introduction to 21:9, refers to "the way of life" and "the way of death" (cf. the choice between "life" and "death" in Deut 30:15, 19). This suggests to the reader that הַחַיִּים ("life") in this context means more than bare survival, and points to Yahweh as promised in Deut 30:15-20.

f...f וָחָי (38:2); καὶ ζήσεται (in both 21:9LXX and 45:2LXX=38:2MT). McKane regards וָחָי as superfluous, in view of יִחְיֶה already present in this verse.[53] However, the textual data may be interpreted differently. καὶ ζήσεται in 21:9LXX points to וָחָי ("and live") as part of the original Hebrew text (retained in some manuscripts), as if to highlight the significance of the guarantee of life. More than prudential action is counseled; certainly not incitement to treason, but in the light of the inevitability of the Babylonian conquest, to accept Yahweh's will and surrender means "life" for those who obey. Jeremiah 38:2 follows the model of 21:9.[54] Jeremiah 39:15-18, the promise to Ebed-melech, according to Holladay "fits poorly in the context."[55] The reason why this passage is found in its present position is not readily determined.[56] However, the redactional insertion of 39:15-18 appears to reflect a tradition that Ebed-melech, like Baruch, was given a special promise which goes beyond survival, as the verbs נצל Hiphil (39:17) and מלט Piel ("I will surely save you," 39:18) imply.[57]

Comment

The role of *inclusio* requires attention in Jeremiah 21-45; the phrase "to have one's נֶפֶשׁ as a שָׁלָל" occurs both near the beginning (21:9) and at the very end (45:5), as well as in 38:2 and 39:18. This suggests that late in the editorial process, this phrase served the purpose of bringing together the narrative portions and prose discourses relating to the destruction of Jerusalem and its aftermath.[58]

Another phrase with נֶפֶשׁ "to long (yearn) to return" (נשא Piel + נפש) is found both in 22:27 and 44:14. Jeremiah 22:27 applies to Jehoiachin (כָּנְיָהוּ) and

---

[53] McKane, *Jeremiah 2*, 948.
[54] For Rudolph (*Jeremia*), "38:2 is a gloss," based on 21:9 (p. 136).
[55] Holladay, *Jeremiah 2*, 281. He proposes a shift to a position after 38:27.
[56] McKane, *Jeremiah 2*, 1992.
[57] Cf. Ps 41:2 (41:1E) and the promises which follow; note expecially the verbs שמר ("protect"), חיה ("keep alive"), אשר ("call blessed"), in 41:3MT.
[58] Cf. Holladay's remarks concerning *inclusio* in *The Architecture of Jeremiah 1-20* (London: Associated Presses, 1976) 169.

his mother, destined for exile in Babylon, never to return.[59] Jeremiah 44:14 has to do with the "remnant of Judah" who fled to Egypt; they also will not return to the land of Egypt, although they yearn to do so, "except some fugitives."[60]

The word "doublet" is perhaps inappropriate as a description of some passages with many phrases in common, such as 24:8–10 and 29:16–19; 25:3b–6a and 35:14b–15. They are not direct parallels, but contain numerous clichés which will be discussed in chapter thirteen. We conclude this chapter with an investigation of four parallel passages which are of exceptional interest: 26:3=36:3; 32:4=34:3; 34:22a=37:8; 39:3=39:13.

16. JEREMIAH 26:3=JEREMIAH 36:3

JEREMIAH 26:3
[a] Perhaps they will listen[a]
[b] and each turn from his evil way;[b]
[c] then I will relent[c] [d] from the disaster which I am proposing to bring about to them [d] [e] for the evil of their deeds.[e]

JEREMIAH 36:3
[a] Perhaps the house of Judah will hear[a] [b] all the disaster that I am proposing to bring about him [d] [b] so that each may turn from his evil way [b]
[f] and that I may forgive their iniquity and their sin.[f]

Textual and Translational Notes

[a...a] אוּלַי יִשְׁמְעוּ בֵּית יְהוּדָה, 26:3; אוּלַי יִשְׁמְעוּ, 36:3. The subject implied in 26:3 is "all the cities of Judah"; in 36:3 "the house of Judah."

[b...b] וְיָשֻׁבוּ אִישׁ מִדַּרְכּוֹ הָרָעָה, 26:3; לְמַעַן יָשׁוּבוּ אִישׁ מִדַּרְכּוֹ הָרָעָה, 36:3. Whereas the phrase in 26:3 is governed by the previous אוּלַי ("perhaps"), 36:3 uses לְמַעַן to express purpose, "to the end that" (cf. LXX ἵνα).

[c...c] וְנִחַמְתִּי (+ אֶל -), 26:3. The meaning of the verb here is "relent" (cf. παύσομαι LXX "cease") rather than "repent."[61]

[d...d] אֶל־הָרָעָה אֲשֶׁר אָנֹכִי חֹשֵׁב לַעֲשׂוֹת לָהֶם, 26:3;
אֵת כָּל־הָרָעָה אֲשֶׁר אָנֹכִי חֹשֵׁב לַעֲשׂוֹת לָהֶם, 36:3.
The phrase and its position in the sentence differ slightly.

---

[59] See W. J. Wessels, "Jeremiah 22,24–30. A Proposed Ideological Reading," *ZAW* 101 (1989) 232–249. Wessels regards 22:27 as an expansion added to 22:25-26 (p. 239).

[60] In view of 42:17, this final phrase is a gloss; cf. McKane (*Jeremiah 2*), "...clearly an adjustment which has been made in the light of the knowledge that some had returned from Egypt to Judah" (p. 1075).

[61] See D. Winton Thomas, "A Note on the Hebrew Root נחם," *ExpTim* 44 (1933), 191–92; Nicholson (*Preaching to the Exiles*) translates, "I will be relieved of my plan" (p. 52).

e...e מִפְּנֵי רֹעַ מַעַלְלֵיהֶם, 26:3. Although this phrase is not in 36:3, it is found in 4:4b=21:12b; 23:22.

f...f וְסָלַחְתִּי לַעֲוֹנָם וּלְחַטָּאתָם ("that I may forgive their iniquity and their sin," 36:3MT and LXX). The verb סלח ("forgive, pardon") occurs also in 5:1, 7; 31:34; 33:8; 50:20 (i.e., six of the thirty-three occurrences in the OT are found in Jeremiah).[62] In 31:34 (the new covenant), סלח occurs in the context of לעונם ולחטאתם. עָוֹן and חַטָּאת are coupled together, both in Jeremiah (e.g., 5:25; 14:10 [חטאת is missing in the LXX]; 16:10; 30:14, 15; 31:34; 50:20) and more frequently elsewhere in the OT (note especially Hos 4:8; 8:13; 9:9; 13:12).[63]

There is clearly a connection intended between Jeremiah 26 and 36.[64] Jeremiah's temple sermon (Jeremiah 26; cf. Jeremiah 7) early in the reign of Jehoiakim and the subsequent threat of the prophet's death finds a parallel in Jeremiah 36 (a few years later) when the scroll containing Jeremiah's words was burned by Jehoiakim, with Jeremiah and Baruch forced to hide to escape punishment. In the doublet 26:3=36:3, the hope is held out that a positive response to Jeremiah's proclamation will avert Yahweh's judgment (cf. 3:12b-13; 3:22; 4:1-2; 18:6-8; 36:7). If Jeremiah entertained such hopes, they were shattered by the obdurate attitude of "the inhabitants of Jerusalem" and "the men of Judah" who "would not hear" (36:31 וְלֹא שָׁמֵעוּ, the response to 36:3 אוּלַי יִשְׁמְעוּ). Jeremiah 26:3 and 36:3 contain a call for each to "turn from his evil way" (cf. 18:11; 25:5; 35:15; 36:7) and repeatedly there is the statement that this call went unheeded (15:7; 23:14; 44:5). An awareness of the tradition that Jeremiah did indeed at one stage put before his hearers "either-or" propositions, became a springboard for "preaching" passages in the Deuteronomistic style (e.g., the exhortation to "walk in my Torah," 26:4).[65]

17. JEREMIAH 32:4=JEREMIAH 34:3

JEREMIAH 32:4
Zedekiah [a] king of Judah [a] [b] will not escape from the hand of the Chaldeans,[b] [c] for he will surely be given into the hand of the king of Babylon [c] [d] and will speak with him face to face and see him eye to eye.[d]

JEREMIAH 34:3
[b] As for you, you will not escape from his hand, [b] [c] for you will surely be seized and given into his hand; [c] [d] you will see the king of Babylon eye to eye and face to face;[d] [e] and to Babylon you will go. [e]

---

[62] See Andersen and Forbes, *VOT*, 348. See Thiel, *Redaktion 2*, 26. Thiel claims that only four occurrences are pre-exilic: 2 Kgs 5:18 (*bis*); Amos 2:7; Jer 5:7.

[63] See Excursus in Hans Walter Wolff, *Hosea* (Hermeneia; Philadelphia: Fortress Press, 1974) 145.

[64] Rudolph (*Jeremiah*), "The original place of Ch. 26 was before Ch. 36" (p. 169).

[65] Jeremiah 26:4-5 and 2 Kgs 17:13; cf. the analysis of Jeremiah 36 and 2 Kings 17 by Nicholson, *Preaching to the Exiles*, 51-52.

Textual and Translational Notes

^{a...a} מֶלֶךְ יְהוּדָה, 32:4MT (missing in the LXX). יְהוּדָה in 39:1LXX (=32:1MT) is also missing. Note also that הַנָּבִיא (32:2MT) is not in the LXX. The process of filling out names and titles has been explored by Janzen.[66] If the LXX *Vorlage* is closer to the original Hebrew text, the somewhat pedantic addition of names and titles in the final form of the Hebrew text calls for an explanation. No compelling reason has been given; possibly this kind of elaboration was related to the reading of brief passages in the synagogue.

^{b...b} (34:3) וְאַתָּה לֹא תִמָּלֵט מִיָּדוֹ; (32:4) לֹא יִמָּלֵט מִיַּד הַכַּשְׂדִּים.
In 34:3, Zedekiah is addressed personally by Jeremiah (second person); in 32:4, the use of the third person is needed in a passage which duplicates 34:3 and provides the setting (Jeremiah kept in the court of the guard) for the incident of the purchase of Hanamel's field (Jeremiah 32). מִיָּדוֹ ("from his [Nebuchadrezzar's] hand") in 34:3, becomes "from the hand of the Chaldeans" in 32:4.

^{c...c} (32:4) כִּי הִנָּתֹן יִנָּתֵן בְּיַד מֶלֶךְ־בָּבֶל
(34:3) כִּי תָּפֹשׂ תִּתָּפֵשׂ וּבְיָדוֹ תִנָּתֵן
Jeremiah 34:3 contains the verb תפשׂ ("to seize"), a verb which occurs frequently in the narrative portions of the book of Jeremiah, e.g., 26:8; 34:3; 37:13, 14; 38:23; 40:10; (cf. Deut 20:10; 21:19; 1 Kgs 13:4; 18:40); in the OAN 46:9; 49:16; 50:4b; 51:32, 41; see also 52:9 (=2 Kgs 25:6) and 2:8.[67] מֶלֶךְ־בָּבֶל (32:4) occurs also in 34:3 (see ^{d...d}).

^{d...d} (32:4) וְדִבֶּר־פִּיו עִם פִּיו וְעֵינָיו אֶת־עֵינָו תִּרְאֶינָה
(34:3) וְעֵינֶיךָ אֶת־עֵינֵי מֶלֶךְ־בָּבֶל תִּרְאֶינָה וּפִיהוּ אֶת־פִּיךָ יְדַבֵּר
Apart from the change in person in the two passages, the order "face to face" and "eye to eye" is reversed. עֵינָו in 32:4 (*kethib*) is to be read as עֵינָיו (*qere*); cf. LXX τοὺς ὀφθαλμοὺς αὐτοῦ. Note also in the LXX 41:3 (=34:3MT) the phrase וּפִיהוּ אֶת־פִּיךָ יְדַבֵּר is missing.

^{e...e} The final phrase in 34:3, וּבָבֶל תָּבוֹא, is not present in 32:4, although 32:5 continues "and he shall take Zedekiah to Babylon." The remainder of the message to Zedekiah (34:4-5) is not paralleled in Jeremiah 32. Jeremiah 32:3 duplicates the statement in 34:2: הִנְנִי נֹתֵן אֶת־הָעִיר הַזֹּאת בְּיַד מֶלֶךְ־בָּבֶל ("Behold, I am giving this city into the hand of the king of Babylon"), but whereas 34:3 adds וּשְׂרָפָהּ בָּאֵשׁ ("and he will burn it with fire"; cf. 34:22; 37:10; 38:18; 39:8; 52:13), 32:3 reads וּלְכָדָהּ ("and he will take it"). Both verbs are combined in

---

[66] Janzen, *Studies*, chap. 4.
[67] The unusual phrase in 2:8, תֹּפְשֵׂי הַתּוֹרָה ("those who handle the law," RSV; "those who interpreted the law," McKane, *Jeremiah*, 30; "the teachers of the law," Tg) represents a specialized use, referring to the priests (Rudolph, *Jeremiah*, 16), the Levites (Craigie, *Jeremiah*, 29), or possibly the scribes (cf. 8:8).

34:22 (cf. 37:8; see 34:22=37:8 below). Nothing is said in Jeremiah 32 about a peaceful death for king Zedekiah.

Comment

The doublet 32:4=34:3, as well as the phrase which 32:3 and 34:2 have in common ("Behold, I am giving this city into the hand of the king of Babylon") prompt an investigation into the introductions to Jeremiah 32 and 34 (32:1-5; 34:1-7), together with the wider question of how Jeremiah 30-35 finally arrived in its present order. The two introductions may indeed preserve a trace of the tradition of actual words spoken to Zedekiah by Jeremiah (e.g., in the doublet), but in their present form they are largely editorial, following the pattern which is so prominent throughout the narrative passages, in which approximate or even precise dates and situations have been supplied (note 32:2; 34:1; 35:1). Clearly, no strict chronological order has been maintained (cf. also 36:1; 37:1; 39:1). Jeremiah 30-33 has reached its present form by bringing together material with a dominant theme: hope for the future and the importance of covenantal relationships Jeremiah 30-31 (the book of Consolation); Jeremiah 32, the purchase of Hanamel's field as a sign of confidence in the future, summed up in 32:15; Jeremiah 33, the restoration of the fortunes of Judah and Israel.

Jeremiah 32 may have stood at one time between Jeremiah 37 and 38.[68] In the case of Jeremiah 34, the connection between 34:1-7 and 34:8-22 is somewhat loose.[69] However, 34:1-7 provides a setting for the incident of the manumission of slaves for a limited time (34:8-22), which goes back to a tradition that this took place during the final months of the siege of Jerusalem.[70] The temporary withdrawal of the Babylonian army (34:21) because of the movement of Egyptian forces (37:5) in no way modified Jeremiah's conviction (34:2, 22) that Jerusalem would fall. Perhaps this time of withdrawal was interpreted as Yahweh's favourable response to the liberation of slaves, but the motivation for their release may have been primarily to provide additional manpower for the defence of Jerusalem.[71] The unit 34:8-22,

---

[68] Seitz (*Theology in Conflict*), "If the core unit of Chap. 32, together with a temporal notice supplied in 32:2, was originally found between Chaps. 37 and 38, the sequence of events is better displayed" (p. 245).

[69] Seitz, *Theology in Conflict*, 242.

[70] Jeremiah 34:6-7 records that at this time, Lachish and Azekah were the only fortified cities that had withheld the Babylonian invasion. For the Lachish Ostraca, see James B. Pritchard, ed., *Ancient Near Eastern Texts Relating to the Old Testament* (2d ed.; Princeton, New Jersey: Princeton University Press, 1955) 321-322. They provide valuable information regarding the siege of Lachish (Ostracon 4 mentions both Lachish and Azekah, under siege).

[71] See Weippert, *Die Prosareden*, 86-106. She has made a thorough investigation of Jeremiah 34 and suggests a double reason, political as well as religious, for the manumission of slaves at this time, pointing out that political considerations, both in releasing and also in

as it now stands, has been heavily edited in the interests of relating this incident to the requirements of the Torah (e.g., 34:14-15 and Deut 15:12-18; Exod 21:2) and the covenant ritual referred to in 34:18-20, which is connected with Gen 15:7-22. The disobedience related in Jeremiah 34 is in sharp contrast to the loyalty of the Rechabites to their promises in Jeremiah 35.

We return to the doublet 32:4=34:3 and the relationship of 32:3-5 to 34:2-5. Jeremiah 34:2-5 seems to be the primary passage, although the original form has been changed by additions and perhaps also by omissions. In the LXX account (41:2-5LXX=34:2-5MT) the phrase "speak with him face to face" in v. 3 is missing and "You shall not die by the sword" in v. 4. The promise of a peaceful death for Zedekiah and funeral honours (34:5) does not readily cohere with the declaration in the doublet of capture and banishment to Babylon. The final phrase in 34:5, "'I have spoken the word,'says Yahweh," is reminiscent of 4:28; 13:15.

The use of the particle אך ("only") at the beginning of 34:4 provides a clue suggesting that the original words to Zedekiah were in the form of an "either-or" proposition.[72] Failure to surrender to the king of Babylon will bring the dire consequences of 34:3. On the other hand, surrender will mean a peaceful death and funeral honours in Jerusalem.[73] The text has suffered during transmission. Selective use of 34:1-5 has been made in 32:1-5, in particular in the doublet 32:4=34:3. Jeremiah 32:3-4 goes back to 34:2-3, with minor changes regarding the capture of the city ("he [Nebuchadrezzar] shall take it" 32:3; cf. "he shall burn it with fire," 34:2; "face to face" and "eye to eye" in 32:4 reverses the order in 34:3). In the case of 32:3-5, Zedekiah is the speaker, quoting Jeremiah's words, indicating that Yahweh will "visit" Zedekiah after he has been taken to Babylon. Any suggestion of contingency in the prophetic oracle has now disappeared. Jeremiah 32:2 also states that Jeremiah "was shut up in the court of the guard," anticipating the imprisonments of 37:15, 21 (cf. 37:4 "he had not yet been put in prison").

18. JEREMIAH 34:22a=JEREMIAH 37:8

JEREMIAH 34:22a
[a] Behold, I am issuing a command, oracle of Yahweh,[a b] and will bring them back to this city, and they will fight against it, [b c] and take it,[c] and burn it with fire ...

JEREMIAH 37:8
[b] The Chaldeans will come back and will fight against this city;[b c] they will take it[c] and burn it with fire.

---

the calling back of slaves, were in play and perhaps even the decisive factors (p. 90).

[72] Norman H. Snaith ("The meaning of the Hebrew אך," VT 14 [1964] 221-225), "...אך always involves restrictions, an element of 'on the contrary,' and sometimes is even adversative" (p. 221).

[73] The use of the phrase הוי אדון in 34:5 is of interest, since the same phrase occurs in 22:18 (Jehoiakim will not be lamented at the time of his death). The lack of direct reference to Zedekiah in Jeremiah 22 is compensated for by 34:2-5.

Textual and Translational Notes

a...a הִנְנִי מְצַוֶּה נְאֻם־יְהוָה, 34:22a. Cf. הִנֵּה + צוה *Piel* participle (with Yahweh as subject) in Amos 6:11; 9:9, and the frequent use of צוה *Piel* participle after אָנֹכִי (Yahweh speaking) in the book of Deuteronomy (e.g., Deut 4:2; 11:13, 22, 27, 28; 12:11; 13:1; 27:1, 4; 28:14). Note also that 34:22b, מֵאֵין יוֹשֵׁב וְאֶת־עָרֵי יְהוּדָה אֶתֵּן שְׁמָמָה ("I will make the cities of Judah a desolation without inhabitant"), has an almost exact counterpart in 9:10b (9:11bE), the only difference being מִבְּלִי rather than מֵאֵין (and in 9:10b many manuscripts read מֵאֵין).

b...b וַהֲשִׁבֹתִים אֶל־הָעִיר הַזֹּאת וְנִלְחֲמוּ עָלֶיהָ (34:22a)
וְשָׁבוּ הַכַּשְׂדִּים וְנִלְחֲמוּ עַל־הָעִיר הַזֹּאת (37:8)

Jeremiah 34:21–22, in referring to the withdrawal and return of the Babylonian army, is drawing on 37:5, 8. Although 33:5a in its present form presents textual problems, in all probability this verse is also dependent on 37:8.

c...c וּלְכָדוּהָ (34:22a); וּלְכָדָהּ (37:8) — a slight difference in orthography. Jeremiah 34:22a and 37:8 bring together the verbs לכד and שׂרף, which occur separately in 32:3 and 34:2.

Comment

The sermonic character of 34:8–22 has often been noted.[74] The concept of בְּרִית ("covenant") is prominent (34:8, 10, 13, 15, 18), which explains the position of Jeremiah 34 after Jeremiah 30–33, where the covenantal formula (30:22; 31:3, 33; 32:38) and the term בְּרִית occur frequently (31:31; 32:40; 33:10, 21).[2][75]

19. JEREMIAH 39:3 = JEREMIAH 39:13

JEREMIAH 39:3
3. ... all the officials of the king of Babylon came and sat in the middle gate: Nergalsarezar of Simmargir, Nebushazban, the eunuch, Nergalsarezar, the rab Mag and all the rest of the officials of the king of Babylon.

JEREMIAH 39:13
13. Nebuzaradan, captain of the guard sent, and Nebushashban, the chief eunuch, Nergal-Sarezer, the Rab Mag, and all the rest of the officers of the king of of Babylon.

---

[74] E.g., Nicholson, *Preaching to the Exiles*, 64–65; Thiel, *Redaktion* 2, 43; Jones, *Jeremiah*, 425.

[75] The covenant formula and the term בְּרִית are discussed more fully below (chap. thirteen, pp. 268–270).

Textual and Translational Notes

In general, I have followed the translation of McKane in dealing with the Hebrew text in both verses.[76] The LXX of 39:13 is missing; in fact, the complete unit 39:4-13 is missing in the LXX. This is to be explained as the result of haplography, since both 39:3 and 39:13 end in מֶלֶךְ־בָּבֶל.[77]

Comment

Jeremiah 39:3 gives the names of the various "princes" and officers of the king of Babylon who "sat in the middle gate" of Jerusalem "to assert and enforce their new authority over the city."[78] Jeremiah 39:13 serves as a gloss correcting the names in 39:3 and adding the name of Nebuzaradan to those of the other officials mentioned in 39:3. Jeremiah 39:13 functions as a link with the probable original form of the narrative (38:28b; 39:3, 14). A fuller account of events at the time of the capture of Jerusalem has been introduced, overlooking the time element (52:12=2 Kgs 25:8) in which Nebuzaradan's actions took place one month later.[79] In view of the detailed and helpful discussion of the names of the Babylonian officials in 39:3 and 39:13 by McKane, I have not considered it necessary to make a detailed comparison of the parallel verses in this doublet.[80]

SUMMARY: DOUBLETS WITHIN THE BOOK OF JEREMIAH

1. JEREMIAH 2:26-28=JEREMIAH 32:32b; 32:32a; 11:13

All three passages (2:26-8; 11:9-13; 32:26-35) in which these doublets are found have to do with apostasy and idolatry. Jeremiah 11:13 and 32:32-33 have borrowed from 2:28b.

2. JEREMIAH 4:4b=JEREMIAH 21:12b

See chap. four, pp. 62-64.

---

[76] McKane, *Jeremiah 2*, 972.
[77] Janzen, *Studies*, p. 118.
[78] Holladay, *Jeremiah 2*, 291.
[79] Axel Graupner, *Auftrag und Geschick des Propheten Jeremia* (Biblisch-Theologische Studien 15; Neukirchen-Verluyn: Neukirchener Verlag, 1991). For him, "39:13 simply serves as a bracket" (p. 124).
[80] McKane, *Jeremiah 2*, 973-976. McKane's *addendum* (pp. 989-992) on the redactional theories of Wanke, Pohlmann and Thiel with regard to Jeremiah 39 is a very useful summary and critique.

3. JEREMIAH 4:5c=JEREMIAH 8:14a
Jeremiah 8:14 is an ironic statement borrowed from 4:5c.

4. JEREMIAH 5:9=JEREMIAH 5:29=JEREMIAH 9:8 (9:9E)
The threefold use of this refrain indicates the care with which the material in these chapters has been brought together in a unified way.

5. JEREMIAH 7:6=JEREMIAH 22:3
Jeremiah 22:3 reiterates the concern with "the alien, the orphan and the widow" and with the oppression expressed in the sermon in Jeremiah 7.

6. JEREMIAH 7:7=JEREMIAH 25:5
Jeremiah 25:5 (and the context in 25:3-7) reflects 7:7 and the temple sermon.

7. JEREMIAH 7:16=JEREMIAH 11:14
The prohibition of intercession in 7:16 is picked up again in 11:14 (cf. 14:11).

8. JEREMIAH 7:30-32=JEREMIAH 19:5-6, 11-12=JEREMIAH 32:34-35
Jeremiah 19:5-6, 11-12 have been added to Jeremiah 19 from 7:30-32. Jeremiah 19 contains much supplementary material, supporting the view of McKane that prose sections of the book of Jeremiah triggered further prose additions in the course of time.[81]

9. JEREMIAH 7:34; cf. JEREMIAH 16:9; 25:10; 23:11a
The view of Thiel that 16:9 is the primary passage may be correct, but 7:34, concluding the temple sermon, may have been used editorially in other parts of the book.[82] In any case, the phrases do not belong to the Deuteronomistic literature.

10. JEREMIAH 8:2b=JEREMIAH 16:4a=JEREMIAH 25:33b
Jeremiah 25:33b draws on both 8:2b and 16:4a.

11. JEREMIAH 8:15=JEREMIAH 14:19b
See chap. one, pp. 7-8.

12. JEREMIAH 13:14b=JEREMIAH 21:7b
Learned scribes made piecemeal additions to the book, such as those found here.

---

[81] McKane, *Jeremiah 1*, lxxxvi.
[82] Thiel, *Redaktion 1*, 197.

13. JEREMIAH 17:10b=JEREMIAH 32:19b

Jeremiah 32:19b shows indebtedness to 17:10b; 32:19b (missing in the LXX) is another indication of the way in which learned scribes completed passages that were already in part parallel.

14. JEREMIAH 17:26; JEREMIAH 32:34; JEREMIAH 33:13

Six regions are referred to, in a different order in each case. We may conjecture that 32:44 was added first (amplifying 32:43), then 33:13, defining "in all its cities" (33:12); finally 17:26, where the post-exilic community is envisaged, was added.

15. JEREMIAH 21:9=JEREMIAH 38:2

The triad "sword, famine and pestilence" has become normative and stereotypical. "He shall have his life as a prize of war" means more than mere survival, pointing to Yahweh's blessing (cf. Deut 30:15-20) and protection. This phrase is also applied to Ebed-melech (39:18) and to Baruch (45:5) and may reflect an authentic saying of Jeremiah. Late in the editorial process, the phrase in 21:9 and 45:5 serves as an *inclusio*, with the purpose of bringing together the narrative portions and prose discourses relating to the destruction of Jerusalem and its aftermath.

16. JEREMIAH 26:3=JEREMIAH 36:3

In this doublet, a hope is held out that a positive response to Jeremiah's proclamation will avert Yahweh's judgment. An awareness of the tradition that Jeremiah did indeed at one stage put before his hearers "either-or" propositions became a springboard for "preaching" passages in the Deuteronomistic style.

17. JEREMIAH 32:4=JEREMIAH 34:3

Jeremiah 34:2-5 seems to be the primary passage; 32:4 adds names and titles in a somewhat pedantic way (possibly this kind of elaboration was related to the reading of brief passages in the synagogue). Selective use of 34:1-5 has been made in 32:1-5; the promise to Zedekiah, "you shall die in peace" (34:5), no longer appears.

18. JEREMIAH 34:22a=JEREMIAH 37:8

Jeremiah 34:22a draws on 37:8.

19. JEREMIAH 39:3=39:13

Jeremiah 39:13 serves as a gloss correcting the names in 39:3 and adding the name of Nebuzaradan as a connecting link with the probable original form of the narrative (38:28b; 39:3, 14), into which the fuller account of the capture of Jerusalem has been inserted.

CHAPTER TEN

DOUBLETS AND PHRASES IN THE BOOK OF JEREMIAH WITH PARALLELS IN OTHER PARTS OF THE OLD TESTAMENT

In our investigation of doublets so far, some passages in the book of Jeremiah have already been found to have parallels in other parts of the OT. Many of these doublets occur in the OAN, especially with the books of Isaiah and Obadiah (see above, chap. seven, pp. 130-137, 139-140; 147-152). Parallel phrases also appear in both Jeremiah and other OT books. I shall examine each in turn.

DOUBLETS IN JEREMIAH AND IN OTHER BOOKS OF THE OLD TESTAMENT

We shall now examine doublets present in Jeremiah and other parts of the OT. There are doublets with eighth-century prophets (Hosea, Isaiah, Amos, Micah), as well as with Obadiah, Habakkuk and Ezekiel. Other doublets occur in Jeremiah and Deuteronomy, and also a number of Psalms. In some cases, the Jeremiah doublets have been drawn from earlier sources; in other instances, the dependency is in the other direction, particularly with some Psalms.[1]

JEREMIAH AND OTHER PROPHETS

1. JEREMIAH 14:10b = HOSEA 8:13b

JEREMIAH 14:10b
Therefore Yahweh does not accept them; now will he remember their iniquity [a] and punish their sins.[a]

HOSEA 8:13b
Yahweh does not accept them, now he will remember their iniquity [a] and punish their sins.[a]

---

[1] Holladay, *Jeremiah 2*, 35-70.

Textual and Translational Notes

a...a וַיִּפְקֹד חַטֹּאתָם, 14:10b; וְיִפְקֹד חַטֹּאותָם, Hos 8:13b. Jeremiah 14:10b and Hos 8:13b are identical, except for the slight difference in orthography (חַטֹּאתָם, חַטֹּאותָם). Hosea 9:9b consistently uses *scriptio plena* in the phrase יִפְקוֹד חַטֹּאתָם יִזְכּוֹר עֲוֹנָם. וַיִּפְקֹד חַטֹּאתָם is missing in Jeremiah 14:10bLXX.

Comment

The communal lament, Jer 14:7-9, is followed by Yahweh's rejoinder in the unit 14:10 (introduced by כֹּה אָמַר יְהוָה), in which Hos 8:13 is quoted. Catchword connections are present in the use of the noun עָוֹן ("iniquity," Jer 14:7, 10b) and the verb חָטָא ("to sin," Jer 14:7, 10b); note also the verb רָצָה ("to accept," Jer 14:10b, 12). Jeremiah 31:34 looks forward to a reverse situation, in which Yahweh will "forgive their iniquity" and "remember their sin no more."

The fact that the final phrase in Jer 14:10bMT is missing in the LXX is not easily explained. Perhaps Hos 8:13b was originally quoted without the final phrase, which was added later to the Hebrew text, both to conform to Hos 8:13b and also to make a more direct connection with Jer 14:7. In any event, 14:10b is somewhat awkward in style.[2]

JEREMIAH AND MICAH

2. JEREMIAH 26:18b=MICAH 3:12

This single doublet in Jeremiah and Micah has been discussed in chap. one, pp. 8—9. Micah 3:12 is directly quoted.

JEREMIAH AND OBADIAH

3. JEREMIAH 49:9=OBADIAH 5
4. JEREMIAH 49:14-16= OBADIAH 4

These doublets have already been considered in chap. seven, pp. 147—152, where the conclusion was reached that each drew on a common source.

---

[2] See Carroll, *Jeremiah*, 311. He states, "The artificiality of the composition becomes clear in v.10; ...v.10 has nothing to do with a drought; ...v.10 comes from a different strand of tradition to that of the lament."

JEREMIAH AND HABAKKUK

5. JEREMIAH 51:58d = HABAKKUK 2:13

See chap. eight, pp. 181-182. Both passages probably rest on a popular proverb.

JEREMIAH AND EZEKIEL

6. JEREMIAH 31:29 = EZEKIEL 18:2

JEREMIAH 31:29	EZEKIEL 18:2
[a] In those days people will no longer say, [a] 'The fathers [c] have eaten [c] sour grapes and [d] the children's [d] teeth are set on edge.'	What do you mean by repeating [b] this proverb [b] concerning the land of Egypt: 'The fathers [c] have eaten [c] sour grapes and [d] the children's [d] are set on edge'?

Textual and Translational Notes

[a...a] בַּיָּמִים הָהֵם לֹא־יֹאמְרוּ עוֹד ("in those days people will no longer say," 31:29). The phrase בַּיָּמִים הָהֵם(ה) occurs in other late passages: 33:15, 16; 50:4, 20.[3] The sequence of oracles beginning with הִנֵּה יָמִים בָּאִים ("behold, days are coming," 31:27, 31, 38) is interrupted by the introductory phrase in 31:29. Jeremiah 3:16 also contains the phrase לֹא־יֹאמְרוּ עוֹד (cf. 23:7 and a similar phrase in 16:14).

[b...b] אֶת־הַמָּשָׁל הַזֶּה ("this proverb," Ezek 18:2). The proverb was doubtless well-known, although it is probable that 31:29-30 is best understood as an intrusive note inserted redactionally by a learned scribe who was aware of the extensive commentary in Ezekiel 18. He may also have had in mind the similar passage, Ezek 14:13-20, regarding the inability of righteous men (Noah, Daniel and Job) to "deliver" (נצל Niphal and Hiphil) "sons and daughters," as well as passages from Deuteronomy, to be discussed below.[4]

[c...c] אָכְלוּ (31:29); יֹאכְלוּ (Ezek 18:2); ἔφαγον in both LXX passages suggests that the original reading was אָכְלוּ in both MT passages.

---

[3] Holladay (*A Fresh Reading* [New York: The Pilgrim Press, 1990]), "...passages in Jeremiah that speak of a change of speech-pattern (3:16; 23:7-8) betray a late date" (p. 132 n. 2).

[4] Hyatt (*Jeremiah*), "It is not probable that vss.29-30 are from Jeremiah. They presuppose the discussion by Ezekiel" (p. 1036). Cf. Rudolph (*Jeremia*), who draws attention to the disparity between 31:30 and 31:34, "composition by Jeremiah is impossible" (p. 201).

d...d בָּנִים (31:29); הַבָּנִים (Ezek 18:2). Some manuscripts omit the definite article in Ezek 18:2.

Comment

Ezekiel 18 refutes the proverb in a sustained discussion of inherited corporate punishment and personal responsibility, in which the key statement is "the soul that sins shall die" (18:4). The responsibility for exile is not to be attributed to previous generations, but must be faced squarely by the exiles themselves. The ethical norms of *torah* establish who is righteous and will therefore live (18:9). Ezekiel 18 ends (18:30, 31) with a call to repentance, resulting in "a new heart and a new spirit."

In Jer 31:29 the proverb is quoted as a fatalistic cry of despair by those who see themselves as victims of the sins of the fathers. This outlook must be refuted (31:30) by insistence on the fact that each person who eats sour grapes will have his own teeth set on edge and will die for his own sin. Certainly, the idea of collective retribution is present in the book of Jeremiah (e.g., 11:21–22; 20:6; 29:32; 32:18; cf. Lam 5:7), as also in Deuteronomy (Deut 5:9=Exod 20:5; 34:7). Personal responsibilities for actions, however, are clearly enunciated in Deut 24:16, "The fathers shall not be put to death for the children, nor shall the children be put to death for the fathers; every man shall be put to death for his own sin" (cf. Jer 31:30a). Jeremiah 31:29–30 has been prompted by 31:28a, where Yahweh's action "to pluck up and break down, to overthrow, destroy and bring evil" has been applied to those now in exile; whereas 31:31–34 concentrates on "building and planting" (31:28b) and a new covenant. The community aspect is prominent in the oracles of hope: 31:23–25, 27–28; 31:31–34; 31:35–37; 31:38–40.

The composition of Jer 31:23–40 is a good example of McKane's view of a rolling *corpus*.[5]

JEREMIAH AND ISAIAH

7. JEREMIAH 31:35c=ISAIAH 51:15b

a... who stirs up the sea a b so that its waves roar; b
c Yahweh of hosts is his name.c

---

[5] McKane, *Jeremiah 1*, lxxxiii.

Textual and Translational Notes

The MT text of each phrase is identical.

ᵃ⁻ᵃ רֹגַע הַיָּם. This phrase, with רגע I *Qal* ("to disturb, stir up"), occurs only in 31:35c=Isa 51:15.

ᵇ⁻ᵇ וַיֶּהֱמוּ גַלָּיו ("so that its waves roar," 31:35c; Isa 51:15; cf. Jer 5:22).

ᶜ⁻ᶜ יְהוָה צְבָאוֹת שְׁמוֹ ("Yahweh of hosts is his name," 31:35c; Isa 51:15). Isaiah 51:15LXX uses the first person (*my* name) in keeping with the introductory phrase "I am Yahweh, your God" (cf. 10:16; 32:18; 46:18; 48:15; 50:34; 51:19, 57; Isa 47:4; 48:2; 51:5). Note also the hymnic refrain in Amos 4:13; 5:8; 9:5. The phrase was well known in Jeremiah's time.

JEREMIAH AND PSALMS

8. JEREMIAH 10:25=PSALM 79:6-7

Jeremiah 10:23-25 reflects other OT passages. The vocabulary of 10:23 includes אָדָם, דַּרְכּוֹ and the verb כּוּן *Hiphil* + צַעֲדוֹ ("direct his steps"), all found in Prov 16:9 (cf. Prov. 20:24). Holladay points out that 10:24 is a variation of Ps 6:2 (6:1E).[6] They have in common the use of the verb יסר *Piel* ("to discipline, correct"), as well as the phrase אַל־בְּאַפְּךָ ("not in your anger").

JEREMIAH 10:25	PSALM 79:6-7
Pour out your wrath ᵃ on ᵃ	pour out your wrath ᵃ on ᵃ
the nations who do not know	the nations who do not know
you, and on ᵇ the peoples ᵇ	you, and on ᵇ the kingdoms ᵇ
who do not call on your name;	that do not call on your name;
for ᶜ they have devoured ᶜ	for ᶜ they (plural) have
Jacob ᵈ (and have devoured him) ᵈ	devoured ᶜ Jacob and have
ᵉ and have destroyed him ᵉ	devastated his habitation.
and have devastated his habitation.	

Textual and Translational Notes

ᵃ⁻ᵃ עַל (10:25); אֶל (Ps 79:6; some manuscripts, עַל). The two prepositions are almost interchangeable in the book of Jeremiah.

ᵇ⁻ᵇ מִשְׁפָּחוֹת ("peoples," 10:25), LXX γενεάς; מַמְלָכוֹת ("kingdoms," Ps 79:6), LXX βασιλείας. Both terms appear in Jer 1:16 as synonyms in a conflate text. Holladay regards מִשְׁפָּחוֹת as more original.[7] Note, however, that some manuscripts read מַמְלָכוֹת in 10:25 (cf. LXX βασιλείας [MSS 534, 613]).

---

[6] Holladay, *Jeremiah. A Fresh Reading*, 102.

[7] Holladay, *Jeremiah 1*, 338.

c...c אָכְלוּ ("they have devoured," 10:25); אָכַל (3d s.), Ps 79:7. LXX has κατέφαγον in both instances.
d...d וַאֲכָלֻהוּ ("they have devoured him," 10:25 only). The verb is redundant here and is the result of dittography or conflation.[8]
e...e וַיְכַלֻּהוּ ("they have destroyed him," 10:25 only). καὶ ἐξανήλωσαν is the LXX equivalent.

For Holladay, 10:25 is a deliberate quotation by Jeremiah from Ps 79:6-7, put into the mouths of the people.[9] In calling on Yahweh to vent his anger on the nations for devouring "Jacob," there is an implicit presupposition on the part of the people that they are innocent victims of aggression and should be vindicated. Jones, however, puts forward another view of the relationship between 10:25 and Ps 79:6-7.[10]

The view I adopt is that Jer 10:25 (=Ps 79:6-7) has been added to 10:23-24 (somewhat awkwardly), picking up the theme of Yahweh's anger (10:24) and referring to the threat in 10:22 from a post-587 BCE perspective. In 6:11, Jeremiah had called for Yahweh's wrath (חֲמַת יְהוָה; cf. חֲמָתְךָ, 10:25) to be poured out (שְׁפֹךְ) on his own people, who had consistently repudiated the message of Yahweh's judgment.[11] Now the language of Ps 79:6-7 (perhaps originally a scribal comment in the margin) is directed against the "nations." The "nations" deserve to have Yahweh's wrath poured out on them, not only because they have devoured "Jacob," but because they do not know Yahweh or call upon his name.[12]

9. JEREMIAH 15:15d=PSALM 69:8a

This doublet has been discussed above (chap. three, pp. 33-35), with the conclusion that the Psalmist used the language of Jer 15:15d as an apt way of describing his own situation.

10. JEREMIAH 20:10a=PSALM 31:14a

See above, chap. three, pp. 48—52. I have argued that Ps 31:14a is derived from Jer 20:10a.

---

[8] Janzen, *Studies*, 11.
[9] Holladay, *Jeremiah 1*, 344; *Jeremiah 2*, 65.
[10] Jones (*Jeremiah*) states, "Jeremiah may well be quoting a well-known formula, which was also used in the exilic Ps 79" (p. 181).
[11] Cf. Isa 42:25 (שְׁפֹךְ + חֵמָה), referring to Yahweh's action against "Jacob" (Isa 42:24); Lam 2:4; 4:11, where Yahweh's anger is poured out (both שׁפך and חמה are used) on Zion (note also the reference to "Jacob" in Lam 2:3).
[12] McKane (*Jeremiah 1*) considers this "an insensitive addition" (p. 233); Hyatt (*Jeremiah*), "narrow nationalism" (p. 904).

JEREMIAH AND 2 KINGS

11. JEREMIAH 19:3b=2 KINGS 21:12

JEREMIAH 19:3b
Thus says Yahweh [a] of hosts, [a] the God of Israel, [b] Behold, I am bringing such a disaster [b] [c] upon this place [c] that the ears of [d] everyone who hears it [e] will ring. [e]

2 KINGS 21:12
Therefore thus says Yahweh, the God of Israel, [b] Behold I am bringing [c] upon Jerusalem and Judah [c] [b] such a disaster[d] that [f] both [f] ears [d] of everyone who hears of it [d] [e] will ring. [e]

Textual and Translational Notes

[a...a] צְבָאוֹת. Jeremiah 19:3 adds "of hosts" to the name of "Yahweh, God of Israel." In Jeremiah 19:3bLXX and 2 Kgs 21:12 (MT and LXX) צְבָאוֹת is missing, yet this term is frequently added to the Hebrew text in Jeremiah.[13]

[b...b] הִנְנִי מֵבִיא רָעָה ("Behold, I am bringing [a] disaster," 19:3b; 2 Kgs 21:12). Cf. 4:6; 11:11; 11:23=23:12; 19:15; 35:17; 42:17; 44:2; 45:5; 51:64; 1 Kgs 14:10; 21:21; 2 Kgs 22:16.

[c...c] עַל־הַמָּקוֹם הַזֶּה ("upon this place," 19:3b); עַל־יְרוּשָׁלַם וִיהוּדָה ("upon Jerusalem and Judah," 2 Kgs 21:12). McKane (*contra* Rudolph) claims that the reference in 19:3b is to Jerusalem (not Topheth or Ben Hinnom).[14]

[d...d] כָּל־שֹׁמְעָהּ (19:3b); כָּל־שֹׁמְעָיו (2 Kgs 21:12; however, *Qere* שֹׁמְעָהּ parallels 19:3b).

[e...e] תִּצַּלְנָה (19:3b; 2 Kgs 21:12)= תְּצִלֶּינָה.[15]

[f...f] שְׁתֵּי (2 Kgs 21:12; LXX ἀμφότερα; a few manuscripts [19:3LXX] add ἀμφότερα). Cf. 1 Sam 3:11.

Comment

The symbolic action in which Jeremiah broke an earthen flask in the presence of some of the elders and senior priests is recounted in 19:1-2, 10-11a. The speech inserted in 19:3-9 has many points of correspondence between 19:5-6 and 7:30-32 (see above, chap. nine, pp. 192—195). The speech is addressed to "kings of Judah and inhabitants of Jerusalem" (19:3; cf. 19:14, "all the people"); the entire dynasty comes under condemnation for idolatrous practices. 2 Kings 21:12 also describes the רָעָה which will fall upon Jerusalem and Judah, in view of the abomination of Manasseh (cf. Jer 15:4; 2 Kgs 24:3).

---

[13] Janzen, *Studies*, 157 (Table B2).
[14] McKane, *Jeremiah 1*, 449.
[15] GKC § 67g.

Carroll states, "The sermon is an amalgam of phrases to be found throughout the Deuteronomistic editing of the tradition."[16] The phrase רָעָה הִנְנִי מֵבִיא ("Behold, I am bringing a disaster") occurs in other Deuteronomistic passages (e.g., 1 Kgs 14:10; 21:21; 2 Kgs 22:16). The striking phrase "that (both) ears of everyone who hears of it will ring" occurs also in 1 Sam 3:11. Jeremiah 19:3 appears to be based on the Deuteronomistic passage 2 Kgs 21:12.

12. JEREMIAH 38:3 = 2 KINGS 18:30

JEREMIAH 38:3	2 KINGS 18:30
Thus says Yahweh, This city shall surely be given into the hand of the army of the king of Babylon and be taken.	... this city will be given into the hand of the king of Assyria.

Comment

In Jer 38:3 Jeremiah is reported as saying that Jerusalem will be captured by the army of the king of Babylon. In 2 Kgs 18:30b the Rabshakeh speaks against heeding the words of Hezekiah that Jerusalem will not be given into the hand of the king of Assyria. Hardmeier has advanced strong arguments in support of his thesis that the account of the events of 701 BCE in 2 Kings 18–20 has been influenced by an awareness of the events of 589–587 BCE and the reports of Jeremiah's speeches at the time of the temporary withdrawal of Babylonian troops from the city of Jerusalem in 588 BCE.[17]

JEREMIAH AND NUMBERS

13. JEREMIAH 48:45–46 = NUMBERS 21:27–29; 24:17c.

The Jeremiah passage has been adapted from the Numbers passages (see above, chap. seven, pp. 140–143).

JEREMIAH AND DEUTERONOMY

The complicated relationship between the books of Jeremiah and Deuteronomy remains central in Jeremiah studies, going back to the initial

---

[16] Carroll, *Jeremiah*, 389.
[17] C. Hardmeier, *Prophetie im Streit vor dem Untergang Judas. Erzählkommunikative Studien zur Entstehungssituation der Jesaja-und Jeremiaerzählungen in II Reg 18–20 und Jer 37–40* (BZAW 187; Berlin: Walter de Gruyter, 1990) 361-362.

question of Jeremiah's attitude to the discovery of "the book of the law" (2 Kgs 22:8) in 622 BCE and Josiah's subsequent reforms motivated by this discovery.[18]

The study since 1943 of the Pentateuch and the former prophets (Joshua to 2 Kings) has been dominated by the theory of Martin Noth, who put forward the view in 1943 that Deuteronomy and the former prophets contain the work of the Deuteronomistic historian, who made use of earlier source materials in providing a sustained history of Israel, beginning with the account of creation down to the fall of Jerusalem in 587 BCE.[19] Subsequent scholars have built upon this thesis and modified it in various ways. A complete bibliography relating to this vast subject would be immense.[20]

Thiel claims that the book of Jeremiah has been subject to a Deuteronomistic redaction (the work of "D" editors), especially in the extensive prose sections.[21] His arguments are frequently "circular" in the sense that he seeks to establish a wide range of characteristics of D and to impose them on many passages in which his initial assumptions may be open to question.[22] Earlier still, Herrmann had drawn attention to phrases in the book of Jeremiah well-known from the Deuteronomistic literature.[23] Carroll does not hesitate to speak of the "Deuteronomistic edition of Jeremiah."[24] Likewise, Nicholson ascribes prose sayings and sermons which contain Deuteronomistic language to "a group of Deuteronomic authors," while acknowledging that some of these passages are based on original sayings of Jeremiah.[25]

---

[18] *Ur*–Deuteronomy (the law-book found in the temple) is usually thought of as containing major sections of Deut 5–26, 28. However, Jack Lundbom follows the chronology in 2 Chron 34:3-7, claiming that Josiah's reforms (based on the already available Deuteronomy) had taken place before the discovery of the "law-book," which was actually Deuteronomy 32, the "Song of Moses." See "The Lawbook of the Josianic Reform," *CBQ* 38 (1976) 293-302. But is Deuteronomy 32 this early? For different views regarding the date of Deuteronomy 32, see Holladay, *Jeremiah 2*, 54. In any case, the use of Deuteronomistic language in the book of Jeremiah requires careful attention.

[19] Martin Noth, *Überlieferungsgeschichtliche Studien I* (Tübingen: Max Niemayer, 1943; *The Deuteronomistic History* [JSOTSup 15; Sheffield: JSOT Press, 1981]).

[20] A helpful bibliography is given by Mark O'Brien, *The Deuteronomistic Hypothesis: A Reassessment* (Göttingen: Vandenhoeck & Ruprecht, 1989) 293-310.

[21] Thiel, *Redaktion 1, Redaktion 2*.

[22] See McKane, *Jeremiah 1*, xlvi-xlvii. Weippert (*Die Prosareden*) has argued that parallels between the prose discourses of Jeremiah and Deuteronomic-Deuteronomistic phrases have differences and nuances that prohibit the view that the prose discourses originated from the hand of a redactor. Holladay (*Jeremiah 2*, 13) supports Weippert's view regarding the fresh contexts in Jeremiah in which stereotyped Deuteronomistic phrases appear. However, McKane's view that the nuances arise from the particular character and orientation of the book of Jeremiah is persuasive.

[23] Herrmann, *Die prophetischen Heilserwartungen*.

[24] Carroll, *Jeremiah*, 66.

[25] Nicholson, *Jeremiah 1*, 11; *Jeremiah 2*.

Although Deuteronomistic phrases are frequently found in the book of Jeremiah, only relatively few doublets between the books of Jeremiah and Deuteronomy occur.[26] The doublets are as follows: 7:33=Deut 28:26; 19:9=Deut 28:53; 22:8-9=Deut 29:23-25 (29:24-26E); 29:13=Deut 4:29.

14. JEREMIAH 7:33 = DEUTERONOMY 28:26

JEREMIAH 7:33
a The corpse(s) of this people a will be food b for the bird(s) of the air, b and for the beast(s) of the earth and c none will frighten them away. c

DEUTERONOMY 28:26
a Your corpse a will be food b for all the bird(s) of the air b and for all the beast(s) of the earth and none will frighten them away. c

Textual and Translational Notes

a...a נִבְלַת הָעָם הַזֶּה, 7:33; נִבְלָתְךָ, Deut 28:26. נְבֵלָה is used collectively, as are עוֹף and בְּהֵמָה. "This people" provides a link with 7:16 and 7:23.

b...b לְעוֹף הַשָּׁמַיִם, 7:33; לְכָל־עוֹף הַשָּׁמַיִם, Deut 28:26. See BHS for textual evidence supporting לְעוֹף in Deut 28:26.

c...c וְאֵין מַחֲרִיד, 7:33; Deut 28:26. This phrase does not appear in the close parallels to 7:33 in the book of Jeremiah, but is found in 46:27=30:10. The phrase occurs elsewhere in the prophetic oracles: Mic 4:4; Nah 2:12 (2:11E); Zeph 3:13; Ezek 34:28; 36:26.

Comment

The relationship between 7:33 and Deut 28:26 has been frequently discussed, with different conclusions reached regarding which is dependent on the other. Thiel has argued strongly that 7:30-8:3 is a Deuteronomistic formulation; 7:33 is dependent on Deut 28:26.[27] Weippert provides a chart which includes not only 7:33 and Deut 28:26 but the various passages where these formulae are found and concludes that Deut 28:26 and Ps 79:2 are dependent on Jeremiah.[28] Do other passages throw any light on this question? Jeremiah 19:7b is slightly different in form: לְמַאֲכָל לְעוֹף הַשָּׁמַיִם וּלְבֶהֱמַת הָאָרֶץ וְנָתַתִּי אֶת־נִבְלָתָם; it provides another example of the use made of 7:30-34 in 19:5-7, 11. Jeremiah 16:4b and 34:20b are identical: לְעוֹף הַשָּׁמַיִם וּלְבֶהֱמַת הָאָרֶץ וְהָיְתָה נִבְלָתָם לְמַאֲכָל. Weinfeld draws attention to the stereotyped nature of these

---

[26] The subject of Deuteronomistic phrases in the book of Jeremiah will be investigated in chapter thirteen.

[27] Thiel, *Redaktion 1*, 128-134.

[28] Weippert, *Die Prosareden*, 185.

formulations and points to their background in extra-biblical texts dating from the ninth to the seventh centuries BCE.[29] He concludes that some of these conventional maledictions "may actually have been proclaimed by the prophet himself, but they cannot be considered his genuine creation so much as conventional formulae prevalent in treaty literature of his time."[30]

15. JEREMIAH 19:9 = DEUTERONOMY 28:53

JEREMIAH 19:9
[a] I shall make them eat [a]
[b] the flesh of their sons and
the flesh of their daughters, [b]
[d] and everyone shall eat the
flesh of his neighbor, [d] [f] in
the siege and in the distress
[g] with which their enemies
[h] and those who seek their
lives [h] afflict them. [g]

DEUTERONOMY 28:53
[a] You shall eat [a] [b] the fruit
of your body, [b] [c] the flesh of
your sons and your daughters [c]
[e] whom Yahweh your God has
given you, [e] [f] in the siege and
in the distress [f] [g] with which
your enemies afflict you. [g]

Textual and Translational Notes

[a...a] וְהַאֲכַלְתִּים, 19:9; וְאָכַלְתָּ, Deut 28:53. Yahweh is the speaker in 19:9; hence, the use of the first person here and in 19:7, 8, followed by objects in the 3d pl. Deuteronomy 28:47-53 uses 2d s. throughout.

[b...b] פְּרִי־בִטְנְךָ, Deut 28:53; cf. Deut 28:4.

[c...c] בְּשַׂר בָּנָיו וּבְנֹתָיו, 19:9 (cf. Lev 26:29); אֶת־בְּשַׂר בָּנֶיהָ וְאֵת בְּשַׂר בְּנֹתֶיהָ, Deut 28:53. Not only are the forms in 19:9 written out in full, but a further phrase is added ([d...d]).

[d...d] וְאִישׁ בְּשַׂר רֵעֵהוּ יֹאכֵלוּ ("and every one shall eat the flesh of his neighbor," 19:9). Cf. Isa 9:19 (9:20E); Zech 11:9.

[e...e] אֲשֶׁר נָתַן לְךָ יְהוָה אֱלֹהֶיךָ. Deuteronomy 28:53 repeats this phrase from Deut 28:52 (preceded by בְּכָל־אַרְצְךָ).

[f...f] בְּמָצוֹר וּבְמָצוֹק ("in the siege and in the distress," 19:9; Deut 28:53). The phrase is repeated in Deut 28:55, 57, but does not occur elsewhere in the OT.

[g...g] אֲשֶׁר יָצִיקוּ לָהֶם אֹיְבֵיהֶם, 19:9; אֲשֶׁר־יָצִיק לְךָ אֹיִבְךָ, Deut 28:53. "Their enemies," 19:9; "your enemy," Deut 28:53; LXX ὁ ἐχθρός σου.

[h...h] וּמְבַקְשֵׁי נַפְשָׁם ("and those who seek their live[s]," 19:9; cf. 19:7). This phrase appears frequently elsewhere in the book of Jeremiah: 4:30; 11:21; 21:7; 22:25; 34:20, 21; 38:16; 44:30 (bis); 46:26; 49:37; cf. Exod 4:19; 1 Sam 20:1; 22:23 (bis); 23:15; 25:29; 2 Sam 4:8; 16:11; 1 Kgs 19:10, 14; Pss 35:4; 38:13; 40:15; 54:5; 63:10; 70:3; 86:14.

---

[29] Weinfeld, *Deuteronomy and the Deuteronomic School*, 185.
[30] Weinfeld, *Deuteronomy and the Deuteronomic School*, 140.

Comment

References to cannibalism are not confined to Jer 19:9=Deut 28:53, but occur also in Isa 9:20 (9:19E); 49:26; Ezek 5:10; 2 Kgs 6:26-29 (the siege of Samaria); Lam 2:20; 4:10; Lev 26:29. Volz treats 19:7-9 as an insert, a mixture of current clichés, pointing to a historical reality.[31]

Although 19:9 and Deut 28:53 are not exact duplicates, they have in common the use of אכל followed by בְּשַׂר involving "sons and daughters" and the striking phrase בְּמָצוֹר וּבְמָצוֹק. For this reason, some comentators have concluded that Jer 19:9 is dependent on Deut 28:52.[32] On the other hand, Von Rad deals with Deut 28:47-57 as a separate unit, in which Deut 28:49 draws on Isa 5:26 and Jer 5:15 for such phrases as "a nation from afar" and "a nation whose language you do not understand."[33] Holladay concludes that Deut 28:53 is dependent on Jer 19:9.[34] Drinkard points to the feature of assonance (מָצוֹר, מָצוֹק) and the use of a noun (מָצוֹק) and verb (צוק) from the same root as indicative of Jeremiah's style.[35] A good example of assonance in the book of Deuteronomy is the phrase גַּם־בָּחוּר גַּם־בְּתוּלָה ("both young man and virgin," Deut 32:25), but Deuteronomy 32 is usually regarded as late.[36] The question of dependency must be left open.

Relationships between the book of Jeremiah and Deuteronomic-Deuteronomistic prose will be pursued in chapter thirteen of this study. Linguistic parallels do not necessarily provide sufficient information to establish whether prose passages in Jeremiah in which Deuteronomistic language is found are Deuteronomistic in origin. McKane's *caveat* regarding Jeremiah 19 needs to be kept in mind: "It is more important to consider carefully how the prose functions in the context of the book of Jeremiah than to be too preoccupied with the not necessarily profitable pursuit of Deuteronomic or Deuteronomistic affiliations."[37]

---

[31] Volz, *Jeremia*, 201.
[32] For example, Driver, *Deuteronomy*, 315; Boadt, *Jeremiah 1*, 145.
[33] Von Rad, *Deuteronomy*, 175.
[34] Holladay, *Jeremiah 1*, 541.
[35] Drinkard, *Jeremiah 1*, 261.
[36] Sellin-Fohrer, *Introduction to the Old Testament*, 190.
[37] McKane, *Jeremiah 1*, 456.

17. JEREMIAH 22:8-9 and DEUTERONOMY 29:23-25

JEREMIAH 22:8-9

8. [a] Many nations will pass [a]
[b] by this city [b] [a] and everyone
will say to his neighbor [a]
"Why has Yahweh dealt like this
with this great city?"
9. [d] And they will say, "Because
they forsook the covenant of
Yahweh their God [d] [f] and worshiped
other gods and served them." [f]

DEUTERONOMY 29:23-25

23. [a] All the nations would
say [a] "Why has Yahweh dealt
like this [b] with this land? [b]
[c] What does the heat of this
great anger mean?" [c]
25. [d] These people would say
"Because they forsook the
covenant of Yahweh, the God
of their fathers, [d] [e] which he
made with them when he brought
them out of the land of Egypt, [e]
26. [f] and went and served other gods
and worshiped them, [f]
[g] gods whom they had not known,
whom he had not allotted
to them." [g]

Textual and Translational Notes

[a...a] וְאָמְרוּ כָּל־הַגּוֹיִם, Deut 29:23; וְעָבְרוּ גּוֹיִם רַבִּים ... וְאָמְרוּ אִישׁ אֶל־רֵעֵהוּ, 22:8. No translation is given for רַבִּים in Jer 22:8LXX. Janzen thinks that רַבִּים is imported from 25:14 (cf. 27:7).[38] גּוֹיִם ("nations, foreigners") in 22:8 and Deut 29:23 is regarded as a sign of lateness by Carroll, as is also the catechetical method of teaching.[39] Jeremiah 22:8-9 follows both Deut 29:23-25 and 1 Kgs 9:8-9; cf. וְעָבְרוּ ... עַל הָעִיר, 22:8; כָּל־עֹבֵר עָלָיו, 1 Kgs 9:8 (cf. Jer 19:8). אִישׁ אֶל־רֵעֵהוּ (22:8) occurs also in 36:16; 46:16.

[b...b] לָאָרֶץ הַזֹּאת, Deut 29:23. Whereas the question raised by "the nations" in Deut 29:23 has to do with "this land," in 22:8 the concern is with "this city." 1 Kings 9:8 combines "this land" and "this house (temple)."

[c...c] מָה חֳרִי הָאַף הַגָּדוֹל הַזֶּה ("What does the heat of this great anger mean?" Deut 29:23). This phrase is not picked up in the Jeremiah passage. חֳרִי־אַף occurs in Lam 2:3, referring to Yahweh.

[d...d] וְאָמְרוּ עַל אֲשֶׁר עָזְבוּ אֶת־בְּרִית יְהוָה אֱלֹהֵיהֶם, 22:9. The only difference in Deut 29:24 is the designation of Yahweh as אֱלֹהֵי אֲבֹתָם ("the God of their fathers"), which introduces the phrase which follows in [e...e] (missing in 22:9). For יְהוָה אֱלֹהֵיהֶם, cf. 1 Kgs 9:9.

[e...e] אֲשֶׁר כָּרַת עִמָּם בְּהוֹצִיאוֹ אֹתָם מֵאֶרֶץ מִצְרָיִם, Deut 29:24. Jeremiah 22:8-9 is selective in the use of source-material and omits this phrase. 1 Kings 9:9 also refers to Yahweh's action in bringing "their fathers" out of the land of Egypt.

---

[38] Janzen, *Studies*, 44.
[39] Carroll, *Jeremiah*, 420, 421.

f...f 22:9, וַיִּשְׁתַּחֲווּ לֵאלֹהִים אֲחֵרִים וַיַּעַבְדוּם
Deut 29:25 ,וַיֵּלְכוּ וַיַּעַבְדוּ אֱלֹהִים אֲחֵרִים וַיִּשְׁתַּחֲווּ לָהֶם
Jeremiah 22:9 reverses the order of the verbs עבד and שחה *Hithpalel*, following 1 Kgs 9:9, and the order in the Decalogue (Deut 5:9=Exod 20:5).

g...g אֱלֹהִים אֲשֶׁר לֹא־יְדָעוּם וְלֹא חָלַק לָהֶם, Deut 29:25. This phrase is omitted in Jer 22:9 (an unnecessary elaboration in the context of Jeremiah 22).

Comment

A typical Deuteronomistic theological reason for the destruction of Jerusalem is given in 22:8-9: the abandonment of the covenant and the worship of "other gods," a phrase used frequently in Deuteronomy and in Jeremiah (e.g., Deut 5:7, 6:14; 7:4; 8:19 *et al*). Jeremiah 21:11-22:7 places the emphasis on ethical activity and righteous actions, setting forth Yahweh's requirements for the monarchy.

Question and Answer Schemata

Long has analysed two question and answer *schemata* in the book of Jeremiah and elsewhere in the OT.[40] The *schema* found in 22:8-9 employs the third person pronoun, following Deut 29:23-25 and 1 Kgs 9:8-9 (=2 Chron 7:21-22).[41] Long maintains that this pedagogical method is typical of rhetorical preaching during the exile. Rudolph draws attention to an Assyrian parallel.[42]

The dependency of Jer 22:8-9 on Deut 29:23-25 and 1 Kgs 9:8-9 is clear, as is also the awkwardness of the construction.[43]

17. JEREMIAH 29:13 = DEUTERONOMY 4:29

JEREMIAH 29:13	DEUTERONOMY 4:29
[a] You will search for me and you will find (me); [a] [b] when you seek me with all your heart.[b]	[a] From there you will search for Yahweh your God and you will find (him), [a] [b] when you seek him with all your heart [b] [c] and with all your soul. [c]

---

[40] Burke O. Long, "Two Question and Answer Schemata in the Prophets," *JBL* 90 (1971) 129-139.

[41] See Thiel, *Redaktion 1*, 297 (Table 10). Thiel compares the texts of 22:8-9; Deut 29:23-27 and 1 Kgs 9:8-9.

[42] Rudolph, *Studies*, 138. Cf. Drinkard (*Jeremiah 1*, 303) regarding an account in the annals of Assurbanipal of treaty breaking and its consequences.

[43] McKane, *Jeremiah 1*. McKane refers to "...the unskillful use of borrowed material; ...a poorly constructed conflation of Deut 29:23-24 (the גוים theme) and 1 K 9:8f (עבר על כל)" (p. 522).

Textual and Translational Notes

a...a וּבִקַּשְׁתֶּם אֹתִי וּמְצָאתֶם, 29:13
     וּבִקַּשְׁתֶּם מִשָּׁם אֶת־יְהוָה אֱלֹהֶיךָ וּמָצָאתָ, Deut 4:20.
Jeremiah 29:12 is expanded by adapting Deut 4:29. In 29:13 Yahweh is the speaker. מִשָּׁם ("from there") in the context of Deut 4:29 speaks of a situation of exile.

b...b כִּי תִדְרְשֻׁנִי בְּכָל־לְבַבְכֶם, 29:13
     כִּי תִדְרְשֶׁנּוּ בְּכָל־לְבָבְךָ, Deut 4:29
Jeremiah 29:13 repeats Deut 4:29 with necessary adaptation in the personal pronominal suffixes. Holladay points out that the usual form for "heart" in Jeremiah is לֵב (fifty-seven instances); לֵבָב is used only eight times (4:4; 5:24; 13:22; 15:16; 29:13; 32:40; 51:46, 50).[44] He concludes that "29:13 is probably late."[45] "All your (their) heart" occurs in Deuteronomy and Deuteronomistic passages (e.g., Deut 6:5; 30:6; cf. בְּכָל־לְבָבָם in 1 Kgs 2:4; 8:48).

c...c וּבְכָל־נַפְשֶׁךָ, Deut 4:29. This additional phrase ("and with all your soul") occurs often in Deuteronomy (e.g., 6:5; 10:12; 26:16; 30:2, 6, 10), but has not been carried over into Jer 19:13.

d...d The additional phrase ἐν τῇ θλίψει σου ("in your tribulation," Deut 4:29LXX) represents the opening words of Deut 4:30(MT): בַּצַּר לְךָ. The language of Deut 4:29 is reflected in Jer 29:13.

18. JEREMIAH 29:14a and DEUTERONOMY 30:3

JEREMIAH 29:14a	DEUTERONOMY 30:3
[a] I will be found by you, [a] Oracle of Yahweh, and I will restore your fortunes [b] and gather you from all the nations and from all the places where I have driven you [b] — Oracle of Yahweh.	Yahweh your God will restore your fortunes [b] and show compassion on you, and he will gather you again from all the peoples where Yahweh your God has scattered you. [b]

Jeremiah 29:14 has sufficient parallels with Deut 30:3 to make this a near-doublet, yet the differences are significant (see below, [b...b]).

---

[44] Holladay, *Jeremiah 2*, 59, 113.
[45] Holladay, *Jeremiah 2*, 59. In the case of לֵבָב in 4:4 and 15:16, "Deuteronomy lies in the background" (p. 59).

Textual and Translational Notes

a...a וְנִמְצֵאתִי לָכֶם (29:14a); LXX καὶ ἐπιφανοῦμαι ὑμῖν (with the rest of the half-verse missing). Deuteronomy 30:3 does not provide a parallel. Jeremiah 36:14LXX (=29:14aMT) suggests that the Hebrew text originally may have been וְנִרְאֵיתִי.[46] The absence of the rest of 29:14 from the LXX is a strong indication that this passage was not in the translator's *Vorlage*. Furthermore, the restoration of fortunes alluded to in 29:14 has a wider application (a gathering from "all the nations and all the places where I have driven you") than to exiles in Babylonia. This late addition may have been prompted by שוב Hiphil in 29:10.[47]

b...b Jeremiah 29:14a, וְקִבַּצְתִּי אֶתְכֶם מִכָּל־הַגּוֹיִם וּמִכָּל־הַמְּקוֹמוֹת
אֲשֶׁר הִדַּחְתִּי אֶתְכֶם שָׁם
Deuteronomy 30:3, וְרִחֲמֶךָ וְשָׁב וְקִבֶּצְךָ מִכָּל־הָעַמִּים
אֲשֶׁר הֱפִיצְךָ יְהוָה אֱלֹהֶיךָ שָׁמָּה

Both passages use קבץ *Piel*. Deuteronomy 30:3 has additional verbs: רחם *Piel* and שוב. Jeremiah 29:14a has מִכָּל־הַגּוֹיִם וּמִכָּל־הַמְּקוֹמוֹת for מִכָּל־הָעַמִּים (Deut 30:3) and נדח *Hiphil* for פוץ *Hiphil* (Deut 30:3). For the combination בְּכָל־הַמְּקוֹמוֹת and נדח *Hiphil*, see Jer 8:3. For פוץ and עַמִּים (Deut 30:3), see Deut 4:27. Jeremiah 30:11 (=46:28) combines בְּכָל־הַגּוֹיִם and פוץ *Hiphil*. נדח *Hiphil* also occurs in 16:15=23:8; 23:3; 32:37; Deut 30:4. פוץ *Niphal* is found in Ezek 11:17; 21:34, 41; 28:25, in conjunction with קבץ *Piel*.

Comment

This survey of the nouns and verbs used in 29:14a and in Deut 30:3 leads to the conclusion that 29:14a is not a direct quotation from Deut 30:3, but is using conventional phrases found elsewhere in the book of Jeremiah in late passages, of which some have parallels in the book of Deuteronomy.

JEREMIAH AND NEHEMIAH

19. JEREMIAH 18:23b=NEHEMIAH 3:37(4:5E)

See chap. three above, pp. 46–47.

---

[46] Rudolph, *Jeremia*, 184. Cf. ראה *Niphal* in 31:3.

[47] Volz, *Jeremia*, 269. The use of מצא in 29:14aMT is probably derived from 29:13 (but cf. Isa 56:6; 65:1 as a possible influence).

SUMMARY AND CONCLUSIONS: DOUBLETS IN JEREMIAH WITH PARALLELS ELSEWHERE IN THE OLD TESTAMENT

1. JEREMIAH 14:10b=HOSEA 8:13

Hosea 8:13 is quoted in Jeremiah 14:10b.

2. JEREMIAH 26:18b=MICAH 3:12

Micah 3:12 is appealed to in order to free Jeremiah from a death-sentence. See chap. one, pp. 8-9.

3. JEREMIAH 49:9=OBADIAH 5

4. JEREMIAH 49:14-16=OBADIAH 1-4

A common source (perhaps oral) has been drawn upon and used in different ways in Jeremiah and Obadiah. See above, chap. seven, pp. 147-152

5. JEREMIAH 51:58=HABAKKUK 2:13

Either Habakkuk is being quoted from memory in Jer 51:58, or both 51:58 and Hab 2:13 are based on a popular proverb. See above, chap. eight, pp. 181-182.

6. JEREMIAH 31:29=EZEKIEL 18:2

A scribal marginal reference to Ezek 18:2 has been copied into the text of Jeremiah. Cf. 31:35c=Isa 51:15.

7. JEREMIAH 31:35c=ISAIAH 51:15b

Perhaps a scribe, familiar with Isaiah 51, has inserted this verse in the margin. Subsequently, a scribe copied this into the text. Cf. Jer 31:29=Ezek 18:2.

8. JEREMIAH 10:25=PSALM 79:6-7

Jeremiah 10:25 is a somewhat awkward addition from Ps 79:6-7; perhaps originally a scribal comment.

9. JEREMIAH 15:15d=PSALM 69:8

The Psalmist uses the language of Jer 15:15d to describe his own situation. See above, chap. three, pp. 33-35.

10. JEREMIAH 20:10a=PSALM 31:14a

Psalm 31:14a is derived from Jeremiah 20:10a. See above, chap. three, pp. 48-52.

11. JEREMIAH 19:3b=2 KINGS 21:12

Jeremiah 19:3b is based on this Deuteronomistic passage in 2 Kings.

12. JEREMIAH 38:3=2 KINGS 18:30b

Hardmeier's thesis that the account of the events of 701 BCE (2 Kings 18-20) has been influenced by an awareness of the events of 589-587 BCE (Jeremiah 38) is convincing.

13. JEREMIAH 48:45-46=NUMBERS 21:27-28; 24:17c

The Jeremiah passage has been adapted from the Numbers passages. See above, chap. seven, pp. 140-143.

14. JEREMIAH 7:33=DEUTERONOMY 28:26

Conventional formulae are found in both passages. The question of dependency remains unresolved.

15. JEREMIAH 19:9 = DEUTERONOMY 28:53
The question of the direction of dependency remains open.
16. JEREMIAH 22:8-9 = DEUTERONOMY 29:23-25
Jeremiah 22:8-9, from Deut 29:23-25, is somewhat awkwardly inserted in the context.
17. JEREMIAH 29:13 = DEUTERONOMY 4:29
Jeremiah 29:13 repeats Deut 4:29, with a necessary change in pronominal suffixes.
18. JEREMIAH 29:14a = DEUTERONOMY 30:3
Although Jer 29:14a is not a direct quotation from Deut 30:3, conventional phrases are used here and elsewhere in the book of Jeremiah, of which some have parallels in the book of Deuteronomy.
19. JEREMIAH 18:23b = NEHEMIAH 3:37(4:5E)
The passage in Nehemiah is an imprecise quotation from Jer 18:23b. See above, chap. three, pp. 46-47.

The conclusions are as follows:
(1) Direct quotations from Hosea and Micah are to be seen in Jer 14:10b = Hos 8:13; Jer 26:18b = Mic 3:12. Jeremiah 19:3b quotes from 2 Kgs 21:12. Numbers 21:27-28; 24:17c are adapted in Jer 48:45. Jeremiah 22:8-9 and 29:13 draw from Deut 29:23-25 and Deut 4:29.
(2) A common source lies behind Jer 49:5, 14-16 and Obad 1-5. Jeremiah 51:58 may be quoting Hab 2:13 from memory, or perhaps both are based on a popular proverb.
(3) Scribal marginal references account for Jer 31:29 = Ezek 18:2; Jer 31:35c = Isa 51:15b and possibly Jer 10:25 = Ps 79:6-7.
(4) Quotations from Jeremiah are present in Ps 69:8 = Jer 15:15d; Ps 31:14a = Jer 20:10a. 2 Kings 18:30b is dependent upon Jer 30:3; Neh 3:37(4:5E) draws on Jer 18:23b.
(5) In the case of Jer 7:33 = Deut 28:26 and Jer 29:14a = Deut 30:3, conventional formulae are used. The direction of dependency remains open for Jer 19:9 = Deut 28:53.

RECURRING PHRASES IN JEREMIAH AND OTHER BOOKS OF THE OLD TESTAMENT

Many phrases in the book of Jeremiah find parallels elsewhere in other books of the OT. A helpful way to examine these recurring phrases is to investigate the parallel phrases in the prophetic literature, in the Psalms, in Deuteronomy and in the Deuteronomistic literature.

JEREMIAH AND HOSEA

Von Rad emphatically states that Jeremiah was dependent on Hosea and had close contacts with Hosea's disciples, possibly even with writings which were to form the book of Hosea eventually.[48] The correspondences are frequently in thought and terminology, for example, the prominence of the terms חֶסֶד ("steadfast love"), בְּרִית ("covenant").[49] Holladay claims that there are "at least fifty points at which Jrm draws on the diction of Hosea."[50] Parallel terms and phrases in the books of Jeremiah and Hosea (following the order in which they occur in the book of Jeremiah) include the following:
(1) Bridal imagery: 2:2, כְּלוּלֹתָיִךְ; 2:32, כַּלָּה (cf. Hos 4:13, 14).
(2) מוּר Hiphil + כָּבוֹד ("change their glory," 2:11); see Hos 4:7; Ps 106:20.[51]
(3) אִשָּׁה זוֹנָה ("harlot," 3:3); see Hos 2:3-15 (2:1-13E), זנה, זנונים.
(4) שׁוּבָה ("turn, return, repent," 3:12); see Hos 14:2 (14:1E);
אֶרְפָּה מְשׁוּבֹתֵיכֶם ("I want to heal your turnings [faithlessness]," 3:22); see Hos 14:5(14:4E).[52]
(5) בגד ("to act treacherously, faithlessly," 3:20); see Hos 5:7; 6:7.
(6) נִירוּ לָכֶם נִיר ("break up your fallow ground," 4:3); see Hos 10:12b.[53]
(7) רוּחַ ... בַּמִּדְבָּר ("a wind ... in the desert," 4:11b); see Hos 13:15b.[54]
(8) עַל־זֹאת תֶּאֱבַל הָאָרֶץ ("for this the earth will mourn," 4,28; cf. תֶּאֱבַל הָאָרֶץ עַל־כֵּן, Hos.4:3.

---

[48] Von Rad, *Old Testament Theology II*, 192. Studies concerning the relationship between Hosea and the book of Jeremiah to which I have not had access are: K. Gross, *Die literarische Verwandschaft Jeremias mit Hosea* (Dissertation; Berlin: 1930); "Hosea's Einfluss auf Jeremias Anschauung," *NKZ* 42 (1931), 241-246; Alfons Deissler, "Das 'Echo' der Hosea-Verkündigung im Jeremiabuch" in *Künder des Wortes, Beiträge zur Theologie der Propheten, Josef Schreiner, zum 60. Geburtstag* (ed. Lothar Ruppert, Peter Weimar, and Erich Zenger; Würzburg: Echter, 1982) 61-75.

[49] For חֶסֶד, see Hos 2:21(2:19E); 6:4, 6; 10:12; 12:7(12:6E); Jer 2:2; 9:23(9:24E); 16:5; 31:3; 32:18; 33:11; Nelson Glueck, *Das Wort Hesed im altestamentlichen Sprachgebrauch als menschliche und göttlich gemeinschaftgemässe Verhaltungsweise* (2d ed.; BZAW 47; Berlin: Töpelmann, 1961). For בְּרִית, see Hos 2:20(2:18E); 6:7; 8:1; 12:2; Jer 14:21; 22:9; 31:31, 32, 33; 32:40; 33:20, 21; Lothar Perlitt, *Bundestheologie im Alten Testament* (WMANT 36; Neukirchen-Vluyn: Neukirchener Verlag, 1969).

[50] Holladay, *Jeremiah 2*, 47. Cf. J.G. McConville, *Judgment and Promise. An Interpretation of the Book of Jeremiah* (Winona Lake, Indiana: Eisenbrauns, 1992) 152-163.

[51] According to Ittmann (*Konfessionen*), Ps 106:20 is dependent on Jer 2:11 (p. 128 n. 451).

[52] Holladay, *Jeremiah 1*, 123.

[53] See above, chap. four, p. 71.

[54] Berridge, *Prophet*, "In 13:15 Hosea is thinking of the Assyrians...If Jeremiah was indeed influenced by Hosea in his formation o 4:11, we may have here a further indication of the fact that Jeremiah undoubtedly had the Babylonians in mind in 4:5-12." (p. 112, n.223).

(9) הֲגָנֹב רָצֹחַ וְנָאֹף ("Will you steal, murder, commit adultery?," 7:9); see וְנָאֹף וְרָצֹחַ, Hos 4:2 (a different order, but also the use of infinitive absolutes).

(10) חֲזוֹן שֶׁקֶר ("a lying vision," 14:14; יְדַבְּרוּ חֲזוֹן לִבָּם, "they speak a vision of their own mind," 23:16; see Hos 12:11 [12:10E]), a general statement regarding visions which needs modification, a statement in which Yahweh declares, "I spoke to the prophets; it was I who multiplied חָזוֹן." In the polemic against false prophets in Jeremiah, a distinction is made between true and false prophets; the latter do not speak a vision from Yahweh (14:14, "I did not send them, nor did I command them or speak to them").[55]

(11) אִם־כְּלִי אֵין חֵפֶץ בּוֹ ("is [he] a vessel no one cares for?," 22:28, cf.48:38b, regarding Moab). See כִּכְלִי אֵין חֵפֶץ בּוֹ, "as a vessel uncared for (useless)," Hos 8:8. Berridge notes the connection between Hos 8:8 (regarding North Israel) and Jer 22:28 (regarding Jehoiachin).[56] However, McKane contends that the appearance of the phrase in Hosea and Jeremiah "demonstrates no more than that it was an idiom which both knew."[57]

(12) וְעָבְדוּ אֶת־יְהוָה אֱלֹהֵיהֶם וְאֵת דָּוִד מַלְכָּם ("they shall serve Yahweh their God, and David their king"). Hos 3:5 has the same phrase with a different introductory verb (וּבִקְשׁוּ, "they shall seek".) Holladay comments: "here is the thought world of those in post-exilic ties, dreaming of the restoration of the Davidic monarchy."[58] McKane draws attention to similar passages in Ezek 34:24 and 37:24.[59]

(13) 31:18, Ephraim (speaking) is "like an untrained calf, כְּעֵגֶל לֹא לֻמָּד. See Hos 10:11, Ephraim was "a trained heifer," עֶגְלָה מְלֻמָּדָה.[60] Although 31:18 is similar to Hos 10:11, עֵגֶל, "calf" has been substituted for עֶגְלָה, "heifer" and the negative לֹא is used, more in keeping with the thought of Hos 4:16. The confessional lament in 31:18-19 expresses the repentance of Ephraim, who has been disciplined "like an untrained calf."

(14) Although the language regarding Ephraim in 31:20 (cf. 31:9) is not an exact duplicate, the love of Yahweh for Ephraim expressed here with emotional intensity is very similar to that of Hos 11:1-4.[61]

---

[55] Meyer, *Jeremia*, p. 62.
[56] Berridge, *Prophet,* p. 180 n. 358. North Israel's decline in Hosea's day finds a parallel in the significance which Jehoiachin's fate had for Judah.
[57] McKane, Prophet 1, p. 549.
[58] Holladay, *Jeremiah 2,* p. 173.
[59] McKane, *Jeremiah 2,* 761; cf. Carroll, *Jeremiah,* "The common elements of 30:9 and Hos 3:5 point to the shared streams of radition which the book of Jeremiah has in common with so many other biblical traditions." Note also 30:18 and Hos 6:11 ("restore the fortunes," שׁוּב/ שְׁבוּת).
[60] Many MSS have יְפֵיפִיָּה. See McKane, *Jeremiah 2,* 1131.
[61] The frequent references to Ephraim in Jer 31 (31:6, 9, 18, 20) have been interpreted as reflecting Josiah's expansionist policies to the north and the expectation of the homecoming of the northern exiles; see Holladay, 2, 156; Lohfink, "Der junge Jeremia."

JEREMIAH AND AMOS

A number of correspondences of ideas and phrases have been found between Jeremiah and Amos.[63]

(1) The verbs בנה "build" and נטע "plant" in 1:10 (cf. 18:9) occur also in Amos 9:14, but the restoration of fortunes promised in Amos 9:14 is a relatively late passage.[64] For נטע, see also 32:41 and Amos 9:15.

(2) כִּי רַבּוּ פְּשָׁעֶיהָ עָצְמוּ מְשֻׁבוֹתֶיהָ, 5:6c ("because their transgressions are many, their apostasies are great"; cf. Amos 5:12: רַבִּים פִּשְׁעֵיכֶם וַעֲצֻמִים חַטֹּאתֵיכֶם כִּי יָדַעְתִּי.

(3) וּבִתְקוֹעַ תִּקְעוּ שׁוֹפָר, 6:1b ("In Tekoa [Amos's city] blow the trumpet"; Amos 3:6, אִם־יִתָּקַע שׁוֹפָר בְּעִיר ("Is a trumpet blown in a city?").

(4) חָמָס וָשֹׁד, 6:7 (cf. 20:8) "violence and destruction"; cf. Amos 3:10. See above, chap. three, pp. 50–51. The word-pair appears also in Isa 60:18; Ezek 45:9; Hab 1:3.

(5) אֵבֶל יָחִיד, 6:26, "mourning for an only son"; cf. Amos 8:10; perhaps a proverbial expression.[65]

(6) חוֹמַת נְחֹשֶׁת בְּצוּרָה ("a fortified wall of bronze," 15:20; cf. 1:18). The views of Beyerlin concerning the relationship between 15:20 and Amos 7:7–9 have been discussed above (chap. three, p. 38).[66]

(7) וְיוֹם אָנוּשׁ לֹא הִתְאַוֵּיתִי ("I have not [recklessly] desired the day of disaster," 17:16); see Amos 5:18: הוֹי הַמִּתְאַוִּים אֶת־יוֹם יְהוָה ("Woe to those who desire the day of Yahweh!"). Jeremiah 17:16 (יוֹם אָנוּשׁ; cf. 17:18, יוֹם רָעָה) avoids repeating the expression "day of Yahweh" (used in Jeremiah only at 46:10). Berridge discusses the unusual use of אוה Hithpael in these two passages and concludes, "It is quite possible that Jer 17:16a is to be considered as

---

However, McKane (*Jeremiah 2*) claims that "'Ephraim' is an apt cipher for Judah, because history is about to repeat itself. Jeremiah was a Judaean prophet who concentrates on Judah, and it cannot be demonstrated that he had a concern for the exiles of 722."(p. 799).

[62] Holladay, *Holladay 2*, "The phraseology is unparalleled in the OT, but the thought of Yahweh's resowing the land must go back to Hos 2:25, where the reference is a word-play on 'Jezreel'." (p. 196. Cf. Weiser, *Jeremia*, 284 n. 3; Scalise, *Jeremiah 2*, 129.

[63] See Berridge, *Prophet*, 321–341; Holladay, *Prophet 2*, 44–45; Beyerlin, *Reflexe der Amosvisionen*.

[64] Mays, *Amos*, "...probably composed in Judah during the exilic period" (p. 166); see also Thiel (*Redaktion 2*, p. 96) who points out that there is insufficient evidence to decide whether the book of Jeremiah points to Amos or whether the revision of he book of Amos points to Jeremiah.

[65] Holladay, *Jeremiah 2*, 45. See also chap. twelve below, B1.

[66] Baumgartner (*Jeremiah's Poems of Lament*) claims, "Both passages are authentic, but have become contaminated with one another at a later stage" (p. 107 n. 32).

representing Jeremiah's working with these earlier words spoken by Amos, with which he was undoubtedly familiar."[67]

(8) אֵשׁ + בְּ, preceded by וְהִצַּתִּי ("I will kindle a fire," 17:27; cf. 11:16; 21:14; 32:29; 43:12; 49:27; 50:32 and Amos 1:14). Regarding 50:32, Holladay states, "Verse 32b is a variation on 21:14; both follow the pattern of Amos 1:14a."[68] Note also in 17:27 the phrase וְאָכְלָה אַרְמְנוֹת יְרוּשָׁלָם ("and it shall devour the strongholds of Jerusalem"), probably derived from Amos 2:5, which also contains the phrase וְשִׁלַּחְתִּי אֵשׁ.[69]

(9) וְשַׂמְתִּי עֵינִי עֲלֵיהֶם לְטוֹבָה ("I will set my eye(s) upon them [i.e, the good figs] for good," 24:6); see Amos 9:4: וְשַׂמְתִּי עֵינִי עֲלֵיהֶם לְרָעָה וְלֹא לְטוֹבָה ("and I will set my eyes upon them for evil and not for good"). For שִׂים + עֵינַיִם + עַל, see also Jer 39:12; 40:4. Holladay thinks that 24:6 is a deliberate reversal of Amos 9:4, but the idiom may be a familiar one (cf. Gen 44:21).[70]

(10) יְהוָה מִמָּרוֹם יִשְׁאָג ("Yahweh will roar from on high," 25:30); יִתֵּן קוֹלוֹ ("... will utter his voice"); see Amos 1:2a and Joel 4:16 (3:16E), וּמִירוּשָׁלַיִם יִתֵּן קוֹלוֹ יְהוָה מִצִּיּוֹן יִשְׁאָג. Volz acknowledges the link between 25:30 and Amos 1:2, with the substitution of Yahweh's dwellingplace "on high" for "Zion" and "Jerusalem."[71]

(11) יְהוָה צְבָאוֹת שְׁמוֹ ("Yahweh of hosts is his name," 31:35c; cf. 10:16; 32:18; 46:18; 48:15; 50:34; 51:19, 57). Similar expressions in Amos 4:13; 5:8 and 9:5 in hymnic passages indicate that this refrain predates Jeremiah (cf. Isa 17:4; 48:2; 54:5).

JEREMIAH AND ISAIAH

Parallel passages in Jeremiah (OAN) and Isaiah have already been discussed in chapter seven.

Detailed examples of phrases found both in Jeremiah and different parts of the book of Isaiah have been collected and commented upon by a number of scholars.[72] Attention is drawn especially to the following:

---

[67] Berridge, *Prophet,* 43.

[68] Holladay, *Jeremiah 2,* 419. For Hubmann (*Untersuchungen,* 236), this is a characteristic phrase.

[69] Holladay, *Jeremiah 1,* 511. The final phrase in 17:27, וְלֹא תִכְבֶּה ("and shall not be quenched"), occurs also in 7:20; 2 Kgs 22:17; see Thiel, *Redaction 1,* p. 206 n. 18. Thiel (p. 207) draws attention to the fact that 2 Kgs 22:17 (like 7:20, referring to Yahweh's wrath) is a Deuteronomistic verse standing in the background.

[70] Holladay, "Prototype and Copies," 364.

[71] Volz, *Jeremia,* 394. Mays (*Amos*), regarding Amos 1:2a, Jer 25:30, Joel 4:16MT, claims that "their similarity is not due to literary dependence but to common use of a significant motif from the Jerusalem cult" (p. 21).

[72] S. Paul, "Literary and Ideological Echoes of Jeremiah in Deutero-Isaiah" in Proceedings of the Fifth World Congress of Jewish Studies (Vol.I; Jerusalem: World Union of Jewish Studies, 1969) 102–120; Umberto Cassuto, "On the Formal and Stylistic

Parallels in Other Parts of the Old Testament

(1) וַיַּגַּע עַל־פִּי ("and he [Yahweh] touched my mouth," 1:9); see Isaiah's call, וַיַּגַּע עַל־פִּי ("and he [one of the seraphim] touched my mouth," Isa 6:7). Other similarities with Isaiah's call narrative include מֵאֵין יוֹשֵׁב ("without inhabitant," Isa 6:11; cf. Isa 5:9; Jer 4:7; 26:9; 33:10; 34:22; 44:22; 46:19; 51:29, 37; Zeph 2:5; 3:6) and מֵאֵין אָדָם ("without inhabitant," Isa 6:11; Jer 4:25; 32:43; 33:10, 12).[73]

(2) עָלָיו יִשְׁאֲגוּ כְפִרִים ("the lions have roared against him," 2:15); cf. Isa 5:29, יִשְׁאַג כַּכְּפִירִים.[74]

(3) נְטַעְתִּיךְ שֹׂרֵק ("I planted you a choice vine," 2:21); see Isa 5:2, וַיִּטָּעֵהוּ שֹׂרֵק. Note also the unusual term in Jer 31:20, שַׁעֲשֻׁעִים ("darling"); see Isa 5:7, נְטַע שַׁעֲשׁוּעָיו ("his pleasant planting"). The only other occurrence of this term is found in Prov 8:30.

(4) וְנָטִיתִי אֶת־יָדִי ("So I will stretch out my hand against [the inhabitants of the land]," 6:12); see וַיהוָה יַטֶּה יָדוֹ (against Egypt, Isa 31:3). Note also the use of the verbs כשל and נפל in Isa 31:3; see Jer 46:6, 12, 16 (regarding Egypt).[75]

(5) כִּפְרִי מַעֲלָלָיו ("according to the fruit of his doings," 17:10); see מַעַלְלֵיהֶם כִּי־פְרִי, Isa 3:10.[76]

In addition to this partial list, attention must be given to the connections between Jeremiah and Deutero-Isaiah. Cassuto lists other examples of verbal parallels, such as:

(6) Jeremiah 10:9, the craftsman as a חָכָם; cf. Isa 40:20.

(7) Jeremiah 30:5, אֵין שָׁלוֹם; cf. Isa 41:8, 10, 13-14; 43:1, 5; 44:2.[77]

(8) Parallel words and phrases in the doublet Jer 30:10-11 = 46:27-28 are found in DI, e.g., 41:8, 10, 13-14; 43:1, 5; 44:2. See above, chap. seven, pp. 119-125, where the conclusion was reached that this doublet in Jeremiah is late and was influenced by DI. Cassuto comes to a different conclusion, i.e., "the Second Isaiah was greatly inspired by chapters xxx-xxxi of Jeremiah."[78] However, in connection with Jeremiah 50-51 (Oracles against Babylon), he assumes that a later writer imitated both DI (to a very large extent) and also Jeremiah himself.[79] In the case of 30:10-11 = 46:27-28 (*contra* Cassuto's views regarding this doublet), a similar conclusion is highly probable.

Relationship between Deutero-Isaiah and Other Biblical Writers" (Biblical and Oriental Studies I; Jerusalem: Magnes Press, 1973) 141-177.

[73] Berridge, *Prophet*, 93. Berridge (p. 175) also finds a relationship between 9:5 and Isa 6:5, but this seems questionable.

[74] Berridge (*Prophet*), "It would be quite understandable that Jeremiah should have applied this older terminology to the Babylonians, who corresponded so closely to Israel's earlier foe, the Assyrians" (p. 81).

[75] See also chap. seven, pp. 116, 117.

[76] Holladay (*Jeremiah 1*), "The expression 'fruit of one's deeds' seems dependent on Isa 3:10" (p. 496). Cf. Holladay, "Prototype," 355-356. See also Jer 17:10b = 32:19b; 21:14.

[77] Cassuto, "Formal and Stylistic Relationship," 143-160.

[78] Cassuto, "Formal and Stylistic Relationship," 152.

[79] Cassuto, "Formal and Stylistic Relationship," 154-155.

JEREMIAH AND MICAH

The phrase וְלֹא־תָבוֹא עָלֵינוּ רָעָה is found in both Micah and Jeremiah (Mic 3:11c; Jer 5:12b; cf. 23:17). Holladay points to Mic 3:5-8 (against false prophets) and Mic 3:9-12 (against Jerusalem) as important sources for Jeremiah (e.g., תעה *Hiphil,* "lead astray," Mic 3:5; Jer 23:13); שָׁלוֹם in the mouth of false prophets, Mic 3:5; Jer 28:9; cf. Mic 3:10, 11; Jer 22:17; 8:19).[80] In 9:23 (9:24E) Yahweh practices (עשׂה) חֶסֶד ("steadfast love") and מִשְׁפָּט ("justice"); in Mic 6:8, Yahweh demands such conduct from אָדָם ("human beings"), who are also to practice (עשׂה) מִשְׁפָּט and חֶסֶד. Jeremiah (cf. Ezekiel) was aware of the oracles of earlier prophets, which he adapted and used in his prophetic ministry.[81]

JEREMIAH AND ZEPHANIAH

Phrases common to Jeremiah and the seventh-century prophet Zephaniah have been documented by Holladay, who notes the use of Zeph 1:2-13a by Jeremiah.[82] Jeremiah 19:13, "all the houses upon whose roofs incense has been burned to all the host of heaven," is reminiscent of Zeph 1:5. The phrase שֶׁבֶר גָּדוֹל ("great destruction") which occurs six times in Jeremiah (4:6; 6:1; 14:17; 48:3; 50:22; 51:54) perhaps harks back to Zeph 1:10.[83] The phrase סָפְתָה בְהֵמוֹת וָעוֹף ("beasts and birds are swept away," 12:4) is similar to Zeph 1:3.

JEREMIAH AND NAHUM

Jeremiah may have been acquainted with the acrostic poem in Nahum 1, as is suggested by the use of הָרִים ("mountains"); גְּבָעוֹת ("hills") and the verb רעשׁ ("quake") in 4:24 and Nah 1:5.[84] Although different verbs are used (חשׂף in 13:26; גלה in Nah 3:5), both 13:26 and Nah 3:5 contain the phrase עַל־פָּנַיִךְ שׁוּלַיִךְ ("your skirts over your face") and the noun + suffix קְלוֹנֵךְ ("your shame").[85]

---

[80] Holladay, *Jeremiah 2,* 51.

[81] Ezekiel 7:2 reflects both Amos and Isaiah, e.g., קֵץ (cf. Amos 8:2); "the four corners of the land," Isa 11:12.

[82] Holladay, *Jeremiah 2,* 51.

[83] Holladay, *Jeremiah 1,* 153; *Jeremiah 2,* 51. Apart from the Jeremiah references, the phrase is found only in Zeph 1:10.

[84] Holladay, *Jeremiah 2,* 52. Cf. יִרְעֲשׁוּ־הָרִים in Ps 46:4.

[85] Holladay, *Jeremiah 2,* 52; Carroll, *Jeremiah,* 303.

JEREMIAH AND HABAKKUK

קַלּוּ מִנְּשָׁרִים סוּסָיו ("his horses are swifter than eagles," Jer 4:13) is similar to קַלּוּ מִנְּמֵרִים ("his horses are swifter than leopards," Hab 1:8).[86] The phrase זְאֵב עֲרָבוֹת ("a wolf from the desert," Jer 5:6) may be patterned on זְאֵבֵי עֶרֶב in Hab 1:8.[87] Holladay draws attention to the resemblance between 8:13 and Hab 3:17 (תְּאֵנָה, גֶּפֶן).[88] The drought situation depicted in Hab 3:17 resembles the drought in Jeremiah 14. These are not strong grounds for establishing dependency, however.

JEREMIAH AND EZEKIEL

The dependence of Ezekiel on Jeremiah has been demonstrated by Miller.[89] The familiar triad in Jeremiah, חֶרֶב ... רָעָב ... דֶּבֶר ("sword, famine, pestilence"), occurs eight times in the book of Ezekiel: 5:12, 17; 6:11, 12; 7:15 (bis); 12:16; 14:21. Note the addition of חַיָּה רָעָה ("evil beasts, wild animals") in Ezek 5:17 and 14:21.

The concept of covenant is also prominent in Ezekiel (e.g., Ezek 16:59–61; note the phrase בְּרִית עוֹלָם ["everlasting covenant"] in 16:60; cf. Jer 32:40; 17:13–21).

The phrase in Ezekiel: לָהֶם לִרְאוֹת וְלֹא רָאוּ אָזְנַיִם לָהֶם לִשְׁמֹעַ וְלֹא שָׁמֵעוּ עֵינַיִם ... ("[they have] eyes to see, but see not, ears to hear, but hear not," Ezek 12:2) is reminiscent of Jer 5:21, a description of "the house of Jacob" (cf. Ezek 12:9, "the house of Israel"). The similar phrases in Pss 115:5-6 and 135:16-17 are descriptions of idols.

Although Jer 49:31 and Ezek 38:11 do not represent a precise doublet, these verses have some common vocabulary: יֹשֵׁב לָבֶטַח ("who dwell securely"); דְּלָתַיִם (literally, "double doors"); בְּרִיחַ ("bar[s]").[90] Jeremiah 49:31MT purports to be a divine oracle, although the intermediate נְאֻם יְהוָה is missing in the LXX. The "king of Babylon" is called to attack a nation at ease, without

---

[86] Saul and Jonathan are described as "swifter than eagles" (מִנְּשָׁרִים קַלּוּ) in 2 Sam 1:23. נֶשֶׁר also occurs in Hab 1:8. Cf. קַלִּים...נְשָׁרִים in Lam 4:19.

[87] Berridge (*Prophet*, 83) surmises that Habakkuk and Jeremiah have appealed to an older tradition, which they have used in different ways.

[88] Holladay, *Jeremiah 1*, 429.

[89] John W. Miller, *Das Verhältnis Jeremias und Hesekiels sprachlich und theologisch untersucht* (Assen: van Gorcum, 1955). Cf. J. Untermann, *From Repentance to Redemption: Jeremiah's Thought in Transition* (JSOTSup 54; Sheffield: JSOT Press, 1987) 167-170; Thomas Raitt, *A Theology of Exile: Judgment/Deliverance in Jeremiah and Ezekiel* (Philadelphia: Fortress, 1977).

[90] Note also the verb חשׁב at the end of 49:30, and Ezek 38:10.

fortifications.⁹¹ Ezekiel 38:11 expresses the determination of Gog to "go up" (note the use of עלה in both Jer 49:31 and Ezek 38:11) against "the land of unwalled villages." Ezekiel 38-39 are of uncertain origin and date.⁹² Although Bright does not find any reason to suppose that either of the two passages (49:31; Ezek 38:11) is dependent on the other, Rudolph, who thinks that any connection is unnecessary, asserts that if there is a connection, the dependency is on the side of Ezekiel.⁹³ On the other hand, Volz points out that the description of the Bedouin in 49:31 is reminiscent of Ezek 38:11.⁹⁴ In my judgment, there is sufficient common vocabulary to suggest dependency; one is tempted to point to a learned scribe who is familiar with both Joshua 11 (Jer 49:30, 33) and Ezek 38:11 (Jer 49:31).

JEREMIAH AND PSALMS

In 1960, Bonnard published a study of thirty-three Psalms which he believed to reflect the literary and spiritual influence of Jeremiah.⁹⁵ Holladay has also discussed the relationship between the books of Jeremiah and Psalms and has concluded that influences exist in both directions.⁹⁶ The difficulty of precise dating in the case of many of the Psalms makes it impossible to be dogmatic about the relationship; furthermore, liturgical language would be familiar to Jeremiah, in view of his priestly background (1:1).

Jeremiah 17:5-8 and Psalm 1

Jeremiah 17:5-8 (cf. 12:1-2) and Psalm 1 are parallel passages which express similar ideas, in some ways using almost identical language, e.g., וְהָיָה כְּעֵץ שָׁתוּל עַל־מַיִם ("He is like a tree planted by water," 17:8a); Ps 1:3a is identical except for עַל־פַּלְגֵי מָיִם ("by streams of water").⁹⁷ Psalm 1 describes the blessedness of the person whose delight is in Yahweh's Torah as contrasted with the fate of the "wicked"; 17:7-8 reverses the order and begins with a curse

---

⁹¹ The Hebrew text includes the name "Nebuchadrezzar," which is missing in the LXX. The preceding "O inhabitants of Hazor" (49:30), implies that Hazor is a city (cf. 49:33). According to Holladay (*Jeremiah 2*, 384), this is a misunderstanding, since the passage deals with sedentary Arabs.
⁹² See Eichrodt, *Ezekiel* (OTL; London: SCM, 1970). He attributes these chapters to an author "from the school of disciples who gathered themselves to Ezekiel" (p. 520).
⁹³ Bright, *Jeremiah*, 336; Rudolph, *Jeremia*, 295.
⁹⁴ Volz, *Jeremia*, 421.
⁹⁵ Bonnard, Le Psautier selon Jérémie. See above, chap. three, p. 34.
⁹⁶ Holladay, *Jeremiah 2*, 65.
⁹⁷ Holladay (*A Fresh Reading*, 99) considers 12:1-2 to be a variation on Psalm 1. He also claims (*Jeremiah 1*), "...Jrm makes use of material from Psalm 1 in v.2a to set forth his accusation" (p. 369); (*A Fresh Reading*), "Psalm 1... is earlier than Jeremiah, and Jeremiah is here [12:1-2] offering a parody of it" (p. 93).

upon the person who trusts in human resources rather than in Yahweh, and then pronounces a blessing on the person who trusts in Yahweh.

There are differences of opinion regarding the relationship between 17:5-8 and Psalm 1. Rudolph claims that the author of Psalm 1 has taken up the Jeremiah passage, while Carroll asserts that "there are sufficient differences between the two poems for there to be no question of borrowing or dependence."[98] The differences show that there is considerable linguistic independence; 17:5 uses the expression אָרוּר הַגֶּבֶר ("cursed is the man"), not found in Psalm 1, and 17:7 has בָּרוּךְ הַגֶּבֶר rather than אַשְׁרֵי הָאִישׁ (Ps 1:1).[99]

Jeremiah 17:5 refers to the man who "makes flesh (בָּשָׂר) his arm"; Cornill saw here a reference to the pro-Egyptian policies of Zedekiah.[100] כְּעַרְעָר ("like a shrub") is not a comparison used in Psalm 1, and may be an "assonant word-play" on אָרוּר ("cursed," 17:5).[101] There may also be a word-play on the verbs רָאָה and יָרֵא (17:8) as suggested by Drinkard.[102]

Jeremiah 17:5-11 is made up of three Wisdom sayings: 17:5-8, 9-10, 11. Jeremiah 17:5-8 states the principle on which 17:4 is based, introduced by the formula כֹּה אָמַר יהוה (missing in the LXX) which implies an editorial transition. The theme of "the two ways" is rooted in the Wisdom literature (cf. The Instruction of Amen-em-opet).[103] The use of אָרוּר ("cursed," 17:5) and בָּרוּךְ ("blessed") immediately brings to mind Deuteronomy 27 and 28, and the *Tun-Ergehen-Zusammenhang* characteristic of the book of Deuteronomy and sapiential literature (e.g., Proverbs). There is much to be said, therefore, for the view that 17:5-8 is the work of a learned scribe who is able to draw on a variety of biblical sources.

Other Parallels with Psalms

Holladay finds correspondences between the thought and language of 31:8-9 and Ps 107:1-7 (see צָפוֹן 31:8; מִצָּפוֹן Ps 107:3 and דֶּרֶךְ יָשָׁר ("a straight path," 31:9); דֶּרֶךְ יְשָׁרָה, Ps 107:7 (cf. Ezra 8:21).[104] The phrases כִּי טוֹב ... הוֹדוּ אֶת־יְהוָה ("Give thanks to Yahweh ... for Yahweh is good," 33:11; cf.

---

[98] Rudolph, *Jeremia*, 115; Carroll, *Jeremiah*, 351.

[99] Cf. Ps 40:5 (40:4E): אַשְׁרֵי הַגֶּבֶר.

[100] Cornill, *Jeremia*, 212. Cf. Jones, *Jeremiah*, 240. Note the use of בָּשָׂר in Isa 31:3; reliance on Egypt (Isa 31:1-3) is futile (cf. Isa 36:6). Robert Davidson ("The Interpretation of Jeremiah XVII 5-8," *VT* 9 [1959] 202-205) claims that the link between 17:5-8 and Isa 31:3 is slender (the two words אָדָם and בָּשָׂר) and that 17:5-8 reflects Jeremiah's criticism of Josiah's policy in opposing Pharoah Neco at Megiddo in 608 BCE; cf. 1 Esdras 1:28.

[101] Carroll, *Jeremiah*, 350.

[102] Drinkard, *Jeremiah 1*, 226.

[103] Pritchard, *Ancient Near Eastern Texts*, 422. In the "Fourth Chapter" a contrast is made between two trees, one growing in the open and the other growing in a protected garden, as representative of two types of individuals.

[104] Holladay, *Jeremiah 2*, 68, 185.

Ps 107:1; 136:1) and כִּי לְעוֹלָם חַסְדּוֹ ("for his steadfast love endures for ever," 33:11; cf. Ps 106:1; 107:1; 118:1; 136 *passim*) are liturgical phrases almost exactly duplicated in Jer 33:11 and Ps 136:1 (cf. Ezra 3:11).

JEREMIAH AND 2 KINGS

2 Kings 24:18–25:30 is the main source of the historical appendix (Jeremiah 52; cf. 39:1–10). Jeremiah 29:2 is based on 2 Kgs 24:14–16; Jer 40:5, 7–9 draws on 2 Kgs 25:23–24 (Gedaliah); Jer 41:1–3 expands 2 Kgs 25:25 (Ishmael).

A nearly identical phrase is found in Jer 2:5b and 2 Kgs 17:15b, in the MT and in the LXX: "They [i.e., your fathers, 2:5; their fathers, 2 Kgs 17:15] went after worthlessness (הֶבֶל) and became worthless." הֶבֶל ("worthlessness") occurs in Jeremiah in 8:19; 10:8, 15; 14:22; 16:19; 51:18 in contexts referring to idolatrous practices (cf. Deut 32:21; 1 Kgs 16:13, 26).

What is the direction of influence? While Holladay maintains that 2 Kgs 17:15 is in imitation of 2:5b, Thiel is convinced that the half-verse in Jeremiah is an insertion from 2 Kgs 7:15, since 2:5a readily moves on to 2:6a without this phrase.[105] Since Thiel acknowledges that the hand of the Deuteronomist is to be recognized in only a few passages in Jeremiah 2–6, the question of the direction of dependency should be left open.[106]

The books of Kings provide source material for various events referred to in the book of Jeremiah. A good example is Jer 29:2 (cf. 24:1), which summarizes 2 Kgs 24:14–16, referring to Jehoiachin and others taken into exile in 597 BCE.[107] Jeremiah 40:7–9 (concerning Gedaliah) represents 2 Kgs 25:23–24 almost *verbatim*. The Jeremiah account of the role of Johanan (Jer 40:13–16) and Ishmael's assassination of Gedaliah is dealt with at great length in 40:13–41:18.[108] Johanan is mentioned without further comment in 2 Kgs 25:23 and the murder of Gedaliah by Ishmael is stated succinctly in 2 Kgs 25:25. Gedaliah's counsel, "Dwell in the land and serve the king of Babylon, and it shall be well with you" (40:9), with one orthographic change, is paralleled in 2 Kgs 25:24; it is preceded by a phrase with only one slight variation: אַל־תִּירְאוּ מֵעַבְדֵי הַכַּשְׂדִּים (40:9); אַל־תִּירְאוּ מֵעֲבוֹד הַכַּשְׂדִּים (2 Kgs 25:24).[109]

---

[105] Holladay, *Jeremiah 1*, 86; Thiel, *Redaktion 1*, 81.

[106] Thiel, *Redaktion 1*, 80.

[107] Graupner, *Auftrag und Geschick*, 77. Graupner also refers to the views of other scholars (p. 77 n. 47).

[108] For a full discussion of 40:7–41:18, see Pohlmann, *Studien*, 108–122. Seitz (*Theology in Conflict*, 199) claims that 2 Kgs 25:22–16 is dependent on the parallel passages in Jeremiah.

[109] A few manuscripts read מֵעֲבֹד in 2 Kgs 25:24 (cf. Vg *servire*).

2 Kings 25:25 (the assassination of Gedaliah by Ishmael) is expanded in 41:1-3. Jeremiah 41:1 adds the phrase וְרַבֵּי הַמֶּלֶךְ ("and [one of the] chiefs of the king"), not present in 2 Kgs 25:25 or 41:1LXX; this text refers as well to Ishmael and Gedaliah sharing a meal together (וַיֹּאכְלוּ שָׁם לֶחֶם יַחְדָּו בַּמִּצְפָּה) before Ishmael's treacherous act.

Baruch or "a circle of traditionists" may have been responsible for the detailed reports in Jeremiah 37-44, which supplement the material in 2 Kings and point to additional sources.[110]

JEREMIAH AND DEUTERONOMY

Because of common themes and ideas, some parallels between Jeremiah and Deuteronomy are to be expected. Holladay has drawn attention to words and phrases in Jeremiah and Deuteronomy.[111] Jeremiah 3:1 metaphorically introduces the subject of divorce, with parallels to Deut 24:1-4.[112] Jeremiah 5:15-17 and Deut 28:49-53 deal with "a nation from afar."[113] Thiel thinks that both texts go back to a common source, perhaps a ritual curse.[114] Jeremiah 7:9 demonstrates familiarity with the Decalogue, Deut 5:6-21.[115] Jeremiah 7:23a quotes the covenantal formula (cf. Deut 29:12MT; 29:13E). Although the word בְּרִית ("covenant") does not occur in Jeremiah 7, this term occurs twenty-four times elsewhere in the book of Jeremiah, twenty-seven times in Deuteronomy.[116] Jeremiah 17:9-27, with references to keeping the sabbath day holy by refraining from bearing burdens, is an obvious reflection of Deut 5:12-15. The choice between "life" and "death" in 21:8 is reminiscent of Deut 30:15, 19. The reference to an "iron yoke of servitude" to Nebuchadrezzar on the neck of the nations (28:14) invites comparison with Deut 28:48. Jeremiah 34:9, regarding liberation of slaves, relates to Deut 15:12.[117]

Many other examples of connections between the book of Jeremiah and the book of Deuteronomy are listed by Holladay, who concludes that "Jrm drew on Proto-Deuteronomy, and exilic redactors of Deuteronomy sometimes drew on Jrm's words."[118] Certainly, many of the parallels are found in the

---

[110] Holladay (*Jeremiah 2*) ascribes 37:1-43:7 to Baruch, "an eyewitness account" (p. 286). Nicholson (*Preaching to the Exiles*) speaks of "a circle of traditionists" (p. 18).

[111] Holladay, *Jeremiah 2*, 53-56.

[112] James D. Martin, "The Forensic Background to Jeremiah III 1," *VT* 19 (1969) 82-92.

[113] גּוֹי מִמֶּרְחָק, 5:15; גּוֹי מֵרָחוֹק Deut 28:49. See J. P. Hyatt, "Jeremiah and Deuteronomy," *JNES* 1 (1942) 172-173.

[114] Thiel, *Redaktion 1*, p. 97, n. 64.

[115] Cf. Hos 4:2 and the comments of C. Levin, *Die Verheissung des neuen Bundes in ihrem theologiegeschichtlichen Zusammenhang ausgelegt* (Göttingen: Vandenhoeck & Ruprecht, 1985) 91-92.

[116] Andersen and Forbes, *VOT*, 295.

[117] See McKane, *Jeremiah 1*, 882-884.

[118] Holladay, *Jeremiah 2*, 53-63. The quotation is from p. 53.

introduction (Deuteronomy 1–4) and from chapters outside of the central core (Deuteronomy 5–26), such as Deuteronomy 28 and 32. Other phrases common to Jeremiah and the Deuteronomic-Deuteronomistic literature will be cited in chapter thirteen.

RECURRING PHRASES: SUMMARY

Many phrases in Jeremiah are found with parallels in the prophetic literature and in other books, especially Psalms and the Deuteronomistic literature. Jeremiah himself is likely to have used conventional prophetic language; those who followed him in the prophetic tradition were familiar with other books of the OT and drew from these books as they expanded the text that they had inherited. A question to be explored in chapter thirteen is whether there was a systematic redaction of the book of Jeremiah.[119]

---

[119] Those who believe that there was a Deuteronomistic redaction include Hyatt, Herrmann, Nicholson, Thiel and Carroll.

CHAPTER ELEVEN

PROMINENT TERMS AND PHRASES IN THE BOOK OF JEREMIAH AND PHRASES THAT ARE UNIQUE TO JEREMIAH

There is wide agreement that the poetry of Jeremiah 1–20 contains material that is authentically Jeremianic.[1] Holladay, in examining twenty-seven phrases that occur in poetic sections, and in somewhat similar form in prose passages, claims that "many of the characteristic phrases of the prose sections of the book of Jeremiah are a reshaping in prose of phrases which either are original to the genuine poetry of Jeremiah, or, though not new to Jeremiah, were employed by him in his poetical oracles in an original fashion."[2] Furthermore, "many of the distinctive phrases in the prose of Jeremiah have no parallel in Deuteronomy."[3]

A cautionary note is sounded by McKane as to the limitations of arguments based on lexicographical and semantic data when comparing poetry and prose in the book of Jeremiah and with the parallels in Deuteronomy and the Deuteronomistic books.[4] Our approach to the problem of authentic Jeremianic language in poetry and prose will be to draw attention in this chapter to (1) some prominent terms or formulae featured in the book of Jeremiah; (2) distinctive vocabulary and unique phrases in the book; (3) phrases with parallels in other OT writings, excluding the Deuteronomistic literature (chapter twelve); and (4) in chapter thirteen, phrases with parallels in the Deuteronomistic literature, parallels frequently also found in other OT books.

1. Terms and Phrases Prominent in the Book of Jeremiah

(1) The Triad: חֶרֶב רָעָב דֶּבֶר ("sword, famine, pestilence")

The triad occurs in the book of Jeremiah fifteen times, always in prose passages (see discussion above, chap. two, pp. 21–23; chap. nine, pp. 201–204,

---

[1] E.g., Rudolph, *Jeremia*, xv; Bright, *Jeremiah*, lxix; Weiser, *Jeremia*, xxxix; Nicholson, *Jeremiah 1*, 10.
[2] Holladay, "Prototype and Copies," 351.
[3] Holladay, "Prototype and Copies," 352.
[4] McKane, *Jeremiah 1*, xlii–xlvii.

espec. p. 201 note ᵇ⁻⁻⁻ᵇ).⁵ The classical triad appears quite often in the book of Ezekiel as well: Ezek 5:12 (a different sequence); 6:11, 12; 7:15; 12:16; 14:21.

The pair "sword" and "famine" occurs first in Jeremiah in poetic passages.⁶ Holladay has argued that the prototype for the triad is found in a poetic passage, 15:2, where מָוֶת takes the place of דֶּבֶר.⁷ Deuteronomy 32:24–25 has the sequence קֶצֶב, רָעָב, and חֶרֶב, although the date of the "Song of Moses" is uncertain.⁸

Weippert's careful study of the triad lays emphasis on the contexts in which the formula appears and on the different way Deuteronomistic phrases are used in Jeremiah in distinction from their use in the Deuteronomistic literature.⁹ She has convinced Holladay, who claims that "she has written the definitive work on the problem of the stereotyped prose in Jeremiah, and though questions remain, I believe that we can consider that this issue is now solved."¹⁰ However, as McKane observes, "Her method does not dispose of the case for important connections between the prose of the book of Jeremiah and Deuteronomic/Deuteronomistic prose."¹¹

The triad is apparently a development from Jeremiah's original word-pair, "sword" and "famine," appearing in three fold form in prose passages during the period of the exile. The process of development is to be seen in the fact that the LXX frequently has the word-pair "sword" and "famine" in prose passages where the MT uses the triad.¹² Expansionist tendencies in the development of the Hebrew text led to the later substitution of the classical triad for the word-pair in these instances.

---

⁵ The triad occurs in 14:12; 21:7; 21:9=38:2; 24:10; 27:8, 13; 29:17, 18; 32:24, 36; 34:17; 42:17, 22; 44:13, but never in the OAN.

⁶ Holladay, *Jeremiah 1*, 435. See 5:12; 11:22; 14:13, 15, 16, 18; 18:21 (+ חַרְבֵי מָוֶת). Leviticus 26:25 contains the pair "sword" and "pestilence" (cf. Exod 5:3, "pestilence" and "sword").

⁷ Holladay, "Prototype and Copies," 362. Cf. McKane (*Jeremiah 1*), "there are good reasons for equating מות in 15:2 with דבר" (p. 506).

⁸ In Ps 91:6, דֶּבֶר ("pestilence") and קֶטֶב ("destruction") are parallel terms. Gerhard Von Rad (*Deuteronomy* [OTL; London: SCM, 1966]) claims that Deuteronomy 32 may belong to the period of the exile (p. 200). On the other hand, Holladay ("A Fresh Look at 'Source B' and 'Source C' in Jeremiah," *VT* 25 [1975] 394–412) thinks that Deuteronomy 32 was available to Jeremiah.

⁹ Weippert, *Die Prosareden*, 148–191.

¹⁰ Holladay, "'Source B' and 'Source C'," 400.

¹¹ McKane, *Jeremiah 1*, 504.

¹² E.g., 21:9=38:2 (LXX 45:2); 27:8 (LXX 34:6); 32:24 (LXX 39:24); 42:17, 22 (LXX 49:17, 22); 44:13 (LXX 51:13).

(2) "To pluck up," "to break down," "to destroy," "to overthrow," "to build," "to plant."

Six verbs recur in various combinations in passages dealing with the message of "breaking down" and "building up" with which Jeremiah was entrusted.

The complete sequence is found in Jer 1:10: נתשׁ ("to pluck up"); נתץ ("to break down"); אבד Hiphil ("to destroy"); הרס ("to overthrow"); בנה ("to build"); נטע ("to plant").[13] Jeremiah's commission is contained in Jer 1:10, in which he is set "over nations and over kingdoms." Holladay claims that אבד Hiphil and הרס are later additions to 1:10, under the influence of 18:7, 9 and 45:4.[14]

Two or more of these verbs occur in 1:10; 12:17; 18:7, 9; 24:6; 31:28, 40; 42:10; 45:4.[15] Since four of the verbs: נתשׁ, הרס, בנה, and נטע are found in 24:6; 42:10; 45:4 (although in different sequence), one is tempted to suggest that these are the basic verbs used to express "judgment" and "salvation."[16] The elimination of נתץ and אבד Hiphil in 1:10 would provide an *inclusio* (1:10 and 45:4). נתץ and אבד Hiphil would have been added to 1:10 from 18:7.

Böhmer considers 45:4 to be the oldest passage using the four principal verbs, the other passages being dependent on 45:4.[17] In any case, there is the probability that these verbs were a *leit-motiv* in Jeremiah's proclamation, preserved in the Jeremiah tradition in passages which are now post-Jeremianic in their present form.

(3) עַבְדִּי ("my servant")

The passages describing Nebuchadrezzar as "my servant" (25:9; 27:6; 43:10) have been discussed above in chap. six, pp. 102–107, where it was concluded that they are late additions. There are also references to "David, my servant" in 33:21, 22, 26 (cf. 1 Kgs 11:13, 32, 34, 36, 38). The Jeremiah references all fall within the passage 33:14–26, which is missing in the LXX and is to be regarded as a late addition, embodying the hope for a restoration of the Davidic monarchy (cf. Ezek 34:23, 24; 37:24, 25) and Levitical priesthood.[18] עַבְדִּי יַעֲקֹב ("my servant Jacob," 46:27, 28 and 30:10) has been

---

[13] Cf. 31:28, in which an additional term (רעע Hiphil "to bring evil") is added.

[14] Holladay, *Jeremiah 1*, 21. Cf. Volz, *Jeremia*, 3; Rudolph, *Jeremia*, 3; O'Connor, *Confessions*, 119, 143. The LXX contains only five of the six terms. Omission of אבד and הרס would restore the chiastic structure. See also the discussion by Carroll, *From Chaos to Covenant*, 55–58.

[15] Weippert (*Die Prosareden*, 194) supplies a chart outlining the passages which contain these verbs.

[16] For the relationship between these themes in Jeremiah, see Kilpp, *Niederreissen und aufbauen*.

[17] Böhmer, *Heimkehr*, p. 117 n. 37. For a contrary view, see Thiel, *Redaktion 2*, 86.

[18] Volz, *Jeremia*, 315. McKane (*Jeremiah 2*) refers to "the lateness of vv. 14–26" (p. clxiii).

discussed above, chap. seven, pp. 119-125. The hope expressed in Isa 44:1, 2; 45:4 (cf. 48:20; Ezek 37:25) is likely to have influenced the author of 46:27-28 = 30:10-11. For the phrase "my/his servants the prophets," see below, chap. thirteen, C60.

(4) עַם הָאָרֶץ ("the people of the land")

This phrase is used over sixty times in the OT, with a range of meanings.[19] The term occurs in Jer 1:18; 34:19 (הארץ is missing in the LXX); 37:2; 44:21; 52:6, 25 (*bis*). This phrase has been regarded as a technical term referring in pre-exilic times to property-owning citizens. Gunneweg, following Würthwein, believes that this technical meaning applies to 1:18; 34:19; 37:2; 44:21.[20] Nicholson claims that עם הארץ is "a comprehensive term for the rest of the population apart from the royal house or the ruling classes and the priesthood."[21] In the case of 1:18, Holladay states that the term "is used here for the citizens of the nation outside the orbit of the palace and temple in Jerusalem" (cf. McKane, "The view that עם הארץ is an allusion to a class should be rejected. The opposition to Jeremiah is to extend to the common people.").[22] Rudolph accepts the non-technical meaning ("the people as a whole") for 37:2 and 44:21.[23] Jeremiah 52:6, 25 are based on 2 Kgs 25:3, 19. Jeremiah 52:6 refers to the severity of the famine, which would certainly apply to the people in general. Seitz points out that "the use of the term "people of the land" in the Books of Kings refers to those populations which did in fact come from the "land" but which had taken up residence in the capital."[24] A military application may be implicit in 52:25, since "the people of the land" are mustered by "the commander of the army." The phrase occurs twice in 52:25, sometimes interpreted in a technical sense, but perhaps referring to ordinary citizens now resident in Jerusalem.[25] In all likelihood, a non-technical meaning of עם־הארץ is to be understood in all the Jeremiah passages.

---

[19] Note especially Ernst Würthwein, *Der 'amm ha'arez im Alten Testament* (BWANT 17; Stuttgart: Kohlhammer, 1936); E. W. Nicholson, "The Meaning of the Expression עם הארץ in the Old Testament," *JSS* 10 (1965) 59-66; Seitz, *Theology in Conflict*, 42-65.

[20] A. H. L. Gunneweg, "עם הערץ — A Semantic Revolution," *ZAW* 95 (1983) 437-440. Cf. Rudolph (*Jeremia*, 13, 224) regarding 1:18; 34:19.

[21] Nicholson, "The meaning of עם הארץ," 65.

[22] Holladay, *Jeremiah 1*, 45; McKane, Jeremiah 1, 23.

[23] Rudolph, *Jeremia*, 236, 262.

[24] Seitz, *Theology in Conflict*, 64.

[25] Bright (*Jeremiah*) takes the first occurrence of the phrase as equivalent to "the populace" but is tempted to translate "sixty men from the landed gentry" for the second occurrence (p. 369). Cf. Weiser (*Jeremia*, 446), "Vollbürgen." Carroll (*Jeremiah*) considers the second occurrence to be ambiguous, perhaps referring to "the conscripted peasants or the landowners forming part of the army" (p. 867).

(5) שׁוּב שְׁבוּת ("restore the fortunes")

This phrase, which occurs eleven times in the book of Jeremiah (29:14; 30:3, 18; 31:23; 32:44; 33:7, 11, 26; 48:47; 49:6, 39) has been the subject of extensive study.[26]

Etymological considerations have been prominent in major discussions of the noun שְׁבוּת. שְׁבִית occurs in the MT in Jeremiah (29:14; 49:39) and elsewhere in the OT (e.g., Ezek 16:53; 39:25; Job 42:10).[27] Preuschen (cf. Baumann) derives שְׁבוּת from שָׁבָה; Dietrich believes the derivation is from שׁוּב. However, etymology is not the decisive factor in establishing the meaning of a word, as Barr has clearly indicated, "...the etymology of a word is not a statement about its meaning, but about its history."[28]

The phrase appears in Hos 6:11, but this verse, regarding Judah, is probably the work of a Judaic glossator.[29] "I will restore the fortunes of my people Israel" (Amos 9:14) occurs in a passage also to be considered late.[30] A key passage in Deuteronomy is Deut 30:3, in which obeying Yahweh's voice will lead to a restoration of fortunes for Israel, in the sense of a return of exiles to the homeland.[31]

In Jeremiah, the phrase sometimes applies to the land and the cities of Judah (e.g., 30:18; 31:23; 32:44; 33:11), rather than to the people *per se*. The passages in which שׁוּב שְׁבוּת is found must all be considered as late, especially the references to Moab (48:47), the Ammonites (49:6) and Elam (49:39).

Seitz, discussing 29:14, prefers the translation "reverse the exile" or "return from exile" for most of the references in Jeremiah, which "point to the likelihood of an exilic author."[32] Although the influence of Deut 30:1-10 and 1 Kgs 8:33-34 is present, rather than assign the Jeremiah passages to D (as Thiel does), "one might better talk about an exilic redactor closely aligned with the Ezekiel traditions."[33] A more general sense, "restore the fortunes" and probably a post-exilic date apply to the phrase שׁוּב שְׁבוּת in the OAN (48:47; 49:6, 39).

---

[26] See esp. Erwin Preuschen, "Die Bedeutung von שׁוּב שְׁבוּת im Alten Testament," *ZAW* 15 (1895) 1-74; Erich Dietrich, שׁוּב שְׁבוּת *Die endzeitliche Wiederherstellung bei den Propheten* (BZAW 40; Giessen: Töpelmann, 1925); Eberhard Baumann, "שׁוּב שְׁבוּת: Eine exegetische Untersuchung," *ZAW* 6 (1929) 17-44; John M. Bracke, "sûb sebût: A Reappraisal," *ZAW* 67 (1985) 233-244.

[27] However, שְׁבוּת is the *Qere* in these passages.

[28] James Barr, *The Semantics of Biblical Language* (Oxford: Oxford University Press, 1961) 109.

[29] Wolff, *Hosea*, 106. He points out that קָצִיר ("harvest") in Hos 6:11 (denoting judgment) is also used in Jer 51:33 in a similar sense, applied to Babylon (p. 123).

[30] Mays, *Amos*, 166-167, regards this oracle of salvation (Amos 9:12-15) as probably composed during the period of the exile.

[31] See McConville, *Judgment and Promise*, 83.

[32] Seitz, *Theology in Conflict*, p. 210 n. 8.

[33] Seitz, *Theology in Conflict*, p. 210 n. 8.

We turn now to consider distinctive and unique words and phrases which occur more than once in the book of Jeremiah, but which do not have parallels in other books of the OT, or in the Deuteronomistic literature. Some of these are found in doublets.

2. Repetitive Words and Phrases that are Unique to Jeremiah

A1. אִשָּׁה pl. (נָשִׁים) in the phrase וְהָיוּ לְנָשִׁים ("that they [the Babylonians] may become women," 50:37; 51:30). The thought is in keeping with 30:6, where every warrior (גֶּבֶר) is like a woman in labor.[34] See chapter twelve, B16.

A2. בָּעַלְתִּי (+ בָּכֶם, "I am your master," 3:14); (+ בָּם, "though I was their husband," 31:32). The verb בעל + בְּ occurs only in these two passages, in the sense "I have been your (real) 'Baal'," in the context of apostasy in 3:12-14 and breaking the covenant in 31:32, the "new covenant" passage.[35]

A3. גּוֹיִם רַבִּים וּמְלָכִים גְּדוֹלִים ("many nations and great kings," 25:14a; 27:7b). Jeremiah 25:14 and 27:7 are missing in the LXX. Both verses in the MT contain עבד + בְּ, referring to the situation of Babylonian servitude to "many nations and great kings," a complete reversal of Babylonian domination of "all these nations round about" (25:9). These verses are clearly secondary.[36] וְשִׁלַּמְתִּי לָהֶם כְּפָעֳלָם (25:14b) is similar to שַׁלְּמוּ־לָהּ כְּפָעֳלָהּ (50:29); Babylon is included among the nations to be requited according to their deeds. The phrase וְעָבְדוּ בוֹ ("and make *him* their slave," 27:7) raises a question regarding the antecedent of בוֹ; the reference is probably to אֶרֶץ נָכְרִיָּה ("his own land") in the preceding clause; בָּהּ would have been more precise, but the use of הוּא would account for בוֹ.[37] גּוֹיִם רַבִּים occurs in 22:8 (LXX ἔθνη, without the adjective).

A4. דָּבָר in *die Wortereignisformel*: וַיְהִי דְבַר־יְהוָה אֵלַי לֵאמֹר ("The word of Yahweh came to me [saying]"). This standard formula occurs in many autobiographical passages: 1:4, 11, 13; 2:1; 13:3, 8; 16:1; 18:5; 24:4; 32:6; 42:12LXX. Herrmann follows Neumann in regarding the phrase as redactional. He does not entirely dismiss the possibility that the formula goes back to Jeremiah himself and then was later used redactionally to introduce passages without Jeremianic authenticity.[38] As Kilpp has pointed out, the formula does not provide a good criterion for determining what is authentic or non-authentic.[39] However, like the formula introducing biographical material (יְהוָה

---

[34] Holladay, *Jeremiah. A Fresh Reading*, 122.
[35] Holladay, *Jeremiah. A Fresh Reading*, 122.
[36] Janzen, *Studies*, 102. Cf. Holladay, *Jeremiah 1*, 663; *Jeremiah 2*, 121.
[37] Rudolph, *Jeremia*, 177.
[38] Herrmann, *Jeremia*, 44.
[39] Kilpp, *Niederreissen und aufbauen*, p. 32 n. 64.

Phrases Unique to Jeremiah

הַדָּבָר אֲשֶׁר הָיָה אֶל־יִרְמְיָהוּ מֵאֵת, see chap. twelve, B11), the phrase is part of the editorial framework.

A5. חֵמָה יָצְאָה ("wrath has gone forth," 23:19=30:23). See above, chap. five, pp. 85–89 (espec. p. 87 [note ᵃ⁻ᵃ]). The combination of חֵמָה and יָצָא found in these doublets seems to be a typically Jeremianic phrase.

A6. חוּצוֹת יְרוּשָׁלַם ("the streets of Jerusalem," e.g., 5:1; 7:17, 34; 11:6, 13; 14:16; 33:10; 44:6, 9, 17, 21) is usually preceded by עָרֵי יְהוּדָה (see chap. twelve, B43). The poetic passage 5:1 may be the prototype, taken up in prose passages found in Jeremiah 7, 11 and 44, where Deuteronomistic phrases abound, but are not drawn directly from a Deuteronomistic source.[40]

A7. וּנְתַתִּיךָ...וּבְיַד אֲשֶׁר־אַתָּה יָגוֹר מִפְּנֵיהֶם ("I will deliver you...into the hand of those of whom you are afraid," 22:25); יָגוֹר מִפְּנֵיהֶם in יָגוֹר. וְלֹא תִנָּתֵן בְּיַד הָאֲנָשִׁים אֲשֶׁר־אַתָּה ("I will not deliver you into the hand of the men of whom you are afraid," 39:17). In the case of Coniah (22:25) this is a threat; for Ebed-melech (39:17) a promise that he will be delivered. Although 39:15–18 (the promise to Ebed-melech) may have a Jeremianic kernel, the passage appears to be composite: e.g., the repetition of "on that day" (39:16, 17); "for evil and not for good" (39:16; cf. 21:10), and the fact that these verses do not readily fit the context.[41]

A8. יטב *Hiphil* ("amend," 7:3, 5; 18:11; 26:13; 35:15, e.g., וּמַעַלְלֵיכֶם הֵיטִיבוּ דַרְכֵיכֶם ("amend your ways and your doings"). For Holladay, "the phrase is not Deuteronomistic," although 7:1–8:3 abounds in Deuteronomistic phrases.[42] If this is truly an authentic Jeremianic phrase, Jeremiah would have held out hope for a positive response to his early preaching, although issuing a sharp warning regarding the consequences of a complacent trust in the temple and the sacrificial system. The issue is whether Jeremiah initially offered salvation or doom and later became disillusioned and saw nothing but doom. For ישב *Qal*, see chap. thirteen, C40.

The sermon in Jeremiah 7 also contains the striking reference to "a den of robbers" (7:11). In all probability, genuine Jeremianic phrases have been combined with Deuteronomistic language in discourses primarily addressed to Judah during the period of the exile.[43]

A9. יָשַׁב in וַיֵּשֶׁב יִרְמְיָהוּ בַּחֲצַר הַמַּטָּרָה ("and Jeremiah remained [stayed] in the court of the guard," 37:21b; 38:13b; 38:28a; cf. 37:16b; בְּתוֹךְ הָעָם + ישב in 39:14b; 40:6b). Graupner draws attention to the formulaic character of this phrase as the concluding sentence of a narrative.[44] Bright's view that 37:11–21

---

[40] Holladay, "Prototype," 356; Thiel, *Redaktion 2*, 97–98.

[41] Thiel, *Redaktion 2*, 57; Holladay places 39:15–18 immediately after 38:27 (*Jeremiah 2*, 290).

[42] Holladay, *Jeremiah 1*, 241; Thiel (*Redaktion 1*), "a treasure-trove of dtrn. and dtr. phrases" (p. 103).

[43] Nicholson, *Jeremiah 1*, 74.

[44] Graupner, *Auftrag und Geschick*, p. 112 n. 1; cf. Wanke, *Untersuchungen*, 92–95.

and Jeremiah 38 are "parallel accounts of the same events" carries weight.[45] The repetitive phrase (37:21b; 38:13b; 38:28a) is a useful editorial device in linking these accounts together.

A10. כַּוָּנִים ("cakes [for the Queen of heaven]," 7:18; 44:19). King considers כַּוָּנִים "...a loanword from the Akkadian *kamanu*. ...*Kawwanim* denote sweetened cakes used in the cult of the mother goddess Ishtar as practiced in Mesopotamia."[46]

A11. מַדּוּעַ ("why, wherefore") is derived from ידע, used frequently (sixteen times) in Jeremiah, a stylistic rhetorical usage, often after a double question introduced by הֲ...אִם. The references cover all parts of the book: 2:14; 2:31; 8:5, 19, 22; 12:1; 13:22; 14:19; 22:28; 26:9; 30:6; 32:3; 36:29; 46:5, 15; 49:1. Otherwise, occurrences in the prophetic literature are few and mostly in Isaiah (5:4; 50:2; 63:2; cf. Mic 4:9). Berridge observes that when מַדּוּעַ is used in Jeremiah's questioning of Yahweh's actions, the tone is reproachful.[47]

A12. מות in the phrase שָׁם תָּמוּתוּ ("there you shall die"), referring to Coniah and his mother (22:26) and those who plan to flee to Egypt (42:16). Cf. וְשָׁם תָּמוּת (20:6, Pashhur); שָׁם יָמוּת (22:12, Shallum). In all these instances, death will take place in exile. As Carroll has indicated, the prose passage 22:11-12 is an editorial commentary on 22:10, reflecting knowledge of 2 Kgs 23:30-34 (note 2 Kgs 23:34, וַיָּמָת שָׁם).[48] Neither Shallum (i.e., Jehoahaz) nor Coniah (Jehoiachin) offer hope for a restored monarchy. This reflects the viewpoint of Jeremiah (22:10; 22:28-30).

A13. מֵי־רֹאשׁ ("poisoned water," only in the doublet 9:14 [9:15E]=23:15a). Since the phrase occurs only in Jeremiah, this may be reminiscent of language used by Jeremiah against false prophets (23:15a), applied to the people in general in a prose passage (9:11-15MT), a commentary on 9:10MT, in the interests of providing a theodicy. See also chap. five, pp. 83-85.

A14. מְלֶכֶת הַשָּׁמַיִם ("queen of heaven"). The title of this West Semitic deity is found in the OT only in Jeremiah (see 7:18; 44:17, 18, 25).[49] The cult of the queen of heaven is alluded to in 7:18 in the context of offerings to "other gods" (cf. 44:3). Jeremiah 44:15-19 is concerned with the revival of the cult

---

[45] Bright, *Jeremiah*, 233. For a careful analysis of Jeremiah 37-45 as a unified narrative with secondary expansion, see Seitz, *Theology in Conflict*, 236-241. He acknowledges that "problems in narrative sequence are confronted in Chaps. 37-39" (p. 238).

[46] Philip J. King, *Jeremiah. An Archaeological Companion* (Louisville: Westminster Press, 103). Cf. Walter Rast, "Cakes for the Queen of Heaven," in *Scripture in History and Theology: Essays in honor of J. Coert Rylaarsdam* (ed. A. Merrill and T. Overholt; Pittsburgh: Pickwick Press [1977] 167-180).

[47] Berridge, *Prophet*, p. 162 n. 257.

[48] Carroll, *Jeremiah*, 424.

[49] See Weinfeld, *Deuteronomy*, 149-154; M. Smith, *The Early History of God: Yahweh and the Other Deities in Ancient Israel* (San Francisco: Harper & Row, 1990) 90.

among "the remnant of Judah" in Egypt, also in the context of the worship of "other gods" (44:15). Although questions of historicity in Jeremiah 44 abound, 44:15-19 constitutes a central element within the homiletical discourse, harking back to 7:18.[50]

A15. מְעוֹן תַּנִּים ("lair of jackals," 9:10 [9:11E]; 10:22; 49:33; 51:37). This phrase is a description of devastated cities — Jerusalem, the cities of Judah, Hazor, Babylon. The OAN contain a number of Jeremianic phrases taken from the poetic oracles. Although this phrase appears only in the book of Jeremiah, "jackals" are referred to in the OAN in Isaiah, e.g., Isa 13:22 (Babylon); 34:13 (Edom).

A16. מִקְוֵה ("hope"). As an epithet of Yahweh, this only appears in Jeremiah (14:8; 50:7). Jeremiah 50:4-7 is introduced in the OAN (Babylon) to provide a strong contrast between the destruction of Babylon and the restoration of Israel and Judah. מִקְוֵה ("hope") in 14:8 may contain a double entendre, since מִקְוֵה can also mean "pool of water" (Exod 7:19) and Jeremiah 14 deals with drought and the need for water.[51]

A17. (a) דבר + מִשְׁפָּט Piel ("speak in judgment," 1:16; 4:12; 12:1; "pass sentence," 39:5=52:9 [cf. 2 Kgs 25:6]).[52]

(b) מִשְׁפָּט + עשׂה ("do justice," 22:3, 15; 23:5=33:15). See above, chap. four, pp. 60, 64.

(c) וְלֹא בְמִשְׁפָּט ("but not by justice," "by injustice," 17:11; 22:13 [Jehoiakim]).[53]

A18. נצל Hiphil: כִּי אִתְּךָ אֲנִי לְהַצִּילֶךָ ("for I am with you to deliver you"; cf. 1:8; 1:19; 15:20).[54] See chap. three, pp. 35-36, espec. p. 36, note d...d.

A19. עֹרֶף ("[back of] neck"); כִּי פָנוּ אֵלַי עֹרֶף וְלֹא פָנִים, 2:27; 32:33 (cf. 18:17). Holladay considers 2:27 the prototype, 32:33 the prose copy.[55]

A20. עשׁק coupled with גזל in 21:12; 22:3: וְהַצִּילוּ גָזוּל מִיַּד עוֹשֵׁק ("deliver from the hand of the oppressor him who has been robbed," 21:3), repeated with a slight variation (עָשׁוּק) in 22:3. See above, chap. four, p. 64. The relationship between 22:1-5 and 21:12 has been much debated; both set forth the ideals of monarchy in similar language.[56] Jeremiah 22:3 is a prose expansion of 21:12, incorporating phrases from 7:6.

---

[50] McKane (*Jeremiah 2*, 1086-1087) questions the historicity of "the great assembly" (קָהָל גָּדוֹל) in 44:15. See also Pohlmann, *Studien*, 181-182.

[51] Holladay, *Jeremiah 1*, 433.

[52] Holladay (*Jeremiah. A Fresh Reading*) translates the phrase in 12:1, "yet I would pass judgment upon you" (p. 96).

[53] See Holladay, *Jeremiah. A Fresh Reading*, 34.

[54] Holladay (*Jeremiah 1*) states, "The formulation...and its variants is evidently a formula confined to Jer" (p. 35).

[55] Holladay, "Prototype," 353.

[56] McKane, *Jeremiah 1*, 514-516, discusses the views of Duhm, Rudolph, Weiser, Thiel. See also the chart comparing 21:11-14 and 22:1-9 in Jones, *Jeremiah*, 286.

A21. צֳרִי ("balm"), as medicinal, associated with Gilead in 8:22; 46:11 (cf. 51:8). Volz holds the view that a late author has used a citation from Jeremiah in 46:11 as a generalized formula).[57]

A22. וְלֹא יִקָּבֵרוּ ("they shall not be buried," 8:2), preceded by לֹא יֵאָסְפוּ ("they shall not be gathered"), and with לֹא יִסָּפְדוּ ("they shall not be lamented") in 16:4, 6. All three verbs in the *Niphal* (קבר, אסף and ספר) occur in 25:33, which also contains the noun דֹּמֶן ("dung," cf. 8:2). This single prose verse, (25:33), inserted in the poetic passage 25:30-38, is a secondary insertion. הָאָרֶץ מִקְצֵה הָאָרֶץ וְעַד־קְצֵה (cf. 12:12) now applies to "those slain by Yahweh" among all the nations.[58]

A23. קטר Piel + עַל־גַּגּוֹת ("burn incense on the roofs"), only in 19:13, 32:29b. In polemical passages against idolatry, קטר occurs nineteen times in the book of Jeremiah, out of a total of forty-two in the OT.[59] Jeremiah 32:29b draws upon 19:13 (concerning incense on roofs and drink-offerings poured out to other gods); 32:19a reflects 21:10.

A24. קְצוּצֵי פֵאָה ("those who cut the corners of their hair, who roam the fringes of the desert" [NEB], 9:25 [9:26E]; 25:23; 49:32).[60]

A25. רֵאשִׁית + מַמְלְכוּת (and variants), "the beginning of the reign" (i.e., "the accession-year"), Jer 26:1; 27:1; 28:1; 49:34.[61] Jeremiah 27:1 contains textual problems (e.g., missing in the LXX); the reference to Zedekiah (see some manuscripts, Syr, and 27:3, 12); the name of Jehoiakim may have been carried over from 26:1 by a scribal error.[62]

A26. עַל־נַפְשׁוֹת in עַל־נַפְשׁוֹתֵינוּ + רָעָה גְדוֹלָה ("great evil, great calamity") נַאֲנַחְנוּ עֹשִׂים רָעָה גְדוֹלָה ("we are about to bring great evil upon ourselves," 26:19b); לָמָה אַתֶּם עֹשִׂים רָעָה גְדוֹלָה עַל־נַפְשֹׁתֵכֶם) ("why are you bringing great evil upon yourselves?" 44:7). The theme in common in the use of the phrase in two quite different contexts is that of self-inflicted disaster caused by wrong actions.

A27. שָׂשׂוֹן in the phrase קוֹל שָׂשׂוֹן וְקוֹל שִׂמְחָה קוֹל חָתָן וְקוֹל כַּלָּה ("the voice of mirth and the voice of gladness, the voice of the bridegroom, and the voice of the bride," 7:34; 16:9; 25:10; 33:11). שָׂשׂוֹן and שִׂמְחָה appear together in 15:16 (second Confession), and elsewhere in the OT (Isa 22:13; 35:10; 51:3; Zech 8:19; Ps 51:10). The twin phrase may have come

---

[57] Volz, *Jeremia*, 112.
[58] McKane, *Jeremiah 1*, 651 (cf. Duhm, Rudolph, Bright, Janzen).
[59] Andersen & Forbes, *VOT*, 411.
[60] Although McKane (*Jeremiah 1*, 639) criticizes the NEB translation on the grounds that קצוצי/פאה followed by הישבים במדבר is a tautology, he also states, "There is no doubt that קצוצי/פאה occurs in the context of desert communities in all three passages" (p. 215).
[61] Holladay, *Jeremiah 2*, 103.
[62] Holladay, *Jeremiah 2*, 115; Janzen, *Studies*, 14, 45.

into prophetic literature first in Isa 22:13, but the extended series is found only in Jeremiah.[63] See above, chap. six, pp. 113-114; chap. nine, pp. 195-196.

A28. שֶׁבֶר גָּדוֹל ("great destruction," 4:6; 6:1; 14:17 [גָּדוֹל is missing in the LXX]; 48:3 [Moab]; 50:22; 51:54 [Babylon]).

A29. שָׁכַם *Hiphil* (a) הַשְׁכֵּם וְדַבֵּר ("rising up early and speaking" [i.e., "speaking persistently"], 7:13; 11:7; 25:3; 35:14). The phrase is missing in 7:13LXX.[64]

(b) הַשְׁכֵּם וְשָׁלוֹחַ ("rising up early and sending" ["persistently sending"], 7:25; 25:4; 26:5; 29:19; 35:14; 44:4). Elsewhere in the OT, וְשָׁלוֹחַ הַשְׁכֵּם occurs only in 2 Chron 36:15, in a context where Jeremiah is mentioned several times (2 Chron 26:12, 21, 22).[65] These phrases, including הַשְׁכֵּם וְהָעֵד ("warning persistently," 11:7) and הַשְׁכֵּם וְהָעֵר ("teaching persistently," 32:33), are found only in Jeremiah and always in prose passages.[66]

A30. שָׁלָל ("booty, prize of war," in the phrase וְהָיְתָה־לּוֹ נַפְשׁוֹ לְשָׁלָל, 21:9=38:2). This word concerns surrender to the Babylonians (see above, chap. nine, pp. 201-204, espec. p. 202 note ᵉ⁻⁻⁻ᵉ). and, with minor vari'ations, it occurs in two other prose passages, 39:18 (regarding Ebed-melech); 45:5 (regarding Baruch). Although these phrases with שָׁלָל are not found elsewhere in the OT, no poetic prototype occurs in the book of Jeremiah.

A31. (a) שָׁלוֹם in such phrases as שָׁלוֹם יִהְיֶה לָכֶם ("it shall be well with you," 4:10; 23:17);

(b) שָׁלוֹם שָׁלוֹם וְאֵין שָׁלוֹם ("'Peace, peace' when there is no peace," 6:14=8:11 [in 8:11 a single שָׁלוֹם comes at the beginning of the phrase]); see above, chap. five, pp. 93-98. These phrases are found in the mouths of false prophets (cf. 4:13).

A32. שַׁעַר ("gate") in such phrases as:

(a) עֲמֹד בְּשַׁעַר ("stand in the gate," 7:2 [cf. עֲמֹד בֶּחָצֵר, 26:2]; 17:19);

(b) הַבָּאִים בַּשְּׁעָרִים הָאֵלֶּה ("those who enter these gates," 7:2 [missing in the LXX]; 17:20; 22:2 [cf. 22:4]).[67]

(c) שַׁעֲרֵי יְרוּשָׁלִָם ("gates of Jerusalem," 1:15; 17:21; 22:19).[68]

---

[63] Bright, "The Date of the Prose Sermons," p. 208 n. 17.

[64] Janzen, *Studies, 37;* Holladay, *Jeremiah 1*, 236.

[65] Bright, "The Date of the Prose Sermons," p. 207 n. 1.

[66] Jeremiah 11:7-8a is missing in the LXX; see Janzen, *Studies*, 39. Cf. Thiel (*Redaktion 1*), "a later expansion" (p. 148). Weippert's conclusions (*Die Prosareden*, 123-127) regarding Jeremiah's authorship of the prose passages, are challenged by McKane (*Jeremiah 1*). However, he allows that "The correct interpretation may rather be that items of vocabulary have been quarried from the poetry of Jeremiah in connection with the subsequent growth of the Jeremiah corpus through prose additions" (p. 167).

[67] Janzen, *Studies*, 36-37.

[68] Holladay ("Prototype," 354) considers 22:19 to be the poetic prototype, but as Weinfeld (*Deuteronomy*) points out, this is "too general a phrase and cannot be considered a cliché" (p. 353). Cf. Lam 4:12; Neh 7:3; 13:19.

A33. שָׁקַט וְשַׁאֲנַן ("have quiet and ease," 46:27=30:10; 48:11 [concerning Moab, in reverse order]). However, שקט by itself occurs frequently in Deuteronomistic literature (Josh 11:23; 14:15; Judg 3:11, 30; 5:31; 8:28) in the sense of "rest from war."[69] Only Jeremiah has the two words in combination.

A34 (a) שֶׁקֶר ("a lie, deceptive words" + בטח "to trust," 7:4, 8; 13:25; 28:15; 29:31).

(b) שֶׁקֶר + נבא *Niphal* ("to prophesy falsely, to prophesy lies," 5:31; 14:14; 20:6; 23:25, 26; 27:10, 14, 16; 29:9, 21).

A35. שֵׁשַׁךְ, *athbash* for Babylon, 25:26; 51:41. Only in Jeremiah (MT), but not in the LXX. See above, chap. eight, p. 171.

A36. תּוֹדָה (collective, "thankofferings"); וּמְבִאֵי תוֹדָה בֵּית יְהוָה ("bringing thankofferings to the house of Yahweh," 17:26; cf. 33:11). The phrase in 17:26 seems to be intrusive, based on 33:11.[70]

A37. תְּעָלָה אֵין לָךְ ("there is no healing for you," 30:13; 46:11 [not elsewhere in the OT]). If the context of 46:11 is taken into account, McKane's judgment carries weight, "The imitative character of v.11 is so striking that its identification with pastiche can hardly be wrong."[71]

Summary

This survey of repetitive phrases (A1 - A37) found in the book of Jeremiah may be summarized as follows:

(1) Certain phrases occur both in poetic and prose sections (e.g., A2, 6, 13, 17b, 18, 19, 20, 21, 24, 28, 31, 35, 36). This gives substance to the claim of Holladay that the prose sections of the book draw on prototypes in the poetic sections, unique phrases characteristic of Jeremiah.[72]

(2) Some of these phrases also appear in the OAN (A1, 10, 15, 16, 21, 24, 25, 28, 33). This raises the question regarding authorship of the prose passages and of the OAN. Major commentaries contain detailed discussions of the research into such questions over the last century, in which the views of Duhm, Mowinckel, Rudolph, Weiser, Hyatt, Bright and Herrmann are prominent. In recent times, Thiel, Thompson, Holladay (influenced by Weippert), Rietzschl, Pohlmann, Carroll, Jones and McKane have all made important contributions to the debate.[73] We may speak of a "Jeremiah tradition," which incorporates Jeremianic language and distinctive phrases into all parts of the book.

---

[69] Holladay, *Jeremiah 1*, 173.
[70] Bright, *Jeremiah,* 119; Rudolph, *Jeremia,* 118.
[71] McKane, *Jeremiah 2*, 1119.
[72] Holladay, "Prototypes."
[73] See also the articles in Leo G. Perdue & B. W. Kovacs, *A Prophet to the Nations* (Winona Lake, Indiana; Eisenbrauns, 1984), esp. Perdue, "Jeremiah in Modern Research," 1-32; T. R. Hobbs, "Some Remarks on the Composition and Structure of the Book of Jeremiah," 175-191.

(3) Many of these unusual phrases, not found elsewhere in the OT, are confined to the prose sections of the book (A3, 7, 9, 12, 14, 17a, 22, 23, 26, 27, 29, 30, 31, 32, 37), and are frequently embedded in a context of Deuteronomistic phraseology. In view of the context, Thiel usually regards such phrases as the work of Deuteronomistic redactors.[74] Is it not probable, however, that some of these phrases would belong to the "Jeremiah tradition"? Examples are A27, 29, 30, 31.

(4) Some distinctive phrases are found only in poetic passages: A15, 17c, 33, 34.

(5) Some phrases occur in doublets: A5, 13, 17(a) (b), 18, 27, 30, 31(b), 33. These may well reflect authentic Jeremianic vocabulary and characteristic speech.

(6) Some phrases serve an editorial function: A4, 8, 25.

Although the phrases listed are unique in the OT, they cannot in themselves give conclusive answers regarding the authorship of the various parts of the book of Jeremiah. We may speak confidently, however, of a "Jeremiah tradition," which serves as a substratum of the book as a whole.

We now turn to a series of phrases which are found both in Jeremiah and other parts of the OT, but not in the book of Deuteronomy or in the Deuteronomistic literature.

---

[74] E.g., Thiel *Redaktion 1*, 91, 113, 119, 123, 243. See also McKane (*Jeremiah 1*, 504) regarding Thiel's view as to the contribution by a Deuteronomistic editor.

CHAPTER TWELVE

PHRASES IN THE BOOK OF JEREMIAH WITH PARALLELS IN NON-DEUTERONOMISTIC BOOKS OF THE OLD TESTAMENT

We now turn to a series of phrases which are found both in Jeremiah and other parts of the OT, but not in the book of Deuteronomy or in the Deuteronomistic literature.

Repetitive Words and Phrases Common to Jeremiah and Other Parts of the Old Testament (excluding Deuteronomy and the Deuteronomistic literature)

B1. אֵבֶל יָחִיד ("mourning for an only son," 6:26; cf. Amos 8:10). Holladay thinks that this may be a proverbial expression.[1]

B2. אָדָם וּבְהֵמָה ("man and beast," in prose passages 7:20; 21:6; 27:5; 31:27; 32:43; 33:10 [*bis*], 12; 36:29; 50:3; 51:62; preceded by מֵאֵין in 32:43; 33:10, 12). Bright notes the use of the phrase in pentateuchal passages, all JE and P.[2] Cf. Zeph 1:3; Ezek 14:13, 19, 21; 25:13; 29:8; 36:11; Hag 1:11; Zech 2:8H; Jonah 3:7, 8; Ps 36:7H; 135:8. Holladay observes that the phrase is a commonplace in the J and P traditions (e.g., Exod 8:13, 14H) and in the prophetic literature, but "wonders whether its occurrence in Zeph 1:3 did not encourage Jrm to use it here" (7:20).[3] The phrase שְׁמָמָה הִיא מֵאֵין אָדָם וּבְהֵמָה אֲשֶׁר אַתֶּם אֹמְרִים ("of which you are saying 'It is a desolation without man or beast,'" 32:43b) finds a close parallel in 33:10, which substitutes חָרֵב for שְׁמָמָה, together with some minor changes. Marx discusses this near doublet, indicating that 33:4-11 follows the same *schema* as 32:36-44; 33:4-11 has the same thematic unity as Ezek 36:33-38.[4] Jeremiah 32:36-44 is related to the symbolic action of 32:6-15, and places emphasis on the new covenant and the taking up again of commercial activities. Jeremiah 33:4-11 reinterprets the passage, putting the emphasis on the cultic side.

---

[1] Holladay, *Jeremiah 2*, 45. Jeremiah 6:26LXX ἀγαπητοῦ probably represents יָדִיד (McKane, *Jeremiah 1*, 153).

[2] Bright, "The Date of the Prose Sermons," p. 210 n. 32.

[3] Holladay, *Jeremiah 1*, 256.

[4] Marx, "A Propos des Doublets," 111, draws attention to the use of the adjective חָרֵב in Ezek 36:33, 35, found in the book of Jeremiah in 33:10, 12.

B3. אָהֳלֵי יַעֲקוֹב ("tents of Jacob," 30:18 [cf. 4:20 "my tents"; 10:20, "my tent," with Yahweh as spokesman). Note the parallel in the oracle of Balaam, Num 24:5 ("how fair are your tents, O Jacob!").[5]

B4. אוֹי־לִי ("Woe is me!" 10:19; 15:10 [second Confession]; cf. Isa 6:5). Cf. אוֹי־נָא לִי, 4:31; 45:3; אוֹי לָךְ, 13:27 (Jerusalem); 48:46=Num 21:29 (Moab); אוֹי לָנוּ, 4:13; 6:4; 1 Sam 4:7, 8. See above, chap. two, p. 26.

B5. אָוֶן ("evil, trouble," 4:15); מַחְשְׁבֹת אוֹנֵךְ ("your evil thoughts," 4:14; cf. Prov 6:18; Isa 59:7). Only these two occurrences are found in Jeremiah, probably involving a play on words.[6] אָוֶן appears frequently elsewhere in prophetic literature: e.g., Mic 2:1; Isa 29:20; 32:6; 58:9; 59:6; Ezek 11:2; Hab 1:3.

B6. אִישׁ רִיב וְאִישׁ מָדוֹן ("a man of strife and contention," 15:10; cf. Hab 1:3). Jeremiah may be using language from Habakkuk (cf. חָמָס וָשֹׁד, see B19), e.g., Hab 1:8 and Jer 4:13; Hab 2:13b and Jer 51:58b.[7] See also above, chap. two, p. 26.

B7. אֶרֶץ צָפוֹן ("land of the north," 3:18; 6:22; 10:22; 16:15=23:8; 31:8; 46:10; 50:9). Cf. Isa 14:31; 41:25; 43:6; 49:12; Zech 6:8. "The north" conventionally denotes the place from which the enemy and danger come.

B8. בּוֹשׁ (Qal "to be ashamed"; Hiphil "to be put to shame"); this is a favorite verb in Jeremiah (thirty-four times), e.g., Qal 2:36; 6:15=8:12; 15:9; 17:13, 18; 20:11; 22:22; 49:23; Hiphil 2:26; 6:15=8:12; 8:9; 46:24; 48:1, 20.[8] The verb is found frequently in prophetic literature, e.g., Isa 1:29; 20:5; 41:11; 45:16, 17; Ezek 16:52; 36:32. Bak draws attention to parallels between 17:18 (third Confession) and Pss 25:2, 3; 31:18 (31:17E).[9] The expression "to be ashamed and confounded" (בּוֹשׁ Qal followed by כלם Niphal) in 22:22 (cf. כלם Hophal 14:3) is found elsewhere in prophetic literature (see Ezek 16:52; 36:32; Isa 41:11; 45:16, 17. Cf. בּוֹשׁ + חפר, 15:9; Mic 3:7).

B9. בַּת־עַמִּי ("daughter of my people," 4:11; 6:26; 8:11, 19, 21, 22, 23; 9:6; 14:17 [cf. Isa 22:4; Lam 3:48; 4:3, 6, 10]). See above, chap. five, p. 94 (note [d...d]).

B10. גְּאוֹן הַיַּרְדֵּן ("majesty of the Jordan, jungle of the Jordan," 12:5; 49:19; 51:44; Zech 11:3). Cf. also גְּאוֹן־מוֹאָב ("pride of Moab," 48:29=Isa 16:6); see above, chap. seven, pp. 131–132.

B11. דָּבָר in the phrase הַדָּבָר אֲשֶׁר הָיָה אֶל־יִרְמְיָהוּ מֵאֵת יְהוָה, 7:1; 11:1; 18:1; 21:1; 25:1; 30:1; 32:1; 34:1, 8; 35:1; 40:1; 44:1. Cf. similar headings in Hos 1:1; Mic 1:1; Zeph 1:1; Joel 1:1 (all minus מֵאֵת יְהוָה). Thiel regards

---

[5] The Balaam oracles in Numbers 24 were probably introduced by J, according to Sellin-Fohrer, *Introduction*, 132, 149.

[6] Berridge, *Prophet*, 77–78.

[7] Holladay, *Jeremiah 2*, 53.

[8] Kilpp, *Niederreissen und aufbauen*, p. 157 n. 105.

[9] Bak, *Klagender Gott*, 160.

this introduction in Jeremiah as a stereotypical Deuteronomist superscription.[10] However, Seitz concludes, "These introductory forms are far too general...to develop a rigid redactional theory."[11] Rietzschel has suggested that the formula introduced readings in the synagogue.[12]

B12. הוֹי ("Ah, Alas"). The interjection is found in 22:13, 18; 23:1; 30:7; 34:5; 47:6; 48:1; 50:27. Cf. Isa 1:4; 5:8; 10:5; 18:1; 55:1; Amos 5:18; 6:1; Hab 2:6, 9, 12, 15, 19; Zech 2:10, 11 (2:6, 7E).

הוֹי אָדוֹן ("Ah,lord!" 22:18; 34:5). Both passages include the verb ספד ("lament"), with a direct contrast between no lamenting for Jehoiakim (22:18) and lamentation for Zedekiah (34:5).[13]

B13. זֶרַע יִשְׂרָאֵל ("offspring of Israel," 23:8; 31:36, 37; cf. 33:26). Cf. Ps 22:24; Neh 9:2; 1 Chron 16:13. Jeremiah 31:36, 37 may date from the fifth century (cf. Neh 9:2; 1 Chron 16:13).[14] The history of 23:8=16:15 is complicated. See above, chap. four, pp. 72-77.

B14. חָזוֹן ("vision"). Infrequently used in Jeremiah (14:14; 23:16; in connection with false prophets), but used in a positive sense elsewhere in the prophetic literature: Hos 12:11 (12:10E); Hab 2:2, 3; Mic 3:6; Isa 1:1; Obad 1; Nah 1:1. The introductions to Isaiah, Obadiah and Nahum may have been added later.[15]

B15. שלם + אֶל־חֵיק Piel (literally, "to requite (repay)...into the bosom," 32:18 [Jeremiah's prayer]); cf. Isa 65:6 (עַל־) ; אֶל־חֵיק Ps 79:12; עַל־חֵיק Ps 35:13.

B16. חִיל כַּיּוֹלֵדָה ("pain as of a woman in travail," 6:24=50:43; 22:23; cf. Mic 4:9; Ps 48:7 [48:6E]).[16] כַּיּוֹלֵדָה alone occurs in 8:21LXX; 30:6 (missing in the LXX); 49:24 (missing in the LXX); cf. Mic 4:10; Isa 13:8; 42:14.[17] See above, chap. eight, p. 176 (note ⁱ⁻⁻ⁱ).

B17. חֵיל מֶלֶךְ בָּבֶל ("the army of the king of Babylon," 32:2; 34:7, 21; 38:3).[18] Cf. 34:1; 39:1; 52:4(=2 Kgs 25:1); Ezek 29:18, 19 (Tyre).

B18. חַלְלֵי־חָרֶב ("those slain by the sword," 32:18a; cf. Isa 22:2; Lam 4:9). This phrase is used in the OAN in Ezekiel (e.g., 31:17, 18; 32:20, 21, 25, 28, 29, 31, 32 [Egypt]; 35:8 [Edom]).

---

[10] Thiel, *Redaktion 1*, p. 50 n. 9.
[11] Seitz, *Theology in Conflict*, p. 230 n. 49; cf. Janzen, *Studies*, p. 228 n. 80.
[12] Rietzschel, *Der Problem der Urrolle*, 113-114; cf. Thiel, *Redaktion 1*, p. 107 n. 16.
[13] Seitz, *Theology in Conflict*, p. 251 n. 114.
[14] Holladay, *Jeremiah 1*, 622.
[15] Meyer, *Jeremia und die Falschen Propheten*, 62.
[16] See Delbert R. Hillers, "A Convention in Hebrew Literature: The Reaction to Bad News," *ZAW* 77 (1965) 86-90, esp. 87.
[17] In 8:21, LXX has an additional phrase, ὠδῖνες ὡς τικτούσης. Janzen (*Studies*, 31, 63) thinks that this has been taken from 6:24.
[18] See Hardmeier (*Prophetie im Streit*, 177) for the historical background of 34:7, 21.

B19. חָמָס וָשֹׁד ("violence and destruction," 6:7; 20:8; cf. Amos 3:10; Ezek 45:9; Isa 60:18; Hab 1:3 [in reverse order]). See above, chap. three, pp. 50-51.

B20. יָצַת + אֵשׁ ("to kindle a fire," 11:16; 17:27; 21:14b; 43:12; 49:2, 27; 50:32; cf. Amos 1:14).[19]

B21. ישׁב in מֵאֵין יוֹשֵׁב ("without inhabitant," 4:7; 26:9; 33:10; 34:22; 44:22 [missing in the LXX]; 46:19; 48:9; 51:29, 37). Cf. Isa 5:9; 6:11; Zeph 2:5; 3:6. Berridge regards this terminology as pertaining to the Day of Yahweh and derived from the practice of "holy war."[20] Volz thinks that the OAN occurrences (46:19; 48:8; 51:29, 37) were expansions to round out these passages when they were read in the synagogue for edification.[21]

B22. כּוֹס ("cup," 16:7; 25:15, 17, 28; 35:5; 49:12; 51:7). Carroll observes, "...the cup metaphor holds together a cluster of different motifs."[22] Cf. Isa 51:17, 22.

B23. עָשָׂה + כָּלָה ("to make a full end," 30:11=46:28; Isa 10:23; Ezek 11:3; Nah 1:8; Zeph 1:18). For the phrase with the negative (לֹא), as in 4:27; 5:10, 18; 30:11=46:28, see above, chap. seven, pp. 122-123.

B24. כְּלִי in אִם־כְּלִי אֵין חֵפֶץ בּוֹ ("a vessel no one cares for," 22:28 [Jehoiachin]; cf. 48:38 [Moab]; Hos 8:8). Berridge claims that the phrase in Jeremiah is derived from Hos 8:8.[23] This phrase may well have been part of the prophetic idiomatic language. See above, chap. seven, p. 137 (note [j...j]).

B25. כְּלָיוֹת וָלֵב ("the kidneys [heart] and the mind," 11:20=20:12 [doublet in the Confessions]; cf. 17:10; Ps 7:10 [7:9E]; 26:2). See above, chap. two, p. 16. Psalm 7 may have been the source of this expression.[24]

B26. לְבוֹנָה ("frankincense," 6:20; 17:26; 41:5; cf. Lev 2:2, 16; Isa 43:23; 60:6; 66:3).[25] In 6:20, Jeremiah rejects the offering of incense as efficacious *ex opere operato*, whereas the prose passages (17:26, 41:5) regard the offering of incense as a normal and acceptable aspect of cultic worship. Isaiah 66:3 speaks against cultic abuses.[26]

---

[19] Holladay ("Prototype," 316) finds the immediate prototype in Jer 11:16.
[20] Berridge, *Prophet*, 93.
[21] Volz, *Jeremia*, 385.
[22] Carroll, *Jeremiah*, 758.
[23] Berridge, *Prophet*, p. 180 n. 358. For McKane (*Jeremiah*, 549) this was simply an idiom that both Jeremiah and Hosea knew. Cf. Wessels ("Jeremiah 22:24-30"), "It does not necessarily imply literary dependence" (p. 240).
[24] Holladay, *Jeremiah 2*, 67-68. Cf. McKane (*Jeremiah 1*, 278). McKane sees a link with the laments in the book of Psalms. For a full discussion of the term לֵב as a metaphor, see Timothy Polk, *The Prophetic Persona* (JSOTSup 32; Sheffield: JSOT Press, 1984) 44-57.
[25] King, *Jeremiah*, 111-113.
[26] Kaiser, *Isaiah 40-66*, 413-414.

B27. מאס ("reject" [Yahweh's action], 2:37; 6:30; 7:29; 14:19; 31:37; 33:24, 26). Cf. Hos 4:6; 9:17; Amos 5:21. Yahweh's rejection of his people for their apostasy and evil deeds is a recognized prophetic theme.

B28. מָגוֹר מִסָּבִיב ("terror all around," 6:25; 20:3, 10a; 46:5; 49:29; cf. Ps 31:14a; Lam 2:22). The phrase (discussed above, chap. three, pp. 48–52) probably originated with Jeremiah himself.

B29. מוּסָר ("discipline, correction, instruction" + לקח in 2:30; 5:3; 7:28; 17:23; 32:33; cf. Zeph 3:2, 7; Prov 1:3; 8:10; 24:32; Ps 50:17). Weinfeld points out that the phrase "seems to be rooted in the didactic sphere."[27] Jeremiah 7:28 and Zeph 3:2 both contain also the phrase לֹא־שָׁמְעוּ בְּקוֹל ("did not obey the voice" [of Yahweh], see chap. thirteen, C99). Jeremiah 7:28 may be dependent on Zeph 3:2 (*contra* Thiel).[28]

B30. מְלָכִים שָׂרִים כֹּהֲנִים נְבִיאִים ("kings, officials, priests, prophets"). This sequence, in full or in part, is found in 1:18; 2:26; 4:9; 8:1; 13:13; 17:25; 25:18; 26:11; 32:32; 44:17, 21. Holladay thinks that 4:9 is the prototype.[29] Cf. similar lists in later books: Neh 9:32, 34; Dan 9:8. See above, chap. three, p. 37.

B31. מְקוֹר מַיִם חַיִּים ("a fountain of living water," 2:13; 17:13; cf. Gen 26:19; Lev 14:5; Ps 36:10 [36:9E]; Prov 10:1; 13:14; 14:27; 16:22). מַיִם חַיִּים, according to Holladay, "is normal idiom for 'running water'."[30]

B32. מַרְפֵּא ("healing," 8:15[=14:19]; 33:6). Cf. Prov 4:22; 12:18; 13:17; 16:24; 2 Chron 21:18; 36:16; Mal 3:20. The noun is not a characteristic prophetic term, although the verb is frequently used in prophetic oracles (e.g., 3:22; 6:14=8:11; 8:22; 15:18; 17:14; 19:11; 30:17; 33:6; 51:9; Hos 6:1; 14:5 [14:4E]; Isa 6:10; 19:22; 57:19; Ezek 47:8, 9; Zech 11:16).

B33. מַשָּׂא II ("burden," 17:21, 22, 24, 27; cf. Neh 13:15, 19). See above, chap. five, pp. 103–105.

מַשָּׂא III ("oracle," cf. Nah 1:1; Hab 1:1; Isa 13:1; Mal 1:1; Zech 9:1; 12:1). Both senses are present in 23:33–40.[31] See above, chap. five, pp. 91–93.

B34. נְאֻם יְהוָה ("oracle of Yahweh"). The formula occurs 356 times in the prophets (Jeremiah, 176 times; Isaiah, twenty-five; Amos, twenty-one; Hosea, four; Ezekiel, eighty-five).[32] The formula is missing in over seventy instances in the LXX in the book of Jeremiah.[33] The addition of the formula

---

[27] Weinfeld, *Deuteronomy*, 352.
[28] Thiel, *Redaktion 2*, p. 90 n. 17.
[29] Holladay, "Prototype," 361.
[30] Holladay, *Jeremiah 1*, 92.
[31] Thiel (*Redaktion 1*) regards 23:33–40 as the work of a later hand (p. 253 n. 78).
[32] Andersen & Forbes, *VOT*, 370. Cf. Rendtorff, "Zum Gebrauch der Formel n°'um jahwe im Jeremiabuch," *ZAW* 66 (1954) 27–37; F. S. North, "The Expression 'The Oracle of Yahweh' as an Aid to Critical Analysis," *JBL* 71 (1952) x.
[33] Janzen, *Studies*, 82–83, lists the passages in the LXX where נְאֻם יְהוָה does not occur.

in the Hebrew text in some instances may be related to synagogue practices.³⁴

B35. נְאוֹת מִדְבָּר ("pastures of the wilderness," 9:9 [9:10E]; 23:10; cf. Joel 1:19, 20; 2:22; Ps 65:13 [65:12E]). Has Jeremiah's phrase been taken up by Joel?

B36. נַחְלָה ("grievous") followed (10:19; 30:12) or preceded (14:17) by מַכָּה ("wound"); cf. Nah 3:19. Is Nahum dependent on Jeremiah for the phrase?

B37. נִירוּ לָכֶם נִיר ("break up your fallow ground," 4:3b; Hos 10:12b). Perhaps both prophets have used a popular proverb. See above, chap. four, p. 64.

B38. (a) נפל ("to fall") + כשל ("to stumble") occurs in 46:6, 12, 16; 50:32; Isa 3:8; 31:3. See above, chap. seven, pp. 116, 117.

(b) נפל ("to fall") + קוּם ("to rise up") occurs in 8:4; 25:27; Amos 5:2; 8:14; Mic 7:8; Isa 24:20, usually "in association with Yahweh's judgment."³⁵

B39. נְקָמָה ("vengeance," 11:20=20:12; 15:15; 46:10; 50:15, 28; 51:6, 11, 36; cf. Lev 19:18; Ps 94:1; and the phrase יוֹם נָקָם in Isa 34:8; 61:2; 63:4).

B40. נְקִיק ("cleft") + סֶלַע ("rock") occurs in 13:4; 16:16; cf. Isa 7:19.

B41. עָבַד + ב ("to make bondmen of, to enslave," 22:13; 25:14; 27:7; 30:8; 34:9, 10). Cf. Isa 14:3; Ezek 34:27; Lev 25:39, 46; Exod 1:14.

B42. עָרֵי יְהוּדָה ("the cities of Judah"). The phrase by itself (often in combination with "Jerusalem") occurs in 1:15; 4:16; 9:10 (9:11E); 10:22; 11:12; 17:26; 25:18; 26:2; 32:44; 33:13; 34:7, 22; 36:9; 40:5; 44:2; Isa 36:1=2 Kgs 18:13; 40:9; 44:26; Zech 1:12. For חֻצוֹת יְרוּשָׁלַם ("streets of Jerusalem"), see chap. eleven, A6; for the combination ("the cities of Judah and the streets of Jerusalem"), see chap. thirteen, C74.

B43. עֵת in בְּעֵת־רָעָה ("at the time of trouble," 2:27, 28; 11:12, 14; cf. Ps 37:19; Amos 5:13); in בְּעֵת־צָרָה ("in the time of distress," 14:8; 30:7; cf. Isa 33:2; Ps 37:39); both phrases are combined in 15:11 (second Confession).³⁶

B44. פלל Hithpael ("to intercede") + בְּעַד ("on behalf of"); prohibition of intercession in 7:16=11:14; 14:11; intercession at the request of Zedekiah in 37:3; cf. 42:2, 4. See also 29:7 (Jeremiah's letter to the exiles in Babylon). פלל Hithpael occurs frequently in the OT (eighty times), but prohibition of intercession is found only in the book of Jeremiah.

---

³⁴ Janzen, *Studies*, p. 217 n. 28.
³⁵ Berridge, *Prophet*, 171. Berridge has overlooked 8:4 and Mic 7:8, however.
³⁶ Talmon ("The Textual Study of the Bible") states, "It...remains evident that the author of 15:11 (and one does not seem to doubt the ascription of the verse to Jeremiah) purposefully retained here a combination of expressions which he uses elsewhere alternately" (p. 355). If so, the author of Psalm 37 may be indebted to Jeremiah for these expressions (e.g., Ps 37:19, 39).

Parallels in non-Deuteronomistic Books

B45. כִּפְרִי מַעֲלָלָיו ("fruit of his [your] doings," 17:10b=32:19b; 21:14).[37] Jeremiah 32:19MT is missing in the LXX. Cf. Isa 3:10; Mic 7:13 (without כְּ). See above, chap. nine, p. 199 (note [b...b]).

B46. פְּקֻדָּתָם in the phrase שְׁנַת־פְּקֻדָּתָם ("the year of their punishment," 11:23b=23:12b; 48:44 [Moab]); in the phrase עֵת־פְּקֻדָּתָם ("at the time of their punishment," 6:15=8:12; 10:15=51:18; 46:21; 50:27).[38] See above, chap. two, pp. 18-19; chap. five, p. 95 (note [h...h]).

B47. קָרָא + ולא ענה ("call") + ("not answer") in 7:13b, 27b; 35:17b (missing in the LXX).[39] Cf. Isa 65:11-12; 66:4 (and 65:24, where by contrast Yahweh says, "Before they call, I will answer").[40]

B48. אַרְבַּע רוּחוֹת ("four winds," 49:36; cf. Ezek 37:9; Zech 2:6; 6:5; Dan 8:8). See above, chap. seven, p. 161.

B49. אִישׁ רִיב וְאִישׁ מָדוֹן ("a man of strife and contention," 15:10 [second Confession]; cf. Hab 1:3, רִיב וּמָדוֹן ["strife and contention"]). See above, chap. two, p. 26 and B6.

B50. רָעָה (a) יוֹם רָעָה ("the day of evil [calamity]," 17:17, 18 [third Confession]; 51:2; cf. Ps 27:5; 41:2).

(b) מֵרָעַת יֹשְׁבֵי־בָהּ ("because of the wickedness of those who dwell in it," 12:4 [first Confession]; cf. Ps 107:32).[41]

(c) לְרָעָה וְלֹא לְטוֹבָה ("for evil and not for good," 21:10; 39:16; 44:27; Amos 9:14).[42]

B51. רעשׁ ("quake, tremble," 4:24; 8:16; 10:10, 22; 49:21=50:46; 51:29). Cf. Judg 5:4 (Song of Deborah); 2 Sam 22:8=Ps 18:7; Isa 13:13; Ezek 38:19, 20; Joel 2:10; Hag 2:6, 7, 21. "The mountains" (4:24) quake at the outpouring of Yahweh's wrath and judgment. Jeremiah 4:24; 8:16; 10:22 are associated with the coming of the enemy from the north. Childs discusses the passages in the OT dealing with "the enemy from the north" and the eschatological passages concerning the return to chaos.[43] For him, "the root רעשׁ appears to have developed into a technical term for the final shaking of the

---

[37] Holladay, "Prototype," 355, considers 17:10 to be the prototype.

[38] בְּעֵת־פְּקֻדָּתִים (6:15), but ἐν καιρῷ ἐπισκοπῆς (6:15LXX; cf. 10:15LXX) supports the reading בְּעֵת־פְּקֻדָּתָם. See above, chap. five, p. 95 (note [h...h]).

[39] According to Janzen, *Studies*, Jer 35:17 is "from 7:13" (p. 52).

[40] Kaiser (*Isaiah 40-66*) regarding Isa 65:11-12, states: "...it is evident that the author has taken up stock-terms used in the announcements of judgment of older days" (p. 405). As to the four verbs in 7:13 (דבר Piel, שׁמע, קרא, ענה), Holladay, *Jeremiah 1*, 248, points out that the sequence is imitated in Trito-Isaiah in 65:12=66:4; 65:24.

[41] Vermeylen, "Essai de Redaktionsgeschichte," thinks that the Psalmist is quoting from Jeremiah and is also dependent on other psalms and DI for much of his material (p. 245).

[42] Holladay, "Prototype," 364, considers Amos 9:14 to be the prototype. Jeremiah 32:42, however, is a striking reversal of this message of doom.

[43] Brevard S. Childs, "The Enemy from the North and the Chaos Tradition," *JBL* 78 (1959) 187-198.

world at the return of chaos."⁴⁴ The passages in Jeremiah where רעש appears must be regarded as post-exilic. Berridge defends the view that both 8:16 and 10:22 are pre-exilic, pointing to a historical "enemy from the north" and that 4:23-26 likewise speaks of a historical judgment.⁴⁵ תהו ובהו ("waste and void," 4:23) indicates a return to the situation depicted in Gen 1:2 (P), which strengthens the argument that 4:23-26 in its present form contains late elements. The hyperbolic language of 8:16 is not out of keeping with a direct reference to the peril from the north; the phrase "lair of jackals" (see chap. eleven, A15) in 10:22 (cf. 9:10 [9:11E]) makes it possible that this verse goes back to Jeremiah himself, although its "kompilatorischen Character" suggests that the verse has been added later by an editor within the "Jeremiah tradition."⁴⁶

B52. שִׂים + עַל + עֵינַיִם ("to set eyes upon," 24:6; 39:12; 40:4). Cf. Amos 9:4, which may be the prototype.

B53. שְׁאֵרִית ("remnant"). Of sixty-six occurrences of שְׁאֵרִית in the OT, twenty-four are found in the book of Jeremiah.⁴⁷ The reference in 6:9 to "the remnant of Israel" (Israel as a whole) offers little hope (*contra* Mic 2:12, regarding the northern kingdom).⁴⁸ There will be no remnant for the men of Anathoth, 11:23 (cf. 50:26).⁴⁹ Jeremiah 8:3 and 15:9 are, at best, a "gloomy depiction of the remnant hope."⁵⁰ Brueggemann finds an incipient doctrine of the remnant in 1:17-19, where later editors understood themselves to share in the "but you" assurances given to Jeremiah and Baruch (cf. 45:5).⁵¹ Supporters of Jeremiah such as Uriah ben Shemaiah (26:20), members of the family of Shaphan (e.g., 26:24, Ahikam), Baruch, Ebed-Melech, and Gedaliah give some substance to the idea that a small nucleus of the faithful would represent hope for the future.⁵² Such a hope for the remnant of the diaspora is expressed in 23:3.⁵³ Other references to "the remnant of Jerusalem" (24:8); "a remnant in Judah" (40:11; 42:15); "the remnant of Judah" (42:15, 19; 43:5; 44:12, 14, 28 [cf. 44:7]), offer little hope for those who go to Egypt, "except some fugitives"

---

⁴⁴ Childs, "The Enemy from the North," 197.

⁴⁵ Berridge, *Prophet*, p. 82 n. 52.

⁴⁶ Volz, *Jeremia*, 127.

⁴⁷ Andersen & Forbes, *VOT*, 428. H. Klassen (*Who are the Remnant in the Book of Jeremiah?*; M.Th.Thesis, Knox College, Toronto, 1952), claims that "remnant" vocabulary is used more frequently in the Book of Jeremiah than in any other OT writing.

⁴⁸ Holladay, *Jeremiah*, 375.

⁴⁹ See above, chap. two, pp. 21-22.

⁵⁰ Raitt, *A Theology of Exile*, 50.

⁵¹ Brueggemann, *To Pluck Up, to Tear Down*, 28-29.

⁵² According to M. A. Kessler ("Jeremiah Chapters 26-45 Reconsidered," *JNES* 27 [1968]), "a responsive remnant was always present" (p. 85).

⁵³ This text is best taken as a late passage, since the exile and dispersion are understood to have taken place (McKane, *Jeremiah 1*, 558). Cf. Jer 31:7-8 regarding "the remnant of Israel."

(44:14).⁵⁴ Although the word "remnant" is not used, "the good figs" (24:4-7), exiles in Babylonia, provide the basis for genuine hope (cf. 50:20). The concept of a "remnant" goes back to prophets earlier than Jeremiah (e.g., Amos 1:8; 5:15; 9:12; Mic 2:12; 5:6, 7 [5:7, 8E]; Zeph 2:7, 9; 3:13) and recurs in later prophetic literature (Ezek 9:8; 11:13; Isa 46:3; Hag 1:12, 14; 2:2; Zech 8:6, 11, 12).⁵⁵

B54. (a) שֶׁבֶר גָּדוֹל ("great destruction," 4:6b; 6:1; 14:17; 48:3 [Moab]; 50:22; 51:54 [Babylon]; cf. Zeph 1:10).⁵⁶ See also above, chap. seven, p. 128.

(b) שֹׁד וָשֶׁבֶר ("desolation and destruction," 48:3; Isa 59:7; 60:18 [cf. Isa 51:9]). See above, chap. seven, p. 128.

B55. יהוה...שְׁמוֹ ("Yahweh...is his name" [and variations, "Yahweh of hosts is his name," "Yahweh God of hosts is his name"]). This usage occurs mostly in late contexts (10:16=51:19; 31:35; 32:18; 33:2; 46:18; 48:15; 50:34; 51:57). As Janzen indicates, "שְׁמוֹ ...יהוה occurs primarily in creation/redemption contexts" (e.g., Exod 15:3; Amos 4:13; 5:8, 27; 9:6; Isa 47:4; 48:2; 51:15; 54:5).⁵⁷ See above, chap. eight, p. 180.

B56. שֶׁקֶר (See also chap. eleven, A35). שֶׁקֶר + דבר *Piel* ("to speak falsely [lies]," 9:4 [9:5E]; 29:23; 40:16 [דבר *Qal*]; 43:2; Mic 6:12; Isa 59:3; Zech 13:3; Ps 63:12 [דבר *Qal*]).

B57. תְּחִנָּה ("supplication"). Although this noun appears frequently in Solomon's prayer (Deuteronomistic; 1 Kgs 8:30, 38, 45, 49, 52, 54; cf. 1 Kgs 9:3), the combination נפל + תְּחִנָּה ("supplication falls," i.e.,"comes," 36:7; 37:20; 38:26; 42:2, 9) occurs elsewhere only in Dan 9:18.

Recurring phrases found in the book of Jeremiah and elsewhere in the Old Testament, but not in Deuteronomy or the Deuteronomistic literature: Summary (B1-B57)

(1) These phrases occur sometimes in poetic passages only; for example: נְאוֹת מִדְבָּר (B31); מְקוֹר מַיִם חַיִּים (B19); חָמָס וָשֹׁד (B9); בַּת־עַמִּי (B35). A popular proverb may be reflected in אָבֵל יָחִיד (B1); נִירוּ לָכֶם נִיר (B37).

(2) The Confessions contain words or phrases which recur in the OAN: עֵת־פְּקֻדָּתָם and שְׁנַת־פְּקֻדָּתָם (B39); נְקָמָה (B28); מָגוֹר מִסָּבִיב (B10); גְּאוֹן הַיַּרְדֵּן (B46). They also occur in other parts of the OT: כְּלָיוֹת וָלֵב (B25); וּבְעֵת צָרָה (B43); יוֹם רָעָה (B50a). Distinctive phrases from the Confessions or in poetic sections may have originated with Jeremiah and have been picked up by those who composed the OAN and by later prophets and psalmists.

---

⁵⁴ See Thiel, *Redaktion 2*, 65, 78-80.
⁵⁵ See Seitz, *Theology in Conflict*, 30-31.
⁵⁶ Berridge (*Prophet*) writes, "... שבר refers to the broken state of Yahweh's people *following* His judgment" (p. 110 n. 207).
⁵⁷ Janzen, *Studies*, p. 216 n. 22.

(3) Some phrases are found in doublets: B7, B8, B10, B23, B25, B32, B39, B44, B45, B46, B55.

(4) Some phrases and terms occur only in prose passages in Jeremiah: e.g., בְּכָל (B11); the introductory heading הַדָּבָר אֲשֶׁר הָיָה אֶל־יִרְמְיָהוּ מֵאֵת יְהוָה (B17) in narrative sections; פלל Hithpael + בְּעַד (B44); נפל + תְּחִנָּה חֵיל מֶלֶךְ (B57).

(5) Some phrases and words in prose passages are also found in the OAN: אָדָם וּבְהֵמָה (B2); כּוֹס (B22); שְׁמוֹ...יהוה (B55).

(6) Phrases in poetic sections also occur in the OAN: אוֹי־לִי (B4); הוֹי (B12); שֶׁבֶר גָּדוֹל (B54a). אִם־כְּלִי אֵין חֵפֶץ בּוֹ (B16); חִיל כַּיּוֹלֵדָה (B24);

(7) A few repeated phrases within the OAN also occur elsewhere in the OT: e.g., כשל + נפל or קוּם (B38);

(8) Some phrases are found both in poetic and prose passages: זֶרַע יִשְׂרָאֵל (B13); ב + מוּסָר (B29); the sequence מְלָכִים שָׂרִים כֹּהֲנִים נְבִיאִים (B30); לקח Piel דבר + שֶׁקֶר (B41); עָרֵי יְהוּדָה (B42); כִּפְרִי מַעֲלָלִים (B45); שְׁאֵרִית (B53); עבר (B56).

(9) In a few instances phrases or words are repeated in poetry, prose and the OAN: צָפוֹן אֶרֶץ (B7); בּוֹשׁ (B8); אֵשׁ + יָצַת (B20); מֵאֵין יוֹשֵׁב (B21).

We may speak with some confidence of a Jeremiah tradition, leading back to the Confessions and the poetic oracles in Jeremiah 1–20. The poetic passages stand within the prophetic tradition, although new and vigorous phrases have been added by the prophet himself. Biographical and narrative sections (including the homiletical discourses) also reflect the language of the poetic oracles, which is frequently highly distinctive. Those who composed the OAN freely drew on the language of the Confessions, as well as on the language of the poetic oracles and prose sections.

By far the largest category to be considered consists of repetitive phrases in the book of Jeremiah which are in common with the book of Deuteronomy or the Deuteronomistic literature. Consideration of these phrases now becomes our major concern in the following chapter.

CHAPTER THIRTEEN

RECURRING PHRASES IN THE BOOK OF JEREMIAH:
PHRASES WITH PARALLELS IN THE
DEUTERONOMISTIC BOOKS
OF THE OLD TESTAMENT

Prose passages in the book of Jeremiah contain many recurring phrases, often with striking parallels to the book of Deuteronomy and the Deuteronomistic literature, some of which also appear in other books of the OT as well.

Mowinckel made a clear distinction between "biographical" passages (Source B), and prose discourses (Jeremiah's "sermons"), ascribed to Source C.[1] In both areas, Deuteronomistic language and a common Deuteronomistic theology are to be found. Nicholson, in his study of the prose tradition in the book of Jeremiah, finds "striking similarities with speeches and sermons in the Deuteronomic corpus."[2] He concludes "that the twofold division of the prose in Jeremiah as held by most commentators cannot be sustained and that the so-called biographical material assumed its present form, like the prose sermons and discourses, at the hands of the Deuteronomistic circle."[3] However, the situation seems to be more complicated, in that the Deuteronomistic component in Source B is less pronounced than in Source C. Williams indicates that Deuteronomistic diction in Source B occurs mainly in the speeches, but to a

---

[1] Sigmund Mowinckel, *Zur Komposition des Buches Jeremia* (Kristiana: Jacob Dybwad, 1914). Subsequently, Mowinckel used the term "tradition complex" rather than "source"; see *Prophecy and Tradition. The Prophetic Books in the Light of the Study of the Growth and History of the Tradition* (Oslo: Dybwad, 1946) 21-23, 28, 49. Among those who have ascribed the biographical passages to Baruch in their commentaries are Duhm, Volz, Rudolph, Hyatt, Bright and Weiser. Wanke (*Untersuchungen*) rejects this view. Holladay ("A Fresh Look at 'Source B' and 'Source C' in Jeremiah," 220), in his review of Wanke's book, concedes that Jeremiah 37-44 cannot be from Baruch. Carroll (*From Chaos to Covenant*) regards "the figure of Baruch as a deuteronomistic creation" (p. 151).

[2] Nicholson, *Preaching to the Exiles*, p. 32.

[3] Nicholson, *Preaching to the Exiles*, p. 36. Cf. McKane (*Jeremiah 1*): "Source C seems to be an additional, critical superstructure which is not functionally necessary and which ought to be demolished in the interests of economy" (p. lxxxv). See also Jones, *Jeremiah*, 18.

lesser degree than in Source C, and concludes that "Source B prose speeches and prose narratives should be regarded as separate corpora."[4]

Thiel, in his exhaustive study of Deuteronomic and Deuteronomistic phrases in the book of Jeremiah (referred to as D), asserts a thoroughgoing Deuteronomistic redaction of Jeremiah 1–45.[5] Some years earlier, Bright had listed a number of characteristic expressions found in the prose sermons which have counterparts in Deuteronomy and the Deuteronomistic history.[6] Weinfeld has also drawn up a comprehensive list of Deuteronomic phrases, many of which are also found in the book of Jeremiah.[7] Weippert has made a careful study of formulaic phrases in Jer 7:1–15; 18:1–12; 21:1–7; 32:29b–32; 34:17–20 and 35:15, in which she concludes that these prose discourses do not stem from a redactor.[8] Another contribution to the exploration of the relationships between Deuteronomistic phrases and phrases in Jeremiah is by Louis Stulman.[9]

Before examining a list of recurring phrases which belong to both the book of Jeremiah and the Deuteronomistic literature, we shall focus attention on the concept of "covenant" and especially the covenantal formula and the fascinating passage Jer 31:31–34, where the burning hope of a new covenant is set forth.

Covenant (בְּרִית) and the Covenantal Formula

ברית and such forms as הברית, בריתי, בריתך occur two hundred and eighty-four times in the OT, twenty-four times in Jeremiah, twenty-seven times in Deuteronomy.[10] Except for 14:21, the occurrences in Jeremiah are in prose passages, mostly in Jeremiah 11 and 31–34.[11] The phrase דִּבְרֵי הַבְּרִית is found in 11:2, 3, 6, 8; 34:18, as well as in Deut 29:1, 9; 2 Kgs 23:2.

---

[4] Michael J. Williams, "An Investigation of the Legitimacy of Source Distinctions for the Prose Material in Jeremiah," *JBL* 112 (1993) 193–210, esp. 209.

[5] Thiel, *Redaktion 1, Redaktion 2*.

[6] Bright, "The Date of the Prose Sermons," 15–35. Thiel (*Redaktion 1*, 20) points out that the phrases listed by Bright are drawn from biographical passages as well.

[7] Weinfeld, *Deuteronomy*, 320–365.

[8] Weippert, *Die Prosareden*, 234.

[9] Louis Stulman, *The Prose Sermons of the Book of Jeremiah. A Redescription of the Correspondences with the Deuteronomistic Literature in the Light of Recent Text-Critical Research* (SBLDS 83; Atlanta: Scholars Press, 1986).

[10] Andersen and Forbes, *VOT*, 295.

[11] Jeremiah 14:21 is part of the composite section, 14:19–22, in which 14:19b is parallel to 8:15 (see chap. one, pp. 8–9) and 14:22 is probably an addition. McKane (*Jeremiah 1*) states, "Verse 22 is not obviously related to the topics of prayer in vv. 20–21" (p. 332). The appeal to Yahweh to "remember" his covenant (cf. Lev 26:40–45; Exod 2:24) in this litany is based on Yahweh's obligation to honor the covenant he has made and to protect his people. See also Thiel, *Redaktion 2*, 27.

An extensive literature has developed regarding the concept of בְּרִית and the covenant formula.[12] The date of origin of the idea of covenant is a matter of speculation. Most of the occurrences of בְּרִית in the prophetic literature are exilic or later (e.g., occurrences in Ezekiel and DI), although the term appears in Hosea five times (Hos 2:20 [2:18E]; 6:7; 8:1; 10:4; 12:2 [12:1E]).[13] Weinfeld has argued that "there was a direct borrowing from Assyrian by Deuteronomy from Assyrian treaty documents," and that such documents may have created conventional formulae which would have been available to Jeremiah.[14]

Whether Jer 31:31-34 (the New Covenant) is Jeremianic or not has been a perennial subject of debate. Two major studies, by Böhmer and by Levin, have been published in recent years.[15] Böhmer states, "The dtr Covenant theology characterizes Jer 31:31-34."[16] In seeking to trace the history of the text, Levin has difficulties with the label "Deuteronomistic" as used by Herrmann, Thiel and Böhmer.[17] For him, "the Covenant theology" did not exist in pre-exilic times.[18] The long introductory statement in 31:33 is a secondary addition; it expresses the law written by Yahweh upon the hearts of his people (cf. Isa 51:7; Pss 37:31; 40:9MT), reflecting "the late Torah-piety" of post-exilic Judaism.[19]

Another recent study of Jeremiah 30-31, a synchronistic approach by Barbara Bozak, points to a thematic unity, developed parallelism and a complex structure in 31:23-40.[20] She places emphasis on בְּרִית in 31:31-34 in relation to the two preceding sections (31:23-26 and 31:27-30), pointing to an unspecified time when Yahweh "will act with and for the entire people."[21]

---

[12] Note esp. K. Balzar, *Das Bundesformular* (WMANT 4; Neukirchen-Vluyn: Neukirchener Verlag, 1960); E. Kutsch, *Verheissung und Gesetz. Untersuchungen zum sogenannten 'Bund' im Alten Testament* (BZAW 231; Berlin: Walter de Gruyter, 1973); D. J. McCarthy, *Treaty and Covenant* (AnBib 21A; Rome: Editrice Pontifico Istituto Biblico, 1978); Lothar Perlitt, *Bundestheologie im Alten Testament* (WMANT 36; Neukirchen-Vluyn: Neukirchener Verlag, 1969); R. Smend, *Die Bundesformel* (Theologisches Studien 68; Zurich: EVZ, 1963). Walter Eichrodt's approach to OT theology is particularly oriented towards the concept of *Bund*. See *Theology of the Old Testament I* (London: SCM, 1961); *II* (London: SCM, 1967).
[13] Perlitt, *Bundestheologie*, 54.
[14] Weinfeld, *Deuteronomy*, 121, 140.
[15] Böhmer, *Heimkehr* (1976); Levin, *Die Verheissung des neuen Bundes in ihrem theologiegeschichtlichen Zusammenhang ausgelegt* (Göttingen: Vandenhoeck & Ruprecht, 1985).
[16] Böhmer, *Heimkehr*, 78.
[17] Levin, *Die Verheissung*, 17-18.
[18] Levin, *Die Verheissung*, p. 82 n. 53.
[19] Levin, *Die Verheissung*, 58, 257, p. 261 n. 15.
[20] Bozak, *Life 'Anew,'* 106-128.
[21] Bozak, *Life 'Anew,'* 118.

Jeremiah 31:31 is the only OT reference to a "new covenant" (חֲדָשָׁה בְּרִית), perhaps introduced here because of the word חֲדָשָׁה in 31:22. The connection with 24:7 should not be overlooked; Yahweh promises to bring the exiles back to the homeland and give them "a heart to know that I am Yahweh," giving substance to the covenantal formula present both here and in 31:33. Knowledge of Yahweh (31:34) is a theme appearing both in Hosea and in Jeremiah.[22]

The covenantal formula in 31:33 ("I will be their God, and they shall be my people") is found with slight variations in 7:23; 11:4; 24:7; 30:22; 30:25 (31:1E); 32:38, as well as in Exod 6:7; Lev 26:12; Deut 29:12 (29:13E).[23] Hosea 2:25 (2:23E; cf. Hos 1:9, "You are my people...You are my God") has as its background the marriage relationship between Yahweh and his people.[24] This early formulation of Yahweh's relationship with his people is overlooked by Thiel in his conclusion that the covenant-formula occurs "apart from the gloss 30:22, only in D-texts, never in the older tradition."[25]

Jones sums up linguistic and theological aspects of 31:31-34 in a trenchant phrase, "...the teaching is Jeremiah's; the precise wording is not."[26] A more accurate way of summarizing 31:31-34 would be to see here an affirmation and development of Jeremiah's hope for Israel's future, expressed by one who stood in the Jeremianic tradition, but was well acquainted with Hosea and Deuteronomy. This applies also to 32:36-41, with reference to "an everlasting covenant," בְּרִית עוֹלָם, 32:40 (cf. 50:5; Hos 2:20, 21 [2:19, 20E]; Isa 55:3; 61:8; 2 Sam 23:5 et al).

---

[22] Hosea 2:22 (2:20E); 5:4; 8:2; Jer 22:16; 31:34; cf. Brueggemann, *To Build, to Plant*, 71-72.

[23] See also Ezek 11:20; 14:11; 36:28; 37:23, 27; Zech 8:8.

[24] Weinfeld, *Deuteronomy*, 82, 327. Cf. Raitt, *A Theology of Exile*, 199; Holladay, *Jeremiah 1*, 262. The phrase וְאָנֹכִי בָּעַלְתִּי בָם "though I was their husband" (31:32) supports this interpretation.

[25] Thiel, *Redaktion 2*, 27. Jeremiah 30:22 is missing in the LXX. Kilpp (*Niederreissen und aufbauen*, 132) considers 30:22 to be a late addition. Cf. Janzen, *Studies*, 49.

[26] Jones, *Jeremiah*, p. 400. Bright ("An Exercise in Hermeneutics. Jeremiah 31:31-34," *Int* 20 [1966] 188-210), however, states "no reason whatever exists to question the authenticity of the passage" (p. 192). Werner Lemke ("Jeremiah 31:31-34," *Int* 37 [1983] 183-187) points out that the phrase "from the least to the greatest" (31:34) also occurs in 6:13=8:10b (p. 185). Cf. Deut 1:17 and see below, C20.

C. Recurring Phrases Common to Jeremiah and the Deuteronomic/Deuteronomistic literature and in some cases with Other Parts of the Old Testament.

C1. אָבוֹת ("fathers") in such phrases as:

(a) לֹא יָדְעוּ + הֵמָּה וַאֲבוֹתָם ("they and their fathers have not known," 9:15 [9:16E] "nations," cf. Deut 28:36; 19:4 "other gods," cf. Deut 28:64; אַתֶּם וַאֲבוֹתֵיכֶם, 16:13 "land"; 44:3, "other gods," cf. Deut 13:7 [13:6E]).

(b) הָאֲרָמָה אֲשֶׁר־נָתַתִּי לָכֶם וְלַאֲבֹתֵיכֶם ("the land which I gave to you and to your fathers," 35:15; 7:7, 14 "place"; 16:15; 23:39 "city"; 24:10; 25:5; 30:3; Deut 26:15; 1 Kgs 8:34, 40, 48; 2 Kgs 21:8; Amos 9:15 (late); Ezek 36:28; 37:25).

(c) אֲשֶׁר יָצְאוּ אֲבוֹתֵיכֶם מֵאֶרֶץ מִצְרַיִם ("that your fathers came out of the land of Egypt"). See below, C11e.

(d) הֵרֵעוּ מֵאֲבוֹתָם ("they did worse than their fathers," 7:26; cf. 16:12; Judg 2:19).

Such references to "the fathers" ("ancestors") are largely restricted to Jeremiah and to the Deuteronomistic literature.

C2. אֲהָהּ אֲדֹנָי יְהוִה ("Alas, Lord Yahweh," 1:6; 4:10; 14:13; 32:17; cf. Josh 7:7 [Joshua]; Judg 6:22 [Gideon]; Ezek 4:14; 9:8; 11:13; 21:5 [20:49E]). According to Meyer, this is a typical phrase with which a prophet, in autobiographical reports, introduces objections in response to Yahweh.[27]

C3. אֹתוֹת וּמֹפְתִים ("signs and wonders [portents]," 32:21; Deut 4:34; 6:22; 7:19; 26:8; 29:2 [29:3E]; 34:11; cf. Exod 7:3; Pss 78:43; 105:27; 135:9; Neh 9:10).[28]

C4. אזר Qal + מָתְנַיִם ("gird up [your] loins," 1:17; cf. 13:2; 1 Kgs 18:46; 2 Kgs 1:8 [Elijah]; 4:29 [Gehazi]; 9:1 [Elisha]).[29]

C5. אִישׁ יְהוּדָה וְיֹשְׁבֵי יְרוּשָׁלָםִ ("men of Judah and inhabitants of Jerusalem," 4:3, 4; 11:2, 9; 17:25; 18:11; 32:32; 35:13; 36:31; 2 Kgs 23:2=2 Chron 34:30; Dan 9:7).[30] Cf. similar expressions in 11:12; 17:20; 19:3; 25:2; 35:17.

---

[27] Meyer, *Jeremia und die Falschen Propheten*, 84.

[28] Weinfeld (*Deuteronomy*), "The phrase is rooted in the tradition of the plagues" (p. 330).

[29] For a discussion of this phrase, see Reventlow, *Liturgie*, 61–62. Berridge (*Prophet*, 198–200) agrees with Reventlow that "holy war" is in mind. "Jeremiah's own life and ministry shall symbolically represent that holy war which Yahweh would wage against his people" (p. 200).

[30] King (*Jeremiah. An Archaeological Companion*, 65) claims that there are more than one hundred references to Jerusalem in the book of Jeremiah.

C6. הָאֵל הַגָּדוֹל הַגִּבּוֹר ("O great and mighty God," 32:18). Weinfeld points out that these attributes appear also in the declaration of Deut 10:17 and later became an opening formula of liturgies (Dan 9:4; Neh 1:5; 9:32).[31]

C7. מֵאֵין כָּמוֹךָ ("there is none like you [i.e., Yahweh]," 10:6, 7; 2 Sam 7:22; 1 Kgs 8:23; Ps 86:8; Isa 45:5). The theme of the incomparability of Yahweh is not restricted to the book of Jeremiah and the Deuteronomistic literature.

C8. אֱלֹהִים אֲחֵרִים ("other gods," 1:16; 7:6, 9, 18; 11:10; 13:10; 16:11, 13; 19:4, 13; 22:9; 25:6; 32:19; 35:15; 44:3, 5, 8, 15 [all prose passages]). Cf. Hos 3:1; Deut 5:7=Exod 20:3 (Decalogue); 11:28; 28:64; 29:27; Josh 23:16; Judg 2:12, 19; 1 Sam 8:8; 26:19; 1 Kgs 9:6,9; 2 Kgs 17:35. Weippert supplies a chart, and discusses the many passages in which the phrase appears, frequently preceded by הלך + אחרי.[32] Knowledge of the Decalogue (7:9) is already present in Hos 4:2, in addition to the reference to "other gods" in Hos 3:1.[33] The references to "other gods" in the book of Jeremiah occur frequently (Jeremiah 7, 11, 16, 19, 25, 32, 35, 44) in passages where other Deuteronomistic expressions are found.[34]

C9. אַף וְחֵמָה ("anger and fury," 7:20; 42:18; 44:6; cf. 21:5; 32:7; Deut 29:27 [28E]; Deut 29:22 [23E]; Nah 1:6). See below, C89.

C10. אָרוּר ("cursed," 11:3). Jeremiah 11:3-5 begins with a curse on the man who does not heed the words of the covenant, ending with Jeremiah's response, אָמֵן ("so be it," 11:5). The parallel is Deut 27:26, a curse on one who does not confirm the words of the law by doing them, to which the people say אָמֵן (cf. the series of curses in Deut 27:15-25, which begin with אָרוּר and end with the response אָמֵן from the people). Jeremiah 11:3-5 consists largely of Deuteronomistic phrases.

C11. (a) אָרֶץ מִקְצֵה־אָרֶץ וְעַד־קְצֵה הָאָרֶץ ("from one end of the land to the other," 12:12; 25:33; Deut 13:8 [13:7E]; 28:64). Cf. 30:4 (הַשָּׁמַיִם); הָאָרֶץ עַד־קְצֵה in Isa 48:20; 49:6; מִקְצֵה אָרֶץ in 10:13=51:16; see above, chap. eight, p. 178 (note [b...b]).

(b) אֶרֶץ זָבַת חָלָב וּדְבָשׁ ("a land flowing with milk and honey," 11:5; 32:22; cf. Exod 3:8; 13:5; 33:3; Deut 6:3; 11:9; 16:9, 15; 27:3; 31:20; Ezek 20:6, 15). Bright concludes, "It seems to be a popular cliché, and one scarcely coined by D."[35] However, as Carroll points out regarding Jeremiah

---

[31] Weinfeld, *Deuteronomy*, 40.

[32] Weippert, *Die Prosareden*, 215-218.

[33] For a discussion of the early date of the Decalogue, see Walter Harrelson, "Ten Commandments" *IDB* 4.569-573.

[34] For example, see the chart (25:3b-6a; 35:14b-15) in Thiel, *Redaktion 1*, 267; cf. Weinfeld, *Deuteronomy*, 320-324 (Appendix A).

[35] Bright, "The Date of the Prose Sermons," 211.

11, "That the language and ideas of vv.1–13 are a Deuteronomistic composition can hardly be disputed."[36]

(c) וַיָּבֹאוּ וַיִּירְשׁוּ אֹתָהּ ("they entered and took possession of it [the land]," 32:23. The phrase appears only at 32:23 in Jeremiah, but see Deut 4:1, 5; 6:18; 7:1; 8:1; 11:8, 31; 28:21, 63; 30:16; Josh 1:11; 18:3; Judg 18:9.

(d) בְּיוֹם הוֹצִיאִי־אוֹתָם מֵאֶרֶץ־מִצְרַיִם ("in the day I brought them out of the land of Egypt," 11:4 and similar expressions in 2:6; 7:22, 25; 11:7; 16:14=23:7; 31:32; 32:21; 34:13). The verb יצא Hiphil is used in 7:22, 25; 31:32; 34:13; Mic 7:15; Ezek 20:9, 10; Deut 5:6; 6:12, 21; 8:14; 9:26; 26:8; Josh 24:6; 1 Kgs 8:16, 21; עלה Hiphil in 2:6; 11:7; 16:14=23:7 (cf. Amos 2:10; 3:1; 9:7; Hos 2:17; Mic 6:4; Isa 11:16; Deut 1:27; Judg 6:8).[37]

(e) אַתָּה עָשִׂיתָ אֶת־הַשָּׁמַיִם וְאֶת־הָאָרֶץ ("you made the heavens and the earth," 32:17 [Jeremiah's prayer]; 2 Kgs 19:15 [Hezekiah's prayer]; cf. Neh 9:6 [Ezra]; 2 Chron 2:11 [2:12E]).

C12. כִּי אֵשׁ קָדְחָה בְאַפִּי ("for a fire is kindled in my anger," 15:14=17:4, second and third Confessions; Deut 32:22a). See above, chap. two, p. 25 ([g...g]).

C13. כִּי אִתְּךָ־אָנִי ("for I am with you," 1:8; 1:19=15:20; 30:11=46:28; Isa 43:5). See above, chap. three, p. 36; chap. seven, p. 120 ([d...d]).

C14. בחר ("choose"). Israel's election is not a major theme in Jeremiah, but is prominent in Deuteronomy and Deuteronomistic literature. See Jer 33:24; Deut 4:37; 7:6, 7; 10:15; 14:2; 1 Kgs 3:8; cf. Ps 33:12; 78:68; Isa 14:1; Ezek 20:5; Isa 41:8, 9; 43:10; 44:1, 2; 49:7.

C15. מִבֵּית עֲבָדִים ("from the house of bondage," 34:13). Holladay writes, "a traditional expression, perhaps originating in prophetic circles."[38] Cf. Mic 6:4; Exod 13:3, 14; 20:2=Deut 5:6 (Decalogue); 6:12; 7:8; 8:14; 13:6, 11 (13:5, 10E); Josh 24:17; Judg 6:8.

C16. נפש + בקש ("to seek life," 11:21 [first Confession]; 19:7, 9; 21:7; 22:25; 34:20, 21; 44:30; 46:26; 49:37; cf. Exod 4:19; 1 Sam 20:1; 2 Sam 16:11; Ps 35:4; 40:15=70:3 [40:14=70:2E]). Janzen draws attention to 19:9b as a key passage, because the reference to cannibalism in 19:9a reflects Deut 28:53, 57.[39]

C17. בָּשָׂר (a) כָּל־בָּשָׂר ("all flesh," 12:12; 25:31; 32:27; 45:5; cf. Deut 5:26 [5:23E]; Gen 6:12, 13 [P]; Ps 65:3 [65:2E]; 145:21; Isa 66:16, 23, 24; Ezek 21:4; Zech 2:17 [2:13E]).

(b) אכל + בשר ("to eat the flesh," 19:9; Deut 28:53 [see C16]; Isa 49:26).

---

[36] Carroll, *Jeremiah*, 267.

[37] See J. Wijngaards, "הוצא and העלה, a Twofold Approach to the Exodus," *VT* 15 (1965) 91–102.

[38] Holladay, *Jeremiah 2*, 241.

[39] Janzen (*Studies*, 41–43) engages in a helpful discussion of the occurrences of the phrase in Jeremiah, in which the passages in the LXX where it is absent are noted.

C18. בְּתוּלַת בַּת־עַמִּי ("virgin daughter of my people," 14:17 [בְּתוּלַת is missing in the LXX]; cf. 8:21, 22, "daughter of my people"; 46:11 [Egypt]; 18:13; 31:4, 21 [בְּתוּלַת יִשְׂרָאֵל]; cf. Amos 5:2, "virgin Israel"; 2 Kgs 19:21; Isa 37:22 ["virgin daughter of Zion"]; 23:12 ["virgin daughter of Sidon"]; 47:1 ["virgin daughter of Babylon"]). The identity of the addressee in the Jeremiah passages is an important exegetical issue. As in the case of 46:27-28=30:10-11, is Israel as a whole being addressed?[40]

C19. גְּבִירָה ("queen-mother," 13:18; 29:2; cf. 1 Kgs 15:13=2 Chron 15:16; 2 Kgs 10:13).[41]

C20. (a) גְּדֹלִים וּקְטַנִּים ("great and small [i.e., old and young]"; 16:6; 2 Chron 31:15; 34:30).

(b) לְמִקָּטֹן וְעַד גָּדוֹל ("from the least to the greatest [i.e., everyone]," 6:13=8:10; 31:34 (new covenant); 42:1, 8; 44:12; Jon 3:5; Ps 115:13; Esth 1:5, 20; Gen 19:11; Deut 1:17 (כַּגָּדֹל כַּקָּטֹן); 2 Kgs 23:2.[42]

C21. גּוֹי ("nation") is applied to Yahweh's people in 5:9 (cf. this refrain repeated in 5:29; 9:8 [9:9E]; 7:28) and applied to other nations in 1:5; 10:25 (=Ps 79:6); 12:17; 22:8 (cf. 5:15; Deut 28:36, 49). Jeremiah 4:2 repeats the promise of Gen 22:18.[43]

C22. גִּלּוּלִים ("idols, fetishes," 50:2; cf. Deut 29:16 [29:17E]); 1 Kgs 15:12; 21:26; 2 Kgs 17:12; 21:11; 23:24; Ezek 6:5, 9, 13; 14:5; 18:6, 15 [*et al*]).

C23. גֵּר יָתוֹם וְאַלְמָנָה ("the alien, the fatherless, the widow," 7:6=22:3; Deut 10:18; 14:29; 16:11, 14; 24:17, 19, 20, 21; 26:12, 13; 27:19; cf. Exod 22:20, 21 [22:21, 22E]; Ezek 22:7; Zech 7:10 [in separate clauses]).[44] See above, chap. nine, p. 188.

C24. (a) כָּל־הַדְּבָרִים הָאֵלֶּה דָּבָר ("all these words," 11:6; 26:10; 26:15; 27:12; 34:6; 36:16, 18, 24; 51:60; Exod 20:1 [introduction to the Decalogue]; 24:8; Num 16:31; Deut 12:28; Judg 9:3; 2 Sam 7:17). This is not a characteristic expression elsewhere in the prophetic literature.

---

[40] For various views, see Holladay, *Jeremiah 2*, 158-159; Böhmer, *Heimkehr*, 70; Bak, *Klagender Gott*, 71; and regarding 31:4, 21, McKane, *Jeremiah 2*, clxi.

[41] See Seitz, *Theology in Crisis*, 52-55. He provides a comprehensive bibliography (p. 52 n. 115). Seitz denies that there was an actual *office* of "Queen Mother."

[42] Holladay ("Prototype," 358) considers 6:13 to be the prototype of the other passages in the book of Jeremiah. Weinfeld (*Deuteronomy*) claims that the expression "occurs *verbatim* in connection with the treaty ceremony in the Esarhaddon treaty (1.5) and in the annals of Assurbanipal" (p. 101).

[43] McConville, *Judgment and Promise*, 46.

[44] Weinfeld (*Deuteronomy*) considers the phrase to be "a deuteronomistic cliché" (p. 277 n. 2).

(b) דבר + קוּם *Hiphil* ("to establish the word [of Yahweh]," 29:10; 33:14; Deut 9:5; 1 Kgs 2:4; 6:12; 8:20; 12:15).[45]

(c) אֶת־הַדְּבָרִים אֲשֶׁר־אֲדַבֵּר ("the words that I have spoken," 19:2; 25:13; 30:2; 36:2, 4). Jeremiah 37:2 adds "through Jeremiah the prophet"; cf. "through Moses" (Josh 20:2; 1 Kgs 8:53, 56); 1 Kgs 12:15; 15:29; 17:16; 2 Kgs 9:36; 14:25; 24:2.[46]

C25. דָּם נָקִי ("innocent blood," 7:6; 22:3, 17; 26:15; cf. 2:34; 19:4; Deut 19:10, 13; 21:8; 27:25; 1 Sam 19:5; 2 Kgs 21:16; 24:4; Isa 59:7; Joel 4:19 (3:19E); Jon 1:14; Ps 106:38; Prov 6:17). See above, chap. nine, p. 188.

C26. דֹּמֶן ("dung"): לְדֹמֶן עַל־פְּנֵי הָאֲדָמָה ("as dung on the surface of the ground," 8:2; 16:4; 25:33; Ps 83:11); כְּדֹמֶן עַל־פְּנֵי הַשָּׂדֶה ("like dung upon the open field," 9:21 [9:22E]).[47]

C27. דֶּרֶךְ in the phrase הלך + בְּכָל־הַדֶּרֶךְ ("walk in all the way," 7:33; Deut 5:33; 10:12; 11:22; Josh 22:5; 1 Kgs 8:58).

C28. הֶבֶל ("vanity, nothingness," 2:5; 8:19; 10:2, 8, 15; 14:22; 16:19; 51:18; Deut 32:21; 1 Sam 12:21; 1 Kgs 16:13, 26; 2 Kgs 17:15).[48] All these passages have to do with idolatrous worship.

C29. זַוֲעָה (*Qere* זְוָעָה), "horror" (15:4; 24:9; 29:18; 34:17). See above, chap. six, p. 113 n. 59. This noun is preceded by נתן and followed by הָאָרֶץ לְכֹל מַמְלְכוֹת in Deut 28:25 (זַעֲוָה). For the noun + נתן only, see Ezek 23:46; 2 Chron 29:8).[49] Sturdy has argued that Deuteronomy 28 contains other expressions found in the Jeremiah prose sermons and concludes that this chapter is later than the prose sermons in Jeremiah, drawing directly on their language, as well as on the language of Lamentations and Leviticus 26.[50] He believes that the prose sermons in Jeremiah have been preserved and developed by those who stood in the Jeremiah tradition (probably in Palestine) and that this material was incorporated into Deuteronomy 28. Holladay also asserts the priority of Jeremiah.[51] The phrase "all the kingdoms of the earth" (see C55)

---

[45] According to Weinfeld (*Deuteronomy*), "In the deuteronomic literature [this verb] occurs always in connection with the fulfilment of a divine promise of a national nature" (p. 350).

[46] Regarding Jer 37:2, see Thiel, *Redaktion 2*, 52–53.

[47] Holladay (*Jeremiah 1*), "Jrm is suggesting that the people are all comparable to Jezebel" (p. 315). McKane (*Jeremiah 1*, 212) suggests that דֹּמֶן may be secondary in 9:21 (imported from 8:2).

[48] For Carroll (*Jeremiah*), "the sermon in 2:5–9 must be associated with Deuteronomistic editing" (p. 124).

[49] See Weippert, *Die Prosareden*, p. 187 n. 360, p. 188 (chart).

[50] J. V. Sturdy, "The Authorship of the 'prose sermons' of Jeremiah," in *Prophecy. Essays presented to Georg Fohrer on his sixty-fifth birthday 6 September 1980* (BZAW 150; ed. J. A. Emerton [Berlin: Walter de Gruyter, 1980] 143–150).

[51] Holladay, *Jeremiah 1*, 440; cf. Weippert, *Die Prosareden*, 187. However, Jer 7:33 and Deut 28:26 may have used conventional formulae drawn from treaty literature (Weinfeld, *Deuteronomy*, 140).

occurs also in 25:26; 34:1; 2 Kgs 19:15, 19; Isa 23:17; 37;16, 20; Ezra 1:2; cf. Ps 68:33 (68:32E). Hezekiah's prayer (2 Kgs 19:15 = Isa 37:16, 20) may be an early occurrence of this Deuteronomistic expression. With the unusual term "horror" preceding it (15:4; 24:9; 29:18; 34:17) this phrase may well be a Jeremianic expression that has been included in Deut 28:25. The parallels with Deut 28:26 (7:33; 9:21; 16:4b; 19:7b; 34:20b) may reflect conventional formulae rather than language originated by Jeremiah (see above, chap. ten, pp. 222-223).

C30. (a) חָטָא + לִיהוה ("sin against Yahweh," 16:10; 40:3; 44:23; cf. Deut 9:16). Jeremiah 40:3; 44:23 and Deut 9:23 also have in common "did not obey his voice" (see C100).

(b) חטא + אֶת־יהוּדָה *Hiphil* ("to cause Judah to sin," 32:35; 2 Kgs 21:16).[52] Cf. "to cause Israel to sin," a characteristic formula describing kings from Jeroboam on (1 Kgs 14:16; 22:53 [22:52E]; 2 Kgs 3:3; 10:29, 31; 13:2, 11; 14:24; 15:9, 18, 24, 28; 23:15).

C31. (a) חַי־אָנִי ("As I live," 22:24; 46:18; Zeph 2:9; Ezek 5:11; 14:16, 18, 20; 16:48; 17:16, 19; 18:3; 20:3, 31, 33; 33:11, 27; 34:8; 35:6, 11; Isa 49:18). Wessels writes, "...the formula is used as a confirmation that Yahweh censures action, a censure with negative consequences."[53]

(b) חַי יְהוָה ("as Yahweh lives," 4:2; 5:2; 12:16; 16:14-15 = 23:7-8; 38:16; cf. 44:26). This formula is also found in Hos 4:15; Judg 8:19; 1 Sam 14:39, 45; 19:6; 20:21; 25:34; 26:10, 16; 28:10; 2 Sam 4:9; 12:5; 14:11; 15:21; 1 Kgs 1:29; 2:24; 17:1, 2; 18:10; 22:14; 2 Kgs 5:16, 20.

(c) הַחַיִּים ... הַמָּוֶת ("life and death," 21:8; Deut 30:19; cf. Deut 30:15).

(d) חַיַּת הַשָּׂדֶה ("wild beasts," literally, "living creature(s) of the field," 12:9; 27:6; 28:14; Deut 7:22; cf. Gen 2:19, 20; Exod 23:11, 29 [Code of the Covenant]; Lev 26:22 [H]; Hos 2:14, 20 [2:12E, 18E]; 4:3; 13:8; 2 Sam 21:10; 2 Kgs 14:9 = 2 Chron 25:18; Isa 43:20; Ezek 38:20; 39:4; Job 5:23; 39:15). The expression is frequently used in the OT; the dominion of mankind over the animal creation (Gen 1:26) is echoed in Nebuchadrezzar's dominion over "the beasts of the field" (Jer 27:6; 28:14).

C32. חֶסֶד in the phrase עֹשֶׂה חֶסֶד לַאֲלָפִים ("showing steadfast love to thousands" [i.e., "to the thousandth generation"], 32:18a [Jeremiah's prayer]; Exod 20:6a = Deut 5:10 [Decalogue]; cf. Exod 34:7; Deut 7:9).[54] Other occurrences of חֶסֶד in Jeremiah are: 2:2; 9:23 (9:24E); 16:5; 33:11. Jeremiah follows Hosea in placing emphasis on Yahweh's חֶסֶד.[55]

C33. (a) חֶרֶב in the expression שָׁלַחְתִּי...אֶת־הַחֶרֶב ("I will send the sword," 9:15 [9:16E]; 24:10 [triad]; 25:27; 29:17 [triad]; 49:37 [Elam]). חֶרֶב

---

[52] הַחֲטִי (*Kethib*). The concluding א has been dropped through haplography.
[53] Wessels, "Jeremiah 22,24-30," 236.
[54] For a bibliography, see Holladay, *Jeremiah 1*, 48.
[55] Holladay, *Jeremiah 1*, 82-83; Craigie, *Jeremiah 1*, 24.

Parallels in the Deuteronomistic Books

+ שלח Piel is not found elsewhere in the OT. This appears to be authentic Jeremianic language and may point to the process by which the triad became the set formula in Jeremiah (see above, chap. eleven, pp. 243-244).

(b) חֶרֶב in the phrase מִפְּנֵי חֶרֶב הַיּוֹנָה ("because of the sword of the oppressor," 46:16 [26:16LXX]; 50:16 [27:16LXX]; cf. 25:38). See above, chap. eight, p. 169.

C34. חרד in the phrase וְאֵין מַחֲרִיד ("without anyone making [him] afraid," 7:33; 30:10=46:27; Mic 4:4; Isa 17:2; Zeph 3:13; Ezek 34:28; 39:26; Nah 2:13 [2:11E]; Deut 28:26; Lev 26:6; Job 11:13).[56] Jeremiah 7:33 and Deut 28:26 are closely parallel (see C29 above for discussion of these verses); this particular phrase occurs often in the prophetic literature. See above, chap. ten, p. 222 ([c...c]).

C35. חָפְשִׁי מֵעִמָּךְ preceded by שלח Piel ("set free from your service," 34:14; Deut 15:12). Deuteronomy 15:12 (cf. Exod 21:2) is reflected in 34:14.[57]

C36. חֲרוֹן אַף ("fierce anger [of Yahweh]," חָרוֹן is missing in the LXX]; 4:26; 12:13; 23:20=30:24; 25:37, 38; 49:37; 51:45; Hos 11:9; Nah 1:6; Zeph 2:3 [2:2E]; 3:8; Isa 13:9, 13; Jon 3:9; Exod 32:13; Num 25:4; 32:14; Josh 7:26; Deut 13:18 [13:17E]; 1 Sam 28:18; 2 Kgs 23:26; 2 Chron 28:11, 13; 29:10; 30:8; Ezra 10:14; Pss 69:25 [69:24E]; 78:49; 85:4 [85:3E]; Job 20:23; Lam 1:12; 4:11). This is a typical prophetic expression which occurs also in the Deuteronomistic literature.[58] See above, chap. five, p. 87 (note [d...d]).

C37. חָשַׁב followed by מַחֲשָׁבָה [s. or pl.] ("to devise schemes," 11:19 [first Confession]; 18:11, 18; 29:11; 49:20b=50:45b [see chap. seven, p. 156 ([e...e])]; 49:30; 2 Sam 14:14; Ezek 38:10; Dan 11:24, 25; Esth 8:3; 9:25). With the exception of Jer 11:19 and 2 Sam 14:14, most of the occurrences are in late texts.[59]

C38. יָד חֲזָקָה ("a strong hand") + זְרֹעַ נְטוּיָה ("an outstretched arm," 21:5 [the adjectives are reversed]; 32:21; Deut 4:34; 5:15; 7:19; 11:2; 26:8; 1 Kgs 8:42; Ezek 20:33, 34; Ps 136:12); cf. בְּכֹחִי הַגָּדוֹל וּבִזְרוֹעִי הַנְּטוּיָה ("my great power and my outstretched arm," 27:5; 32:21; Deut 9:29; 2 Kgs 17:36). Both phrases have a Deuteronomistic background.

C39. יוֹם (a) בַּיּוֹם הַהוּא ("in that day," 4:9; 25:33 [LXX ἐν ἡμέρᾳ κυρίου]; 30:8; 39:10, 16, 17; 48:41=49:22; 49:26=50:30 [the phrase is missing in the LXX]; Amos 8:3; 9:11; Hos 1:5; 2:18; 2:20 [2:21E]; Isa 2:11,

---

[56] For Jer 30:10=46:27, see above, chap. seven, pp. 119-125.

[57] Holladay, *Jeremiah 2*, 237, 238; Thiel, *Redaktion 2*, 40. McKane (*Jeremiah 2*) claims, "There is no effective defence of vv.13-14" and questions the integrity of these verses (p. 879).

[58] Brian Peckham views this as "a favorite Dtr² expression." See *The Composition of the Deuteronomistic History* (HSM 35; [Atlanta: Scholars Press, 1985] 102-120) esp. p. 93 n. 183.

[59] Thiel, *Redaktion 1*, p. 216 n. 21.

17, 20; 3:7, 18; 4:1, 2 *et al*; Mic 2:4; 5:9 [5:10E]; Zeph 1:10; 3:11, 16; Deut 21:23; 31:17, 18, 22; Josh 6:15; 8:25; Judg 3:30; 4:23; 5:1; 6:32; 1 Sam 3:2, 12; 6:15, 16; 2 Sam 3:37; 1 Kgs 8:64; 22:25; 2 Kgs 3:36). This is only a partial list. Bright claims that since the phrase occurs so frequently in the OT, nothing can be proved concerning its use in Jeremiah.[60] In a major study, Munch (*contra* Gressmann), argues that the expression when referring to the future means no more than "then" (i.e., an editorial link).[61] In a detailed study, DeVries provides a table listing all OT occurrences of the phrase which relate to the future, including the Jeremiah references.[62] Jeremiah 4:9 is understood as epexegesis to a judgment oracle, 4:6-8 (cf. 25:33).[63] Jeremiah 30:8 and 39:17 are salvation oracles; 39:16; 48:41=49:22; 49:26=50:30 are scribal glosses.

(b) (הָהֵם) בַּיָּמִים הָהֵמָּה ("in those days," 3:16, 18; 5:18; 31:29; 33:16; 50:4, 20; Deut 17:9; 19:19; 26:3; Judg 17:6; 18:1; 21:25; Ezek 38:17; Joel 3:2 [2:28E]; 4:1 [3:1E]; Zech 3:8, 23; Esth 1:2; 2:21; Dan 10:2; Neh 6:17; 13:15, 23; 2 Chron 32:24). Sometimes the reference is to the past (Ezek 38:17), or to the present (Esth 2:21). In most cases the phrase refers to the future, as in the book of Jeremiah).[64] Joel 4:1MT and Jer 50:4, 20 are probably the result of conflation.

(c) כַּיּוֹם הַזֶּה ("as at this day," 11:5; 25:18 [missing in the LXX]; 32:20; 44:6, 22, 23; Gen 50:20 [E]; Deut 2:30; 4:20, 38; 6:24; 8:18; 10:15; 29:27 [29:28E]; 1 Kgs 3:6; 8:24, 61; Dan 9:7, 15; Ezra 9:7, 15; Neh 9:10; 1 Chron 28:7). DeVries claims that this is "a characteristic Deuteronomic-Jeremianic locution."[65] Weinfeld understands the phrase as a reference to "the 'this day' of the author."[66]

(d) הַיּוֹם הַהוּא ("that day," 30:7; 46:10). Böhmer sees in these verses a reference to the "Day of Yahweh."[67] However, in the case of 46:10, the battle of Carchemish seems to be the point of reference (46:2).

---

[60] Bright, "The Date of the Prose Sermons," 210.
[61] P. A. Munch, "The Expression Bajjôm Hahu. Is it an Eschatological Terminus Technicus?" (AUNVAO 2, Hist.-Filos Klasse 2; Oslo: Dybwad, 1936); Hugo Gressmann, *Der Ursprung der israelitisch-jüdischer Eschatologie* (FRLANT 42; Göttingen: Vandenhoeck & Ruprecht, 1905).
[62] S. J. DeVries, *Yesterday*, 326-329. Only Jer 39:10 relates to the past, "ultimately from some kind of memoir or annalistic report" (p. 114 and Table 2, p. 132).
[63] DeVries, *Yesterday*, 327, 329. For Rudolph (*Jeremia*, 34) the phrase is not eschatological. McKane (*Jeremiah 1*) also sees here no reference to a distant future (*contra* Duhm), but more probably a reference to "the historical moment which the prophet has just been describing" (p. 93).
[64] DeVries (*Yesterday*, p. 52 n. 78) considers the passages in Jeremiah to be secondary material introduced into salvation oracles.
[65] DeVries, *Yesterday*, p. 52 n. 77.
[66] Weinfeld, *Deuteronomy*, p. 175.
[67] Böhmer, *Heimkehr*, 57-58; cf. Carroll, *Jeremiah*, 574-575.

(e) עַד הַיּוֹם הַזֶּה "this day," 3:25; 7:25; 11:7; 32:20, 31; 35:14 [missing in the LXX]; 36:2; Deut 2:22; 3:14; 10:8; 11:4; 29:3 [29:4E]; 34:6; 1 Sam 8:8; 2 Kgs 21:15). Childs notes that this expression, which occurs eighty-four times in the OT, often has an etiological function, but frequently serves as a non-etiological idiom simply expressing the *terminus ad quem* of a temporal system.[68] He does not comment specifically on the phrase in Jeremiah, but the non-etiological use seems paramount.

(f) בְּאַחֲרִית הַיָּמִים ("in the latter days," 23:20=30:24; 48:47; 49:39; Gen 49:1; Num 24:14; Deut 4:30; 31:29; Hos 3:5; Isa 2:2=Mic 4:1; Ezek 38:16; Dan 2:23; 10:14). Although the phrase has eschatological overtones, the reference in 23:20=30:24 seems to have a more immediate reference.[69] See above, chap. five, p. 89.

(g) הִנֵּה יָמִים בָּאִים ("Behold, days are coming," 7:32=19:6; 9:24; 16:14=23:7; 23:5=33:14; 30:3; 31:27, 32, 38[Q]; 48:12; 49:2; 51:47, 52; Amos 4:2; 8:11; 9:13; Isa 39:6=2 Kgs 20:17; 1 Sam 2:31). See above, chap. four, p. 62 (ᵃ⋯ᵃ).

(h) יָרֵא + כָּל־הַיָּמִים ("to fear [Yahweh] all the days" [i.e. "forever"], 32:39; cf. Deut 4:10; 6:2; 14:23; Josh 4:24; 1 Kgs 8:40).

C40. יָטַב *Qal* in phrases such as "that it may be well with you," 7:23; 38:20; 40:9; 42:6; Deut 4:40; 5:16 (Decalogue); 5:29; 6:3, 18; 12:25, 28; 22:7; Gen 12:13; 40:14; 2 Kgs 25:24; Ruth 3:1.

יטב *Hiphil* ("to do good, deal well with, cause to prosper," 32:41; Deut 28:63; 30:9).

C41. יעל *Hiphil* ("that which does not profit," 2:8, 11; 7:8; 12:13; 16:19; 23:32; Hab 2:18; Isa 44:9, 10; 57:12; 1 Sam 12:21).

C42. יָרֵא ("to be afraid"); אַל־תִּירָא ("do not be afraid," 1:8; 30:10=46:27; Isa 41:10, 13, 14; 43:1, 5; 44:2).

יָרֵא + חתת ("to be dismayed," 23:4; 30:10=46:27; Deut 1:21; 31:8; Josh 8:1; 10:25; cf. 1 Sam 17:11). See above, chap. seven, p. 119 (note ᵃ⋯ᵃ).

C43. יָשָׁר + עשׂה ("to do what is right," 26:14; 34:15; Deut 6:18; 12:25, 28; 13:19 [13:18E]; 21:9; 1 Kgs 11:33, 38; 14:8; 15:5, 11; 22:43; 2 Kgs 10:30; 12:3 [12:2E]; 14:3; 15:3, 34; 16:2; 18:3; 22:2).

C44. וְלֹא תִכְבֶּה ("and not be quenched," 7:20; 17:27; 2 Kgs 22:17=2 Chron 34:25).

C45. כּוּר הַבַּרְזֶל ("iron furnace," 11:4; Deut 4:20; 1 Kgs 8:51).[70] עֳנִי כֻּר ("furnace of affliction," Isa 48:10) refers to the exile.

---

[68] Brevard S. Childs, "A Study of the Formula, 'Until This Day'," *JBL* 82 (1963) 278-282.

[69] Rudolph (*Jeremia*) claims that "in the latter days" is "not an eschatological term" (p. 153). Duhm had given the phrase an eschatological interpretation. McKane (*Jeremiah 1*) refers to Kimchi's view that the phrase means "in the days of the Messiah" (p. 583).

[70] According to Thiel (*Redaktion 2*), this is a "designation for Egypt" (p. 93).

C46. כעס *Hiphil* in such phrases as:

(a) לְמַעַן הַכְעִסֵנִי ("to provoke me to anger," 7:18; 25:7). לְהַכְעִסֵנִי (11:17; 32:32; 44:3; cf. 32:29). See also 8:19 (poetry). For similar phrases see Hos 12:15 (12:14E); Isa 65:3; Ezek 8:17; 16:26; Neh 3:37 (4:5E); 2 Chron 28:25; Deut 4:25; 9:18; 32:16; Judg 2:12; 1 Kgs 14:9, 15; 15:30; 16:2; 21:22; 22:54 (22:53E); 2 Kgs 21:15; 23:26. Cf. Ps 78:58; 106:29.

(b) כעס + בְּמַעֲשֵׂה יְדֵיכֶם (יְדֵיהֶם) *Hiphil* ("to provoke to anger with the work of your hands," 25:6; 32:30; 44:8; Deut 31:29; 1 Kgs 16:7; 2 Kgs 22:17).

C47. כרת *Niphal;* לֹא־יִכָּרֵת אִישׁ לְ ("shall never lack a man," 33:17 [Davidic dynasty]; 33:18 [the Levitical priests]; 35:19 [Rechabites]; 1 Kgs 2:4; 8:25 [=2 Chron 6:16]; 9:5 [=2 Chron 7:18]).

C48. לֵב (a) בְּכָל־לִבִּי וּבְכָל־נַפְשִׁי ("with all my heart and with all my soul," 32:41; similar phrases in Deut 4:29; 6:5 [*Shema*]; 26:16; Josh 22:5; 1 Kgs 2:4; 2 Kgs 23:3). For 29:13=Deut 4:29, see above, chap. ten, pp. 226–227.

(b) כִּי־יָשֻׁבוּ אֵלַי בְּכָל־לִבָּם ("for they shall return to me with their whole heart," 24:7; cf. 3:10; 1 Kgs 8:48; 2 Kgs 23:25).

(c) עַל־לֵב preceded by עלה ("to enter [Yahweh's] mind, come into the mind," 7:31; 19:5; 32:35; 44:21; cf. 51:50; Ezek 14:3, 7; Isa 65:17; 2 Kgs 12:5).

C49. לַיְלָה וְיוֹמָם ("night and day," 14:17; Deut 28:66; Isa 34:10). יומם and לילה in parallel clauses: 31:35; cf. Isa 21:8; 2 Sam 21:10; Ps 22:3 (22:2E); 42:9 (42:8E); 91:5 (reverse order); 121:6.

C50. לָשׁוֹן + ידע (or שמע) ("a language you do not know [or understand]," 5:15; cf. Deut 28:49; Isa 33:19). Jeremiah 5:15LXX is an abridgment of 5:15MT. McKane claims that "Deut 28:49 has exercised some influence on the abridgment. תשמע has been adopted as the verb and תדע has been dropped."[71] Jeremiah 5:15LXX is more in keeping with Deut 28:49. Jeremiah 5:15 may represent a conflation of two readings; but since the metre is regular (3 + 3), it seems probable that the MT text is sound. Perhaps a curse-ritual lies behind 5:15, but Thiel finds the assumption of such a common source to be improbable.[72]

C51. מול II ("to circumcise") in the phrase לַיהוָה וְהָסִרוּ עָרְלוֹת לְבַבְכֶם הִמֹּלוּ ("Circumcise yourselves to Yahweh, remove the foreskin of your hearts," 4:4a).[73] Compare 9:25 [9:26E]: "all the house of Israel is uncircumcised in heart." Compare also וּמַלְתֶּם אֵת עָרְלַת לְבַבְכֶם ("Circumcise the foreskin of your

---

[71] McKane, *Jeremiah 1*, p. 123. For another view, see Janzen, *Studies*, 97. According to Rudolph (*Jeremia*), Jer 5:15-17 has influenced Deut 28:49-53 (p. 39).

[72] Thiel, *Redaktion 1*, p. 97 n. 64.

[73] Robert Althann considers the *lamedh* in Jer 4:4a to be the *lamedh* of agency, "be circumcised by Yahweh." See "mwl, 'circumcise' with the *lamedh* of Agency," *Bib* 62 (1981) 239–240.

heart," Deut. 10:16). Although Jer 4:4a uses the *Niphal* of מוּל, לֵבָב (rather than the more usual לֵב in Jeremiah) suggests a direct reference to Deut 10:16.[74]

C52. מוֹרָא ("fear, terror, awe-inspiring spectacle"); מוֹרָא גָּדוֹל ("great terror," 32:21; cf. Deut 4:34[pl.]; 26:8; 34:12).

C53. מְלָאכָה ("work"). Prohibition of "all work" (כָּל־מְלָאכָה) on the Sabbath: 17:24; cf. Deut 5:14=Exod 20:10 (Decalogue).

C54. מלט *Piel* (a) וּמַלְּטוּ אִישׁ נַפְשׁוֹ ("let every man save his life," 51:6, 45; cf. 48:6; Amos 2:14, 15; Ezek 33:5). The phrase appears in prophetic literature and also in Deuteronomistic passages (1 Sam 19:11; 2 Sam 19:6; 1 Kgs 1:12).

(b) לֹא יִמָּלֵט יָד ("shall not escape from the hand," 32:4; 34:3; see chap. nine, p. 206 (note [b...b]).

C55. כֹּל מַמְלְכוֹת הָאָרֶץ ("all the kingdoms of the earth," 15:4; 24:9; 25:26; 34:1, 17). Frequently preceded by זַעֲוָה (Qere זְוָעָה) ["horror"; cf. Deut 28:25]. See above, C29.

C56. בְּמָצוֹר וּבְמָצוֹק ("in the siege and in the distress," 19:9; Deut 28:53, 55, 57). See above, chap. ten, p. 223 (note [f...f]).

C57. בַּמָּקוֹם הַזֶּה ("in this place," 7:3, 6, 7, 20; 14:13; 16:2, 3; 19:7; 22:3; 33:10, 12; 44:29). Other references to "this place" are 16:9; 19:3, 4 (*bis*), 6, 12; 22:11; 27:22; 28:3 (*bis*), 6; 29:10; 32:37; 40:2; 42:18. Cf. Deut 1:31; 9:7; 11:5; 26:9; 29:6 (29:7E).

C58. מָשָׁל ("proverb, by-word") + שְׁנִינָה "taunt," 24:9; Deut 28:37; 1 Kgs 9:7=2 Chron 7:20).

C59. מִשְׁפָּט וּצְדָקָה ("justice and righteousness," 9:23 [9:24E]; 22:3, 15; 23:5=33:15; Isa 9:6 [9:7E]; Ezek 45:9; Ps 99:4). See above, chap. four, p. 60.

C60. (a) נָבִיא. Jeremiah is designated as "the prophet" thirty-one times in prose passages: 20:2; 25:2; 28:5, 6, 10, 11, 12, 15; 29:1, 29; 32:2; 34:6; 36:8, 26; 37:2, 3, 6, 13; 38:9, 10, 14; 42:2, 4; 43:6; 45:1; 46:1, 13; 47:1; 49:34; 50:1; 51:59 (cf. 2 Chron 36:12). Only four of these instances are in the LXX (42:2; 43:6; 45:1; 51:59).[75] Jeremiah was looked upon as *the* prophet *par excellence* by the scribes who expanded the Hebrew text.

(b) נְבִיאֵיכֶם ("your prophets," 2:30; 27:9, 16; 29:8; 37:19; cf. "their prophets," 32:32). Yahweh's exhortations, "do not listen to your prophets" (27:9, 16) and "do not let your prophets deceive you" (29:8), occur in polemical passages against false prophets which Thiel ascribes to D.[76]

---

[74] According to Holladay (*Jeremiah 1*), "the choice of לֵבָב here would remind the hearer of Deuteronomy" (p. 130).

[75] Janzen, *Studies*, 145–148 (Appendix A).

[76] Thiel, *Redaktion 2*, 53.

(c) עֲבָדַי הַנְּבִיאִים ("my servants the prophets," 7:25; 26:5; 29:19; 35:15; 44:4; 2 Kgs 9:7; 17:13; Ezek 38:17; Zech 1:6).[77]

(d) עֲבָדָיו הַנְּבִיאִים ("his servants the prophets," 25:4; Amos 3:7; 2 Kgs 17:23; 21:10; 24:2; Dan 9:10); cf. "your [s.] servants the prophets," Ezra 9:11; Dan 9:6).

C61. נְבֵלָה ("corpse") as "food for the birds of heaven and the beasts of the earth," 7:33; 16:4; 19:7; 34:20; Deut 28:26; cf. 2 Kgs 9:37 (Jezebel's corpse). See C75 below. Is this a conventional formula?

C62. נדח Hiphil + שָׁם (or שָׁמָּה), with Yahweh as speaker: 8:3; 16:15=23:8; 23:3; 24:9; 29:14, 18 (29:16-20 not in the LXX, by haplography); 32:37; 46:28.[78] For נדח without שָׁם, cf. 27:10 (missing in the LXX); 27:15 (missing in the LXX); נדח Niphal 40:12 (missing in the LXX); 43:5. Elsewhere in the OT: Deut 30:1, "where Yahweh your god has driven you"; Ezek 4:13; Dan 9:7. Janzen notes: "In all these instances, the sentence refers to the dispersion proper, whether the connotation is return or punishment."[79]

C63. נחל Hiphil ("to give the land as a heritage," 3:18; Deut 32:8); נַחֲלָה (Israel as Yahweh's "heritage," 3:19; 10:16=51:19; 12:7, 8, 9, 14; 17:4; Isa 19:25; Mic 7:18; Deut 4:20; 9:26, 29; 32:9; 1 Sam 26:19; 2 Sam 20:19; 21:3).

C64. נטה Hiphil + אֹזֶן ("to incline the ear" [usually preceded by the negative לֹא], 7:24, 26; 11:8; 17:23; 25:4; 34:14; 35:15; 44:5; Isa 55:3; 2 Kgs 19:16=Isa 37:17 [Hezekiah's prayer]; Dan 9:18; Ps 116:2; Prov 4:20; 5:1, 13; 22:17). The references outside of Jeremiah are mostly without the negative and apply to prayer or receiving instruction; the Jeremiah references point to a long history of Yahweh's people as irresponsive to him. Although the phrase may not be Deuteronomistic, the Jeremianic occurrences are found in sermonic passages in which Deuteronomistic phrases abound.[80]

C65. שמר + נֶפֶשׁ Niphal, הִשָּׁמְרוּ בְּנַפְשׁוֹתֵיכֶם ("Take heed for the sake of your lives," 17:21; cf. Deut 4:9 [Qal + sing.]; 4:15; Josh 23:11).

C66. נשא + נֵס ("set up a standard [banner]," 4:6; 50:2; 51:12, 27; Isa 5:26; 11:12; 13:2; 18:3). The phrase implies impending judgment.

C67. סְדֹם וַעֲמֹרָה ("Sodom and Gomorrah," 23:14; 49:18=50:40; Isa 1:9, 10; 13:19b; Amos 4:11; Zeph 2:9; Gen 19:24; Deut 29:22 [29:23E]. See above, chap. seven, p. 153 (ᵃ⋯ᵃ). Mays, commenting on Amos 4:11, states, "The catastrophe like that which befell Sodom and Gomorrah is not included in the preserved lists of covenant curses. But its repeated occurrence in the Old Testament, often as part of a malediction, shows that it belonged to a traditional

---

[77] McConville (*Judgment and Promise*, 120) draws attention to the fact that Jeremiah 44 has affinities with 2 Kings 17, a protest against idolatry.

[78] The parallel passage to 46:28 (30:11) has the verb פוץ Hiphil; see above, chap. seven, p. 120 (note ᶠ⋯ᶠ); pp. 123–124.

[79] Janzen, *Studies*, 53.

[80] Weippert, *Die Prosareden*, 128; Carroll, *Jeremiah*, 215.

reservoir of curses."[81]

C68. (a) סוּר *Hiphil* in the phrase לַהֲסִירָהּ מֵעַל פָּנָי ("so that I will remove it [Jerusalem] from my sight," 32:31; cf. 2 Kgs 17:23; 23:27; 24:3).

(b) סוּר ("to turn away" [in the sense of "apostasize"], 5:23; Deut 11:16; 1 Sam 12:21).

(c) סוּר מֵעָלָי ("to turn away from me [Yahweh]," 32:40; cf. 1 Sam 12:20; 2 Kgs 18:6).

C69. סָלַח ("to forgive" [with Yahweh as subject], 5:1, 7; 31:34; 33:8; 36:3; 50:20). Thiel claims that only four of the thirty-three occurrences of this verb in the OT are pre-exilic, namely, Amos 7:2; 2 Kgs 5:18 (*bis*); Jer 5:7.[82] See also Deut 29:19 (29:20E); 1 Kgs 8:30, 34, 36, 39, 50 (Solomon's prayer); 2 Kgs 24:4.

C70. דִּבֶּר + סָרָה *Piel* ("to utter rebellion, entice to apostasy," 28:16; 29:32; Deut 13:6 [13:5E]; cf. Isa 1:5; 31:6 [without דבר]). In both 35:16LXX (=28:16MT) and 36:32LXX (=29:32MT) this phrase is missing; Graupner considers the phrase to be a postdeuteronomistic gloss.[83] For Janzen, these additions in MT "are clear examples of scholarly glossing as one would wish to find."[84]

C71. עבר in the phrase כָּל־עֹבֵר עָלֶיהָ ("every one who passes by it," 18:16; 19:8; 49:17; 50:13; Zeph 2:15; Lam 2:15; 1 Kgs 9:6 [=2 Chron 7:21]). See above, chap. seven, p. 152 (note ᵇ...ᵇ).

C72. עֲוֹן אָבוֹת ("the guilt [iniquity] of fathers," 32:18; Deut 5:9=Exod 20:5 [Decalogue]; Exod 34:7; Num 14:18).

C73. עזב in the clause כַּאֲשֶׁר עֲזַבְתֶּם אוֹתִי ("as you have forsaken me," 5:19; cf. 1:16; 9:12 [9:13E]; 16:11; 19:4; 22:9; 2 Kgs 22:17).[85] Forsaking Yahweh or his תּוֹרָה (9:12H) is the reason for Yahweh's judgment upon his people.

C74. בְּעָרֵי יְהוּדָה וּבְחֻצוֹת יְרוּשָׁלָיִם ("in the cities of Judah and in the streets of Jerusalem"). For עָרֵי יְהוּדָה see chap. twelve, B43; for חֻצוֹת יְרוּשָׁלָיִם see chap. eleven, A6. The two phrases are combined in 7:17, 34; 11:6; 33:10; 44:6, 17, 21. Weinfeld concludes that two authentic expressions have been combined by the Deuteronomistic editor and raises the question, "Is it not natural to expect that the editor of the prose sermons would adopt phraseology from the authentic

---

[81] Mays, *Amos*, 80.

[82] Thiel, *Redaktion 2*, 26. Thiel (following Duhm) excludes 5:1, which he regards as an insertion. Yahweh is the speaker in 5:1 (וְאֶסְלַח לָהּ and LXX λέγει κύριος), but the other 2d pl. verbs in 5:1 militate against the view that Jeremiah is being addressed. See McKane, *Jeremiah 1*, 114–115; Carroll, *Jeremiah*, 175. Holladay's view (*Jeremiah 1*, 175) that witnesses at a cosmic law court are being addressed (cf. 2:10) is a reasonable assumption.

[83] Graupner, *Auftrag und Geschick*, p. 68 n. 32. McKane (*Jeremiah 2*, 714) claims that the gloss is very late.

[84] Janzen, *Studies*, p. 48.

[85] See discussion of this and other phrases by Thiel, *Redaktion 1*, 74 and Table 1 (p. 75).

prophecies of Jeremiah which he was editing, just as he adopted phraseology from Dtr which antedated him?"[86]

C75. עוֹף in the phrase לְעוֹף הַשָּׁמַיִם וּלְבֶהֱמַת הָאָרֶץ ("for the birds of the air and for the beasts of the earth," 7:33; 16:4; 19:7b; 34:20; Deut 28:26; Ps 74:14; 79:2). עוֹף הַשָּׁמַיִם, Hos 2:18 (2:20E); 1 Kgs 4:11; 16:4. See above, C61 (נְבֵלָה).

C76. עַם in (a) עַם־הַזֶּה ("this people").

(b) אֶת־עַמְּךָ אֶת־יִשְׂרָאֵל ("your [s.] people Israel," 32:21; Deut 21:8 [bis]; 26:15; 2 Sam 7:23, 24; 1 Kgs 8:33, 34, 38, 43, 52; cf. Deut 9:26). All of these occurrences are in a liturgical context.[87] Cf. also Isa 10:22 (non-liturgical).[88]

C77. עֵץ in עַל־כָּל־גִּבְעָה גְבֹהָה וְתַחַת כָּל־עֵץ רַעֲנָן ("upon every high hill and under every green tree," 2:20; 1 Kgs 14:23; 2 Kgs 17:10; and with variations, Jer 3:6b, 13; 17:2; Hos 4:13; Isa 30:25; 57:5, 7; 65:7; Deut 12:2; 2 Kgs 16:4 = 2 Chron 28:4; Ezek 6:13; 20:28; 34:6). Holladay claims that Jeremiah standardized the phrase in the form in which it occurs in Jer 2:20.[89] For Thiel, the phrase in 2:20 is a D insertion.[90] McKane is critical of both views; he believes that the phrase is not an insertion in 2:20, but is integral to the text; however, he finds the resemblance in vocabulary to Hos 4:13 to be too slight to justify Holladay's view that "the line of influence...runs from Hosea to Deut 12:2 to Jeremiah."[91] The interest in Deut 12:2 is in the centralization of the cult and the destruction of Canaanite places of worship. Although centralization of the cult is not a Jeremianic theme, there is no reason to deny that Jeremiah was concerned about idolatrous and syncretistic practices and inveighed against them. At the same time, there is need to acknowledge that references to Baal and the Asherim (e.g., 7:9; 9:14; 11:13; 17:2), the Queen of Heaven (7:16-20; 44:15-30) and "other gods" (see C8 above) occur in contexts together with Deuteronomistic phrases.

C78. עֹרֶף preceded by קשׁה Hiphil ("to stiffen the neck," 7:26; 17:23; 19:15; Deut 10:16b; 2 Kgs 17:14; 2 Chron 30:8; 36:13; Neh 9:16, 17, 29; Prov 29:1).

C79. עֵת in the phrase בָּעֵת הַהִיא ("at that time," 3:17; 4:11; 8:1; 31:1; 33:15; 50:4, 20; Amos 5:13; Mic 3:4; Zeph 1:12; 3:19, 20; Deut 1:9, 16, 18; 2:34; 3:4, 8, 12, 18, 21, 23; 4:14; 5:5; 9:20; 10:1, 8 and frequently in Joshua, Judges and 1-2 Kings. In Jeremiah, the phrase serves as a redactional transition (8:1; 31:1) or as an introduction to a literary addition (3:17; 4:11; 33:15; 50:4,

---

[86] Weinfeld, *Deuteronomy*, p. 7 n. 4.
[87] Weinfeld (*Deuteronomy*), "a stylized parenetic formula" (p. 32; see esp. n. 3).
[88] Kaiser (*Isaiah 1-12*, 147) considers Isa 10:20-23 to be a secondary interpolation.
[89] Holladay, "On every high hill and under every green tree," *VT* 11 (1961) 170-176. See also "Prototype," 359.
[90] Thiel, *Redaktion 1*, p. 42 n. 39, p. 82.
[91] McKane, *Jeremiah 1*, p. 41; Holladay, "On every high hill," 176.

20).⁹² Future events are in mind (cf. Mic 3:4; Zeph 1:12; 3:19, 20). In the book of Deuteronomy, the references are retrospective, pointing to past events.

C80. פֶּה ("mouth") in the expression נָתַתִּי דְבָרַי בְּפִיךָ ("I have put my words in your mouth," 1:9b [cf. Deut 18:18b]; 5:14). Jeremiah 1:9 reflects both Isa 6:7 (Isaiah's call) and Deut 18:18 (Yahweh will raise up a prophet like Moses and will put his words in his mouth). שִׂים rather than נָתַן is used in other passages: Num 22:38; 23:5, 12; Isa 51:16; 59:21.⁹³

C81. פוץ Hiphil ("to scatter," 9:15 [9:16E]; 30:11 [cf. 13:24; 18:17]; Deut 4:27; 28:64; 30:3; 32:26; Ezek 11:16; 12:15; 20:23; 36:19; Neh 1:8). In 30:11=46:28, 30:11 has פוץ Hiphil; 46:28 has נדח Hiphil. See C62 and chap. seven, p. 120 (note ᶠ⋯ᶠ); pp. 123–124.

C82. פָּנִים ("face [of Yahweh])," preceded by various verbs:

    (a) שלח ("send," 15:1; 1 Kgs 9:7=2 Chron 7:20);
    (b) שלך ("cast out," 7:15; 52:3; 2 Kgs 13:23; 17:20; 24:20=Jer 52:3);
    (c) סיר Hiphil ("remove," 32:31; 2 Kgs 17:18, 23; 23:27; 24:3);
    (d) נטש ("cast away," 23:39 [cf. 23:33]).

C83. (a) פָּקַד + עַל ("to visit upon [punish]," 9:24 [9:15E]; 11:22; 21:14; 23:2, 34; 25:12; 27:8; 29:32; 30:20; 36:31; 44:13 [bis], 29; 46:25; 50:18 [+ אֶל, bis]; 51:44, 47, 52; Amos 3:2, 14; Hos 1:4; 2:15 [2:13E]; 4:9, 14; Isa 24:21; 26:21; Zech 10:3; Deut 5:9=Exod 20:5 [Decalogue]; Exod 34:7; Num 14:18; 16:29; Lev 18:25). The phrase is widespread in the prophetic literature, but not in Ezekiel, DI or Zechariah 1–8.⁹⁴

    (b) פקד + חַטֹּאת ("he will punish their sins," 14:10; Hos 8:13; 9:9). **C84.** צְבָאוֹת ("[Yahweh] of hosts"). A frequent epithet in the book of Jeremiah, often followed by "the God of Israel." צְבָאוֹת is often missing in the LXX.⁹⁵ Detailed information is given above (chap. two, p. 13 (ᵇ⋯ᵇ). Cf. Isa 21:10; 37:16; Zeph 2:9; 1 Sam 17:45; 2 Sam 7:27.

C85. צוה Piel (a) in the phrase אֵת כָּל־אֲשֶׁר אֲצַוְּךָ תְּדַבֵּר ("all that I command you, you shall speak," 1:7b; Deut 18:18b). פֶּה (see C80) and the phrase in 1:9b are also found in Deut 18:18. Lundbom claims that "Jeremiah understands himself to be the prophet of Deut 18:18." Whether this is the case or not, equation of Jeremiah with a prophet like Moses (Deut 18:18) is reflected in the account of Jeremiah's call, where 1:7b, 9b point to Deut 18:18. Those who preserved the Jeremiah traditions saw Jeremiah in this light.

    (b) אֲשֶׁר לֹא צִוִּיתִי וְלֹא עָלְתָה עַל־לִבִּי ("which I did not command, nor did it come into my mind," 7:31 [closely parallel to 19:5 and 32:35]); see above C48(c): עַל־לֵב preceded by עלה.⁹⁶

---

⁹² DeVries, *Yesterday*, 41.
⁹³ For both phrases, see Thiel, *Redaktion 1*, 67–68.
⁹⁴ Bright,"The Date of the Prose Sermons," 211.
⁹⁵ Janzen, *Studies*, 79–80.
⁹⁶ See also Meyer, *Jeremia und die Falschen Propheten*, 57–58 (צוה Piel).

(c) צוה *Piel* + דבר *Piel* or שלח: 1:7, 17; 7:22; 14:14; 23:32; 26:2; 29:23; cf. Exod 7:2; 25:22; 34:34; Deut 18:20; all these passages deal with authentic or non-authentic prophecy.

C86. צלל I ("tingle," in the phrase אֲשֶׁר כָּל־שֹׁמְעָהּ תְּצִלֶּינָה אָזְנָיו "that the ears of everyone who hears it will tingle," 19:3; 2 Kgs 21:12; cf. 1 Sam 3:11).

C87. קטר *Piel* + לֵאלֹהִים אֲחֵרִים ("to burn incense to other gods," 1:16; 19:4; 44:3, 5, 8, 15; 7:9 [to Baal]; cf. 11:12, 13; 32:29; 44:17, 18, 19, 25 [to the queen of heaven]. See 2 Kgs 22:17 (to other gods); 2 Kgs 23:5 (to Baal).[97] See also chap. eleven, A23.

C88. קְלָלָה ("curse") in the phrase לִקְלָלָה לְכֹל גּוֹיֵי הָאָרֶץ ("as a curse to all the nations of the earth," 26:16; 44:8; cf. 24:9; 25:18; 42:18; 44:12, 22; Deut 11:26, 28; 28:15, 45; 2 Kgs 22:19).

C89. קֶצֶף גָּדוֹל ("great wrath," 21:5; 32:37; Deut 29:27 [29:28E]). All three texts contain אַף ("anger") and חֵמָה ("fury"). See C9. Jeremiah 21:4–6 sets out the striking view that Yahweh is now *against* Israel in holy war. The triad "anger, fury and great wrath" is matched by the triad "pestilence, sword and famine" in 21:7 (cf. these two triads in Jeremiah 32: "sword, famine and pestilence" in 32:36; "anger, fury, great wrath" in 32:37). Is this triad original with Jeremiah?[98] Jeremiah 21:5LXX contains only two of the three terms (μετὰ θυμοῦ καὶ ὀργῆς μεγάλης). Janzen suggests that 21:5MT may have added אַף, in keeping with the coupling of אַף and חֵמָה elsewhere in the book of Jeremiah (see C9) or that the MT may be original.[99] All three terms appear in 39:37LXX(=32:37MT) and in Deut 29:27LXX. Deuteronomy 29:27MT uses the verb נתש ("to uproot"), which is not found elsewhere in Deuteronomy, but which occurs in 1 Kgs 14:15 (in both cases followed by מֵעַל הָאֲדָמָה; cf. Jer 12:14).[100] We conclude that Jer 21:4–6 echoes authentic Jeremianic terms and ideas, but also witnesses to the expansionist tendencies of the MT. Deuteronomy 29:27MT reflects the influence of the book of Jeremiah. The final form of the books of Deuteronomy and of Jeremiah demonstrate interaction between the two books during the process of revision.

C90. ראה in the phrase אַתֶּם רְאִיתֶם ("you have seen," 44:2; Exod 19:4; Deut 29:1 [Deut 29:2E]; Josh 23:3). Thiel considers these to be Deuteronomistic texts.[101]

---

[97] Thiel (*Redaktion 1*, 74–75) has a chart comparing 2 Kgs 22:16–17; Jer 1:16; 19:3–4; 44:3; 44:7, 8 and containing comments on 1:16, to which he ascribes a Deuteronomistic origin.

[98] This is the view of Holladay, *Jeremiah 1*, 570, 572; cf. Weippert, *Die Prosareden*, 82. According to Thiel (*Redaktion 1*, 234), 21:5b and 32:37 are derived from Deut 29:27.

[99] Janzen, *Studies*, 43.

[100] נתש as a key verb in Jeremiah is discussed above, chap. eleven, p. 245.

[101] Thiel, *Redaktion 2*, 70.

C91. רִנָּה וּתְפִלָּה ("cry" or "prayer," i.e., a prayerful cry [hendiadys], 7:16; 11:14). Both nouns occur in 1 Kgs 8:28=2 Chron 6:19; Pss 17:1; 61:2; 88:3. Thiel regards the expression as belonging to D.[102]

C92. (a) רֹעַ מַעַלְלֵיכֶם ("the evil of your doings," 23:22; 26:3; cf. Isa 1:16; Hos 9:15; Deut 28:20; Ps 28:4). See above, chap. five, p. 90. The phrase belongs within the prophetic tradition.

(b) לְרַע לָכֶם ("to your own hurt [injury]," 7:6; 25:7). Jeremiah 25:7LXX has only the opening words: καὶ ἠκούσατέ μου. Janzen concludes that Jer 25:6-7MT represent a conflation of two variants.[103] Cf. Ps 56:6 [56:5E]; Eccl 8:9. Deuteronomy has the opposite phrase: לְטוֹב ("for good," Deut 6:24; 10:13; 19:13). Cf. Jer 24:6; 32:39; and both phrases in 21:10; 39:16; 44:27 and Amos 9:4; see above, chap. twelve, B51c.

(c) הָרַע, following עשׂה, ("to do evil [in Yahweh's sight]," 7:30; 18:10; 32:30; 52:2). It appears frequently in Deuteronomy and Deuteronomistic books: Deut 4:25; 9:18; 17:2; 31:29; Judg 2:11; 3:7, 12; 4:1; 6:1; 10:6; 13:1; 1 Sam 15:19; 2 Sam 12:9; 1 Kgs 11:6; 14:22; 15:26 (and repeatedly throughout 1-2 Kings and 2 Chronicles, recounting the evil deeds of the kings); Isa 65:12; 66:4; cf. Mal 2:17.

(d) רָעָה + מֵבִיא אָנֹכִי (הִנֵּה): ("[Behold] I am bringing evil," 4:6b; 6:19; 11:11; 19:3; 35:17; 42:17; 45:5; 51:64; cf. 11:23b=23:12b [see above, chap. two, p. 19 (ᵇ...ᵇ)]; 1 Kgs 14:10; 21:21; 2 Kgs 21:12; 22:16=2 Chron 34:24).[104]

(e) קָרָא + הָרָעָה הַזֹּאת ("this evil...to fall upon," 32:33; 44:23; Deut 31:29).

(f) הָרָעָה + נחם Niphal ("to repent of the evil [Yahweh]," 18:8; 26:3, 13, 19; 42:10; Exod 32:12, 14; 2 Sam 24:16=1 Chron 21:15; Jon 3:10; 4:2; Joel 2:13). Thiel ascribes the phrase to D.[105] See above, chap. nine, p. 204 (note ᶜ...ᶜ, נִחַמְתִּי, meaning "I will relent").

(g) הָרָעָה in the phrase שׁוּב + מִדַּרְכּוֹ הָרָעָה ("turn from his evil way," 18:11; 23:22; 25:5; 26:3[=36:3]; 35:15; 36:7; 1 Kgs 13:33 [Jeroboam]; cf. 2 Kgs 17:13; Ezek 13:22; 33:11; Jon 3:8, 10; Zech 1:4; 2 Chron 7:14).[106]

---

[102] Thiel, *Redaktion 2*, 93.

[103] Janzen, *Studies*, 13. McKane (*Jeremiah 1*, 622–623) gives reasons why the MT text should be retained.

[104] According to Thiel (*Redaktion 1*), this phrase is used "almost exclusively in dtr texts" (p. 100).

[105] Thiel, *Redaktion 1*, 215. McKane (*Jeremiah 1*), regarding Jer 18:7-11, states: "there can be little doubt that they embody Deuteronomic theology" (p. 426). Cf. McKane (*Jeremiah 2*). He refers to "the theme of conditional doom...as a leading idea of the redaction" (p. 675).

[106] According to Thiel (*Redaktion 1*), the phrase occurs "extraordinarily frequently in dtr. or D-texts" (p. 252).

C93. שבע *Niphal* in the phrase הַשְּׁבוּעָה אֲשֶׁר־נִשְׁבַּעְתִּי לַאֲבוֹתֵיכֶם ("the oath which I [Yahweh] swore to your fathers," 11:5; cf. 32:22; Deut 1:8; 7:8; 8:18; 9:5; Josh 1:6; 5:6).

C94. שׁוּב שְׁבוּת ("restore the fortunes"). See above, chap. eleven, p. 247.

C95. שָׁכַח ("to forget [Yahweh]," 2:32; 3:21; 13:25; 18:15; cf. 23:27; Hos 2:15 [2:13E]; 8:14; 13:6; Isa 17:10; Deut 8:19; Judg 3:7; 1 Sam 12:9).

C96. שָׁכֵן + לָבֶטַח ("to dwell securely," 23:6 [Israel]=33:16 [Jerusalem]; cf. 49:31 [Hazor]; Lev 26:5; Deut 33:12 [Benjamin]; Ezek 34:25).

C97. שֵׁם (a) in the phrase בַּיִת + אֲשֶׁר נִקְרָא־שְׁמִי עָלָיו ("the house which is called by my name," 7:10, 11, 14, 30; 25:29 [עִיר, "city"; cf. 2 Sam 12:28; Dan 9:18, 19]; 32:34; 34:15; 1 Kgs 8:43=2 Chron 6:33; Amos 9:12 [גּוֹיִם, "nations"]). Cf. 14:9, "we are called by your name"; 15:16, "I am called by your name"; Deut 28:10, "you are called by the name of Yahweh"; Isa 63:19, "those who are not called by my name"; 2 Chron 7:14, "my people who are called by my name."[107]

(b) in the phrase אֲשֶׁר שִׁכַּנְתִּי שְׁמִי שָׁם ("where I made my name dwell," 7:12; cf. Deut 12:11; 14:23; 16:2, 6, 11; 1 Kgs 9:3 [+ שׁוּם, cf. 1 Kgs 11:36; 14:21; 2 Kgs 21:4, 7]). Weinfeld observes: "The expression קרא שם על (in the sense of ownership and protection...) is itself ancient (2 Sam 6:2 12:28 Isa 4:1 Ps 49:12) and as such cannot be considered deuteronomic."[108] However, the contexts in which the phrase is found in Jeremiah contain Deuteronomistic phrases. Berridge states, "This formula is undoubtedly to be considered as being dependent upon the Deuteronomic conception of the dwelling of Yahweh's name."[109]

(c) שֵׁם combined with תְּהִלָּה and תִּפְאֶרֶת ("a name, a praise and a glory," 13:11; cf. 33:9; Deut 26:19). Regarding 13:11, Stacey writes, "The similarity between the latter part of v.11 and Deut 26:19 is unmistakable, which leads to the conclusion that a Deuteronomic editor is responsible for vv.10f."[110] Jeremiah 13:10-11 provide a Deuteronomistic interpretation of the incident of the spoiled waist-cloth.

C98. שַׁמָּה ("horror, that which evokes horror") is a characteristic word in Jeremiah in both poetry and prose, frequently combined with other similar terms. For details, see above, chap. seven, p. 152 ([a...a]). Cf. Hos 5:9; Isa 13:9; Deut 28:37 (cf. Deut 28:25); 2 Kgs 22:19. Weippert has shown that some of the terms with which שַׁמָּה is combined in Jeremiah are not characteristically Deuteronomistic (חָרְבָּה ,חֶרְפָּה and שְׁרֵקָה).[111]

---

[107] Holladay ("Prototype," 358) considers the poetic passages 14:9 and 15:16 to be the prototypes.

[108] Weinfeld, *Deuteronomy*, 325.

[109] Berridge, *Prophet*, 121; cf. Nicholson, *Jeremiah 1*, 77.

[110] Stacey, *Prophetic Drama*, 133; cf. Carroll, *Jeremiah*, 294.

[111] Weippert, *Die Prosareden*, 187-191 (see Table, p. 188).

C99. שִׁמְעוּ בְּקוֹלִי ("obey my voice," 7:23; 11:4, 7; 18:10). Cf. 12:17; 26:13; 32:32; 35:8, 14; 38:20; 40:3; 42:6 (bis), 13; 44:23; Deut 4:30; 13:4; 27:10; 28:62; 30:2, 8, 20.

C100. שִׁקּוּצִים ("detestable things, abominations" [associated with idolatry], 4:1; 7:30=32:34; 13:27; 16:18; Hos 9:10; Deut 29:16 [29:17E]; 2 Kgs 23:24; Ezek 5:11; 11:18, 21; 20:7, 8, 30; 37:23; Dan 9:27).

C101. שְׁרִירוּת לֵב, preceded by הלך ("to walk in stubbornness of heart," 7:24; 11:8; 23:17; cf. 3:17; 9:13 [9:14E]; 13:10; 16:12; 18:12; Deut 29:18 [29:19E]; Ps 81:13 [81:12E]). Holladay calls this "a stock phrase in the tradition."[112] Rudolph attributes 3:17 to a glossator (who follows Jeremiah's use of language), since this verse points to a post-exilic situation (cf. Isa 2:2-4=Mic 4:1-4); the promise would apply to Israel (as elsewhere in Jeremiah), rather than to "the nations," if the text were emended to מִכָּל־הַגּוֹיִם.[113] However, the versions do not support a change in the text, and the MT should be retained.

C102. תּוֹעֵבָה ("abomination") occurs 117 times in the OT; eight times in Jeremiah (2:7; 6:15=8:12; 7:10; 16:18; 32:25; 44:4, 22); seventeen times in the book of Deuteronomy (e.g., 7:24; 12:31; 17:4; 18:9; 20:18; cf. 1 Kgs 14:24; 2 Kgs 21:2, 11); forty-three times in Ezekiel.[114] Compare Proverbs, where the term has an ethical connotation, e.g., Prov 3:32; 8:7; 13:19; 16:12; 29:27.[115] Thiel draws attention to the combination of עשׂה תועבה with the verb שׂנא ("hate" [with Yahweh as subject] in Deut 12:31 and Jer 44:4b).[116]

C103. תּוֹרָה in the phrase הָלַךְ בְּתוֹרַת יְהוָה ("to walk in the law of Yahweh" [and minor variations], 26:4; 32:23; 44:10, 23; cf. 2 Kgs 10:31; Ps 78:10. Commenting on 26:4, Nicholson states: "this reference to the law (Torah)...is evidence that this narrative was composed by Deuteronomistic authors."[117]

---

[112] Holladay, *Jeremiah 1*, 121.

[113] Rudolph, *Jeremia*, 27.

[114] Andersen and Forbes, *VOT*, 444. See above, chap. five, p. 98.

[115] Weinfeld (*Deuteronomy*) claims that "the book of Deuteronomy was influenced by the ancient sapiential ideology that found expression in the book of Proverbs and the wisdom literature of the ancient Near East" (p. 297).

[116] Thiel, *Redaktion 2*, 71.

[117] Nicholson, *Jeremiah 2*, 21. Cf. McKane (*Jeremiah 2*), "the anti-cultic stance of the historical Jeremiah has faded into the background and another model of the prophetic office, attached to Jeremiah, has taken control" (p. 672).

Conclusions

How are we to interpret the data contained in this review of characteristic terms and repetitive phrases (C1–103) in the book of Jeremiah?[118] Data to be interpreted include the following:

I. All parts of the book of Jeremiah (poetry, prose, the OAN) yield phrases and terms with parallels in Deuteronomy and the Deuteronomistic literature, sometimes also with the prophets and with other parts of the OT. However, the following facts emerge:

(1) The Confessions (11:18–12:6; 15:10–21; 17:14–18; 18:18–23; 20:7–18), although showing signs of redaction (see chaps. two and three above), have minimal parallels with Deuteronomy and the Deuteronomistic literature, with the exception of מחשבות + חשב (11:19; 18:18; see C37) and the prose insertion 11:21–23 (C16; C83) and 15:12 (C12).

Other passages with few parallels include:

(2) Jeremiah 30–31, except for 30:1–8, the doublets 30:10–11 (=46:27–28), 30:23–24 (=23:19–20), 31:8 (see C11b) and 31:31–40.

(3) Jeremiah 41; 43; 45.[119]

(4) In the OAN, 46:2–9; 47:1–7; most of Jeremiah 48; 49:1–16.

II. With the exception of Deuteronomy 20, 23 and 25, every chapter of the book of Deuteronomy has phrases found also in Jeremiah. Deuteronomy 4 and 28 (both Deuteronomistic) present numerous parallels.[120] In particular, prose passages such as Jeremiah 7; 11:1–17; 16; 18; 23:1–8; 25:1–7; 32:17–41 and 44 offer an amalgam of phrases found in the book of Deuteronomy and in the Deuteronomistic history. The composition of these passages with such a plenitude of Deuteronomic and Deuteronomistic phrases and idioms must have been undertaken by authors who were thoroughly acquainted with the Deuteronomistic literature.

III. Many of the repetitive phrases are also found throughout Joshua and Judges and especially in the books of Samuel and Kings. Parallels with 1 Kings 8 and 2 Kings 17 are especially numerous. Terms and phrases in common (sometimes with minor variations) include:

(1) **Jeremiah and 1 Kings 8 (Solomon's Prayer)**
(a) "the land which you gave to their fathers," 1 Kgs 8:34, 40, 48 (C1);
(b) "there is no God like you," 8:23 (C7);
(c) "the day that I brought them out of the land of Egypt," 8:16, 21 (C11e);

---

[118] To construct tables with the relevant data would be a complicated undertaking. Parallel phrases in C1–C103 provide the basis for the factual observations which require interpretation. Twenty-two of these phrases occur in the doublets.

[119] Jeremiah 44, concluding the section chaps. 37–44, has numerous parallels with Deuteronomy and the Deuteronomistic literature.

[120] Note especially Deut 4:20 (C45, 63, 39c); 4:34 (C3, 38); 28:25, 26 (C29, 61, 75); 28:49 (C11, 50); 28:64 (C81, 11a, 8, 1b).

(d) "the words that I (he) have spoken," 8:53, 56 (C24c);
(e) "your mighty hand and outstretched arm," 8:42 (C38);
(f) "on that day," 8:64 (C39a);
(g) "that they may fear you all the days," 8:40 (C39h);
(h) "Egypt as "the iron furnace," 8:51 (C45);
(i) appeal for Yahweh's forgiveness, 8:30, 34, 36, 39, 50 (C69);
(j) "your people Israel," 8:33, 34, 38, 43, 52 (C76);
(k) "prayer" and "supplication," 8:28 (C91);
(l) "this house...called by your name," 8:43 (C97a).

(2) **Jeremiah and 2 Kings 17**
(a) "other gods," 2 Kgs 17:35 (C8);
(b) גִּלּוּלִים "idols," 17:12 (C22);
(c) הֶבֶל, 17:15 (C28);
(d) "great power and outstretched arm," 17:3b (C38);
(e) "my (his) servants the prophets," 17:13, 23 (C60c);
(f) "Yahweh removed Israel out of his sight," 17:23 (C68a Jerusalem);
(g) "upon every high hill and under every green tree," 17:10 (C77);
(h) "they were stiff-necked," 17:14 (C90);
(i) "turn from your evil ways," 17:13 (C92g).

    IV. Phrases which occur in the prophets prior to Jeremiah's day are numerous enough to suggest that these phrases (also found in the Deuteronomistic literature) are part of the stock of conventional phrases used by the prophets generally. Examples include, turning to "other gods" Hos 3:1 (C8); Yahweh's bringing his people out of the land of Egypt, Amos 2:10; Hos 2:17; Mic 6:4; Isa 11:16 (C11e); "the house of bondage," Mic 6:4 (C15); "virgin Israel," Amos 5:2 (C18); "without anyone making them afraid," Mic 4:4; Isa 17:2; Zeph 3:13 (C34); "fierce anger," Hos 11:9; Zeph 2:3 (C36); "like Sodom and Gomorrah," Amos 4:11; Zeph 2:9 (C67); "to visit upon (punish)" (i.e., Yahweh's action); Amos 3:2; Hos 1:4 (C83a); "the evil of your doings," Isa 1:16; Hos 9:15 (C92a).

    V. Terms and phrases which are found in later prophets (especially in Ezekiel) are numerous and testify both to the influence of Jeremiah and the Deuteronomistic literature. Examples include, "the land which I gave to them," Ezek 20:15; Amos 9:15 (C1c); "there is none like you [Yahweh]," Isa 45:5 (C7); "for I am with you," Isa 43:5 (C13); גִּלּוּלִים, "idols," Ezek 6:5; 14:5 (C22); "the alien, the fatherless, the widow," Ezek 22:7; Zech 7:10 (C23); "innocent blood," Isa 59:7; Joel 4:19; Jon 1:14 (C25); "that which does not profit," Hab 2:18; Isa 44:9; 57:12 (C41); "to enter (Yahweh's) mind," Ezek 14:3; Isa 65:17 (C48c); "justice and righteousness," Isa 9:6; Ezek 45:9 (C59); "turn from his evil way," Ezek 13:22; Jon 3:8, 10; Zech 1:4 (C92g); שִׁקּוּצִים, "detestable things," Ezek 5:11; Dan 9:27 (C100).

    VI. Phrases which occur also in other parts of the OT are frequently found in books later than Jeremiah and the Deuteronomistic literature, although there can be no certainty about the date of some Psalms and phrases in the sapiential literature (e.g., in Proverbs), which may go back in origin to an early period.

A Deuteronomistic Redaction

Although the evidence given above is not sufficient to provide conclusive proof that a Deuteronomistic redaction took place, the preponderance of Deuteronomistic phrases in large sections of the book of Jeremiah leads on to the strong probability that such a redaction occurred. Many passages and additions to the book testify to scribes and editors who were thoroughly grounded in the Deuteronomistic literature.

In the following chapter, I arrive at some further conclusions regarding the frequent use of doublets and parallel phrases in the book of Jeremiah, with proposals regarding how the book evolved over several centuries.

CHAPTER FOURTEEN

CONCLUSIONS

In the course of this study, nearly fifty doublets or near-doublets have been examined, as well as almost two hundred recurring terms and phrases which are found within the book of Jeremiah and in many cases also elsewhere in the OT, especially in the Deuteronomistic literature. Doublets occur both in poetic passages and in prose narratives and discourses. Many of the recurring phrases appear in the doublets. The book concludes with an historical appendix (Jeremiah 52) based on 2 Kgs 24:18-25:30 as well as on other sources (e.g., 52:28-30).

In our investigation of doublets we have discovered a variety of reasons for their inclusion in the MT of Jeremiah. In some instances, passages have been borrowed and inserted in a new context with a different addressee in mind. For example, the poetic passage 6:22-24 reappears in 50:41-43, where the "foe from the north" is ironically reinterpreted to represent another foe which is to bring about the downfall of Babylon. Jeremiah 10:12-16, a late passage composed by an author who was heir to the Jeremianic tradition, has been reintroduced in 51:15-19; in both cases it is a polemic against idolatry and a witness to the incomparability of Yahweh. The late passage 23:5-6 has been adapted in 33:14-16, with the "righteous Branch" to be raised up for David now as the guarantee of security for Jerusalem. Jeremiah 33:17-18 interprets the passage not only as restoration of the Davidic monarchy but as an assurance that the Levitical priesthood will be a permanent institution.

On occasion, a passage from elsewhere in the OT is directly quoted (e.g., 26:18b quotes Mic 3:12; 14:10b quotes Hos 8:13b; 29:13 adapts Deut 4:29). Sometimes quotations are from memory (e.g., 18:23b quotes Neh 3:37 [4:5E] with a change in the initial verb; 51:58d quotes Hab 2:13b, unless both go back to a common source [cf. "the sour grapes" passage in 31:29 and Ezek 18:2]). Jeremiah 48:34-39 is dependent on Isa 15:2-7 (OAN), while Jer 48:29-33 draws on Isa 16:6-10 with considerable freedom. On the other hand, a part of the Isaiah apocalypse, Isa 24:17-18ab, is dependent on Jer 48:43-44.

There is a possibility that some marginal references have been written later into the main body of the text during the course of transmission. Examples would be 15:13-14=17:3-4 and 10:25=Ps 79:6-7, where a scribal comment in the margin, taken from Ps 79:6-7 has been incorporated as an *addendum* (10:25) to 10:23-24.[1]

Our contention (see chaps. two and three above) has been that the Confessions should not be assigned arbitrarily to specific occasions in the prophet's life and ministry. They have been inserted with some skill in the enlarged collection of poetic oracles and sayings, once many additions had been made to the *Urrolle* (36:32). In the process, doublets have been used as a form of cross-referencing.[2] For example, the doublet 11:20=20:12 serves as an *inclusio*; 11:23b in the prose editorial passage 11:21-23 intentionally reflects 23:12b. Jeremiah 18:20a=18:22b, "for they have dug a pit," has been repeated intentionally, with the introductory כִּי serving a different function in each instance.[3]

Our examination of terms, duplicated phrases, and wordstrings (chaps. eleven, twelve and thirteen) leads to the following conclusions:

I. All parts of the book of Jeremiah contain phrases which were already in use by prophets earlier than Jeremiah himself. Jeremiah and others who contributed to the book which bears his name stood within the prophetic tradition. Examples of phrases belonging to this tradition include אֵבֶל יָחִיד ("mourning for an only son" [B1]); חִיל כַּיּוֹלֵדָה ("pain as of a woman in travail" [B16]); יָצַת + אֵשׁ ("to kindle a fire" [B21]); כְּלִי אֵין חֵפֶץ בּוֹ ("a vessel no one cares for" [B25]); נְאֻם יְהוָה ("oracle of Yahweh" [B35]); נִירוּ לָכֶם נִיר ("break up your fallow ground" [B38]); נפל ("to fall") + כשל ("to stumble" [B39a]); נפל + קום ("to fall" + "to rise up" [B39b]); בְּעֵת רָעָה ("at the time of trouble" [B44]); שׂימוּ...יְהוָה ("Yahweh...is his name" [B56]); עָלָה Hiphil + מֵאֶרֶץ מִצְרַיִם ("bring up...from the land of Egypt" [C11e]).[4] See also: וְאֵין מַחֲרִיד ("without anyone making [him] afraid" [C34]); בַּיּוֹם הַהוּא ("in that day" [C39a]); בָּעֵת הַהִיא ("at that time" [C79]); בָּאִים הִנֵּה יָמִים ("Behold, days are coming" [C39g]); וּמִלְּטוּ אִישׁ נַפְשׁוֹ ("let every man save his life" [C54]); נָשָׂא + נֵס ("to set up a standard [banner]" [C66]); וַעֲמֹרָה סְדֹם ("Sodom and Gomorrah" [C67]); עַל + פקד ("to punish" [C83a]); פקד + חַטֹּאת ("to punish sins" [C83b]); רֹעַ מַעַלְלֵיכֶם ("the evil of your doings" [C92]); שׁכח ("to forget [Yahweh]" [C95]); תּוֹרָה ("Torah" [C103]).

II. A large majority of the repeated phrases listed in C1-103 have parallels in Deuteronomy and/or the Deuteronomistic literature. Jeremiah would be familiar with proto-Deuteronomy and may well have used some expressions from this source. Jeremianic language may also have influenced some sections

---

[1] For 15:13-14=17:3-4 see Janzen, *Studies*, 133, and above, chap. two, pp. 23-31. For Jer 10:25=Ps 79:6-7, see above, chap. ten, pp. 217-218.

[2] Diamond, *The Confessions*, 181.

[3] See above, chap. three, p. 43.

[4] According to Wijngaards (" הוֹצִיא and הֶעֱלָה, a Twofold Approach to the Exodus," *VT* 15 [1965] 91-102), this formula is well attested in the pre-deuteronomistic and early prophetic texts.

of the book of Deuteronomy (e.g., Deuteronomy 28; see C29). Nevertheless, the very large number of phrases with direct parallels to the Deuteronomistic literature lead to the conclusion that many passages in Jeremiah were composed by later authors who were thoroughly acquainted with this literature. Much of this material is very different from the poetic oracles and consists of prose passages which lack the "sparkle" of the poetry and are monotonously repetitive, e.g., Jer 7:23-26; 11:1-8; 19:3-9; 32:16-23; 44:1-10. To illustrate how Deuteronomistic phrases permeate Jer 7:23-26, attention is drawn to the following: 7:23 ("obey my voice" [C99]; "walk in all the way" [C27]); 7:24 ("they did not obey or incline their ear" [C64]; cf. 7:26; "stubbornness of their evil deeds" [C101]); 7:25 "your fathers came out of the land of Egypt" [C11e]; "to this day" [C39e]; "my servants the prophets" [C60c]); 7:26 "stiffened their neck" [C78]). The covenantal formula, "I will be your God, and you shall be my people" (7:23: see above, chap. thirteen, p. 270), occurs mostly in contexts in which Deuteronomistic expressions predominate (11:4; 24:7; 32:38). The phrase, "I have persistently sent" (A29b), belongs to the Jeremiah tradition.

To reconstruct the history of the development of the book of Jeremiah from early beginnings to the finished canonical MT text is a formidable task. Any theory as to the various stages contributing to the process must inevitably be tentative. There are few areas in which certainty can be attained; we can only speculate regarding the steps that led to the book in its final form.

The tragic collapse of Jerusalem in 587 BCE (a sequel to the episode a decade earlier, when the first group of exiles was taken to Babylonia) meant that a sizeable number of leading citizens were transplanted to a foreign environment many miles away. This would lead to a great concern to preserve all the traditions, oral and literary, belonging to a people denied normal temple worship and forced to deal with an entirely new situation and to discover new norms for community life and worship.

The concern for the preservation of oral traditions and writings and for maintaining some degree of continuity with the past would apply not only to those who remained in Jerusalem and Judea, but to the three groups of exiles in Babylon (52:28-30) as well as to the exiles (including Jeremiah and Baruch) who fled to Egypt (43:5-7).[5] We can speculate that in each of these locations scribes would have in their possession written material and records stemming from Jeremiah's prophetic ministry.

---

[5] Jeremiah 40:6 records that Jeremiah had allied himself with Gedaliah at Mizpah. His intention was to remain in the land rather than to respond affirmatively to Nebuzaradan's invitation to go to Babylon. According to 42:7-22, Jeremiah spoke strongly in Yahweh's name against flight to Egypt, indicating (42:10) that "the remnant of Judah" (42:15, 19) should remain in the land. Since Jeremiah and Baruch were taken to Egypt by Johanan (43:5-7), one can only assume that they went involuntarily (cf. Volz, *Jeremia*, "against their will" [p. 362]).

There are good reasons for believing that Jeremiah's early oracles were written down as early as 605 BCE, if the tradition of the *Urrolle* (36:2) and its subsequent expansion (36:28, 32) is substantially correct. The problem of what is historical and what is the result of the artifice of a compelling narrative (an example of superb story-telling) is a primary consideration, especially in the light of the probability that Jeremiah 36 contains the work of Deuteronomistic editorial activity.[6] If we accept the LXX reading in 36:2 (43:2LXX; cf. 36:31MT=43:31LXX), which states that the words of the scroll were "concerning Jerusalem and Judah" (the MT states "Israel and Judah"), and that the reference to "all the nations" is a late addition (as McKane asserts), then Rietzschel's view that the *Urrolle* consists of oracles of doom within Jeremiah 1–6 is reasonable.[7] In spite of all the difficulties of Jeremiah 36, there do not seem to be adequate grounds for rejecting the tradition that an original scroll dictated by Jeremiah was later expanded, again at his dictation, and that the scribe Baruch wrote down Jeremiah's words.[8]

The rewriting and expansion of the *Urrolle* would have taken place largely within the period from the situation depicted in Jeremiah 36 down to the fall of Jerusalem in 587 BCE. Poetic material within Jeremiah 8–18; 22 (critique of the monarchy) and 23 (critique of the prophets) may have been added during this time. After the first deportation in 597 BCE, the preservation of oracular material would become increasingly important, especially oracles addressing those who remained in Jerusalem and Judah during this decade.

We have speculated (chaps. two and three) that the Confessions already existed in written form, and that they were "memoirs" from the prophet himself, reflecting on his life and ministry as well as the persecution and suffering which he had faced. Characteristic Jeremianic expressions and terms include גְּאוֹן הַיַּרְדֵּן ("majesty of the Jordan," 12:5; B10); כְּלָיוֹת וָלֵב ("the heart and mind," 11:20=20:12; B26); חָמָס וָשֹׁד ("violence and destruction," 20:8; B19); מָגוֹר מִסָּבִיב ("terror all around," 20:10; B29); נְקָמָה ("vengeance," 11:20=20:12; 15:15; B40); אִישׁ רִיב וְאִישׁ מָדוֹן ("a man of strife and contention," 15:10; B50). At some stage Baruch or someone else inserted them in various contexts in the expanded *Urrolle*.

We now draw attention to the two visions recorded in 1:11-12 and 1:13-14 and the vision of two baskets of figs in 24:1-3. Although the word חָזוֹן ("vision," B14) is not actually used in these passages, Jer 1:11 and 24:1, 3 use

---

[6] Rietzschel (*Der Problem der Urrolle*, 105–109) discusses the question of historicity. Rietzschel treats Jeremiah 36 as an originally independent single narrative, in which the art of the narrator precludes treating the events narrated as a strictly historical account.

[7] McKane, *Jeremiah 2*, 901; Rietzschel, *Der Problem der Urrolle*, 136.

[8] Carroll's conclusion (*Jeremiah*, 45) that Baruch is a fictional creation seems too extreme. On the other hand, Muilenburg ("Baruch the Scribe") appears to move too far in the opposite direction in considering it probable "that Baruch had a major hand in the compilation and editing of the original work extending from 1:1 to 45:5" (p. 237).

the verb ראה ("see") in much the same way as this verb is used in the "visions" of Amos (7:1, 4, 7; 8:1-2; 9:1; cf. Zech 5:1-4). These "visions," preserved in the Jeremianic tradition, are to authenticate Jeremiah as a true prophet of Yahweh, and also to provide an *inclusio* at the beginning and end of a significant block of tradition (Jeremiah 1-24). Another link between Jeremiah 24 and Jeremiah 1 is the use of the verbs בנה ("build"), הרס ("tear down"), נטע ("plant") and נתש ("uproot," 24:6; 1:10); see above, chap. eleven, p. 245.

Jeremiah 24 is of particular interest in that the vision of the good and bad figs is reported to have taken place after Jeconiah with his officers, craftsmen and smiths had been deported to Babylon by Nebuchadrezzar in 597 BCE. The interpretation of this vision identifies these exiles as the good figs (24:5), while identifying the bad figs as Zedekiah, his officers, and the remnant of Jerusalem who remained in Judah (24:8; cf. 29:16-17), as well as those who had fled to Egypt to dwell there.[9] McKane claims "...Chapter 24 is a later schematizing of a theory or dogma."[10] In the case of the good figs, the exiles of 597 BCE are to return to "this land" (Judah) to become the nucleus of a restored covenant community (24:6-7). The fate of the bad figs (24:8-10) is seen from a perspective later than that represented in 27:12-15, where Jeremiah had offered hope to Zedekiah and those who remained in the land, subject to their submission to Nebuchadrezzar.

When and by whom were the prose passages in Jeremiah 1-24 added? The temple sermon (Jeremiah 7), the dire predictions of 8:1-3, the passage concerning the broken covenant (11:1-17), the incident of the linen waist-cloth (13:1-14), the command that Jeremiah must not marry (Jeremiah 16), the passage regarding Sabbath observance (17:19-27), the visit to the potter's house (18:1-12), the symbolic action of breaking the flask (Jeremiah 19), the judgment pronounced against Passhur the priest (20:1-6), Jeremiah's reply to the embassy when Jerusalem was under siege (21:1-10), passages directed against false prophets (14:11-16; 23:16-17; 23:23-40), and the vision of the baskets of figs (Jeremiah 24), have certain features in common. They reflect traditions concerning Jeremiah: his opposition to false reliance on the temple and on cultic practices, the reminder of the fate of Shiloh, symbolic actions such as those involving the spoiled waistcloth and the breaking of the flask, the interpretation of the siege of Jerusalem as holy war against Israel (21:5), Jeremiah's vision of the rod of almond (1:11-12), the boiling pot (1:13-14), and the two baskets of figs (Jeremiah 24). These passages preserve a few traces of Jeremiah's language, e.g., "amend your ways and your doings" (7:3, 5); "a den

---

[9] The reference to "those who dwell in the land of Egypt" (24:8) indicates that although according to tradition Jeremiah may have experienced the vision of the two baskets of figs after the event of 597 BCE, the interpretation of the vision belongs to a later post-Jeremianic period. McKane (*Jeremiah 1*, lxxx) considers the reference to the Egyptian diaspora to be secondary.

[10] McKane, *Jeremiah 1*, 610.

of robbers" (7:11); "poisoned water" (9:14 [9:15E]; "the voice of mirth and the voice of gladness, the voice of the bridegroom and the voice of the bride" (7:34; 16:9); "persistently speaking" (7:13; 11:7); "persistently sending" (7:25). Nevertheless, the phrases and wordstrings in these prose passages are predominantly Deuteronomistic (C1-103, in chap. thirteen). The language is pedantic, repetitive, and different from that of the poetic oracles. The circles in which these passages were composed can rightly be termed "deuteronomistic." Weippert's important study (1973) regarding the linguistic nuances of phrases in the prose passages in Jeremiah, which differ from the way in which these phrases are used in the Deuteronomistic literature, may not convince us that her conclusions are necessarily inevitable. As Carroll observes, "Perhaps within Deuteronomistic circles there were those who worked specifically on a production of Jeremiah, or post-Deuteronomistic sources contribute nuances of language which went beyond the Deuteronomistic lexical range."[11]

The various blocks of prose in Jeremiah 1-24 were not necessarily added *in toto* at one time by those within the Deuteronomistic circles. In all likelihood, an initial Jeremian Deuteronomistic redaction was supplemented by many later prose additions, along the lines suggested by McKane, that is, a rolling *corpus* in which some parts of the prose text "triggered" commentary.[12]

In my view, substantial blocks of prose were indeed inserted by the Jeremian Deuteronomists at the time of the Deuteronomistic redaction, but these in turn generated further prose additions. A good example would be 8:1-3, introduced by "at that time" and adding to the concept of "the dead bodies of this people" (7:33), by referring to "the bones of the inhabitants of Jerusalem" (8:1) "spread before the sun and the moon and all the host of heaven which they have loved and served" (8:2; cf. 7:18, idolatrous worship of the "queen of heaven"). Another example is Jer 11:9-13, which spells out the breaking of the covenant. Jeremiah 11:1-18 follows Deuteronomistic linguistic patterns and form. Jeremiah 11:13 reflects Jer 2:28b. An additional example is Jer 13:12-14, introducing a new subject, "Every jar shall be filled with wine" (13:12). This passage ends with the statement, "I will not pity or spare, or have compassion when I destroy them" (13:14; cf. 21:7). Yet another example is Jer 23:33-40, where a question posed by one of "this people" (23:33; cf. 23:32) leads to a lengthy treatment of the subject of "the burden of Yahweh," with its *double-entendre*.

The Jeremian Deuteronomists, who preserved the traditions recorded in the prose passages, had two major purposes in mind: one, theodicy, a justification of Yahweh's action in bringing about the fall of Jerusalem, the destruction of the temple, and exile at the hands of the Babylonians because of

---

[11] Carroll, *Jeremiah*, 42.
[12] McKane, *Jeremiah 1*, lxxxiii.

Israel's idolatry and apostasy; two, a reapplication and reinterpretation of Jeremiah's preaching (in Deuteronomistic language) to address a post-Jeremianic situation.

Nicholson has argued that the circle of traditionists responsible for the prose passages throughout the book of Jeremiah were located in Babylon rather than in Judah.[13] Hyatt, on the other hand, locates the work of the Jeremian Deuteronomists in Egypt.[14] Thiel asserts that the place of origin of the D-texts "is undoubtedly the land of Judah."[15]

I believe that Judah is the most likely *locus*. Ackroyd, commenting on the relatively modest numbers of those deported to Babylon (according to 52:28-30), thinks that the depopulation was not extensive.[16] Ackermann, in her study of popular religion in Judah in the sixth century, concludes, "Certainly the bulk of the Judahite population remained in the land during the exile."[17] The reference to the "poor people who owned nothing" (39:10; cf. 52:16=2 Kgs 25:12) is not to be interpreted to mean that only the poor remained in Judah, but that the rural poor were given vineyards and fields, a Babylonian policy aimed at providing for the economic security of those who remained in the land.[18]

Thiel's argument for Judah as the location of those who produced the Deuteronomistic book of Jeremiah is that the passages which speak of the scattering abroad of the people of Judah ("among all the nations where I [Yahweh] have driven them," e.g., 8:3; 9:15 [9:16E]; 16:13; 22:26; 23:3, 8; 24:9; 29:14, 18; 32:37), and which promise a return "to this place" (27:22; 29:10, 14; 32:37), are formulated from a Judean standpoint. The origin of such passages would be the homeland. Those who produced these passages were deeply immersed in the language and thought forms of the Deuteronomistic literature and at the same time were in close contact with the Jeremianic tradition.

We now turn to consider Jeremiah 25-52, best considered in terms of blocks of tradition (25-36; 37-45; 46-51 [OAN] and the concluding historical appendix, 52).

The first section, Jeremiah 25-36, does not really constitute a unity, but consists of disparate elements that needed to be included as part of the developing book. Jeremiah 25:1-13MT expands 25:1-13LXX. The shorter LXX

---

[13] Nicholson, *Preaching to the Exiles*, 133.
[14] Hyatt, *Jeremiah*, 788-789.
[15] Thiel, *Redaktion 2*, 113.
[16] Ackroyd, *Exile and Restoration*, 21, p. 22 n. 24.
[17] Susan Ackermann, *Under Every Green Tree. Popular Religion in Sixth-Century Judah* (HSM 46; Atlanta: Scholars Press, 1992), p. 216.
[18] Leslie, *Jeremiah*, 254; but see Seitz, *Theology in Conflict*, p. 270 n. 180. Volz (*Jeremia*, 347) sees a partial fulfilment of 6:12 in fields being turned over to others. Cf. Weiser, *Jeremia*, 348.

version serves as an introduction to the OAN. In both MT and LXX versions, 25:1-13 provides a summary of the work of the prophet up to "the fourth year of Jehoiakim," a date that coincides with the superscription in 36:1MT. Jeremiah 25 and 36 provide an appropriate beginning and end of this section, as does the reference to "this book" (25:13), referring to the scroll containing the OAN and providing a link with the two scrolls in 36:2, 32. The removal of the OAN from a position immediately after 25:13 in the LXX to a position at the end of the book (Jeremiah 46-51MT) has been discussed above (chap. six, pp. 111-112). Jeremiah 25:14MT (not in LXX) makes the transition to the subject of "Yahweh's cup of the wine of wrath" (25:15), followed by the list of the nations (25:18-26, with an addition in 25:26bMT to include the Babylonians). Throughout Jeremiah 25, the references to the "nations" ("all these nations," 25:9; "all the nations," 25:13, 15, 17; "many nations," 25:14; an indictment "against the nations," 25:31; "evil is going forth from nation to nation," 25:32; "from one end of the earth to the other," 25:33) account for the piecemeal way in which this chapter has been put together. The OAN contain numerous doublets and additional material added at various times over a period of many years.

Jeremiah 26 reverts to the incident of the temple sermon and selective use is made of the material in Jeremiah 7. The temple will be destroyed as was Shiloh (7:14; 26:6; cf. Ps 78:60). The reference to "all the nations" in 26:6 provides a link with Jeremiah 25. This sermon has been repeated in order to give a reason for the sentence of death, finally revoked, which is recorded in the biographical narrative (26:7-24). The narrative also demonstrates that Jeremiah was not without support from various quarters (26:16, 24) during this stage in his prophetic ministry.

Jeremiah 27-29 represents an independent cycle of tradition (with variations in the spelling of names, e.g., Nebuchadnezzar with *nun*, and shortened forms of the names Zedekiah and Jeremiah).[19] Biographical material is included: the sign of the yoke to the envoys from Edom, Moab, Ammon, Tyre and Sidon; the conflict with Hananiah; Jeremiah's letter to the exiles in Babylon. The subject is true and false prophecy, in which Jeremiah's hearers are exhorted not to listen to their prophets (27:9, 14, 16, 17); Hananiah has not been sent by Yahweh (28:15); Ahab, Zedekiah and Shemaiah have prophesied a lie (29:21, 31).

Jeremiah 30-33 contain mostly oracles with a common theme of hope, brought together as a collection. Jeremiah 30-31 (Book of Consolation) are a cycle of oracles, some from Jeremiah (e.g., 31:15-20), but others from a later period (e.g., 30:10-11= 46:27-28).[20] Jeremiah 32 rightly belongs to this

---

[19] See above, chap. six, p. 102 n. 5.

[20] See above, chap. seven, pp. 119-125. Although some early material is included in this collection, most of the oracles point to a period later than the time of Jeremiah. Carroll (*Jeremiah*) attributes Jeremiah 30-31 to "the anonymous circles during and after the exile

section of the book. The purchase of Hanamel's field was a mark of hope for the future, epitomized in 32:15, "Houses and fields and vineyards shall again be brought in this land."[21] Carroll points out that Jeremiah 32 is heavily edited and should not be considered to rest on an historical event; McKane also expresses some reservations concerning historicity.[22] Deuteronomistic phrases are found throughout 32:16-25 (Jeremiah's prayer), as well as in 32:26-35, in which judgment is pronounced on Jerusalem in view of the idolatrous practices of its inhabitants. The note of hope is sounded again in 32:36-44, in which the renewal of the covenant and the restoration of fortunes are promised, themes which are reasserted in Jeremiah 33 (33:19-22; 33:7, 26). The view that seems most probable to me is that members of the Deuteronomistic circle were drawing on the Jeremiah traditions that had been handed down. The purchase of Hanamel's field by Jeremiah and his statement regarding its significance for the future is recorded in 32:15. Jeremiah 33 takes up previous passages and reapplies them, especially in the case of 33:14-16=23:5-6, now specifically applied to Jerusalem.[23]

Jeremiah 34 is loosely connected with the preceding chapters, e.g., 34:2-3 and 32:2-5 have some phrases in common ("Behold, I am giving this city into the hand of the king of Babylon," 34:2; 32:3; "eye to eye" and "face to face," 34:4; and in reverse order, 32:4). McKane draws attention to links between 34:2-5, 21:3-10 and 37:5-10.[24] Jeremiah 34:4b-5a, "You shall not die by the sword, You shall die in peace," is best taken as a conditional promise to Zedekiah (cf. 38:17, "If you will surrender to the princes of the king of Babylon, then your life shall be spared"). The subject of 34:8-11 is Zedekiah's edict regarding the manumission of slaves (to assist in the defence of the city?); this was adhered to only for a brief time by the slave-owners, who took back their slaves when the Babylonians withdrew, perhaps mistakenly thinking that relief from Egypt was imminent. Again, Deuteronomistic language is in evidence, with appended references to the Deuteronomic law (34:13-14; Deut 15:1, 12) and to Gen 15:10-21 (34:18-19) as later commentary on the incident.[25]

---

which cherished expectations of restoration" (p. 569).

[21] Jeremiah 32:15 is widely accepted as an authentic saying of Jeremiah. Bright (*Jeremiah*) states, "the authenticity...is unquestionable" (p. 239). Cf. Thiel (*Redaktion 2*), "an authentic autobiographical report" (p. 31); Holladay (*Jeremiah 2*), "a turning point in Jrm's message" (p. 216). See above, chap. four, p. 77.

[22] Carroll, *Jeremiah*, 620-621; McKane, *Jeremiah 2*, 841.

[23] See above, chap. four, pp. 55-60.

[24] McKane, *Jeremiah 2*, 877.

[25] Weippert's careful treatment of 34:8-22 (*Die Prosareden*, 86-106, 148-149) leads her to the conclusion, "the linguistic usage is not demonstrated to be deuteronomistic, but at most is dependent on Deuteronomy" (p. 106). But phrases such as "I will make you a horror to all the kingdoms of the earth" (34:17; 15:4; see C29, C55) and "Their dead bodies shall be food for the birds of the air and beasts of the earth" (34:20; 7:33; 16:4; 19:7b; see C75)

The connection of Jeremiah 35 to the foregoing chapters is very loose, especially since the superscription in 35:1 places this encounter with the Rechabites in the days of Jehoiakim. Those who preserved this tradition were concerned to make a strong contrast between the fidelity of the Rechabites to their vows and the disobedience and idolatry of "the men of Judah and the inhabitants of Jerusalem." Jeremiah 35:15-17 contain a series of Deuteronomistic wordstrings (see C60c, C92g, C8, C1c, C64, C92d), for which there are parallels in many other prose passages in Jeremiah (cf. Jeremiah 7, 16, 18, 19, 25:3-6, 26, 44).[26]

Jeremiah 36 provides an appropriate conclusion to the block of tradition, Jeremiah 25-36. Both 25:1 and 36:1 have superscriptions containing a reference to the fourth year of Jehoiakim (cf. 35:1, "in the days of Jehoiakim"); 25:13 ("this book," an incipient collection of OAN) and 36:2, 32 have as their focus various scrolls (cf. 45:1) which have contributed to the book of Jeremiah in its present form.

The next block of tradition, Jeremiah 37-45, is made up of a series of narratives recounting events during the final months prior to the fall of Jerusalem (587 BCE). A second wave of exiles went into exile in Babylon in 587 BCE. This dramatic event is followed by an account of Gedaliah's brief governorship of the cities of Judah at Mizpah and the subsequent flight to Egypt of another group of exiles, under Johanan, including Jeremiah and Baruch. Jeremiah 44, which contains many Deuteronomistic phrases and wordstrings (cf. especially the parallels with Jeremiah 7), is largely sermonic. Jeremiah 45 not only concludes this section but serves as the conclusion of Jeremiah 1-45.

Noteworthy features of these chapters include:

(1) the use of the phrase וַיֵּשֶׁב יִרְמְיָהוּ בַּחֲצַר הַמַּטָּרָה ("and Jeremiah remained in the court of the guard," 37:21b; 38:13b; 38:28a; see A9);
(2) the phrase בְּתוֹךְ הָעָם ("in the midst of the people," 39:14b; 40:6b);
(3) formulaic phrases concluding various parts of the narrative;
(4) duplications in the narrative (e.g., 37:11-21 and Jeremiah 38; 39:11-24 and 40:1-6);
(5) two versions of Jeremiah's imprisonment in Jeremiah 38 and 39, which suggest that parallel accounts have been brought together;
(6) no mention of Jeremiah in a sizeable section of the narrative (40:7-41:18), the account of Gedaliah and his murder by Ishmael (cf. no mention of Jeremiah in Jeremiah 52);
(7) Jeremiah 39:1-10 follows 52:4-16 in recounting the fate of Zedekiah, with an addition, 39:11-14 (not present in Jeremiah 52 or in 2 Kings 25), which

---

are typically Deuteronomistic.

[26] Weippert (*Die Prosareden*, 121-148) concludes that the phrases in 35:15 are Jeremianic, but with the exception of the phrase הַשְׁכֵּם וְשָׁלוֹחַ, "persistently sending" (see A29b), the wordstrings in 35:15-17 are Deuteronomistic. For further discussion of 35:15, see above, chap. six, p. 111.

recounts Nebuzaradan's action in entrusting Jeremiah to the care of Gedaliah, another version of 40:1–6;

(8) the role of Ebed-melech (38:7–13) in his rescue of Jeremiah from the cistern, and subsequent commendation by Jeremiah (39:15–18). He is to have his life as "a prize of war" (לְשָׁלָל, 39:18; see A30), using a term found in 38:2=21:9 (see above, chap. nine, pp. 201–204) and also in 45:5 (regarding Baruch), serving as a connecting link in bringing together various portions of the narrative.[27]

Pohlmann argues that Jeremiah 37–44 reflect a Babylonian Gola orientation and that the author of Jeremiah 24, with this same orientation ("the good figs" are the exiles in Babylon in 597 BCE) is also responsible for the present version of Jeremiah 37–44.[28] He proposes three stages in the development of Jeremiah 37–44: (1) an original kernel, consisting of 37:11–16, with some sections of Jeremiah 38, 39, 40, 41, 42; (2) a *gola*-oriented redaction: 37:1–10; 38:1–6; 39:1–2, 4–13; parts of Jeremiah 41, 42, 44 and Jeremiah 43 *in toto*; (3) later additions, 37:17–21, 38:15–18 (regarding Ebed-melech), and sections of Jeremiah 40, 42 and 44.[29] He is undoubtedly correct in his view that the process by which Jeremiah 37–44 reached its present form is complicated and represents several stages. The impression given by 39:9–10, that a substantial part of the population was taken to Babylon in 587 BCE (cf. 52:15–16) is offset by 52:28–30, which indicates that the several deportations did not constitute a majority of the citizens. Jeremiah 24:5–7 has the exiles of the first deportation to Babylon (597 BCE) in mind and looks forward to their return (or the return of their descendants), when they will become the basis of the post-exilic community in the homeland (the verbs בָּנָה ["build"] and נָטַע ["plant"] in 24:6 provide a link with 1:10).

Our survey of Deuteronomistic phrases (C1–C103, chap. thirteen) indicates that Jeremiah 37–43 is remarkably free of such phrases.[30] Jeremiah 44, on the other hand, is replete with Deuteronomistic phraseology, including many parallels to Jeremiah 7.[31] Traditions regarding this crucial time-period at the end of Zedekiah's reign and subsequent events, including the flight to Egypt of "the remnant of Judah" (43:5) under Johanan and their subsequent residence at Tahpanes (43:7–44:30), were probably brought together at an early period during the exile. Amplifications would have been made at a later stage (e.g., Jeremiah 39, in part dependent on Jeremiah 52, and ultimately on 2

---

[27] For formulaic phrases referred to in (1) above, see Wanke, *Untersuchungen*, 94–95; Holladay, *Jeremiah 2*, 282.

[28] Pohlmann, *Studien*, 30.

[29] Pohlmann, *Studien*, 225.

[30] Even Thiel (*Redaktion 2*, 52–68), who tends to manufacture D phrases, finds few examples in these chapters.

[31] Jeremiah 7 and 44 have references to worship of the "queen of heaven" (see A14), not found elsewhere in Jeremiah.

Kings). Statements such as 37:1 (cf. 2 Kgs 24:17) and 39:1-10 (cf. 2 Kgs 25:1-12) may have been added at the time that Jeremiah 44 was composed by the Deuteronomistic circle.

The OAN (46-51) have been examined in detail in chaps. seven and eight above. This collection grew and expanded over the years, very much along the lines of McKane's "rolling *corpus*."[32] Many of the additions are very late, the work of learned scribes who were well-acquainted with other OT writings. There are anomalies and inconsistencies which were not of great concern to those who added to these chapters over the years. No attempt was made to reconcile Jeremiah's pro-Babylonian attitude expressed in the letter to the exiles in 29:4-9 with the harsh statements against Babylon in Jeremiah 50-51.[33] Likewise, the universalizing tendency which promises restoration of fortunes to Moab, the Ammonites and Elam (48:47; 49:6, 39), represents a much later addition to passages which make such promises as "Moab shall be destroyed and be no longer a people" (48:42); "with none to gather the fugitives" (49:5); "until I have consumed them" (49:37).

Jeremiah 1 has been edited with care in order to make connections with other parts of the book, including the OAN, and with other parts of the OT. Although Jeremiah 1 contains an account of Jeremiah's call based on an authentic tradition, the present form of 1:5-10 shows indebtedness to the account of the call of Moses and his subsequent remonstrances (1:5-8; Exod 3-4), to Isaiah's call (1:9 and Isa 6:7) and to Deut 18:18 (1:7b, 9b).[34] A second introduction (1:3) has been inserted, which goes beyond "in the days of Josiah" (1:2) and includes subsequent kings "until the captivity of Jerusalem," thereby covering the entire period of Jeremiah's prophetic activity (Jeremiah 2-45). The commission to "pluck up and to break down...to build and to plant" (1:10) includes prophecy to "the nations" (1:5, 10). Jeremiah 46-51 are therefore seen by the editors as stemming from the prophet. Brueggemann has indicated how the "but you" passages (1:17; 45:5) provide an envelope for Jeremiah 1-45.[35] Jeremiah 1:17-19 are dependent on 17:18b and 15:20 and have been composed with these Confessions in mind.

The text of the book of Jeremiah found in the Septuagint represents a stage in the development of the book. The LXX is some 2,700 words shorter than the MT.[36] In this study, we have consistently put forward the view that the final form of the Hebrew text (the MT) is an expansion of the LXX. Some omissions in the LXX are the result of haplography.[37] Other "omissions" are

---

[32] McKane, *Jeremiah 1*, lxxxiii.
[33] See above, chap. eight, p. 166.
[34] Herrmann, *Jeremia*, 44-45; Thiel, *Redaktion 1*, 71.
[35] Brueggemann, *To Pluck up, To Tear down*, 28-29.
[36] Giesebrecht, *Jeremia*, xxv.
[37] Janzen, *Studies*, 117-120.

best explained as examples of conflation in the Hebrew text.[38] We are unable to date the Hebrew *Vorlage* of the LXX. In the course of time a number of Hebrew manuscripts emerged with variant readings. A process of collation took place in order to preserve texts which might otherwise have been lost. In view of this, the MT has material not found in the LXX.

So far as the doublets which the LXX "omits" are concerned, Janzen's observation that "more than half the time the large doublets were rendered both times" in the LXX makes any view of deliberate omission by LXX, in the interest of conserving space or for any other reason, highly questionable.[39] Explanations such as haplography or texts added in the margins of Hebrew manuscripts can account for the LXX "omissions" in the doublets; see espec. discussions above on 17:3-4 (chap. two, p. 28); 33:14-26 (chap. four, p. 61 n. 26); 39:4-13 (chap. nine, p. 210); 48:40b, 41b (chap. seven, p. 139); 48:45-46 (chap. seven, p. 143).

The inclusion of names in the MT is another example of expansion, e.g., Nebuchadrezzar or Nebuchadnezzar (see chap. six, p. 102 n. 5). Frequently, צְבָאוֹת ("of hosts") is added to Yahweh's name. Jeremiah is designated as "the prophet."[40]

The MT uses the phrase נְאֻם יְהוָה very frequently; in over seventy instances the phrase is not present in LXX.[41] Janzen follows the suggestion of A. Scholz, who thinks that the phrase occurred frequently in synagogue homiletical practice, an explanation which may also account for the repetition of names and titles.[42]

Additions in the MT should not be regarded as merely secondary. The text of the Septuagint should not be considered to be definitive for exegesis of the book of Jeremiah. McKane's discussion of the text of the LXX and the final shape of the MT leads him to an important conclusion, "along with the assertion that the Hebrew *Vorlage* of Sept. represents an earlier and more cohesive text than MT there goes the counter-assertion that it is the duty of the commentator on the Hebrew text to maintain the final form of that text in MT."[43]

Our study of doublets and repetitive phrases in the book of Jeremiah contributes only in a limited way to resolving questions concerning the process by which the book of Jeremiah reached its extant form. A thorough study of the superscriptions that occur frequently throughout the book might throw

---

[38] Janzen, *Studies*, 10–33.

[39] Janzen, *Studies*, 92.

[40] Janzen (*Studies*, 75) notes that צבאות occurs eighty-two times in Jeremiah (MT), but only ten times in the LXX version. See above (chap. two, p. 13 [ᵇ⁻⁻ᵇ]) and see also C60 (chap. thirteen).

[41] See above, chap. twelve, B35.

[42] Janzen, *Studies*, 83; Scholz, *Der Masoretische Text*, 101.

[43] McKane, *Jeremiah 1*, 622.

additional light on this complicated and perplexing problem. In view of the long history of the development of the book, decisions as to what sayings are authentically Jeremianic or post-Jeremianic are difficult to make. Those who stood in the Jeremiah tradition undoubtedly sought to preserve the words and message of the prophet, interpreting his words in the process and applying them to later contemporary situations. Doublets which we have considered to be post–Jeremianic, e.g., 30:10–11=46:27–28 (see chap. seven, pp. 119–125); 23:5–6=33:15–16 (see chap. four, pp. 55–60); and 16:14-15=23:7-8 (see chap. four, pp. 72–77) express a vibrant hope for the future, couched in language that is comparable to the finest oracles to be found anywhere in the OT.

BIBLIOGRAPHY

COMMENTARIES ON JEREMIAH

Boadt, Lawrence, *Jeremiah 1-25* (Old Testament Message 9; Wilmington, Delaware: Glazier, 1982).
—— *Jeremiah 26-52, Habakkuk, Zephaniah, Nahum* (Old Testament Message 10; Wilmington, Delaware: Glazier, 1982).
Bright, John, *Jeremiah: Introduction, Translation, and Notes* (AB 21; Garden City, New York: Doubleday, 1965).
Brueggemann, Walter, *To Pluck Up, to Tear Down: A Commentary on the Book of Jeremiah 1-25* (ITC; Grand Rapids, Michigan: Eerdmans, 1989).
—— *To Build, to Plant: A Commentary on Jeremiah 26-52* (ITC; Grand Rapids, Michigan: Eerdmans, 1991).
Carroll, Robert P. , *Jeremiah: A Commentary* (OTL; London: SCM, 1986).
Clements, Ronald E., *Jeremiah* (Interpretation; Atlanta: Knox, 1988).
Condamin, Albert, *Le Livre de Jérémie: Traduction et Commentaire* (3d ed.; Echter Bibel; Paris: Gabalda, 1936).
Cornill, Carl Heinrich, *Das Buch Jeremia* (Leipzig: Tauchnitz, 1905).
Craigie, Peter C. , Kelley, Page H. and Drinkard, Jr., Joel F. , *Jeremiah 1-25* (WBC 26; Dallas: Word, 1991).
Cunliffe-Jones, Hubert, *The Book of Jeremiah: Introduction and Commentary* (TBC; London: SCM, 1960).
Drinkard, Jr., Joel F. See Craigie, *Jeremiah 1-25*.
Duhm, Bernard, *Das Buch Jeremia* (Kurzer HandKommentar zum Alten Testament 11; Tübingen: Mohr, 1901).
Freedman, Harry, *Jeremiah. Hebrew Text & English Translation and Commentary* (Soncino Books of the Bible; New York: Soncino, 1949; rev. by Rabbi A. J. Rosenberg, 1985).
Giesebrecht, Friedrich, *Das Buch Jeremia* (2d ed.; HKAT 3/2; Göttingen: Vandenhoeck & Ruprecht, 1907).
Hitzig, Ferdinand, *Der Prophet Jeremia* (KEH 3; Leipzig: Weidmann, 1841).
Holladay, William L., *Jeremiah 1: A Commentary on the Book of the Prophet Jeremiah Chapters 1-25* (Hermeneia; Philadelphia: Fortress, 1986).
—— *Jeremiah 2: A Commentary on the Book of the Prophet Jeremiah Chapters 26-52* (Hermeneia; Minneapolis: Fortress, 1989).
Huey, Jr., F. B. , *Jeremiah, Lamentations* (The New American Commentary 16; Nashville: Broadman, 1993).

Hyatt, James Philip, *The Book of Jeremiah: Introduction and Exegesis* (IB 5; New York: Abingdon, 1956).
Jones, Douglas R., *Jeremiah* (NCB; Grand Rapids: Eerdmans, 1992).
Kelley, Page H. See Craigie, *Jeremiah 1-25*.
Keown, Gerald G., Scalise, Pamela J. and Smothers, Thomas J., *Jeremiah 26-52* (WBC 27; Dallas: Word, 1995).
Kidner, Derek, *The Message of Jeremiah: Against Wind and Tide* (The Bible Speaks Today; Leicester, England: Inter-Varsity, 1987).
Leslie, Elmer A., *Jeremiah: Chronically Arranged, Translated, and Interpreted* (Nashville: Abingdon, 1954).
McKane, William, *A Critical and Exegetical Commentary on Jeremiah. Volume 1. Introduction and Commentary on Jeremiah 1-25* (ICC; Edinburgh: T. & T. Clark, 1986).
—— *A Critical and Exegetical Commentary on Jeremiah. Volume 2. Commentary on Jeremiah 26-52* (Edinburgh: T. & T. Clark, 1996).
Nicholson, Ernest W. , *The Book of the Prophet Jeremiah: Chapters 1-25* (CBC; Cambridge: Cambridge University Press, 1973).
—— *The Book of the Prophet Jeremiah: Chapters 26-52* (CBC; Cambridge: Cambridge University Press, 1975).
Rothstein, J. W., *Das Buch Jeremia* (4th ed.; HSAT 1; Tübingen: Mohr, 1922).
Rudolph, Wilhelm, *Jeremia* (3rd ed.; HAT 12; Tübingen: Mohr, 1968).
Scalise, Pamela J. See Keown, *Jeremiah 26-52*.
Smothers, Thomas G. See Keown, *Jeremiah 26-52*.
Thompson, John A., *The Book of Jeremiah* (NICOT; Grand Rapids: Eerdmans, 1980).
Volz, Paul, *Der Prophet Jeremia: Übersetzt und Erklärt* (2d ed.; KAT 10; Leipzig: Deichert, 1928).
Weiser, Artur, *Das Buch Jeremia: Übersetzt und Erklärt* (5th ed., ATD 20/21; Göttingen: Vandenhoeck & Ruprecht, 1966).

GENERAL BIBLIOGRAPHY

Abba, Raymond, "Priests and Levites," *IDB* 3.876-889.
Ackermann, Susan, *Under Every Green Tree. Popular Religion in Sixth-Century Judah* (HSM 46; Atlanta: Scholars Press, 1992).
Ackroyd, Peter R., "Jeremiah 10:1-16," *JTS* 14 (1963) 385-90.
—— *Exile and Restoration* (OTL; London: SCM, 1968).
Ahuis, Ferdinand, *Der klagende Gerichtsprophet. Studien zur Klage in der Überlieferung von den alttestamentlichen Gerichtspropheten* (Calwer Theologische Monographien 12; Stuttgart: Calwer, 1982).
Albertz, Rainer, "Jer 2-6 und die Frühzeitverkündigung Jeremias," *ZAW* 94 (1982) 452-467.

Allen, Leslie C., "More Cuckoos in the Textual Nest: At 2 Kgs 23:5; Jer 17:3, 4; Micah 3:3; 6:16(LXX); 2 Chr 20:25 (LXX)," *JTS* 24 (1973) 70-71.
Althann, Robert, "*mwl*, 'circumcise' with the *lamedh* of Agency," *Bib* 62 (1981) 239-240.
—— *A Philological Analysis of Jeremiah 4-6 in the Light of Northwest Semitic* (Biblica et Orientalia 38; Rome: Biblical Institute, 1983).
Andersen, Francis I. and Forbes, A. Dean, *The Vocabulary of the Old Testament* (Rome: Editrice Pontificio Istituto Biblico, 1989).
Anderson, A. A., *The Book of Psalms, Volume 1* (NCB; London: Oliphants, 1972).
Anderson, Bernhard W., "Lord of Hosts," *IDB* 3.151.
—— "Hosts, Host of Heaven," *IDB* 2.654-656.
Andreasen, Niels-Erik A., *The Old Testament Sabbath: A Tradition-Historical Investigation* (SBLDS 7; Missoula: Scholars Press, 1972).
Andrew, Maurice E., "The Authorship of Jer 10 1-16," *ZAW* 94 (1982) 128-130.
Auld, A. Graeme, "Prophets and Prophecy in Jeremiah and Kings," *ZAW* 96 (1984) 66-82.
Avigad, Nahman, *Hebrew Bullae from the Time of Jeremiah. Remnants from a Burnt Archive* (Jerusalem: Israel Exploration Society, 1986).
Bak, Dong Hyun, *Klagender Gott - klagender Menschen. Studien zur Klage im Jeremiabuch* (BZAW 193; Berlin: Walter de Gruyter, 1990).
Baldwin, Joyce G., "Semah as a Technical Term in the Prophets," *VT* 14 (1964) 93-97.
Balzar, Klaus, *Das Bundesformular* (WMANT 4; Neukirchen: Neukirchener Verlag, 1960); *The Covenant Formulary in Old Testament, Jewish and Early Christian Writings* (Philadelphia: Fortress, 1971).
Barnes, W. Emery, "Prophecy and the Sabbath (A Note on the Teaching of Jeremiah)," *JTS* 29 (1928) 386-390.
Barr, James, *The Semantics of Biblical Language* (Oxford: Oxford University Press, 1961).
Bartlett, J. R., *Edom and the Edomites* (JSOTSup 77; Sheffield: JSOT 1989).
Batten, L. W., *The Books of Ezra and Nehemiah* (ICC; Edinburgh: T. & T. Clark, 1913).
Baumann, Eberhard, "שוב שבות: Eine exegetische Untersuchung," *ZAW* 6 (1929) 17-44.
Baumgartner Walter, *Die Klagedichte des Jeremias* (BZAW 32; Giessen: Töpelmann, 1917); *Jeremiah's Poems of Lament* (Sheffield: Almond, 1988).
—— "Das Aramäische im Buche Daniel," *ZAW* 45 (1927) 81-133.
Begrich, J., "Das priesterliche Heilsorakel," *ZAW* 52 (1934) 81-92.

Berridge, John M., *Prophet, People, and the Word of Yahweh. An Examination of Form and Content in the Proclamation of the Prophet Jeremiah* (Basel Studies of Theology 4; Zürich: EVZ, 1970).
Beyerlin, Walter, *Bleilot, Brecheisen oder was sonst? Revision einer Amosvision* (OBO 81; Göttingen: Vandenhoeck & Ruprecht, 1988).
—— *Reflexe der Amosvisionen im Jeremiabuch* (OBO 93; Göttingen: Vandenhoeck & Ruprecht, 1989).
de Boer, P. A. H., "An Inquiry into the Meaning of the Term מׂשּא," *OTS* 5 (1948) 197-214.
—— "Notes on the Text and Meaning of Isaiah 38:9-20," *OTS* 9 (1951) 170-186.
Bogaert, P.-M., "De Baruch à Jérémie: Les deux Redactions conservées du livre de Jérémie," *Le Livre de Jérémie: Le Prophète et son Milieu, les Oracles et leur Transmission* (ed. P.-M. Bogaert; BETL 54; Leuven: Leuven University Press, 1981) 168-173.
—— "Les mécanismes rédactionnels en Jér 10:1-16 (LXX et TM) et les signification des suppléments," *Le Livre de Jérémie* (ed. P.-M.Bogaert, BETL 54; Leuven: Leuven University Press, 1981) 222-238.
Böhmer, Siegmund, *Heimkehr und neuer Bund. Studien zu Jeremia 30-31* (Göttinger Theologische Arbeiten 5; Göttingen: Vandenhoeck & Ruprecht, 1976).
Bonnard, Pierre, *Le Psautier selon Jérémie. Influence littéraire et spirituelle de Jérémie sur trente-trois psaumes* (Lectio Divina 26; Paris: Les Editions du Cerf, 1960).
Bozak, Barbara, *Life 'Anew.' A Literary Study of Jer 30-31* (AnBib 122; Rome: Editrice Pontificio Istituto Biblico, 1991).
Bracke, John M., "Sûb sebût: A Reappraisal," *ZAW* 67 (1985) 233-244.
Brettler, Marc Zvi, *God is King: Understanding an Israelite Metaphor* (JSOTSup 76; Sheffield: Sheffield Academic, 1989).
Bright, John, "The Date of the Prose Sermons of Jeremiah," *JBL* 70 (1951) 15-35.
—— "An Exercise in Hermeneutics. Jeremiah 31:31-34," *Int* 20 (1966) 188-210.
Brown, F., Driver, S. R., and Briggs, C. A., *A Hebrew and English Lexicon of the Old Testament* (Oxford: Clarendon, 1906).
Brown, Raymond E., *The Birth of the Messiah* (New York: Doubleday, 1977).
Brueggemann, Walter A., "Jeremiah's Use of Rhetorical Questions," *JBL* 92 (1973) 358-374.
Buchanan, G. W., "Eschatology and the 'End of Days'," *JNES* 20 (1961) 188-193.
Carroll, Robert P., *From Chaos to Covenant. Uses of Prophecy in the Book of Jeremiah* (London: SCM, 1981).

Cassuto, Umberto, *A Commentary on the Book of Exodus* (The Hebrew University, Jerusalem: The Magnes Press, 1967).
—— "On the Formal and Stylistic Relationship between Deutero-Isaiah and Other Biblical Writers," in *Biblical and Oriental Studies 1* (Jerusalem: Magnes Press, 1973) 141-177.
Cazelles, Henri (1951) "Jérémie et le Deutéronome," *Recherches de Science Religieuse* 38 (1951) 5-36.
—— "Sophonie, Jérémie, et les Scythes en Palestine," *RB* 74 (1967) 24-44.
Childs, Brevard S., (1959) "The Enemy from the North and the Chaos Tradition," *JBL* 78 (1959) 187-198.
—— "A Study of the Formula, 'Until This Day'," *JBL* 82 (1963) 278-282.
—— *The Book of Exodus: A Critical Theological Commentary* (OTL; Philadelphia: Westminster, 1974).
Christensen, Duane L., "'Terror on Every Side' in Jeremiah," *JBL* 92 (1973) 498-502.
Clines, D. J. A. and Gunn, D. M., "Form, Occasion and Redaction in Jeremiah 20," *ZAW* 88 (1976) 390-409.
—— "'You tried to persuade me' and 'Violence! Outrage!' in Jeremiah 20:7-8," *VT* 28 (1978) 20-27.
Conrad, E. W., *Fear not Warrior: A Study of 'al tîra Pericopes in the Hebrew Scriptures* (Brown Judaic Studies 75; Chico: Scholars Press, 1985).
Cooke, G. A., *A Text-Book of North-Semitic Inscriptions* (Oxford: Clarendon, 1903).
Cowley, A. E., ed., *Gesenius' Hebrew Grammar* (Oxford: Clarendon 1910).
Cross, F. M. and Freedman, D. N., "A Royal Song of Thanksgiving: 2 Samuel 22=Psalm 18," *JBL* 72 (1953) 15-34.
Czerny, Ladislav, *The Day of Yahweh and Some Relevant Problems* (Prague: Nákladem Filosofické Fakulty University Karlovy, 1948).
Dahood, Mitchell, "Hebrew-Ugaritic Lexicography II," *Bib* 45 (1964) 393-412.
Davidson, Robert, "The Interpretation of Jeremiah 17 5-8,"*VT* 9 (1959) 202-205.
Dearman, J. A., "My Servants the Scribes; Composition and Content in Jeremiah 36," *JBL* 109 (1990) 403-421.
Deissler, Alfons, "Das 'Echo' der Hosea-Verkündigung im Jeremiabuch" in *Künder des Wortes. Beiträge zur Theologie der Propheten, Josef Schreiner, zum 60. Geburtstag* (ed. Lothar Ruppert, Peter Weimar, and Erich Zenger; Würzburg: Echter, 1982) 61-75.
DeRoche, M., "Yahweh's *rîb* Against Israel. A Reassessment of the So-Called 'Prophetic Lawsuit' in the Preexilic Prophets," *JBL* 102 (1983) 563-574.
DeVries, S. J., *Yesterday, Today and Tomorrow* (Grand Rapids, Michigan: Eerdmans, 1975).
Diamond, A. R., *The Confessions of Jeremiah in Context. Scenes of Prophetic Drama* (JSOT 45; Sheffield: Sheffield Academic, 1987).

Dietrich, Erich, שוב שבות *Die endzeitliche Wiederherstellung bei den Propheten* (BZAW 40; Giessen: Töpelmann, 1925).
Driver, Godfrey R., "Linguistic and Textual Problems: Jeremiah," *JQR* 28 (1937) 97-129.
—— "Two Misunderstood Passages of the Old Testament," *JTS* 6 (1955) 82-87.
Driver, S. R., *Deuteronomy* (2nd ed.; ICC; Edinburgh: T. & T. Clark, 1896).
Eaton, J. H., *Psalms* (TBC; London: SCM, 1967).
Ehrlich, Arnold B., *Randglossen zur Hebräischen Bibel: textkritisches, sprachliches und sachliches, 4-5, Jesaia, Jeremia* (Leipzig: J. C. Hinrich's, 1910, 1912).
Eichler, Ulrike, *Der klagende Jeremia. Eine Untersuchung zu den Klagen Jeremias und ihrer Bedeutung zum Verstehen seines Leiden* (unpublished dissertation, University of Heidelberg, 1971).
Eichrodt, Walter, *Theology of the Old Testament I* (London: SCM, 1961).
—— *Theology of the Old Testament II* (London: SCM, 1967).
—— *Ezekiel* (OTL; London: SCM, 1970).
Eissfeldt, Otto, *Einleitung in das Alte Testament unter Einschluss der Apokryphen und Pseudepigraphen* (Tübingen: Mohr, 1934).
—— *The Old Testament: An Introduction* (Oxford: Blackwell, 1965) Emerton, John A., "A Problem in the Hebrew Text of Jeremiah 6:23 and 50:42," *JTS* 23 (1972) 106-113.
Ewald, H., *Die Propheten des Alten Bundes* (Stuttgart: Krabbe, 1841).
Fahlgren, K.Hj., *S^edaka, nahestehende und entgegengesetze Begriffe im Alten Testament* (Uppsala: Almquist & Wiksell, 1932).
Fishbane, Michael, "Revelation and Tradition. Aspects of Inner-Biblical Exegesis," *JBL* 99 (1980) 343-361.
Fischer, Georg, *Das Trostbüchlein. Text, Komposition und Theologie von Jer 30-31* (Stuttgarter Biblische Beiträge 26; Stuttgart: Verlag Katholisches Bibelwerk GmBH, 1993).
Fleischer, G., "ראש," *TWAT* 7.285-286.
Freedman, D. N., Forbes, A. D., Andersen, F. I., *Studies in Hebrew and Aramaic Orthography (Biblical and Judaic Studies 2;* Winona Lake, Indiana: Eisenbrauns, 1992).
Gerstenberger, E., "Jeremiah's Complaints: Observations on Jeremiah 15:10-21," *JBL* 82 (1963) 393-403.
Glueck, Nelson, *Das Wort Hesed im alttestamentlichen Sprachgebrauch als menschliche und göttlich gemeinschaftgemässe Verhaltungsweise* (2d ed.; BZAW 47; Berlin: Töpelmann, 1961).
Gosse, Bernard, "Le malédiction contre Babylone de Jérémie 51,59-64 et les rédactions du livre de Jérémie," *ZAW* 98 (1986) 383-399.
Gottwald, Norman K., *Studies in the Book of Lamentations* (SBT 14; London: SCM, 1954).

Graupner, Axel, *Auftrag und Geschick des Propheten Jeremia* (BTS 15; Neukirchen-Vluyn: Neukirchener Verlag, 1991).
Gray, G. B., *Numbers* (ICC; Edinburgh: T. & T. Clark, 1903).
—— *Sacrifice in the Old Testament* (Oxford: Clarendon, 1925).
Gray, John, *I & II Kings. A Commentary* (OTL; London: SCM, 1964).
Greenberg, Moshe, "The Hebrew Oath Particle Hay/He," *JBL* 76 (1957) 34-39.
Gressmann, H., *Der Ursprung der israelitisch-jüdischer Eschatologie* (FRLANT 6; Göttingen: Vandenhoeck & Ruprecht, 1905).
Gross, Karl, *Die literarische Verwandschaft Jeremias mit Hosea* (Borna-Leipzig: Universitatsverlag von Robert Noske, 1930).
—— "Hosea's Einfluss auf Jeremias Anschauung," *NKZ* 42 (1931) 241-256, 327-343.
Gunkel, H., *Die Psalmen übersetzt und erklärt* (HKAT; Göttingen: Vandenhoeck & Ruprecht, 1926).
Gunneweg, Antonius H. J., "עם הארץ — A Semantic Revolution," *ZAW* 95 (1983) 437-440.
Hardmeier, Christof, *Prophetie im Streit vor dem Untergang Judas. Erzählkommunikative Studien zur Entstehungssituation der Jesaja-und Jeremiaerzählungen in II Reg 18-20 und Jer 37-40* (BZAW 187; Berlin: Walter de Gruyter, 1990).
Harrelson, Walter, "Ten Commandments," *IDB* 4.569-573.
—— *Interpreting the Old Testament* (New York: Holt, Rinehart and Winston, 1964).
Hayes, John H., "The Tradition of Zion's Inviolability," *JBL* 82 (1963) 419-426.
—— "The Usage of Oracles Against Foreign Nations in Ancient Israel," *JBL* 87 (1968) 81-92.
Hayward, Robert, *The Targum of Jeremiah* (The Aramaic Bible 12; Edinburgh: T. & T. Clark, 1987).
Herrmann, Siegfried, *Die prophetischen Heilserwartungen in Alten Testament. Ursprung und Gestaltwandel* (BWANT 5; Stuttgart: Kohlhammer, 1965).
—— *Jeremia* (BKAT 12/1; Neukirchen-Vluyn: Neukirchener Verlag, 1986).
—— *Jeremia. Der Prophet und das Buch* (Erträge der Forschung 271; Darmstadt: Wissenschaftliche Buchgesellschaft, 1990).
Hertzberg, H. W., "Die Entwicklung des Begriffes משפט im A. T.," *ZAW* 40 (1922) 256-287; *ZAW* 41 (1923) 16-76.
Heschel, Abraham, *The Prophets* (New York: Harper & Row, 1962).
Hillers, Delbert R., "A Convention in Hebrew Literature: The Reaction to Bad News," *ZAW* 77 (1965) 86-90.
—— *Lamentations* (AB 7A; New York: Doubleday, 1972).
—— *Micah* (Hermeneia; Philadelphia: Fortress Press, 1984).

Hobbs, Trevor R., "Some Remarks on the Composition and Structure of the Book of Jeremiah," *CBQ* 34 (1972) 357-275.
—— "Jeremiah 3:1-15 and Deuteronomy 24:1-4," *ZAW* 86 (1974) 23-29.
Höffken, Peter, "Zu den Heilszusätzen in der Völkerorakelsammlung des Jeremiabuches," *VT* 27 (1977) 398-412.
Holladay, William L., *The Root SÛBH in the Old Testament, with Particular Reference to its Usages in Covenantal Contexts* (Leiden: Brill, 1958).
—— "Prototype and Copies: A New Approach to the Poetry-Prose Problem in the Book of Jeremiah," *JBL* 79 (1960) 351-367.
—— "'On every high hill and under every green tree,'" *VT* 11 (1961) 170-176.
—— "Style, Irony and Authenticity in Jeremiah," *JBL* 81 (1962) 44-54.
—— "The Background of Jeremiah's Self-Understanding: Moses, Samuel and Psalm 22," *JBL* 83 (1964) 153-164.
—— "Jeremiah and Moses: Further Observations," *JBL* 85 (1966) 17-27.
—— "Once more 'anak=tin,' Amos 7:7-8," *VT* 20 (1970) 492-494.
—— "The Covenant with the Patriarchs Overturned. Jeremiah's Intention in 'Terror on Every Side' (Jer 20:1-6)," *JBL* 91 (1972) 305-320.
—— *Jeremiah, Spokesman Out of Time* (New York: Pilgrim, 1974).
—— "A Fresh Look at 'Source B' and 'Source C' in Jeremiah," *VT* 25 (1975) 394-412.
—— *The Architecture of Jeremiah 1-20* (London: Associated Presses, 1976).
—— *Jeremiah. A Fresh Reading* (New York: Pilgrim, 1990).
Honeyman, A. M., "Magôr Mis-sabîb and Jeremiah's Pun," *VT* 4 (1954) 424-426.
Hubmann, Franz D., *Untersuchungen zu den Konfessionen Jer 11,18-12,6 und Jer 15,10-21* (Forschung der Bibel; Echter, 1978).
Hyatt, J. P., "Jeremiah and Deuteronomy," *JNES* 1 (1942), 156-173.
—— "The Deuteronomic Edition of Jeremiah," *Vanderbilt Studies in the Humanities* I (ed. R. C. Beatty, J. P. Hyatt and M. K. Spears; Nashville: Vanderbilt University Press, 1951), 71-95.
Ittmann, Norman, *Die Konfessionen Jeremias. Ihre Bedeutung für die Verkündigung des Propheten* (WMANT 54; Neukirchen-Vluyn: Neukirchener Verlag, 1981).
Janzen, J. G., (1973) *Studies in the Text of Jeremiah* (HSM 6; Cambridge: Harvard University Press, 1973).
Joüon, Paul, *A Grammar of Biblical Hebrew, Part 3, Syntax* (Subsidia Biblica 14/11; Rome: Editrice Pontificio Istituto Biblico, 1991).
Jüngling, Hans W., "Ich mache dich zu einer ehernen Mauer, Literarkritische Überlegungen zum Verhältnis von Jer 1:18-19 zu Jer 15:20-21," *Bib* 54 (1973) 1-24.
Kaiser, Otto, *Isaiah 1-12: A Commentary* (OTL; London: SCM, 1972).
—— *Isaiah 13-39: A Commentary* (OTL; London: SCM, 1974).

—— *Isaiah 40-66: A Commentary* (OTL (London: SCM, 1969).
Kelley, Page H., Mynatt, Daniel S., Crawford, Timothy G., *The Masorah of Biblica Hebraica Stuttgartensia* (Grand Rapids: Eerdmans, 1998).
Kessler, Martin A., "Jeremiah Chapters 26-45 Reconsidered," *JNES* 27 (1968) 81-88.
Kilpp, Nelson, *Niederreissen und aufbauen. Das Verhältnis von Heilsverheissung und Unheilsverkündigung bei Jeremia und in Jeremiabuch* (Biblisch-Theologische Studien 13; Neukirchen-Vluyn: Neukirchener Verlag, 1990).
King, Philip J., *Jeremiah. An Archaeological Companion* (Louisville: Westminster, 1993).
Kissane, Edward J., "Who Maketh Lightnings for the Rain," *JTS* NS 3 (1952) 214-216.
Klassen, H., *Who Are the Remnant in the Book of Jeremiah?* (M.Th. Thesis, Toronto: Knox College, 1984).
Knierim, Rolf, *Die Hauptbegriffe für Sünde im Alten Testament* (Gütersloh: Mohn, 1965).
Knights, Chris H., "The Structure of Jeremiah 35," *ExpTim* 106:5 (1995) 142-144.
Köhler, Ludwig, *Hebrew Man* (London: SCM, 1956).
Kraus, Hans-Joachim, *Psalmen I* (BKAT 15/1; Neukirchen-Vluyn: Neukirchener Verlag, 1961).
Kutsch, E., *Verheissung und Gesetz. Untersuchungen zum sogenannten "Bund" im Alten Testament* (BZAW 131; Berlin: Walter de Gruyter, 1973).
Labuschagne, C. J., *The Incomparability of Yahweh in the Old Testament* (Pretoria Oriental Series 5; Leiden: Brill, 1966).
Landes, G. M., "The Fountain at Jazer," *BASOR* 144 (1956) 30-37.
Lauha, Aare, "ZAPHON: Der Norden und die Nordvölker im Alten Testament" in *Annales Academiae Scientiarum Fennicae*, (Helsinki: Suomalainen Tiedeakatemia, 1943) 1-96.
Lemke, Werner E., "Nebuchadnezzar, my servant," *CBQ* 28 (1966) 45-50.
—— "The Near and the Distant God. A Study of Jer 23:23-24 in its Biblical Theological Context," *JBL* 100 (1981) 541-555.
—— "Jeremiah 31:31-34," *Int* 37 (1983) 183-187.
Leslie, Elmer A., *The Intimate Papers of Jeremiah* (Boston: Boston University Press, 1953).
Levin, Christoph, *Die Verheissung des neuen Bundes in ihrem Theologiegeschichtlichen Zusammenhang ausgelegt* (Göttingen: Vandenhoeck & Ruprecht, 1985).
Levinson, B. M., "Recovering the Lost Original Meaning of ולא תכסה עליו (Deuteronomy 13:9)," *JBL* 115 (1996) 601-620.
Lindblom. J. *Prophecy in Ancient Israel* (Oxford: Basil Blackwell, 1963).

Lindhagen, Curt, *The Servant Motif in the Old Testament* (Uppsala: Lundequistska Bokhandeln, 1950).
Lipinski, E., " באחרית הימים dans les textes pre-exiliques," *VT* 20 (1970) 445-450.
—— "Études sur des textes 'messianiques' de l'Ancien Testament," *Semitica* 20 (1970) 41-57.
—— " נקמה," *TWAT* 5.603-604.
Liwak, Rudiger, *Der Prophet und die Geschichte. Eine literar-historische Untersuchung zum Jeremiabuch* (BWANT 121; Berlin: Kohlhammer, 1987).
Loader, J. A., *A Tale of Two Cities. Sodom and Gomorrah in the Old Testament, early Jewish and early Christian Tradition* (Kampen: J. H. Kok, 1990).
Lohfink, Norbert, "Der junge Jeremia als Propagandist und Poet, zum Grundstock von Jer 30-31" in *Le Livre de Jérémie: Le Prophète et son Milieu; Les Oracles et leur Transmission* (ed. P.-M. Bogaert; BETL 54; Leuven: Leuven University Press, 1954) 351-368.
—— "Die Gotteswortverschachtelung in Jer 30-31" in *Künder des Wortes. Beiträge zur Theologie des Propheten: Josef Schreiner zum 60 Geburtstag* (ed. Lothar Ruppert, Peter Weimar and Erich Zeuger; Würzburg: Echter, 1982) 105-119.
Long, Burke O., "Two Question and Answer Schemata in the Prophets," *JBL* 90 (1971) 129-139.
—— "The Stylistic Components of Jeremiah 3:1-5," *ZAW* 88 (1976) 386-390.
Lundbom, Jack R., *Jeremiah. A Study in Ancient Hebrew Rhetoric* (SBLDS 18; Missoula: Scholars Press, 1975).
—— "The Lawbook of the Josianic Reform," *CBQ* 38 (1976) 293-302.
—— *The Early Career of the Prophet Jeremiah* (Lampeter, Wales: Edwin Mellen, 1993).
Lys, Daniel, "Jérémie 28 et le problème du faux prophète ou la circulation du sens dans le diagnostique prophétique," *RHPR* 59 (1979) 453-482.
Macchi, Jean-Daniel, "Les Doublets Dans le Livre de Jérémie," in *The Book of Jeremiah and Its Reception* (ed. A. H. W. Curtis and T. Romer; BETL 128; London: London University Press, 1997) 110-150.
Margoliot, M., "Jeremiah 10:1-16. A Re-examination," *VT* 30 (1980) 295-308.
Martin, James D., "The Forensic Background to Jeremiah 3:1," *VT* 19 (1969) 82-92.
Marx, Alfred, "A Propos des doublets du livre de Jérémie: Reflexions sur la formation d'un livre prophetique" in *Prophecy: Essays presented to Georg Fohrer on his sixty-fifth Birthday 6 September 1980* (ed. J. A. Emerton; BZAW 150; Berlin: Walter de Gruyter, 1980).
Mays, James L., *Amos* (OTL; London: SCM, 1969).

McArter, Jr., P. Kyle, *2 Samuel* (AB 9; Garden City, New York: Doubleday, 1984).
McCarthy, D. J., *Treaty and Covenant* (AnBib 21A; Rome: Editrice Pontifico Istituto Biblico, 1978).
McConville, J. Gordon, *Judgment and Promise. An Interpretation of the Book of Jeremiah* (Winona Lake, Indiana: Eisenbrauns, 1992).
McKane, William, "Poison, Trial by Ordeal and the Cup of Wrath," *VT* 30 (1980) 474-492.
—— "משא in Jeremiah 23:33-40" in *Prophecy, Essays Presented to Georg Fohrer on His Sixty-Fifth Birthday, 6 September 1980* (ed. J. A. Emerton; BZAW 150; Berlin: Walter de Gruyter), 35-54.
—— "Relations Between Poetry and Prose in the Book of Jeremiah with Special Reference to Jeremiah 3:6-11 and 12:14-17" in *Congress Volume: Vienna 1980* (ed. J. A. Emerton; Leiden: Brill, 1979) 220-237.
—— "Jeremiah and the Rechabites," *ZAW* Supplement 100 (1988) 106-123.
—— "Jeremiah 27:5-8, especially 'Nebuchadrezzar, my servant'" in *Prophet und Prophetenbuch. Festschrift für Otto Kaiser zum 65 Geburtstag* (ed. Volkmar Fritz, Karl-Friedrich Pohlmann and Hans Christoph Schmitt; *BZAW* 185 Berlin: Walter de Gruyter, 1989) 98-110.
Meyer, Ivor, *Jeremia und die Falschen Propheten* (OBO 13; Göttingen: Vandenhoeck & Ruprecht, 1977).
Michaelis, Johann D., *Observationes Philologicae et Criticae in Jeremiae Vaticinia et Threnos* (Göttingen: Vandenhoeck & Ruprecht, 1793).
Miller, John W., *Das Verhältnis Jeremias und Hesekiels sprachlich und theologisch untersucht* (Assen: van Gorcum, 1955).
Mitchell, H. G., Smith, J. M. P., and Bewer, J. A., *A Critical and Exegetical Commentary on Haggai, Zechariah, Malachi and Jonah* (ICC; Edinburgh: T. & T. Clark, 1912).
Morrow, Stanley B., "Hamas ('violentia') in Jer 20:8," *VD* 43 (1965) 241-255.
Mowinckel, Sigmund, *Zur Komposition des Buches Jeremia* (Kristiana: Jacob Dybwad, 1914).
—— *Prophecy and Tradition. The Prophetic Books in the Light of the Study of the Growth and History of the Tradition* (Oslo: Dybwad, 1946).
Muilenburg, James, "Baruch the Scribe" in *Proclamation and Presence. Old Testament Essays in Honour of Gwynne Henton Davies* (ed. J. I. Durham and J. R. Porter; London: SCM, 1970) 215-238.
Munch, P. A., *The Expression 'Bajjôm Hahu.' Is It an Eschatological Terminus Technicus?* (AUNVAO 2, Hist.-Filos Klasse, 2; Oslo: Dybwad, 1936).
Myers, Jacob, *Ezra-Nehemiah* (AB 14; New York: Doubleday, 1965).
—— *I Chronicles: Introduction, Translation and Notes* (AB 12; New York: Doubleday, 1965).

―――― *II Chronicles: Translation and Notes* (AB 13; New York: Doubleday, 1965).
Nestle, Eberhard, "Pashhur=Magor-missabib," *ExpTim* 18 (1905) 382.
Neumann, Peter K. D., "Das Wort, das geschehen ist...Zum Problem der Wortempfangsterminologie in Jer 1-25," *VT* 23 (1973) 171-217.
Nicholson, Ernest W., "The meaning of the Expression עם הארץ in the Old Testament," *JSS* 10 (1965) 59-66.
―――― *Deuteronomy and Tradition* (Philadelphia: Fortress, 1966).
―――― *Preaching to the Exiles* (Oxford, Basil Blackwell, 1970).
Niehr, H., "שפט," *TWAT* 8.408-428.
North, Frank S., "The Oracle Against the Ammonites in Jeremiah 49:1-6," *JBL* 65 (1946) 37-43.
―――― "The Expression 'The Oracle of Yahweh' as an Aid to Critical Analysis," *JBL* 71 (1952) x.
Noth, Martin, *Überlieferungsgeschichtliche Studien I* (Tübingen: Max Niemeyer, 1943); *The Deuteronomistic History* (JSOTSup 15; Sheffield: JSOT, 1981).
―――― *Exodus: A Commentary* (OTL; London: SCM, 1974).
―――― *Numbers: A Commentary* (OTL; London: SCM, 1968).
Nötscher, F., "Zum emphatischen Lamed," *VT* 3 (1953) 372-380.
O'Brien, Mark, *The Deuteronomistic Hypothesis: A Reassessment* (Göttingen: Vandenhoeck & Ruprecht, 1989).
O'Connor, Kathleen M., *The Confessions of Jeremiah. Their Interpretation and Role in Chapters 1-25* (SBLDS 94; Atlanta: Scholars Press, 1988).
Odashima, Von Taro, *Heilsworte im Jeremiabuch. Untersuchungen zu ihrer vordeuteronomistischen Bearbeitung* (BWANT 125; Stuttgart: Kohlhammer, 1989).
Orlinsky, H., "Haser in the Old Testament," *JAOS* (1939) 22-37.
Overholt, Thomas W., "The Falsehood of Idolatry. An Interpretation of Jer 10:1-16," *JTS* 16 (1965) 1-12.
―――― "King Nebuchadnezzar in the Jeremiah Tradition," *CBQ* 30 (1968) 39-48.
―――― *The Threat of Falsehood* (SBT 16; London: SCM, 1970).
Parke-Taylor, Geoffrey H., *Yahweh, The Divine Name in the Bible* (Waterloo, Ontario: Wilfrid Laurier University Press, 1975).
Paterson, Robert M., "Reinterpretation in the Book of Jeremiah," *JSOT* 28 (1984) 37-46.
Paul, Shalom M., "Literary and Ideological Echoes of Jeremiah in Deutero-Isaiah," in *Proceedings of the Fifth World Congress of Jewish Studies* (Vol. 1; Jerusalem: World Union of Jewish Studies, 1969) 102-120.
Peckham, Brian, *The Composition of the Deuteronomistic History* (HSM 35; Atlanta: Scholars Press, 1985).
Pedersen, Johs., *Israel: Its Life and Culture I-II* (Oxford: Blackwell, 1965).

Perdue, Leo G., "Jeremiah in Modern Research: Approaches and Issues" in *A Prophet to the Nations* (ed. Leo G. Perdue & B. W. Kovacs; Winona Lake, Indiana: Eisenbrauns, 1984) 1-32.
Perles, Felix, "A Miscellany of Lexical and Textual Notes on the Bible," *JQR* 2 (1911-1912) 97-132.
Perlitt, Lothar, *Bundestheologie im Alten Testament* (WMANT 36; Neukirchen-Vluyn: Neukirchener Verlag, 1969).
Pohlmann, Karl-Friedrich, *Studien zum Jeremiabuch. Ein Beitrag zur Frage nach der Entstehung des Jeremiabuches* (Göttingen: Vandenhoeck & Ruprecht, 1978).
—— *Die Ferne Gottes. Studien zum Jeremiabuch* (BZAW 179; Berlin: Walter de Gruyter, 1989).
Polk, Timothy, *The Prophetic Persona* (JSOTSup 32; Sheffield: JSOT Press, 1984).
Preuschen, Erwin, "Die Bedeutung von שוב שבות im Alten Testament," *ZAW* 15 (1895) 1-74.
Pritchard, James B., ed., *Ancient Near Eastern Texts Relating to the Old Testament* (2d ed., Princeton: Princeton University Press, 1955).
Rahlfs, Alfred, *Septuaginta* (3d ed.; Stuttgart: Priviligierte Württembergische Bibelanstalt, 1949).
Raitt, Thomas M., *A Theology of Exile. Judgment/Deliverance in Jeremiah and Ezekiel* (Philadelphia: Fortress, 1977).
Rast, Walter, "Cakes for the Queen of Heaven" in *Scripture in History and Theology: Essays in Honor of J.Coert Rylaarsdam* (ed. A. Merrill and T. Overholt; Pittsburgh: Pickwick Press, 1977) 167-180.
Rendtorff, R., "Zum Gebrauch der Formel n^e'um jahwe im Jeremiabuch," *ZAW* 66 (1954) 27-37.
Reventlow, H. Graf, *Liturgie und prophetisches Ich bei Jeremia* (Gütersloh: Mohn, 1963).
Rietzschel, Claus, *Der Problem der Urrolle. Ein Beitrag zur Redaktionsgeschichte des Jeremiabuches* (Gütersloh: Mohn, 1966).
Robinson, T. H., "The Structure of the Book of Obadiah," *JTS* 17 (1916) 402-408.
Rowley, H. H., "The Text and Interpretation of Jer 11:18-12:6," *AJSL* 42 (1926) 217-227.
—— "The Early Prophecies of Jeremiah in Their Setting," *BJRL* 45 (1962) 178-234.
Rudolph, Wilhelm and Rüger, H. P., *Biblia Hebraica Stuttgartensia* (2d ed.; Stuttgart: Deutsche Bibelgesellschaft, 1984).
Saggs, H. W. F., *The Greatness That Was Babylon* (2d ed.; London: Sidgwick & Jackson, 1988).
Schenker, Adrian, "Nebukadnezzars Metamorphose vom Unterjocher zum Gottesknecht. Das Bild Nebukadnezzars und Einige mit Ihm

zusammenhängende Unterschiede in der beiden Jeremia-Rezensionen," *RB* 89 (1982) 498-527.

Schmuttermayr, G., *Psalm 18 und 2 Samuel 22. Studien zu einem Doppeltext* (SANT 25; Munich: Kösel, 1971).

Scholz, A., *Der Masoretische Text und die LXX-Uebersetzung des Buches Jeremias* (Regensburg: G. J. Manz, 1875).

Schwally, Friedrich, "Die reden des Buches Jeremia gegen die Heiden, 25, 46-51," *ZAW* 8 (1888) 177-217.

Seidl, Theodor, *Texte und Einheiten in Jeremia 27-29* (Arbeiten zu Text und Sprache im Alten Testament, 2; St. Ottilien: EOS, 1977).

Seitz, Christopher R., *Theology in Conflict: Reactions to the Exile in the Book of Jeremiah* (BZAW 176; Berlin: Walter de Gruyter, 1989).

Sellin, Ernst and Fohrer, Georg, *Introduction to the Old Testament*, (New York: Abingdon, 1968).

Seybold, Klaus, *Der Prophet Jeremia. Leben und Werk* (Stuttgart: Kohlhammer, 1993).

Skinner, John, *Prophecy and Religion* (Cambridge: Cambridge University Press, 1922).

Smend, R., *Die Bundesformel* (Theologisches Studien 68, ed. K. Barth und M. Geiger; Zurich: EVZ, 1963).

Smith, J. M. P., Ward, W. H. and Bewer, J. A., (1911) *A Critical and Exegetical Commentary on Micah, Zephaniah, Nahum, Habakkuk, Obadiah and Joel* (ICC; Edinburgh: T. & T. Clark, 1911).

Smith, M., *The Early History of God: Yahweh and the Other Deities in Ancient Israel* (San Francisco: Harper & Row, 1990).

—— *The Laments of Jeremiah and Their Contexts. A Literary and Redactional Study of Jeremiah 11-20* (SBLMS 42; Atlanta: Scholars Press, 1990).

Snaith, Norman H., *The Distinctive Ideas of the Old Testament* (London: Epworth Press, 1944).

—— "The meaning of the Hebrew אך," *VT* 14 (1964) 221-5.

Soggin, J. Alberto, "La negazione in Geremia 4,27 e 5,10a, cfr. 5,18b," *Bib* 46 (1965) 56-59.

Stacey, W. David, *Prophetic Drama in the Old Testament* (London: Epworth Press, 1990).

Streane, A. W., *The Double Text of Jeremiah (Massoretic and Alexandrian) Compared, Together with an Appendix on the Old Latin Evidence* (Cambridge: Deighton Bell, 1896).

Stulman, Louis, *The Prose Sermons of the Book of Jeremiah. A Redescription of the Correspondences with the Deuteronomistic Literature in the Light of Recent Text-Critical Research* (SBLDS 83; Atlanta: Scholars Press, 1986).

Sturdy, John V. M., "The authorship of the 'prose sermons' of Jeremiah" in *Prophecy. Essays presented to Georg Fohrer on his sixty-fifth birthday*

6 September 1980 (ed. J. A. Emerton; BZAW 150; Berlin: Walter de Gruyter, 1980), 143-150.

Swetnam, James, "Some Observations on the Background of צדיק in Jeremias 23,5a," Bib 46 (1965) 29-40.

Talmon, Shemaryahu, "Double Readings in the Text of Jeremiah," *Textus 1 (1960) 144-184.*

—— *"An Apparently Redundant MT Reading in Jeremiah 1:18," Textus 8* (1973) 160-163.

—— "The Textual Study of the Bible — A New Outlook," in *Qumran and the History of the Biblical Text* (ed. F. M. Cross and S. Talmon; Cambridge: Harvard University Press, 1975), 321-400.

Taylor, Marion Ann, "Jeremiah 45: The Problem of Placement," *JSOT* 37 (1987) 79-98.

Thackeray, H. St.John, *The Septuagint and Jewish Worship* (2d ed.; Schweich Lectures, 1920; Oxford: Oxford University Press, 1923).

Thiel, Winfried, *Die deuteronomistische Redaktion von Jeremia 1-25* (WMANT 41; Neukirchen-Vluyn: Neukirchener Verlag, 1973).

—— *Die deuteronomistische Redaktion von Jeremia 26-45* (WMANT 52; Neukirchen-Vluyn: Neukirchener Verlag, 1981).

Thomas D. Winton, "A Note on the Hebrew Root נחם," *ExpTim* 44 (1933) 191-192.

Tov, Emanuel, "L'Incidence de la critique textuelle sur la critique littéraire dans le livre de Jérémie," *RB* 79 (1972) 189-199.

—— "Some Aspects of the Textual and Literary History of the Book of Jeremiah" in *Le Livre de Jérémie: Le Prophète et son Milieu, les Oracles et leur Transmission* (ed. P.-M. Bogaert; BETL 54; Leuven: Leuven University Press) 145-167.

—— *The Text-Critical Use of the Septuagint in Biblical Research* (Jerusalem Biblical Studies 3; Jerusalem: Simor, 1981).

Tsevat, M., "בּחן," *TDOT* 2.69-72.

Untermann, J., *From Repentance to Redemption* (*JSOT* 54; Sheffield: JSOT, 1987).

Vaggione, Richard P., "Over all Asia? The extent of the Scythian domination in Herodotus," *JBL* 92 (1973) 523-530.

Vermeylen, Jacques, "Essai de Redaktionsgeschichte des 'Confessions de Jérémie'" in *Le Livre de Jérémie* (ed. P.-M. Bogaert; BETL 54; Leuven: Leuven University Press, 1981) 239-270.

Volz, Paul, *Studien zum Text des Jeremia* (BWAT 25; Leipzig: Hinrichs, 1920).

Von Rad, Gerhard, "The Origin of the Concept of the Day of Yahweh," *JSS* 4 (1959) 97-108.

—— *Old Testament Theology* (2 vols.; London: Oliver and Boyd, 1962-1965).

—— *Deuteronomy* (OTL; London: SCM, 1966).

Wambacq, Bernard N., "Jérémie, X.1-16," *RB* 81 (1974) 57-62.
Wanke, Gunther, *Untersuchungen zur sogenannten Baruchschrift* (BZAW 122; Berlin: Walter de Gruyter, 1971).
Ward, J. M., "Pashhur," IDB 3.662.
Watson, Wilfred G. E., "Gender-Matched Synonymous Parallelism in the Old Testament," *JBL* 99 (1980) 321-341.
—— *Classical Hebrew Poetry* (JSOTSup 26; Sheffield: JSOT 1984).
Watts, J. D. W., *Obadiah. A Critical Exegetical Commentary* (Winona Lake, Indiana: Eerdmans, 1969).
—— "Text and Redaction in Jeremiah's Oracles Against the Nations," *CBQ* 54 (1992) 432-447.
Weinfeld, Moshe, *Deuteronomy and the Deuteronomic School* (Oxford: Oxford University Press, 1972).
—— "The Worship of Molech and of the Queen of Heaven and Its Background," *UF* 4 (1972) 149-154.
Weippert, Helga, *Die Prosareden des Jeremiabuches* (BZAW 132; Berlin: Walter de Gruyter, 1973).
Weiser, Artur, *Das Buch Hiob* (ATD 13; Göttingen: Vandenhoeck & Ruprecht, 1957).
—— *The Psalms. A Commentary* (OTL; London: SCM, 1962).
Weiss, M., "The Origin of the 'Day of the Lord' — Reconsidered," *HUCA* 37 (1962) 29-71.
Weiss, Raphael, "On Ligatures in the Hebrew Bible (מ=נו)," *JBL* 82 (1963) 188-194.
Welch, Adam C., *Jeremiah. His Time and His Work* (Oxford: Oxford University Press, 1928).
Wessels, Walter J., "Jeremiah 22:24-30. A Proposed Ideological Reading," *ZAW* 101 (1989) 232-249.
Westermann, Claus, *Isaiah 40-66* (London: SCM, 1969).
—— *Prophetic Oracles of Salvation in the Old Testament* (Louisville: John Knox Press, 1991).
Wevers, John, *Ezekiel* (The Century Bible; London: Thomas Nelson, 1969).
Whitley, Charles F., "The Term Seventy Years Captivity," *VT* 4 (1954) 60-72.
—— "The Date of Jeremiah's Call," *VT* 14 (1964) 467-483.
Wijngaards, J., "הוציא and העלה, a Twofold Approach to the Exodus," *VT* 15 (1965) 91-102.
Wildberger, Hans, *Yahwewort und prophetischer Rede bei Jeremia* (Diss. Theological Faculty of the University of Zürich; Zürich: Zwingli, 1942).
—— *Jesaja* (BKAT 10/1-2; Neukirchen-Vluyn: Neukirchener Verlag, 1972, 1978).
Wilke, Fritz, "Das Scythenprobleme in Jeremiabuch" in *Alttestamentliche Studien Rudolf Kittel zum 60. Geburtstag dargebracht* (ed. Albrecht Alt et al; BWANT 13; Leipzig: Hinrichs, 1913) 222-254.

Williams, Michael J., "An Investigation of the Legitimacy of Source Distinctions for the Prose Material in Jeremiah," *JBL* 112 (1993) 193-210.
Williams, Ronald J., *Hebrew Syntax: An Outline* (Toronto: University of Toronto Press, 1967).
Wiseman, D. J., *Chronicles of Chaldaean Kings (626-556 B.C.) in the British Museum* (London: British Museum Publications, 1956).
—— "The Vassal Treaties of Esarhaddon," *Iraq* 20 (1958) 521-522.
Wolff, Hans Walter, *Hosea* (Hermeneia; Philadelphia: Fortress Press, 1974).
Würthwein, Ernst, *Der 'amm ha'arez im Alten Testament*, (BWANT 17; Stuttgart: Kohlhammer, 1936).
Zevit, Ziony, "The Use of עֶבֶד as a Diplomatic Term in Jeremiah," *JBL* 88 (1969) 74-77.
Ziegler, J., *Septuaginta Vetus Testamentum Graecum 15: Jeremias, Baruch, Threni, Epistula Jeremiae* (Göttingen ed. of LXX; Göttingen: Vandenhoeck & Ruprecht, 1957).
—— *Beiträge zur Jeremias-Septuaginta* (Mitteilungen des Septuaginta — Unternehmens der Akademie der Wissenschaften in Göttingen 6; Göttingen: Vandenhoeck & Ruprecht, 1958).
Zobel, H.-J., "הוֹי," *TDOT* 3.359-364.
—— "צְבָאוֹת," *TWAT* 6.876-892.

INDEX OF DOUBLETS IN THE BOOK OF JEREMIAH

	DOUBLETS	PAGES
Jeremiah	1:17b = 17:18b	40–42
	1:18–19 = 15:20	35–40
	2:26b = 32:32b	185–186
	2:27b = 32:33a	185–186
	2:28b = 11:13	185–186
	4:4b = 21:12b	62–64
	4:5c = 8:14a	187
	5:9 = 5:29 = 9:8(9:9E)	187–188
	5:29 = 5:9 = 9:8(9:9E)	187–188
	6:13–15 = 8:10b–12	93–98
	6:22–24 = 50:41–43	174–176
	7:6 = 22:3	188–189
	7:7 = 25:5	189–190
	7:16 = 11:14	190–192
	7:30–32 = 19:5–6 = 32:34–35	192–195
	7:33 = Deut 28:26	222–223
	7:34 = 16:9 = 25:10 = 33:10a, 11a	195–196
	8:2b = 16:4a = 25:33b	196–197
	8:10b–12 = 6:13–15	93–98
	8:14a = 4:5c	187
	8:15 = 14:19b	7–8
	9:8(9:9E) = 5:9 = 5:29	187–188
	9:14(9:15E) = 23:15a	82–85
	10:12–16 = 51:15–19	177–180
	10:25 = Ps 79:6-7	217–218
	11:14 = 7:16	190–192
	11:20 = 20:12	13–18, 52
	11:23b = 23:12b	18–21
	13:14b = 21:7b	197–198
	14:10b = Hos 8:13b	213–214
	14:19b = 8:15	7–8
	15:13–14 = 17:3–4	23–31
	15:15d = Ps 69:8a	33–35
	15:20 = 1:18–19	35–40
	16:4a = 8.2b = 25:33b	196–197
	16:9 = 7:34 = 25:10 = 33:10a, 11a	195–196
	16:14–15 = 23:7–8	72–77
	17:3–4 = 15:13–14	23–31
	17:10b = 32:19b	198–199
	17:18b = 1:17b	40–42
	17:25 = 22:4	65–68

	DOUBLETS	PAGES
Jeremiah	17:26=32:44=33:13	199–200
	18:16=19:8=49:17=50:13	152–153
	18:20a=18:22b	42–46
	18:22b=18:20a	42–46
	18:23b=Neh 3:37(4:5E)	46–47
	19:3b=2 Kgs 17:15b	219–220
	19:5–6=7:30–32=32:34–35	192–195
	19:8=18:16=49:17=50:13	152–153
	19:9=Deut 28:53	223–224
	20:10a=Ps 31:14a	48–52
	20:12=11:20	13–18, 52
	21:7b=13:14b	197–198
	21:9=38:2	201–204
	21:12b=4:4b	62–64
	21:14b=50:32b	171–172
	22:3=7:6	188–189
	22:4=17:25	65–68
	22:8–9=Deut 29:23–25	225–226
	23:5–6=33:14–16	55–60
	23:7–8=16:14–15	72–77
	23:12b=11:23b	18–21
	23:15a=9:14(9:15E)	82–85
	23:19–20=30:23–24	85–89
	25:5=7:7	189–190
	25:10=7:34=16:9=33:10a, 11a	195–196
	25:33b=8:2b=16:4a	196–197
	26:3=36:3	204–205
	26:18b=Mic 3:12	8–9
	29:13=Deut 4:29	78, 226–227
	29:14a=Deut 30:3	227–228
	30:10–11=46:27–28	119–125
	30:23–24=23:19–20	85–89
	31:29=Ezek 18:2	215–216
	31:35c=Isa 51:15b	216–217
	32:4=34:3	205–208
	32:19b=17:10b	198–199
	32:32b=2:26b	185–186
	32:33a=2:27b	185–186
	32:34–35=7:30–32=19:5–6	192–195
	32:44=17:26=33:13	199–200
	33:10a, 11a=7:34=16:9=25:10	195–196
	33:13=17:26=32:44	199–200
	33:14–16=23:5–6	55–60
	34:3=32:4	205–208
	34:22a=37:8	208–209
	36:3=26:3	204–205
	37:8=34:22a	208–209
	38:2=21:9	201–204

Index of Doublets

	DOUBLETS	PAGES
Jeremiah	38:3 = 2 Kgs 18:30b	220
	39:3 = 39:13	209–210
	39:13 = 39:3	209–210
	46:27–28 = 30:10–11	119–125
	48:5ab = Isa 15:5bc	130–131
	48:29–33 = Isa 16:6–10	131–135
	48:34–39 = Isa 15:2–7	135–137
	48:40–41 = 49:22	137–139
	48:43–44 = Isa 24:17–18ab	139–140
	48:45–46 = Num 21:27–29; 24:17c	140–143
	49:9 = Obad 5	147–149
	49:14–16 = Obad 1–4	149–152
	49:17 = 50:13 = 18:16 = 19:8	152–153
	49:18 = 50:40	153–155
	49:19–21 = 50:44–46	155–157
	49:22 = 48:41	137–139
	49:26 = 50:30	158–159
	50:13 = 49:17 = 18:16 = 19:8	152–153
	50:16b = Isa 13:14b	170–171
	50:23b = 51:41b	171
	50:30 = 49:26	158–159
	50:32b = 21:14b	172–173
	50:39–40 = Isa 13:19–22	173–174
	50:40 = 49:18	153–155
	50:41–43 = 6:22–24	175–177
	50:44–46 = 49:19–21	155–157
	51:15–19 = 10:12–16	177–179
	51:39b = 51:57b	181
	51:41b = 50:23b	171
	51:57b = 51:39b	181
	51:58d = Hab 2:13b	182–183

www.ingramcontent.com/pod-product-compliance
Lightning Source LLC
Chambersburg PA
CBHW020639300426
44112CB00007B/168